THE COMPLETE
UNIVERSITY
WORD HUNTER

THE COMPLETE

UNIVERSITY

WORD HUNTER

John T. Gause

THOMAS Y. CROWELL COMPANY

New York

Established 1834

PUBLISHER'S FOREWORD

The Complete University Word Hunter has the word you want when you want it. It is a constant source of unusual and exciting words—words which will enlarge your vocabulary and increase the effectiveness of your writing. This book is a new idea in publishing: it finds, it defines, it discriminates, combining a thesaurus, a dictionary, and a book on word usage.

A thesaurus is arranged according to subject categories, and *The Complete University Word Hunter* has some ninety categories, such as FRIENDSHIP, GRAMMAR, LITERARY TERMS, TRAVEL, and THE WEATHER. For example, under FRIENDSHIP are such words as "affable," "amity," "amiable," "convivial," "fellowship" and "pal." If you want to find a new word, turn to the category that represents the subject you have in mind and select the word you want.

As a dictionary, *The Complete University Word Hunter* includes two types of definitions. First, most of the words listed under each subject category have appropriate, easily grasped definitions, especially written to show the proper use of each word within that category. For example, under LOGIC you will find the word "thesis" defined as "the general direction or significance of an argument, as 'You don't prove your thesis that all men are naturally good.'" Second, for each of the more difficult words or phrases an extended discussion about its origin, its development in our language, and its precise meaning is added. Thus every word in *The Complete University Word Hunter* is carefully defined in terms of its use.

These discussions are very important. They really constitute in themselves a work on word usage. For example, under COLOR you can find a clear discussion of how to use "grey" and "gray." Or under GOVERNMENT there is a careful analysis of the distinctions between "administrative" and "executive." In this way *The Complete University Word Hunter* discriminates words of similar meanings. But it is not only these discussions that are so valuable. The grouping together of words with related meanings helps you see their subtleties and their differences one from another. You cannot fail to find at a glance the pertinent word.

For many years Mr. Gause has been interested in philology (he is the author of two earlier books about words), and he has a wide and original knowledge of our language. Mr. Gause's style is free and easy: you can quickly understand even the most complicated discussions of complex words.

The Complete University Word Hunter is an indispensable word book. It gives you exactly the right word in the shortest possible time. The words and phrases are defined with respect to each other in such a way that you always choose the word of maximum expressiveness. Subtle meanings are carefully explained and proper usage discussed and demonstrated. And constant use of this book will incalculably enrich your vocabulary.

The sources of *The Complete University Word Hunter* are various but, of course, largely lexical. The author wishes to acknowledge most freely and gratefully his appreciation of aid and counsel from other books about words, especially from the larger dictionaries. The author also wishes to acknowledge the aid of Gorton Carruth, who edited the manuscript and wrote most of the shorter definitions in the text.

CONTENTS

Appendix

THE COMPLETE
UNIVERSITY
WORD HUNTER

AILMENTS

See also Health and Remedies

AFFECTION *n.* an abnormal or morbid bodily or mental condition; a disease.

AGUISH *adj.* pertaining to ague or malarial chills and fever.

ALOPECIAN *adj.* pertaining to baldness (from a Greek word that meant fox-mange and also baldness). The spelling of this adjective is not formalized.

Amnesia see Aphasia & Amnesia

Aphasia & Amnesia

BACILLAR or **BACILLARY** *adj.* pertaining to **BACILLUS**, a rod-shaped bacteria.

CARCINOMATOUS or **CANCEROUS** *adj.* pertaining to cancer.

CARIOUS *adj.* pertaining to tooth or bone decay.

CHIRAGRIC *adj.* pertaining to gout in the hand.

Comatose

COMPLAINT *n.* a cause of bodily pain or uneasiness; a malady; a disease or ailment.

COSTIVE *adj.* pertaining to constipation, or to its causes.

CROUPOUS *adj.* pertaining to the croup.

DAMAGE *n.* injury in general; harm; hurt.

DIARRHEAL *adj.* pertaining to **DIARRHEA**.

DISEASE *n.* a morbid physical condition, acute or chronic, that may result in death.

    ALLERGIES

    APPENDICITIS

    ARTHRITIS

    ATHLETE'S FOOT (EPIDERMOPHYTOSIS)

    BRIGHT'S DISEASE

    CANCER

    CHICKEN POX (VARICELLA)

    DIABETES

    DIPHTHERIA

    DYSENTERY

    ECZEMA

    GALL BLADDER DISEASE (CHOLECYSTITIS)

    GALL STONES

    GOUT

    INFANTILE PARALYSIS (POLIOMYELITUS)

    MALARIA

    MEASLES

    MUMPS

    POISON IVY

    RABIES (HYDROPHOBIA)

    RESPIRATORY DISEASES

        ASTHMA

        BRONCHITIS

        INFLUENZA

1

PNEUMONIA

SINUSITIS

STREPTOCOCCAL NOSE & THROAT INFECTIONS

TONSILLITIS

TUBERCULOSIS

RHEUMATIC FEVER

RINGWORM

SCARLET FEVER & STREPTOCOCCAL INFECTIONS

SMALLPOX (VARIOLA)

TETANUS (LOCKJAW)

TRENCH MOUTH (VINCENT'S INFECTION)

TYPHOID FEVER

TYPHUS FEVER

UNDULANT FEVER (BRUCELLOSIS)

VENEREAL DISEASES

GONORRHEA

SYPHILIS

WHOOPING COUGH (PERTUSSIS)

DISTEMPER *n.* a disease, malady, or indisposition. Most commonly applied to diseases of animals.

DISTRESS *n.* pain or suffering in body or mind. *v.* to cause pain and suffering.

DIURETIC *adj.* causing urination.

EMETIC *adj.* causing vomiting. ANTIEMETIC refers to any remedy for vomiting.

FEBRILE, PYRETIC or PYREXIAL *adj.* pertaining to fever. see HECTIC

FLATULENT *adj.* pertaining to gas in the alimentary canal or stomach.

FRAMBESIAL *adj.* refers to yaws, a contagious skin disease prevalent in certain tropical regions.

GERATIC or, in biology, GERONTIC *adj.* pertaining to decadent old age.

HARM *n.* physical or material injury. *v.* to damage or to hurt.

HECTIC *adj.* pertaining to fever, esp. to the fever of consumption, with its flushing of the face; hence, to a gay or wild time.

HEMORRHOIDAL *adj.* pertaining to piles or HEMORRHOIDS.

HERNIAL *adj.* pertaining to a rupture or HERNIA.

HURT *n.* an injury, esp. one that gives physical or mental pain; a wound, an insult. *v.* to injure, harm, wound; to cause pain and suffering.

HYDROPIC or DROPSICAL *adj.* pertaining to DROPSY.

ICTERIC *adj.* pertaining to jaundice.

ILL *adj.* in a disordered state physically; diseased; impaired.

INJURY *n.* that which inflicts damage, hurt or harm. A broken leg is an INJURY. Battle fatigue may also be considered an INJURY.

Lesion & Trauma

LETHARGIC *adj.* morbidly sluggish or drowsy; dull; torpid.

MALADY *n.* a physical disorder or disease, esp. a chronic, deep-seated or dangerous disease.

Malaise

Mal de mer

MIASMAL or MIASMIC *adj.* pertaining to pollution originally, then to malarial swamp mists, then to malaria itself—now, any foul and noxious vapor.

MORBIFIC *adj.* pertaining to disease or its causation, or to morbidness.

MYOPIC *adj.* pertaining to nearsightedness.

NAUSEOUS *adj.* pertaining to seasickness, from Greek *naus*, 'ship.'

NOSTALGIC *adj.* pertaining to homesickness, esp. to an acute or morbid desire for one's native land.

ODONTALGIC *adj.* pertaining to toothache.

OTALGIC *adj.* pertaining to earache.

PAIN *n.* bodily or mental suffering.

PANDEMIC *adj.* pertaining to a widespread epidemic. Hence, it sometimes means general, or universal.

PARAPLEGIC *adj.* pertaining to paralysis from the hips down. Also a *n.*

PAROTITIC *adj.* pertaining to mumps.

PHRENETIC *adj.* pertaining to frenzy, brain fever, or phrenitis.

PHTHISICAL *adj.* pertaining to consumption, or tuberculosis of the lungs.

PNEUMONIC *adj.* pertaining to pneumonia, or simply to the lungs.

PODAGRIC *adj.* pertaining to gout, esp. of the foot.

PUERPERAL *adj.* pertaining to the state or condition of a woman at childbirth or following it.

SABURRAL *adj.* pertaining to foulness of stomach or mouth or, thus, of breath.

SCABROUS or SCABIETIC *adj.* pertaining to mange, scabies. But MANGY is the better adjective.

SCIRRHOUS *adj.* pertaining to hardness, as in cancer.

SCLEROTIC *adj.* pertaining to hardening of the tissues.

SCORBUTIC *adj.* pertaining to scurvy. *n.* one having scurvy.

SENESCENT *adj.* pertaining to growing old.

SEPTIC *adj.* pertaining to putrefaction, sewage. ASEPTIC is the antonym. PUTREFACTIVE is a synonym, and so also is PUTRID, which includes the idea of a bad smell or of moral foulness.

SICK *adj.* pertaining to physical or mental disorder; indisposed. *n.* in distinction to MALADY, SICKNESS may be more or less temporary.

SPASTIC *adj.* pertaining to SPASM, esp. tonic spasm.

SPHACELOUS or GANGRENOUS *adj.* pertaining to gangrene.

STERNUTATIVE *adj.* sneeze-causing.

STRUMATIC or STRUMOUS *adj.* pertaining to a goiter.

SUDORIFIC or DIAPHORETIC *adj.* causing sweat.

TOXIC *adj.* poisonous.

Trauma see **Lesion & Trauma**

TUSSAL or TUSSIVE *adj.* pertaining to cough.

URTICARIAL or URTICARIOUS *adj.* pertaining to hives.

VARICOSE *adj.* pertaining to an

enlarged (literally 'bent by dilation') condition, as of tumors, veins, ulcers.

VESICANT *adj.* causing blisters. VESICATORY is the medical version, extended to include capability of causing blisters.

VOMICOSE *adj.* pertaining to ulcerous cavities. Hence, also, pockmarked.

Aphasia and **Amnesia**   APHASIA weakens or destroys your use or comprehension of speech and writings. AMNESIA impairs or purloins your memory. If you are suffering from AMNESIA and cannot remember who you or your antecedents are, it is said that a familiar tune or perfume may evoke a single recollection that will bring back all of your past with it.

APHASIA requires a word or two more. There are several kinds arising from different causes. Usually it is the result of brain injuries. Without paralyzing your vocal chords it may strike you dumb or so obfuscate you as to make you unable to talk or follow a conversation clearly. It does not impair your other intellectual powers.

Comatose   This is an adjective that means 'stupefied'—and not because it suggests commas and grammar, which may also stupefy. This coma is Greek, and some say it comes from *komē*, the hair of your head, and others that from the beginning it meant 'slumber,' *koma*. In medicine a coma is a stupor or an unnaturally heavy sleep, as if from drugs. On the other hand, the silvery-haired head of a comet is a coma. So there you are! For laymen the chief virtue of the word is that it sounds pretty nice. Like comical it is clear and full-measured in your mouth. It even has a whimsical sound. Some slothful clerks have a COMATOSE look about them. They are almost comically lethargic.

Lesion and **Trauma**   A LESION is an 'injury' or 'loss.' Physiologically, it is a damaged organ or tissue. Legally, LESION is the relative loss you suffer when you don't get your money's worth or your service's worth. A TRAUMA is simply a 'wound.' The adjective is TRAUMATIC.

Malaise   In varying degrees of hyperbole we can be scared to death or merely feel uncomfortable in our bones. Neither discomfort can really be called a malady. But the second of the two is MALAISE, and is described by the medicos: 'an indefinite feeling of uneasiness, or of being ill; also, generally, a feeling of discomfort.' When we are afflicted with MALAISE we are distressed in our feelings, which is exactly what the French meant by *malaise*, 'ill ease.' The 's' in it sounds like a 'z,' and the whole word slides off our tongues with a sibilant suggestion of sickness.

Mal de mer   Interesting as an illustration of fluctuations of usages, MAL DE MER in the sedate '80's and even in the comparatively gay '90's was esteemed as an 'elegant' term. Its English equivalent 'seasickness' was thought to be too physically expressive for refined tastes. In the preceding century the purists had begun attacking words that bordered on slang: such words as 'jilt,' 'shabby,' 'touchy' and 'humbug,' and even 'fun,' 'flirtation,' 'enthusiasm' and 'sham' have had to fight for their lives. As for the word 'sick' it is probably a thousand years old, even in English; but at length in England it has come to mean only 'nauseated.' In America it retained its broader meaning of 'ill' or 'ailing,' so that now when we are not polite enough to use the Greek word 'nausea' we usually explain: "I was sick to my stomach." But such expressions were offensive to the Victorians. But how could they speak of a 'nausea from the ship's motion' when 'seasickness' was so much shorter? A soft French phrase proved to be euphonious, and became fashionable: *mal de mer,* meaning 'illness caused by the sea.' But fashions do not always endure. In the hurly-burly of successive World Wars people quite forgot about MAL DE MER, and now you can buy pills for seasickness.

ANGER

See also War

Abhor   see **Detest, Despise,** etc.

Acrimonious

Aggressor   see **Assailant & Aggressor**

Altercation & Dispute

Anger & Wrath

ANIMOSITY   *n.* ill will, often resentment, tending toward hostile action.

ANNOYANCE   *n.* act of disturbing, irritating, molesting, or harassing someone; a nuisance.

Antagonism   see **Pugnacity & Antagonism**

ANTIPATHY   *n.* aversion or dislike; repugnance; distaste.

Assailant & Aggressor

Avenge & Revenge

BAD HUMOR   *n.* a disagreeable or unpleasant state of mind or mood.

Bellicose & Belligerent

Belligerent   see **Bellicose & Belligerent**

BITING   *adj.* sharp, cutting; sarcastic, caustic.

BITTER   *adj.* stinging, caustic, acrimonious.

CONTENTIOUSNESS   *n.* quarrelsomeness; the quality of being given to brawls or wrangling.

CROSSNESS   *n.* ill humor.

Deplore   see **Deprecate, Depreciate,** etc.

Deprecate, Depreciate, Deplore

Depreciate see **Deprecate, Depreciate**, etc.

Despise see **Detest, Despise**, etc.

Detest, Despise, Abhor, Loath, Hate

Diatribe, Invective, Vituperation. See also **Philippic, Tirade**, etc.

DISCORD *n.* disagreement; dissension; conflict.

DISLIKE *n.* antipathy or aversion to something.

DISPLEASURE *n.* the feeling of one who is displeased; also, that which gives offense or injury.

Dispute see **Altercation & Dispute**

ENEMY *n.* a foe; one hostile to another.

Enmity & Inimicalness

Expostulate

FERVESCENT *adj.* becoming hot, even 'hot under the collar.'

Flaunt & Flout

Flout see **Flaunt & Flout**

FRICTION *n.* disagreement that tends to slow progress.

FURY *n.* violent anger; rage.

GRUDGE *n.* cherished ill will. *v.* to give reluctantly.

Hate see **Detest, Despise**, etc.

HATRED *n.* strong aversion coupled with ill will.

HOSTILITY *n.* an act of open enmity; a hostile deed; an act of warfare.

ILL HUMOR *n.* a disagreeable mood; an unwholesome, sick or painful state of mind.

INDIGNATION *n.* anger resulting from what is unworthy or base; righteous wrath.

Inimicalness see **Enmity & Inimicalness**

Intransigent see **Recalcitrant & Intransigent**

Invective see **Diatribe, Invective**, etc.

IRASCIBILITY *n.* state of being testy, cranky, cross.

IRE *n.* anger; wrath.

IRRITATION *n.* annoyance; anger.

Lampoon

Leer & Sneer

Loath see **Detest, Despise**, etc.

MALEVOLENCE *n.* ill will.

MIFF *n.* a petty quarrel; tiff.

Militate

NIPPY *adj.* biting.

OFFENSE *n.* a hurt or damage; act of attack or assault; breach of conduct or law.

Opprobrium

PASSION *n.* a violent or intense emotion, for example, rage or wrath, lust, deep love or zeal.

Philippic, Tirade, Diatribe

PIQUE *n.* an offense taken by one slighted. *v.* to nettle or offend by slighting.

Pugnacity & Antagonism

Quarrel & Querulous

Querulous see **Quarrel & Querulous**

RAGE *n.* anger accompanied with raving; fit of fury.

RANCOR *n.* vehement ill will; intense spite.

Recalcitrant & Intransigent

REPUGNANCE *n.* deep rooted antagonism; aversion, antipathy.

RESENTMENT *n.* indignation because of a wrong or insult.

Retort

Revenge see Avenge & Revenge
Sneer see Leer & Sneer
STRIFE *n.* altercation; conflict; fight; contest for superiority.
SURLY *adj.* ill-natured; abrupt; rude; cross.
TANTRUM *n.* a fit of ill temper.
Thwart
TIFF *n.* a slight fit of anger; a petty quarrel.

Tirade see **Philippic, Tirade**, etc.
UMBRAGE *n.* offense or resentment.
VEXATION *n.* trouble; irritation; state of annoyance or anger.
VIRULENCE *n.* bitter enmity; malignity.
Vituperation see **Diatribe, Invective**, etc.
Wrath see **Anger & Wrath**

Acrimonious Perhaps the best of our adjectives for 'sharpness, bitingness, extreme tartness' of a person's manner or disposition. It combines the qualities of two small companion words, 'acerb' (soft 'c') and 'acrid' (hard 'c'). All three words derive from the Latin *acer*, 'sharp, fierce, piercing.' Acerb means sour and astringent; acrid means sharp and cutting (or burning). ACRIMONIOUS—a bigger word packed with more meaning—suggests also a note of 'human bitterness.' It suggests, besides sharpness, the bite of a sarcastic temper and the corrosion of a sullen mood. Unlike its two small companion words, ACRIMONIOUS can modify only persons.

Altercation and **Dispute** You can ALTERCATE probably more easily than you can DISPUTE since to DISPUTE always requires some mind-work while to ALTERCATE is only 'to bicker, to accuse back-and-forth, to quarrel thoughtlessly.' When a debate, for example, grows angry, and points are wrangled over rather than reasoned through, it is no longer a debate, nor even a DISPUTE. To DISPUTE is 'to reckon' or 'to reason,' often in a contentious and aggressive way. But DISPUTE, no matter how heated or biased it may be, is always of the mind. The main idea in ALTERCATION is simply that of 'taking turns,' like in the word 'alternate.' The beauty of ALTERCATION is in its rhythm, which suggests the bandying back and forth of words. "He blocked the whole road and I stepped over to his car to tell him so. Quite an altercation followed." We might more often say, "Quite an argument followed." But in this case 'argument' is probably not as precise a word as ALTERCATION. 'Argument,' like DISPUTE, suggests some mind-work. 'Argument' is often used to indicate the persuasive content of an essay or an editorial.

Anger and **Wrath** WRATH suggests a blast or, the old meaning of blast, a blowing; but ANGER means something harder, deeper, fiercer—a clangor, almost, of hard hate. WRATH, like the wind, may blow beyond you and be gone. But ANGER is poised, with a throaty yet metallic growl, to crush you and to hold you beneath its weight until you are dead. An ANGRY sea smashes and sinks the ships which a wild or rough sea only buffets or flings upon a shore. An ANGRY sore in your body festers until it devours you. ANGER swells from the depths of a man and is lasting. WRATH flashes quickly from a man's mind or emotions, and may soon pass.

In the Old Norse, ANGER means 'trouble,' and in Chaucer's day 'affliction.' ANGER is the steadier and deeper word. WRATH is authentic Anglo-Saxon and it means ANGER in the hostile sense. WRATH stems from the root of 'wroth,' which in the Anglo-Saxon is a form of the verb meaning 'writhe' or 'twist.' The force of your hostility makes your enemy writhe, or perhaps in your excitement you writhed yourself.

It is perhaps a good practice that we say so often "That makes me mad," or "He was mad at me," presumably reserving such deeper or more stirring adjectives as ANGRY, 'furious' and 'infuriated' for really important occasions. Incidentally, 'to be angry *at*' refers to the *reason* for your ANGER: "I was angry at all the delay that might be costing lives." But 'to be angry *with*' refers to the *object* of ANGER: "I was so angry with him I couldn't see straight!"

Assailant and **Aggressor**   Today we have come to know AGGRESSOR too well and we have too many occasions to use it with its fullest implications. Our Victorian grandparents probably used it sparingly in polite references to thugs and holdup men. For us it now intimates war and signifies how most of our big troubles begin. ASSAILANT, and especially its verb, to ASSAIL, are softer words and less used. They are expressive. To ASSAIL suggests the expression "I sailed right into him," which implies high courage and lofty purpose but which does not convey blood and thunder. There is, therefore, a certain insouciance in to ASSAIL; its soft sounds are not misplaced.

You do not admit that your ASSAILANT in a dark and narrow thoroughfare subdued you. He did sail into you, it is true; but whether or not he knocked you down and captured your purse is not implied or stated. Had he *assaulted* you, the story would be blunter. Had he *attacked* you, it would be sharper. 'Assault' suggests both 'insult' and 'injury,' perhaps 'slaughter.' 'Attack' indicates 'suddenness,' and you are thrown back astoundedly on your heels. Each word has its implications of your discomfiture. But if you are ASSAILED, there is nothing to show your defeat. To ASSAIL is simply 'to essay, to attempt a conquest with vigor and élan.'

Avenge and **Revenge** Melodious words that ring softly with anger. Grammatically, REVENGE is the intensive of AVENGE, or rather the iterative, as 'reiterate' is of 'iterate.'

They are cousins of our verb 'to vindicate,' which means that one 'defends,' rather than 'destroys,' an object of blame or suspicion. The originator of all three words was the Roman *vindex*, 'righter of wrongs.' The verb deriving from *vindex* took on all the meanings that could arise from the righting of a wrong: 'to defend,' hence 'to preserve or restore'; 'to free, save or deliver from danger or wrong'; 'to maintain,' and before that 'to lay claim to'; 'to excuse' and 'to vindicate' but also 'to punish'; finally 'to avenge, revenge.' Nevertheless the idea of 'redressing a wrong,' rather than 'satisfying a hatred' dominated these meanings. Today even an avenger in a blood feud has, or feels he has, a clear conscience since he is vindicating his own honor, or his clan's honor, or a wronged friend.

In usage there are two sharp distinctions between AVENGE and REVENGE not always observed even by the best speakers. AVENGE means 'one's vindication of someone else's wrong.' REVENGE is 'one's vindication of one's own wrong.' This distinction was recognized when we derived from 'vindicative' (the adjective for 'vindicate') a new adjective, 'vindictive.' 'Vindictive' has invariably a grim meaning suggesting personal retaliation. A 'vindictive' action is essentially REVENGEFUL though sometimes 'vindictive' is used impersonally, e.g., a vindictive fate. 'Vindicative' action, on the other hand, describes the action of the AVENGER, who wishes to see justice done.

With two words so similar we expect their meanings to become to some extent reciprocal. We expect REVENGE should seem sometimes righteous, or an AVENGE often less than ideal. It is possible to be more unjust or bloodthirsty in AVENGING the death of a friend than in taking REVENGE for a personal wrong.

There is in REVENGE a strong suggestion of 'retaliation.' Just as wars are sometimes said to have no excuse, so REVENGE connotes the wreaking of vengeance for its own sake. 'Vengence,' itself, from Tudor times on, has identified itself in colloquial phrases with the horror of plagues and poxes. It has no relation to justice. As for AVENGE it is good that we have it. It is good to have a word that suggests the freeing of a friend from blame or unjust wrong.

Bellicose and **Belligerent** Both of these adjectives derive their warlike meaning from Latin *bellum*, 'war.' BELLIGERENT usually implies actual participation in hostilities, or an actively hostile frame of mind.

BELLICOSE suggests a constant readiness or willingness to fight or to stir up a fight, and it is more often applied to a mood or temper. A soldier is a BELLIGERENT man; a baseball fan who loudly protests an umpire's decision is a BELLICOSE man.

Deprecate, Depreciate, and **Deplore**   DEPLORE means 'to bewail'; DEPRECATE means 'to pray away or against.' DEPLORE is an earnest and a strong word. When you DEPLORE something you really pour out your grief or your regret about it. But DEPRECATE is a more useful word because it has no good synonym. You can pray *for* rain or good fortune, but when you beg or plead for something *not* to happen, or for someone *not* to do something, you DEPRECATE the event or the act. When you DEPRECATE an evil you strongly want deliverance from it, and you also express disapproval of it. When you DEPLORE an evil you are telling the world how bad it really is in the hope you can avert or deter it.

The words DEPRECATE, DEPRECATORY, and DEPRECATIVE are often confused with DEPRECIATE, DEPRECIATORY, and DEPRECIATIVE. To DEPRECIATE means 'to disparage' or 'to belittle' someone or something. A truck DEPRECIATES, or loses value, when it is parked continually in an open lot.

Detest, Despise, Abhor, Loath, and **Hate**   Let us see how these five old stand-bys can serve to express our dislikes effectively. First of all, what is HATE? It is the old Anglo-Saxon word for the fierce dislike which is 'malignity.' HATE is a rudimentary word, too strong for mere sniping and lampooning. DETEST, ABHOR, and LOATH convey in part HATE. DESPISE may be free of HATE. (DESTEST, DESPISE and ABHOR are all Roman.) DETEST originally meant a 'calling on the gods to witness against someone.' To DETEST is now 'to dislike intensely, to hate intensely.' A DESPISER originally looked down his nose at you (*de* for 'down,' *spectare* for 'to look'). He now regards you as contemptible, and scorns and disdains you. So does the ABHORER, but in doing so he also HATES you. ABHOR has a suggestion of repugnance (*ab* for 'from,' *horrere* for 'to shrink'). The first LOATHER was an Anglo-Saxon HATER. But now he regards you with mingled HATRED and 'disgust.'

Diatribe, Invective, and **Vituperation**   A DIATRIBE is a 'protracted scolding.' It is Greek for 'a wearing away, a rubbing in of abuse'—abrasive verbal abuse, as it were. Today DIATRIBE is even rougher, more a knocking and a tearing. 'To INVEIGH against' is 'to launch a verbal assault' or 'to assail with words.' You may be vehement and even abusive with this INVECTIVE; but when you become vicious or defamatory, and extremely personal, you are descending to VITUPERATION.

VITUPERATION is 'excoriating,' and especially aimed at all tender spots where the skin is thin and easily scored off. It is 'raillery directed against the faults of a single individual.' In other words, VITUPERATION is a meanly calculated and viciously vulgar form of abuse, reserved especially for persons—and persons only—who rile you.

Enmity and **Inimicalness** ENMITY is your state of being if you are INIMICAL to someone or to someone's ideas or actions. It would therefore be synonymous with INIMICALNESS except that it acquired more force somewhere in its evolution. INIMICAL is a rather weak negative of 'friendly.' The Latin *amicus*, 'friendly,' with a negative prefix, produced it. ENMITY, with the same origin but a more various history, has more character. It grew from the original *inimicus* to *inimicitia*, and then gathered strength and sound as it drew itself together into ENMITY. We can say it is a 'dignified or formal kind of animosity.' But where animosity is spiteful, ENMITY is broad and perhaps grim. It also cuts deeper than animosity. But notwithstanding its formal uses and, in fact, by virtue of its formal flavor we often use the word playfully. The ENMITY existing between gridiron rivals is a favorite theme of sports writers.

Expostulate A useful word with a delicately balanced multiple meaning. Its emphasis may be shifted according to the situation. When you EXPOSTULATE with a friend your discussion and arguments are designed to make him understand and correct his errors. If your friend looks kindly on your good offices, then your EXPOSTULATION approaches mere remonstrance or complaint. But if your friend continues stubbornly in his errors, your EXPOSTULATION is likely to veer towards exasperation or vehemence.

Flaunt and **Flout** Truly a treacherous pair. Each is constantly inveigling us into using it for the other. This is because the two can approach each other in meaning; but they are never one and the same.

FLOUT is probably Dutch and meant merely 'to play the flute.' How flute-playing, unless it was impudently done, became synonymous with 'jeering' has not been exactly explained. But FLOUTING now means 'to mock, to insult,' or 'to fly obnoxiously in the face of.' FLAUNT is probably Swedish, and at first meant 'to waver.' To FLAUNT has now come to mean 'to wave,' as to wave a banner. If you wave a red flag in a bull's face, you are FLOUTING or insulting the bull. That is one way the two words approach each other.

But FLOUTING has less to do with what you say or do than with your manner or attitude. If you FLOUT either someone's opinion or the person himself, you are showing your contempt for it or him in an openly insolent manner. You are, in fact, provocative, as the matador provokes the bull. In this way FLOUTING also approaches 'taunting.' And if the bull were to think that the matador was impudent, or was conceited and making a show of himself, it might say: "That man is flaunting that rag in my face just to flout me." FLAUNTING is never a mere waving but is always an ostentatious and often an impudent display. A FLAUNTING of something is like vaunting one's self.

When we simply FLAUNT (used intransitively) we make a vulgar showing as publicly as we can of ourselves or of our possessions. This FLAUNTING is another way of FLOUTING something, in this case the feelings of persons of good taste. We can also just FLOUT (used intransitively); that is, simply sneer or fleer without FLAUNTING anything, unless it be, figuratively, our insolence.

Lampoon A literary word meaning a written satire designed expressly to bring down ridicule upon someone you are 'against'; it is also used as a verb, as to LAMPOON someone. The classical examples are found in Italian history. In Rome there was a statue on which anonymous and often nastily satirical papers were posted as publicly as ads are nowadays plastered on the walls of subway platforms. Since the statue, after it was unearthed in probably Columbus' day, was set up in a square near Pasquino's tailor shop, the French today call such LAMPOONS *pasquinades*. This French word is sometimes used in English. The French also gave us the word LAMPOON for the same literary ribaldry. LAMPOON once meant a certain drinking song because the refrain in that song was *lampons*, 'let's drink.' The verb *lamper* means actually 'to guzzle.' Evidently, the song was a rabid slam at some other fellows not of the party. At any rate, we have from it an excellent word.

Leer and Sneer The dictionaries tell you that a SNEER is supercilious while a 'taunt' is defiant and a 'scoff' is, of course, just scurrilous, as against things that should be respected. It has been said that nothing can refute a SNEER. Perhaps that is because a SNEER is historically (in the Dutch) a 'snarl,' and sometimes the better part of verbal valor is silence. SNEERS are not, however, only implied and silent snarls but are also covert and cowardly attacks. In a SNEER the mouth apes a silent, LEERING expression, copying its sly and mean maliciousness.

LEERS were once cheeks, in Saxon England, and they engendered a verb meaning 'to look askance.' Possibly the cheeks were in profile, as of a thwarted and resentful person looking back at you obliquely, saying "Just you wait!" At any rate the idea was graphic and undoubtedly it later colored our dialectal adjective 'leary,' though 'leary,' being connected with learning, originally meant 'clever.' But LEERS which were cheeks also referred in due course to complexion. From complexion LEER extended its meaning to describe the whole face. And in such a way a LEER retreated eventually to the eyes. LEER became bold and amorous. Today instead of being sidelong and swift, a LEER is more often insolent and lustful.

Militate MILITATE is an intransitive verb meaning simply 'to fight' or 'to have influence.' But that doesn't limit its usefulness. You can add 'against' and then you can fight or influence whatever opposes you. The early suffragettes MILITATED against oppressive conceptions of women's rights, and they were called MILITANTS. MILITANCY is found in all societies and ranks, from school children with antipathies to Latin to gloom-oppressed miners in coalpits. On one hand, MILITANCY of the present against the past is perpetual; on the other, conservatism MILITATES forever against innovations and reform.

Opprobrium An antonym for 'encomium (praise).' 'Disgrace' is the central idea in OPPROBRIUM. If you heap OPPROBRIUM on someone you reproach him to the point of abuse, you disdain him too intensely to remain silent, and your contempt colors and completes your recriminations. If it is heaped on you, you are in OPPROBRIUM—in 'ignominy' or 'disgrace.' Usually, and more broadly, it is that which most often causes disgrace—'public scorn.'

Philippic, Tirade, and **Diatribe** PHILIPPICS are eponymous of Philip of Macedon, but most unflatteringly so. Demosthenes, the Greek orator, declaimed the first PHILIPPIC. Fearing Philip's invasion of Greece, he spoke to rouse the Athenians. He stirred them by excoriating (literally, 'taking the skin off') Philip. In fact, he did it three times in three bitter and inflammatory speeches, or PHILIPPICS.

Each to a certain degree was a DIATRIBE, none was a mere TIRADE. DIATRIBES and TIRADES are lengthy. DIATRIBES, while professing to be critical, are often malicious to the point of abuse. TIRADES are the tireless and vulgar abuse of irate persons who hold grievances or grudges. Both seek to wear someone down with a torrent of words, harsh in the one case and miscellaneous or mean in the other. DIATRIBE comes from the Greek verb 'to rub away, waste.' The noun was a 'wearing away, a waste of time, even a pleasant pastime.' The beginnings of TIRADE are also deceptive. When you retire to the quiet of your bed you draw yourself back from the day's activity. From the French derivative *tirer*, 'to pull,' came TIRADE. In Italy, from the pulling of a bow-string or trigger which releases an arrow, this pulling became a shot, then a volley. In France, the word came suggestively to mean a 'continued blasting with words'—a TIRADE.

Pugnacity and **Antagonism** PUGNACITY is a combination of 'impudence, self-assertiveness, impulsive enterprise, love of excitement, war-likeness.' Professional soldiers and pugilists are seldom PUGNACIOUS. Fighting is their business, not their personal pleasure or recreation. A PUGNACIOUS person is not necessarily ANTAGONISTIC in a broad sense. Anyone will resent being baited though he may be riled reluctantly by an impulsive person who likes arguments and fist fights for the excitement in them. But ANTAGONISM implies scheming. It goes about making you mad under your skin. It may employ propaganda. It may instigate devious hostilities. If you are ANTAGONISTIC to, let us say, some business project, you are not merely averse to it or reluctant to support it. You are *against* it, you will fight it down, and you may ANTAGONIZE its defenders by your beliefs.

Quarrel and **Querulous** Certainly QUARREL requires today no defining; but its origin and development cast an interesting light on its character. It may take two to make a QUARREL but, historically, both must be QUERULOUS—that is, 'quarrelsome,' in that word's original sense. The Latin word *queri* means 'to complain' as well as 'to bewail, lament.' The Latin adjective *querulus* produced our present adjective QUERULOUS, meaning 'fretfully disposed to find fault.' At one time QUERULOUS also had the quite contrary meanings of 'chirping, warbling, even cooing'—adjectives have always been notoriously free in their habits. The Latin noun *querela* had no such soft meanings. It originally meant a 'complaint,' but soon came to mean also an 'accusation.' This Latin *querela* produced our forceful word QUARREL. And though it may take at least two to make a QUARREL, presumably one of them must commence it—unless it is a case of QUARREL at first sight, and both accuse simultaneously.

Recalcitrant and **Intransigent** RECALCITRANT is pure Latin (*re* plus *calcitrare*) for 'kicking back or backwards.' INTRANSIGENT is Latin too, for 'not coming to an agreement'; but it was sharpened and given a specific meaning in Spain where it was applied to extreme Republicans, and later in France it was modified again before it came to us. Now INTRANSIGENT means 'uncompromisingly unreconcilable.' It is still chiefly a political word applied especially to extreme or radical parties.

Naturally, anyone who is INTRANSIGENT and doesn't conform to ideas that many other people regard as important is likely to be RECALCITRANT too. But a youngster desperately objecting to a return to school in the fall is more likely to be called RECALCITRANT than INTRANSIGENT. The latter word is the more grandiose, and its emphasis is less on kicks and squawks than on "Give-me-liberty-or-give-me-death." Patrick Henry, from the British viewpoint, was also INTRANSIGENT. Besides, the RE-CALCITRANT objector is usually opposed to some specific proposal while the INTRANSIGENT person rebels against a cause, a policy, or a course of events.

Retort A reply in kind. You can imagine the report and counter report of two pistols. A rebuttal is an argumentative RETORT, that is, it tries to refute. But a RETORT need *not* be a rebuttal. It may be only an insult presumably answering an insult.

Thwart Kind of a tongue-twister, this, but as effective as a 'road-block.' And that is what THWART really is—to put something 'athwart' or 'across' another fellow's path. It comes to us from Iceland where ice ridges probably THWARTED the first colonists.

ANIMALS

AMPHIBIUM *n.* an animal living both on land and in water, though not able to breath under water, such as a frog, turtle, crocodile, seal. *pl.* AMPHIBIA. *adj.* AMPHIBIAN or AMPHIBIOUS. The *sing. n.* is sometimes spelled AMPHIBIAN.

ANTHROPOID *adj.* manlike; human or simian in a zoological sense; *n.* an anthropoid ape or similar Primate.

BEAST *n.* a living being; an animal, esp. any four-footed animal as distinguished from fowls, insects, fishes and man. Applied chiefly to large animals.

Behemoth, Mastodon, Mammoth

BOVINE *adj.* pertaining or belonging to oxen or cows; hence, ox-like, stolid, inert, dull.

BRUTE *n.* a beast, esp. one of the higher quadrupeds.

CARNIVOROUS *adj.* eating or subsisting on flesh, as "The tiger is a carnivorous animal."

DINOSAUR *n.* one of a group of extinct gigantic reptiles. DINO-SAUR comes from the Greek for terrible or mighty lizard.

Dromedary

EQUINE *adj.* of or pertaining to or resembling a horse.

FELINE *adj.* catlike in form and structure. *n.* in popular usage, a house cat.

Gavials

HERBIVOROUS *adj.* herb or grass eating, as distinguished from carnivorous.

INVERTEBRATE *adj.* not vertebrate, having no backbone; hence, *n.* an animal with no backbone, like an amoeba.

KINE *n.* plural of cow. Often seen in print though it is an archaic word.

MAMMAL *n.* an animal which suckles its young; the highest class of vertebrates, in which man is included.

Mammoth see **Behemoth, Mastodon,** etc.

Mastiff

Mastodon see **Behemoth, Mastodon,** etc.

Mongrel

Monkey

MONSTER *n.* any very large animal. *adj.* MONSTROUS, unnatural, and usually large, as a MONSTROUS tree.

ONTOGENY *n.* the life history or development of any single organism.

PHYLOGENY *n.* the ancestral history of any type of organism. It considers in part the evolution of a type of animal or plant.

Poodle

PRIMATES *n. pl.* the first and highest order of mammals, including man, monkeys and lemurs.

QUADRUPED *n. & adj.* four-footed [animal], as distinguished from biped, like man or a bird.

REPTILIAN *adj.* of or pertaining to a reptile, which is a creeping animal, one that goes on its belly or on small, short legs.

RODENT *n.* one of the gnawing animals that possess large, strong incisor teeth, like the rat, mouse, rabbit and squirrel.

SERPENTINE *adj.* of or pertaining to serpents or snakes; thus, twisting and turning.

SIMIAN *adj.* like an ape or monkey. *n.* an ape or monkey of any kind.

Spaniel

Terrier

VERTEBRATE *n. & adj.* possessing backbone, like a dog or man. *n.* such an animal.

ZOOLOGY *n.* the science which studies animals.

ENTOMOLOGY *n.* the branch of zoology that treats of insects.

HELMINTHOLOGY *n.* the study of worms, esp. parasitic worms.

HERPETOLOGY *n.* the branch of zoology which treats of reptiles and amphibians, like snakes, lizards, frogs.

ICHTHYOLOGY *n.* the branch of zoology which treats of fishes.

MALACOLOGY *n.* the branch of zoology which treats of mollusks.

MAMMALOGY *n.* the branch of zoology which deals with mammals.

OPHIOLOGY *n.* the branch of zoology which deals with snakes or serpents.

PROTOZOOLOGY *n.* the study of protozoa, mostly microscopic one-celled animals.

TAXONOMY *n.* the science of classification, esp. of animals and plants.

ZOOGRAPHY *n.* the description of animals, their habits and form.

ZOOTOMY *n.* the science which treats of the anatomy of animals.

Behemoth, Mastodon, Mammoth (1) A colossal Biblical beast, probably a hippopotamus. (2) A gigantic elephant-like animal now long extinct, but plentiful in America during the Miocene and Pliocene ages. (3) A similar extinct beast, with two tremendous curled tusks, whose bodies are still found in northern Asia, frozen in the ground and still edible after eons. The name comes from the Russian.

Dromedary A one-humped camel. The name is Greek for 'running.'

Gavials The great Indian crocodiles. Their jaws are unusually long and slim, and one has a nob on it.

Mastiff Large dogs, looking like bulldog-ized great Danes, as popular in the '90's as cocker spaniels are now. To the medieval French a MASTIFF was a mongrel. But he lived to lord it over dog shows, and like the last Mohican, his luster was brightest before his extinction.

Mongrel The word was applied first to dogs by the uneducated fellow. There was in Old English a common word *mong*, a 'mixture,' which occurred in various forms, including *gemong*, now our 'among.' Some people think the first MONGREL was a *small* mixed-breed dog, but others think he was a *miserably* mixed-breed dog from the start. That is, the suffix 'el' might have been a diminutive, as in 'pickerel,' a 'little pike'; or it might have been depreciatory, like the 'el' in 'wastrel' and the 'ard' in 'drunkard.'

Monkey An excellent example of how animals, especially those closely associated with humans, have enlivened our vocabularies. There are some curious facts about this word's relationship with English and American English.

It was inevitable that animals like the simians, that seem to caricature people, should give us words. At first soubriquets, these words soon graduated to more general use. But the simians do not come from England or even Europe. How and when 'ape' got into our language has never been explained. Probably the children of the Anglo-Saxons were sometimes chided for 'aping' their elders since the early English had the word *apa*, 'ape.' Where the exact word MONKEY originated is doubtful, but it owes its present expressive usage to America.

Very occasionally we use MONKEY in the sense of 'aping' or 'imitating,' but the bigger animal is too well established in the verb 'to ape' to be pushed out by the smaller. By its nature MONKEY is more suited to the sense we give it. Its meddlesome and humorously inquisitive activity, as when we MONKEY with delicate machinery, or just MONKEY around, fit our idea of the animal. In fairness to the word's history, we should remember that even in Medieval Europe its imagery was appreciated. One version of its origin has it as a diminutive of *monna*, a popular contraction of *madonna*, 'my lady.' Thus MONKEYS and women were compared. Another version has it, in the north, as *moneke*, probably meaning the son of Martin. Animals were often given such names in folk-tales. Note, for example, *Renard le goupil*. *Renard* is now the standard French word for 'fox,' but *goupil* is forgotten. Since MONKEY cannot help being an expressive word, it will probably always belong to our everyday speech.

Poodle German, from *pudel*, 'puddle.' POODLES were sporting dogs in Germany. They can thank the court ladies of France for their social status.

Spaniel From the old French *Espanol*, 'Spaniard.' Spain is their mother country.

Terrier His derivation is interesting. Ancient Frenchmen adopted the low Latin *terrarius* for his name because it meant 'of the earth.' Fox TERRIERS were once used to follow the fox where the hounds couldn't—into his hole—when he had been run to earth, as the saying goes.

AREAS AND MEASUREMENTS

Acre see **Hectare, Are, etc.**

AMPLITUDE *n.* fullness; width; extent.

Are see **Hectare, Are, etc.**

AREA *n.* any open, though usually bounded, space. *adj.* AREAL.

ARENA *n.* an amphitheater; esp. the portion of ground where the contests take place.

BELT *n.* a zone; a long strip of land distinguished for a particular characteristic, as the cotton BELT; a looping route.

COMPASS *n.* area; space within bounds; scope.

COUNTRY *n.* a regional or national designation, as "The United States is a country," or "The country in New England is rocky."

Cubit see **Fathom, Cubit, etc.**

Diminish & Lessen

DISTRICT *n.* part of a territory, carefully bounded and usually designated for administrative purposes.

DOMAIN *n.* a district or territory considered as a possession, as "The farmer's domain extended from river to river."

Ell see **Fathom, Cubit, etc.**

Extension

EXTENT *n.* the reach of an area; scope; length; etc. *adj.* EXTENSIVE, pertaining to EXTENT; broad, distant. See also **Extension.**

Farther see **Further & Farther**

Fathom, Cubit & Ell

FIELD *n.* a section of cleared land, esp. an area used for pasture or tillage.

Further & Farther

GROUND *n.* a particular piece of land, as the rocky GROUND of Tulliver's farm.

Hectare, Are, Stere & Acre

HORIZON *n.* the visible boundary between earth and sky.

KEN *n.* view; esp. the extent of sight permitted by the nature of the land.

Knot see **Parasang & Knot**

LENGTH *n.* the extent of anything measured from end to end.

Lessen see **Diminish & Lessen**

Little

LOCALITY *n.* a region; a small sized part of a country; spot; as the LOCALITY for blueberries.

Long

MAGNITUDE *n.* size; extent.

NEIGHBORHOOD *n.* vicinity; the area close or about one or several things, as in the NEIGHBORHOOD by the oak tree.

Parasang & Knot

PATCH *n.* a very small field used for cultivation, as the vegetable PATCH.

PLOT *n.* a patch; a small piece of land, esp. one of only sufficient size for a house or grave.

PRECINCT *n.* usually a walled or fenced area that surrounds a building, as the PRECINCT of the parsonage.

PROVINCE *n.* a region of a country designated for administrative purpose, as the PROVINCES of Canada.

Purview

RADIUS *n.* any circular area; thus, the extent or range of operations, as "The hunters covered a radius of about five miles."

RANGE *n.* compass; scope; the reach of one's operations, as the RANGE of the local police.

REACH *n.* the extent or scope of anything.

REALM *n.* domain.

REGION *n.* any territory usually with carefully fixed boundaries. *adj.* REGIONAL.

SCOPE *n.* ken; range; field of one's activities, as "The scope of our patrol mission was limited to a square mile."

SECTION *n.* a district of one mile square. *adj.* SECTIONAL.

SPACIAL or SPATIAL *adj.* pertaining to space.

SPAN *n.* a short distance of space.

SPHERE *n.* the globe; a field of activity.

Stere see **Hectare, Are,** etc.

STRETCH *n.* a reach or extent of land, as "That stretch of marsh

over there is dangerous to cross."

SWEEP *n.* an extent or continuous stretch of land.

TERRITORY *n.* a section of land usually belonging to one jurisdiction.

TRACT *n.* a piece of land; a stretch.

VICINITY *n.* neighborhood.

ZONE *n.* belt.

Diminish and Lessen DIMINISH and DIMINISHMENT are euphonious words which fill a need. So too are their shorter synonyms, LESSEN and LESSENING. But brevity is often unsatisfying and sometimes crude, especially as short words are usually common and colloquial. Longer words are capable of more accentuation. Compare "What to my surprise," with "What to my astonishment." Note the inevitable emphasis on 'ton' and consequently on the speaker's emotion. Compare "The lessening of our pain," to "The diminishment of our anxiety." The meaning lingers in the longer word, and it matches 'anxiety' which is slow and continuous compared to 'pain.' The sound of DIMINISHMENT is almost stately, as with measured steps. There is also the suggestion of a musical diminuendo and of an impending vanishment.

Though DIMINISH meant exactly LESSEN from its start—*de,* 'from,' plus *minus,* 'less'—it has outgrown the shorter word in connotations. Today DIMINISH can mean 'to belittle' and even 'to degrade.' A man is DIMINISHED in our eyes when he loses standing or respect. Unlike LESSEN, DIMINISH can suggest 'shrinkage' rather than a simple 'waning' of force or effect. Our holdings in stocks and bonds DIMINISH rather than LESSEN. Areas as well as volumes DIMINISH rather than LESSEN. The number of your dollars may LESSEN but your wealth DIMINISHES.

Extension We do not remember all figurative uses of words, however picturesque or striking. The word EXTENSION is an example. If we forget its strictly linear meaning, we find EXTENSION useful to express almost any 'furtherance' or 'enlargement.'

For example, "The problem of worker efficiency in a large factory may be simply seen in the extension of the personnel problems in a small shop." Or, "The extension of the President's remarks today lead logically to a declaration of peace."

Fathom, Cubit, and Ell A FATHOM has a foot for each of its letters. It is a measure six feet long. A CUBIT (from elbow to end of middle finger) is now a foot and a half, though the Roman CUBIT was an inch less and the ancient Jewish and Egyptian CUBIT was twenty inches. An ELL, however, is forty-five inches (in Flanders twenty-seven inches). It is an obsolescent cloth measure.

Further and Farther FURTHER is the figurative form of FARTHER. You approach FARTHER toward New York, but you approach FURTHER toward the point of your argument.

Hectare, Are, Stere, and Acre A HECTARE is an Asian and East European metric land measure equal to 2.471 acres. An AR or ARE is an old land measure coming to us via the French from the Latin word *area*, 'area,' and equivalent to about $\frac{1}{40}$th of an ACRE. An ACRE, from Latin *acer*, 'field,' is about seventy yards square, or about 4900 square yards. It is about the size of a small city block. A God's ACRE is a grave-yard. STERE, meaning 'solid' in Greek, comes via France, and is either one cubic metre (a metre is about thirty-nine inches) or 1000 litres.

Little There is a colloquialism, a 'big little man,' which has immense implications. For while LITTLE is one of our commonest diminutives, it is also one of the most adaptive of them all. A man who is LITTLE need not be small in size. Likewise, do we not sometimes say, "I love him not a little," in which LITTLE helps us avoid committing ourselves to a 'very' or 'much'? Or, 'my poor little friend,' whose smallness may not be physical at all but just some lack of show, of selfishness or of assertiveness that endears him to us? Or, "Little did I think (not at all did I think) that you would be there," with LITTLE obliterating its own meaning so that we might have an attractive absolute for negation?

LITTLE is active as an adjective or adverb. It can express size, amount, number and degree. It can shuffle its meanings with dexterity. "This daredevil thought little of risking his neck"; nevertheless, he probably thought LITTLE (had no high opinion of) having his neck broken. And a man can be LITTLE not only when he is small ('miserly, mean'), but also when he is spiritually shrunk in any way. You can be LITTLE about something which requires, really, magnanimity. This is quite different from being merely LITTLE in importance. When we ask for a LITTLE of that grape salad, LITTLE even becomes a noun.

LITTLE is so alert we can hardly blame ourselves for using it too much. But we do use it too much. After all, there are other words that deftly particularize a reference to size and importance. There is 'trivial,' for example, meaning 'small' in the same sense as 'gossip' is small. Trivial is 'of no estimation,' coming from the 'crossroads,' *tri viae*, where everybody met, mingled and gabbled. There is 'petite' which, as only the French can express it, says 'little and dainty.' There is 'diminutive,' suggesting 'comparison, relativity.' There is Scotch 'wee,' a playful intensive, and its south-of-Ireland variant, 'weeny.' There is 'tiny,' once followed always by LITTLE and meaning 'small in quantity'; but now, like the Scotch 'a bit laddie,' it means 'small in size.' There is 'minute,' which is the scientist's word for the child's 'tiny (very small).' There is 'miniature,' denoting something done on a 'small scale.' Finally, and always, there is 'small.' 'Small' is more concerned than LITTLE with lack of size, the plain and the paltry. Louisa Alcott wrote of LITTLE women, and not of 'small women.' A LITTLE learning is a dangerous thing, but still it's a more intimate thing than the 'small knowledge' of which pedants, rehearsing the age of Johnson and Pope, still speak.

Long This word stems with almost its full force from the Old English adjective *lang*, or 'LONG.' We use it now not only as an adjective but also as a noun, verb, adverb and even conjunction. But these latter usages are either elliptical or parings-down of earlier elaborations of the old form. For example, the Anglo-Saxons themselves had *lange* for the adverb and *langian*, to 'seem long to,' and hence to 'yearn for,' as the verb. Our noun, as in 'the LONG and the short of it,' is simply an adjective substituting for a qualified noun. The true noun for LONG is, of course, 'length.' The present abverb, as in 'long before this,' 'stay too long,' and 'all my life long,' is merely a paring-down of, and internal tinkering with, the old *lange*, though it may be, as in 'all my life long,' aphetic for 'along,' which the Old English had as *gelang*. 'Longshoreman,' for example, was originally 'alongshoreman.' The conjunctional usage is now rare, being confined usually to certain regions. This use includes a tagging preposition, 'of'; "Along of this (or simply, 'long of this') I would like to say. . . ," that is, "In connection with, or on account of this, I would like to say . . ."

LONG's flexibility is shown in its compounds. In 'long-suffering' LONG is clearly an adverb in an adjectival compound. Though we have a comparable compound in 'long-drawn,' we seldom use that one without adding 'out' to it. In 'long-winded' LONG is vaguely adverbial, referring first to lineal and then to temporal length. But in 'long-headed' it takes us back to the very beginning of itself, before even Latin *longus* that preceded English *lang*. There we find the true root, a lumpish *dlongho,* an element of many early words. It appears in Greek *dolichos,* whence our 'dolichocephalic' (long-headed), referring to the skull. But in *dlongho* there was peculiarly a sense of 'slowness'; through the noun 'length,' this slowness may have descended both to 'lenten,' to indicate the spring of the year when the days are slowly growing longer, and to 'lentamente (slowly),' a musical term. So also the 'longheaded' man is deliberative; he is the opposite of 'headlong.' 'Headlong' has nothing to do with length. Its LONG was originally an adverbial suffix, *ling,* indicating 'direction' or 'condition,' as in 'darkling.' Thus 'headlong' meant 'headfirst.' The 'longheaded' man compares with the levelheaded man, well-balanced and of sound judgment.

LONG is deeply expressive. Even the broken English expression, "Long time, no see," conveys the idea of waiting, and perhaps of longing. And one philologist in particular has pointed out the poignant difference, to us, between a 'longing' (English) and a 'desiring' (Latin). The deep expression in LONG may somehow derive from its ultimate source, which has not yet been fully traced. Incidentally, the Latin *longus* and the English LONG are simply cognates. Somewhere there is a common source for the both of them.

Parasang and **Knot** A PARASANG is a Persian and Turkish 'road measure,' usually about four miles, though it differs with localities and has changed with time. A Chinese mile is a *li,* about equal to ⅝ of a mile, or a kilometre. The Japanese marine 'mile' is a *ri.* Our own marine mile is a KNOT, almost exactly 800 feet longer than the land mile. But only landlubbers speak of the KNOT as a measure of distance. To seafarers it is a rate of speed.

Purview PURVIEW is the sphere or scope of an extensive and exalted point of view, as the PURVIEW of a history book, of law or of philosophy.

ASSEMBLAGE AND DISPERSION

ACCUMULATION *n.* an amassing; a collecting together; growth by continuous additions. *v.* ACCUMULATE, to heap up; to collect or bring together.

AGGREGATION *n.* the act of collecting or the state of being collected into an unorganized whole; a combined whole.

AMASSMENT *n.* a collection of individuals or things. See also Assemble, Collect, etc.

Assemble, Collect, Collate, Compile

ASSORTMENT *n.* a collection of things assembled according to some definition, as distinguished from an aggregation.

Cluster   see **Clutter, Cluster, etc.**

Clutter, Cluster & Huddle

Collate   see **Assemble, Collect, etc.**

Collect   see **Assemble, Collect, etc.**

Compile   see **Assemble, Collect, etc.**

Comprehend   see **Comprise, Comprehend, etc.**

Comprise, Comprehend, Include

Concerted

CONGLOMERATION *n.* a collection into a mass or ball; a mixture; a mass of any indiscriminate form.

Consist & Constitute

Constitute   see **Consist & Constitute**

DIASPORA   *n.* the dispersion of the Jews.

DISBAND   *v.* to break up, or destroy, the organization of something, as "The general disbanded his army on the order of his superiors."

DISMEMBER   *v.* to separate limbs from the trunk or main body; to cut in pieces, as "The hawk dismembered his prey in a matter of seconds."

Dispel & Disperse

Disperse   see **Dispel & Disperse**

DISPERSION   *n.* the state of being scattered. See also **Dispel** and **Disperse.**

Disrupt

DISSIPATION   *n.* a passing or wasting away, esp. by misuse.

DISTRIBUTE   *v.* to divide or allot; to apportion; to spread, scatter, disperse.

Divest & Invest

FASCICULAR   *adj.* pertaining to a small bunch or bundle.

Gather

Huddle   see **Clutter, Cluster, etc.**

Include   see **Comprise, Comprehend, etc.**

Integrate

Invest   see **Divest & Invest**

Mingle & Mix

Mix   see **Mingle & Mix**

SCATTERING   *n.* the act of sprinkling, sowing or strewing.

SYMPOSIUM   *n.* a witty or lively party. Hence, any collection of opinions or articles. *pl.* SYMPOSIA or SYMPOSIUMS.

Assemble, Collect, Collate and **Compile**   To ASSEMBLE is 'to bring a number of things together into more or less a group,' like, for example, data for a report. This group is an ASSEMBLAGE, and when it is exclusively of people it is called an ASSEMBLY. These people are called in political terms ASSEMBLYMEN.

COLLECT comes from Latin *collecta*, 'ASSEMBLAGE.' To COLLECT is consequently a synonym for 'to ASSEMBLE.' COLLECTION is a synonym for 'ASSEMBLAGE.' But you do not usually use COLLECT or COLLECTION for people.

COLLATE is a critical word. Just as ASSEMBLYMEN may convene to study or compare plans, so when you COLLATE notes or papers you COLLECT and arrange them for systematic use. The word means literally 'borne together,' and is not specifically related to 'collateral,' which means 'along with, side-by-side with.'

We continually COLLECT all sorts of things, but tend foolishly to feel that we can ASSEMBLE only our military forces and COLLATE only the cards in an index file. Both ASSEMBLE and COLLATE are, as a matter of fact, more connotative than the indefinite (though for that reason very useful) COLLECT. ASSEMBLING your scattered wits or mentally COLLATING your ideas are certainly descriptive phrases.

COMPILE is also expressive. Its primary idea is 'to acquire' (originally it was 'steal') facts, information, etc. But this sense of acquisition has through usage been complemented by a reference to the actual information acquired, and now this excellent verb means 'to compose or to build with acquired materials.' There is, in COMPILE, a suggestion of systematic arrangement of material, such as in the meaning of COLLATE. For example, statisticians COMPILE tabular reports. But when you COMPILE information taken from other books into one of your own, your COMPILATION ceases to be a mere process. It takes on the aspects of a structure. The word was once used frankly in the sense of 'piling up' or 'building,' but that usage is now obsolete.

Clutter, Cluster and Huddle   The streets are CLUTTERED with everything under the sun; your mind is CLUTTERED (literally, 'clotted and clotted,' the frequentative of 'clot') with a thousand miscellaneous thoughts. More happily, congenial people CLUSTER together; the right words CLUSTER in your mind when you want to say something significant. Unlike HUDDLE CLUSTER suggests harmony and peaceful purpose. HUDDLE implies a 'coming together for conspiratorial purpose,' like a football HUDDLE. Each of these words is both a verb and a noun.

Comprise, Comprehend and Include   Structurally, COMPRISE is an abbreviation of COMPREHEND. Both derive from French *comprendre,* but COMPRISE comes from *comprendre's* short past participle, *compris,* often conveniently expanded in colloquial English to a whole verb: "Oh yes, I compree," ('I comprehend, I understand'). Sometimes we use COMPRISE to express basically the idea of 'compreeing.' "What you have just said about this matter comprises your opinion of it." In other words, there is a hint that your opinion COMPREHENDS, or understands, the matter under discussion. But fundamentally the sentence means that what you said 'is, constitutes, composes' your opinion, as stones compose a stone wall.

Both COMPRISE and COMPREHEND fundamentally connote a 'laying hold of something.' We still utilize that idea when we use COMPRISE to mean to include. "Your hand is comprised of fingers, palm, wrist, etc." When we use COMPREHEND we imply that a variety of things 'are laid hold of,' helter-skelter. For example, the President's annual report COMPREHENDS a variety of unrelated items that constitute the year's work.

In the Middle English COMPREHEND began to assume a highly important but specialized meaning. It began to mean the 'grouping of things with the mind.' Here the modern use of COMPREHEND begins. While it retained its idea of 'containment,' as COMPRISE also did, COMPREHEND became an intellectual word. Now COMPREHENSION implies both physical grasp and mental understanding. It is consequently a more subjective word than COMPRISE. A book may COMPRISE much wisdom, but it is our mind that COMPREHENDS the wisdom.

Coming then to INCLUDE we find comparatively little life in it. It quite unemotionally expresses the idea of 'containment.' It does not even have any suggestion of 'grasping,' but rather the contrary, since INCLUDE comes from the motionless Latin word for 'to shut in.' But in common diction there is one juncture where INCLUDE refuses to be subordinate and competes with COMPRISE. When should we say INCLUDE and when should we say COMPRISE in referring to parts of a whole? Opinion seems to differ but probably *either* usage *can* be right, except that COMPRISE in this numerical emphasis implies 'constituent parts' and thus '*all* parts.' An axe COMPRISES a head and a handle, a house COMPRISES a living-room, dining-room, etc. The fact that we add *et cetera* does not imply that the other rooms are not considered; but on the contrary, they are well understood, and we are only saving breath in not naming them. But the same *et cetera* after INCLUDE, and its list, might well imply that the additional things are 'accessory,' and too numerous both to mention *and* to consider individually. In short, though COMPRISE has long since ceased to mean simply to compose, the things which something COMPRISES do constitute that thing. See also CONSIST and CONSTITUTE.

Concerted A CONCERT is a CONCERTED effort of musicians to please us with their art. One football team makes a CONCERTED assault upon the opposite line. CONCERTED means not only 'united' but also 'planned and agreed upon in advance.'

Consist and **Constitute** Your car CONSISTS of many parts, and the parts CONSTITUTE the car. But the CONSTITUTION of the car, aside from its parts alone, might refer to something like the CONSTITUTION of the human body when we speak of it from the physician's point of view. The inference is that a CONSTITUTION is well put together, equally strong in all its parts, and therefore resistant to wear. The Constitution of the United States put the country, i.e., the 13 colonies, 'together,' into a State or Republic. In the same way, your opinion of a matter may CONSIST of many ideas you have on the subject. But these ideas compiled in a systematic way CONSTITUTE your opinion, just as bits of evidence looked at in a certain way can CONSTITUTE proof of a crime.

Dispel and **Disperse** DISPEL is a pretty word and DISPERSE isn't. Both mean, fundamentally, to scatter. The teacher DISPERSES the class but the sun DISPELS the clouds. Something rudely DISPERSES our thoughts, but glad tidings DISPEL our anxieties. The joke of it is that historically DISPEL is the harsher word. It meant 'to drive apart,' while DISPERSE comes from *spargere,* 'to scatter.'

Disrupt This word says what 'disturb' or 'break-up' can't. DISRUPT is a powerful word. Whatever is DISRUPTIVE bursts asunder your plans, your orderly course of thinking, your life.

Divest and **Invest** An expressive word meaning 'to cast off,' as you would cast off a vest in warm weather. To DIVEST your mind of worries is a real joy. Trees paradoxically DIVEST themselves of foliage in the fall, and stand naked to the bleak winds of winter.

The opposite of DIVEST can be INVEST. Trees INVEST themselves with new clothing in the Spring. When you INVEST your money you of course expect the profits to be gathered unto you.

Gather GATHER is a good, everyday word. In fact, it may once have meant 'good,' or derived with good from a common ancestor. Even in Anglo-Saxon times it was both transitive and intransitive. "He gathered flowers for a peace offering." "The men gathered quickly to discuss the outrage." The Old English *gaed* was a 'company' or 'society,' and *gaedeling* a 'comrade.' *Ge-gada* was a 'companion,' or perhaps a 'cousin,' called by the ancient Goths a *gadiliggs.* A Dutch 'spouse' today is a *gade,* and the German 'husband' a *gatte.* These are all worthy components of a GATHERING. When a train GATHERS speed the word GATHER is cruelly stretched. The usage is common now, but once it must have been a purple spot that caught an editor's eye.

Integrate INTEGRATE means 'to embody' when the 'body' is a 'summation of totality.' Thus when you INTEGRATE some good ideas into a plan, the plan is brought nearer to a state of completion. The idea behind INTEGRATE is that something new is brought into or combined with something already existing. In the army it is sometimes said that men are INTEGRATED into regular outfits when these recruits have become fully trained and accepted as competent soldiers.

Mingle and **Mix** When compared with its stodgy synonym MIX there is in MINGLE 'motion, music and merriment.' When you MINGLE with a crowd you join the crowd, you move about within it, you are 'among' it. In fact, 'among' is, at bottom, the same word as MINGLE. But when you MIX with a crowd, there is a suggestion less of the crowd's having attracted you than of finding yourself in a fix.

Likewise, transitively, when you MINGLE shades of color you 'blend' them while when you MIX them they are merely a MIXTURE, 'a medley, a confused collection.' Moreover, MINGLE is a pretty word, while MIX sounds like tricks or even bricks. MINGLE is designed for art or pleasure, and MIX is made for commerce or industry.

And yet MINGLE came from common beginnings. The Anglo-Saxons had a word for a MIXTURE, and hence for an assembly or crowd: the word was *mang*. The verb was *mengan*, which in the Middle English became both *mengen* and *mingen*. These gave way to *mengelen*, a frequentative form meaning practically 'to MIX' *and* 'to stir.' From its contraction *mengel* we got MINGLE. But the roots are all common Teutonic, and appear also in other Continental words. 'Costermongers' and 'ironmongers' once MINGLED, as dealers, with the populace, and now 'warmongers' tangle with the world.

BAD BEHAVIOR

Abase see **Abash & Abase**

Abash & Abase

ANNOY *v.* to disturb, molest, or irritate; to be troublesome to (a person).

ARRANT *adj.* unquestionably bad, as an ARRANT coward.

ARROGANT *adj.* very haughty; immoderately proud; affected by an unwarranted sense of self-importance.

BAD *adj.* not good; hurtful; offensive.

BITTER *adj.* harsh; sarcastic; hateful. "She has only bitter words for her former lover."

CARELESS *adj.* negligent; inconsiderate; weak.

CAUSTIC *adj.* biting; malicious; as a CAUSTIC joke.

COLD-HEARTED *adj.* without human warmth; ruthless; aloof.

COWER *v.* to crouch or stoop with shame and fear.

CRABBED *adj.* cross; peevish; sour; as "She is a crabbed old librarian."

CRINGE *v.* to cower; to shrink from fear and cowardice.

CRUSTY *adj.* testy; peevish; harsh; as "The general has a crusty manner of exerting his authority."

Fawning

GRIM *adj.* painfully serious; very stern; sullen.

HARASS *v.* to pester; to annoy; to cause persistent trouble to (a person).

HARSH *adj.* severe; unfeeling; unkind.

HEARTLESS *adj.* cold; without human warmth; ruthless.

INTRACTABLE *adj.* stubborn; uncontrollable; as an INTRACTABLE child.

Mope, Sulk & Pout

OILY *adj.* unctuous; smooth; pertaining to talk or behavior which has a concealed purpose.

ORGY *n.* wild, drunken revelry; unrestrained self-indulgence. *adj.* ORGIASTIC.

PERVERSE *adj.* obstinate; intractable.

PESTER *v.* to annoy continually; to torment.

PLAGUE *v.* to harass; to pester.

Pout see **Mope, Sulk, etc.**

RASH *adj.* inconsiderately hasty in behavior.

REFRACTORY *adj.* intractable; sullen.

SERVILE *adj.* slavish; base; esp. in the sense of cringing or being cowardly.

SLAVISH *adj.* servile; imitative, in the sense of lacking independence.

SOUR *adj.* caustic; crabbed; pertaining to a short, disagreeable disposition.

STINGY *adj.* selfish; niggardly; never sharing.

STUBBORN *adj.* intractable; being fixed and unyielding in manner and opinion.

STUFFY *adj.* obstinate, straight-laced; self-important; esp. in the sense of believing oneself to be of superior intelligence or virtue.

SUBSERVIENT *adj.* servile.

Sulk see **Mope, Sulk, etc.**

Tease

THOUGHTLESS *adj.* careless; inconsiderate.

TOADY *v.* to flatter; to act in a servile manner. *n.* a TOADY.

TRUCKLING *adj.* slavish.

UNCTUOUS *adj.* oily; servile.

UNFEELING *adj.* insensitive; cold-hearted.

WILD *adj.* uncontrollable or unrestrained; rash; inconsiderate, but often in the sense of implied enthusiasm.

WORRY *v.* to annoy persistently; to make (someone) feel anxious or unhappy.

Abash and **Abase**   ABASHMENT is mingled 'astonishment, shame, humility.' You are usually rattled. You may be awed, as when beholding a king in his royal splendor. You may even be painfully embarrassed and show it.

ABASEMENT is a 'lowering,' and you can be lowered in a thousand ways, showing it variously. A military man reduced in rank, is ABASED. Loose living may ABASE you, and here the word takes on a sinister significance.

When you 'abase yourself' before others you are either exhibiting your baseness quite unconcernedly, or, with callousness, you are fawning for favors. It is said you can not ABASH a cat before a king; neither can you ABASE her, nor will she ABASE herself. But men are not cats. They are plainly and quite commonly ABASABLE and self-ABASABLE.

Fawning   This is *no* relation to a 'fawn.' In fact, the two words come from almost half a world apart. 'Fawns' come to us via the Old French (which beautified it) from Latin *fetus*, bluntly meaning 'offspring.' But a FAWNER was 'fain (glad)' to please his lord in early Iceland. The word started as *fagna;* the Anglo-Saxons built a verb from their corresponding *faegen,* 'fain.' It became a very adaptable word. It could mean anything from 'reluctant' to 'overjoyed.' Today a FAWNER can still artfully pretend unwillingness in his effort to ingratiate himself.

Mope, Sulk and **Pout**   MOPE is Dutch for POUT; POUT is Welsh for 'protrude,' specifically, of the lips; and SULK is English for 'languid.'

But a MOPER is now unsociably melancholy, not mournful like a POUTING child. A SULKER is stubbornly if not crossly sullen. And though a POUTER is always a spoilt child, regardless of his age, he is also sullen from that kind of ill-humor which is covertly cunning and looking for a reward. A POUT is an inaudible but a very visible whine.

All are expressive words, especially MOPE. You can almost see a MOPER hugging his own concocted gloom.

"If a man is too much of an introvert, he mopes around his house and office, never making many friends." "The convict who thinks all the world is against him, sulks day after day in his cell." "Some girls, spoiled all their lives by their families, simply pout if their escorts do not take them to expensive restaurants." MOPE is rarely used transitively, "Life in tropical jungles will often mope a man." POUT is frequently used transitively, "The baby pouts his lips." "Old people pout their dissatisfaction with the way the world is run."

Incidentally, the bike-wagons called SULKIES on the trotting-tracks were so named because they hold only one man, who rides by himself, a kind of SULKER.

Tease   If someone pulls your hair playfully, he is TEASING you. In the Anglo-Saxon TEASE meant 'to comb out flax and wool,' and today the word is still used in that specialized sense. Perhaps 'pulling' and 'plucking' wool reminded people of the 'pulling' and 'plucking' a child does when he begs, or TEASES, you for a nickel. Anyhow, to TEASE means 'to beg, vex, trouble, bother.' "He teased the dog so much that finally it turned and bit him."

BEGINNINGS

See also Ends; Series

Advent & Arrival
APPEAR   *v.* to come or be in sight; to become visible by approach or by emerging from concealment. *n.* APPEARANCE, the state of being visible; the act of presenting oneself.

APPROACH   *n.* the act of drawing near. *v.* to come or to go near in place or time; to come into presence.

ARISE   *v.* to come into existence or play; to start into prominence or activity; appear; to have a beginning or origin; to originate.

Arrival   see Advent & Arrival

Begin   see Commence & Begin

Cause

COMING   *n.* arrival.

Commence & Begin

COMMENCEMENT   *n.* the act or fact of commencing; beginning; rise; origin; first existence; inception.

EMBARKATION   *n.* the act of going aboard ship; the act of setting out on water; *v.* EMBARK, to go on board ship; to set out; to venture.

EMERGE   *v.* to come forth, appear, as from concealment. *n.* EMERGEMENT something that rises suddenly into view (see LOOM); an unexpected occurrence.

ESTABLISH   *v.* to appoint, ordain; to fix permanently.

FOUND   *v.* to lay the basis of; to fix, set, or place; to establish.

Inaugurate   see Institute, Initiate, etc.

Inception, Incipient, Inchoate

Inchoate   see Inception, Incipient, etc.

Incipient   see Inception, Incipient, etc.

Incunabula

Initiate   see Institute, Initiate, etc.

Install   see Institute, Initiate, etc.

Instigate

Institute, Initiate, Inaugurate, Install

LAUNCH   v. to send out into another sphere of duties; to enter upon a different career or course.

LOOM   v. to come dimly into view; to rise up before one's eyes (often used figuratively, as "The prospect of war loomed in men's minds").

Maiden

NASCENT   adj. beginning to grow, or coming into existence.

OPENING   n. a beginning, an initial stage; commencement.

ORGANIZE   v. to make a systematic functioning whole out of several parts.

ORIGIN   n. beginning of existence; fountain, source. v. ORIGINATE, to give rise or ORIGIN to; to initiate; set going.

OUTSET   n. a setting out; beginning; start.

OUTSTART   n. to start out; to start up.

PRIMAL   adj. pertaining to beginning or origin. Hence, also, of first importance.

Project

PROVENANCE   n. origin; source or quarter from which anything comes.

ROOT   n. that from which anything springs.

SOURCE   n. a spring; a fountainhead; a first cause, origin.

SPRING   v. to take one's birth; rise, origin; to come into view or notice.

START   n. a setting out on some course; beginning; outset; departure.

STARTING POINT   n. the place, point, or position at which something begins.

Advent and Arrival   ADVENT announces a 'beginning' and ARRIVAL an 'ending.' When a ship ARRIVES in port it completes its voyage, and the ARRIVAL stresses this completion.

An ADVENT, on the other hand, is definitely a 'birth' or a 'beginning.' For example, the ADVENT of printing made books available to a large number of people. While it is true that we do speak of the ARRIVAL of a new baby, apparently from nowhere, perhaps it is only because we are imagining a large bird conveying the infant to us. An ADVENT, at any rate, is definitely, not just predominantly, a 'beginning,' while an ARRIVAL is predominantly, though not entirely, an 'ending.'

Cause   This verb is sometimes helpful, especially as a substitute for 'make,' which is terribly overworked. It emphasizes 'motive power' rather than compulsion. "This book causes me to think," instead of "This book makes me (compels me to) think."

Commence and **Begin** These words excellently illustrate our Latin and Anglo-Saxon heritages. Today they work side by side, meaning the same thing but saying it with a slightly different emphasis.

BEGIN is the simpler word, and its first meaning was 'to open,' from *ginnan;* the 'be' was simply intensive. When the day BEGINS it opens upon us. But when a day COMMENCES all its activities are 'set in motion.' COMMENCE is an intricate word, such as the Romans delighted in. The 'com' was, of course, their *cum,* meaning 'together,' and it now suggests a complexity of events. The 'mence' was once a built-up Latin word for 'initiating' or 'going into,' which has given us 'initiating.' So, with that background, COMMENCE is the more formal word, though the senses in which we now use it are almost as simple as BEGIN. Perhaps we now use COMMENCE when we wish to appear rather literate. Actually, however, BEGIN, being abrupter, is more appropriate to the first step in any action, which is probably the commonest sense in which we use both words.

The words are both intransitive and transitive; you can BEGIN or COMMENCE *to* work, or BEGIN or COMMENCE *a* work. But in the transitive usages there is more meaning in COMMENCE. You COMMENCE building a house, which refers to the very first spadeful of dirt that originates all the work that goes into house-building. But you BEGIN work on the house each day. See also INSTITUTE, INITIATE, etc.

Inception, Incipient and **Inchoate** INCEPTION means 'a start, a beginning, the first part of any development including its conception.' For example, a reformatory idea is conceived, it is born; and the beginning of the development of this idea is its INCEPTION. But the reformatory idea may cause the INCEPTION of the reform itself. The word is thus a little abstract. You would be less likely to speak of the INCEPTION of a walk than of a talk. Walks don't generally develop, they are linear affairs; but talks usually develop and may generate lots more talk.

The adjective INCIPIENT is also a little abstract. The INCIPIENT stages of a disease are the ones in which it gains a hold. INCIPIENT suspicions are the dawning of a doubt—provided the doubt ultimately develops.

As a plain adjective INCEPTIVE pertains to a beginning where INCIPIENT would not always sound right. For example, where INCIPIENT is a reportorial or after-the-event word, INCEPTIVE can have the force of instigating: an INCEPTIVE desire may be one that causes, and so commences, an evil deed.

But INCIPIENT coalesces a little with INCHOATE, which refers to the 'elemental state of something.' The earth itself, before its crust had cooled, was not yet completely formed or in operation. The earth was at that time in an INCHOATE stage of development, but perhaps INCIPIENT life had its INCEPTION during this very early period.

Incunabula From Latin *cunae,* 'cradles,' this word is a curious contraction and expansion of that object's significance. As usual, the word lengthened as the diminutive of the object, *cunabula* was adopted. Then the meaning and figurative use of the word grew. A cradle is a beginning, a beginning is a birthplace, a birthplace is one's native land, his home. Homes are sanctuaries, and objects associated with the home personify them in minds and hearts. They are little household idols, they are concrete childhood recollections. Along these lines the word INCUNABULA grew. History is marked by certain inevitable changes, which persisted to form an historical period. Everything typically related to the beginnings of such periods are INCUNABULA, whether artistic, economic, racial or what. Concretely, books printed about 1500 A.D. are INCUNABULA. The swords of our 18th century admirals are INCUNABULA, not of the era of hand-to-hand fighting, but of our navy, which was then beginning. Independence Hall in Philadelphia is an INCUNABULUM—a cradle of independence. Bird sanctuaries are INCUNABULA: homes or refuges for birds.

Instigate 'To start something by incitement.' Its root presumably is Latin *stigo,* 'goad.' Like 'incite,' it has quite commonly taken on a sinister meaning, as in INSTIGATING ('plotting, causing') a crime or in INSTIGATING ('stimulating, goading') someone to commit one. But this stigma need not invalidate the word for other uses. People can be incited to fight righteous wars, and so preparedness for such wars can be INSTIGATED by indignation against aggression.

Institute, Initiate, Inaugurate and **Install** In the beginning there was the Word—but for humans a beginning is seldom that simple. In fact, beginnings are as complex as are the myriads of things that can be begun and as the still more numerous and perplexing ways in which they may be begun. Consequently, when the ancients were about to undertake an important enterprise they consulted the gods. As a result we have today a large handful of words all more or less expressing this ancient dilemma, and resolving it always with seriousness and usually with ceremony.

The root of to INSTITUTE is 'to set'; prefixed with an 'in' it enveloped an idea at once definite and expansive. When you 'set' something 'in' you 'establish' it, or 'set it up.' You have, in effect, caused it to exist, or have originated it. Further, once 'set up,' it can be changed or improved. Whatever you 'set up' quickly achieves complexity and organization.

That is the commonest meaning of INSTITUTE today, as when we INSTITUTE a government or a society. But such things are not INSTITUTED without toil and care, and consequently when we INSTITUTE an inquiry into a crime there is more meaning in the expression than there is in its equivalent, 'to begin an investigation.' For the word INSTITUTE is formal, and suited to serious or formidable things. But, unlike many formal words, it is not hollow but solid. Its root *statuere*, 'to set,' having taken another prefix *cum*, 'together,' gave us 'constitute,' a definitely constructive word meaning 'to set together' or 'to give integrity and substance to.'

"I received all the data you sent me, but haven't yet gone into it." The late Romans fashioned from the verb 'to go' and the preposition 'in' the new and figurative verb INITIATE. That verb, being figurative, was naturally unstable and used with variable senses. We INITIATE either a freshman in college or, at an opposite pole, a series of moral reforms.

The logic of this phenomenon lies exactly in the multiplicity of things that can be done, and the diversity of ways in which they can be begun. The freshman is INITIATED in (we usually say 'into' now) his college life by certain instructions in the virtues of discipline in general. Later, he may be INITIATED into a secret society by more serious ceremonial instruction. Or, anyone may be INITIATED into the mysteries of science or the secrets of art. Such is one meaning of INITIATE.

The *first* person to propose or to promote any activity is the INITIATOR of it. Hence, we have our adjectives INITIAL, meaning 'the very first,' and INITIATIVE, meaning 'having the ability or the disposition to start things.' This, then, is the second meaning of INITIATE.

But INITIATE is essentially a special and formal word. In the sense of introducing someone into an office or society, with ceremonies, the word came into English late in Shakespeare's lifetime. That was the meaning that had predominated among the Romans, though the ceremonies were then religious rites, first pagan consecrations, then Christian baptism. Even with the Romans, however, the word had begun to take on the more general secular sense which Shakespeare knew.

The collateral idea of originating something has come down to us from the Latin adjective to our own INITIAL. INITIATIVE was adopted from the French *after* Elizabethan times. Consequently, both meanings of the word came from the Latin, but were introduced into our language at different times.

The significant fact is that the two senses have combined. Just as the heathens were afterwards regarded as being reborn when they were baptised, so the ceremonies of an INITIATION imply a birth or a beginning.

In INAUGURATION is also a consecrated beginning, and today INAUGURATE, like INSTITUTE, is usually specific in its application. But it is an even more formal word than INSTITUTE, expressing the impressiveness of high authority. In fact, in its origin it represented the awesomeness of the gods and of the mysterious fates, and this emphasis is still reflected in its usage. To INAUGURATE a president is to INSTALL him in office with appropriate and impressive ceremonies. Nothing ever really INAUGURATES bad times or misfortunes. To the ancients the word pictured the actions of the augurs or diviners, whose reading of omens indicated approval or disapproval from the gods of a candidate for office. These prophets had established religious ceremonies which preceded or included the rites of INSTALLATION.

When, therefore, we INAUGURATE a man we solemnize his INSTALLATION by the INAUGURAL ceremony. When we INAUGURATE a public building the ceremony becomes a kind of dedication.

Finally, an INSTALLATION is also a beginning. A man is INSTALLED in a public office; he becomes a new officeholder. Literally, he is put 'in a stall.' Politics and business have put the word on a rather low level, in spite of the fact that a stall, in itself, is by no means a simple thing. Most dictionaries will give you the impression that it is Latin. Actually, the Romans took it from the Germans. It meant 'a fixed place, hence a standing place.' INSTALL and 'stand' are cognate words. A 'stalemate' in chess is the point where the game comes to a 'standstill.' A 'stall' for cattle or for produce-dealers is their 'standing place.' INSTALL came also to mean 'to enthrone,' as to enthrone a church dignitary, or in modern times 'to seat,' as to seat a new incumbent in office. Thus INSTALL conveys the idea of a beginning. An idea that has been INSTALLED in your head not only has a place 'to stand,' but can also INITIATE a whole series of thoughts.

Maiden As an adjective, MAIDEN was given certain highly figurative connotations which now denote specific ideas. A new member's MAIDEN speech in the Senate is simply his first speech as a Senator. The idea of 'first' derives from MAIDEN's sense of 'virginity.' Virgin soil, for example, is fresh or untouched soil. A related meaning occurs in horse races called MAIDEN races. These are not for fillies (young female horses) or for elderly but unmated mares. MAIDEN races are run by any horses, of any age, and of either sex, who have never won a race, no matter how many times they have previously tried. And, in racing, the term is extended to the jockeys, none of whom are females. This reference to the male sex is not, historically, so unusual as it might seem at first, for etymologically the word MAIDEN is only one of several words that grew out of an Old Teutonic word for a 'boy.' Even in Middle English both MAIDEN, and its abbreviation MAID, could be an unmarried man. Chaucer said he was sure a certain Apostle was a *mayd*.

Project A PROJECT is 'a plan to do something in the future,' or it is the activities that carries out the plan. Hence the word is overworked: PROJECTS range from paper Utopias to real bridges being built. We squeeze even more use out of the verb PROJECT, and out of the noun PROJECTION. Literal-minded people correctly think of a PROJECTION as something 'sticking out' from a house onto the pavement. The 'ject' in the word was once the Roman *jacere*, 'to hurl.' Today we speak easily of PROJECTING our thoughts or our hopes, as if we were flinging them into the future.

BLAME

(*adjectives*)

ABSURD obviously false or, esp. foolish.

ACID sour; tart; as "He has an acid disposition."

BANAL trite; trivial; as a BANAL play.

BATTERED knocked-about; bruised; damaged.

BIZARRE odd; fantastic; queer; as "Those bizarre paintings she has on her wall!"

BLEMISHED stained; spotted; imperfect; flawed.

BLIGHTED withered; diseased.

BROKEN-DOWN ruined; shattered; not functioning.

BURDENSOME difficult; heavy; oppressive.

COARSE ordinary; common; rough; rude.

CORRUPT tainted; spoiled; blemished; depraved.

CROOKED not honest.

CRUDE rough; coarse; rude.

DECAYED rotted; moldy.

DECOMPOSED decayed.

Decrepit & Dilapidated

DEFECTIVE faulty; imperfect.

DEVIOUS roundabout; crooked; remote.

Dilapidated see **Decrepit & Dilapidated**

DILATORY pertaining to delay, as "His dilatory methods lost money for the business."

EXTRAVAGANT exceeding the dictates of common sense.

FADED without color; pale; insipid; dull.

FANTASTIC elaborately or fancifully unreal; eccentric; wild.

FAULTY imperfect.

FEEBLE weak.

FLAWED faulty; imperfect.

FOOLISH banal; unwise; silly.

FRAGILE delicate.

FRAIL weak; small; thin.

FRAYED worn.

FURTIVE secretive; in a thief-like manner.

GARISH glaring; distastefully bright.

GAUDY showy; ostentatious.

GAUNT haggard; emaciated; grim.

Grandiose

GROSS coarse; indelicate; indecent.

GROTESQUE odd; bizarre.

HACKNEYED commonplace; trite.

HAGGARD gaunt; wild-looking, esp. from over-exposure.

HUMDRUM tedious; everyday; dull; monotonous.

IMPAIRED flawed; faulty.

INANE silly; empty-headed.

INFIRM weak.

Insipid

Irksome see **Tedious & Irksome**

LAUGHABLE ridiculous; comic.

LUDICROUS ridiculous; absurd.

OBSCENE foul; loathsome; repulsive; dirty; indecent; offensive.

ONEROUS burdensome.

OSTENTATIOUS showy; flagrant; pretentious.

POMPOUS overly dignified; ostentatious show, as in manners or speech.

Preposterous

PRETENTIOUS ostentatious; characterized by a show of false importance, dignity or knowledge, as a PRETENTIOUS book.

PUTRID in a state of decomposition and decay; rotten; esp. with a suggestion of stench.

RAGGED tattered; pertaining to cloth ripped and torn.

RAMSHACKLE ready to fall apart; unsteady; shaky.

RANCID pertaining to the unpleasant taste or smell that comes from spoiled foods, as RANCID butter.

RIBALD obscene or off-colored; offensive; coarse.

RIDICULOUS preposterous; laughable; absurd; outrageous.

ROTTEN putrid; decomposed; corrupt, as "He has a rotten mind."

Scrawny

SEEDY not new or fresh; thus, shabby, worn; sometimes in the sense of a run-down physical condition, as "I'm sure feeling seedy today."

SHABBY worn; not in repair; seedy; ramshackle.

SHOWY flamboyant; gaudy; ostentatious.

SICKLY unhealthy; unwholesome; weak; pallid.

SKINNY thin.

SOUR pertaining to an acid taste; tart; as a SOUR lemon or grapefruit.

SPARE lean; thin.

Stain see Tarnish & Stain

STALE not fresh, like STALE bread; dry and tasteless.

Stiff

Tacky or Tackey

Tarnish & Stain

Tart

Tawdry

Tedious & Irksome

THREADBARE worn; shabby.

TIRESOME dull; boring; unstimulating.

Tortuous

Trite

UNSOUND weak; faulty; imperfect; as "He looks healthy but he has an unsound heart."

UNSTEADY shaking; swaying; wobbly.

Vapid

VULGAR obscene; coarse; not tasteful, as a VULGAR dress.

WASHED-OUT vapid; pallid; tired; played-out.

WASTED thin; emaciated.

WEAK frail; not strong; indicating deficiency.

WEARISOME tedious; tiresome.

WISHY-WASHY pallid; vapid; without strength or resolution.

WORN much used; old; tired; as "The woman's face was lined and worn."

Decrepit and **Dilapidated** A DECREPIT state is not a 'worn-out-ness' so much as a 'broken-down-ness.' It comes from Latin *crepare*, 'to crack.' DECREPIT is sometimes incorrectly spelled 'decrepid.'

DILAPIDATED has lost strength by long sentimental association with old houses and old hats. Actually, the word has more force. It should picture a 'fallen house, a broken hat.' The *lapid* is Latin for 'stone,' the *de* means a 'tearing apart.'

Grandiose A GRANDIOSE person has 'exaggerated grandeur' and probably some 'bombast.' This word is the Italian development of Latin *grandis*, which gave us our much abused word 'grand.' GRANDIOSE implies a big gesture of lavishness without the authenticity of true grandeur. An 'affected splendor' or simply a 'meaningless bigness' is a GRANDIOSE style in literature, music or architecture.

Insipid Flat, unseasoned food is INSIPID. An INSIPID girl has no get-up-and-go in her manner, or spark in her eye.

Preposterous The 'pre' in the word is itself PREPOSTEROUS. It of course means 'before,' and, like the newspaper headline that blurts the outcome at the outset, it proclaims that the Latin *posterus*, or 'coming after,' comes 'first.' At once the meaning of PREPOSTEROUS becomes re-markable, if not impossible, like a cart before the horse. So the whole word, and especially with its explosive second syllable, becomes a wonderful one to remember when you want to shout your mingled surprise and disbelief in one burst of breath: "PREPOSTEROUS!"

Scrawny This descriptive word probably comes from a Swedish dialectal word, *scrag*, meaning a 'great dry tree.' Children, cattle and stray cats are often SCRAWNY, that is, 'weak-and-skinny-looking.' Trees among our larger living things are often SCRAWNY. This is an expressive word. If you call a man SCRAWNY, he's pegged and fitted, for everyone immediately thinks of Ichabod Crane in the famous *Legend of Sleepy Hollow* by Washington Irving.

Stiff This word, only five letters long and one of them superfluous, can talk on many subjects. And with supple ease, though in the be-ginning it was a rigid enough 'stem' or 'stake.' The word is cognate with Latin *stipes*, 'stem,' and with other similar Aryan relatives. Its synonyms are now amazing: 'affected, ceremonious, immoderate, ex-cessive, rigorous, harsh, severe, strong, stilted, inflexible, inelastic.' Stakes and stems may be inelastic, but would you expect them to be 'harsh, immoderate, ceremonious or affected?' Yet we certainly have manners that are STIFF and formal, prices that are STIFF and immod-erate, and examinations so STIFF they are painfully severe. And con-strained writing is called STIFF. There is also a STIFF drink that is strong, and a STIFF breeze that you have to push against. And though a STIFF person is undoubtedly wooden, like a stake, a 'big stiff' is simply rough and clumsy, an unmannered lout. And STIFF is under-world slang for 'corpse.'

Tacky or **Tackey** TACKY is the opposite of 'swanky.' TACKY has come to mean, with slight gradations, 'toughly raffish, cheaply dowdy, neg-ligently shabby'—and all three meanings usually combine. It was first applied to the poor whites of the South, in the mid 'Eighties, and be-fore that to poor or cheap horses, without breeding. Now it is a con-temptuous term for the vulgarly cheap. TACKY company need not be obscenely vulgar, but they are far from being personable.

Nevertheless the word is slang. It is a loose one-word phrase slung at inferiors. It has been taken up by these same inferiors and used in new ways. A TACKY party may be, in general, a rough party; but it can be, specifically, just a whacky party, with the guests arriving in ri-diculous costumes. In some circles TACKY has come to mean 'offensively common, mean or contemptible.' It is even used for 'sickness.' A TACKY cow is a sick cow.

Where the word came from, no one knows. There is an older TACKY meaning 'sticky,' like molasses or partly-dried varnish. It obviously has some connection with the little nail which attaches (make the 'ch' hard and it sounds like TACKY) things together.

Tarnish and **Stain** In common usage the word TARNISH certainly has a definite, though not quite a simple, meaning. A TARNISHED reputation is definitely a 'damaged reputation,' but the damage is clearly understood to have been done by STAINS. TARNISHED goods are also understood to be 'blotched.' And yet the TARNISHING is really a larger matter than 'sullying or soiling.'

STAIN, contracted from 'distrain,' is a Latin word meaning literally 'to take the color or dye from.' But removing a color may often mar former color. So the meaning extended to a change of color, especially the defacing of a color by foreign matter. Now we can STAIN clothes ('change their color'); but clothes can also, to our dismay, be STAINED by spilled coffee. Even in Shakespeare's time a STAIN could be a natural spot different from the surface color. And huntsmen speak technically of a fox's scent being STAINED by too many hounds running back and forth over the trail.

TARNISH comes from the Old French, which probably had it from Teutonic sources. It means broadly 'to darken,' and hence, intransitively, 'to lose color, become dull or dingy.' When rust TARNISHES bright metal it causes it to lose luster. The whole surface may not be rusted, it may be STAINED only in blotches. But fundamentally when it, or a reputation, is TARNISHED, it is darkened or faded all over.

Tart A TART tongue is sometimes considered to be smart. But the real meaning of the word is more cutting than you might think. The origin of TART was among the fierce Anglo-Saxons where it meant 'to tear.' TARTNESS in your manner may now be a crisp and invigorating kind of sophistication, but TART talk can do some awful things.

Tawdry In Old England the village fairs celebrating St. Audrey were markets for cheap finery. The name St. Audrey was corrupted; at the same time perhaps the finery deteriorated to showy and gaudy trinkets. Today, as a result, we have a useful word. The wares of many modern emporia, like penny arcades, are TAWDRY; so also are the tastes and the manners of tenpenny sports.

St. Audrey (St. Ethelreda as she is ecclesiastically known) was a princess. She was born in present-day Suffolk in the 7th century and became the Abbess of Ely. The story is that she died of a throat tumor and remorsefully attributed her affliction to her own inordinate love of fine necklaces. Subsequently at the fairs in her honor necklets of lace, called Saint Audrey's lace, were sold. At any rate in Shakespeare's time they were still talking of "tawdry lace and a pair of sweet gloves." Thus TAWDRY at that time may not have meant 'cheap and showy.'

One should note, moreover, that lace, the fabric, as distinguished from laces (compare 'necklace') was rare in England before the Elizabethan period, and for a long time was not a common or domestic article. It was imported from abroad for the courtiers and the ladies.

Tedious and **Irksome** In English usage there is a distinction between these two words. IRKSOME implies some slight 'petulance on our part.' Something IRKS us when it is distasteful to us and yet has to be done or endured, like an IRKSOME task or obligation. But if the IRKSOME thing is long drawn out it becomes TEDIOUS, with the implication that anything that is *that* IRKSOME must be IRKSOME to *anybody*. And since petty feelings exhaust themselves after a while, the continuously IRKSOME thing becomes simply 'wearying,' which is the basic meaning of TEDIUM. Nevertheless, the original Latin *tedium* conveyed a sense of 'personal disgust' or even 'loathing.' Today TEDIUM is tiring largely because it is trying to the feelings; it is not necessarily fatiguing to mind or body.

Tortuous Absolutely consanguineous (same-blooded) with 'torture,' but retaining the original pure meaning of 'twisted.' A winding road, a devious business policy, a twisted dead leaf are all TORTUOUS. A TORTUOUS argument is a round-about one, employing maneuvers and circuitous approaches to the main contention, often to confuse the opponent, to tire him out, or most particularly to dodge his own argument. Thus the word took on a bad odor from the start. Even today we speak of a TORTUOUS man as a crook. The root also gave us 'tort,' the legal term for a 'wrong.' There once was a separate adjective, 'tortious,' meaning 'harmful or wrongful.' Its meaning has been absorbed in the growing implications of TORTUOUS. And as torture is associated with the wrack and thumbscrew, so also TORTUOUS has its intimations of 'writhing.' A TORTUOUS mind may be writhing in confusion.

Trite Yesterday's news, if people talked it to shreds, is TRITE today. It is 'threadbare, commonplace, banal, empty.' Trivialities become TRITE overnight, and larger matters more slowly.

At the bottom of TRITE is a busy little Latin verb, *terere*, 'to rub.' It

also gave us 'termites (grind-worms, as the Romans saw them), detriment and contrite.' A 'detriment' is an injury or damage that 'upsets (rubs away)' values. 'Contriteness' is that bruised feeling you may have when your sorrow 'rubs away' your sins, leaving you penitent or humble.

Vapid Words are like people. When they resemble each other we don't always ask ourselves why. The words VAPID, 'insipid' and 'trite' all mean flat to us. But the 'trite' is flat because it is 'shopworn,' the 'insipid' is flat because it has 'lost its taste,' the VAPID is flat because it has 'lost its vim.' *Vappa* was the Latin word for 'dead wine.' *Vapidus* meant 'having lost life and spirit.'

BUSINESS AND MONEY

Accrue

Affluence & Opulence

Afford

Appraise

ASSETS   *n. pl.* property in general; all that one owns; any portion of one's property that has value, as "That farmer's biggest asset is his fine cattle." When a portion of one's property is meant, the sing. form is used; but when all of one's property is meant, the plural form is used. "On his death the banker's assets were considerable."

BOND   *n.* an interest-bearing certificate issued by a corporation that shows ownership of a portion of the assets of that corporation.

BROKER   *n.* an agent, or middleman, in the sale of stocks, bonds, or property.

CAPITAL   *n.* the wealth of a business that is used for further production or increased productivity.

Chap, Customer, Cheap

Cheap   see Chap, Customer, etc.

COMMERCIAL   *adj.* pertaining to COMMERCE or trade. *n.* COMMERCE, the interchange of goods or property; trade, traffic.

COMMODITY   *n.* an article of merchandise; anything movable that may be sold, traded or acquired.

Consolidate & Liquidate

Constrain   see **Distrain & Constrain**

CREDIT   *n.* trust or confidence extended by seller to buyer in a business transaction so that the latter may defer payment. *v.* to extend such trust or confidence.

CURRENCY   *n.* whatever is generally used as a medium of exchange; spec. the money in use in any particular country.

CUSTOM   *n.* the trade or traffic a

merchant possesses; a buyer, purchaser, customer. See also **Chap, Customer,** etc.

Customer see **Chap, Customer,** etc.

DEBIT *n.* in accounting, that which is entered as a debt.

Distrain & Constrain

Dollar Crisis & Dollar Gap

Emolument & Remuneration

Excise Tax

FINANCE *n.* revenue, funds in a treasury; resources of money; an individual's income or resources.

Fiscal

FUNDS *n. pl.* the accumulation of wealth or resources that can be set aside for a specific purpose.

GOODS *n. pl.* movable property or belongings; articles of portable property; merchandise.

Gratuity & Tip

Kudos & Lucre

Liquidate see **Consolidate & Liquidate**

Lucre see **Kudos & Lucre**

MARKET *n.* an occasion on which people meet for buying and selling; a public place where goods are displayed for selling.

MERCHANT *n.* one engaged in buying and selling commodities.

MONETARY *adj.* pertaining to money.

NOTE *n.* a written acknowledgement of debt.

Opulence see **Affluence & Opulence**

Proposition

Remuneration see **Emolument & Remuneration**

STOCK *n.* a share of the fund used to form and run a business. SHARES are owned by individuals who organize a corporation.

SUMPTUARY *adj.* pertaining to expenditures.

Tip see **Gratuity & Tip**

WARES *n. pl.* the goods or commodities a merchant has for sale.

Accrue In a broad sense ACCRUE means 'to accumulate, to increase through a natural course of events.' But custom shows that the usual application is not so general. Business and finance have taken over the word. Profits ACCRUE as time passes and business prospers. Benefits and even opportunities ACCRUE. It's a neat little word that we could use more. However, its formal association will probably prevent its becoming popular.

Affluence and **Opulence** AFFLUENCE means 'wealth, abundance,' from the Latin *ad,* 'to,' plus *fluere,* 'to flow.' Thus, if you are AFFLUENT, wealth has flowed upon you. OPULENCE, though it comes directly from Latin *opes,* 'riches,' conveys no suggestion of a wealth poured liberally over someone. OPULENCE connotes 'luxuriance,' and it thus suggests material wealth: big house, flashy cars, rich clothes, and all the things that money can buy. AFFLUENCE, on the other hand, connotes a kind of divine bestowal. It does not refer only to material wealth. An AFFLUENT man may be rich in natural talents: in intelligence, physical beauty, or artistic power. These two words, making such a fine but important distinction, are excellent additions to your vocabulary.

Afford From the Old English *forthian*, 'to further' or 'to promote,' this word AFFORD has enjoyed several changes that help explain a modern use of it. The original meaning of 'to further' and 'to promote' has left the word, and now AFFORD means 'to yield, to produce, to furnish.' AFFORD, however, also has now an additional meaning illustrated by the sentence, "If you don't want to live beyond your income, you can't afford to be lavish." A clue to the derivation of this sense may be discovered in an etymological analysis of this word. The Old English *forthian* was prefixed by the intensive *ge*. This intensive was later replaced by the Latin *ad*, 'to.' But 'ad' in English often changed to 'af,' and at this point it is easy to see how AFFORD came into being. Accompanying all these changes, however, was the persistent idea of progress, which evolved from the Anglo-Saxon root *fore*, 'before,' and which we see in the word *forthian*. The root *fore* produced 'forth,' meaning forward, and with the addition of the intensive *ge* and the Latin *ad* the concept of forward movement was strengthened at the same time the word AFFORD was created. The modern use of the word in, "We can't afford to be lavish," shows this persistent idea of progress. We can AFFORD much; that is, we can progress in our spending up to a certain point. Beyond that point, which is defined by lavish, we can not AFFORD to go.

Appraise Through the Old French from the Latin for 'price,' APPRAISAL comes to us with soft overtones in spite of its official use as a cold 'reckoning of values.' In the Middle English it replaced the verb 'to praise' (cognate with it in the Latin). Thus, like 'appreciate, praise and esteem,' which express our spiritual sense of values, APPRAISE still reflects some of this softness. It is true that when we APPRAISE an article of commerce we usually set a price in hard money upon it. But when we APPRAISE a palace the act of estimating its worth necessarily engages our sense of human values on a vast scale. Moreover, when we APPRAISE a great painting, a beautiful poem, or a human being we usually are involved in sentiments that they say have no place in the business world.

Chap, Customer and **Cheap** It may be helpful to reflect that these three words have a bearing upon one another. They are all quite practical, and illustrate humanity in trade. CUSTOMER is Roman, apparently going back to *suos,* 'one's own,' and probably to the idea of having one's own way about something. Having your own way about a thing quickly 'accustoms' you to it. If the 'custom' is buying, you become a CUSTOMER. In early England another name for CUSTOMER was 'chapman.' Abbreviated to CHAP, it became a term of derogation. They said, "She will buy but she will be a bad chap." Eventually the derogatory sense disappeared, and CHAP referred simply to a fellow, especially to a young fellow. Now we can call quite affectionately almost any masculine friend 'old chap.'

CHEAP was at first a noun meaning 'barter,' and it lingers still in London's Cheapside. The Anglo-Saxons spelled it *ceap,* probably from the ancient German for 'huckster,' and gave us chapman, CHAP, Scottish *scallant,* for 'lad,' and our own chaffer, which originally meant to trade before it meant to haggle. But as CHAP and CUSTOMER turned bad ('a queer customer,' etc.), CHEAP turned good, and *then* bad. A 'good CHEAP,' like the French *bon marché,* was good business. Thus 'to CHEAPEN' was at first to buy advantageously, and our adjective CHEAP took on that sense before it became predominantly derogatory.

Consolidate and **Liquidate** CONSOLIDATE means 'to make solid, to strengthen, to form into a whole.' It is used figuratively of unsubstantial things, like gains, results of any sorts, and positions taken. In this figurative use CONSOLIDATE usually means 'to strengthen.' "The president of the company is consolidating his position," means that the president is securing his power. LIQUIDATE is the opposite of CONSOLIDATE. Curiously, while we can CONSOLIDATE our profits, we always LIQUIDATE losses. LIQUIDATE means 'to discharge a debt, to settle the accounts of a business, or simply to remove completely.' A ruthless killer LIQUIDATES his victim. Just as frozen funds in a bank are CONSOLIDATED but may later be LIQUIDATED by returning them to circulation, so also personal or intellectual resources can be either CONSOLIDATED or LIQUIDATED.

Distrain and **Constrain** DISTRAIN means 'to seize personal property for debt.' It is a much narrower, and a drastically legal, sense of the verb 'to CONSTRAIN,' which broadly means 'to compel by physical or moral means.' The sentence, "I am constrained to dispossess you," means that I have no choice but to dispossess you. In earlier times DISTRAIN meant 'to coerce' or 'punish' by distraint, but it also meant to seize chattels as a pledge of reparation. Now this pledge is called an indemnification: when the landlord DISTRAINS your household furniture for back rent the furniture is an idemnification.

Dollar Crisis and **Dollar Gap**   The first dollar (German *thaler*) was coined in a Bohemian valley in Shakespeare's time, and we must admit our modern dollars still have some Bohemian traits. They have a careless and light-hearted way of comporting themselves by never being around when we want them. A DOLLAR CRISIS is a condition brought about by the failure of exports to keep up with imports, causing a shortage of dollars. For purposes of exchange this crisis is called a DOLLAR GAP.

Emolument and **Remuneration**   'Recompense for labor' may be called EMOLUMENT. Specifically, income from an office to the office-holder, and, more generally, profit, gain, or any advantage accruing from a position is EMOLUMENT. It refers also to honors and favor as well as money. REMUNERATION is an 'exact return for work done,' reckoned only in money. EMOLUMENT is a reward, largely monetary, for attaining and creditably occupying a high position.

Excise Tax   An EXCISE TAX is a domestic tax on the manufacture, sale or consumption of commodities. A domestic tax is one levied within a country's own borders.

Fiscal   An adjective deriving from Latin *fiscus,* 'state treasury,' and hence referring to 'governmental finances.'

Gratuity and **Tip**   GRATUITY is a dignified and more gracious word for TIP. TIP is said to have originated on a placard, reading "To Insure Promptitude," placed beside a bowl in an inn. TIPS also include rake-offs and hand-outs of many sorts that may not be genteel expressions of gratitude, as GRATUITIES are supposed to be.

Kudos and **Lucre**   KUDOS is Greek for 'fame' and LUCRE is French-Latin for 'riches.' But KUDOS embraces glory and acclaim, like our word celebrity, while LUCRE is—well, we often call it filthy though we may be amassing it industriously at the time.

Proposition   Fortunately, even in practical America we tend to reject words whose meaning becomes too cold and hard. Who, for instance, in love would make a matrimonial PROPOSITION, instead of a 'proposal?' Unfortunately a good word is sometimes lost to general use in this way. For, though PROPOSITION has narrowed and hardened in usage, it still means simply 'the offering of something for discussion or consideration.' "The proposition is, gentlemen, that we adjourn to the coffee room, and continue our deliberations there," is the kind of use the word should get more often. Our chief errors in usage lie in the habit, not of restricting, but of dispersing the sense of a word. We overwork a word. Continually we say we 'make a proposition' when we actually mean to make only a 'suggestion.' Sometimes we let PROPOSITION take the place of recommendation. At other times we use PROPOSITION as a synonym for plan. This overworking of a word is as much a loss to our vocabulary as its restriction to, say, business or sports.

CELEBRATION

Accolade

ANNIVERSARY n. the annually recurring date of some past event; a day set apart in each year to commemorate a past event.

ARRAY n. an orderly collection or assembly of articles or people; a display; an imposing layout of things exhibited.

Bacchanals & Bacchantes

Bacchantes see **Bacchanals & Bacchantes**

BALL n. a social assembly for the purpose of dancing.

BLOWOUT n. a feast; an entertainment; a spree. (Slang)

CARNIVAL n. the feast or season of rejoicing before Lent; feasting or revelry in general.

Cavalcade

CELEBRATION n. a commemorative or distinguishing ceremony.

Ceremonial & Ceremonious

Ceremonious see **Ceremonial & Ceremonious**

CIRCENSIAN adj. pertaining to circus.

Conjugal see **Nuptial, Matrimonial**, etc.

Connubial see **Nuptial, Matrimonial**, etc.

DEBUT n. beginning; first attempt; thus, in society, the first appearance of a young lady, or in the theater, the first appearance of a player.

DEMONSTRATION n. a manifestation; a show; a public exhibition.

DISPLAY n. an exhibition, an opening or unfolding to public view; an imposing show, as "The runners made a great display of physical stamina."

EPULARY adj. pertaining to feast.

EVENT n. an occurrence of some importance; a specially observed incident.

EXEQUIES n. pl. funereal rites.

EXHIBIT v. to display; to show conspicuously. n. any collection of things EXHIBITED publicly. Also, n. EXHIBITION, the act of EXHIBITING or displaying.

FEAST *n.* a sumptuous entertainment or repast.

FESTAL *adj.* refers to holiday.

FESTIVAL *n.* a feast; a festal day; a time of celebration.

FETE or FÊTE *n.* a feast; a holiday.

FIELD DAY *n.* a day of unusual exertion or of display; a gala day; an outdoor occasion.

FIESTA *n.* a saint's day; a holiday; any festivity.

FUNCTION *n.* an official ceremony.

FUNERAL *n.* the ceremony of burying a dead person. *adj.* FUNEREAL.

GAME *n.* a contest.

HOLIDAY *n.* a religious day; a day of exemption from work.

Hymeneal see **Nuptial, Matrimonial,** etc.

JAMBOREE *n.* a spree; any noisy merrymaking. (Slang)

JUBILEE *n.* in general, the celebration on completion of any fiftieth year of continuous course.

JUNKET *n.* a feast, or merrymaking; a picnic; an excursion at public cost.

Matrimonial see **Nuptial, Matrimonial,** etc.

Nuptial, Matrimonial, Hymeneal, Conjugal, Connubial, Spousal

OBSEQUIES *n. pl.* funeral rites or processions. Sometimes used in the singular, OBSEQUY. See also OBSEQUIOUS & OBSEQUIES under the category CONDUCT.

OBSERVANCE *n.* a rite or ceremony.

PAGEANT *n.* a spectacle; a show; an entertainment.

Parade

POMP *n.* a procession of much splendor; a pageant; a display.

PRESENTATION *n.* a representation, exhibition, appearance.

PROCESSION *n.* a parade; a succession of persons walking or riding; a formal march, as an academic PROCESSION.

PROMENADE *n.* a place for walking. *v.* to walk about, or up and down.

REGATTA *n.* a boat race.

REVELRY *n.* a merrymaking.

REVIEW *n.* a formal inspection of military forces.

RITE *n.* a formal act or series of acts of a religious or other solemn nature.

RITUAL *n.* a prescribed set of rites.

ROUT *n.* a large social assemblage.

SALUTE *n.* a ceremonial salutation. *v.* to thank a hero publicly for service rendered to the nation; to greet or welcome.

SATURNALIA *n.* any wild or noisy revelry.

SPECTACLE *n.* a public show or display, esp. designed to attract the eye.

Spousal see **Nuptial, Matrimonial,** etc.

SPREE *n.* a frolic; a prank; a blowout.

TRIUMPH *n.* a public festivity, often to salute a popular victory.

WAKE *n.* a watch throughout the night, often over a corpse.

Accolade 'To acclaim' something or someone is to shout applause. Naturally in an age abounding in baseball and military heroes 'acclaim' is a popular word. ACCOLADE, though an old and ceremonial word concerned with chivalry, is, today, any ritualistic gesture in a public event, the ceremony itself or, in commoner circumstances, high praise. It is not shouted praise, like 'acclaim,' but serious and fervent praise—and intimate. Ceremonial sentiment permeates its meaning. Even in Shakespeare's time ACCOLADE was described as an 'embracing' or 'colling' (literally, 'necking'), and referred especially to the dubbing of a knight. The knightly salutation used to be a kiss or an embrace, but it has become a light, affectionate tapping on the shoulder with the flat of a sword. In France, however, honors are still bestowed with a light kiss on each cheek.

Bacchanals and **Bacchantes** 'Male and female votaries of Bacchus, Greek god of wine.' The Bacchantes used in their revelries a peculiar cry: Evoe! It was an interjection, and perhaps had no meaning except as an expression of exhilaration. The masculine two-syllable form of the French BACCHANTE—i.e. 'bacchant'—can be used for BACCHANAL. Both are from the original Bacchae, the Maenads, or raving maidens, who fled to the woods to celebrate the mysteries Bacchus had taught them. BACCHANAL is also an adjective referring to wild feasting, flowing, and a return to the liberating aspects of a natural life. Incidentally, Dionysus is another name for Bacchus.

Cavalcade From Latin *caballus,* 'horse,' and hence referring properly to 'a procession of persons on horseback.' CAVALCADE is loosely used now for 'any parade.' But you see the word 'motorcade' in our newspapers more and more now as demonstration by our language that automobiles are here to stay for a while.

Ceremonial and **Ceremonious** As 'astronomical' is to 'astronomy,' so CEREMONIAL is to a CEREMONY. It is the plain and regular adjective for its noun. But CEREMONIOUS is a derivative adjective referring to 'manners.' CEREMONIOUS describes any 'air, behavior, appearance or speech that suggests ceremony.' CEREMONIAL suggests everything appropriate to the *specific* occasion or ritual of a CEREMONY. "Not only the whole setting, but especially the solemn mien of the chairman, were oppressively ceremonial." CEREMONIOUS is strong and general enough to describe any elaborate manner or solemn occasion. "The ceremonious man in black is the head waiter."

Nuptial, Matrimonial, Hymeneal, Conjugal, Connubial and Spousal
The nub of NUPTIAL is Latin *nubo*, 'I marry.' We use the word chiefly in connection with weddings. The source of MATRIMONY is Latin *mater*, 'mother.' HYMENEAL is a lighter word, celebrating Hymen, god of marriage. CONJUGAL is figurative and synthetic, meaning 'joined together,' and referring to marriage as a 'joint enterprise.' CONNUBIAL is the emphatic of NUPTIAL, but referring especially to life after the wedding. Like NUPTIAL it is related to *nubo*, but is prefixed with *con*, 'together.' SPOUSAL refers to the pledge at the altar, and hence to marriage.. An 'espousal' is a 'wedding,' or, figuratively, your 'acceptance of an idea, a cause, a plan.' "I espoused his opinions, for they represented a good cause."

Parade PARADE is typical of some colorful and restless words we can use with effect in figurative ways. Sunlit streets and applauding crowds are essential to PARADES. If, then, you PARADE your own knowledge, you are either making a public show of yourself, or you are advertising ideas with a splurge. Or that girl ahead of you on the street who PARADES her charms, has at the least an open manner. We instinctively distrust a man who makes a PARADE of his wealth wherever he goes. Used as either a noun or a verb this word is an excellent addition to your vocabulary.

CHANCE AND NECESSITY

ACCIDENT *n.* in general, anything that happens without design; an unforeseen effect; the operation of chance.
Adventitious & Fortuitous
CASUAL *adj.* happening without apparent cause or without design; occasional.
CHANCE See **Adventitious & Fortuitous** for a general discussion of the ideas involved in CHANCE
CONTINGENT *adj.* due to chance, or a free agent; accidentally happening; dependent on a person's decision, and thus an effect of free will.
Determinate see **Determined & Determinate**
Determined & Determinate
ESSENTIAL *adj.* involved in the nature or definition of a thing, as "An essential factor in classical art is symmetry."
Exigent
FLUKE *n.* any unexpected, or accidental, advantage or turn. (Slang)

Fortuitous see **Adventitious & Fortuitous**

FORTUNE *n.* chance; hap; luck.

HAP *n.* a fortuitous event; fortune; luck.

HAZARD *n.* a fortuitous event; chance; accident.

HIT-OR-MISS *adj.* reckless; haphazard.

IMPERATIVE *adj.* peremptory; absolute, as IMPERATIVE commands; hence, obligatory, binding, as IMPERATIVE duties.

Inadvertent

INCIDENTAL *adj.* occurring fortuitously; happening in conjunction with something else of greater importance.

INDISPENSABLE *adj.* requisite; not to be omitted; absolutely necessary or requisite.

INEVITABLE *adj.* unavoidable because destined.

LOT *n.* share or portion in life that befalls in a casual manner.

LUCK *n.* fortune; hap; whatever happens by chance.

Necessary

NECESSITY *n.* the condition or quality of being necessary or needful; a condition requisite for the fulfillment of a goal.

NEEDFUL *n.* necessary; requisite.

PREREQUISITE *n.* previously required; a condition necessary for the fulfillment of something following, as "A prerequisite for social success is good manners."

RANDOM *adj.* aimless; fortuitous; haphazard; casual.

Required & Requisite

Requisite see **Required & Requisite**

UNAVOIDABLE *adj.* cannot be shunned; as an UNAVOIDABLE calamity.

Adventitious and Fortuitous FORTUITOUS means much more than 'chance.' It refers to unexpected events that happen entirely by chance and *without known cause*. Columbus accidentally discovered America when he was looking for India. Miscalculations may have contributed to the discovery. Nevertheless the discovery itself was FORTUITOUS because it was completely unexpected. No one suspected the existence of a Western Continent, and lo and behold! it was there. Things that are FORTUITOUS are like that: they are bolts from the blue. FORTUITOUS events are sometimes unfortunate developments we couldn't possibly anticipate or entirely understand. FORTUITOUS derives from Latin *fors*, 'chance.' Generally, the difference between 'chance' and FORTUITOUS is that the latter is an unexpected event while the former is half expected at the least. A coin 'by chance' lands heads or tails up, and we *expect* either heads or tails though we don't *know* which.

ADVENTITIOUS can also mean 'accidental,' but the accident is not essential to the event. ADVENTITIOUS is a narrower word than FORTUITOUS, and is used specifically in botany and biology. It comes practically intact from the Latin *adventicius*, meaning 'foreign, extraordinary, coming from abroad.' An exotic plant is ADVENTITIOUS in that original sense. But today we say scientifically a plant is 'adventive' (the more technical form of the word) when it has not become perfectly naturalized. Weeds that grow profusely in our garden are also 'adventive.' Diseases that are not inherited, but acquired, are ADVENTITIOUS. Buds that appear irregularly in wrong places are ADVENTITIOUS. Anything that appears to be natural and spontaneous, but occurs sparsely or accidentally, is ADVENTITIOUS. ADVENTITIOUS things are not inherently essential, but imposed by chance or circumstances, such as spangles on a dress or campaign buttons. The 't' in the word 'against' is ADVENTITIOUS because it wasn't originally in that word at all. These examples define ADVENTITIOUS as it is generally used, and they are cited because the use of this word is often confused with the use of FORTUITOUS and 'chance.' While FORTUITOUS things happen without design, because we don't understand them well enough to have a hand in them, ADVENTITIOUS things can be brought in from the outside by human intervention. ADVENTITIOUS things are not only incidental to a subject, as a spangle is to a dress, or outside the regular course, as casual things are. Sometimes they are intrinsically acquired. An odd phrase or mannerism that is so spontaneous we can't believe it was deliberately assumed, is thus ADVENTITIOUS. An ADVENTITIOUS advantage has an aspect of unexpected luck, or of an unusual interposition in our favor from the outside.

Determined and **Determinate**   You should know the difference between these two words as well as the various meanings of the second. The senses of both are almost inextricably entangled with all the intensive ('de'-prefixed) derivatives of their common Latin root, *terminus*, 'end.' 'Determinant' and 'determinative,' upon which both popular and academic usage has heaped so many meanings, have become too confused for even dictionaries to treat adequately.

Both meanings of DETERMINED are quite simple. One comes from its use as a participle, and the other as an adjective. Whether you say, "I have determined the truth," or "I am determined to discover the truth," no one will seriously misunderstand you. But both these meanings have carried over into DETERMINATE where they can easily be confused with the meaning of that word.

The main and oldest meaning of DETERMINATE is 'limited' or 'clearly defined,' and hence 'definite, fixed, distinct, specific, established.' Examples can best indicate how this principal meaning of DETERMINATE is expressed. A concept of limits 'reached and defined,' and hence both 'distinct outlines' and 'a fixed integrity' persists in each of these examples.

"The clear and determinate meaning of my letter was . . ." "The ensuing intervals of peace were determinate." "Just as the physiques of children are not yet determinate, so their minds and spirits are still facile and volatile." In mathematics, there is a DETERMINATE quantity, which is known or fixed. There is also a DETERMINATE problem, admitting of only one solution. In botany, certain fungi which, in spite of their fleshiness, are clearly defined in their outlines, illustrate DETERMINATE growth. The shoots of many trees, that stop, as if their job were completed, before the season is over, or, more often, a flowering outward, called also 'centrifugal, cymose or definite growth,' in which the main stem of a plant produces a flower, first, at its top, with the secondary axes or stems beneath it flowering in turn at their tips—these are examples of DETERMINATE growth. In biology, there are DETERMINATE or orthogenic variations in which certain tendencies persist in new types developed by natural selection.

The hard core of this meaning was so opposed to vagueness and chance that DETERMINATE came to mean 'not arbitrary.' 'Arbitrary' refers to the results of a will or force that is not controlled by rule or government. An 'arbitrary' command comes not from law but from dictators. So we can speak either of the DETERMINATE opinion of mankind that atrocities should be outlawed, or of the ultimate, or crystal, shape which each mineral inevitably assumes for itself as its DETERMINATE form. But words follow men's needs as polo ponies the ball, and in Shakespeare's age DETERMINATE sheered off some of its meaning. Applied to the multifarious affairs of men, it did not adhere solely to its meaning of inflexibly established and hence *not* 'arbitrary.' Certain decrees which *are* 'arbitrary' in representing an exercise of the will rather than the application of a principle, came to be called DETERMINATE, and now we can speak of a DETERMINATE order of procedure, meaning one that is agreed upon, definite and formal. Thus DETERMINATE came to suggest 'pre-determination,' or 'an agreed conclusion,' and hence to imply or state that a thing is 'final' and 'definitive,' as a DETERMINATE judgment. A DETERMINATE judgment is one that either has been arrived at beforehand and is, as we would say, cut and dried, or one that is intended to be permanent. There is even a meaning of invariability in the word which seems still to be extant. Monks used to write of a "determinate form of praying." Formerly DETERMINATE even meant 'intended.'

It is easy to see how DETERMINATE, as it lost its meaning of 'not arbitrary' and assumed its meaning of 'pre-determination,' was gradually confused with DETERMINED. Being 'fixed in mind and purpose,' or being 'resolute in decisions and actions' is the same as being DETER-

MINED; being 'fixed in mind and purpose,' or being 'resolute in decision' we have just seen is involved in the meaning of 'DETERMINATE judgment.' At this point, the meanings of the two words merge.

Exigent This word means either 'urgent' or 'exacting.' EXIGENT circumstances either 'urge' you to do something or 'force' you to do it. The usual implication is that the action demanded is some sort of aid, either to others or to yourself. "In this exigent circumstance he appealed to the home office." Very often we use the noun, EXIGENCY or EXIGENCE, to mean 'pressing necessity.' Incidentally, EXIGENT comes from Latin *exigere*, 'to require, exact.'

Inadvertent 'Momentarily absent-minded' is the meaning of this word. An INADVERTENT mistake may cost many soldiers their lives. Its base is the verb 'advert' ('to turn toward') made into a negative. If you advertise your wares, you turn the minds of others to them. If you act INADVERTENTLY, you 'fail to turn' your own mind properly to your own affairs. The rabbit which INADVERTENTLY hopped into a trap did not watch where it was going. The word is naturally useful to businessmen. "I didn't at once sense the importance of your letter and so neglected to answer it sooner. I hope you will pardon this inadvertence."

Necessary There is a certain philosophic logic in the word NECESSARY that may escape our consideration. For example, precept, which prescribes what is NECESSARY in moral conduct, is only personal. We don't apply precepts to *things*. You might teach a child by precepts, but you may arouse in his mind certain precepts counter to your own. That is where the word NECESSARY comes in. Whatever is NECESSARY 'has to be,' whether you like it or not. But its use is softened by the grammatically passive form, 'it is necessary' instead of 'you must.' The trouble with 'you must' is that it also throws you back on your personal inclination. When somebody says, "You must do this," you are inclined to answer, "Must I?" When someone says, "It is necessary to do this," well then you just go ahead and do it. You must not forget, though, that 'must' is short and powerful. Sometimes the force with which a person can say, "You must," is more effective than the long-way-around in "It is necessary."

Required and Requisite REQUISITE is a synonym for REQUIRED, but it has uses for which REQUIRED is inadequate. Their bases are the same. Both mean literally 'to seek again,' and what you seek a second time you 'need.' You can speak of either the REQUIRED or the REQUISITE means of doing something, and each time the inference is that these means are 'essential.' But REQUIRE is reserved for the particular needs of one situation or one person. "This job requires tact." "Courtship requires money."

But REQUISITE is used for the permanent nature of things, and for *all* the circumstances of a certain time or purpose. REQUISITE thus becomes nearly a synonym for 'indispensable.' "High office requires us to respect the incumbent; such respect is, in fact, a requisite of good government." However, the words are commonly used interchangeably, with only a difference in phraseology. Good weather is REQUIRED for our enjoyment of an outing: it is REQUISITE to our enjoyment.

The nouns are REQUISITION and REQUIREMENT. A REQUISITION is often simply a 'REQUIREMENT' or a 'need.' But it can also refer to the 'state of being needed.' A store keeper who has run out of shirts, has a REQUISITION for a new supply. You may use the verb, "He requisitions new shirts." The verb means 'to order what is needed,' or 'to press into service.' "During the flood the mayor requisitioned all the beds he could find."

CHARACTER

ABILITY *n.* talent; mental gift or endowment; usually in the *pl.* ABILITIES, as "The natural abilities of an artist eventually determine the direction of his genius."

APTITUDE *n.* a capacity or propensity for a certain course, career, result, as "That child already has an aptitude for petty crime."

BENT *n.* inclination; disposition; propensity. "A juvenile delinquent possesses a bent for contrariety."

CAPABILITY *n.* the quality of being able to do something, of being fitted to assume some responsibility.

CAPACITY *n.* active power; ability, as "His genius has the capacity to display itself in several fields of art."

CAST *n.* manner; outward appearance; air; style.

CELEBRITY *n.* fame; renown; distinction; also, a famous person.

Character & Reputation

COMPLEXION *n.* the general appearance of anything; aspect, as "The complexion of the political convention was clearly turbulent."

CONSTITUTION *n.* the composition or make-up of anything, as "The athlete's constitution was strong and in tone."

DISPOSITION *n.* aptitude, inclination; tendency.

ÉCLAT *n.* renown; glory.

FACULTY *n.* a specific power, mental or physical.

FAME *n.* renown; notoriety; reputation. "The fame of his last book spread over the English-speaking world."

FORTE *n.* that in which one excels; a particular talent.

FRAME *n.* the general form or composition of anything.

Genius & Talent

GIFT *n.* a special talent or aptitude.

GLORY *n.* éclat; fame; praise or honor afforded by the public to a person or thing.

HONOR *n.* respect mixed with reverence; esteem persons afford to another person or an event.

INDIVIDUALITY *n.* the particular or distinctive character of a person.

KNACK *n.* a specific ability; dexterity.

MOOD *n.* a display of certain temperament; state of mind; disposition.

NATURE *n.* essential character, quality or kind of anything.

NOTORIETY *n.* the state of being widely or publicly known, esp. in the sense of ill fame.

PERSONALITY *n.* the character of a person as distinguished from that of a thing.

PRESTIGE *n.* reputation for excellence; the power of getting respect, praise and honor.

RENOWN *n.* fame.

Reputation see **Character & Reputation**

Talent see **Genius & Talent**

TEMPER *n.* disposition or frame of mind; mood; the character of one's emotions.

TEMPERAMENT *n.* that part of a person's personality that has been formed by physical or deep-seated psychological factors; thus, the relatively constant part of personality.

Character and **Reputation** REPUTATIONS reflect CHARACTER. REPUTATIONS are what people think *and* say *and* hear *and* repeat about CHARACTER. However, since the nature of man is what it is, REPUTATIONS are not usually accurate representations of CHARACTER. Besides, the best of REPUTATIONS can be ruined in an hour, but CHARACTER, as Horace Greeley said, endures. The CHARACTER of a man, or of anything, is 'his, or its, true nature.' If one can really learn the true CHARACTER of a man, he can correct the distortions of his REPUTATION. The CHARACTER of Christ is beyond dispute. And the CHARACTER, the aggregate and unalterable physical characteristics, of the atomic bomb we are sure of.

Genius and **Talent** In general, TALENT is low-grade GENIUS. TALENT can be trained while GENIUS is a law unto itself. GENIUS has been defined laconically as 'hard work.' GENIUS is like our will power, which on the one hand enables us to do astounding deeds without premeditation or preparation, and on the other hand supports us while we achieve distant goals. Many inspired definitions of GENIUS have been made, and some good ones of TALENT, because the comparison appeals to the imagination.

TALENT is marked by unusual *mental* ability, combined with such special skills as that ability needs. GENIUS is exceptional, or exalted, *intellectual* ability, combined with any power that derives from it. TALENT may be brilliant and amazing, but it lacks that imposing imagination and power to create new things that point to a link between the Divine and GENIUS. This is implicit in the origin and history of the word GENIUS itself. GENIUS is undoubtedly touched by madness, on which is perhaps built part of its reputation. Its genesis is shrouded in prehistory, probably Aryan, in a root *gan* that gave us many other powerful words, like 'kindred' and 'king.' The first recognizable GENIUS was an immaterial spirit, part of the Roman religion, born severally in every individual, like our soul. Sometimes it was even worshipped, especially when it lodged in the person who headed a home, family, or locality. Thus it became associated with destiny, and each locality had its own familiar spirit or GENIUS, of which we still speak as the spiritual character of a place. Likewise in Rome the personal GENIUS was objectified as TALENT and wit, these springing from one's inborn nature.

Thus far GENIUS was practical and sane. But in its Latin root *gens*, 'a clan' or 'race,' there was a power. It begat a verb *gignere*, meaning 'to beget,' or 'to create.' When GENIUS came into English in the 16th century it was associated with man's mind. Derived from the Latin suggestion of TALENT and wit, in English it referred to natural ability and, after Dr. Johnson's time, to intellectual power. But in the meantime, and this is important, something else had happened to it—something touched with real madness and magic.

In Arabian demonology there are powerful nature spirits called *jinn*. The singular is *jinni*, and the French used their own word, *genie*, which referred to the Roman GENIUS, to translate this nature spirit from Arabian tales. Likewise the English used GENIUS to translate *jinni*, though later they adopted (and we still use) the French *genie*. (For the plural *jinn* we now use the Latin *genii*, but GENIUSES is the plural of GENIUS.) This Oriental imp of the air was not unfamiliar to the English. Since medieval times they had known him, and had confused him with the demons or evil spirits of the New Testament. These New Testament spirits were originally the Greek daimons or demi-gods.

Even the Latin GENIUS was eventually corrupted by the Greek daimons so that the Romans began to think of their individual spirits as ghosts or demi-gods who influenced their destiny. So in the English word GENIUS a sense of the demon came from both the Latin GENIUS and especially from the Arabian *jinni*. The demons had warred with the angels, and the jinn inhabited fire and air, exercising fantastic influences over persons and only controllable by magic. Finally we find Kipling speaking of the demon who initiated and directed his writing. With that, the two meanings in GENIUS unite.

In contrast TALENT has maintained its stability. Once it was nearly on a par with GENIUS. In post-Roman Europe some small difference was felt between the two words, but it was the German writers of the 18th century who first emphasized the distinctions. Where GENIUS assumed the inscrutable character of a seemingly irresponsible will, TALENT became a capacity which we could analyze.

TALENT did not, like GENIUS, come vaguely out of an obscure antiquity. It began (in Greece) concretely, as a weight, its root being in a Sanskrit word meaning 'to lift.' So it became a balance, and then in New Testament times, the metal coin weighed in a balance. Since a balance is tilted, TALENT began to mean an inclination, a human disposition, and at last an aptitude. Only, as in the case of GENIUS, something else happened to it also. There is, in Matthew's gospel, a parable in which a 'TALENT of money' became a gift and, incidentally, a great gift since the 'gold TALENT' was worth some thirty thousand dollars, and the silver one over two thousand. While the word TALENT, then, began more and more to take on the meaning or ability, it began also to be thought of as a great gift, or endowment. Today TALENT signifies both a 'bestowal of ability,' and the 'skill to make use of it.'

CHARITY

ALTRUISM *n.* the benevolent instincts and impulses in general. *adj.* ALTRUISTIC.

BENEFACTION *n.* the act of doing good, of giving benefits.

BENIGNITY *n.* goodness of disposition; kindness of nature.

BOUNTEOUS *adj.* full of goodness to others; generous; disposed to giving.

CHARITY *n.* good will; love for everyone; spec., philanthropy.

CLEMENCY *n.* mildness of temper; disposition to forgive; leniency.

Commiseration see **Compassion & Commiseration**

**Compassion & Commiseration
Eleemosynary & Philanthropic**

FORBEARANCE   *n.* restraint of passions; indulgence; patience.

HUMANITARIANISM   *n.* the belief that man's obligations are to man alone, rather than to God; hence, generally a regard for man; benevolence.

KIND   *adj.* pertaining to a sympathetic nature; good-hearted; considerate.

LIBERALITY   *n.* generosity; bounty; freeness in giving.

MAGNANIMOUS   *adj.* great of mind or heart; liberal and honorable; unselfish.

Philanthropic   see **Eleemosynary & Philanthropic**

PITY   *n.* a sympathetic sorrow for others in distress; an impulse to relieve other people's sufferings.

RUTH   *n.* compassion; pity; mercy; tenderness.

SYMPATHETIC   *adj.* pertaining to the common feelings one person has with another. *n.* SYMPATHY.

Compassion and **Commiseration**   COMPASSION is a noble word, and COMMISERATION is a rather miserable one. Both speak of suffering, but the second speaks of misery. The 'ess's' in COMPASSION were once a 't'; perhaps through suffering the word has softened. Componently it means, like COMMISERATION, 'suffering together.' But COMPASSION means more. The philosophy that 'misery loves company' has given us COMMISERATE. But a COMPASSIONATE person is selfless. He suffers with another in order to help. His sympathy is a pity that helps and supports.

Eleemosynary and **Philanthropic**   The first is as long as an eel, almost, and about as repulsive and useless. But you do find it in newspapers occasionally. It was the Greek way of saying 'alms.' Today it refers principally to 'institutional charity.'

PHILANTHROPIC is also Greek, meaning literally 'love of man.' The millionaire who takes two and a half seconds of his time to sign a check for charity lest he be thought niggardly may be ELEEMOSYNARY (or an ELEEMOSYNARY) but he is not PHILANTHROPIC.

COLORS

ACHROMATIC   *adj.* free from color; uncolored.

ASHEN   *adj.* like ashes; gray; pale.

BLANCH   *v.* to whiten; to cause to lose color; also, to lose color.

BLEACH   *v.* to whiten; to blanch; also, to grow pale.

BRILLIANCE or BRIGHTNESS *n.* luminosity; value. With SATURATION and HUE or TINT one of the three qualities of COLOR.

CANESCENT *adj.* becoming white.

COLOR *n.* hue, tint.

AERUGINOUS *adj.* green, as of verdigris.

ARGENT *n.* silver. *adj.* like silver, esp. in color.

CERULEAN *adj.* azure; sky-blue.

Fulvid

FULVOUS *adj.* tawny; dull yellowish-grey or brown.

GLAUCOUS *adj.* light greenish-blue; sea green.

Gray & Grey

HYACINTHINE *adj.* bluish-blue-red; or of hyacinth blue, hyacinth violet or hyacinth pink in hue.

ICTERITIOUS *adj.* jaundiced yellow.

Magenta & Solferino

Pinto

RUFOUS *adj.* dull red.

Sable

Sepia

Shot

Solferino see Magenta & Solferino

STRAMINEOUS *adj.* in botany, straw-colored.

Tawny

Viridiscent

XANTHIC *adj.* yellow. Used esp. of flowers.

Colorful see Colorless & Colorful

Colorless & Colorful

ERUBESCENT or RUBESCENT *adj.* reddening, blushing.

ETIOLATE *v.* to whiten; blanch; esp. by loss of sunlight.

FLAVESCENT *adj.* turning yellow, as the leaves of an old book.

HUE *n.* color.

Kaleidoscope

LUTESCENT *adj.* tending toward yellow. LUTEOUS means of a deep reddish yellow.

NIGRESCENT *adj.* turning black.

PALE *adj.* dim; ashen; without strong color.

SATURATION *n.* amount or intensity of color; also called CHROMA.

TINT *n.* pale color; delicate color. Also used to mean hue, or variety of color. *adj.* TINCTORIAL, of or relating to color or colors.

WAN *adj.* pale; ashen.

WHITEN *v.* to become white; to lose color; to blanch.

Colorless and Colorful Though everything really has color, COLORLESS can figuratively describe about one half of everything. COLORFUL describes the other half. Perhaps it is the powerful impression the outdoors and the weather makes on us which has most contributed to the figurative use of these two words. After all, if the day is bleak and grey, so are we gloomy; but, if the day is sunny and bright, so are we cheerful. Perhaps also, since one half of our life is spent in the day, and one half of it in the night, we can quite naturally conceive of everything in terms of color. And so there are such images as COLORFUL music, COLORLESS personalities, COLORFUL ideas, and COLORLESS philosophies, etc.

Fulvid Means 'reddish-yellow.' Like another word, 'turgid,' which means 'swollen,' FULVID is most often used to describe flood waters. 'Fulvous' is a weak variant of FULVID.

Gray and **Grey** Only of horses is GREY necessary: a pair of GREYS. Plenty of race horses bear names like Gray Fox and Gray Goose, but the equine himself should be a GREY. Here in America even that distinction is not always the rule. Either spelling is in all cases logically correct, for the two words mean and sound the same. The English still prefer GREY and we prefer GRAY. 'Greyhound' is an exception. The GREY might have been Latin *grae*, 'Greek,' or Old English *grig*, 'bitch.' GRAY is the more sensible since by analogy GREY could rhyme with 'key.' No one is tempted to mispronounce GRAY.

Among the fastidious there are objections to any arbitrary preferences. It is claimed that usage has made the signification vary with the spelling. It is claimed that GREY is more truly GREY than GRAY is. They say GREY is a lighter and more delicate color. GRAY, on the other hand, is said to be a warm color, with a touch of brown, or even of red, in it. But this simply confuses the words needlessly. We had better take our pick of GRAY or GREY, and stick to our choice for good.

Kaleidoscope KALEIDOSCOPES today are often heard of, but seldom seen. Probably many of us who use the adjective KALEIDOSCOPIC, which promotes the instrument's fame, have never peered into the tube of this optical toy and beheld the inter-tumbling cataracts of brightly colored crystals that fascinate the eye by their color and the mind by their symmetry. The crystals are only bits of glass, but their images are caught up, reflected and thrown into symmetrical and ever-changing patterns by a system of miniature mirrors within the tube. The tube itself is bulbous at one end like that of a modern giant flashlight; but the KALEIDOSCOPE's objective is art, not utility. The word itself means literally in the Greek 'beautiful forms to behold,' and inevitably its adjective now means not merely 'picturesquely diversified,' as some dictionaries may give you, but 'bewilderingly colorful.' It conveys also the ideas of motion and continuous change, and an over-all suggestion of multiple design.

Magenta and **Solferino** These brilliant red dyes came to us in 1859. That was when the French and the Sardinians were fighting the

Austrians in northern Italy. At Magenta they checked the Austrians and at Solferino they routed them. Both battles were hard fought and bloody. At Solferino alone, on the plains of Lombardy, the combined losses were thirty-eight thousand men—more than twenty-five times the entire population of the little town which has provided a name for both the battle and the color. The association of so much blood with the crimson shades of these two colors was inevitable. Specifically, MAGENTA is 'purplish,' and SOLFERINO is 'bluish-red.' Both are variants of fuchsine, a dye named for the usual color of fuchsia, a flower named for a German botanist, Fuchs, which means 'fox.'

Pinto A 'mottled' or 'piebald' color is PINTO. In the Western United States a horse or pony is often called simply PINTO. Etymologically, 'piebald' and PINTO are the same. The 'pie' is French from the Latin *pica,* a 'magpie.' The root is *pingere,* 'to paint.' 'Pinto' in Spanish means 'painted,' and comes from the same Latin verb. The 'bald' is not exactly what it seems to be. 'Bald' used to be spelled 'balled,' and probably referred to 'white spots.'

Sable SABLE is a poetic word for 'black.' Symbolically, it suggests 'mourning.' SABLE is the fur of the little Russian weasel-like flesh-eater whose coat is really dark brown. Perhaps merchants darkened the fur because it sold better that way. Because of its costliness and richness, SABLE was often worn with snow-white ermine, and perhaps was dyed black to make a better contrast. In heraldry, at any rate, SABLE means 'positively black.' It bears connotations more regal and romantic than 'ebon' or 'raven.' SABLE sounds at least as black as 'jet-black.'

Sepia SEPIA is a 'reddish dark-brown color,' prepared from the ink of a cuttlefish, which is a big-eyed, meat-eating mollusk.

Shot This word means 'many colored,' as a cloth is when the warp and weft are of different colors. Silk of any tint is SHOT with silver when it is twisted in the light. A favorite expression to describe a sunset is, "The sky is shot with crimson."

Tawny TAWNY means 'brownish-yellow.' It is a wonderful old word predating the Normans and the Saxons, going all the way back to the Britons and their word *tann,* 'oak-tree.' A tall, TAWNY man has a mystery about him since no mere sun-bathing produced his color. TAWNY still has a sound of the primitive in it, and old hunters probably sit around and talk about that man-eating TAWNY cat they shot in the darkest, loneliest part of the jungle.

Viridiscent 'Beginning to be green,' and hence 'slightly green.' "Boy, are you viridiscent!" might be a good way to tell your friend next time that he looks sick.

COMPARISON

AFFINITY *n.* inherent likeness or agreement, as between things.

AGREEMENT *n.* a state of similarity or resemblance, as between things; thus, concord; harmony; conformity.

ALIKE *adj.* having resemblance or similarity.

Analogy

APPROACH *v.* figuratively, to come near to in quality or character; to become nearly equal to.

As see Like & As

COMMENSURATE *adj.* corresponding in amount, degree, magnitude; proportionate to the purpose; as "To be a success you must make an effort commensurate with your goal."

COMPARABLE *adj.* worthy of comparison, as "In her beauty she was comparable to any of the most famous women of history."

CORRESPONDENCE *n.* a parallel relationship; similarity; as "There is a correspondence between the eye of the modern painter and the vision of the twentieth-century scientist." *adj.* CORRESPONDENT.

DIFFERENCE *n.* the condition of being other; dissimilarity in general; the relation between unlike things.

DISCONGRUITY *n.* disagreement; inconsistency.

DISCREPANCY *n.* difference; disagreement; variance or contrariety, esp. of facts or sentiments.

DISSIMILARITY *n.* unlikeness; want of resemblance.

DISSONANCE *n.* inharmoniousness; mixture of sounds.

EQUAL *adj.* having the same measurement in all respects as another.

Equate

EXAMPLE *n.* a sample; a specimen; an exemplar.

EXEMPLARY *adj.* serving as a model of imitation. *n.* EXEMPLAR. See also the category CONDUCT.

HETEROGENEITY *n.* state of dissimilarity; unlikeness.

IDENTICAL *adj.* pertaining to what is the same; to what is absolutely indistinguishable.

Ilk

INCONGRUITY *n.* unsuitability; unharmoniousness; anything out of keeping or having inappropriate parts.

KIND *n.* a class; individual ob-

jects having common characteristics; as, "They are all the same
kind of birds."

Less & Lesser

Lesser   see **Less & Lesser**

Like & As

Match

Model   see **Standard & Model**

OTHER *adj.* second, as every
OTHER day; additional; further,
as "All other peoples are mostly
like us too!" *n.* OTHERNESS. See
also the example under RESEM-
BLANCE.

PARADIGM *n.* an example; a
model; in grammar, an illustration of a word with all its inflections.

PARALLEL *adj.* having the same
direction or tendency; continuing a resemblance through
many particulars; like; similar.

PATTERN *n.* an original or a
model used for copying or making more of the same.

RECIPROCAL *adj.* mutually ex-
changed or exchangeable; given
in exact return.

Replica

RESEMBLANCE *n.* likeness; similarity; *v.* RESEMBLE. "Identical
twins often resemble each other
so closely that one is continually mistaken for the other."

SAME *adj.* not other; identical.

SIMILARITY *n.* likeness; perfect or
partial resemblance.

SORT *n.* kind; the quality or character of something. "He's the
sort of man everyone likes."

Standard & Model

TOUCHSTONE *n.* a test or criterion
by which the qualities of things
are judged.

TYPE *n.* a definitive example or
standard; an exemplar; pattern;
model.

YARDSTICK *n.* a measure; thus,
any standard of model against
which something is compared.

Analogy ANALOGY, though an important word, is a difficult one to
define. Roughly, it means 'resemblance of parts in a proportion.' The
derivation is from the Greek 'according to proportion.' The resemblance, though partial, portrays a relationship which is, for the moment, all-important. Ordinarily, most resemblances are simple and
superficial. For example, superficially a rat resembles a mole. But a rat
and a rabbit, though they don't obviously resemble each other, both
possess big, sharp front teeth. We know that a rat is a rodent. Because
a rabbit's front teeth are analogous (that is, make an ANALOGY) to the
rat's teeth, we learn the rabbit is also a rodent. ANALOGY takes into
account relations and, what is more important, it does so *for a purpose*. The purpose of an ANALOGY is to help us learn something new
about the parts involved in the resemblance. In an ANALOGY the resemblance is not lightly used as an example from which to argue or
illustrate, but deliberately.

ANALOGIES are 'meaningful comparisons of parts.' If you say a shrewish woman is a tigress, the comparison does not mean that the woman is literally, or actually, a tiger. The comparison is made to point an ANALOGY—she is like a tiger *in part*, in her tigerish temper.

An ANALOGUE is the part of an ANALOGY that is being compared for a purpose to the other part. In the example above, the rabbit's teeth are the ANALOGUE. In philology an ANALOGUE is a word that is the same in meaning, function and use in one tongue as another word is in another tongue, as English 'and' is the same as French *et*.

In biology an ANALOGUE is a structure having the same function, but not the same biological origin, as another structure. An ANALOGUE to the lungs in man are the gills in fish. ANALOGUE should not be confused with 'homologue,' which in biology refers to structures having the same evolutionary origin but possibly having different functions, like the wings of a bird and the forelegs of a horse.

Equate This word means 'to make equal.' If you EQUATE roast beef with steak, then you are making them equal in taste. Because EQUATE is a verb, it is frequently more direct and forceful than the adjective 'equal.' If you say, "I equate all politicians with gangsters," you have a stronger sentence than if you say, "All politicians are equal to gangsters."

Ilk A little vestigial English word we still thoughtlessly bandy about. ILK simply meant 'the same.' It has survived in Scotland for several uses, but reaches us via one, which we have wrongly expanded. We ought not to speak of two things being of the same ILK, meaning 'of the same breed or kind.' ILK properly refers to 'one of the same name or place,' as, for example, Mr. Carroll of that ILK, namely, Carrolltown. By extension, this ILK has become equivalent to a 'race' or a 'kind.'

Less and Lesser These sound like 'little' and 'littler,' but they are really both *equivalents* of 'littler.' Originally they were variants, although LESSER was generally used only as an adjective and before a noun, as "He was a LESSER man," or "That is a LESSER house." This division of labor still generally holds. LESS generally indicates a comparative smallness of *only* amounts; but LESSER may mean comparative smallness in *other* respects. Even as an adverb, as "You weigh less this week than last," LESS suggests amount. The present tendency is to use other words for LESS or LESSER when the context permits. You may have LESS courage than the next man, but 'fewer' (instead of LESS) enemies. Something may cost 'fewer' (not LESS) dollars than something else. The price may be LESS, though it is usually 'lower.' You may have LESS opportunity than your neighbor, and consequently a 'slighter' (not LESS) chance of success. LESS abjures singular nouns preceded by 'a' or 'an.' We never refer to 'a LESS splendor' or 'a LESS gloom.' LESS seldom refers to plurals, unless they are conceived of as bulked amounts. You don't have LESS motor cars, though you *might* wear LESS clothes.

LESSER is more qualitative. A LESSER prize may represent LESS money value, but it inevitably implies also a degree of value other than monetary. It has, however, an archaic flavor, and the trend is to pass it by and to substitute more modern and specific comparatives.

Like and As As conjunctions, both of these words are in common use not only here but also in England. "Do as I say," or "Do like I do," are both now permitted. AS is still the preferred usage; but LIKE is popular, and is shouldering its way into even the topmost circles. The asset of LIKE is its adverbial activity. "Do like I do" suggests "Look, do like this." This pictorial force, this vivid suggestion of action, is genuine today. In the beginning LIKE was a still-life picture from the Anglo-Saxon *lic,* a noun meaning 'a form.' It took a prefix, and became *gelic,* meaning 'of the form of.' It then lost that prefix, and became our LIKE. The point is that the formal meaning of 'similarity' has expanded today into *active* similarity. In contrast AS has shrunk from 'all' and 'so' into a soft little lump suggesting 'all in this manner.'

Nevertheless we are all used to the soft AS, and the harder LIKE is loud and awkward. To educated ears LIKE still jars. What the outcome will be is anybody's guess.

Incidentally, some regard the conjunctional function as adverbial. Surely the conjunction has the force of an adverb and is close to a preposition. "Do as others do," is "Do in the common manner," or is "Do like others." These usages suggest adverbs.

Match The MATCH of 'matchstick' has nothing to do with 'matching one thing with another.' The latter derives from a different noun that was *gemaecca,* a 'companion' in early English. The match you strike was Old French *mesche,* modern French *meche,* a 'wick.'

Replica As Italian as 'regatta' is, and meaning, specifically, 'a painting copied by the original artist himself from his own work.' Hence

REPLICA loosely refers to 'a duplicate, an exact copy.' Still more loosely, it is used in music to denote a passage to be played again, that is, the musician copies his own work.

Standard and **Model** (see also NORM and CRITERION) Gold is a STANDARD of monetary values, and determines the *relative* values of dollars and pounds. A beach beauty is a MODEL of pulchritude. Both the gold and the girl are visible examples which enable us to compare and determine values mechanically, like the grocer's scales and a tape measure. Generally speaking, STANDARDS and MODELS are lower than 'criteria,' which involve very formal comparisons. Even if Miss America is selected by distinguished artists, she is hardly a 'criterion' of eternal beauty. Wealth may, in some people's minds, be a STANDARD of success but it is more exactly a STANDARD of security or position. A STANDARD is a 'value which is absolutely attainable,' but a MODEL is a more or less 'ideal value' which we strive to attain. A MODEL of virtue is what we want to be; a STANDARD of virtue is what we are expected to be.

CONDUCT

ACQUIT ONESELF *v.* to behave; to bear or conduct oneself, as "The women in the French *Résistance* acquitted themselves with soldierly bravery."

ADDRESS *n.* manner of speaking with people; personal behavior in society.

AIR *n.* general character or complexion of a person; appearance.

Aloof　see **Distant & Aloof**

Apology & Excuse

BEAR ONESELF *v.* to behave; to act; as, "The prince bore himself in a kingly manner."

BEARING *n.* the manner in which a person comports himself; carriage; behavior.

Behave　see **Comport & Behave**

CARRIAGE *n.* behavior; conduct; deportment; manner.

Comport & Behave

Congee & Obeisance

Conventional

CUSTOM *n.* established manner or way of doing things, as "It was the custom for young women to curtsy on greeting gentlemen."

Decorum　see **Deportment & Decorum**

Demean

Deportment & Decorum

Distant & Aloof

Excuse　see **Apology & Excuse**

Exemplary

GUISE *n.* way; manner; mode; fashion.

Importune

MANNER *n.* personal bearing or behavior, as "Lincoln's manner always betrayed great personal dignity." See also example under BEAR ONESELF.

MIEN *n.* a person's manner or appearance; expression, as "Our banker's mien is always sour."

Obeisance see Congee & Obeisance

Obsequious & Obsequies

PRACTICE *n.* habit; usage, custom. See also the category WORDS OFTEN CONFUSED.

PRESENCE *n.* the aspect or appearance of a person; mien; air; as, "The speaker's presence dominated the audience."

Suave

Thanks

Willing

WONT *n.* custom; habit; practice; way.

Apology and **Excuse** An APOLOGY is a kind of gift while an EXCUSE is an asset. You give and receive an APOLOGY, but an EXCUSE is your own property. Of course, you give your EXCUSE, in a way, to others; but only as justification of your actions. APOLOGIES usually come after your thoughtless behavior, but EXCUSES sometimes serve as pretexts for it.

Moreover, APOLOGIES are entirely unselfish. They are sincere expressions of your regret for unintentionally committing an offense. But an EXCUSE, since it is primarily an explanation instead of an acknowledgement of your offense, is thus usually a rationalization. In short, APOLOGIES, in our present usage, come from the heart, and EXCUSES are a product of reason.

APOLOGY came to us from the Greek via the French. Originally, it meant more what EXCUSE does today. APOLOGY used to be a formal defense or plea, like the famous APOLOGY of Socrates. The literal translation would be 'speaking away.' It was of course an intellectual and philosophic word. In this old use, an APOLOGY tried to extenuate faults by rationalization, as EXCUSES do today; but the process was closer to objective analysis and explanation, with a commendable interjection of feeling, than our modern EXCUSE, which is characteristically selfish, biased.

The verb EXCUSE has a more dignified use than the noun. When a boy is EXCUSED from school it means that he will not be blamed for his absence. Likewise, when a defendant is EXCUSED by the court he knows that the charge against him has been dropped. In this usage the word goes back to the original Latin, *ex* plus *causa*, literally 'out or free from the charge.' It is easy to understand how this Latin meaning gradually changed into the meaning of the modern noun. "My excuse for being late is that I overslept," simply means that I have taken upon myself the authority to EXCUSE, or to free my own person from the charge.

Comport and **Behave**   COMPORT literally means 'carry with,' that is, you 'agree or act compliantly with something.' But in general BEHAVE means 'any kind of action, without reference to an external standard.' "The moon behaves according to celestial principles," implies that the principles are once and for always part of the moon's nature. BE-HAVE has of course the same limitation when used about children. "Behave yourself!" means inexorably, "Be good!" "He comports him-self like a college boy," infers that the boy is acting after the fashion of a sophomore.

Congee and **Obeisance**   A CONGEE is a 'farewell' or, if we wish to harshen the inference, a 'dismissal.' The word is French and formerly meant a 'curt or formal bow.' It is still sometimes used in that old way, but more often it is simply a leave-taking. OBEISANCE also means a 'bow or curtsy'; but in this case, instead of farewell, the gesture signifies 'homage, overemphasized respect, submission.' It connotes 'servility.' Its origin is in the word 'obey,' and formerly it meant obedi-ence.

Conventional   CONVENTIONAL means 'formally commonplace.' The word is directly connected with a CONVENTION, a coming-together of people to discuss and decide things. CONVENTIONAL customs or manners suggest the way large numbers of people act. CONVENTIONAL is an ad-jective: "His conventional courting did not please her because she had dreamed so often of the noble knight sweeping her away on his white charger." A CONVENTION is either the normal, average way of doing something, or a meeting of people. "It is a convention at con-ventions to elect a chairman."

Demean   This is a word that has had its ups and downs, has almost fizzled out, has been crossbred or copied in its own image and in the images of other words to arrive at its most useful modern reflexive meaning, namely, 'of lowering one's self in one's own estimation and, consequently, in the estimation of others.' "I will not demean myself by accepting such an offer." That sense is aspersed by scholars, who call it vulgar, hybrid and originally a misusage. Yet this modern mean-ing appears in all dictionaries. The process by which it originated, a mixing of fanciful slang with imitation of other words, is one that has formed many of our best words. DEMEAN in the modern sense was an innovation in Shakespeare's day, a day of many lasting, as well as brilliant, verbal innovations.

The original verb, which was straight transitive (not the reflexive remnant we still use), outlasted Shakespeare's day by a little. Originally it was Roman and connoted 'action.' It meant 'to threaten,' and then 'to drive with threats, to herd cattle, to deal with and manage, finally to employ people.' But these meanings fell away from the old verb. The adjective 'mean,' with its sense of underhand dealing, had come to take over the usefulness of DEMEAN. But there was the word 'debase.' What is more natural than to join the meanings of 'mean' and 'debase' to make a substitute for the old, dying sense of DEMEAN? At length George Eliot's heroine spoke of DEMEANING herself to a common carpenter, which illustrates the word's modern reflexive use.

This sense of degrading oneself, which is one of the modern meanings of DEMEAN, is not the word's preferred meaning. Strictly, DEMEAN is a synonym for 'behave' and 'comport.' "Well brought up girls demean themselves courteously." But this use of the verb sounds unnatural; everywhere DEMEAN today is a synonym for 'degrade.' "The famous author was forced to demean himself by hack writing when he was a young man." The strict sense of DEMEAN has survived in the noun DEMEANOR. "Her demeanor was courteous," is formally correct, and it sounds more natural than "She demeans herself courteously." DEMEANOR connotes some of the action that the very old verb DEMEAN had. DEMEANOR refers not merely to behavior but also to the carriage and bearing of a person. "He has the demeanor of a gentleman," means that he is not only courteous and mild but also walks and dresses after the gentlemanly fashion.

But note that there is a difference in emphasis between 'degrade' and DEMEAN. "He degrades himself by his continual drinking," implies that he knows and doesn't care that he is hurting himself. But "He demeans himself by his continual drinking," suggests that he isn't aware of the damage he is doing to himself, and that we can expect his pride to awaken him eventually so that he can right himself.

Deportment and **Decorum**   During school days DEPORTMENT became formidable in our minds. DEPORTMENT represents 'good behavior' in school where good behavior is expedient because it is compulsory. Actually, the word simply means 'bearing, how you carry yourself, your conduct, good or bad, including your demeanor.' See DEMEAN.

DECORUM, however, refers only to the good side of behavior. DECORUM signifies the 'suitable, befitting, conformable.' "The decorum of the Princess' parties made her the social leader of Parisian society that season." The adjective DECOROUS is a lighter word. There is a suggestion of delicacy or daintiness in it. DECOROUS manners are almost delightful, they are tactful as well as correct. What is personally courteous in formal manners belongs to the DECOROUS person. The word *décor*, borrowed from the French, is no blood relation to DECOROUS, but 'décor' has a spiritual kinship with it. The 'décor' of a stage, a ballroom or an apartment is presumably tasteful and correct. Our own word 'decoration' can also mean 'décor,' but usually it refers to whatever trimmings something may have, whether or not they are in taste.

Distant and **Aloof** These are two expressive words that describe manners. They are not precisely synonymous. The ALOOF person may be shy or socially timid. He is perhaps pathetically cautious, like the stray dog we speak to on the street, torn between affection and fear. Sensitive wild creatures like deer are ALOOF. But the DISTANT man is cold or inscrutable. You cannot approach him mentally or spiritually.

ALOOF is the more delicate word. It comes from the Dutch. *Loef* is a part of a ship, probably the windward side; the 'a' means 'apart, but not out of sight.' DISTANT means literally 'standing apart from.' ALOOF means approximately the same. But DISTANCE has extended its connotations. A DISTANT object may now be so far apart from us it is invisible. The DISTANT person is rather awesome or annoying. The ALOOF person can be interesting or indescribably appealing.

Exemplary EXEMPLARY is a rather austere word, reminiscent of the days when we were exhorted by our elders to be examples to our younger brothers. EXEMPLARY conduct is both specific and superlative, like 'best behavior' and 'perfect manners.' It is a precise word, and should be added to our everyday vocabularies.

Importune This is a very useful word. It is a polite word for 'pester.' People who dun you all the time for payment of bills IMPORTUNE you. Formerly the word meant 'to annoy.' Now it means 'to urge persistently and insistently, to press a demand, to request relentlessly.'

If you are IMPORTUNED too long, if life itself is too pressing, you may in your turn become IMPORTUNATE. Then your personality will be impatiently demanding or forward. You may press your personal opinions on others. You may be rashly impulsive or thoughtlessly inconsiderate.

Obsequious and **Obsequies** An OBSEQUIOUS man ought to be accommodating (the word originally meant 'compliant'), but he is invariably a pest. An OBSEQUIOUS man has fawning manners and an oily, submissive personality. The word itself is genuine enough, having come without alteration from the Latin original, *obsequium*, 'compliance.' Until modern times it served as the adjective for its ill-fated half brother, OBSEQUIES, which are 'funeral and burial ceremonies.' OBSEQUIAL is the present adjective for OBSEQUIES. OBSEQUIES, in fact, is a spurious production. Its sire is the same *obsequium* alluded to above. Its dam is *exsequiae*, 'a funeral.' The two words were confused and thus telescoped together physically, like smoke and fog in 'smog,' or breakfast and lunch in 'brunch.'

Suave The Romans had two words for SUAVITY: *suavitas* and *dulcedo*, whence our 'dulcet.' The first meant 'agreeableness' and the second meant 'sweetness, delightfulness.' Even then, their meanings combined in the case of *suavitas*, to produce 'graciousness.' Then the French added to SUAVITY a note of 'personal politeness.' And today we have more impersonally added 'urbanity,' and an unflattering implication of 'smooth glibness.' Our SUAVE man today is quite a little bit too polite. He is polite mechanically. Perhaps only in music has SUAVE retained its full dignity. In music SUAVITY matches more closely the Roman feeling of graciousness.

Thanks In a way, THANKS are 'thoughts.' 'Think' and THANK are cognates, just as German *denken* and *danken* are. "I thank you," suggests "I am thinking of you."

Though THANK is harsh in sound, like a clanking, as compared with 'think,' in which there is a tinkle, it is still a more expressive word than the soft and gracious *merci* of the French. The latter is not related to 'mercy,' but derives from the Latin *merces*, 'reward,' and is therefore cognate with our prosaic, rather hard words 'merchant' and 'commercial.' But there is still another undertone in THANKS, audible in the quaint 'methinks.' The early English had, besides *thancian*, two closely related verbs, *thencan*, 'to think,' and *thyncan*, 'to seem.' The former was simply the more active or causal form of the latter. Later they merged into our 'think.' But still we say "I think that's so," "Methinks it is," "It seems to me it is." Whether this undertone ever reaches our THANKS, only listening can tell.

Willing This word has listened to us, and learned that the exercising of one's own will is unpleasant to others. When someone asks you if you are WILLING to lend him your lawnmower or fountain pen, you are not much expected to 'will' the transaction. You are simply expected to oblige. Nowadays WILLING implies 'graciousness' rather than an act of the mind. The demonstration of this lies in the synonymous requests "Will you be good enough to lend me . . . ," or "Will you kindly . . ." Even WILLING hands are now predominately more 'gracious helpers' than 'determined doers.'

CO-OPERATION

Accede, Concur, Acquiesce, Assent & Consent

Accord

Acquiesce see **Accede, Concur,** etc.

ACQUIESCENCE *n.* a silent submission; submission with apparent consent. See also the *v.* ACQUIESCE.

AGREEMENT *n.* the act of coming to a mutual arrangement; a bargain; contract; covenant.

ALLIANCE *n.* the state of being connected, as by an agreement or a treaty.

APPROBATION *n.* approval; sanction; commendation; as, "In order to promote domestic co-operation, Mrs. Jones gave her approbation to everything her husband proposed."

Approval

Assent see **Accede, Concur,** etc.

ASSOCIATION *n.* a union or fraternity of persons or ideas. "The men formed an association in order to advance their political fortunes."

Collaboration

COLLUSION *n.* a secret agreement for a harmful purpose.

COMBINATION *n.* a union of two or more persons for the attainment of a common end.

Compatible

COMPLICITY *n.* the state of being an accomplice; thus, esp. a partnership in wrong doing.

COMRADESHIP *n.* fellowship; the state of close companionship.

CONCERT *n.* agreement of two or more in a plan, as "They arrived at a concert which they all swore to carry out."

CONCOMITANCE or CONCOMITANCY *n.* state of being together, of being in intimate connection.

CONCORD *n.* agreement; harmony.

Concur see **Accede, Concur,** etc.

CONCURRENCE *n.* joint approval. See also the *v.* CONCUR.

CONFEDERACY *n.* a contract between persons, organizations or states for the purpose of mutual support or joint action.

Consent see **Accede, Concur,** etc.

CONSONANT *adj.* harmonious; agreeing.

CO-WORKING *n.* a working together.

ENDORSE v. to approve; to sanction; to give one's support to.

FELLOWSHIP n. the state of mutual relationship among persons; the state of sharing in common.

FRATERNITY n. a state of fellowship characterized by a brotherly regard for each other.

FUSION n. an intimate joining.

Harmonious

LIKE-MINDEDNESS n. agreement, esp. approval of a common venture.

MUTUAL ASSISTANCE n. all for one and one for all.

PARTICIPATION n. a sharing in work, or anything, with others.

RAPPORT n. agreement; harmony; accord.

SANCTION n. public approval of a proposal.

UNION n. two or more things joined into one; a coalition; a combination.

UNISON n. togetherness; union; concord. adj. (in music) identical in pitch.

Accede, Concur, Acquiesce, Assent, and Consent ACCEDE is a rather formal word, but one that we can afford to use more exactly than we do. When you ACCEDE to a point you 'grant it, admit it.' When you ACCEDE to a cause you 'accept, adopt and adhere to it.' When you ACCEDE to any proposition you 'agree to it.' To ACCEDE is an admitted 'yielding' in order to reach an agreement.

ACCEDE is just one of perhaps a dozen words we commonly use to indicate agreement. Circumstances suggest which word is appropriate. First, ACCEDE usually concerns an opinion, faith, purpose, cause or plan, rather than actual active complicity in a deed or act, a meaning conveyed, for example, when you CONCUR with others in a policy or plot. You may CONCUR in opinions, too; but the essence of CONCUR is 'to join a majority by contributing your opinion or by lending your influence.' The essence of ACCEDE is quite the opposite. You don't join in an opinion or plan as you do when you CONCUR. When you ACCEDE you are accepting for yourself alone a new opinion or a new plan which has been submitted for your consideration. To ACCEDE is not to ACQUIESCE, for ACQUIESE implies 'your submission to necessity,' or simply 'your indifference.' When you ACQUIESCE to something you are probably wishing you could CONCUR to something else.

Having ACCEDED to a view, you then customarily ASSENT to it, that is, you 'signify your agreement with it.' To ASSENT, be it understood, is not expressing yourself so strongly as to CONSENT, which implies 'positive approval' and a willingness to assist in action. This positive meaning of CONSENT carries the word closer, of course, to the meaning of 'granting permission,' a sense of complicity not a part of ACCEDE at all. In addition, CONSENT suggests also its own original meaning of

'feeling together' and of 'co-operation,' while ASSENT and ACCEDE remain essentially unilateral. To CONSENT has a little of the sense of
CONCUR: it means that you will be partly responsible for whatever is
submitted for your CONSENT.

Accord This word comes from the Latin *ad* plus *cor, cordis,* 'heart.'
Some of the 'heart' in the original word remains in the modern meanings, especially in that of the noun, which basically means 'harmony.'
Sometimes the noun ACCORD implies an 'enthusiastic unanimity,' as in
the expression, 'with one accord.' But the noun came from the verb,
which was a Gallic build-up of the Latin elements. Today the noun
represents only one part of the verb's present double meaning. The
noun and the verb coincide in to 'reconcile, adjust.' In this sense the
verb's full force is felt in the intransitive form, with a supplementary
'with.' "These colors accord with those," that is, they all harmoniously
correspond.

It seems that not much of the 'heart' in ACCORD is responsible for the
verb's second meaning—the sense of 'awarding, bestowing.' When
praise or approval is ACCORDED it is allowed as something due. Certainly there is not much good will or good heart in obligated praise.
ACCORD in this sense is an intellectual rather than an emotional word
because we have other words, like 'grant' and 'bestow' which have
kept a good heart in their meanings. If something is 'granted,' there
is a suggestion of human compassion. And if something is 'bestowed,'
it is a token of benevolence, but with a strong hint of condescension.
The meanings of ACCORD are confusing, but that's the price we pay for
the word's rather urbane flexibility.

Approval The word APPROVAL has a schoolroom flavor, but it has
its indispensable uses. Where a dictatorial bias exists, as it invariably
does in a schoolroom, APPROVAL loses its benign sense of 'agreement,'
and takes on an antagonizing 'must.' If a teacher says to a student, "You
have my approval for that project," the student had better complete
that project whether he wants to or not. But where the use is more
general, and where the authority is respected or venerated, APPROVAL
may be a boon and a blessing. You have, for example, a scientific paper
which you have prepared, but which now needs the APPROVAL of the
experts. And what does this APPROVAL mean? It does not mean that
these gentlemen have issued you a permit to publish. Rather, it means
that they have read your paper without bias, and have acknowledged
its value. Their APPROVAL is then their support. If it is a matter of
swearing, and a friend does not APPROVE your conduct, it does not

mean that he is forbidding you to swear. It simply means that your action does not look good to him. You may or may not pay attention to your friend's opinion.

Collaboration COLLABORATION is not exactly 'co-operation.' It is a narrower and more intense term. 'To co-operate' is to 'operate (work) in conjunction with others,' either in act, in spirit or both. On the the other hand COLLABORATION has always, and still does, imply *real* toil, and in usage it has been limited chiefly to the mutual efforts of a very few toilers at a time. For example, two scenario writers COLLABO-RATE (toil together) on a movie, or a team of scientists COLLABORATES in the search for a new drug.

The root of COLLABORATION is 'labor,' and the root-meaning of 'labor' is 'struggle'; whence come the 'labors of childbirth,' 'hard labor' and the 'laboring' of a point in an argument. Consequently COLLABORATION, which is literally 'laboring shoulder to shoulder,' is more intense and particular than 'co-operation.'

But unfortunately the devil has been tampering recently with this word. Several decades of global warfare have produced COLLABORA-TIONIST. A COLLABORATIONIST co-operates with his country's enemies. And by association this taint has infected COLLABORATOR itself, and now COLLABORATION is fast being ruined. A COLLABORATOR is in danger of being taken, not for a literary or scholarly partner, but for a national traitor, and COLLABORATION hints less of close association in work than of perfidious defection from native standards of conduct.

Though this debasing of a word may be inevitable in an age where change is generally so rapid and widespread, the old word, or a good substitute, is still needed. The whole original meaning can, of course, be expressed pretty well with phrases or loose compounds, like 'working together' or 'joint efforts'; but to find a single word that is comprehensive enough will be a task. Such words as 'business associates' and 'to work in concert with' do not imply the 'sweat, toil, mutual aid and benefit' that COLLABORATION expresses.

But there *is* a word, 'co-adjuvancy,' that has some vigor and purpose. An 'adjuvant' is someone who aids another person. He is more important than an auxillary, who may not be an intimate co-operator at all. Hence, like COLLABORATION, 'co-adjuvancy' can mean co-operation but like COLLABORATION also emphasizes shoulder to shoulder work. So if we could get used to it, and separate it in our minds from 'adjutancy,' referring to a commanding officer's adjutant or aide, it might be useful. It is cogent: barbitals added to certain ordinary medicines have 'adjuvant (working-with)' effects that quicken their action, enough, in some cases, to kill you. The trouble is, 'co-adjuvancy is not easy to pronounce. If it were possible, it would be better to resurrect COLLABORATION.

Compatible Thanks to Reno, and other dissolving centers, we hear much of COMPATIBLE's antonym 'incompatible.' But COMPATIBLE is a good word, and could be more generally useful in our everyday talk. The accent is appropriately and honestly on the 'pat.' We don't have to mumble the other syllables as we do when we expend our breath on the first syllables of such words as 'comparable, corrigible, and dirigible.' Many things are COMPATIBLE besides honeymooners. Thoughts, colors, cats, actions, intentions can all be COMPATIBLE among themselves, and with any number of other things. If you add this word to your vocabulary, you will be surprised how often you use it.

Harmonious This word was vastly popular with the Victorians. Even the telephone was at first called the harmony-telegraph. Imagine saying: "I'll harmony-telegraph you this afternoon"! HARMONY is always reminiscent of music, but there is no reason why the sweetness of music cannot prevail in society. HARMONIOUS social relations are governed by agreement and tolerance. But many things may have HARMONY besides people and music. Colors, poetry, clothes—anything, in fact, that is susceptible to aesthetic judgment may have HARMONY, which means simply 'an excellent relation of parts.' This is a good practical word.

DEATH

See also Eradicate

DEAD *adj.* pertaining to death. See also **Demise, Death,** etc.

Death see **Demise, Death,** etc.

DECEASE *n.* departure from life; death. *adj.* DECEASED, departed from life; dead.

DEFUNCT *adj.* dead; deceased; extinct.

Demise, Death & Dismiss

DEPARTED *adj.* dead; gone; vanished.

Dismiss see **Demise, Death,** etc.

ETERNAL REST *n.* death; the sleep in the grave.

ETERNAL SLEEP *n.* synonym for eternal rest.

EUTHANASIA *n.* an easy tranquil death; thus, the act or practice of painlessly putting to death a person suffering extreme pain from a mortal disease. See also ERADICATE.

EXTINCTION *n.* a going out of existence; destruction; death.

FINAL SUMMONS *n.* death.

INANIMATE *n.* without life, like a stone.

LAST BREATH *n.* death.

LAST GASP *n.* death.

LIFELESS *adj.* without life, like a corpse.

Macabre

Noxious & Obnoxious

Obnoxious see **Noxious & Obnoxious**

PASSING *n.* death, spec. a reference to the removal from earthly life to another life.

Perish & Vanquish

QUIETUS *n.* death; eternal rest; a final finishing; a final quittance, as from an obligation.

Sepulchral

Vanquish see **Perish & Vanquish**

Demise and Death and Dismiss We never speak of a living DE-MISE though we do speak of living DEATH. In common usage DEMISE is more dead than DEATH. It more exclusively pertains to mortal extinction itself. It is the formal word for DEATH, and used often in obituaries, where the fact that someone has died cannot be controverted.

But the origins of the word DEMISE indicate that it means more a 'transference' or a 'dispatch' than it does 'extinction.' DEATH is commonly thought to be a removal to another world, and DEMISE supports this connotation. DEMISE comes from the French *desmettre,* which in turn derives from Latin *dimittere,* 'to send away.' Originally in English it meant 'to displace, transfer.' In England DEMISE referred also to the transference of kingship when a king died. Ordinarily, the subjects of a king may be DECEASED, but the death of the king is his DEMISE. The statement, "The king is dead, long live the king," refers to the DEMISE of the old king and the transfer of his royal state to the new king. In this sense, DEMISE is used today in legal language when an estate is conveyed by a will or lease. When DEMISE is used this way it has a suggestion of less dead than DEATH, for a king, like a piece of property, never dies.

The little word DISMISS helps clarify the connotations of DEMISE. It also derives from the French word *desmettre.* But it was coined from that word's *past participle,* meaning 'sent.' So nowadays when a teacher DISMISSES a class, she is thinking of the children as already 'sent away,' in much the same way as DEATH refers to a 'sent away' to another world. Even the very act of DISMISSAL presupposes an absence. Thus the word DEMISE suggests not only 'extinction' but also 'rejection or dismissal.' DEMISE is a word of subtle connotations, and we have to observe carefully how a man uses it before we know what he means.

Macabre Looks a little like a Scotch patronymic, especially in its variant spelling, 'macaber'; but it is far from being Gaelic. It is an adjective vividly describing the spectral aspect of death. Thus, without pathological or religious allusion, it evokes death itself in the form of a skeleton, close at hand and about to snatch us away. It evokes, therefore, horror or terror. At the least it suggests an eerie, creepy sense of ghastly awfulness. Its own far-flung history, which is practically a panoramic allegory of death, accounts for MACABRE's power.

In the late Middle Ages the fanciful idea of Death as a bony person, who mingled freely with crowds or hovered at someone's elbow, looking for persons to lead away, or who conducted a long funereal dance or procession, was widespread in Europe. In both art and in certain dramatic representations Death, as a skeleton or a corpse, conversed intimately with all comers, from the Pope down.

Artists were encouraged by medieval culture to make continually visible, as a warning, the presence of Death. Thus the power of Death was exhibited on the walls of churches and cemeteries, and in symbolic skits, stories and dances. The theme demonstrated the equality of all men before Death, and thus the futility of earthly pride.

The intimate connection of Death with Life was, in those days of sudden plagues and catastrophes of all kinds, an emphatic fact. The conception of Death as a visitor, who knew his way about and who was present behind every shadow or curtain, became universal. He was seen leading the plowman's horse up the furrow, or standing close, perhaps between, the newly-wedded couple at the altar. Even in our own day such pictures would still be MACABRE.

How the word MACABRE itself became attached to the Dances of Death is a matter of doubt. These medieval dances swept Germany in the fourteenth century, and spread to France and over Western Europe. In Germany they were the Totentanz and in France they became known, as early as 1376, as the *danse Macabré*. Who this Macabré was, or whom or what the proper name commemorated, is the question. It has been said he was a contemporary artist who probably painted the first Dance of Death. Evidently the name was first Macabé, a French form of Maccabaeus, meaning literally 'The Hammer,' which was the surname acquired by an early leader in the Biblical revolt of the Jews against the Syrian kings, and later applied to the whole Hasmonean dynasty, or the Maccabeans. In the fifteenth century there was a popular dramatic representation called the *Chorea Machabaeorum*, which apparently portrayed in a dance the story of seven Hasmonean brothers murdered, with their mother, by a Syrian king. This term is said to have become the name, in Latin, for the Dances of Death.

There is the possibility that Macabé was a corruption of (Saint)

Macarius the Hermit, identified in art posed with a finger pointing at a decaying corpse. Perhaps it was not a proper name at all, but came from the Arabic word *magbarah*, meaning a 'cemetery' or a 'funeral chamber.' Thus from all directions death impregnates this word; but it is the spectral idea, with its chilly horror, that has survived, not the mawkish, the gory, or, on the other hand, the ethical. And yet some of the grotesquery of the old paintings also survives—a grotesquery that was only too painfully real. It undoubtedly reflected the violent exertions of persons who, struck by the paralyzing plague, ran out of their houses and tried desperately to keep themselves alive in the streets: a veritable Dance of Death.

Noxious and **Obnoxious** NOXIOUS means 'poisonous.' OBNOXIOUS is the 'pseudo-poison that merely annoys.' An OBNOXIOUS mosquito, no matter how annoying, is not poisonous; but NOXIOUS fumes from your gas stove are not simply bothersome but deadly.

Perish and **Vanquish** These are bookish words, perhaps. To PERISH means 'to die,' and to VANQUISH means 'to defeat.' Bookish words do possess the attribute of novelty in conversation, especially if their synonyms, like 'die' and 'defeat,' are shopworn. Moreover, if they are high-sounding or vain glorious, they may display a welcome tinge of humor. To say, "I am simply perishing from hunger," is a nearly impossible exaggeration that makes us laugh. Or to boast, "I really vanquished him at cards," is to make your victory sound that much bigger. These are two good words for general use.

Sepulchral The noun SEPULCHRE is a dull and formal name for a 'tomb.' But the throaty sound of the adjective SEPULCHRAL makes this word very appropriate to gloomy descriptions.

DEJECTION

Anguish see **Anxious & Anguish**
Anxious & Anguish
APPALLED *adj.* full of horror or dismay; greatly upset.
APPREHENSIVE *adj.* fearful, as an APPREHENSIVE feeling.
Dejected

DOLE *n.* sorrow; lamentation; grief. (Archaic.)
GRIEF *n.* regretful or remorseful sorrow; affliction; woe; misery.
HEARTACHE *n.* anguish; sorrow; a feeling of deep regret.

LACHRYMATORY *adj.* causing tears.

LACHRYMOSE *adj.* weeping; also, weepy.

Lugubrious see **Mournful & Lugubrious**

MISERY *n.* distress or extreme unhappiness. *adj.* MISERABLE.

Morose

Mournful & Lugubrious

PROSTRATION *n.* extreme mental or emotional dejection.

REGRET *n.* a feeling of loss or disappointment. *n. pl.* feelings of sorrow over what is lost or has happened.

SAD *adj.* unhappy; mournful; as a SAD face.

Saturnine

SORROW *n.* grief; sadness; a feeling of loss and disappointment.

Taciturn

TERRIFIED *adj.* full of fear; frightened.

Weep

WOE *n.* grief; distress; great trouble.

Anxious and **Anguish** In one way it seems strange to say you are ANXIOUS to please someone, for ANXIETY means 'trouble' and it doesn't naturally go with 'pleasure.' But, in another way, it is very appropriate, for ANXIOUS is, from its roots, such an urgent word that it means you can hardly wait to please him, that you are 'in torment' until you do.

To the Romans ANXIETY was ANGUISH. Specifically, it was also a name for 'quinsy,' a swelling and throttling of the throat. ANGUISH itself refers to a 'choking' or 'strangling' in the throat. From it sprang a number of ideas about pain, and hence of vexation, concern, disquietude and disturbance, provided they were intense, like the excruciating effects of the quinsy. Even our word 'anger,' though its origin was in the ancient North, is probably cognate. Its first sense was 'affliction, pain.'

Coming to the present, ANXIETY separates from ANGUISH, though in the Latin they were twins, both born of *angere,* 'to choke.' It loses its sense of 'trepidation' and 'dread.' When we are ANXIOUS we are not without hope, though still we are tormented by uncertainty. What we are ANXIOUS about is always impending. It worries us deeply; but we need not be despairing.

ANGUISH, on the other hand, has kept its primitive force. It conveys perhaps a sense of 'affliction' more terrible than any other word in our language can suggest. ANGUISH is pain that comes not so much from physical affliction as from spiritual trial. Job felt more ANGUISH in his spirit than he did pain in his body. To the psychologist, ANGUISH comes from a denial of life itself, from a compulsion to suicide.

Dejected Literally, this word means 'cast down.' The word itself has become DEJECTED. It has lost ambition, and is apparently good only for describing people's looks or feelings. You apply for a job, a cold 'No' from the prospective employer stops you. You feel and look DEJECTED. But, in fact, you *are* DEJECTED. It is not only your features and your feelings, but the 'total you,' the applicant, that has been cast down.

Morose A word that should be used much more often since it is richly suggestive. In the beginning, in the Latin, it meant above all, 'fretful' and 'particular'; but already it was used imaginatively to refer to 'stubborn things.' Since then its precocity has burgeoned into a word that volubly and variously means today 'ill-natured or ill-humored, crabbed, bitter, gloomy, churlish, acrimonious or sour, doggedly severe, dour, surly.' But, as some dictionaries will tell you, MOROSENESS is no passing mood, like 'sulkiness' or 'sullenness,' but a bitterness of nature, with a disposition to growl or complain menacingly.

Mournful and **Lugubrious** Richly onomatopoetic words, respectively from the Anglo-Saxon and Latin words for 'grieving,' but both now meaning 'gloomy.' Since grief largely shows in lamentation, both adjectives are usually used of sounds. "The mournful wailing of a distant hound is music to the ears of certain sportsmen." "The lugubrious sounds of a foghorn at sea turn even the jolliest personality towards funereal thoughts."

Saturnine It has nothing to do with the Satyrs, genealogically, and is only incidentally connected with Saturn, the Italic god of agriculture. Incidentally, Saturnalia is a harvest festival celebrated in Saturn's honor, occurring, in Italy, in winter, so that some say it eventually grew into our Christmas. SATURNINE achieved its gloomy content from the planet Saturn. Astrologists thought that the planet was supposed to exert a gloomy influence on mortals, and chemists used to use the sign for the planet to represent that heavy element lead. SATURNINE thus meant, and still specifically means, pertaining to 'lead.'

The SATURNINE man today is dull and heavy. But if you want to imply 'stupidity,' then you are using the wrong word. SATURNINE is the opposite of 'mercurial,' as that word refers to personality, just as 'lead' is the opposite of 'quicksilver.' SATURNINE still implies 'graveness' in that word's elementary meaning of 'heaviness,' but the forceful connotation is of 'unsociability,' or 'sourness,' in contrast to the volatile person.

Taciturn Straight from the Latin, meaning 'silent with respect to persons.' But as now understood, TACITURN means 'silent' with a touch of 'austerity,' sometimes of 'contempt,' or at least of 'superiority.' Commonly, however, the word just means 'silent, reserved.'

Its connotations come from the beginning, from the Latin *taciturnus* and *tacitus,* or 'taciturn' and 'silent.' For *taciturnus* meant also 'close,' in the sense of 'guarded' and 'cunningly kept,' as well as 'secluded' or 'concealed.' And *tacitus* meant many things to the Romans, such as 'mute' in its various senses, 'kept (as a secret), noiseless, hidden, not mentioned.' All these are echoed in the nature of a TACITURN man. Hence, a TACITURN man today is not just habitually silent, whether from shyness or from prudence. Rather, he is holding back more than mere words, for in his reserve there is a positive quality, a quality that discourages others from talking as well. TACITURNITY may result from 'diffidence'; but, at its extreme, it is 'sour, calculating and forbidding.'

Weep Nobody, not even a child, likes to be called a cry baby. It is felt that only infants cry, for they are still only little animals, and know no better.

We have in this word an illustration of the evolution of manners. To cry the way a baby does is to WEEP. It is a 'bawling,' exactly what all WEEPING was originally, a 'crying out,' an 'outcry.' With more civilization and better manners, we softened the sense. You can find instances in our own American history where Indian sachems nobly chided the white men for their uncouth failure to understand the ways of others; and perhaps, in this connection, it is significant that Indian squaws WEEP, not softly, but almost silently. But even the colonizers knew the difference between a cry baby and a WEEPING woman. Centuries earlier when the Anglo-Saxons WEPT they raised a clamor, but the pilgrims to Canterbury could '*wepen* unnoisily,' from reverence or sorrow. And so could the Pilgrims who came here.

Nevertheless, WEEP has not wholly purified itself. Along the New York waterfront disgruntled dock workers recently bore a placard on which they derisively named a disliked boss 'Weeping Joe,' because he had not defended their rights as they thought he should have. For WEEP now connotes a 'pusillanimous softness.' Even humorously we are none too respectful of WEEPING: "Read that," we say, "and weep!" There is no word depicting grief that is entirely sacred anymore. Note the heart-rending word 'sob,' Chaucer's *sobben,* which probably arose from a sincere word among the rough Anglo-Saxons that meant 'to lament, bewail.' But we debase the word in 'sob-stuff' and 'sob stories.' We turn what can really be a profound emotion into sickly sentimentality.

DISCOURTESY

(*adjectives*)

ACRIMONIOUS caustic; bitter; extremely scolding, etc.; as ACRIMONIOUS language.

BEARISH gruff; uncouth; ill-mannered.

BITING bitter; cutting; sarcastic.

Brash

BRUSQUE abrupt; rude; as "His brusque manner offended gentle people."

CHURLISH rude; sullen; surly; ill-mannered.

COARSE rude; common; indelicate; obscene; offensive.

CONTEMPTUOUS scornful, esp. as applied to actions and emotions, as CONTEMPTUOUS language, or a CONTEMPTUOUS dislike.

CURT sharp; brusque.

CUTTING biting.

DISCOURTEOUS ill-mannered; unpleasant; uncouth.

DISDAINFUL scornful; contemptuous; showing a haughty or condescending regard, as a DISDAINFUL glance.

DISRESPECTFUL discourteous; uncivil; having lack of proper respect toward people.

Dour, Glum & Sullen

FLIPPANT boldly discourteous; pert; shallow and bold in manner; as "Now that he had come to a new country he was flippant toward all his native customs."

FRIVOLOUS lighthearted and gay to an inconsiderate or displeasing degree.

Glum see Dour, Glum, etc.

GROSS coarse; very fat; vulgar in manner and taste.

GRUFF rude; very outspoken; inconsiderate of other people's feelings.

HAUGHTY very proud and unbending; arrogant.

HEEDLESS careless; ill-considered.

IMPERTINENT meddling or interfering; saucy; rude.

INCONSIDERATE careless; not attentive to other people's feelings.

INDIFFERENT apathetic; unconcerned.

INSENSITIVE not sensitive; indifferent; unresponsive.

INSOLENT impertinent; referring to an overbearing, haughty manner; insulting.

INSULTING abusive; referring to an affronting or offensive manner.

MORDANT biting; caustic; as a MORDANT personality.

NEGLECTFUL careless; inattentive; indifferent.

Pert see Petulant & Pert

Petulant & Pert

SARCASTIC bitter; cutting; esp. in an intentionally insulting way.

Saucy

SHORT curt; abrupt; as "Being irritated, she was very short with him."

Slouch

Smug

Sullen see **Dour, Glum,** etc.

Supercilious

SURLY sullen; morose; churlish; esp. in the sense of being disrespectful.

TART pert; biting.

UNCOUTH ignorant; esp. in the sense of not knowing correct manners.

Vulgar

WANTON discourteous, esp. in the sense of foolish indulgence of one's own desires; hence, reckless.

Brash A slangy, self-made word, rhymingly constructed from rash and splash. No doubt BRASH still conveys some of its Scottish meanings, a 'bout' or 'set-to,' an 'upset stomach, acid mouth.' Thus, we now use it to mean 'tactlessly or foolishly impetuous,' and hence 'saucy, forward, impudent.' Visibly it suggests a mingling of 'brassiness' and 'rashness,' and in fact there is a strong strain of 'recklessness' in it. 'Recklessness,' in the sense of 'thoughtlessness.' A freshman home from college who is obnoxiously slangy in polite company is BRASH.

Dour, Glum and **Sullen** Don't think these words are insignificant because they are little. Each is very expressive.

DOUR people don't talk much. They are morose but not moody. Their outlook on life is stern but unheroic. They are realists looking at the world with dark glasses. DOUR is from Scotland where it means 'hard, unyielding, stubborn, SULLEN.' Its roots are in the Latin word *durus*, 'hard,' whence our 'endure.' A DOUR individual is hard and intractable, difficult to work with and unmanageable. His aspect is dreadful or gloomy. A DOUR assent is reluctantly and surlily given. DOUR weather is hard weather. DOUR farmland is unproductive.

GLUM is Swedish and, though it now means 'moodily and SULLENLY silent,' it must originally have implied a kind of stupidity because it meant 'to stare.' In DOUR there is considerable habitual GLUMNESS. If a person is GLUM all the time, then he may also be DOUR; but usually one is GLUM by fits and starts.

SULLEN is from Latin *solus*, 'alone,' and thus it is a melancholy commentary on the pernicious effects of a solitary life.

The beauty of these words is their shortness and their sound. See MOPE, SULK and POUT. Anyone who has a feeling for words will automatically use these quick, expressive terms very often. After all, they describe very common aspects of life. Today SULLEN means 'being alone through ill-humor,' 'unsociable, sulky, dismal, gloomy.' Sometimes a SULLEN person goes so far in his antihuman attitude that he becomes dangerous and threatening to his community. Criminals are usually SULLEN.

Petulant and Pert PETULANCE is 'fretful ill-humor.' It is nothing to be proud of, but is only a petty, childish offense. It started out as an offense in antiquity: Latin *petere*, 'to attack.' When you are PETULANT, you are irritable. You think you are always right and that you are being abused. A child is often PETULANT.

But PERT is something else again. How it ever came about is not at all clear. In Wales it was once 'comely, handsome.' In Old France it was 'open, candid, *apert.*' Until recently it was, at least occasionally, 'of fine appearance.' But, however strangely, it has definitely become 'bold' and 'saucy' today. "Susan is certainly a pert child; she answers you right back with a saucy tongue."

Saucy A salty word we could use more fancifully than we do. SAUCY comes from sauce, and sauce comes from salty food. In that sense even a catchy, peppy tune is SAUCY—it is highly seasoned.

Slouch This is certainly an expressive word, since it indicates an inner feeling by an outward gesture. From earliest Scandinavian times there was a 'droop' in SLOUCH. Flowers SLOUCH on their stems when they droop. A SLOUCH is a languid person, and this languidness probably comes less from weariness than from sluggishness. 'Sluggard' is a related word. Today, as in Shakespeare's time when a SLOUCH was a 'lout,' SLOUCH is associated with a tramp or loafer in contrast to an alert soldier. When someone SLOUCHES down on your couch he is not too tired to be polite. Rather, he is too impolite to control his tiredness.

Smug SMUG is a word you must observe over a long period of time before you can even attempt to define it. Exactly what you think SMUG-NESS is will depend upon your perception. Dictionaries define it with synonyms: 'complacent; highly self-satisfied; affectedly precise, prim.' But such an approach to its definition leaves much to be desired.

In the beginning the word was a verb in central Germany meaning 'to don, to put on.' Webster says it was an Old Swedish word for 'elegant.' So it came to mean 'to adorn,' then, as a noun, 'ornament,' finally 'affectation.' Through the Netherlands it came to us from the Low German *smuk*, meaning 'smooth.' The 'affectation' is thus clearly connected with 'vanity,' the kind of pleasure we feel while preening ourselves. It suggests not only self-indulgence but self-satisfaction. A SMUG person is a smooth and smart fellow, who wears an air of superiority he is loath or unable to conceal. He is a polite but unctuous prig. What little he says he firmly believes is edifying for everyone. He is cagey and contemptuous. The SMUG person is always hugging himself. So, also, is the SMUG cat who has surreptitiously swallowed a canary.

Supercilious *Cilia* is Latin for 'eyelids.' So the whole word refers literally to the lifting of the eyebrows, which are 'above,' *super,* the lids. SUPERCILIOUS refers to the way you look when you are trying to express haughtiness by mixing indifference and condescension. But you usually end up suggesting a silly or simpering arrogance.

Vulgar Words, like people, must fight to maintain their social standing, and some, like VULGAR, lose the fight. Something VULGAR is today something 'disgusting,' though originally VULGAR was a synonym for 'common.' Of course, whatever is used by most people is often considered disgusting by aristocrats. A common thing receives their contempt, and that is why the English language itself was still VULGAR even in Chaucer's England. Hardly anyone who could write would have thought of composing a personal letter in common English. The language of the people was beneath them; they used the more cosmopolitan French or Latin.

The great bard Shakespeare introduced into our still-new literary language many words in their literal Latin sense, and VULGAR was one of them. He speaks of "driving away the vulgar from the streets." But this VULGAR did not yet suggest the 'disgust' that Alexander Hamilton, the exacting little aristocrat of our Revolutionary times, felt for the 'commoner.' VULGAR has now slipped down the scale till it is a companion word of 'lewd.' Only reminiscently does it connote a 'commonness' like that in which Lincoln saw something divine: God must have loved the common man, He made so many of him. When Dr. Johnson called Milton's "Lycidas" VULGAR he meant only that it was 'commonplace,' and so he added, "and therefore disgusting." But 'disgusting' itself has slipped down the scale. To Johnson it meant only 'distasteful,' rather as we would say today that a work of art is artificial, not in good taste. A hundred years before Dr. Johnson, King James the Second had looked at the new St. Paul's Cathedral and called it amusing, awful and artificial. But he meant only that it was designed with true art, and therefore it not only pleased his royal self but awed him. When we now say that something is VULGAR we need no interpreter. Everybody knows where VULGAR stands, and we are surprised only when it tries to speak like its former self.

DISCUSSION

ACKNOWLEDGE v. to recognize (openly concede) the truth, existence or fact of something, as "I acknowledge what you are saying." n. ACKNOWLEDGEMENT.

Actualities

ANALYSIS n. the separation of a compound thing, such as a conception or argument, into its parts, as "Your analysis of the preceding discussion clarifies the issues for us."

Apparent & Obvious

ASSUMPTION n. the act of taking something for granted; a thing supposed; as "It used to be an assumption that the earth is flat."

BIAS n. an undue propensity toward something; a prejudice; a one-sided tendency of the mind. "M. Carnot's mental bias appears in all his discussions: he believes no one but a Frenchman is intelligent."

Cause & Reason

CONCLUDE v. to arrive at an opinion; to form a final judgment; as "From his wild argument I concluded he was not quite sane."

Criterion see **Norm & Criterion**

CRITICISM n. the art of defining, judging and declaring the merits of a thing. "My criticism of your point is that you do not take enough facts into account."

CRYPTIC adj. hidden; secret; as, "No one understands his cryptic argument."

Data

DISCURSIVE adj. passing rapidly from one subject to another; digressive.

DOCTRINE n. a principle or principles relating to religion, science, politics, art. "The doctrine of equality in America is no longer literally believed."

Dogmatic

EFFECT n. the general intent, purpose or consequence of something, as "The sudden effect of his announcement stunned us all."

FACT n. a real, or historically true, event or situation, as distinguished from personal belief, as "It is a fact, in spite of what a child believes, that the earth is round."

IDEA n. an opinion; a thought; a mental picture or image; as "The idea of his discussion is that justice and wisdom are identical."

INFERENCE n. reasoning from effect to cause.

INTELLIGIBLE adj. that which can be understood or grasped by the mind, as "His argument was intelligible but not complete."

INTERPOLATION n. the act of verbally interrupting or of

changing the subject for a moment, as "The speaker's joke was an interpolation in his talk: it has almost nothing to do with his subject."

INTERPRETATION n. the act of expounding or explaining, as "The chairman's interpretation of my badly put objections to the main discussion was understood by everyone."

Norm & Criterion

Obvious see **Apparent & Obvious**

PEDANTRY n. an inappropriate or exaggerated display of learning.

PREJUDICE n. a bais, or leaning, of mind, favorable or unfavorable, to something to the extent that the truth or facts are obscured. adj. PREJUDICED.

PSEUDO a prefix meaning false or sham. Thus, PSEUDOlogy is the science of lying, of false speech, and PSEUDOnym is a false name.

Reason see **Cause & Reason**

Relevant & Significant

Significant see **Relevant & Significant**

Specific

SPECIOUS adj. outwardly showy, beautiful, charming, pleasing; deceptively just, fair, plausible.

SUBJECT n. that which is treated, spoken about or written about, as the SUBJECT of a book.

SYNTHESIS n. the putting together of known ideas or facts in usually a new and intelligible way.

THESIS n. a proposition; an idea or subject stated in advance which is later proven, as "The speaker's thesis was that the gold standard would be good for the country, but he didn't stay on his subject, and so failed to prove it."

Thing

VALIDITY n. the truth of something.

Version

VIEWPOINT n. the perspective, or attitude of mind, which a person has about a subject.

Actualities ACTUALITIES are hard and fixed. ACTUALITIES are those 'stark facts' and 'condensed realities' that require no emphasis or exposition. No two persons should see opposite sides of ACTUALITIES. ACTUALITY denotes a practical reality, a factual reality confined to one subject no matter how extensive that subject may be. For example, the ACTUALITY of the human passions of love and hate is beyond dispute and beyond measurement.

Apparent and Obvious That which is APPARENT is 'visible to all,' like a pole-sitter in an open square. But sometimes APPARENT is used more narrowly. Sometimes the APPARENT thing is simply the most obvious of two or more obscure things. If you say, "The apparent point to your argument is . . . ," you really mean that nothing in his argument is clear, but it seems as though he meant this. . . . In this narrow usage it is the adverbial form, APPARENTLY that is most commonly used. "Apparently that man is a fool," you say, because so far as you have observed him he acts more foolishly than wisely. By using the word APPARENTLY you guard yourself against an outright assertion about something you are not sure of.

Though OBVIOUS also refers to what is 'plainly visible,' it has a more positive and unalterable meaning. In the Latin its prefix *ob* meant 'before,' and the rest of the word meant 'way.' So an OBVIOUS thing today is something that stands bluntly in your way. You can't help but see it. Naturally, the word is also used figuratively for something that is 'plain' to the mind's eye, though it has no physical reality. You say, "It is obvious that man is a fool," when you are certain of his foolishness.

Cause and **Reason** A CAUSE produces an effect that a REASON explains by showing the CAUSE. An effect may become in its own turn a CAUSE of a new result. For example, if you are late to a dinner date because you forgot to look at your watch, the effect is your lateness, the CAUSE is your forgetting to look at your watch, and the *simple* REASON is the same as the CAUSE, that you forgot to look at your watch. But the *complete* REASON for your lateness is probably more complex. Perhaps you were out so late at the opera the night before that you were stupid this afternoon and lost all track of time. You might even feel it necessary to mention many circumstances, real or fictitious, to account for your lateness. All these explanations are the REASONS for your lateness; but the CAUSE, which is the most immediate REASON, is that you forgot to look at your watch. Sometimes, according to our present usage, REASONS may be fictitious; but a fictitious REASON can never be a true CAUSE.

But when all this has been said, a good deal still remains to be said. The above generalization is both incomplete and, in part, erroneous. For the colloquial use of these words has combined meanings so much that valuable distinctions have been lost. Would you not have CAUSE (it ought to be REASON) to be afraid of a lion on the loose, and have good REASON (it ought to be CAUSE) to run to cover?

The fact is, CAUSES and REASONS habitually combine because immediate CAUSES are sometimes *magnified* to include every possible explanation or REASON, while, on the other hand, we *reduce* our REASONS for something to such logic and cogency that they assume the appearance of immediate CAUSES. Let us consider the first clause in our illustrative sentence. The immediate CAUSE of your fear of the lion is not the lion himself but your love of life, which the lion has placed in jeopardy. But the REASONS for your fear of a loosed lion is, of course, that he is loose, that he is coming toward you, that he is bigger and stronger than you are, etc. These REASONS help explain the CAUSE of your fear, because, after all, it wouldn't make any difference if the lion is bigger and stronger if you didn't love your life, which is the most important and immediate point about your whole situation. Consequently the first clause would be more accurate if it read, "Would you not have reason to be afraid of a lion on the loose . . ." The REASON why one tends to substitute CAUSE for REASON in this clause is because all your REASONS are so logical and cogent that you turn them into a CAUSE.

Such confusion more often occurs when the effects of a CAUSE are human actions, because then we are so intent on providing good, rational REASONS that we forget and call them CAUSES. We forget the intrinsic inflexibility of all sequences of 'CAUSES and effects.' That is the best way of indicating a CAUSE: it is the REASON *closest* and most *necessary* to the production of an effect. "He fell down and hurt himself." All CAUSES are, strictly speaking, of that sort. They are inevitably followed by effects, regardless of what other explanations sometimes append.

Thus much for qualifying the generalization, which still needs completion. For even in good parlance the words CAUSE and REASON do possess practically perfect equivalence in some senses. The connecting link is the idea in the word 'enough.' Because having 'enough' of anything implies a RESULT. If you should think about something which you want to do and decide that, having done it, you will be able to adduce facts or circumstances that will make your having done it appear 'reasonable'—that is, that you will 'justify' or 'excuse' it—then you have possessed your REASONS 'in advance,' and you have 'enough' to proceed to action. In other words, if you have 'enough' REASONS, you are furnished with a motive, which is, of course, a kind of CAUSE.

Consequently, you will find in the dictionaries that a REASON can be any fact or circumstance that leads you to a course of action or to a belief. On the other hand, a CAUSE similarly can be something that moves you to action, like a motive or REASON. Moreover you will find that the idea of 'enough' positively obtrudes itself in an exacter usage: when a CAUSE, especially a legal 'just cause,' becomes 'sufficient' grounds for action, or when a REASON serves as a means of 'justifying,' not merely 'explaining,' an action. But this usage applies only to CAUSES and REASONS referring to human actions. When we apply our REASONS to those causes which are beyond our personal selves we are still modest enough to regard them merely as 'explanations,' instead of 'justifications,' of nature.

Data Both DATUM and DATA, which is the plural of DATUM, meaning 'fact,' are Latin words taken over by English. As little grains of earth make up a garden plot, so DATA is material you use for arguing a case, drawing a conclusion or an inference, writing a book or a report, or calculating the result of any action. Each DATUM is an assumption given or furnished as a basis for your efforts, because in the beginning DATUM came from the Latin verb *dare,* 'to give.' So the question often arises now, whether DATA is a collective noun constituting a single mass of facts, or whether it refers simply to a number of facts that do not make a unit?

Authorities differ. All admit that a single DATUM is seldom mentioned nowadays, but some refuse to accept the transference of meaning in the plural form from the assembled objects to the unal mass. They insist we must say, "The data are . . . ," just as we say, "The people are . . ." This is logical, until you reflect that we also say, "The peoples of the earth are numerous," meaning there are many large groups of people on earth. Big dictionaries rather beg the question. They admit that we "not infrequently" use DATA as a singular, as "This data isn't complete enough." But the implication seems to be that, while this usage is too formidable to be denied, it still warrants disapproval. It is a question of usage versus authority, and probably the former will soon have general approval.

Dogmatic DOGMAS are opinions promulgated by authority and accepted by adherents to a creed, political party, society, government, etc. Less rigidly they are the 'tenets' of a doctrine which may or may not be enforceable upon those whom it could concern. But DOGMATIC, the adjective, branches out still more, as descriptive words usually do. Literally, a DOGMATIC individual, considered apart from any creed or party, should be solemn but assertive and positive, with some air of authority. Actually, he is just 'stubbornly or even churlishly assertive.' There is something unnatural in his persistence, and a strong hint of an inferiority complex in his manner.

Norm and **Criterion** (see also STANDARD and MODEL) CRITERIA (the still-accepted plural of CRITERION) are more than models or standards of measurements. CRITERIA are principles, ideals, or requirements from which intelligent persons not only deduce conclusions but acquire comparisons useful in guiding themselves.

A NORM (this little word has filtered to us through the Spanish from the Arabic) is scientifically a 'typical specimen,' and consequently becomes generally a valid, wholly real, normal example of anything. The comparison of NORMS, or the comparison of an individual object with a NORM, produces CRITERIA.

The word CRITERION comes from the Greek for 'judge' and so differs from its approximate synonyms, 'standard' and 'model.' A CRITERION provides a way of testing the 'rightness' of conclusions or judgments. Precedents, if they are well-established and credited, may become CRITERIA. Against them we can check our present opinions. For example 'kindness' is universally one CRITERION of 'virtue.' In other words, we test an action against the CRITERION of kindness to see whether it can be virtuous.

Relevant and **Significant** RELEVANT is an adjective that refers to whatever is 'pertinent,' or whatever 'applies' or is 'relative' to anything. In some way everything is RELEVANT to everything else in a world as complex as ours. But only the most 'immediately relative' things are SIGNIFICANT. A man writing a short story has many immediately RELEVANT thoughts and facts to choose from. He chooses only those that are SIGNIFICANT, only the ones that signify something that is not simply immediately connected with the story but that is especially vital to the progress and the purpose of it.

Literally SIGNIFICANT means 'making signs.' A SIGNIFICANT fact, for example, is a sign, or pointer, that indicates a very essential meaning, a SIGNIFICANT novel is a milestone in the history of novel writing. Whatever is SIGNIFICANT must 'define something new.'

The negative of SIGNIFICANT is catchy. An 'insignificant' person is 'notoriously unimportant.' He is no personage. This derived and derogatory meaning has engulfed the authentic negative meaning, 'of no import,' which is the simple antonym of SIGNIFICANT. Some differentiation might be obtained by using the alternate 'unsignificant,' though the larger dictionaries suggest it is obsolete or nearly so, and lesser lexicons ignore it unanimously.

Specific This word means 'particular,' especially in the sense of 'specifying precisely.' A SPECIFIC thing is pointed, clear and exact. "His specific answer to my request was 'No!'" But watch out for this word! It does not mean 'detailed.' A very detailed report on the transactions of your last committee meeting might not contain a single SPECIFIC detail. In other words, this report was filled with lots of extraneous information, but with nothing on what the committee actually did.

Thing The real THING, the right THING, "That's all the thing now," (in other words, it's the 'rage' or 'fashion'), and "That is quite a different thing," as well as 'thingamerees, thingamabobs, thingamajigs' and all the ordinary indeterminate THINGS in careless talk that save us the trouble of fumbling for exact names or terms—all these suggest that we are crazily overworking the word THING. And the fact is, we are. For the first THING in our language, as also in several Scandinavian tongues, was a 'judicial meeting' where one subject or another was laboriously debated and resolved. Inevitably the debated subjects came to be called THINGS also. These THINGS ultimately were loosed on the air in such numbers they became 'anything' that anybody could discuss or mention—that is, 'anything' at all.

Version VERSION is related to a number of words which, like itself, are derived from the Latin *vertere*, 'to turn.' It depends on several of its relatives for co-operation in expressing its present meanings. The classical meaning of version is simply 'translation,' the turning of one language into another, as in the various VERSIONS of the Bible. But VERSION has drawn from the meanings of 'controversy' and 'inversion' to the point of suggesting today an argument or a rebuttal: "His version of the story was that no such warnings were given at all, but that he was taken completely by surprise." Each person, you see, may have a different 'translation' of the same original story.

DISLIKE

Affront

Aggravate & Annoy

ANIMOSITY *n.* hatred, or ill-will, usually manifested in active opposition.

ANIMUS *n.* hostile spirit or angry temper, as "The animus in his book against foreigners spoiled his thesis."

Annoy see **Aggravate & Annoy**

ANTAGONISM *n.* state of being mutually opposed; opposition.

Antipathy

BADGER *v.* to bait; worry; pester.

"He was so badgered by the chairman during the investigation that he could hardly think."

BAIT *v.* to harass, annoy; nag. "A man placed in the stocks was baited by the whole populace."

BOTHER *v.* to give trouble to; to annoy; pester. *n.* trouble, vexation.

CHAFE *v.* to warm by rubbing; to annoy; vex; anger; irritate.

ENMITY *n.* dislike; hatred.

EXASPERATE *v.* to irritate; to provoke; enrage; as "The many, continual, unwanted attentions exasperated her." n. EXASPERATION.

FRET v. to be worried; to complain; to act peevishly; as "The girl frets if her friends don't give her presents."

GALL v. to fret; vex; irritate.

HECKLE v. to question continually and antagonistically in order to embarrass or annoy someone.

Hector

HOSTILITY n. state of antagonism; open opposition; as "The senators used to be friends; but they joined opposing parties, and now have only the deepest hostility for each other."

HOUND v. to pursue or harass someone or something, as "The children hounded their mother until she gave them cookies to get rid of them."

IGNORE v. to shun; avoid; to disregard; as "She ignored everyone but Jack at the dance."

INDIGNITY n. any base act committed against someone.

INSULT n. an affront or hurt against a person's dignity or sensibility.

IRK v. to annoy; to pain. "Now that he was rich he was irked by requests for help."

IRRITATE v. to vex or exasperate someone.

Molest

NETTLE v. to upset or annoy someone.

OUTRAGE n. an attack; a violent wrong; maltreatment. v. to assault violently or brutally; to wrong.

PEEVE v. to irritate; to become peevish. adj. PEEVISH, fretful; ill-natured; petulant.

PERTURB v. to disturb greatly; agitate. n. PERTURBATION.

PESTER v. to annoy; irk.

PLAGUE v. to bother; badger; vex; harass.

PROVOKE v. to arouse or to stimulate, esp. to anger or to vex.

SLIGHT v. to disregard intentionally; to make little of; as "He was so angry with his girl friend that he slighted her by forgetting her birthday."

TEASE v. to vex; annoy; disturb.

UPSET v. to discompose someone, as "She was obviously upset by the bad news."

WORRY v. to annoy; tease.

Affront When you feel insulted perhaps there is nothing more satisfying than to say simply: "That is an insult." Common words are often strong by virtue of their familiarity. But unfortunately this familiarity can lead also to vulgar harshness. Sometimes it also happens that a common word loses its edge from overwork. AFFRONT is no weak word. It carries the two meanings of the word 'offensive': 'insulting' and 'aggressive,' and it has a strong suggestion of 'insolence' thrown in. A person who offends you may not know all this exactly, but he can sense the word's strength when you use it. "That is an affront,' gives you the advantage by throwing the offensive person back on his heels.

Aggravate and Annoy AGGRAVATE means 'to make something more serious' and hence, since it is used only of bad things, 'to make it worse —more seriously bad.' In its origin AGGRAVATE meant to make things heavier in the sense of graver, or more serious: the root of 'grave,' in that sense, means 'heavy.'

We erroneously tend to use AGGRAVATE in the sense of 'agitate' or 'irritate,' as if the evil were excited, driven or provoked to worseness. It is incorrect to say that something is AGGRAVATING you.

'To ANNOY' is quite a different thing from 'to AGGRAVATE.' To ANNOY means 'to irritate, provoke.' It is, today, a mild or petty vexing. The word ANNOY came through the Old French, and thence through our forebears and through centuries of cumulating mispronunciations from Latin *in odio*, 'in hatred.'

Antipathy This word means 'mental or spiritual allergy, instinctive, often involuntary and sometimes intense dislike,' the very opposite of 'affinity.' ANTIPATHY is also opposed radically to 'sympathy': the root of both is the Greek *pathos*, 'feeling,' in one case prefixed with *anti*, 'against' and, in the other, with *sym*, 'with.' To emphasize the contrast we use two different prepositions after them: ANTIPATHY uses 'to' and sympathy 'with.' ANTIPATHETIC is a particularizing adjective. It is concerned with particular things and personal prejudices. ANTIPATHIES cling like grudges to little things, and thus are in contrast both with 'sympathies,' and with many ordinary dislikes.

Hector HECTOR means to dominate or domineer other people in a bullying way. It can be used either as a noun or a verb. The word comes from the famous Trojan hero, Hector, who slew many Greeks during the Trojan war.

Molest In the beginning it meant 'to burden.' Now MOLEST means 'to annoy hurtfully' or perhaps 'to disturb harmfully.' It nicely describes pestering. Mosquitos, for instance, certainly MOLEST us. Unpleasant thoughts MOLEST us when we are trying to forget them.

DRESS

Attire, Garments, Raiments, Habiliments, etc.

BONNET *n.* a form of hat that can be pulled down over the back and sides of the head, now worn usually by women.

BOOTS *n. pl.* heavy shoes with high tops, or leg coverings, usually reaching to just below the knees.

CEREMENT see Attire, Garments, etc.

CHEMISE *n.* an undergarment, like a shirt, worn by women.

CHIC *adj.* stylish; fashionable; very smartly dressed.

CRINOLINE *n.* a stiff cloth; also a hoop skirt.

DAMASCENE *adj.* pertaining to damask.

Dapper see Spruce, Natty, etc.

DASHING *adj.* chic.

Décolleté, Dishevelled, Dishabille

Dishabille see Décolleté, Dishevelled, etc.

Dishevelled see Décoleté, Dishevelled, etc.

Doff & Don

Don see Doff & Don

Fillet

FROCK *n.* a smock; an outer garment covering the whole body and worn by either sex; a dress; robe.

Garb see Attire, Garments, etc.

Garments see Attire, Garments, etc.

GAUNTLETS *n. pl.* gloves; esp. medieval armored gloves; now, gloves that cover a large portion of the forearm.

GREATCOAT *n.* an overcoat; topcoat.

Habiliment see Attire, Garments, etc.

Hosiery

Kilt see Tartan, Kilt, etc.

LINEN *n.* thread or cloth made of flax; shirts, sheets, etc., which were formerly made of LINEN.

LIVERY see Attire, Garments, etc.

MILLINERY *n.* the articles made by a MILLINER; the industry of making women's hats. MILLINER, one who makes and sells ribbons, stuffs, for women's hats.

Minever see Samite, Vair, etc.

Moire

MUFFLER *n.* a large, warm scarf used to wrap the throat in cold weather.

Natty see Spruce, Natty, etc.

NEGLIGEE *n.* an informal dressing gown worn by women; thus, informal loose-fitting clothes.

PELISSE *n.* a coat or cloak, usually trimmed with fur.

Plaid see Tartan, Kilt, etc.

Raiments see Attire, Garments, etc.

SLACKS *n. pl.* loose, casual trousers worn by men and women.

Samite, Vair, Minever

SMART *adj.* chic, as SMART clothes.

SMOCK *n.* a light outer garment used to protect clothes, as a carpenter's SMOCK.

Sombrero

Spruce, Natty, Dapper

Tartan, Kilt & Plaid

TIDY *adj.* neat; orderly.

TRIM *adj.* neat; well-dressed; well-groomed.

Vair see **Samite, Vair,** etc.

WARDROBE *n.* one's total amount of clothes.

Worsted

Yarn

Attire, Garment, Raiments, Habiliments, etc. We have some interesting words for our clothes. GARMENT comes from the Old French, relating back to the word 'garnish,' and meaning 'a fringe of ornaments around a plate.' It was a whimsical warning, it seems, to guests because *garnir* is related to a Teutonic word meaning to warn. RAIMENTS are traceable to 'array'—again Old French from a Teutonic stem built on by Romans and passed into Middle English. APPAREL came into the French as a verb, from the common talk of the Romans. It meant roughly 'to put things together, to put them on a par'—compare our adopted French word *nonpareil,* 'without equal.' But it soon took on the sense of 'equipment,' and appeared in the Old French and in Chaucer's England as a noun, often aphetically without the first syllable, meaning then as now, GARMENTS. HABILIMENTS are Old French from *habiller,* 'to dress'; compare 'riding habit.' DRESS is what the French did to the Latin word for 'to direct'—the original meaning which remains in the 'dressing' of a line in military drill, and in the 'address' (manner, bearing or, in speaking, delivery) of a man. GARB, the whole clothing, is an Old High German word for APPAREL. COSTUME is 'customary GARB'—Roman via French. But more often today COSTUME is 'special GARB,' as the dress for a COSTUME ball. CLOTHING is Anglo-Saxon, and from cloth. ROBES were originally 'plunder' or 'booty.' The word is cognate with 'rob.' LIVERY, now a special COSTUME, especially for servants, was in Late Latin days a 'master's gift'—that is, free provisions —to his household help. It comes from *liber,* 'free.' ATTIRE itself (via Old French) is 'adornment.' Its base is probably Teutonic. From 'equipment' and 'arrangement' its meaning spread to 'arraying' and 'adorning.' ATTIRE is usually gala or stylish dress, though in a broader sense anything is ATTIRE if it serves as a garment. Lastly, CEREMENTS comes from the Latin *cera,* 'wax.' CEREMENTS are the waxed or any other wrappings of a corpse. See SINCERE.

Décolleté, Dishevelled and Dishabille What with innumerable plunging necklines today, DÉCOLLETÉ is becoming *passé.* You hear it almost as seldom as its grim companion, 'decollation,' a 'beheading.' The

'col' in them both is from Latin *collum*, 'neck,' whence later 'collar.'
DÉCOLLETÉ means 'low, or no, collar,' that is, a neckline free to plunge.
But the word in its prime, in America, at the turn of the century, meant
more. It commonly meant 'with bare shoulders and neck.'

DISHEVELLED is also from France, but via earlier English 'dishevely.'
It fares better today, except we use it carelessly. Its root is *chevel*,
'hair'; so we needn't, though we often do, say someone's hair is DI-
SHEVELLED. But since good descriptive words are naturally ambitious
there is no sin in letting this one refer also to clothes, which, like hair,
can be tousled. But in that case it is better to mention the garment,
and not to say simply that someone is DISHEVELLED. By extension DI-
SHEVELLED can well refer to many other things, like feelings or plans.
It is used not only as an adjective, but also as a transitive verb, "the
wind dishevelled her summer dress."

DISHABILLE or DESHABILLE (either form is correct) is a more serious
word in its associations. It comes from the French word, *habiller*, 'to
dress' or, originally, 'to make ready.' The orientation of the word towards clothing was like 'habit' in riding habit—it was first a condition,
then a customary condition. So DISHABILLE means literally 'undressed,
unprepared'; but the 'dis' is now a mere scattering negative as in
DISHEVELLED. DISHABILLE refers to 'any loose, careless attire,' like a
wrapper or morning dress.

Doff and **Don**   You DOFF your hat to the ladies, you DON your best
clothes. The rush age is not modern, as witness these words. They are
contractions of 'do-off' and 'do-on.' Pure time savers! We could DOFF
and DON a lot of things we don't. We could for instance DOFF our bad
manners and DON a smile.

Fillet   This word comes via Old French from the Latin for 'thread.'
Most commonly now it means a narrow ribbon used as a head band.
But many filar (thread-like) things are FILLETS, as a strip of lean meat,
an engraved line, a narrow molding, or gold lines on a book-cover.
And sometimes the thread expands, as in a square of meshed lace called
a FILLET or in a FILLET of meat or fish, a boneless slab. When the expansion includes granulation we have the doubly delicate filigree
work. 'Filigree' comes from the Latin for both 'thread' and 'grain.'

Hosiery   This is a dignified word for 'stocking.' To the Anglo-Saxons
it meant 'underclothing.' HOSE, the abbreviated form, does not use 's' in
the plural: HOSE means 'stockings.' HOSIERY and the garden 'hose' are
cognate words.

Moire This word refers to metal or cloth, especially silk, that has a watered appearance.

Samite, Vair and **Minever** SAMITE was a precious silk fabric in the Middle Ages. The word is Old French from the Greek meaning 'six-threaded.' VAIR was fourteenth century fur used on noblemen's garments. In Latin the word meant 'spotted,' but later it meant 'ermine.' MINEVER (also spelled MINIVER) is literally French *menu vair*, 'dainty fur,' and specifically the white winter coat of the ermine. More probably MINEVER included a mixture of furs, with a preference for the soft, spotlessly white ones used for trimming courtly robes in the Middle Ages. However, the Siberian squirrel, and its fur, are called MINEVER. The Old French *ver* traces to Latin *varius*, 'spotted.' The *menu* meant 'little.' Rows of tiny shields represent *vair* in heraldry.

Sombrero The term for the Mexican broad-brimmed hat meant, to Shakespeare, a 'parasol.' It is Spanish from Latin for 'shade,' *sombra*. Its idea has settled down more broadly in our word 'somber,' meaning literally 'dismal with shade, darkly gloomy.' But 'somber' came to us through the French. The SOMBRERO may still be a 'sunshade'; but it is hardly 'somber,' being associated with the wide open spaces of our own vast South West.

Spruce, Natty and **Dapper** Fops and dandies are not content to be SPRUCELY dressed. Their clothes are not only SPRUCED and slicked, but new and of the latest cut. But everyone, from a laborer to a lord, who SPRUCES up his attire for holidays, is SPRUCELY dressed. In medieval England Prussia was called SPRUCE, a variant of the Old French *Pruce*, from the late Latin rendition of German *Preussen*, 'Prussia.' At that time resplendent Prussian leather, doubtless worn by dashing cavalry officers, was by abbreviation called SPRUCE. Finally, any articles of finery became SPRUCES, from which the adjective and the verb were naturally evolved. Today you can SPRUCE up your mind, your spirits or your English, making them bright and smart. Incidentally, the 'spruce tree' is also Prussian.

NATTY is much the same as SPRUCE—only more so. It was the diminutive of 'neat,' so to be NATTY you must be neat and tidy. But today a NATTY dresser is also a snappy dresser. He is smart and up-to-date in his fashions.

DAPPER is a word of more character. It was Dutch, and meant 'brave.' Just as we speak of making a brave appearance, we see valiancy in a DAPPER person. We must admit he carries himself with an air. "The generals, dapper in their square cut uniforms, marched in and out of the Pentagon carrying important looking briefcases."

Tartan, Kilt and Plaid TARTAN is *not* a kind of cloth from which kilts are made, but it *is* a pattern of colors on that cloth. The material may vary in any clan's TARTAN, but the pattern is distinctive. A KILT was once a mantle. When it was wound about the body, including the thighs, it became a KILT. Sometimes trews (tight breeches) are worn under the KILT. PLAIDS are not properly TARTANS. They were the careless ends of the mantled TARTANS thrown over the shoulders. A filibegs is the common modern KILT in the Highlands, as distinguished from the older great or overall KILT.

Worsted Generally speaking, WORSTED is any cloth made from wool. Originally it was a kind of fine wool textile fabric made in Worsted, England. Now it is any fabric woven from a certain kind of yarn with usually a little finishing. But to the ordinary eye this divides into two kinds of WORSTED: the hard, tight-twisted goods tailors sell you, and the softer, loosely twisted yarn used for knitting, crocheting, etc., which may be mixed with other yarn. The characteristic of true WORSTED is that it is spun from pure, long-fibered wool, combed so as to make the fibers lie parallel with one another.

Yarn YARN is any thread spun from natural fibers, whether animal, vegetable or mineral. The 'spun' is probably deeply rooted in this supposed Ancient Aryan word. Sometimes the fibers are not spun or twisted to make the YARN. In asbestos YARN, for example, the fibers are compressed or specially treated in other ways. In some YARN the fibers are not natural. Nylon, rayon and other new textiles are woven from synthetic YARNS. Some nylon fibers are now called 'threads' because they are drawn like wire. But in all instances, whether artificial or natural, YARN consists of fibers.

The purely figurative spinning of YARNS (tales) is really occupational slang. The word was used in this way by sailors at sea, who made their tedious sit-down jobs, like the winding of YARN, endurable by the telling of stories.

EMOTIONAL EXTREMES

ARDOR (or ARDOUR) *n.* warm or intense affection; desire; zeal.

CARNALITY *n.* sensuality; a preoccupation with things of the flesh.

CRAZE *n.* mania; a widespread fad.

DELIRIUM *n.* a mental or emotional disorder, usually temporary, marked by wild talk and delusions. *adj.* DELIRIOUS.

ECSTASY *n.* an extreme emotion, usually joy or happiness. "I have an ecstasy of hate for that man!"

ENTHUSIASM *n.* zeal; eagerness. *adj.* ENTHUSIASTIC.

EXCESSIVE *adj.* extreme; immoderate. See also **Ordinate & Inordinate.**

FANATICISM *n.* extreme zeal; extravagant ideas, esp. in the realms of religion and politics.

FERVOR (or FERVOUR) *n.* strong enthusiasm; a strong passion for some cause, idea or business. ZEAL. "His fervor convinced his audience that at least he was sincere in his strange ideas."

FIXED IDEA *n.* an idea which completely dominates a person's thinking, and consequently his behavior.

FRENZY *n.* wild excitement; extreme anger; fury; delirium. *adj.* PHRENETIC.

FURY *n.* a violent anger or rage against someone or something.

HYSTERIA *n.* morbid or senseless emotionalism; a psychoneurosis marked by bodily disturbances as well as emotional outbreaks. In popular usage, loss of emotional control characterized by fits of weeping and laughing.

IMMODERATE *adj.* excessive; more than necessary or usual. "He has an immoderate craving for chocolate."

Incubus, Obsession, Mania

INFATUATION *n.* an extravagant and often unreal love or affection for someone.

Inordinate see **Ordinate & Inordinate**

Jealous

LECHERY *n.* carnality; the indulging of one's lusts; obscenity.

LUST *n.* an excessive desire to possess and enjoy something; as a LUST for gold, LUST for power.

Mania see **Incubus, Obsession,** etc.

Masochism & Sadism

MONOMANIA *n.* fixed idea; as MANIA for one fixed thing. See also **Incubus, Obsession,** etc.

Obsession see **Incubus, Obsession,** etc.

Ordinate & Inordinate

PARANOIA *n.* an insanity distinguished by delusions, esp. of grandeur and persecution.

PASSION *n.* intense or overwhelming emotion; esp. an intense desire or love, as a PASSION for literature.

PHOBIA *n.* a morbid fear or dread, which often generates exaggerated hatred of the thing feared.

AGORAPHOBIA *n.* morbid dread of crossing or being in open places.

ANGLOPHOBIA *n.* dread and dislike of Englishmen or things English. Often used in overstatement.

BACTERIOPHOBIA *n.* morbid fear of disease germs.

CLAUSTROPHOBIA *n.* morbid fear of enclosed places.

DEMONOPHOBIA *n.* morbid dread of spirits.

FRANCOPHOBIA *n.* fear of France or Frenchmen.

GALLOPHOBIA *n.* fear of France or Frenchmen.

GERMANOPHOBIA *n.* fear of Germany or Germans.

HERESYPHOBIA *n.* dread of heretical belief.

LYSSOPHOBIA *n.* fear of hydrophobia.

NEOPHOBIA *n.* morbid dread of, or aversion to, novelty.

PANTOPHOBIA *n.* a morbid fear of everything.

PHARMACOPHOBIA *n.* morbid dread of drugs or medicine.

PHOBOPHOBIA *n.* fear of one's own fears.

PHOTOPHOBIA *n.* morbid fear of light.

PYROPHOBIA *n.* morbid fear of fire.

RUSSOPHOBIA *n.* morbid dread of Russia or Russians.

SITIOPHOBIA *n.* morbid dread of food.

SYPHILOPHOBIA *n.* morbid dread of syphilis, or fear that one is infected with it.

THANATOPHOBIA *n.* a morbid fear of death.

TOXICOPHOBIA *n.* a morbid fear of poison.

ZOOPHOBIA *n.* morbid fear of animals; fear of spirits in animal forms.

PRURIENCY *n.* carnality; sensuality; lust for bad or lewd things.

RAGE *n.* intense anger; fury.

RAPTURE *n.* ecstasy; extreme pleasure or happiness.

RULING PASSION *n.* fixed idea; monomania.

Sadism see **Masochism & Sadism**

SALACITY *n.* lewdness; obscenity; lust.

TRANSPORT *n.* rapture; a carrying away by strong feeling.

ZEAL *n.* intense devotion to a cause or idea.

Incubus, Obsession and **Mania** Literally, an INCUBUS is something that 'lies upon your mind,' from the Latin root for 'to lie upon.' Actually, it is a nightmare that besets your mind even when you are awake, an ugly or indigestible idea that presses on your mind, a mental demon that perches there. Etymologically, this is an understatement. The *incubo,* like his companion of the opposite sex, the *succubo,* was in late Latin times a lecherous fiend seeking prey.

An OBSESSION is a milder and less lurid affliction, but a larger one, usually more persistent and in the end achieving greater domination. OBSESSION is now, as revised by usage in the nineteenth century, a mental conception, often a delusion, that besets your mind—literally, it besieges it, from the Latin 'to sit down before' and 'to besiege'— and ends by possessing it. Sometimes intellectual OBSESSIONS possess a despotism which circumvents our free thinking, as when an OBSESSING bias blindly prejudices one's mind. But usually OBSESSIONS are characterized by a powerful emotion for which there is no rational excuse. When an OBSESSION, an infatuated idea, begins to 'rage,' it becomes a MANIA. If the MANIA drives the individual to mad action, he is a 'maniac.'

Jealous No need to explain this much used word, except in one sense which you may occasionally encounter. "The captain was jealous of his knowledge of seamanship." This means that the captain could not tolerate anyone whose seamanship rivaled his own. "The mother was jealous of her child's manners," means that she would not admit any child had better manners than her own child. The usual meaning of JEALOUS is quite the opposite. "I am jealous of that man's attentions to my girl," means, not that I think his attentions are the best, but that they are very bad, hurting me, and should be removed. Specifically, in this common meaning of JEALOUSY you are afraid that the goodwill or love someone shows you will be diverted to someone else.

Masochism and Sadism Two real persons gave us these important words, from their surnames, one in the early and one in the late nineteenth century. MASOCHISM distils from the elements of self-pity an unsavory and often sexual pleasure from the suffering of pain, torment, abuse or humiliation at the hands of others, as originally illustrated by a glaring instance in the novels of Leopold von Sacher-Masoch, an Austrian. SADISM represents an abnormal or inhuman love of inflicting cruelty, described in the books of Count de Sade of France. He was usually called the Marquis de Sade, but that was only what he, in spite of the facts, called himself. Before he was thirty-three he was sentenced for sodomy and poisoning; he spent years in the Bastille, and at seventy-four died in a lunatic asylum. Both words thus intrinsically represent perversions, and so are analogous and can be compared. But they are also sharply in contrast with each other, and for that reason have proved particularly useful to the medical profession.

But their chief importance derives from their wide applicability to all things that represent 'self-pity,' on the one hand, and 'cruelty' on the other, accompanied by any degree of personal pleasure in both cases. For human nature is so full of unrealistic quirks that it often confuses the lines between pleasure and pain. Even self-immolation, for example, can become an inordinate pleasure.

If you have ever sat in a subway car and observed a person opposite you, reading a newspaper, with two strangers on either side of him, reading it too, and then seen him flick the pages rudely, to suit his own pleasure, have you never thought: Is that fellow really a SADIST, or are those uncomplaining perusers both MASOCHISTS?

Though the sense of SADISM is now well understood, because it was so well illustrated in German concentration camps, MASOCHISM is still vaguely comprehended. The term is often used loosely, especially in the sense of self-torture. This, however, is the essence of its meaning: If you like to be dominated by others, you naturally enjoy abusing yourself: the others are, after all, only proxies.

Ordinate and **Inordinate** Everyone knows what an ordinance is: specifically, a 'municipal or city law,' or, more broadly, any 'authoritative rule.' Consequently, an ORDINATE thing is a 'regular' thing in the sense that it is 'orderly.' We use this adjective surprisingly little, but what is worse we virtually misuse its expressive negative, INORDINATE. The flavor of that word is not merely 'excessive.' An INORDINATE desire is not simply a great big desire. It is not necessarily rash or overweening, but it must be 'crudely or rudely immoderate.' No methodical man can possess it. Because even if an INORDINATE desire is excessive or unrestrained, it became so because it is 'unregulated.' From being 'unregulated' it has gradually dispensed with all rules. Its greed and grasp impress us most, because they are offensive; but we have forgotten their cause. Our present usage has run away with almost all the meanings.

ENDS

See also Beginnings; Series

ACME *n.* the top or highest point, as the ACME of beauty.

AIM *n.* mark or target; the goal to be reached, as "His aim was to be the best player on the team."

AMBITION *n.* an eager or inordinate desire; the pinnacle of one's wishes. "His ambition was to be the most famous writer of his generation."

APEX *n.* the tip, point or summit of anything.

APOGEE *n.* the highest or most distant point, as "The apogee of her desires was not attainable by any mortal woman."

Aspiration

CAP *v.* to go one better; finish off; crown; consummate. "He even capped his own effort, by beating his record of a year previous."

CLIMAX *n.* a culminating point of intensity; acme; as, the CLIMAX of his career.

CLOSE *n.* the end of something, as the CLOSE of the holidays.

COMPLETE *v.* to finish; end; conclude; as "She completed her unmarried life by burning all her old love letters the night before her marriage."

CONCLUDE *v.* to bring to an end; to finish; terminate; as "He concluded the business deal by writing a check." *n.* CONCLUSION.

CONSUMMATION *n.* the completion of anything; end; esp. in the sense of fulfillment. "The consummation of a devout man's life is his death." *v.* CONSUMMATE.

CROWN *v.* to cap; terminate; complete; esp. in the sense of consummate.

Culminate see **Eventuate & Culminate**

DESTINATION *n.* the goal; end; the ultimate purpose, design or end; as "Her destination in life is to be a mother."

END *n.* the conclusion or termination of anything.

Eventuate & Culminate

EXPIRATION *n.* the last breath; cessation; death.

FINAL *adj.* pertaining to the end or conclusion; ultimate; last; etc.

FINALE *n.* the last piece on any program of entertainment.

FINIS *n.* end.

GOAL *n.* destination.

Last & Latest

Later see **Latter & Later**

Latest see **Last & Latest**

Latter & Later

LIMIT *n.* in general, a terminal line or point.

MERIDIAN *n.* a great circle of the earth; midday; hence, the highest point or culmination; *adj.* at midday; pertaining to a MERIDIAN.

OBJECTIVE *n.* destination; end; target; goal. "The army's objective was Berlin."

OMEGA *n.* the last of anything. OMEGA is the last letter in the Greek alphabet.

PEAK *n.* summit; acme.

Penultimate

PINNACLE *n.* acme; topmost point, as the PINNACLE of success.

SENESCENT *adj.* growing old

Summation

SUMMIT *n.* the highest point; top; apex.

Target

TERM *n.* limit; completion; boundary.

TERMINAL *adj.* pertaining to the end; *n.* destination; goal.

TERMINATE *v.* to end; complete; finish. *n.* TERMINATION.

ULTIMATE *adj.* last; esp. in the sense of the last of a series.

WINDUP *n.* conclusion.

ZENITH *n.* pinnacle; meridian.

Aspiration 'Soaring hopes,' not designing ambitions, are ASPIRATIONS. You may ASPIRE to high office, but you do so for altruistic or romantic reasons. You may paradoxically ASPIRE to humility, to anything that endears you to others or ennobles you, though it may mar your worldly hopes. ASPIRATIONS are the ambitions of the heart or spirit. If these ambitions become corrupted, you may hold evil ASPIRATIONS. The desire to be the undoing of your business rival is perhaps an evil ASPIRATION.

Eventuate and **Culminate** EVENTUATE is a useful though solely intransitive verb. You can say, "All your speeding on the parkway will certainly eventuate in a crash." But it is incorrect to say, "All your speeding will eventuate a crash." Things EVENTUATE either forward or backwards. A quarrel can EVENTUATE *in* a fight, or a fight can EVENTUATE *from* a quarrel. The noun 'event' thus has its useful verb, meaning 'to happen ultimately as a result.' And don't forget its useful adverb: "Eventually, why not now!" A quarrel, of course, may terminate in a fight; but 'terminate' is a muted verb. EVENTUATE has some motion in it.

Still more has CULMINATE, which suggests the combing tops of sea breakers. And, in fact, the final curve and crash of surf combers is a vivid illustration of CULMINATION. The word comes from Latin *culmen*, 'top.' A quarrel graphically ends in a fight when it CULMINATES in flying fists, like the tumultuous spray of the breaking comber.

Last and **Latest** LAST is a contraction of LATEST. But that statement is partly untrue since LAST was first a contraction of Old English *latost*, the superlative of 'late,' long before the form LATEST came into being. But in meaning LAST now has more emphasis than LATEST, largely, no doubt, because it is the handier word. Only occasionally, and probably in old books, can you find LATEST used for LAST. For example, "It was his latest (meaning his last) wish to spare his friends sorrow." But nowadays LAST replaces LATEST frequently: "Last night I heard him saying . . . ," "I said it in my last letter," or "For the last three weeks it has been raining." In these examples LAST implies not finality but a particular place of a thing in a series, which is properly the function of LATEST. "The latest (most recent) bit of news to come in was . . ."

But everyday words sometimes pick up too many trick usages to catalogue. For example, "He had his last look at the sea before he died," or "The latest basket of apples from the store was wormy." Generally speaking, LAST means 'coming after all others,' and LATEST means 'most recent *in the order of time.*' But LAST is sometimes used to emphasize the *very* latest. The same intensive use of LAST is carried on enthusiastically to mean 'the least' or 'the most unlikely.' "The last thing on earth that I would do, would be to . . ." which doesn't mean that you would do that thing with your LAST breath but that you would probably not do it at all. LAST thus means 'the most remote' from your intentions; quite at odds with LATEST's 'the most recent.' In saying what we would have them say, words sometimes contradict themselves. Silk tropicals may be the LAST (best) word in fashions, but bare legs for grandmothers are the LATEST (worst).

Latter and **Later**   LATTER is simply a variant of the adjective LATER. It is confined to a few usages, notably as a substantive equivalent to the 'later one' of two things compared. "The latter appeals to me more than the former," which is saying simply that the second appeals to me more than the first. In this case, LATTER is still really an adjective, because there is nothing to prevent us from uttering the noun it qualifies, "The latter *proposition* appeals to me. . . ." In its other chief use the noun *is* retained, and we say, "I'll see you in, or during, the latter part of the week." In either of these usages there is no important reason we shouldn't say LATER instead of LATTER. But custom makes LATTER sound better to us, and that is not unjust. After all, LATTER arrived in our language long before LATER did. It was the Old English *laetra*, the comparative degree of 'late.' Now LATTER has surrendered most of the field, but as a correlative of 'the former' it still has an advantage over LATER. This is because in using 'the former' and 'the LATTER' the important distinction is *not* one of different times but of different things. It is good to have a special word set aside for this since the use of 'earlier' and LATER in this way would be confusing.

In some rare usages LATTER approaches 'latest,' as when we speak of the 'latter end of the day,' and hence of 'latter days,' and the 'Latter-Day (literally Latest-Day) Saints.' It can even go beyond 'latest,' as in 'lattermath,' meaning 'aftermath.' LATER has, of course, a wider field, and is common as an adverb. "I'll see you later"; "Later, he changed his mind." LATTER occasionally enters this field by donning a suffix, LATTERLY, meaning 'lately' or, in a more literary sense, 'toward the end of life,' or 'some other period of time.' The differences between LATER and LATTER should not be hard to remember, since the uses of LATTER are prescribed by custom. We should remember that 'the LATTER' always refers to one thing of *only* two things, and that the two things should be of a kind easily compared.

Penultimate This long word means 'next to the last.' In the word 'declaration' you accent the PENULTIMATE syllable. The semi-finals in a tournament are also PENULTIMATE.

Summation It means either a 'summing-up' or a 'summed-up result or total.' SUMMATION may be the 'process' of finding the sum of a number of things, especially a number of numbers, as in arithmetic. Similarly, it can be a 'review' of acts in order to present a final total effect, as when a lawyer rehearses his facts at the conclusion of his argument. Or it may be a 'total' of effects, amounts or numbers. Thus, "The summation of all his remarks was, that he didn't care to go." Here the context tells us that SUMMATION means the substances of all his remarks, lumped together for a conclusion, the sum-and-substance of all he had said.

Target In all fields where words are impressive and where actions are important this word is used. For example, official Washington, where there is plenty of activity, has taken up TARGET. There are TARGET figures to be shot at, and TARGET groups that do the shooting. Sometimes a TARGET group represents an ideal for other groups to emulate. There is even the practice of TARGETING a project or activity.

It would be a pity to spoil the profitable picture with a few historical notes on TARGETS, but the fact is that TARGETS were prosaic *things* and not ideal *goals*. The first TARGETS were 'shields' or, as often as not, merely the 'frames, sides, edges' of things like boats and walls. The early French got them from the ancient Germans, and the early English got them from both the Germans (later the French) and the Scandinavians. The French shrunk them to 'little shields' (adding the diminutive *ette,* now 'et'), and hardened the 'g.' But not till the eighteenth century were 'shield-like marks' in archery called TARGETS, and soon thereafter visible arrows gave way to invisible bullets. Now a TARGET is anything to shoot at or to aim for, which accounts for its use in the District of Columbia.

ERADICATE

See also Death

ABOLISH *v.* to do away with; put an end to; destroy; efface or obliterate; annihilate.

ANNIHILATE *v.* to reduce to nothing; to destroy, esp. to efface a specific thing, as to ANNIHILATE an army.

Atrociter & Genocide

BLOT OUT *v.* to destroy; annihilate; as "He blotted out his past by destroying his possessions and moving to a new town."

CANCEL *v.* to blot out; obliterate; destroy; make void; set aside.

Defunct see **Extinct, Defunct,** etc.

DELETE *v.* to blot out; expunge; erase.

DEMOLISH *v.* to destroy generally; put an end to; ruin completely; lay waste; as DEMOLISH the dinner.

DERACINATE *v.* to pluck up by the roots. See also ERADICATE.

DESTROY *v.* to pull down; demolish; to overthrow; to kill; slay; extirpate.

EFFACE *v.* to erase or obliterate, as to EFFACE bad memories.

Eradicate

ERASE *v.* to remove; strike out; obliterate; as "The passage of time erased all the writing from the tombstone."

Euthanasia

Expunge

Extant see **Extinct, Defunct,** etc.

EXTERMINATE *v.* to bring to an end; destroy utterly; root out; extirpate.

Extinct, Defunct, Extant

EXTINGUISH *v.* to put out; quench; stifle; as to EXTINGUISH fire.

EXTIRPATE *v.* to pull up by the roots; destroy utterly.

Genocide see **Atrociter & Genocide**

OBLITERATE *v.* remove completely; erase; efface.

RAZE *v.* to destroy; annul; tear down; demolish.

UPROOT *v.* to pull out by the roots; as "Many refugees were uprooted from their homes and forcibly settled in new places."

WIPE OUT *v.* kill off; exterminate; erase; destroy.

Atrociter and **Genocide** This generation coined GENOCIDE as a word for the 'mass murder of a population.' But GENOCIDES were perpetrated even in the ancient past. Genghis Khan eradicated whole peoples of North China in the thirteenth century, yet the Chinese delegates to the United Nations had to admit there was no Chinese word for this atrocity. The delegates were at a loss how to translate the new coinage, coming up at last with something like 'man-sheep butcher-kill.' Etymologically the word is simply an expansion of the meaning in homicide, the killing of a single man, to the killing of a whole race.

Atrocities, of course, are no recent phenomena. The perpetrators of them must be beginning to wonder why they have not yet been accorded a one-word designation. Or, at least, it is odd that we ourselves have not noticed the lack, since we must cumbersomely say 'a perpetrator of atrocities.' The improvisation ATROCITER is therefore submitted. You won't find it in the dictionaries, and perhaps someone else will come up with a better word. But you might find some use for it now.

Eradicate　This word is pure Latin. Most of us know that radicals are roots, and can appreciate the real force of ERADICATE. It means 'to root out,' not merely to pull out or remove. Thus it means 'to kill, exterminate.'

Euthanasia　This word refers to an 'easy death,' or a way of inducing it. More specifically, EUTHANASIA may be the public practice of killing human beings mercifully when they are afflicted with incurable diseases. Without the sanction of law, it is murder.

Expunge　EXPUNGE means 'to sponge out, efface, blot out.' This in spite of the fact that while *ex* did mean 'out,' the original *pungere* meant 'to prick.'

Extinct, Defunct and **Extant**　EXTINCT and DEFUNCT are useful words for people who like to make an effect with their talk: "Good manners are now extinct," says someone, or, "Alas, the simple virtue of modesty is long since defunct." The very sound of these words indicates the force of the observations.

EXTANT, the antonym of EXTINCT, is also effective. "No man extant is more illustrious than he." Etymologically, the two words are connected only by the ring through their noses, the *ex* for 'out.' EXTINCT means 'to quench out'—it came from the past participle of Latin *extinquo,* 'extinguish.' EXTANT means 'to stand out,' as the living from the dead. Latin DEFUNCT means literally 'discharged' or 'finished.'

EULOGY

ACCLAIM *n.* a shout of joy. *v.* to applaud; to salute by shouts or other demonstrations. Also *n.* ACCLAMATION.

Adulation

ALLELUIA *interj.* same as HALLELUJAH.

APPLAUD *v.* to praise or show approval by clapping hands; commend; cheer.

BRAVO! *interj.* Well done! Good!

CELEBRITY *n.* fame; renown; distinction; also, a famous person.

CITATION *n.* specifying points of distinction, for the purpose of eulogy, as a military or academic CITATION.

COMMEND *v.* to praise; to mention with approval. *n.* COMMENDATION.

COMPLIMENT *n.* a statement of praise or admiration. "Girls especially thrive on compliments." *v.* to praise, as "To keep a friend, compliment him."

DISTINCTION *n.* eminence; superiority; high social status; as "His distinction is being mayor."

ÉCLAT *n.* a burst of applause or acclamation; renown; glory.

Encomium

ENCORE! *interj.* literally, again. ENCORE is an exclamation of approval, said after any performance done well enough to be repeated.

Esteem, Repute, Prestige

EULOGY *n.* high commendation, esp. a formal expression of praise and approval. *v.* EULOGIZE, to pronounce an EULOGY upon. "The young man eulogized her beauty."

EXALT *v.* to praise, extol, glorify; to raise someone to a position of high distinction.

Extol see Laud, Extol, etc.

FAME *n.* renown; notoriety; public opinion about someone.

FLATTERY *n.* false or insincere praise.

GLORY *n.* exalted praise, honor, or distinction given by many to one. *v.* GLORIFY, to magnify and exalt with praise.

GRATULATORY *adj.* pertaining to congratulations.

HALLELUJAH! *interj.* praise ye the Lord; used esp. in songs of praise.

HEAR! HEAR! *interj.* exclamations of approval, esp. after someone has spoken.

HOMAGE *n.* respect; reverence; esp. formal expression of submission.

HONOR *n.* respect; reverence; esp. freely given respect to one whose virtues are outstanding. *v.* to respect; to show reverence for.

Laud, Extol, Plaudit

NOTABILITY *n.* the state of being notable; a notable person. *adj.* NOTABLE, memorable; remarkable; distinguished.

PANEGYRIC *n.* an eulogy, written or spoken. *adj.* PANEGYRICAL.

Plaudit see **Laud, Extol**, etc.

PRAISE *n.* an expression of approval, honor, commendation. *v.* to extol, approve, honor.

Prestige see **Esteem, Repute,** etc.

RENOWN *n.* fame; notoriety.

Repute see **Esteem, Repute,** etc.

RESPECT *n.* feeling of esteem, regard. In *pl.* RESPECTS, expressions of esteem and deference, as to give one's RESPECTS.

TRIBUTE *n.* a mark of devotion, gratitude or respect.

Adulation It is insulting to ADULATE whatever you adore. An ADULATOR has always been a 'fawner.' Today we sometimes use the word ADULATION in a sense of 'great public praise.' But its plaudits are more extravagant than sincere.

Encomium Greek scholars are about as numerous among English-speaking peoples as naval captains are among the Swiss. Instinctively we handle words derived from the Greek with formality. ENCOMIUM in Greek meant 'in revel,' so to us it should properly mean 'profuse praise.' But we use it to mean a 'formal expression of praise,' usually a 'single compliment, an individual bit of a eulogy.'

Esteem, Repute and Prestige If you are of good REPUTE, everybody speaks well of you, you have a 'good reputation.' If you are ESTEEMED, you are 'admired' and 'appreciated,' you are valued as a friend. But a man of PRESTIGE is not necessarily ESTEEMED or of good REPUTE. The word is French, but it has deep and ramifying roots in the Latin. PRESTIGE is related to 'prestidigitation,' trick artistry. In the beginning PRESTIGE was 'illusion,' hence 'delusion.' Then it was 'deception,' like dazzling juggler tricks. To the French it meant 'éclat.' Then PRESTIGE added to itself 'charm' and the talent to 'cause homage.' It identified itself at last with the 'status' that a man of power and public talent has. We have tamed the word down some today, but still a man can have a good name but little PRESTIGE.

Laud, Extol and Plaudit Though it is Latin, LAUD sounds English. Even the Latinish noun LAUDATION enables us to avoid the florid Greek word 'panegyric.' To LAUD is 'to praise' in the sense of eulogy or panegyric—sometimes sung, always vocal, and often highly rhetorical. EXTOL is as Latin as a Caesar. It means literally 'to raise up and out.' When you EXTOL someone, you praise him to the skies. PLAUDITS are simply 'individual bits of applause,' associated with laurel, which imply 'recognition' and 'reward.'

FATE

Chance *n.* see the category
CHANCE AND NECESSITY

CONSEQUENCE *n.* an effect
or result, as "The conse-
quence of poverty is usually
apathy."

DESTINY *n.* the future that is to
come; one's lot; a predeter-
mined course of events.

DOOM *n.* fate or destiny.

EFFECT *n.* consequence; whatever is produced by something
else, as "One of the effects of
sunlight is heat."

FATE *n.* destiny; the power or
force which predetermines
events, as "Fate saved him from
drowning by casting him on
shore."

FOREORDAIN *v.* to predetermine.

FORTUNE *n.* chance; lot; one's
destiny in the world.

ISSUE *n.* consequence.

LOT *n.* chance; a random draw.

Nemesis

OMINOUS *adj.* pertaining to good
or bad fortune, as the OMINOUS
outlook. *n.* OMEN.

OUTCOME *n.* result; consequence.

PORTENTOUS *adj.* ominous; fate-
ful; pertaining to what is about
to happen, usually calamitous.
n. PORTENT.

PREORDAIN *v.* to predetermine; to
cause in advance a certain effect.

RESULT *n.* consequence.

UPSHOT *n.* consequence; conclusion; end.

Victim

Nemesis The NEMESIS of most writers is popularity. NEMESIS is a
'personal fate' that frustrates and dooms. It is not a general and retributive fate; but familiar, like a shadow that mysteriously intends to be a
master in the end.

A NEMESIS may not only seem human but *be* a human. Uriah Heep
was the NEMESIS of the family into which he was adopted. Moreover,
in classical times there was only one NEMESIS, and she was a goddess—
the goddess of 'chastisement' and 'vengeance.' Vicariously her name
is kept alive by the shadow of retributive justice that follows each
mortal from infancy to death, chalking up and toting up his cumula-
tive missteps.

Victim Victors may be outstandingly conspicuous in their triumphs,
but VICTIMS are overwhelmed not only by human adversaries but by
everything from earthquakes to diseases. In the beginning VICTIMS were
slaughtered like beasts on an altar to propitiate the gods. In fact, before man's conceptions of divine vanity had suggested the appropri-
ateness of human VICTIMS, VICTIMS were animals.

So it seems a little queer that the Romans extended such a bloody word to 'everyday sufferers.' VICTIM found no popularity in English until the Bible featured it in sixteenth century translations. But it steadily grew in colloquial usage until now dictionaries generally agree it can equally designate someone who gets hurt or killed trying to accomplish some particular purpose, or someone who gets hurt or killed by bad luck or malevolence. Even so, the word remained a noun all through our Colonial period. 'To victimize' was still crude slang long after the founding of this Republic, and some dictionaries still call it a colloquialism.

FOODS

ABSINTHIC *adj.* refers to absinthe or to wormwood, used in its manufacture.

ACESCENT *adj.* tending to turn sour, or else somewhat sour.

ALLIACEOUS *adj.* pertaining to such vegetables as onions, garlic, leeks.

AMYGDALATE or AMYGDALINE *adj.* pertaining to almond.

AQUEOUS *adj.* pertaining to water.

BIBULOUS *adj.* addicted to alcoholic drinking.

BUTYRACEOUS *adj.* pertaining to butter.

CASEOUS *adj.* pertaining to cheese.

COFFEIC *adj.* pertaining to coffee.

COLLATION *n.* a light meal; thus, sometimes food and drink served at an entertainment.

Comestible see Condiment & Comestible

Condiment & Comestible

Culinary & Gastronomic

ENTRÉE *n.* a dish served before the main course or between courses. In U.S., a main dish other than a roast.

FARE *n.* food; menu, as a bill of FARE.

FARINACEOUS *adj.* pertains to meal or flour. Hence, also, starchy.

FRAPPÉ *n.* an iced or frozen mixture served in glasses.

FRIJOL or FRIJOLE *n.* a bean much used in Latin-American cookery, *pl.* frijoles.

FRITTER *n.* a cake made of batter which often contains corn, clams, etc., fried in a deep fat.

GALACTIC, LACTIC or LACTEAL *adj.* pertaining to milk. LACTEAL also means milky, and LACTEOUS either milky or resembling milk.

GALANGAL *adj.* pertaining to ginger.

Gastronomic see Culinary & Gastronomic

Grist & Meal

GRUEL *n.* a thin liquid food, usually made by boiling oatmeal in milk or water.

Mace see **Nutmeg & Mace**

Maize

MALIC *adj.* pertaining to apples.

MASTICATORY *adj.* pertaining to chewing.

Meal see **Grist & Meal**

MELLIFLUOUS *adj.* pertaining to honey; flowing with or like honey.

MENU *n.* a French word for bill of fare.

Mushroom

NECTARIAL or NECTAREOUS *adj.* pertaining to nectar. NECTARINE, meaning deliciously sweet, is the name of a downless peach.

Nutmeg & Mace

OLEAGINOUS *adj.* pertaining to oil.

Pabulum see **Papescent & Pabulum**

Papescent & Pabulum

Potable

Pumpernickel

RAGOUT *n.* a seasoned meat and vegetable stew.

Rasher

SALINE *adj.* pertaining to salt.

Salmagundi

SAPOROUS *adj.* imparting flavor.

Scrapple

SOUFFLÉ *n.* a very light dish, made of beaten eggs and other, variable ingredients, baked in an oven.

SUSTENANCE *n.* food; nourishment.

Taffy, Toffy or **Toffee**

TANNIC *adj.* pertaining to tan (not the color) as TANNIC acid, found in tea and certain other plants.

Tenderloin

Tipple

TITBIT or TIDBIT *n.* choice morsel of food.

Toast

Usquebaugh

VIANDS *n. pl.* articles or dishes of food.

VINOUS or VINACEOUS *adj.* pertaining to or like wine.

WELSH RABBIT *n.* a melted cheese dish, properly made with beer and poured over hot toast.

Condiment and **Comestible** CONDIMENTS are 'relishes,' sometimes 'sauces' or 'spices.' For example, the little Basque herring, or anchovy, is a CONDIMENT. COMESTIBLES are 'eatables.' A COMESTIBLE bird is an edible bird.

Culinary and **Gastronomic** Kitchen in Latin is *culina.* CULINARY means 'pertaining to the kitchen and to cooking.' GASTRONOMIC comes from Greek fragments amounting to the 'law of the stomach.' It therefore refers to the art of preparing and serving appetizing food and to the art of good eating.

Grist and **Meal** GRIST is grain destined for grinding at the mill; MEAL is ground grain.

Maize Like 'potato' and 'tomato,' MAIZE (Aztec) is an American Indian word. It means 'corn.' It is the original name for corn, the kind of grain we eat off the cob or feed to cattle. The word 'corn' itself is Anglo-Saxon, and means 'grain.' 'Corn' originally referred to crops that bear granular seeds, like wheat and rye. The English still use 'corn' in this broad and true sense. We apply it commonly to MAIZE, and when we want to designate other kinds of corn, we use 'grain.'

Mushroom The word MUSHROOM is derived from the French *mousseron,* in which the *mousse* represents 'moss.' Generally, MUSHROOMS are any edible fungi. They are commonly used in sauces, but they may provide a dish in themselves. The poisonous varieties, called toadstools, are very similar; it takes an experienced man to gather them wild. Nowadays most MUSHROOMS we buy in the stores are cultivated.

In most dictionaries you may not find MUSHROOM as a verb. Nevertheless, the verb exists and like the fungus is prolific. As a verb, MUSHROOM conveys a graphic image because of its umbrella shape and because of its quick growth. There is no other word that so aptly describes the expanding shape of an atomic cloud. In earlier ballistics there was a soft bullet, named from a military post in India, that MUSHROOMED when it struck its target. 'Dum dum,' it was called. But MUSHROOMING like that is not the same thing as the majestic unfolding of a bomb cloud in the skies, or as the MUSHROOMING of evil ideas in the minds of conspirators. Given a little more time, we may expand the verb usages still more. Already in slang a 'parvenu,' or 'upstart,' as well as an umbrella, is a MUSHROOM. The fact is inescapable that the word is already used almost *ad nauseam;* which suggests that it could be, without our detecting it in time, something of a toadstool.

Nutmeg and Mace The NUTMEG is the seed of an East Indian and Caribbean tree. The fruit is pear-sized but round, and the shell, opening in halves, encloses the nut. The nut is enclosed in a fibrous seed-covering, which is MACE.

Papescent and Pabulum PAPESCENT means 'of or like pap,' a milky juice. 'Pap' is food for babies, but PABULUM is simply 'food or nourishment.' Both come from the Latin, *pappa,* representing a babe's cry for food.

Potable This word means 'drinkable.' "The water from your well is the most potable I ever had!"

Pumpernickel This is the coarse bread of the German peasant, made from unbolted (unsifted) rye.

Rasher A RASHER is a 'thin slice' of any meat, but especially now it is a slice of bacon. It is so called because a RASHER is rashly, or hastily, cooked.

Salmagundi This is a French word from the Italian for 'seasoned salt meat' dish, which contains such tidbits as anchovies, eggs, onions, etc. It is in fact such a medley that SALMAGUNDI can mean 'medley.'

Scrapple SCRAPPLE is made of scraps of pork. Compare 'scrap iron,' 'scraps of iron.' Only the iron is unadulterated, while the pork is mixed with cornmeal, and fried.

Taffy, Toffy or Toffee TAFFY means 'flattery' or 'blarney,' the dictionaries say; it is colloquially derived from the candy made of brown sugar or molasses, with probably butter and perhaps nuts added. Flattery is a very devious and often elaborate thing, and blarney is a humorous, coaxing kind of flattery, mixed with cajolery. Perhaps in the colloquial meaning of TAFFY there is a suggestion of the old-fashioned candy pulls, wherein much 'kidding' and horse play occurred. Farther back, when most candy was homemade, and molasses was more common than commercial sugar, such occasions were to a degree matchmaking affairs. Even in the gay 'Nineties there was an uncouth but romantic saying, "He's stuck on her," meaning he thinks he is going to be in love with her, and reminiscent of the taffy-pulls when boy and girl worked as a pair and were literally all stuck together with candy. At any rate, now there is some facetiousness in TAFFY, and sometimes some romance.

TAFFY is American, TOFFY and TOFFEE British; or rather TAFFY is the original north-of-England British and TOFFY or TOFFEE is its later all-English form. Philologists connect it not too confidently with a curiously widespread word, *tafia* or *taffia*, occurring natively in both the East and West Indies, and in both places serving for an 'ersatz rum' distilled from crude molasses or refuse cane. It probably appears also as an element in French *ratafia*, either a 'cordial' or a 'sweet biscuit.'

Tenderloin Though 'tender-hearted,' with its sublimated emotional meaning, comes from the Bible (the Coversale translation, nearly a century before the King James Version), TENDERLOIN is probably a butcher's invention. It is the tender flesh of cattle cut from under the

short ribs in the loins. The British call it the 'undercut,' or 'fillet.' TEN-
DERLOIN is the opposite piece to the 'sirloin,' in which the 'sir' was Old
French *sur,* for Latin *super,* 'over.'

The extension of the term as a proper noun designating a part of a
town where night-life abounds, began in a midtown section of Manhattan several generations ago. In the old 29th Police Precinct west of
Broadway vice flourished so lavishly and brazenly the police couldn't
handle it. They couldn't, or didn't, at least, without sharing in its
profligacy, and accepting graft. The story therefore is that they came
to call this juiciest section of the city 'The Tenderloin.' More specifically, one captain, on being assigned to it, is said to have exclaimed:
"I've been eating chuck (neck or shoulder) steak all these years, now
I'll eat tenderloin!"

Tipple   In an age in which alcoholic drinking has so much increased, it is a wonder more words have not been coined or unearthed for our social drinking. But TIPPLE seems to have been unanimously ignored, probably from its sounding ridiculously old fashioned.
But in fact it has qualifications worth noticing. A TIPPLER is now taken
to be a little different from a 'toper,' a slightly old-fashioned and
jocular name for a 'steady drinker.' This slight may be justified, since
some dictionaries, asked where TIPPLE came from, answer laconically,
we don't know. But possibly it began in Scandinavia with a mere
'sipping of liquids,' as the frequentative of a word meaning 'to drip
from the tip' of something, like water from a melting icicle. Its present
proper meaning 'to drink habitually but in small quantities,' is con-
sistent with that derivation. Thus to TIPPLE is a different thing from
drinking heavily, as a toper does. Perhaps 'topple' would be a better
verb for 'heavy drinking.'

The word is very old. Surnames prove there were TIPPLERS in the
times of King John and the Magna Charta. But those TIPPLERS were
no more drinkers than tobacconists are smokers. They were simply
'keepers of alehouses.' This suggests that the 'tips' in their names were
somehow connected with 'taps.' But it has not been settled—you may
take your choice, or the derivation that pleases your understanding
of TIPPLE.

Toast   Literally, TOAST is not so much 'roasted bread' as it is 'parched
bread.' The Old French had *toster,* 'to roast' or 'grill'; but the original
was Latin *torrere,* 'to parch.' 'To torrefy' something today is either 'to
roast it' or 'to dry it' by exposure to heat. This is interesting because in
the Middle Ages dried bread was often stuffed with spices and sopped

in drinks, whence supposedly came today's 'toastmasters' at formal dinners, and the drinking of TOASTS.

There was a story told in 1709 of a celebrated English beauty whose health was drunk by a gallant admirer, in the fashionable Cross Bath, his glass having been filled from the water in which she had just sopped herself. A cynical wag who was present promptly remarked, that he cared not for the liquor but did covet the TOAST. However, it is quite possible that the drinking of TOASTS was more bibulous than that, in its origin. For at a very early date drinks already were 'tossed off (drunk at one draught),' as witness the antiquated synonym for a 'toper': a 'toss pot.' So the TOASTS which have come to be drunk and not eaten, may have been 'tosseds' or 'tosts,' with no actual relation to parched bread.

Usquebaugh All this is to say 'whiskey.' But the original Irish form of the word disarmingly meant only 'water of life,' while the clipped English version means still less, merely 'water,' as does also the Russian vodka. All of which is quibbling, since anything as expressive as these hard liquors has no trouble in convincing everyone of its real character.

Nevertheless, USQUEBAUGH does contain the answer to something you may have wondered about: how it came that Frenchmen purse up their lips and sound their 'u's' so peculiarly? For the Irish or Celtic 'u' was like that, as witness the Englishman's crude efforts to render it in 'whiskey.' But the Gauls who mingled with Germans to become Frenchmen took more pains, and though the exact resulting sound is now a headache for outsiders to learn, it is apparently no trouble to the French themselves.

USQUEBAUGH is now archaic even in Ireland. In Elizabethan England it was the name of the finest whiskey to be had, comparable with the later Scotch. The British drank it like brandy, and the Irish like beer. The original native term was *uige heatha.*

FORCE AND DESTRUCTION

Baleful   see **Baneful** & **Baleful**
Baneful & **Baleful**
CATACLYSMIC or CATACLYSMAL
   adj. pertaining to vast disaster, to CATACLYSM.
COERCION   *n.* force; rule by force; compulsion. *v.* COERCE, to com-

pel or force, as "They coerced the captives into confessing."
COMPULSION   *n.* constraint; coercion; state of being forced to do something. *v.* COMPEL, to force someone to do something.
CONVULSION   *n.* tremendous or vi-

olent upheavals, often in reference to the human body. *v.* CONVULSE, "The comedian convulsed his audience with laughter."

DEMOLISH *v.* to break up or utterly to smash or ruin something, esp. a building or city. *n.* DEMOLISHMENT.

DESOLATION *n.* ruin; wastes; areas uninhabited because of demolishment. "Desolation reigned throughout the bombed cities." *adj.* DESOLATE.

Destroy *n.* see the category ERADICATE

DEVASTATION *n.* desolation; ruin. *v.* DEVASTATE, as "The hurricane devastated the Long Island village."

DURESS *n.* imprisonment; constraint; compulsion. "As a suspect he was held under duress for a week until the culprit was caught."

FIERCE *adj.* furiously and fearlessly savage; violently cruel.

FIERY *adj.* of or pertaining to fire; hence, hot, quick-tempered, rash.

FORCE *n.* coercion; violence; power. *v.* FORCE, as "The bully forced the boy into a corner."

FRENZY *n.* violent mental or emotional derangement; tremendous, unrestrained excitement.

FURY *n.* anger; rage; wrath. *adj.* FURIOUS.

Havoc

Iconoclast

INJURIOUS *adj.* of or pertaining to injury or wrong. *n.* INJURY, hurt; wrong; esp. in the sense of an injustice.

MALIGNITY *n.* evil; malevolence. *adj.* MALIGN, having evil designs against someone.

MIGHT *n.* power; force; strength.

Pernicious

RAGE *n.* fury; violent anger; violence. *v.* to rave; to be uncontrollably upset or agitated, as "The wild beast raged within his cage."

RAVAGE *v.* to devastate or lay waste.

RAZE *v.* to demolish; to destroy; to break or pull down.

RIOT *n.* tumult; a wild public outburst; loose, wild behavior. *v.* to act without restraint; sometimes also used in the sense of indulging one's appetites.

RUIN *n.* anything destroyed or demolished. *v.* to destroy or demolish.

STORM *n.* a more or less violent disturbance of the atmosphere. *v.* to attack with violence; to rage.

TUMULT *n.* a noisy crowd of people; uproar, as the TUMULT of the battle guns.

Tumultuous see **Turbulent & Tumultuous**

Turbulent & Tumultuous

VIOLENCE *n.* a great force, often uncontrolled.

WASTE *n.* a stretch of barren land; desolation.

WILD *adj.* pertaining to unrestrained behavior.

WRECK *v.* to destroy; raze.

Baneful and **Baleful** BANEFUL means 'harmful'; BALEFUL means 'gloomy.' BANE is a strong word. It means 'death, ruin, woe.' "Beowulf was the bane of all monsters," means that he was the 'death' or the 'ruin' of all monsters. 'Ratsbane,' for example, is rat poison, and 'wolf's-bane,' 'badger's-bane,' 'bear's-bane,' or 'hare's-bane' all refer to the same plant, which is poisonous and which presumably destroys these animals. In the noun BALE, which is now a poetic and archaic word, there is a touch of evil and destruction. But the word mostly conveys woe and sorrow. The adjective BALEFUL, the form now generally in use, is a good word to add to your vocabulary. 'A baleful look' not only suggests 'sorrow' and 'gloom' but also 'evil.'

Havoc HAVOC in the beginning was the furious destruction a hawk caused—*hafoc*, the Anglo-Saxon's 'hawk.' Someday we may have a new and more awful word for HAVOC, something like 'bomboc,' from the atom bomb; but for many generations HAVOC has served expressively for 'wild, sudden and devastating ruin.'

Iconoclast An 'icon' is an 'image or likeness,' as a holy picture or statuette in the Greek church. The 'clast' means in Greek 'to break.' In early Greece the ICONOCLASTS were Carry Nations who destroyed venerated images. Modern ICONOCLASTS are less openly ruthless, but they will deliberately assail any outdated ideals, obsolete beliefs or traditions.

Pernicious That which is PERNICIOUS is 'harmful.' But it is by suggestion a whole lot more. It has the power 'to injure, kill, destroy.' Thus PERNICIOUS can refer to almost anything that is really bad. Besides, it looks vicious and sounds venomous. In the beginning it meant something like 'to kill through-and-through.'

Turbulent and **Tumultuous** Both words mean the same, only a TUMULT seems to 'rise or swell upwards,' like an uproar, while a TURBULENCE seems to 'swirl,' and is sometimes silent. Both, however, are violent commotions. A TUMULTUOUS mob is noisy, but may not mill around. TURBULENT waters are muddy and in motion, and so are TURBULENT thoughts and emotions. Both words are powerful. TUMULTUOUS is the nobler word, it has a triumphant sound. It doesn't heave up from the bottom among the dregs, but rises rapidly and swellingly from its own elevation. TURBULENCE is a deep down confusion.

Still, they are sometimes awe-inspiring. The TUMULT of our thoughts and the TURBULENCE of our souls—adjectives are known by the company they keep.

FRIENDSHIP

AFFABLE *adj.* easy-going; gracious; conversationally fluent.

AGREEABLE *adj.* pleasing.

Amenity, Amity, Enmity

Amiable & Amicable

Amicable see Amiable & Amicable

Amity see Amenity, Amity, etc.

CHUMMY *adj.* intimate; sociable. (Colloq.)

Comity

COMPANIONSHIP *n.* fellowship.

COMPLAISANT *adj.* affable; agreeable; obliging; compliant.

COMRADERY or COMRADESHIP *n.* fellowship.

CONCORDANT *adj.* harmonious; agreeing; consonant.

CONVIVIAL *adj.* pertaining to the fellowship of eating and drinking together.

Enmity see Amenity, Amity, etc.

FAMILIARITY *n.* intimacy; good social terms.

FELLOWSHIP *n.* mutual social intercourse.

FRATERNIZATION *n.* social intercourse, in a brotherly spirit.

GOOD-NATURED *adj.* likable; easy-tempered.

GOOD WILL *n.* good disposition toward people.

GREGARIOUS *adj.* sociable; companionable.

HARMONIOUS *adj.* agreeable.

HOSPITABLE *adj.* showing a ready and warm welcome.

INTIMACY *n.* close social or personal relationship.

OBLIGING *adj.* accommodating; agreeable; complaisant.

PACIFIC *adj.* pertaining to peace & calm.

PAL *n.* chum; friend. (Colloq.)

Amenity, Amity, and Enmity AMENITIES can produce AMITY, and AMITY can breed AMENITIES. AMITY is 'friendliness' in social or political relations, and AMENITIES are those 'civilities' which make life pleasant and people friendly.

AMITY cannot depend entirely upon AMENITIES, since the latter may be only acts of gentility performed for the sake of social form. True AMITY is a 'mutual peaceableness,' particularly between nations, and implies a disposition to be *really* friendly. But the word has been so much broadened in usage from the intimate relationships between individuals that it has become principally a noun of attitude and appearances. Two nations may be said to be in a state of AMITY when their relations are ostensibly friendly, when they exchange diplomatic notes and economic goods.

These uses are in keeping with the history of AMITY, as a word, and consequently of AMENITY, which is cognate. Their origins, though uncertain, both point back toward the Latin words for a 'friend' and for 'love.' Both flourished, however, in the Old French, AMENITY from an isolated Latinish word meaning 'pleasant,' and AMITY presumably from the Vulgar Latin noun meaning 'comity': *amicitas*. The exact antonym of Latin *amicus*, a 'friend,' was *inimicus*, an 'enemy.' Therefore, ENMITY, from *inimicus*, is still etymologically all that AMITY is not. Our adjective for ENMITY is 'inimical,' and ENMITY is either a state of being an enemy 'toward an enemy,' or the action of mutual enemies, for the implication is 'mutually active antagonism.'

AMENITIES is usually plural, referring to little acts or collective effects, rather than to states or conditions. The French love the AMENITIES of life, and they have given us *an* AMENITY as an 'act, trait, quality, feature' making for agreeableness. 'Reading,' for example, is an AMENITY or life, just as passing an attractive girl is an AMENITY of walking in the park. In time AMENITIES paled the meaning of AMITY. When the word AMENITY came into English it referred to 'places,' as we might still speak of the AMENITY of a residential section of a town as compared with its factory area. But AMENITY's importance dwindled and in self-defense, as it were, it gathered its forces into the plural, where they have become an asset to social behavior. AMITY has, in the meantime, likewise spread its implications, and in doing so somewhat abandoned its position as the antithesis of ENMITY. Conversely, ENMITY has narrowed its meaning to the 'ill-well' that exists between personal enemies and that actuates anger. See COMITY.

Amiable and **Amicable** Both words go back to the late Latin adjective, *amicabilis*, meaning 'friendly or kind.' In early Elizabethan times this adjective was adapted for English use, giving us our AMICABLE.

Much earlier the French *amiable* had been adopted whole for *our* AMIABLE, but its meaning soon steered away from 'full friendliness' toward 'pleasantness.' The reason for this was, that the influence of the still-existing pure Old French, distinct from the Norman French that had come in with the Conquest, was still active in England. Somehow the French *amiable* became confused in England with a very similar old French adjective, *amable*, which had come not from the Latin *amicabilis*, but from *amabilis*, meaning 'pleasant, affable.' Later on even this mixed word fell under the influence of a third, the French *aimer*, 'to love,' so that today, in modern French, it is spelled *aimable*. All these words, whether Latin or French, go back to Latin *amare*, 'to love.'

Thus we have the distinction between the two words. AMIABLE refers to 'affable kindliness,' AMICABLE to 'friendliness.' But until the Pilgrims sailed the ocean AMIABLE meant 'friendly and kind,' and in a new land the old meaning clung, or within recent generations returned, and we still take AMIABLE to mean 'kindly disposed'—a quality more of the heart than of manner.

Comity This word means 'mutual courteousness, kindly consideration for others,' as when nations respect each other's laws and customs. But even in its broadest sense it amounts to much more than 'politeness.' It is a real understanding which depends upon courtesy. Nor is the understanding quite what we commonly mean by 'understanding.' It is more an 'understanding between equals.' And while COMITY implies a 'friendly disposition,' as 'amity' also does, it also suggests 'action.'

For, if we look further, we can find among its etymological relatives such animated words as 'smile, marvel, mirror, admire.' From such actions true courtesy is compounded. When the word is applied, as it commonly is, to international relationships it retains this significance of a 'courteous understanding.' See AMITY.

Etymologically there is good reason why COMITY is unique among words expressing friendship. The beginning of COMITY was the Latin adjective *comis*, meaning not only 'kind' and 'friendly' but also 'loving.' But there is now a tendency to use COMITY, in another way, which depends on another source. The other word is Latin *comes*, which means a 'companion, partner.' Thus COMITY suggests 'the company of,' as in the COMITY of nations practicing (true) COMITY.

There are some who defend this new meaning because it is useful. They say, thus all languages grow. But granting that, we can still ill afford to wrench the roots of words, especially important words. While companions and partners are often personal or intimate friends, and COMITY should exist between them, still companionship is often casual. Partners are usually business companions, and their association is on a material, rather than personal, basis. The word has gained nothing by this narrower meaning. It is better to be conservative in this case, and to keep in the word the suggestion of 'courtesy' and 'mutual understanding.'

GEOGRAPHY

See also Areas and Measurements; Social, Political and Cultural Designations

AGRARIAN *adj.* pertaining to land, esp. to farm or public land.

Ait

ALLUVIAL *adj.* pertaining to riverside mud.

AQUATIC *adj.* living on or near water, as AQUATIC birds (water birds).

ARCHIPELAGO *n.* any broad strip of sea where many islands are located.

ARENACEOUS *adj.* pertaining to sand. ARENOSE means sandy in the sense of gritty.

ARGILLACEOUS *adj.* of the nature of clay; containing clay.

ATOLL *n.* a ring-shaped coral island enclosing a lagoon.

AUTOCHTHONOUS *adj.* referring to the status of nativity, as of rocks originally formed where they now are, or of indigenous flora and fauna. It has also the sense of aboriginal, as of the 'first' thing.

BOG *n.* a section of soft, wet ground; marsh; quagmire.

BOLAR *adj.* clayey; esp. in the sense of wet, earthy, reddish clay (BOLE).

BUSH *n.* uncleared country; waste; wild land; forest; esp. wild scrubland.

CAMPESTRAL *adj.* relating to or growing in level, open country. Compare PELAGIC.

CATACLINAL *adj.* running with the slope of the land, as a valley.

COAST *n.* shore; the land that adjoins the ocean.

Col

CRAG *n.* a cliff; a steep rock; a high promontory.

DELTA *n.* the often triangular piece of alluvial land through which the diverging branches of the mouth of a river pass before emptying into the ocean.

DIVIDE *n.* a ridge or upland range which separates two areas of drainage; a watershed.

EURASIAN *adj.* refers to Eurasia, or Europe and Asia considered as one land mass.

FEN *n.* marsh; bog.

FLUVIAL *adj.* pertaining to or produced by a river.

Gat

GEAL *adj.* pertaining to the earth.

GEODESIC *adj.* pertaining to GEODESY, or the measurement of the earth's face in areas large enough to be affected by the global curvature. The *adj.* GEODETIC refers to the mathematics of GEODESY.

Geopolitics

Glade

GRANITIC *adj.* pertaining to granite. Often used figuratively of a human personality.

GULF   *n.* a large body of water that extends within a land area, as the GULF of St. Lawrence, the GULF of Mexico.

HALIMOUS   *adj.* pertaining to the sea.

HEATH   *n.* bush; waste; esp. uncultivated land covered with bushes or low trees.

INSULAR   *adj.* refers to island.

LACUSTRAL or LACUSTRINE   *adj.* pertaining to lakes.

LAGOON   *n.* an area of shallow water, separated from the sea by narrow strips of land. See also ATOLL

LAPIDARY   *adj.* refers to stones or to stone-cutting.

LITTORAL   *n.* shore; coast. *adj.* LITTORAL.

LOCH   *n.* lake; small inlet from the the sea, mostly landlocked. (Scot.)

MACROCOSMIC   *adj.* pertaining to big-worldness; hence, universal. *n.* MACROCOSM. Change the 'a' to an 'i' and the reference is to a world in miniature; *adj.* MICROCOSMIC. *n.* MICROCOSM.

MARINE   *adj.* pertaining to the sea.

MERIDIONAL   *adj.* pertaining to the meridian.

MESA   *n.* a relatively small plateau situated in mountainous country and possessing steep approaches.

MOOR   *n.* heath; waste; esp. when overgrown with heather.

MUNDANE   *adj.* pertaining to the earth; thus, often, worldly or earthy.

PALUDIC   *adj.* pertaining to marsh.

PELAGIC   *adj.* pertaining to open or deep sea. compare CAMPESTRAL

PLATEAU   *n.* a flat section of land; a tableland; a level area higher than surrounding land.

REEF   *n.* a ridge or pile of rocks which rises from the ocean floor to a peak near the surface.

RIPARIAN   *adj.* pertaining to a river or to shores or banks.

Seascape

SEISMIC   *adj.* pertaining to an earthquake.

STEATITIC   *adj.* refers to soapstone.

STRAITS   *n. pl.* a narrow passage of water connecting two large sections of lake, ocean, or other bodies of water.

TERRAQUEOUS   *adj.* pertaining to land and water together.

TERRENE   *adj.* pertaining to the earth, as *terra firma;* mundane.

TERRESTRIAL   *adj.* pertaining to the earth or land.

TERRICOLOUS   *adj.* pertaining to the inhabiting of land.

TERRIGINOUS   *adj.* earth-born, in distinction to heavenly; also means land derived, like certain sea deposits, from disintegrating shores. Also AUTOCHTHONOUS, in the sense of 'in the very earth of.'

THALASSIC   *adj.* pertaining to seas and bays. Sometimes it equates with oceanic.

Tor

TRANSMARINE   *adj.* overseas.

TRANSMONTANE   *adj.* the other

side of the mountain; hence, **Valley**
also, strange, wild, or foreign. WATERSHED *n.* an area of land
TUMULAR *adj.* pertaining to from which water drains away,
mound. TUMULOSE means full of as the two sides, generally, of a
mounds or hills. mountain chain. See also DIVIDE.

Ait AIT is a little island in a river. The final 'ey' in some surnames
has this meaning.

Col A pass between mountain peaks is called a COL, from Latin *collum,* 'neck.'

Gat This word is a Scandinavian or Low German word meaning
an 'opening or hole,' used by us now with a specific meaning: a shallow, inland channel winding between sandbanks or rocky capes. The
channel may be natural or artificial. The word is related to 'gate.'
The latter was commonly used not so very long ago in Northern England to mean 'street.'

Geopolitics 'Politics' originated in the Greek *polis,* 'city.' The Greek
word for the world, *gē,* meant more generally the 'earth,' which at that
time was supposed to be stationary and flat, with the sun and the stars
sashaying around it. This word gave us our 'geography,' which is the
science and description of the earth, and GEOPOLITICS. The science of
GEOPOLITIK arose in Germany to consider the dependence of a people's
politics, both at home and abroad, upon physical environment.

But unfortunately the Teutonic mind has not always been exclusively
interested in peoples as such, or even the German people as a whole.
The new science provides a method of studying geography and power
politics together. Upon these depend the national security of any people. Who and how situated are our neighbors, reasoned the German
geopoliticians? What is their political and industrial strength, how
does it depend upon their geographical situation, and how does that
affect us? Finally, as the argument of *lebensraum,* or living space, was
advanced, the word GEOPOLITIK began to denote a doctrine. This doctrine holds that the domination of land area and natural resources is
the best guarantee of, first, national security and, second, world power.

Now the word has come to us. There is an idea in GEOPOLITICS that is
bigger than Germany, and bigger than any amoral doctrine of world
domination. For it is the duty of all politicians in the higher sense to
study the influences of all conditions whatsoever, upon the people
whom, whether by delegation or assumption of power, they govern.

The significance of vast features of topography in encouraging people to develop themselves assuredly warrants a political science embracing geography. So with all its recent evil connotations GEOPOLITICS may someday imply the elevation of Secretaries of Interior, Commerce and State into important offices in a universal organization.

Glade If you have ever made your way through a deep woods and come suddenly to a sunlit opening, you will appreciate the old meaning of this word, 'bright.' GLADE comes from Early English and was pronounced more like 'glad.' Today GLADE is an open place in a wood or forest.

Seascape This is a companion word to 'landscape.' It refers of course to the view the sea gives to us. In a museum marine pictures are called SEASCAPES.

Tor TOR means variously a prominent craggy hill, a jutting rock, a rugged knob, etc. It comes from the Anglo-Saxon *torr*, with the same meanings.

Valley This word comes from the French, *vallée*, diminutive of *val;* but it quickly grew larger and took over *val's* whole meaning, besides holding on to its own. 'Vale,' an English poetic word, denotes a 'broad, low-sided VALLEY.' VALLEY also drove out the native English *dean*, for a 'dale or VALLEY.' 'Dale' is now poetically used for 'glen,' occurring often in the hackneyed expression, 'up hill and down dale,' which suggests a good-sized VALLEY, or 'vale.' A variant of 'dale' is 'dell,' with a still more poetic suggestion of remoteness. 'Glen' is a Gaelic word that denoted a 'mountain VALLEY,' but to us 'glen' now suggests any narrow, unfrequented VALLEY.

No doubt all these terms have always been used rather indiscriminately. But the course of running water is implicit in them all: a 'vale' or VALLEY is, essentially, a drainage area. But when the action of rushing water becomes more marked in its results, cutting through cliffs or digging out steep-sided valleys, the names are more descriptive. 'Gorges' were first 'whirlpools' or 'abysses (immeasurable pits),' to the Romans; and they gave the later Latin a word for the human throat which is still occasionally heard in English. 'Gullies' also probably represent the throat, from old French *gole*. 'Gulches' are American, but probably are companions in sense with those others, from an obsolete word meaning 'to swallow.' 'Ravines' represent the 'rapine' of a raging flood. The Latin 'p' changed to French 'v,' as in 'river.'

GOVERNMENT
See also Law; Rule; and Politics

Administrative & Executive
Annualize
COUNTRY *n.* the land or territory that constitutes a nation.

> BODY POLITIC *n.* collectively, the constituents of a politically organized state or community.
>
> DOMAIN *n.* that territory over which one power rules.
>
> DOMINION *n.* domain; esp. in the sense of a country that belongs to a larger federation, as the DOMINIONS of the British Commonwealth of Nations.
>
> LAND *n.* territory; often, figuratively, a country, as the LAND of the brave.
>
> NATION *n.* any group of people which exists as a community for any reasons, political, racial, or other.
>
> REPUBLIC *n.* a nation, state or country where the power ultimately rests with a certain portion of the people.
>
> REALM *n.* country; domain.
>
> STATE *n.* the body politic, esp. with reference to the government that controls the body politic.

DIPLOMACY *n.* the art of managing the affairs one country has with other countries.

Enact
Executive see **Administrative & Executive**
Forum
GOVERNMENT *n.* the established institutions of control a state possesses.

> AUTOCRACY *n.* a government where all the power is in the hands of one ruler.
>
> AUTONOMY *n.* a self-governing state; thus, a state existing without higher control over it.
>
> DEMAGOGY *n.* a government that maintains its power by capitalizing on social discontent and popular ignorance.
>
> DEMOCRACY *n.* a government that derives its power from the consent of a nation. See also NATION.
>
> FEDERALISM *n.* a system of political organization established by the union of formerly autonomous states.

Hagiarchy
> HETERONOMY *n.* a state which is partly controlled by a superior power.
>
> LIMITED or CONSTITUTIONAL MONARCHY *n.* a monarchy whose power is limited, more or less severely, by a constitution or by the na-

tion itself through a parliament.

MONARCHY   *n.* a state ruled by a king.

MONOCRACY   *n.* an autocracy.

OLIGARCHY   *n.* a government in which the power is held by a few people.

REPRESENTATIONAL, or CONSTITUTIONAL, GOVERNMENT   *n.* a government whose power is limited by a constitution and by the voice of the people expressed through their chosen representatives.

Technocracy

THEOCRACY   *n.* a government directed by the command of God; thus, a government by priests.

Legal & **Legislative**

Legislative   see **Legal** & **Legislative**

Mandate

MAYOR   *n.* the highest officer of a village or city government. *adj.* MAYORAL.

MINISTRY   *n.* a department of government headed by a minister, who is an official appointed usually by the highest authority. *n.* MINISTER. *adj.* MINISTERIAL.

Political & **Politic**

Politic   see **Political** & **Politic**

Polity

PRESIDENT   *n.* in the United States, the chief executive officer of the federal government.

Protocol

REGIME   *n.* government, esp. its way, system or period of duration. "A dictator's regime is usually tyrannical." *adj.* REGIMINAL.

SENATE   *n.* a body of national representatives that has the highest legislative function in government. *n.* SENATOR, a member of a SENATE, esp. a member of the United States SENATE. *adj.* SENATORIAL.

STATESMAN   *n.* one who is especially wise and experienced in the art of government.

Administrative and **Executive**   Most officials like to be called EXECUTIVES. The word suggests 'power' and, although an ADMINISTRATOR is generally recognized as a competent man in a position of great trust and importance, an EXECUTIVE nevertheless has a higher status. The reasons for this are, broadly, three: first, the etymological histories of these two words support the popular distinctions; secondly, the wide use in local, state, and national government helps maintain the differences; and thirdly, the psychological nature of man urges him to give superior status to an EXECUTIVE.

The essential difference between ADMINISTRATIVE and EXECUTIVE can be illustrated by the use of two small prepositions. Let us say that ADMINISTRATIVE means carrying *on* business, government, etc., and that EXECUTIVE means carrying *out* a provision, general business plans, law, etc. At the beginning, ADMINISTRATIVE meant 'serving,' from Latin *ad-*

ministrare, and EXECUTIVE meant 'following through to the end,' from Latin *sequor,* which also produced our 'sequence' and 'consequence.'

Government, for example, will illustrate this distinction. The President of the United States is not called an ADMINISTRATOR. He is our Chief EXECUTIVE. He is required by the Constitution to direct the application of our federal laws—he must carry them 'out.' Ultimately we, the voters, throw him out of office if he doesn't properly fulfill this responsibility. Of course, there must be a plan, or way, for the President to function. This plan he, in a sense, gives to various government officials, primarily cabinet officers, who then become ADMINISTRATORS of this plan. These men carry 'on' the President's plan. If they fail, they are dismissed; but the plan remains, and new ADMINISTRATORS are found. If the President fails, the plan is a failure, and the continuity of government is, in a sense, temporarily destroyed.

Obviously the terms overlap. For example, an ADMINISTRATOR has to have a plan in order to carry out the plan of the Chief EXECUTIVE. Is this ADMINISTRATOR then an EXECUTIVE? Yes, if one wants to so name him. But the point is that he is already named an ADMINISTRATOR by the Chief EXECUTIVE, and so we all accept that designation. And when we compare the ADMINISTRATOR to the Chief EXECUTIVE he does not, of course, have as much power or status. This brings us to the psychological grounds for distinguishing the two words.

How often have you heard that a man would rather be the first bullfrog in a small pond than a second bullfrog in a big lake? In other words, he wants to be an EXECUTIVE. We all know that the second bullfrog in the big lake is much more powerful than the first bullfrog in the pond, but most of us really admire the chief, wherever he is. If we keep this psychological perspective in our minds, we shall never confuse the meanings of EXECUTIVE and ADMINISTRATIVE when we see in the newspapers that our Secretary of State is called an ADMINISTRATOR, and our local gas company's president is called an EXECUTIVE.

These inner distinctions are felt not only in public affairs but in private. An ADMINISTRATOR is appointed by a court to manage the estate of a man who has died intestate. But an EXECUTOR of an estate is identified with the testator himself, who while still living, in his own written will designates him the posthumous EXECUTIVE of his affairs. This EXECUTOR, however, may not attend to the technical legal details of carrying out the will; he will probably leave those to an ADMINISTRATOR. His own job is to see that all the terms are carried out. Prior to this the will itself was EXECUTED: it was signed, sealed and delivered—that is, it was completed. The EXECUTION of its terms then becomes a second EXECUTION. When we speak of EXECUTING a criminal, we are using a recent figurative usage, accentuating 'finality.' Actually, the criminal is not EXECUTED but the law is, just as *it* is (and not you) when you are fined for speeding.

Again, a 'stewardship' is not properly an EXECUTIVE job; it is the regulating of a process by which an estate, a household, a club or a hotel is maintained. On the other hand, though a secretary is clearly an ADMINISTRATIVE unit, we now have EXECUTIVE secretaries, with managerial abilities plus delegated EXECUTIVE powers. Likewise, we have EXECUTIVE sessions of not exclusively top EXECUTIVES. On the other hand, we have, though this again is in public affairs, ADMINISTRATIVE law, in which even minor ADMINISTRATORS become not only EXECUTIVES but judges and legislators as well. Enmeshed in the complexities of a vast routine they must be decisive and incisive, to cut all the Gordian knots. Even Lincoln recognized such difficulties during the Civil War. He said his generals were such that he was obliged to be both Commander-in-Chief (head EXECUTIVE) and General-in-Chief (head ADMINISTRATOR)—until he found Grant and made him generalissimo (trusted judge, lawmaker and EXECUTIVE, within his own field).

Annualize This is an old word that has almost forgotten its inherited meaning and is now appearing in Washington's officialdom with an entirely new one. The word can still mean simply 'to write for or to publish an ANNUAL,' but in its new sense it is far more pretentious. It now means, apparently, 'to project the findings of a few months over the period of a year.' For example, the early operational expenses of a new commission are imaginarily extended for a longer period so that a budget, or estimate, of total expenses can be arrived at.

Enact One of the highly useful 'en' prefix words. You can, of course, 'act' a part as well as ENACT it. But the little 'en' is far from insignificant. Its gesture is vague but sweeping. A panorama can be ENACTED in the sense that all the scenery, circumstances and actors are represented. But an 'acted' scene lays emphasis only on the actors. Such a scene RE-ENACTS itself in your mind when all the details are recalled.

And then, of course, a law can be ENACTED. It comes definitely into being by reason of an act. Many things come into being that way, such as newspapers every morning; but the act is usually so common we don't take the time to describe it with an emphatic verb. Nevertheless we can, for example, ENACT democracy simply by acting democratically.

Forum Roman mass meetings, as well as public tribunals, were held in FORUMS. These were open spaces in towns where the crowds could come, see, hear and speak. So, today, when you attend a FORUM you have a right to speak whether you are an important, or unimportant, member of the assembly. Without FORUMS, without the public interest they generate, true democratic government can not exist.

Hagiarchy 'A sacerdotal government, government by priests.' 'Hagio' is a combining form, from the Greek, meaning 'sacred.' It recurs in 'hagiology,' a list of saints.

Legal and **Legislative** LEGISLATIVE refers to the 'enacting of laws, to the political body that enacts them, to the members of that body, to laws in general.' This still leaves something over for LEGAL, even though its subject, law itself, has still other adjectives for more broad, or even more specific, meanings. For example, admitting that law is broader than LEGISLATION (since nature also has its laws, which can hardly be said to have been *enacted*), nevertheless the law which is human has its LEGISLATIVE aspect, quite distinct from its simply LEGAL aspect. For LEGAL refers first 'to law as a human institution governing the conduct of persons collectively,' while LEGISLATIVE speaks of a matter-of-practice relating to such law, namely, 'law-making.'

The word LEGAL has hardened in a specific usage to the point where it excludes all thoughts of law not backed by the authority of the LEGISLATURE. When we say something is LEGAL we mean, and everyone knows we mean, that the books say it is lawful and that nothing else counts. This concentration of meaning has unfortunately ruined both LEGAL and 'lawful' for general usages. Anything relating to the laws of God or of nature, for example, cannot be said to be either LEGAL or 'lawful,' and yet what other adjective can we use here?

Mandate A MANDATE is a 'command.' A dictionary will tell you that the Roman word *mandatus* means a 'command'; but it will give you as modern synonyms 'law, decree, edict, ordinance, statute.' It will go on to show you how the term is used legally, as of judicial directives or of royal or authoritative decrees and behests. It will explain that even in these circumstances a MANDATE will sometimes be the equivalent of a 'request.' In international law a MANDATE is, in substance, the same as a 'protectorate.' For, at bottom, a MANDATE is *not* just a 'command.' A tyrant can command you, if he has the power to do so; but the essential of a MANDATE is 'entrustment.' Literally, the word means 'that which is given by hand,' that is, that which is personally entrusted to someone. The sense of MANDATE has recently extended to mean an 'authorized rule or domination.' For example, the United Nations has given our country a MANDATE to rule certain Pacific Islands. Perhaps the related word, 'mandatory,' meaning 'officially obligatory,' has exercised an influence on MANDATE.

Though MANDATE is used only figuratively in informal personal affairs, it has real force in those usages. We collectively, as voters, may correct evils or enjoin good by our sovereign MANDATE. So also life itself may enjoin us in our various activities. Thus life gives us a MANDATE, or we ourselves, our own will or conscience, give MANDATES about how to act.

Political and **Politic**   POLITICAL possesses applications other than those relating to machinations of our POLITICAL parties. It may refer to the broader and calmer practices of a government, specifically denoting the 'policies' a government pursues in fulfilling its duty as a managing agency. A POLITIC man is a 'wise and tactful man.' He is tactful because he knows that tact, involving considerate judgment, pays off. He is prudent but urbane, and he is still playing POLITICS.

Polity   'An organized system of government.' Probably every state and church as well as any smaller organization has one. 'Policies' form the strategy, and 'politics' the tactics within a POLITY.

Protocol   As commonly understood, PROTOCOL is the working out of a formulary covering the conduct of diplomatic and official affairs of a national government. (A formulary is a collection of 'forms, formulas, treaties and precedents.') Hence, in practice, it refers to the official pattern of diplomacy. In particular, PROTOCOL regulates official and diplomatic etiquette, specifying, for example, who sits next to the President and who next to his wife at a state dinner.

But this sense is derivative. It comes from the European meaning of PROTOCOL as a 'code of international politeness,' affecting primarily kings and their heads of government. The word itself is Greek, and means literally 'first glue.' The first glue was the first page, you might say, of a papyrus rolled on a cylinder. That first roll was then the official one, the first draft of a document. Today, it is still the 'first draft' or perhaps the 'original copy' of a diplomatic agreement or official transaction. It is the authentic inception of such things.

But the collective diplomatic PROTOCOLS of Europe are 'ceremonial rules' governing all written or personal intercourse between rulers and their ministers, and prescribing, in particular, official phraseology and diplomatic courtesies, with meticulous regard to gradations of rank, honor, traditional precedents, etc. That is why in Washington today PROTOCOL is primarily not a pestiferous collection of red tape but an awesome etiquette.

But sometimes a PROTOCOL may be merely a 'social convention.' Or it may be a 'preliminary discussion' that leads to a convention (agreement), or an 'extra clause' or 'statement' explaining a treaty or extending its terms. Or it may be only a 'codicil' to a will.

Technocracy There is a punning witticism that all governments need more pruning and less grafting, which was apparently taken to heart by a certain scientist soon after the first World War. He had been tremendously impressed by this country's war effort, which had produced, as he said, the first Industrial Democracy. So, in contemplating the achievement, he conceived a type of government that should be effective in all times, peace or war, conducted by managers recruited from all the fields of applied or theoretical science. For such a government he coined the term TECHNOCRACY.

The idea held forth a promise of political efficiency and, in fact, efficiency in all kinds of management; and so it became popular to the public. But unfortunately the exact nature or method of technology is not generally clear in the layman's mind. Thus its precise implications and whole meaning remained vague. Too vague, as it turned out, to support TECHNOCRACY's propositions when they encountered objections from established systems. So TECHNOCRACY is now not much more, to most of us, than a word in the dictionary.

All this can be read between the lines of the texts the lexicographers themselves wrote. For some word experts regard TECHNOCRACY as a 'theory' by which scientists and technicians would administer government, while others call it a school of thought stressing the need of technicians in modern society and especially of engineers in the control of economy, with no specific mention of government. Other experts see it more positively as a social and economic system in which capital, resources *and* advanced technological knowledge are all used to the utmost. Some word men speak of it matter-of-factly, as if it already existed officially, "Government by technological experts." Still others view it with two separate eyes: one eye sees it broadly but appraisingly as a proposed political community controlled by experts or as actually a government by organized technologists. The other eye envisages something smaller and nearer at hand, a nonpolitical fact-finding body of experts in all the various departments of science, aiming to revaluate industrial output in terms of energy factors—which is still not too clear to most minds. Finally, Webster's, the king of definers, says: Government or management of the whole society by technical experts or in accordance with principles established by technicians; (hence), an organization of technicians that studies the possibilities of such management.

GRAMMAR

See also Language

ALPHABET *n.* the letters from which words are constructed, such as "A," "B," "C."

Anonym see **Synonym, Antonym,** etc.

Antonym see **Synonym, Antonym,** etc.

Clause

DIACRITIC or DIACRITICAL *adj.* pertaining to distinguishment, as by a mark or sign; for example the dash, or macron, over a long vowel in phonetic spelling.

Eponym see **Synonym, Antonym,** etc.

Grammatical

Paradigm

Paronym see **Synonym, Antonym,** etc.

PARTS OF SPEECH *n.* the various categories under which all words fit according to their grammatical use.

> ADJECTIVE *n.* any word that somehow modifies a noun, like a GRAY house. *adj.* ATTRIBUTIVE or ADJECTIVAL.

> ADVERB *n.* any word that somehow modifies a verb, as to jump QUICKLY. *adj.* ADVERBIAL.

CONJUNCTION *n.* any word that connects phrases or sentences together, like AND, BUT, OR.

INTERJECTION *n.* any exclamatory word, like OH.

NOUN *n.* any word that specifies some thing, like HOUSE, IDEA, LOVE. *adj.* NOMINAL or NOUNAL.

PREPOSITION *n.* a word, like BY, AT, IN, that shows a relationship between other words, esp. nouns. *adj.* PREPOSITIONAL.

PRONOUN *n.* any word that substitutes for a noun, like HE, SHE, IT. *adj.* PRONOMINAL or PRONOUNAL.

VERB *n.* any word that expresses action or condition, and is combined with a subject to form a sentence, like DO, MAKE, PLAN. *adj.* VERBAL often refers simply to words. Hence it often means oral.

Prosody & Syntax

Pseudonym see Synonym, Antonym, etc.

Purism

SUBSTANTIVE *n.* noun. *adj.* SUBSTANTIVAL.

Synonym, Antonym, Paronym, Eponym, Pseudonym & Anonym

Syntax see Prosody & Syntax.

See also Linguistics, under the category LANGUAGE.

Clause From the Latin *claudere*, 'to close.' A CLAUSE differs from a phrase by having a subject and finite verb. The following example contains three clauses, but it ends with a phrase: "The man, who was busy reading, finally looked up, and then he said, with the beginning of a smile . . ."

Grammatical There is some question whether a GRAMMATICAL error can exist, on the grounds that, if it did, it wouldn't be GRAMMATICAL. But good dictionaries generally give GRAMMATICAL two senses: good GRAMMAR, with the implication that all GRAMMAR is good; or just pertaining to GRAMMAR, whether or not it be good or bad.

Together with 'graphic' and 'carve' this word is derived from a Greek word meaning 'to write.' In the Middle English *grammere* narrowed to the study of Latin GRAMMAR, which to the masses was so occult it engendered in Scotland our word 'glamour,' connoting all the mysterious powers of magic. Even today it has uncommon meanings transcending the principles of words and sentences. The GRAMMAR of an art or a science is its 'methodic principles.' Yet the word has cleaved closely to a meaning of 'correct verbal construction.' If your speech is GRAMMATICAL, you are at least next door to being a grammarian.

Paradigm A PARDADIGM is not often a word. It is a 'model, example or pattern,' from the Greek for 'beside' plus 'show.' In grammar, it is a complete illustration of a word's inflections, whether a 'declension' for a noun or adjective, or a 'conjugation' for a verb.

Prosody and Syntax PROSODY is the 'science of verse,' and SYNTAX is the 'rules of diction.' It is the poet who needs to know the rules of PROSODY; it is any writer, you and I, who needs to know the rules of SYNTAX. See LINGUISTICS, PHILOLOGY, ETYMOLOGY, etc.

Purism This word refers to the extreme principle that diction should always be precise and decent. PURISM emphasizes what has been traditional in our language often at the expense of what is fresh and vivid.

Synonym, Antonym, Paronym, Eponym, Pseudonym and Anonym

'Jet-black' is SYNONYMOUS with 'ebony.' A SYNONYM is a word, or phrase, equivalent in meaning to some other word, or phrase. The phrase 'chalk-white' is an ANTONYM of both 'jet-black' and 'ebony.' Conversely, 'jet-black' and 'ebony' are ANTONYMS of white. 'Darkness' and 'light,' 'fat' and 'thin' are mutual ANTONYMS. ANTONYMS are 'opposites.' The 'nym' stems from Greek *onama*, 'name.' The 'an' is a Greek negative. Certain ANTONYMS may be 'privatives.' See PHILOLOGICAL TERMS.

A PARONYM is one of two or more 'conjugate' words, that is, words of the same derivation or root, like 'animus' and 'animal.' It is also any one of several words that sound alike, but differ in meaning and spelling, like 'ant' and 'aunt.' Also, a PARONYM is a word built from a foreign one. A rough-and-ready PARONYM of this sort is 'Idaho.' The Indians used to say "ee-dah-how," meaning 'hello.'

The 'ampere,' 'Washington Avenue' and the 'Victorian period' were all named for persons. An EPONYM is the person whose name has been taken to designate something else, and it is also the thing so named.

A PSEUDONYM is of course a 'false name.' An ANONYM, whence 'anonymous' and 'anonymity,' is a person who is 'unknown,' that is, whose 'name is not known.' If all we know of a man is his PSEUDONYM, then he is an ANONYM.

HEALTH AND REMEDIES

See also Ailments

ADIPSOUS *adj.* thirst quenching.

ANTHELMINTIC *adj.* purging parasitic worms.

ANTIPHLOGISTIC *adj.* reducing inflammation. See also FEBRIGUGAL

APHRODISIAC *adj.* stimulating sex passion.

CATHARTIC *adj.* purging, from the Greek for purifying. See also PURGATIVE

EUPEPTIC *adj.* pertaining to good digestion.

FEBRIFUGAL *adj.* acting to reduce fever. See also ANTIPHLOGISTIC.

FINE FETTLE *n.* in good state or condition; full of energy.

FIT *adj.* in good physical condition, as players FIT to play ball.

GUTTATE *adj.* pertaining to or like a drop.

HALE *adj.* robust; free from disease or injury; vigorous, as a HALE old man.

Healthful & Healthy

Healthy see **Healthful & Healthy**

HEARTY *adj.* hale; full of life.

HYGIENIC *adj.* clean; free of disease, as a HYGIENIC restaurant; good; tending to promote good health.

IATRIC or MEDICINAL *adj.* pertaining to medicine.

LECTUAL *adj.* pertaining to long confinement in bed.

LONGEVOUS or MACROBIOTIC *adj.* pertaining to long life.

NARCOTIC *adj.* pertaining to sleep producing, and thus often beneficial, drugs.

NERVINE *adj.* quieting to the nerves. Like 'nervous' it also refers to nerves generally.

NUTRITIOUS *adj.* pertaining to foods that are good for the body.

PANACEAN *adj.* pertaining to PANACEA, or cure-all.

PINK *n.* in good shape, as to be in the PINK of condition.

PURGATIVE *adj.* refers to purging, from Latin for cleansing. See also CATHARTIC.

REMEDIAL *adj.* affording a cure.

Robust

Salubrious & Salutary

Salutary see **Salubrious & Salutary**

SANITARY *adj.* of or pertaining to health, as SANITARY conditions.

SEDATIVE *adj.* soothing pain or quieting the nerves.

SOPORIFIC *adj.* causing sleep.

STRENGTH *adj.* physical power, as "The blacksmith displayed great strength."

STYPTIC *adj.* pertains to the stopping, or clotting, of flowing blood.

SUTURAL *adj.* pertains to the sewing up of wounds.

VERMIFUGINOUS *adj.* purging parasitic worms.

VIGOR *n.* active strength or force, esp. of mind or body.

WELL *adj.* of or pertaining to good health.

WHOLESOME *adj.* promoting well-being; nutritious.

Healthful and **Healthy** HEALTHFUL means 'giving,' and HEALTHY means 'having,' health. We do speak of a HEALTHY climate in the sense of the climate's 'giving' health. Usually, though, HEALTHY is used to describe a state of health, like "He is a healthy man." But "Apples are a healthful food," clearly means that an apple a day keeps the doctor away.

Robust 'Strong' is its fundamental meaning. It suggests anything bursting with life. To emphasize this exploding quality we have the longer adjective 'robustious.' But ROBUST itself means, very broadly, 'strong with health' or 'of healthy strength.' Virile writing is manly, but a ROBUST style can certainly be feminine, if it is vigorous, for women as well as men can be strong and healthy.

Salubrious and Salutary Both words come from the Latin *salus,* 'health.' But SALUTARY is the broader word. SALUBRIOUS means 'conducive to health,' and therefore 'healthful' or 'wholesome,' as mountain air is, by its very nature, SALUBRIOUS. SALUTARY means fitted to bring about a sound condition by offsetting or removing bad influences. SALUTARY laws are designed to bring about peace and prosperity. SALUTARY measures are adopted to correct evils, and since evils include diseases, such beneficial results are also SALUBRIOUS.

HUMAN BEHAVIOR

(*Adjectives*)

ADVENTUROUS bold; daring.

AGILE nimble; active; as an AGILE mind or imagination.

ALERT watchful; very attentive.

ANIMATED lively; full of movement and life, as an ANIMATED face.

ARTLESS without art or skill; hence, unsophisticated; sincere; simple; as an ARTLESS smile.

ASSURED confident; bold; certain.

ASTUTE shrewd; keenly intelligent; as "That was an astute remark."

AUSTERE severe; stern; harsh; esp. in the sense of sober and very serious.

AVID eager, as an AVID reader of books.

BASHFUL excessively modest; timid; very shy.

BLUNT rough or rude in manner; plain-spoken; direct and open in manner.

CANDID open and sincere; frank; honest; free from malice.

CANNY artful; full of prudence, often resulting from special knowledge.

CAUTIOUS very prudent and watchful; timid.

Childish & Childlike

Childlike see **Childish & Childlike**

Clumsy

COLLECTED showing control over one's emotions; sober; tranquil.

CONFIDING of a trusting disposition or manner, as "A confiding person tells all his intimate thoughts."

COOL calm; collected; composed; without passion.

DASHING showy; spirited; bold; as a DASHING suitor.

DEMURE modest; quiet and sober; as DEMURE behavior.

DETACHED reserved; withdrawn; unconcerned; as a DETACHED manner.

DISCREET prudent; very careful not to offend others, as a DISCREET remark.

DISMAYED awed; referring to a quick loss of courage, as "The bombs scattered the dismayed population."

EAGER characteristic of keen desire or excitement, as "The eager lecturer did not see that most of his hearers did not understand what he was saying."

FAMILIAR confiding; being friendly, esp. when friendship is not desired by the other person.

FASTIDIOUS excessively proper; very difficult to please.

FERVID eager; impassioned; full of burning emotions.

GARRULOUS talkative.

GUARDED wary; very watchful; prudent; as a GUARDED speech.

GAWKY awkward, esp. in the sense of physical clumsiness, as a GAWKY youth.

HARDHEADED stubborn; experienced, esp. in the matters of business.

HUMBLE submissive; overly modest; insignificant.

IMPASSIONATE moved by strong emotions.

IMPATIENT quick-tempered; eager for a change.

IMPERTURBABLE calm; incapable of being upset, as "Fortunately her imperturbable husband paid no attention to her silly remarks."

IMPULSIVE pertaining to one who acts suddenly, emotionally and without thought.

INDIFFERENT detached; unconcerned; the opposite of eager.

Inebriate see Sober & Inebriate

INNOCENT free from sin or any harmful thought or intention.

INEXCITABLE calm; imperturbable; even-tempered.

KEEN eager; ardent.

LIVELY gay; sprightly; full of fun; animated.

LOQUACIOUS talkative.

LUSTY full of spirit; keen; strong.

MEEK very shy; modest; humble.

Modest

Naive

NIMBLE agile; lively; quick; as the NIMBLE feet of a dancer.

NONCHALANT indifferent; careless; casual.

Obtuse

OPEN candid; frank; as an OPEN face.

PATIENT submissive; being able to endure misfortune without strong protest.

PHILOSOPHICAL pertaining to the calmness and wisdom of a philosopher; judicious; even-tempered.

PROUD haughty; confident and pleased with oneself, as "He was proud of his success."

PRUDENT sensible; wary; thoughtful; careful.

RATIONAL pertaining to reason; hence, wise; sensible, esp. in the sense of conforming to the rules of reason or logic, as a RATIONAL argument.

REASONABLE rational; sensible; esp. in the sense of not exceeding moderate limits, as a REASONABLE manner.

RESERVED modest; quiet; distant; cold.

RETICENT quiet; withdrawn; untalkative.

ROUGH crude; coarse in manners; without social refinement.

SAGACIOUS wise.

Selfless

SELF-POSSESSED in command of oneself at all times.

SENSIBLE reasonable; having good sense.

Serious see **Sincere & Serious**

SHREWD canny.

SHY very modest; bashful.

Sincere & Serious

SMART quick-witted.

Sober & Inebriate

SPIRITED full of life; vigorous; keen.

STALWART bold; stout; sometimes in the sense of being loyal.

STEADY sober; quiet; respectable.

STERN grim; unyielding; strict.

Stodgy

STRONG having strength; powerful.

SUBTLE clever; tricky; crafty; artful.

TALKATIVE prone to talk a great deal; loquacious.

UNASSUMING unpretentious; modest.

UNOBTRUSIVE reserved; withdrawn; quiet.

UNPRETENTIOUS not having large opinions of one's self-importance; unassuming.

UNRUFFLED calm; self-possessed.

Unruly

VERECUND shy; modest.

VOLATILE full of spirit; quick to come out of an emotional depression; changeable.

WARY watchful; cautious.

Childish and **Childlike** Both words mean 'like a child,' though CHILDLIKE is the more specific, referring to 'children themselves,' while CHILDISH can also suggest 'childhood.' But children are nice or not so nice. So CHILDLIKE is the optimistic word, seeing the artlessness, genuineness and youthful spontaneity in children. CHILDISH adopts the opposite key, seeing them as silly, unreliable, and nasty. CHILDISH emphasizes troublesome pettiness. But CHILDLIKE stresses the appealing confidence and simplicity of a child. It looks at spiritual qualities, like a child's love, rather than at intellectual qualities, like inanity.

Clumsy CLUMSY is a wonderful word for figurative usage. Its origin is a Swedish word meaning 'benumbed'; essentially CLUMSY is a 'benumbed awkwardness.' What is a more expressive word for our minds when we wish to make bright remarks in society and come out instead with inanities?

Modest A 'MODEST request' is a 'moderate request,' one that is kept within measure, is decent. That is the underlying sense also in

MODEST behavior, and in MODEST dress. 'Model, moderate and MODEST' all relate back to Latin MODUS, 'a measure,' and, figuratively, 'a manner.' 'Moderate' literally means 'halfway up the hill,' or 'midway to the peak,' hence 'half-and-half, fifty-fifty, so-so and, probably, cheap.' MODEST is therefore a way of putting a better face on cheapness. When we say the prices at a certain shop are MODEST we imply usually that the store is a good one but that it doesn't have exorbitant prices. A MODEST proposal suggests that the proposal isn't the most important ever made but that it is good enough for your attention. A MODEST girl neither hides nor flaunts herself. "If you eat modestly, you will never become fat."

Naive   This is one Latin word which the French have made their own. It comes from Latin *nativus*, 'natural, innate, native'; but they tailored it to their taste, tincturing it with their own inimitable ideas. Consequently, when the English Cavaliers came to France to escape Cromwell they immediately recognized that the very expressive NAIVE had no counterpart in English. So when they returned to England they took it with them, and at once the smart set of London adopted it. NAIVE then became elite, and it should have remained so, but it didn't.

The reason for this sad fact probably is, that NAIVE means 'natural,' as a child is. But children have so many ways of being natural, some appealing, some baffling, some embarrassing. This mixture tempts us to misuse this word. Only the French know how to combine fancy with precision.

For example, the NAIVETE of a debutante, her unspoiled freshness, preserves the Gallic flavor of the word because the debutante is, like a child, artless and unsophisticated. Her innocent vivacity provides a vivid example of what the French had in mind. But if you look up the synonyms of artless, unsophisticated, or freshness, you will be led far astray. Our word 'ingenuous' comes the closest to NAIVE, especially as it is influenced by the French *ingénue*, an 'innocently frank girl.' But the fact is that NAIVE is a more sprightly word than 'ingenuous,' and it is quite free of any moral implications. NAIVE sometimes suggests to us ideas of 'cunning' and of 'pretended innocence.' "His insistence on his own innocence struck me as being rather naive," you might say. There is a subtle reason, certainly, behind his insistence. NAIVE is often extended to mean 'untutored' or 'unwise.' "Well, sirs, I think this gentleman is just a little too naive for our purposes," that is, he is too infantile or blunt for our smooth and subtle projects. Only among the erudite has NAIVE gone back beyond the French to mean simply 'natural' in the sense of 'uninstructed.' "The professor believes that the best way to teach is to capitalize on a freshman's naive point of view."

What words we can use to correct NAIVE's misuse are not easy to find. Most often 'ingenuous' will serve, or sometimes 'coy,' which is really a shy, half-concealed joy or desire, tinctured with cunning. 'Uninhibited,' 'unaffected,' and even 'natural' are prosaic, and therefore out of tune with NAIVE. 'Frank,' 'open,' 'simple,' and 'artless' are plain synonyms that lack the fanciful explicitness of NAIVE. If we still prefer to use NAIVE, we must remember that it should never suggest 'plain stupidity,' any kind of 'depravity,' or 'sordidness.'

Obtuse Literally, OBTUSE means 'beaten against'; but it is the effect, instead of the art, that gives us the meaning of our adjective OBTUSE. Hence, OBTUSE means 'blunt,' like the round end of a leaf, and also 'dull,' like a person when his mind is blunted. If you are OBTUSE, something like a fit of blind rage may have made you so. You are thickheaded, stupid; your thoughts are indistinct.

OBTUSE angles are 'thick or broad.' Even a low, heavy thud somewhere down in the cellar in the dead of night may be called an OBTUSE sound.

Selfless Probably any good sized dictionary you look into will tell you this word means 'without regard to one's self; unselfish.'

But, analogously, 'endless' might mean simply 'without regard to an end, unshortish.' But its usual connotation is 'full of weariness,' 'monotony,' or else 'limitless or unexhaustible joy.' So also of SELFLESS. SELFLESS devotion to a cause is more than unselfish in that it not only has *no* regard for one's self but has *every* regard, and in the whole scope of things, for this cause. That is, SELFLESS, is not, like 'unselfish,' a negative word. It is a positive one.

Sincere and **Serious** These two words are sometimes synonyms. But SINCERE means 'genuine,' and SERIOUS means 'grave,' from Latin *serius,* 'grave' or 'serious.' SINCERE arose from Roman wax, *sine;* 'without,' plus *cere,* 'wax.' That is, certain vessels without wax in them were 'genuine.' Thus it was at first an attribute of lifeless things. Even today our grandfather's clocks are still SINCERE. A hundred or two hundred years of toil have not broken their faithful service.

Sober and **Inebriate** INEBRIATE, or 'drunkenness,' must have been deprecated almost from its beginning. For the word SOBER, which was the Roman *sobrius*, and the opposite of their *ebrius*, became almost immediately a word of general commendation, in the sense of 'sedate, earnest, decent.' Today we say, "It is the sober truth," suggesting not only temperance in drink but also all else that temperance implies: 'deliberation, earnestness, dispassionateness, and calm objectivity.'

The roots of SOBER and INEBRIATE ('inebrious' is now rare) are probably the same. The 'so' in SOBER represents Latin *se*, 'away,' equivalent here to a negative; the Latin *brius*, shrunk in France to *bre*, English 'ber.' Since *brius* itself meant 'drunken,' the prefixes in INEBRIATE look contradictory. Normally the 'e' would represent Latin *ex*, 'from,' and have the same force as, the *se* in SOBER. But it was placed in front of the verb, *ebriare*, meaning 'to make drunk,' so INEBRIATED would refer to 'someone made drunk.' Normally the prefix 'in' would be a negative, like in 'inactive,' in which case an INEBRIATE would be a drunkard who has taken the cure. In this case 'in' is only an intensive, equivalent to 'very.' INEBRIATED means not only 'made drunk' but '(sunk) *in* drunkenness' as well. But the English verb 'ebriat' is now obsolete, and the noun 'ebriety' is archaic, so INEBRIATE, serving both their weaker meanings and its own, has lost some of its force.

Stodgy This is a useful word, whose origin is dubious. Some say it represents colloquial 'stogy,' meaning 'stocky.' 'Stocky' things are usually heavy, and STODGY, applied to foods, certainly means 'thick and heavy.' But STODGY has a collateral meaning of 'clumsiness,' which is worth bearing in mind.

There is another word, 'stodge,' perhaps coined in the seventeenth century from 'stow' or 'stuff,' meaning 'to cram.' Though STODGY food is merely 'coarse and heavy,' a STODGY book, discourse, manner or personality, suggests 'stuffing.' STODGY books or persons are dull and uninspiring not only because their ingredients are coarse but also because they are unsifted. They fill us up like unstrained oatmeal, they are lumpy and heavy. An old STODGER is an old fogey, full of wearisome tales.

So we are prejudiced against STODGERY. We feel that STODGY people are self-satisfied. We even use STODGE contemptuously to mean 'to trudge through mud' or 'to get stuck in it,' like a lumbering lout.

Unruly Don't forget this expressive word, soft and short yet sufficiently strong. "His unruly tongue will be his undoing." It has the disadvantages as well as the advantages of being informal. It grew from its now deceased antonym, 'ruly,' which doubtless did sound too careless to preserve, like saying an attorney is 'lawy.' But look in your dictionaries at the unwieldy or exaggerative alternates of UNRULY: 'intractable, refractory, ungovernable, contumacious.'

HUMAN STATES

(*Nouns*)

ABHORRENCE detestation; loathing; intense dislike.

Acquisitiveness see **Cupidity & Acquisitiveness**

ADMIRATION respect and wonder for something or someone, as "Our admiration for Lincoln knows no bounds."

AFFECTION strong liking; attachment; fondness.

ALIENATION the feeling of separation, as "An unloved child feels his alienation from security, from all that belongs to a happy home."

ALLEGIANCE the state of being in freely chosen obligation, as "I swore allegiance to my country."

AMOUR-PROPRE self-love; self-respect.

ANGER & RELATED WORDS see the category ANGER

ANTIPATHY strong aversion or dislike for something or someone, as "Many women have an antipathy for weakness."

ANXIETY state of profound worry; deep unrest.

APATHY an absence of feeling; lack of emotion, excitement, eagerness. "Profound apathy is a denial of life."

APOSTASY the giving up of principles one had formerly pledged allegiance to. "A good example of political apostasy is a senator changing his party."

Ardency see **Ardor & Ardency**

Ardor & Ardency

ASSURANCE complete confidence; lacking timidity; as, a salesman's ASSURANCE.

AVARICE greed; an insatiable desire for wealth; a lust for wealth.

AVERSION a strong dislike; repugnance; as an AVERSION to oysters.

AWE great wonder or admiration, usually mixed with fear or dread, as "The beauty and power of the sea has always filled me with awe." *adj.* AWED.

BEATITUDE the highest bliss; extreme happiness; as "They enjoyed rare beatitude the first year of their marriage."

BELIEF a conviction or persuasion of the truth or power of anything, as "He possessed unshakeable belief in his prejudices."

BLESSEDNESS being in the favor of God; happiness; in general, being highly favored.

BLISS great joy; intense delight; blessedness.

BLUES depression; gloomy spirits.

BOREDOM tedium; the feeling that everything is tiresome or uninteresting, as the BOREDOM of ceremonial dinners.

BRAVERY courage; heroism; fearlessness; as the BRAVERY of the soldiers.

CAUTIOUSNESS prudence; being wary or watchful, as "The cautiousness a good soldier always has keeps him alive in battle."

CERTAINTY belief; the state of being sure or convinced of something, as "He displays in his business the certainty that comes from long experience."

CONCEIT an exaggerated opinion of one's own importance, as "He has the conceit that he is very wise."

CONCUPISCENCE lust; sensual desire.

CONFIDENCE trust in or reliance upon something, as "He has confidence in his rattling old car."

CONSTANCY unshakeable, in the sense of not breaking one's allegiance, as "Lovers exchange vows of constancy."

Consternation

CONTEMPT disdain or scorn for something, as "A proud man has contempt for the humble man."

CONVICTION certainty.

COURAGE bravery; valor; esp. boldness and resoluteness, as "Bravery can confront anything; courage can do anything."

Credence, Credible, Creditable & Credulous

Credible see **Credence, Credible, etc.**

Creditable see **Credence, Credible, etc.**

Credulous see **Credence, Credible, etc.**

Cupidity & Acquisitiveness

Defection, Dereliction, Derogation & Denigration

DEJECTION depression; low spirits; the blues.

Delight

Denigration see **Defection, Dereliction, etc.**

DEPENDENCE needing support or help from an outside source, as "The dependence of a child on its mother's love is the first fact of social development."

DEPRESSION dejection; the blues.

Dereliction see **Defection, Dereliction, etc.**

Derogation see **Defection, Dereliction, etc.**

Derring-Do

DESIRE an emotion deriving from the want one has for something, as the DESIRE for success.

DETESTATION intense dislike.

DEVOTION state of giving oneself up to some cause or person, as "His devotion to science is well known," or "Her devotion to his well-being is the real basis of their marital happiness."

DISCONTENT unhappiness; dissatisfaction; uneasiness; as "Discontent is the source of most crime."

Discretion

Disdain

DISPLEASURE the state of being annoyed or displeased; uneasiness; discomfort.

Docility

Doldrums

DOUBT state of uncertain belief; unsureness; as "Conflicting evidence must cause doubt."

DREAD profound fear; terror or apprehension toward something expected to happen, as DREAD of a flood.

DUMPS the blues. (Colloq.)

EAGERNESS state of being anxious or desirous, esp. in an impatient manner, of doing something.

ECSTASY extreme joy; bliss; state of being out of rational control of a strong emotion, as a very ECSTASY of hate.

ELATION the expansion of one's spirits because of happiness or success.

ENCHANTMENT bewitchment; the state of being in a spell; as, the ENCHANTMENT a beautiful woman casts.

ENNUI boredom; tedium.

ENTHUSIASM eagerness; passion for a cause, or subject, as an ENTHUSIASM for hunting.

ENVY ill will or discontent, usually stimulated by another's success or advantages.

ESTEEM respect; honor; as "He earned the public's esteem."

FAITH an acknowledgement of the truth or existence, of something, without doubt or intellectual questioning; blind certainty.

FEALTY allegiance; in general, faithfulness.

FEAR apprehension; uneasiness of mind; an emotional apprehension that something evil or dreadful is going to happen.

FELICITY happiness; good fortune.

FERVOR or FERVOUR zeal; intense interest or desire to promote the success of anything; ardor.

FIDELITY the state of keeping allegiance or faith.

FORTITUDE the strength and resolution to withstand adversity.

FRIGHT sudden fear.

GLEE delight; merriment; mirth.

GLOOM depression; dejection; the blues.

GREED an unnatural or extreme longing for wealth.

HAPPINESS the feeling one gets from good fortune, from pleasure, from contentment.

Hardihood

HATE intense dislike; aversion; detestation.

HILARITY laughter; glee.

HOPE an expectation for something good.

HORROR fright mixed with aversion or repugnance.

IMPATIENCE eagerness, often mixed with irritation.

INDEPENDENCE needing no support or help. Compare DEPENDENCE.

INDIFFERENCE the state of regarding something as unimportant.

JOLLITY merriment; glee; state of laughter.

JOY intense delight for something; great gladness.

LOYALTY state of being faithful or of keeping one's allegiance.

LUST greed; inordinate desire.

MIRTH glee; merriment; laughter.

MISTRUST doubt; lack of trust; suspicion.

PANIC terror, esp. as it affects a crowd.

PASSION intense emotion of any kind, such as hate, love, fear, anger.

PLEASURE the feeling that accompanies a gratification of desire.

PRIDE an inordinate opinion of one's own superiority.

PRUDENCE cautiousness.

Pudency

Pulchritude

RAPTURE extreme joy or exaltation.

RELIANCE trust; faith; dependence; as "Modern man hardly walks at all, so great is his reliance on his automobile."

REPUGNANCE aversion; dislike; a deep distaste for something, as REPUGANCE to dirt.

SCORN open contempt for something; derision; an emotion combining anger and disgust.

Self-Esteem

SUSPICION an uncertain belief that something is guilty or false, as "His suspicion is that the girl has an unsavory past."

TEDIUM tiresomeness.

TERROR panic; intense fear that drives one beyond the control of reason.

Trance

TRANSPORT joy; bliss; esp. in the sense of being carried away by some emotion.

TRUST fidelity.

VALOR courage, esp. in the sense of making a decision and of carrying it out in the face of danger.

Vanity

ZEAL fervor; the devotion of all one's passions and energy to a cause; intense enthusiasm.

Ardor and **Ardency** Unlike fervor, ARDOR includes most of the emotions, affections, passions and other feelings which distinguish the heart from the head. It is spiritual warmth, both that which you feel and that which you express. ARDOR implies 'intense enthusiasm,' like the ARDOR which animates a military march, expressing the composer's spirit and awakening our own. But it may vary from the heat of passion, as in poetry, to the common, sometimes almost arduous enthusiasm, with which we pursue our hobbies.

But ARDOR can be seen, felt or possessed in almost any field: love, friendship, work, hobbies, art, anywhere. But it cannot be used for eagerness in 'evil' enterprises. If we must speak of the ARDOR of criminals, we always qualify: the 'malign ARDOR.'

Such an expressive word as ARDOR naturally implies a state of being and a condition or quality of heart. That state or condition is ARDENCY. The ARDENCY of military marches is the collective ARDOR of all the marches. ARDENCY is the common quality of all true lovers.

'Fervor' incidentally, is one kind of ARDOR. See FERVENT and FERVID.

Consternation A long, completely self-contained noun. It has no verb, and gives us no adjectives. It impresses us with its length, and it means an 'overwhelming and confusing fright.' Individuals may be dismayed, but it is usually a crowd or a group that is struck with CONSTERNATION.

Credence, Credible, Creditable and **Credulous** CREDIBLE means 'believable,' and CREDITABLE means 'praiseworthy.' But the roots are the same. When you 'credit' an account you 'certify' it, make it 'believable.' What can be 'credited' to your account or to your character is 'believable, CREDIBLE.' CREDULOUS means 'believing,' or 'overready to believe.' A CREDULOUS person is as likely to believe what is *not* CREDITABLE about you as he is to believe what *is* CREDITABLE. He may even believe what is *in*credible.' CREDENCE is 'belief.' If all the rumors in the world were condensed into one report, the noise would surpass CREDENCE, it would be beyond belief.

Cupidity and **Acquisitiveness** CUPIDITY is a word very insulting to Cupid, the god of love. Love, after all is more than mere desire, but CUPIDITY means a desire carried to the point of avarice. Both words come from Latin *cupere*, 'to long for, desire.'

ACQUISITIVENESS is 'mild CUPIDITY.' To begin with, the word 'acquire' is pleasantly indefinite. When you 'acquire' property it is not asked whether you bought, stole or were given it. ACQUISITIVE persons simply want to acquire things. If the things are bits of gossip, the ACQUISITIVE persons are simply 'inquisitive.' If the things are solid pieces of knowledge, they are on their way to wisdom. If the things are pieces of money and the ACQUISITIVE persons are miserly, then their ACQUISITIVENESS becomes CUPIDITY.

Defection, Dereliction, Derogation and **Denigration** DEFECTION refers to a man's deflection from duty 'on purpose.' An arrow may be deflected from its course by the wind, or a man may be deflected from his duty by an unavoidable accident. To make an error, is to wander from the morally right course; but a DEFECTION from duty is less a wandering from it than a 'disregard' of it. The implication in DEFECTION is that, if the DERELICTION is discovered, the defaulter is exposed to criticism or condemnation. In usage it is significantly followed by the preposition 'from.' "Defection from the cause of liberty is treason." 'Defects,' incidentally, are particularizations of DEFECTION. For example, "The defect in your automobile is a faulty sparkplug," quite plainly says that "Your automobile's defection caused you to find out the trouble."

A DERELICTION is a specific instance of your DEFECTION. It is a 'neglect of duty.' The word means 'utterly relinquished,' from *de*, 'thoroughly' plus *relinquere*, which gave us our word, 'relinquish.' The hulk of a wrecked ship at sea is a DERELICT; it has been 'utterly abandoned' to the waves and wind. A bum on the Bowery is a DERELICT.

When you call someone a bum who isn't one, you DEROGATE him, your characterization of him is DEROGATORY. You 'depreciate him, disparage him, pull him down'—there are plenty of synonyms, so the verb itself is little used. The noun DEROGATION, referring to the 'act of defaming,' is common in the phrase 'derogation of character.' It is legalistic. In law DEROGATION is not only the 'belittling' and, thus, the 'damaging' of an individual, but also the lessening of the force of a law, by speaking first of 'proposing a law,' *rogare*, and then of thinking better of it, *de*, 'from.' But there are two adjectives, with slightly different connotations. 'Derogatory' usually refers to persons and personal remarks. "The senator's observations about his opponent's wisdom were plainly derogatory." 'Derogative' usually has a broader application. "The senator today made a derogative speech about the bill his opponent offered," doesn't mean he made personal remarks or emotional statements. It means he talked against a bill.

If DENIGRATION conveyed its first full meaning, it would speak only of chimney-sweeps and coal miners. It evolved from the Latin *niger*, 'black.' But it jumped, as it were, from Italy to England, and from coal miners to mires. Now it means 'to sully,' a word from the Old English *sol*, 'mire.' Malicious propaganda DENIGRATES (blackens) the names of illustrious leaders.

Delight A DELIGHT is forever a dainty but an exhilarating joy. It is too fine and too spiritually alive to share the common connotations of mere pleasure. Because of its own spirit and being, the word is elite.

Derring-do It is a pity to prick the bravado of a dashing word that adds color and animation to our diction but DERRING-DO is, historically, as empty as an egg shell. For it was first used, rather carelessly, by a poet ages ago, and two centuries later was garbled by another poet. It has so far lost its wits that today it is more or less garbled by everybody. The very fact that its obsolete spelling seems to make fun of valorous 'daring' often makes us lend it a mock-heroic meaning, especially in the comics where it often appears. Some dictionaries call it archaic and others obsolete; but this doesn't matter. It seems to be finding a place in our mad, modern world.

Some dictionaries say the word means simply 'bravery, valor or daring.' To others it means, literally, 'courageous deeds,' or the capability of doing such deeds. Hence it is what we call 'virility,' or 'redblooded manhood.' In the beginning it was used by Chaucer in speaking of Troilus, a great knight, who was second to none "in durring don that longeth to a knight," that is, "in daring to do what belongeth to a knight." But unfortunately a printer's hand was unsteady, and in a copy that came later to the poet Spencer the 'durring don' came out as 'derrynge do.' In the course of succeeding centuries much more of the original sense escaped into other meanings. Nevertheless, it is not so unfortunate in this age of ruthless daring, to have even an archaic word that still connects 'courage' with 'chivalry.'

Discretion DISCRETION comes etymologically from 'discerning.' If you are DISCREET, you 'discern (perceive)' what is proper and improper, and you act accordingly. Usually, DISCRETION implies a 'do-nothingness' for a very good reason. DISCRETION must have a 'reason or purpose' behind it. This reason distinguishes it from 'caution,' which may be the result of a good reason but may also have completely unexplainable or irrational causes. DISCREET is sometimes falsely spelled 'discrete,' but this is another scientific word with several meanings.

Disdain 'Silent and restrained scorn,' and 'unexpressed but considered contempt' is DISDAIN. "The passion of my soul is scorn," says the poet; but DISDAIN, though quiet and cultured, can also be intense. It usually implies a righteous and proud sense of superiority. Just as a 'reproach' is more intimate and spiritual than a 'reproof,' which pertains mainly to manners, so DISDAIN is more subtle and profound than 'scorn' and 'contempt.' DISDAIN, moreover, usually conveys the high and cultured man's disgust for the low and vulgar. "That man has disdain for quibbling—he pays whether he can afford to or not," means that the man thinks bargaining is beneath his dignity.

Docility This is a useful word because of its softness, because of the matching of its sound with its sense. Unfortunately, DOCILITY also has connotations of 'meekness' and 'tameness.' Sometimes a man noted for his DOCILITY has been beaten by life into submission in the same way a mule is often beaten to tame its spirit. A DOCILE manner need not always humiliate a virile character. The DOCILITY of April breezes after the blustering winds of March is a positive virtue.

Doldrums The DOLDRUMS are the 'blues, the jimjams, the dumps.' But where did they come from, what were they first?

Probably, we're told, they came from 'tantrums'—but dull ones. This means a kind of telescoping of the word 'dull' into the word 'tantrum.' But 'tantrums' are an emotional blow-out, which is certainly a contradiction in terms, for 'dumps' and 'blues' are depressingly dull. A clue comes from the equator, where winds are variable and baffling but where calms on the seas are frequent, stalling many sailing vessels. Sailors called these calms the DOLDRUMS. There is another suggestion, also from the tropics. What is more typical of equatorial natives than their monotonous beating of drums, on one note, in one continuous rhythm? 'Dull' and 'drum.' Moreover, there is a word, 'humdrum.' Some dictionaries have it built up from 'hum' and 'drum,' though most of them say it was a reiteration of the one word 'hum,' with a 'd' butting into it. But if the 'drum' is authentic in DOLDRUMS the meaning is still a contest between 'dullness' and 'sudden impulses.' Can they be joined? Probably only on the seas, along the equator; and apparently the calms won out, for now we apply the word to ourselves, when we are 'mentally and emotionally becalmed.' Nevertheless, some great authorities believe that a human 'dullard,' called also a DOLDRUM, gave rise to both the nautical term and our plural, the DOLDRUMS.

Hardihood Only now and then does it mean 'hardiness.' Usually it is not a state of being, but an attribute, and rather a reprehensible one at that. HARDIHOOD customarily implies 'boldness' mixed with 'brashness, impudence'; 'blunt audacity; presumptuousness or effrontery.' "He had the hardihood to tell me that I was indebted to him!" In a somewhat better sense it means 'rash enterprise, foolish daring.' "Mountain climbers must have plenty of hardihood." In its best sense HARDIHOOD suggests a temperamental quality associated with physical hardiness, that is, a slightly ersatz 'moral courage, stamina.' "That young man had the hardihood to ask for a raise when his wife gave birth to their first child."

Pudency In Latin it meant 'bashful,' in English it means 'modesty,' in which both sexes can share. PUDENCY may be stretched to mean 'shamefacedness.' As an adjective, there is only PUDENDAL (or 'pudical'), referring primarily to the generative organs.

Pulchritude An ugly, vulgar-looking word meaning 'beauty.' Hard-sounding as it is, PULCHRITUDE also means 'grace' and 'physical charm.' The Latin tongue sometimes sounded harsh even when the word meant the opposite.

Self-esteem What it means to say is, 'a proper self-respect,' 'a due pride in one's self.' But then ESTEEM by itself has come so close to 'praise' in common diction, that we use SELF-ESTEEM at times like 'self-praise.' So today you will find the word broken in two in the dictionaries, with the second part meaning 'conceited.' It does seem that we need not be professional purists to defend the word's proper meaning.

Trance There is an etymological link between 'death' and TRANCE. We think of a TRANCE as a state either of 'rapture' or of 'dazed, soulless bewilderment,' of 'vacancy of mind.' But to the French, who had the word first from the Romans, it still denotes something close to death, a 'deathly anxiety, a mortal fright.' When they took it from its origins TRANCE literally meant a 'passing from life to death.' But even in Chaucer's time, in English, TRANCE had the two-fold suggestion of 'downright death' and of 'dazed rapture.'

Vanity The literal meaning of VANITY is 'emptiness.' But it shows how words collect meanings they didn't originally have. VANITY's modern sense can be best understood in a certain satirist's definition: "Vanity is the tribute of a fool to the nearest ass."

So VANITY has come to mean self-admiration carried to the point of paying tribute to one's own silliest self. But the connotations are as numerous as the stars. If you begin admiring yourself continually you inevitably become an exhibitionist, and then the word connotes everything exhibitionism involves. But the satirist was thinking far beyond the obvious; perhaps he means we too are asses when we accept a fool's compliment. You have only to recall how some people get themselves talked about, to realize all that VANITY inaugurates. For the vain person is not so much empty as afflicted with internal chaos, which he must spread about him.

HUMAN TYPES

Amateur, Novice & Dilettante
Apostate & Apostle
Coward
Creole
Crone & Crony
Dandy & Fop
Dastard
Dunce
Gentleman & Lady
Martyr
Mulatto
Nincompoop & Dunderhead

Paragon
Scamp
Scapegoat
Scoundrel
Stooge
Termagant
Wiseacre
Wretch
Xanthippe
Yokel
Zealot

Amateur, Novice and **Dilettante** 'Love' makes an AMATEUR and 'inexperience' a NOVICE. The Romans used both words: AMATEUR is merely the French version of Latin *amator*, a 'lover'; NOVICE is our own rendition of Latin *novicius*, 'new,' from *novus*, 'new' or 'young.' A NOVICE is now a 'beginner' in anything, whether a freshman in college or a budding professional ball player. In the church, specifically, a NOVICE in a monastery has not yet taken his vows.

An AMATEUR may be a lifelong devotee of an art, science or sport, and may surpass in knowledge and skill a professional. The essence of his devotion is 'love.' In a slightly derogatory sense, a DILETTANTE is an 'arty or effeminate dawdler.' Once he was a real AMATEUR, and still is in France. The French equivalent of our AMATEUR is DILETTANTE. Originally he was what we would call an 'enthusiast,' someone who has a particular interest in something, or a taste for it. This is the sense which the French have preserved.

Apostate and **Apostle** If you are a member of good standing in a society, you are etymologically the opposite of an APOSTATE. An APOSTATE, from the Greek words for 'away' and 'standing,' is one who has 'abandoned' his faith, his principles or his party. On the contrary, an APOSTLE is something more than a loyal follower or member in good standing. In the beginning he was, in the Greek, a 'messenger, one sent away.' Now an APOSTLE 'hears and teaches a creed.' An APOSTATE is a 'recanter,' an APOSTLE is an 'expounder'—they are diametrical opposites.

Coward COWARD, meaning to be 'scared' or 'unmanly, timid,' comes from Latin *cauda*, 'tail.' This meaning apparently derives from two images. The first is that of the timid hare, which dashes off with its tail showing conspicuously. But this image became confused with a dog's behavior when it is frightened—it slinks away with its tail between its legs. If you have a friend whose last name is Coward, you will want to know that, in this case, the word means the same as Shepard (shepherd)—that is, cow-herd.

Creole To Creoles themselves, this word is vulgar, though in common usage it has no such connotations. In America true CREOLES are white people descended from the Spanish, Portuguese or French settlers in the old territory of Louisiana, which included all the Gulf states of today. But now we extend the term loosely to anyone, black, white or intermediate shade, who speaks the CREOLE patois. Sometimes American-born Negroes, as distinguished from any other Negroes, are called CREOLES. The pale brown offspring of whites and mixed races, especially mixed Spanish and Indian, are sometimes called CREOLES. Finally any native West Indian with European, Negro or Creole blood may be designated CREOLE. To Europeans the word is more specific, referring to the descendants of Frenchmen and Spaniards who are born and brought up in distant, probably tropical, countries. But to the true CREOLES of our South it is a word in which their history, speech and culture is typified and preserved, and to hear it encrusted with miscellaneous associations derived from mixed blood and from often antipodal life is an affront.

And yet, etymologically, the CREOLES have slight claim to their word. A London dictionary of Shakespeare's time says: *criollos*, 'those that are born of a Spaniard and Indian.' That was its original meaning over here: any West Indian with European (practically speaking, Spanish) blood in his veins. Authorities differ as to the word's exact origin, but trace it variously through the Negroes, the Spanish and the French to the Latin word, *creare*, 'to create': and specifically, though still uncertainly, to the term supposedly applied to 'indoor slaves,' *creatus*.

Crone and **Crony** This word comes from the Danish for 'old ewe,' which is a 'female sheep.' CRONE means an old withered woman though today the word is popularly used for 'side-kick, pal, a CRONY.'

Dandy and **Fop** You may not meet these little words often in your reading; but since one of them has been imbedded classically in Yankee Doodle, you should know something of its origin and meaning.

FOP arose from the Dutch word *foppen*, 'to prate' or 'to cheat.' Soon it referred to a man inordinately proud of his good clothes. Meanwhile, in Shakespeare's youth there was a small English coin called a DANDY. How it acquired its name, or how and why it was used to name a FOPPISH Englishman, this book doesn't know. But there are two clues. DANDY was a rhyming alternate for 'Andy.' As we call donkeys and rabbits 'Jacks,' so perhaps Shakespeare's contemporaries called half-groat pieces ANDIES. Moreover, such pieces were probably small to the point of insignificance. Perhaps the first DANDY was a ten-penny sport— or less, since a half-groat amounted only to tuppence. Even today 'groat' is still figuratively used for 'trifle,' at least in literature.

In slang, DANDY does not mean a FOP. In "I had a dandy time at the party," or "You sure got a dandy blister on your hand" DANDY means 'top-notch,' of the 'first water,' or 'first-rate.' Originally it probably derived, in this sense, from the Low German, for the Danish word *dande* today means 'excellent' or 'brave.'

Dastard Today we seldom use the word DASTARD though quite often we speak of DASTARDLY insults meaning 'offenses' that are 'base, contemptible, cowardly, sly.' DASTARDS in Middle English were 'pitiable dullards.' Perhaps they were simply 'contemptible sluggards.' The 'dast' in their name had originally meant 'dazed,' or 'winded, exhausted, weary.' Now a DASTARD is a 'cowardly, base person,' who does sneaky things.

Dunce He was a real man, John Duns Scotus, a pedantic pedagogue. Seldom do victimized pupils effect such an enduring vengeance.

Gentleman and Lady Probably GENTLEMAN has never been defined well enough to cover all that it implies and all that it excludes. One trouble is, that though GENTLEMAN is in itself one word, its component parts defy definition. For if a man is in reality 'gentle,' what still does his 'gentleness' imply; and what after all is a man? Much the same trouble arises daily concerning LADIES, especially since the modern LADY considers herself simply a woman when she is on the job in her office, say, or factory.

Socially, the word GENTLEMAN has suffered more vicissitudes than has LADY. Men have gotten around more, and both generally and socially they have had to represent more types and degrees. Nevertheless, GENTLEMAN has more aristocratic foundation, than has LADY. The latter was at first the designation of a woman who 'kneaded bread' (Old English *hlaf*, 'bread' plus *dige*, 'to knead'). She was a female baker, or baxter—the words still survive in surnames. But she was lifted by chivalry, uplifted by the knights of old who devoted all their services to the particular woman who represented their ideal. Thus men still speak of their 'lady-loves'; but realizing that GENTLEMEN belong to the world, a woman would not dream of saying my 'gentleman-love.'

GENTLEMEN were independent from the beginning. They were of gentle birth and noble degree. Whereas today a LADY is commonly defined as a 'woman of courtesy and refinement,' a GENTLEMAN is defined more broadly, as a man 'well-bred and honorable.' In English law he is still any man of established repute who is well enough off not to work, and who doesn't work. He is a kind of king in his own garden, with many worldly interests, distinguished sharply from any busy baker who might have married a Baxter.

Nevertheless, the word GENTLEMAN has acquired a cheap usefulness in business, where it is used for just about everyone whose name you don't know. As an expression of politeness it sometimes means really nothing at all. From which arises the question: just what is a man? To which the only adequate answer seems to be: He is just a male adult. This is another way of saying that perhaps all men can be GENTLEMEN, which is no doubt an excellent state of affairs. Perhaps we should pay respects to the profound quality of a GENTLEMAN, as it was once known. The 'gentility' goes back through the Old French gentil to the sacred Roman gens, 'clan,' with always an implication of revered rank and character. As for the LADY, who was lifted to high rank, she has achieved an integrity that has weathered better than the integrity of GENTLEMAN. When after Prohibition, women were first admitted to bars a barkeep was asked: "Will women now become as rowdy as men?" He answered: "No. Most girls will stop at some point, lest it be said they're no lady."

Martyr This is a Greek word meaning a 'witness,' which epochal events have made immortal and universal. Adopted in Rome, MARTYR was applied to the Christians who were massacred for their beliefs. They 'witnessed' their faith ('testified' to it) by dying. Today the word may have social as well as spiritual significance. A good cause can be MARTYRED to the greed of politicians, for example, or the virtues of a simple soul to the demands of a sophisticated life.

Mulatto MULATTOES, or persons with a Negro and a white parent, are usually light brown in color, like young mules. This is not said to asperse the MULATTOES. For though the name does probably come from a Spanish or Portuguese word for a 'young mule,' mulata, there was, in the idea behind it, no color association. It is simply the idea of a mixed parentage, like in the mule's case.

Nincompoop and **Dunderhead** A NINCOMPOOP is a DUNDERHEAD or 'dunce.' It comes from the Latin *non compos mentis*, 'not possessing a sound mind.' DUNDERHEAD first meant 'thunderhead'; a 'thunderhead' is full of noise and wind, just like a blockhead or dunce.

Paragon This is an old French word envisaging a 'peerless knight,' a model of unsurpassable virtue and excellence. Now PARAGON is used almost scornfully to describe a 'noble goody-goody.' A martyred but imperturbable and undaunted spouse is a PARAGON of all virtues.

Scamp SCAMP is essentially a playful word. It is a by-product of a wayward Old French verb meaning 'to decamp.' In England the word literally ran wild. Its first meaning was to 'take to the highway,' then 'to run wild.' Its frequentative form, SCAMPER, means 'to run wild friskily.' Then it engendered a noun, and the noun, as you might suppose, was as wayward. In fact, it used to be pure slang. People began to call rogues and highwaymen SCAMPS, and even in Elizabethan times the waggish word 'scampant' appeared in a burlesque of the traditional 'rampant' of heraldry. But the old verb SCAMP, unlike the sedater 'tramp,' which gave us our formal word for 'hobo,' has now passed into oblivion, except as its spirit still animates our SCAMPER or as it makes of today's SCAMPS something less businesslike than burglars or assassins.

Scapegoat This is a common word we could appreciate more. In its make-up it is the kind of word all advertisers dream of, being reasonably short but hinting at diverting stories. The 'scape' is for 'escape,' which is a moving picture in itself of a cornered man's slipping from his cape and saving himself by flight (Latin *ex cappa*, 'out of one's cape'). But here this action is overlooked in our modern usage. For the SCAPEGOAT no longer escapes. He is the goat on which everything is heaped. In the Bible, a Hebrew priest confessed the sins of his people over the goat's head and then drove the animal into the wilderness. There it probably starved, but at least it was supposed to carry away the people's sins. When the King James Version of the Bible was composed much of the phraseology of the earlier Version by Tyndale was retained. Tyndale was no poet, but he knew his vernacular, and he was something of a genius at phrase-making. He coined SCAPEGOAT, along with many others that have rolled or sprung off our tongues ever since.

Scoundrel We have softened the word SCOUNDREL; but through the ages it has represented, either as a noun or as an adjective, a 'thoroughly bad' or an 'utterly worthless' fellow. Webster's will tell you that the origin of the epithet is uncertain, yet its antecedents are undoubtedly involved in early expressions for 'disgust, reproach, fearing, avoiding' —surely a shady enough background for any term of opprobrium. Besides that, the word has a Viking-like sound, like the word 'scathing.' By the sixteenth century it was commonly used to designate a 'mean fellow.' But the archetype of the word seems to have been used by the old Norsemen to express their contempt for a 'coward,' who was, therefore, to them 'loathsome.' The fact probably is that the word grew not only from the qualities of the culprit but still more from the contempt of the users. In spite of, or just possibly because of, our softening it toward 'scamp' and 'rascal,' SCOUNDREL remains one of our most expressive words.

Stooge STOOGE is of uncertain, but assertedly American, origin. He is a 'comedian's foil,' but not in as active a sense as is a Charlie McCarthy, who can hit back unmercifully. The connotation has drifted in the opposite direction, and the STOOGE on the stage is more often either a compliant dummy, who answers only 'yes' or 'no,' or else an innocent-looking but not-so-dumb subordinate, who feeds material to the real performer. But all STOOGES are not hired butts for professional jokers. They are also useful tools and potential scapegoats for confidence men. Unprofessionally, a STOOGE may be any one willing to be a mirror for another's wit, humor or wisdom. He may also be the assistant who does all the dirty work. Simply, he is a 'yes-man.'

The word is not labeled as slang in newer dictionaries though as slang it has run riot. This slang may ultimately determine new, legitimate uses. The starting point is the STOOGE on the stage, asking dumb questions which enable the comedian to make a fool of him.

Though a subordinate, he is also a 'helpmeet' and 'confederate.' Thus, a STOOGE loses a prearranged prize fight. He also plays second fiddle to a pal. He gives reporters news and gossip. He covers up a confederate's crime. He is a straw-bidder in an auction and a fake-buyer in a boardwalk concession. He runs errands or does business for a bootlegger or a dope peddler. But if he does any such things for someone who is not a team mate or a pal, his character changes. To his former pals, he becomes a bootlicker, handshaker, toady, or cringing footwiper, or dumb doormat. But a STOOGE may also be a strawboss, a subordinate foreman, or in the army an assistant to any superior. Also, more generally, he is a 'valet,' an aristocrat's STOOGE. With mild contempt he is sometimes a 'student.'

Termagant This is nothing good to be said about a TERMAGANT. She is always potentially loud, violent and quarrelsome. Viewed as an etymological product of her past, she apparently suffers from a dangerous inferiority complex, a relentless and distracting frustration, an imperial will thwarted in its destiny. For in the beginning she was not only a creature of fiction, at the disposal of the imagination of dramatists, but she was also connected with the gods. But now she is only a shrew.

In the medieval romances of Europe she was supposed to be a despised deity, not a woman at all, worshipped by the Saracens. This masculine god was pictured as a boisterous, brawling and vociferous troublemaker. When he was presented on the stage in morality plays he wore a long robe, supposedly indicating his Orientalism but proving to be his undoing. For the wholly Occidental English took him to be a woman, and so he has remained ever since. But he (or she) has fallen from another high estate: a TERMAGANT has nothing to do with the theater anymore. For a time, in the puppet shows, he attempted the role of a roving rascal. TERMAGANT, the god's name, meant the Thrice Roving One. But that didn't last, and there was nothing for her to do but to become a 'virago,' a 'shrew' of the first magnitude, with a tart, fault-finding tongue and a terrible temper.

Wiseacre He is beginning to be confused with our ubiquitous 'wisecracker,' but when he arrived here from abroad he was already beginning to become a 'dunce.' A WISEACRE is a dunce who thinks that he knows everything and that everybody wants to know what he thinks. Originally, in the Old High German, he was a 'soothsayer,' *wizago*. Later, in Germany and among the Dutch he remained a 'wise-sayer,' and is still given credit for it, humorously, among us.

Wretch Like honey on tart fruit, humor sometimes mixes well with unpleasantness, creating an effect not unpleasantly poignant. And though we do use the word WRETCH in its unpleasant sense, like the 'vile WRETCH' in the prisoner's dock, or our own 'WRETCHED ('bad') health,' there are times when we add humor, and say, perhaps, "And then this wretch came up behind me and slapped me familiarly on the shoulder." But intrinsically there is nothing funny about a WRETCH, and we are right in ordinarily regarding him as either unfortunate or evil. The word WRETCH is very old. It probably began in the ninth century as the proper name of someone who had been exiled. In early English the WRETCH, or *wraecca*, was still an 'outcast, a miserable creature.' As in other Teutonic tongues, he was the product of a verb that had come to mean not only 'to drive out' but also 'to avenge.'

Hence an odium clung to the WRETCH in his misery. In those uncouth times an 'avenging' was the execution of a curse, and the 'blood-wreaker' relentlessly pursued the WRETCH until he was a 'wreck'—that is, one whom vengeance has ruined. So when we now speak of 'wreaking vengeance' we are really making WRETCHES, wrecks or worse.

Xanthippe The great philosopher who drank hemlock, and stoically died when his State had condemned his teachings and him, had no doubt been prepared by his wife to pass away so philosophically. All during their life together she had been nagging and scolding him with all the vicious vigor of which she was capable, and her name XANTHIPPE is now a synonym for a 'shrew.' He, on the other hand, is immortal in an opposite way, for Socrates has given us the adjective 'socratic,' almost synonymous with 'philosophic.'

Yokel A YOKEL is what we call a 'rube' or a 'hick,' but with emphasis not on his 'ignorance' but on his 'native boorishness.' Persumably he was at first a 'ploughboy,' and the 'yoke' in his nickname was the wooden yoke on the necks of an ox team. The 'el' is a playful diminutive. But no one really knows where the word came from, and some fanciful derivations have been produced. Undoubtedly he was always rural. Etymologists are cautious but very investigative. One of them can't help pointing out that one kind of woodpecker, the 'hickwall,' is sometimes colloquially called, exactly, a YOKEL. Another recalls that owls were not always considered to be 'wise,' but were sometimes thought to be 'stupid' or 'nutty': 'plumb loco' stems from the Spanish *alocco*, 'owl,' and 'goofy' traces to Old English *gofish*, 'stupid,' undoubtedly connected with the owl's old name in the Shetland Islands: *yuggle*. (Compare Anglo-Saxon *ule*.) So the owls might have produced YOKEL, though the term is much less likely to have been ornithological than agricultural. Webster's tells you a YOKEL is a typical 'rustic' or 'country bumpkin'; but since the type is fast fading the word is reserved chiefly for figurative usage: 'slow-wittedness, gullibility, ignorant earthiness, physical clumsiness, laziness, coarseness.'

Zealot A ZEALOT boils with fervor: the Greek for 'boiling' is *zeo*. He is almost always a patriot or a worker for some cause.

HUMOR

Agog
Antic
Arch
BUFFOON   *n.* a clown; one who entertains with jokes, tricks, and gestures; a fool.
CAPER   *n.* a gladsome leap or spring; a gay jump. *v.* to skip about in a merry way; to cavort.
CHESTNUT   *n.* an old joke or tale; a standard jest.
CLOWN   *n.* a professional funnyman, esp. one in a circus who dresses bizarrely and plays the buffoon.
COMEDIAN   *n.* a man who makes you laugh by his talk and antics, esp. a professional actor who specializes in comic roles.
COMIC   *n.* a comedian. *adj.* of or pertaining to whatever makes one laugh.
DROLL   *adj.* funny; amusing; laughable.
FACETIOUS   *adj.* droll; waggish; comical, as a FACETIOUS remark.
FARCICAL   *adj.* ludicrous; absurd; of or pertaining to a farce. *n.* FARCE, a fast-moving drama with a comic plot and highly exaggerated comic characters.
FOOL   *n.* a buffoon.
FROLIC   *n.* a merry or delightful performance. *v.* to perform a FROLIC, as "The children frolicked."
Fun   see **Humor & Fun**
Funny   see **Humorous & Funny**
Harlequin
Humor & Fun

Humorous & Funny
Jaunty
JEST   *n.* a joke or trick.
JESTER   *n.* a clown; buffoon.
JOCOSE   *adj.* of or pertaining to joking or jesting, as a JOCOSE manner.
JOCULAR   *adj.* jocose; but esp. referring to witty or facetious jokes or jests.
JOKE   *n.* a trick or saying that produces laughter.
LUDICROUS   see the category UN-PLEASANTNESS
Merry
MERRY-ANDREW   *n.* a clown; fool.
Pun
QUIP   *n.* a humorous or sarcastic remark.
Quixotic
REPARTEE   *n.* a witty reply; talk full of such sallies.
Riant
RIDICULOUS   *adj.* pertaining to whatever creates laughter or derision, as a RIDICULOUS situation.
RISIBLE   *adj.* laughable; also, of a person, given to laughter.
RISORIAL   *adj.* causing laughter.
SALLY   *n.* a retort; a clever or humorous response or remark.
Sprightly & Spry
Spry   see **Sprightly & Spry**
WITTY   *adj.* wise; intelligent; esp. in the sense of intellectual humor, or the ability to see two sides.
ZANY   *adj.* pertaining to anyone who behaves absurdly; clownish.

Agog AGOG means 'excited with curiosity or expectation.' Its original meaning in the Old French was 'in fun,' *en,* 'in,' plus *gogue,* 'fun.'

Antic An ignoramus might confuse ANTIC with 'antique.' Etymologically, he would be exactly right. Originally, ANTIC meant 'ancient' in Latin; in France it was spelled 'antique.' At an early date it came to mean 'clownish' or a 'clown,' perhaps because the grotesque capers of clowns suggest the jerky movements of old people. Today it means 'fantastic in a ludicrous way,' or as a noun, an 'awkward and consequently ridiculous caper,' loosely, any 'funny action or trick.'

Arch Mix 'merriness' and 'slyness' together, without fuss, and you miraculously have ARCHNESS. It is much more than 'coyness,' which, after all, is only silly or sentimental, and much less than 'cold cunning,' which is a cerebral kind of slyness, associated with evil scheming. ARCH, an adjective, is mischievousness in tone and manner. "Mary suspected from John's arch expression that he was about to play a joke on her, and she prepared herself for anything ridiculous and fantastic."

Harlequin A HARLEQUIN used to be a pantomime buffoon in motley (varicolored) garb, like a jester's, with fake wand and sword, playing fantastic tricks. Nowadays he is a pantomiming clown. In Old French HARLEQUIN meant a 'demon.' Formerly he *and* the clown played a part of the pantomime called a 'harlequinade.' Today we use 'harlequinade' to mean 'fantastic and facetious pageantry.'

Humor and **Fun** The distinction between these two words is not the same as the distinction between their adjectives, humorous and funny. See HUMOROUS and FUNNY. If you need a literal adjective for FUN you will probably have to improvise one, such as 'funful.' HUMOR and FUN in their present usage represent a combination of meanings from widely different sources. But this development has been marked by side leaps and new starts, so that now to distinguish nicely between them we should really know their histories.

FUN, as we know it, was unheard of before late Colonial times, nor was HUMOR used in the modern sense before the 18th century. Shakespeare's 'humorous' Hamlet was not 'amusingly lighthearted' but 'distressfully moody.' Shakespeare also uses 'humorous' in the sense of 'damp,' because it came from the Latin word, *humus,* 'moisture or liquid.' But though both FUN and HUMOR took on abstract meanings through association with other ideas, by the 18th century HUMOR had

acquired an associated sense from certain classical conceptions of body
fluids. The Greek physician and philosopher Galen in the second century had perceived four fluids, or HUMORS, in the composition of the
human body. They were blood, phlegm, yellow bile and black bile.
The yellow bile was associated with choler, and the black bile with
melancholy. Blood produced the Latin *sanguis,* and phlegm the Greek,
phlegma. These fluids, mixed in our bodies, tempered them, and gave
each a temperament, specifically, various moods or tempers. When we
were full of blood (sanguine) we were active and cheerful; full of
phlegm (phlegmatic), slow and dull; full of bile (bilious), ill-
tempered, splenetic; full of black bile (melancholy or atribilious), depressed, despondent. Good HUMOR suggests a right balance or good disposition of the four HUMORS. When we HUMOR someone, giving way
to his whims and wishes, we indulge one of those four aspects of personality.

But while nearly all this was happening to HUMOR, FUN was unborn.
Its early idiomatic use probably did not begin until long after the Norman conquest of England in the eleventh century. Then, apparently,
the word appeared as *fon,* a 'foolish person,' perhaps from the Old
English *faeme,* 'virgin,' and still earlier, on the Continent, from a *fone,*
'maid,' used sometimes as a 'simpleton' because such is often the conclusion of a housewife regarding her serving maid. At any rate, an
adjective was derived from a *fonned* or 'befooled' person. Originally
the word 'fond,' in English, meant 'foolish': "By reason of his age the
the old man was a little fond."

But in the Middle English the active verb, by this time spelled with
a 'u' but still meaning 'to befool' and 'to cheat,' produced our noun
FUN. At this stage FUN meant a 'trick.' It remained an inelegant word
for some centuries, being termed cant, and low cant, by old Dr. Johnson. Already in his time the trick was becoming 'amusing' and
'merry.' Since mirth, high spirits and good HUMOR cannot exclude some
jocularity, FUN is even today sometimes a 'joke.' But the joke must
be playful, or it ceases to be merry sport. We can poke FUN at some
one, it is true; but if this becomes contemptuous and we *make* FUN
of that person, then FUN reverts to the crude hoaxing or knavery of
its earlier meaning.

Nevertheless, FUN in its full stature is now indispensable to our
language. HUMOR can express only part of FUN's meaning. The HUMOR
that we find in the sayings of Lincoln is fundamental, since HUMOR
grew from the classical attempts to understand the origins of human
moods and temperament. But FUN is more virile. It not only signifies
the things and the qualities we laugh at, but also their effect upon us.

Certain things *are* FUN, and we *have* FUN. HUMOR is as broad and almost as profound as the heart, but FUN in one way exceeds HUMOR. It is more active, infectious and invigorating than HUMOR, which has come down to us mostly as good HUMOR. Even in their modern senses of a capacity of perceiving what is laughable or odd, there are distinctions. A 'sense of HUMOR' enables us to see what is 'funful.' But a 'sense of FUN' grasps at all the opportunities for a laugh, it goes out of its way to make more gay ordinary existence.

Humorous and **Funny**   Under HUMOR and FUN we see that a sense of humor enables us to perceive what is full of fun. The humor we see in two small dogs eyeing each other intently and weighing the expediency of battle, can make us laugh. If we say that their seriousness is FUNNY, we still do not mean that it is a joke. And that is what HUMOROUS means: it is an adjective that describes whatever can make us really laugh.

This is the point where HUMOROUS leaves off and FUNNY often begins. Not all jokes are HUMOROUS. But all jokes are FUNNY. For example, the spectacle of the two dogs debating battle in their minds, is HUMOROUS, as we have seen, *and* it is FUNNY. But some jokes are bitter: they are twists of fate in which there is nothing HUMOROUS. If we say "Something funny is going on here," we are prepared *not* to laugh. It may be a strange, unfortunate thing indeed. Something FUNNY may be sheer incongruity or oddness. We laugh wryly, but not *really* laugh, at many queer things. So what we call FUNNY may be only ridiculous or even foolish, even while what is HUMOROUS retains contact at all times with all that disposes us to laugh.

Jaunty   Oddly, the origin of this lively word is domestic. In Old French it was *gentil*, which derives from Latin *gentilis*, 'of the same family.' The JAUNTY person today has a certain sprightliness and buoyancy, a bounciness reminiscent of an earlier meaning of our word JAUNT, 'to bounce' or 'to jolt' (or 'be jolted'), as in a JAUNTING cart. A troop of cavalrymen passing smartly by at a trot bounce JAUNTILY in their saddles. The rolled curls at the nape of a young girl's neck bounce JAUNTILY as she walks, quite regardless of whether she is going on a JAUNT ('a roving pleasure trip'), which today does not suggest JAUNTINESS. A JAUNT perhaps acquired its meaning from a word in Swedish dialect that meant merely 'foolish.'

Merry   Aside from its gay, genuine humor and charm, MERRY has played on us one little trick which maltreats the truth. When we read or speak of 'merrie England' we think of the 'merrie men' of Robin Hood, or of a 'MERRY population' of Englishmen. But the persons who originated the phrase had in mind the comfortable English country-side, with its pleasant fields, hills and hedgerows. MERRY once described such warm delights, but it gave over the job. Now it refers normally only to creatures that can play: man, bird, animal. So it is no longer correct to talk about 'merry trees' or 'merry hills.' Figuratively, the word may refer to the works of man, "That is a very merry tune."

Pun This is an unpedigreed word. The Standard Dictionary thinks it probably comes from an English provincial word meaning 'to beat' or 'to mash,' in turn from the Anglo-Saxon 'to pound.' Webster's thinks it comes from Italy, and is akin to 'punctilio,' a 'quibble or fine point.' Perhaps it is crossbred. Certainly some PUNS are blunt enough to pound your senses, and others are so fine pointed as to be almost invisible. It is tough, says a newspaper comic, to pay eighty cents a pound for meat, but it is tougher if you pay sixty. Thus you can "make a PUN on almost any subject, except a king, who is not a subject."

Quixotic The most famous Spanish writer, Miguel de Cervantes Saavedra, ridiculed knight-errantry to our everlasting amusement. His symbol for it was a crazy old knight on a ridiculous horse, whose pathos, ludicrous ideals, and real humanity we love, and laugh at. Don Quixote tried to be a knight in an age when it was no longer practical to fight dragons and save ladies from distress. But at the least he succeeded in giving us a useful adjective, QUIXOTIC. A QUIXOTIC person is still somewhat crazy, as Don Quixote was; but his queerness, though usually amusing, need no longer be an absurd and obsolescent attachment to chivalrous ideals. If you are QUIXOTIC today, you are just 'peculiarly impulsive' in action. You have notions which you impractically put into effect without proper regard for consequences. "My friend has the quixotic idea that if he laughs all the time, other people will always laugh with him."

Riant Since it has a lilt and means 'laughing,' RIANT is a pretty word, and expressive. It comes from French *rire*, 'to laugh.' But RIANT doesn't sound as if it could mean 'guffaw,' so you had better save it for a real joyful, lyrical laugh, like the laugh of a happy child.

Sprightly and **Spry** The spelling of SPRIGHTLY is what philologists call barbarous, meaning false, since the word comes from 'SPRITE,' from

French *esprit,* and from Latin *spiritus,* 'spirit.' SPRIGHTLY has no doubt been influenced by a lively little word of no known origin, namely SPRY, which, though it may also have once denoted 'spirit,' now produces a down-to-earth image in our minds. A SPRY person is inevitably 'nimble,' at the direction of a quick and active mind. SPRIGHTLY refers usually to manners, like SPRIGHTLY talk, and it is just its connotation of 'spirit,' or dancing fairies, that makes it suitable for abstract things. SPRIGHTLY means 'brisk, vivacious, lively'; SPRY means the same, but it refers to the body. "The little old woman looked very spry walking down the street with her granddaughter, who chattered with sprightly enthusiasm about all they saw."

IDIOMS

Get	Hot
Had	Kick
Hand	Let & Leave
Happen	Make
Hardly	Must
Have	Take
Head	Turn
Help	Whip

Get GET is perhaps the most used, and the most misused word in the English language. To no avail philologists have pointed out that GET has strength and character. It should not be expected to be a mere jack-of-all-jobs. Even literati pay it scant respect and jingle it in their diction like coins in their pockets. In *The American Thesaurus of Slang* nearly three pages are devoted merely to *indexing* the slang uses of GET. A distinguished scholar recently said: "This word has a wide range but definite boundaries." What he meant was, that GET has a perfectly definite meaning. It means the 'attaining possession by voluntary exertion.' To say, "I've got a book (or a cat)," is a barbarism, not simply because it wastes breath, but because it is like telling a carpenter's helper, in the carpenter's presence, to do a job. The GOT is an unnecessary helper, because the abbreviated 'have' is enough to proclaim possession. "I have a book," tells you all you want. We have (possess) many things only because we go after them and GET them. Other things we have only because they are given us or thrust upon us.

GET is an important Scandinavian word, possibly cognate with a Russian word and the Latin *prendere*, 'to grasp,' remaining in our 'apprehend' and 'comprehend.' It came into English with the Danes, and was terribly kicked about, even in early times. It developed especially wildly in the intransitive use, which derived principally from its reflexive nature in 'get you gone' and 'getting one's self disliked.' This, no doubt accounts to some extent for the freedom of our slang; for how otherwise could we by voluntary effort 'GET stuck with something we don't want,' or 'GET rusty in our French or German,' or 'GET snooty?'

Yet to give slang its due, it often illustrates vividly the true meaning of GET. 'Go-getters' GET riches, they 'GET rich.' A problem is 'get-at-able,' or its solution is 'getable.' We 'GET religion'; the parson doesn't stuff it into us. We 'GET a shoe shine'; no one transports us to the shoe parlor against our will. We (ourselves) 'GET up' in the morning and 'GET on with' the day's work. Even when we are advised to 'GET wise' to ourselves the meaning may be less 'don't be ridiculous' than 'recognize your own interests.' Only, if someone should then say, "Get out of here," we might literally be unable to do this by *voluntary* exertion. Still, we will 'GET his idea'—and make our 'getaway.'

Had Grammarians take pride in the exactness of their science, but they often overlook a fact that sometimes sets their principles at naught—the fact that we haven't enough common words. Some philologists have suggested that we have deliberately stinted ourselves in order to avoid an unwieldy stock for daily employment. Whether or not that is true, we do most assuredly wring the utmost usage out of what we do possess. We assign absurdly various and numerous meanings and functions to individual words. This results in whimsical and peculiar senses, and finally in idioms that have no more respect for science or grammar than an elf has.

Take, for example, the word HAD. Usually HAD is used as a synonym for 'possessed.' "I had a hat," or "I had money," or as an auxiliary verb to form the past absolute tense, "I had found your hat before you came," or "I had done my work before I was paid." If we say, "You had better have done it," that doesn't mean that you HAD (in the past) done it better. In this case, the verb 'to do' already has an auxiliary, 'have.' Consequently, HAD assumes the role of a whole verb itself, and that verb means 'to find.' 'Had better,' therefore, is an idiom. The whole sentence really means: "We find it would have been better if you had done it." Or, to be literal: "You would find to-have-done-it better." Worse yet, as Fowler points out, is the passive version: "It had better have been done," for who then can be doing the 'finding out,' unless it is the very thing itself that was to have been done?

However, this peculiar idiom is probably more noticeable in British English than in American. Where the British might say "That sum had been spent better on other projects," we would say "That sum would have been spent better on other projects." When we do use the idiomatic 'had better' we use it usually in the simpler present tense, which is really a simple future with the force of either an admonition or a threat: "You had better wear your raincoat (you will find it will be better to wear your raincoat)," or, reversing the word-order for emphasis, "You better had wear your (own) raincoat (and not mine)."

But idiom will not down. For there is also 'had rather' and 'would rather.' The sense is recognizably conditional in the second idiom which is analogous to the old "I would liefer (I would hold dearer) . . ." Hence, now, 'I would rather' means 'I prefer.' And 'Had rather' is merely a more idiomatic rendering of 'would rather.' Here HAD again has its old verbal meaning 'to find,' but it is in the subjunctive tense: "I would find . . . ," or, "I would hold preferable . . ." The 'would' in 'had rather' is unexpressed, whereas in the variant 'would rather' it is expressed. "I had rather you go home before Father catches us."

Hand Next to the head, which we frown with, smile with and speak from, the HAND is the most eloquent part of our body. It may even have been our mouthpiece, in a sense, before sign language was supplanted by speech. So it is not surprising that the word HAND enters into so much of our phraseology as a picturesque or expressive element.

"All hands on board, sir," reports the mate to the captain. Handwriting, hand shaking and handiwork (things made by HAND) all indicate the activity and utility of HANDS. 'Handfuls' are units of more-or-less cubic measurement everyone uses. "By George, they're a handful," can refer to anything from uproarious children to wildcats. HAND, of course, gave us our word 'handles.' "To fly off the handle," as an ax-head off its helve, is accounted an Americanism; but Americans only added, vividly, the verb 'fly' to an old saying. Centuries earlier, the aimlessness of anything without its handle, and the danger of anything suddenly coming off it, was recognized in similar expressions. 'Handsome' first meant 'easy to handle.' "Handsome is as handsome does," means you are good-looking to the extent that you act well. The second 'handsome' is an adverb. Chaucer's 'coverchief' (from French *couvrechef*, or 'cover-head') turned into 'handkerchief' after it became less a cap than a nose cloth, and was carried in the HAND. Pocket handkerchiefs did not appear until late Colonial times. 'Hand over hand' is a nautical expression describing how a sailor hauls on a rope. Then Americans speeded up the image by inserting a fist, 'hand over fist,' which refers to something being done very quickly. 'Handmaidens' came into English very early in imitation of the Anglo-Saxon *handthegns*, 'attendants.' 'To wash one's HANDS' of something, or of someone, was a symbolical cleansing act after passing judgment, and is illustrated in the Bible by Pilate, after he delivered Christ to the Jews. 'Handcuffs' is a quite recent word, since the 'cuffs' were at first mittens. HANDS are extremely useful in card games, aside from the deals or HANDS (cards dealt or handed to you) themselves. Hence we 'play into the hands of others,' or 'show our hands,' in many ways. 'Handbills' are distributed by HAND, and 'handbooks' and 'handbags' are carried about by HAND. A 'four-in-hand' is a tandem of two pairs of horses, managed by HAND. If they break into a 'hand gallop,' they are still 'in hand'; but if they get out of control, they are 'out of hand.' 'Hand in glove' (or 'hand *and* glove,' as Washington probably said in his boyhood, means 'very compatible,' as a glove with the HAND in it. To be a 'good hand' at anything, or a 'green hand' or an 'old hand,' again personifies the HAND. And there is really a HAND in 'handicap,' though it was really 'hand in cap,' meaning 'cap in hand' or, still more exactly, '*in* cap in hand.' 'Cap in hand' was the pool in an old bartering game in Queen Anne's time, when English horse racing was inaugurated. So the term got into racing, with respect to the arrangement of stakes and imposts.

Slang offers the greatest profusion of 'hand-picked' and 'hand-raised' products of HAND. There is first of all the prized 'handout.' To the hobo that is a basic word, signifying a whole free meal, including meat. 'Handouts' are also prepared statements for the press, and soft jobs, graft, mooch, swag and rackets in both politics and the underworld. In baseball a base-on-balls is a 'handout,' and elsewhere almost anything free is a 'handout.' 'Hand-me-downs' are clothes or tokens from elder brothers and sisters or from ancestors. The expression 'hands down,' means easily or utterly, like "He won that race hands down." And don't forget the 'glad hand' we give our friends, and the '(noisy) hand' we give a matinee idol.

Happen Some say we use this word too much because every occurrence we mention must in one way or another HAPPEN, and so there is no sense in our saying it did HAPPEN: "It happened to be a frightfully hot day and I almost died," instead of "It was a frightfully hot day." But this redundancy is due to our making the word mean more than it naturally does. If we think it means 'occur' the error is ours. Some dictionaries grant this secondary meaning, and some even place it first. HAPPEN came from the Old Norse word *hap*, which even in the Old Norse meant not only 'chance' but 'good chance,' or 'luckiness.' So the only things that really HAPPEN today should be those things that occur 'by chance.' We are justified from time immemorial in considering HAPPENINGS lucky for us. If we say, "As it happened, I missed the curbstone by an inch on the turn," we might be drawing rather freely on the meaning of HAPPEN. We might be trying to shift the blame for our recklessness upon fate. This may be overworking poor HAPPEN, but there is after all much reason to be thankful for words by which we can condone our own foibles. Haven't we done as much for the 'happy?' It is another one we inherited from the same Old Norse *hap*, and it really means 'lucky.' "Happily," we say, "the front wheels missed the curb by an inch."

Hardly Just as we shouldn't say 'different than' for 'different from' so we shouldn't say 'hardly . . . than' for 'hardly . . . when.' But we sometimes do, reasoning something like this: A parasol looks like an umbrella, so I'll use it for one. 'Hardly . . . than' looks like 'hardly . . . when,' as in: "Hardly had I reached the house when the storm broke," meaning quite correctly, "No sooner had I reached the house than the storm broke." Consequently we form the habit of saying, incorrectly, "Hardly had I reached the house than the storm broke." Likewise we misuse 'scarcely,' and say 'scarcely . . . than.'

HARDLY in the use here indicated is idiomatic anyhow. The adverb HARDLY usually means simply 'in a hard way' or 'with difficulty.' "The handle turns hardly." But when something can be done only with difficulty it is human to think that it is HARDLY possible to do it. Hence HARDLY (as it has just been used in the previous sentence) takes on the meaning of 'almost not,' and when we can HARDLY do something, the idea is that perhaps we can and perhaps we can't. This usage has become so common that to avoid confusion we usually drop the adverbial 'ly' in HARDLY when we want it to express 'with difficulty.' Thus it sounds more natural to say, "The handle turns hard."

But when HARDLY assumes the sense of 'almost' we must be careful not to use it with a negative. Though it is true that we can 'hardly do something,' it is false that we can 'hardly *not* do it.' "There isn't hardly a chance of my going," is incorrect English. We must say, "There is hardly a chance . . ."

Have "Eureka!" cried Archimedes in his bath, "I have found it!" meaning the relation that exists between volume and weight. Nowadays we don't cry "Eureka," nor even "I've found it!" We say emphatically "I have it." "I have it, we'll go fishing!" Here lies the full force of the old Indo-European word HAVE.

For the main meaning of HAVE is 'possession.' 'Possession' is, we feel, almost everything, for don't we say, "Finders keepers, losers weepers," or "Possession is nine-tenths of the law." Is not the world divided between the 'haves' and the 'have-nots?' And can you not ring all the changes on the figurative uses of HAVE today, and find 'possession' at the root of every one? We 'HAVE a good time,' or we 'HAVE a headache.' We 'HAVE the goodness' to thank someone, or else we 'HAVE ill will' and don't thank him. A woman 'HAS three sons,' but three times previously she 'HAD (she produced) one son.' Logically she produced only what she already possessed. When we sail down a coast we 'HAVE the land' on one side. In this case we don't really 'possess' it, but it is part of our surroundings at the moment. We make a point in argument and say, "I have you there." HAVE is no unambitious word. It tends incessantly toward 'acquirement': the more we HAVE, it seems, the more we go after. "I have this man on the hip," says the ruthless man. He 'HAS him' where he wants him, he controls him. He 'possesses' an advantage. If the underdog in such a relationship struggles and 'HAS his leg broken,' misfortune may seem to possess him, but still it is *his* misfortune. If then he goes to a doctor, and 'HAS the leg set,' he grasps his evil possession with both hands and makes of it an order—to the doctor. Here HAVE reasserts the ancient meaning now waning, in "I'll have at him!" We 'HAVE Greek,' 'HAVE a knowledge or understanding' of that language; or, still more broadly, 'HAVE *it*' (meaning practically anything) our own way; or, less aggressively, 'HAVE merely an idea,' that this or that thing is so; or again 'HAVE *it* (perhaps anything) in mind.' In these cases the 'possession' is concrete, but the object is vague. When we say, "Have a seat," the object becomes concrete but the 'possession' is vague. Finally, "I will have no more of your nonsense," where 'possession' is rejected but still is alluded to quite fiercely.

And here we might leave the hero of this entry, the pan-European HAVE, probably cognate with Latin *habere* that gave us 'habits' and 'habitations.' But how HAVE began as the auxiliary verb used to form the perfect and pluperfect past tenses is hard to say. Perhaps the idea behind the use developed like the idea behind these sentences: "I have this inveterate foe of mine at my feet, as you see, and lifeless." "I have him lifeless—that is, killed." Many generations later: "I have killed him." And after more generations, even with an intransitive verb: "They have died."

But watch these pitfalls: 1) Don't say, "I meant to have written you" for "I meant to write you," since at the time you intend to refer to, you meant 'to write' not 'to *have* written.' However, there are times in the past when you doubtless intended to 'have done' something still earlier: "I intended to have 'phoned you *before* I left." 2) In the early stages of its use as an auxiliary HAVE remained the main verb, definitely denoting possession of something. The second verb entered the equation only by contributing its past participle to indicate, like an adjective, what state the thing possessed was in. For example, "I have him conquered" eventually became "I have conquered him." Many generations came and went before 'conquered' was regarded as the main verb, and HAVE its humble helper. Even today we are likely to credit the auxiliary with chief importance and say: "I never *do* that"—entirely ignoring the main verb in the syncopated first clause. Grammatically correct, it is "I never have *done* that and I never will *do* it." 3) While 'do' can also be used with the verb HAVE itself, as in "Do fishes have lungs," the unison should be only used for clarity or emphasis. Fowler points out that "Do you have coffee for breakfast?" is not exactly the same as "Is there coffee in your house at breakfast time to make a drink of?" But to say, "Do you have a cigarette (i.e. that I can have)" when emphasis is not needed, and when "Have you a cigarette" is quite clear enough, is just careless word-work.

Head The HEAD is the body's watchtower, and the office of its manager. Thus we have our 'headquarters,' and thus whoever is the HEAD of a concern is its director and commander. The HEAD also gives us our 'headlands' and our HEADS, or sources, of streams, because in these cases the geographical sites correspond in function or prominence to our HEAD. By a somewhat similar analogy 'fifty head' of cattle condenses the plural into one commanding figure.

In English, words that derive from that part of the body we call HEAD came from both the Germanic tongue and the Latin. The former provided words like 'hat' and 'heed.' The Latin *caput*, 'head,' provided 'cap,' 'captain,' 'chieftain,' and 'cape,' which once had a hood covering the HEAD.

Less logical are such colloquial expressions as 'to head for home,' 'to head him off,' and "You can't make a long-headed man headlong." 'Headway, heady, headstrong' are colorful words whose relation to HEAD is obvious. If, for example, the HEAD is the source of our greatest power, then being 'headstrong,' which means 'unruly' or 'willful,' is understandable. 'Heady,' which means 'rash, intoxicating,' is a good adjective referring to anything that goes to the HEAD. A train gains 'headway (momentum)' as it increases speed. And the time interval between train departures is also called a 'headway.' The old nautical meaning of 'headway' refers to the ship's forward motion compared to its leeway, or divergence from its true course compelled by the winds. 'Headway' is also the clear space under an overhead crossing.

The riotous expression 'head over heels' used to be 'heels over head.' A 'head wind' is probably nautical—a wind that strikes the HEAD of a ship 'head on.' 'Head off' means 'to swerve something' by getting in front of it. 'To make head or tail of something' does *not* mean to understand completely a mystery. It simply means to know a little something about a puzzle—to distinguish one end of it from the other. The sense in 'headlong' no more implies linear length than a 'levelheaded' person means a 'flathead.' The original form was 'headling,' analogous to 'sideling' that gave us sidelong. 'Headling' meant 'moving head foremost'; 'headlong' means 'plunging head fore-most.' To 'head up' means simply forming into a HEAD. In 'to come to a head' there is some association with the French *venir à chef,* 'to come to a head,' whence, via Old French, *achever,* and our 'achieve.' 'Achieve' is a magnificent word utilizing the powerful significance of HEAD. Shakespeare used it in three ways: "Achieve me," he said; that is, 'kill me,' or 'bring my life to a HEAD, to an end.' "He does achieve with his sword," an obscure reference to the sword being as mighty as the HEAD. And "Some achieve greatness," or some arrive at the HEAD of great things.

HEADS are held high when we are proud, but it is not necessarily our pride that is addressed when someone shouts, "Heads up!" He simply means "Watch out!" But in every idiom and colloquialism we come back to the fact that HEADS are very important. When we lose our HEADS and act like agitated geese we are certainly very confused, and when we keep our HEADS we are cool and collected.

Help As a youngster, Shakespeare probably never asked for a 'second helping,' or a second HELP, at the table. But he couldn't HELP that; the word didn't come into English in that sense until he was grown up, or perhaps dead. This special meaning came from the knowledge of the French translation in 1611 of *servir,* 'to help, stead, avail.' Within the next generation this meaning, conveyed in the word HELP, was applied in the comparatively democratic Colonies to the 'helpers,' for the humane purpose of not hurting their feelings by calling them servants.

But the matter of a 'second helping' is a minor idiosyncrasy of HELP. Where the word really acts up is in certain idiomatic negative or negative-sounding usages that followed from the comparatively simple "I can't help it":

If we 'can't HELP doing' something, we aren't strong enough to resist doing it—'HELP' is common Teutonic and originally meant 'strong.' An example of this is, "I couldn't help laughing at him." But beyond that we slip into distorting idioms, to the horror of some scholars. The two 'it's' in "Don't do it if you can help it" don't refer to one and the same thing: the second one refers to 'doing' the first one. We often correct this confusion carelessly, by omitting the second 'it' and saying, "Don't do it if you can help." But this doesn't sound well because HELP ought to have an object. It shows what sort of mischief we are up to. From saying "Don't do it if you can help," we go on to say "Don't do it any more than you can help," which, if we analyze it, as Fowler's *Modern English Usage* does, really means: "Don't do it any more than you can't help doing it." Then, "Do it as little as you can help," is really monstrously illogical, because not only do we again use 'can help' for the logical 'can't help'; but, in this usage, 'can't help' doesn't HELP to correct the sense anyhow. For the HELP itself, at the phrase's end, is of no HELP to the meaning since the real sense is already and exactly expressed in, "Do it as little as you can."

For this, and more of it, see Fowler, H. W., *A Dictionary of Modern English Usage.*

Hot   Without wishing in the least to appear sacrilegious, it may be remarked that in everyday life the devil does seem to have one advantage over the Lord: he is a more spectacular showman. It may have been that he breathed his HOT breath into this word, HOT, and gave it its astonishing and fiendish effectiveness. For have we not 'hot-heads,' 'hotbeds,' 'Hotspurs,' and 'blows hot and heavy' in a fist fight, 'hot mammas,' 'hot tempers,' 'hotboxes,' and things 'too hot to handle'? And what about the devil-spurted HOT water that scalds you suddenly in your shower, and all the other HOT waters we get into? Or, turning to slyer and more deceitful slang, there are all our 'hotshots' who are magnates in business and experts in sports, yet convert so easily into 'stuffed-shirts,' 'dudes,' 'sensualists' or 'crooks.' Even 'hotcakes' and 'hot tamales' may be lures of the devil since they derived from the griddle or are peppery HOT. 'Hotstuff' is not commonly in the dictionaries yet, though 'hot rods' have ridden in. And all these things suggest in the offing a malignant spirit, grinning satisfaction. The slang adjective HOT bespeaks 'luck,' since a man who is in a 'run of luck' is said to be HOT. With the same implications HOT bespeaks an eagerness or a fitness that arouses suspicion: a race horse that is HOT may be stimulated with dope. HOT is a handy word but no trifle. 'Hot talk' is profanity—surely the devil's own speech.

All of which is, of course, only facetiously significant. The word HOT is no slang in itself. In fact, it existed in English before 'heat' did. 'Heat' derived from HOT. HOT is Teutonic; it was *hoot*, pronounced 'hawt,' in the Middle English. It is interesting to follow HOT's history. Five hundred years ago Sir Henry Percy, harassing the Scottish border, was called a 'hotspur'; today we might call him 'hotstuff,' something 'fast' and 'hard-hitting.' And Percy is pictured principally as 'hot-headed'—his temper was HOT and perhaps his liver—'hot-livered' meant 'violent' and 'rash.' 'Hotspurs' had been plentiful in England long before Percy. Horses in turn were 'hot-spirited' or 'headstrong.' The chase became HOT when the 'HOT scent' was strong. The heat increased up to and including the kill: today we are HOT when we are about to run down a quarry, an answer to a problem. A 'hotbed' of flowers was used enough in the eighteenth century to give us our figurative 'hotbeds,' which are sometimes exceedingly unpleasant. But as far back as medieval times HOT water was probably called HOT water. And in provincial English today 'hotshots' are neither big shots or sporting aces: they are persons who are impetuously foolish. Finally, HOT has gone aloft in warfare. 'Hot missions' are perilous bombing missions.

Kick This word is an example of how busily a word can get about in (or KICK about in) a language. No one knows exactly how KICK got into our language; but, once in, it lost no time making itself handy. So handy, in fact, particularly in rough usage, that today it may be actually more often slang than legitimate. We don't discharge an employee—we 'KICK him downstairs,' or we rid ourselves of him by 'KICKING him upstairs,' by way of a promotion. We 'KICK (complain)' about the weather. We 'KICK up our heels' when we go on a spree, and then 'KICK up our toes' when we die. Or perhaps, in the latter instance, we just 'KICK in, off or out.' The remarkable thing is that our ancestors, back beyond, say, Geoffrey Chaucer, got along without this little word altogether. But it is not at all remarkable that by this time we have found so many uses for it, with its vigor, its adaptability to the tongue and its suggestion of the hard hitting hoof of a mule.

As long ago as Shakespeare's time KICK illustrated its popularity. A

'kickshaw' today is some trifle inclined to be fantastic. When Elizabethans had trouble with the French *quelque chose*, 'some thing,'
they thought in their dilemma first of KICK and then perhaps of 'pshaw.'
Thus 'kickshaw' for some odd thing not usually on the menu became
common English.

And KICK has been obliging us ever since. Note 'kickback,' any 'unexpected and disconcerting result,' and hence that particular 'kickback' which is a quick restoration of booty to a victim in order to
head off prosecution. Or the 'kickback' that is a payment back of fees
in order to keep a job. Note also our 'KICKING about' a neighborhood
when we are aimlessly rambling around it. A pilot KICKS his plane
when he swishes its tail to lessen speed. Whatever KICKING may lack
in dignity, it always makes up for in energy. While we are alive, we
are 'alive and KICKING.'

Let and Leave   Little words like LET are lively and double-talking.
They may even contradict themselves, as this one sometimes seems
to do. We could say, "Let him do that without let or hindrance," which
might be read as "Allow him to do that without not allowing him
to do it." The catch is in the second LET, which is an archaic noun
from an obsolete verb *letten*, 'to hinder.' The first LET comes from another obsolete verb *leten*, meaning the opposite of 'hindering'—that is,
meaning 'to allow.' The basis of *letten* is 'late,' which runs back to
Latin *lassus*, 'weary.' But the other verb, *leten*, 'to allow,' may also be
cognate, ultimately, with 'late,' though in its early English meaning it
suggested less 'weariness or tardiness' than 'looseness or weakness.' It
evidently runs back not to Latin *lassus*, 'weary,' but to Latin *laxus*,
'lax.' So it came to mean 'to allow.' When you LET your hair down you
'allow' it to come down. When physicians formerly LET blood from
persons they 'allowed' the blood to run out. Similarly, land was LET
out to hire in England long before the Conquest. Figurative uses of
this LET have followed in great numbers, some elaborate and elliptical.
For example: "Let's do this," a vague and playful imperative amounting only to a suggestion. "Let X represent the unknown quantity,"
allows X to represent that quantity. And note the expressions 'let off a
broadside,' 'let a prisoner off,' 'let go,' 'let be,' 'let know,' and a 'let-
down' or a 'let-up.'

LET often works hand in glove with 'LEAVE,' which itself does some
double-talking. Originally transitive, LEAVE meant 'to LEAVE something
behind.' But since you can't LEAVE anything behind you without going
away, LEAVE came also to mean in reference to persons 'to depart.'
This 'to depart' is the present intransitive meaning of LEAVE. When a

train LEAVES it is, of course, figuratively endowed with life, like a person.

Sometimes we have incorrectly permitted LET to take over the transitive use of LEAVE. For example, unless you are very careful, you will think that 'let something alone' means exactly the same as 'leave something alone.' "I let the cat alone," does *not* mean the same as "I leave the cat alone." The description of the first example is that the cat has my permission to be alone; the description of the second example is that I am going away from the cat, the cat is going to stay behind. Totally different ideas are behind these two examples. If you remember that LET signifies a granting of permission, given of your own free will, and if you remember that LEAVE always involves a sense of physical removal, you will never confuse the use of these words. Then you will never say "I leave my lessons slide," because you know that that is physically impossible in the first place and in the second you are really trying to say that, by an act of my own will, I simply LET my lessons slide. In a sense, your lessons had your permission to slide.

In tennis 'LET ball' is more clearly called a 'net ball.' That LET is not the allowing LET, but the hindering LET. The LET ball goes over the net, but touches it, and is sometimes partly checked. In other words, it is not wrong to say "Let ball"; but, since this use of LET is now archaic, perhaps it is better to say "Net ball."

Make If we are all made in the image of our MAKER, that perhaps explains how we are ourselves such good MAKERS. Webster's gives fifty-nine senses of the word MAKE, and then adds over a hundred phrases in which we MAKE such diverse things as terms, haste, peace, war, tracks, a living, bones (adding 'about'), mountains (out of molehills), long arms, headway, the most (of anything), books (of betting data), much (adding 'of') and game or fun (also adding 'of'). And with a finer touch of dexterity, emulating our own MAKER, we MAKE 'out,' 'over,' 'off,' 'up,' 'believe,' 'ready,' 'shift,' 'good,' and now, as the columnists say of the smalltown girls who go astray in the big cities, 'bad.' It all shows not only that we are inventive geniuses but that, given a good idea to begin with, a word can multiply indefinitely.

MAKE is historically what is called Common Teutonic: it existed in the Anglo-Saxon, the Old Frisian, Old Swedish and Old High German. It exists today in Dutch *maken* and German *machen*. It had kindred in Old Irish and in ancient Greek. Trace it back and you will find it meant 'to build, to form, to fit together,' but, first of all, 'to knead.' It is perhaps one of the first words, like 'mother' and 'tree,' that our primitive forefathers used.

Must "For all who love the great outdoors, this book is a must."
Well, probably it is. But the great outdoors is always fresh and free, and MUST is becoming a little 'musty' from overwork. It does seem that we could find another word without weakening our point. And yet, can we?

"For all who love the great outdoors, this book is literally necessary." Here the point is undoubtedly weakened. 'Compelling' and 'demands admiration' have, of course, been worked out already. Unfortunately, brevity is an advertiser's MUST, and two or three syllables are not so good as one. It is the one-punch-and-out theory that makes MUST a MUST.

And there is another difficulty in finding a relief noun for this new but rapidly aging substantive. Its parent, the auxiliary verb, is almost unique. Its principal usefulness, of course, comes from its blunt force— 'you must go' means 'you have to go,' and that's all there is about it! But MUST was not originally that harsh. It meant 'may' or 'is permitted.' And that leniency lingers in a secondary use of MUST, in the sense of merely 'logical necessity or truth.' We scratch our heads thoughtfully and conclude: "He must mean he doesn't *want* to go." It is probably impossible to find a synonym that combines this sense of 'by logic' and of 'willful necessity.' What other possible synonyms are there, anyhow? The loose 'have to' and the passive 'is necessary' and 'are obliged to' obviously won't do. If we are over-blessed with a bonanza, where to find a new bonanza?

Take Like Mark Twain's Captain Stormfield, who found on arriving in Heaven that angel wings are mostly ornamental and not to fly with, many of us discover as we grow older that long, fancy words are more decorative than useful. It is then that we appreciate those busy little words like TAKE, which are forever combining with others, like flakes in a kaleidoscope, to sprinkle our speech with idiomatic excitement. It has been estimated that fully one-half of our usages are figurative. A large portion of these are highly idiomatic.

Few idiomatic words have been busier than TAKE. It not only combines with much small fry, as in 'TAKE in' and 'TAKE aback,' but sometimes conspires with a single particle to coin many new or divergent meanings: 'TAKE up' has thirty different meanings. In addition, its own sense development has been remarkable. In the Old Norse it was simple and direct enough, meaning 'to lay hold of, seize, grasp, or TAKE.' In English it took over bodily the meaning of Anglo-Saxon *niman*, 'to capture, TAKE, and, thus, to marry.' So when the minister asks you at the altar if you TAKE this woman for your wife, you are at the moment following a historically savage rule. An unabridged dictionary may give you half a hundred meanings of TAKE itself, and as many more phrasal distinctions. There are probably twice as many more than the dictionary lists.

Thus you may 'TAKE care' of yourself. You may 'TAKE' a date home from a party, but here there is no hint of violence. You make 'TAKE it' into your head to say something, when, in reality, the impulse to say it TAKES you. You may 'TAKE after' a thief who has 'TAKEN (seized) your satchel.' You may resemble your grandparent whom, in looks or ways, you 'TAKE after.' After a great excitement, you may 'TAKE a long breath.' A superior may 'TAKE you down' for an impertinence, and his doing so may be a form of violence. But you can also 'TAKE yourself' downtown in your car.

In one primitive usage TAKE has remained loyal to itself. When we kill we 'TAKE life'; also, the game laid out on the ground in a row is the 'hunter's TAKE,' and a fisherman's total catch is his 'day's TAKE.' The gate-receipts or the 'gate' are also the 'TAKE (more fully, the 'intake').' 'Intake' is used also in gambling houses, where the patrons may be victims, and 'TAKEN in.' And surely in the underworld when you are 'TAKEN for a ride' the verb reverts to its primitive meaning, for you are murdered.

Turn   When the worm TURNS it should, by historical rights, TURN in a circle, round and round. That was the first intransitive meaning of TURN, 'to revolve,' like a wheel. But now we have 's-turns' that emulate the worm when it is merely wriggling, weather that TURNS cold when the thermometer drops straight downward, and lights we TURN off and on by flipping a tab up or down or by pushing a plug horizontally inward. But the wheels of cars still TURN in the old Roman fashion, even though we sometimes find it necessary to add 'around.' We can TURN on the hot water by revolving the spikes of a wheel. But in this case the wheel doesn't turn all the way around. And it is this incompleted action, this gesture, as it were, that gave us our many metaphorical meanings of TURN. The first TURN was a Grecian 'carpenter's compass' or a 'TURNER's chisel' that became in Rome that useful wheel itself, the 'lathe,' *tornus*. From this we still have the 'well-TURNED' phrase, and the 'well-TURNED out' young lady of fashion. The handicrafts, which rounded things off, gave fanciful analogies to our minds.

Now a desk dictionary may give you three dozen meanings of TURN, and an unabridged that many for the transitive verb alone, and eighty-five for both the verbs and the noun. More than that, you will find traces of it in many other words, such as 'attorney,' 'contour,' 'return' and even 'turnip,' because it is round. And in TURN, TURN itself was influenced by related words.

Whip   For some 250 years we have had 'whippersnappers' among us—literally, 'snappers-of-whips,' though for the sake of double emphasis the agency of both the noun and the verb are cited, much as we waste breath but gain force by saying 'cutter-uppers' for 'cut-uppers.' But these 'whippersnappers,' these little persons who have to crack WHIPS to attract attention to themselves, are only one example of many figurative uses of the word WHIP. 'Whippersnapper' is said to be imitative in its origin of quick motion within a narrow space, as we speak also of the 'swish' of a whip, imitating its sound. Even the object itself, the WHIP, was so named from the quick turning of binding strands around a cord to give it strength. And since the original motion was either a swinging, a bobbing up and down, a sudden movement in any direction or a darting to and fro, we now have the 'whippletree' ('swingletree,' 'wiffletree'), which is the swinging bar for traces in a team of horses, and the 'whipsaw,' which cuts from either edge. In slang 'to whipsaw' someone is to get the better of him in no matter what he does. In Wall Street they speak of the 'whipsawing process,' in which the speculator gets stung (or WHIPPED) twice when he buys high and has to sell low. A hostess 'WHIPS up' a quick meal, perhaps WHIPPING eggs and cream into a froth for a fruit dessert. The fox 'WHIPS out of sight' before the WHIP (the huntsman's alert assistant who controls the hounds) can WHIP the pack onto the scent. The WHIP in Congress keeps the members posted on affairs and, if possible, present at proceedings. An agitator 'WHIPS up' public sentiment in favor of new or radical ideas. In an old-fashioned brawl the protagonist 'WHIPS out' a razor and carves his opponents; nor in some towns did the populace care a 'whipstitch' (a quick overhand stitch, figuratively amounting to almost nothing) how many were carved. In the underworld 'to WHIP it' means to junk something quickly, such as a gun when arrest is imminent.

All these usages and many more, like the WHIPPING of a stream with a fisherman's line or fly, may well remain with us though the original WHIP, and its spectacular lash, is disappearing. Gone are the days when cart horses were flogged daily through the streets with long rubber rat-tails, or WHIPS. In those days to be a WHIP (an expert driver of a four-in-hand) was the height of social distinction among gentlemen. But all this vividness of WHIP makes one thing seem odd, that the half-humorous use of WHIPPING for 'defeating' is losing popularity. Now and then a sportscaster speaks of one team's WHIPPING another.

But 'beat,' perhaps because it has somewhat the same meaning of 'to lash,' is replacing WHIP in this usage.

Etymologically WHIP is not very old in English. It appears in Middle English as *whippen*, 'to overlay a cord,' and as *whippe*, 'scourge'; also as *wippen*, 'to jump up or down,' or 'jig.' Its sources are Low German and Scandinavian.

INDIVIDUALITY

BEING *n.* a person; the state of existing; life.

BODY *n.* the main part, or the general whole, of anything, as the BODY of people; person.

Entity

ESSENCE *n.* the fundamental, inner nature of a thing or person.

EXISTENCE *n.* life; being; entity.

Identity

OBJECT *n.* a thing; a single entity, usually lifeless, as "The object is a box."

PERSON *n.* an individual; a human being.

SOMETHING *n.* an unspecified thing.

THING *n.* an object; a specified thing, as "Bring me that thing on the table."

UNITY *n.* having the character of one; the state of being wholly integrated.

Entity An ENTITY is a 'being,' whether breathing, inanimate, imaginary or immaterial. It is anything that 'exists,' big or little, real or vague. A cat is an ENTITY, and so is your own soul. ENTITY comes from the participial form of Latin *sum*, 'I am,' 'I exist.' It is a very useful word.

Identity Everyone knows what 'identify the corpse' means. Everybody knows what IDENTICAL twins are. But the word IDENTITY seldom slips into conversation. It arrives from the perfectly simple little Latin word *idem*, 'the same.' It enables us to avoid using the awkward word 'sameness,' which would often be inadequate anyhow since 'same' is often confused with 'similar.' "What is the identity of this flower? It is a buttercup." From this we know a particular flower has a 'sameness' to buttercups. Therefore it is a buttercup.

IDENTITY is a positive and versatile word. It denotes not only the 'sameness' but the 'self-sameness' of two or more entities. IDENTITY suggests the 'likeness' of an entity with respect to its former appearance, or of an original to its copy, providing the copy is a facsimile, a replica, a duplicate.

IDENTITY has taken on a certain philosophical quality concerned less with physical similarities than with distinctive characteristics. IDENTICAL twins are presumably just alike, though we know they are not. But when we come to IDENTIFYING a corpse we look at once for a characteristic or distinguishing mark. When we speak of the IDENTITY of a living person we take either a broad or a selective view, or sometimes both. The IDENTITY of a man is properly his whole entity. If we are a detective and the man is a crook, his IDENTITY will consist of what will legally establish it, a reasonable number of distinctive characteristics.

KINSHIP

Affinity

AGNATION *n.* kinship; blood relationship established only through the male members of a family; any relation on the father's side, whether through males or females.

AVITAL *adj.* pertaining to grandfather. It sometimes refers simply to antiquity.

AVUNCULAR *adj.* pertaining to uncle.

BLOOD-RELATION *n.* a kinsman; a person related by birth to another.

BROTHERLY or FRATERNAL *adj.* pertaining to brother; of or like relations between brothers.

COGNATION *n.* blood relationship.

Consanguineous

COUSINLY *adj.* pertaining to cousin; of or like relations between cousins.

ENATION *n.* blood relationship established only through the female members of a family. Compare AGNATION.

German & Germane

Germane see **German & Germane**

KINDRED *n.* all of one's family relationships, including blood, marriage, and step relationships.

    AUNT
    BROTHER
    BROTHER-IN-LAW
    COUSIN
    DAM
    DAUGHTER
    DAUGHTER-IN-LAW
    FATHER
    FATHER-IN-LAW
    FIRST, SECOND, THIRD, COUSIN
    FOSTER DAUGHTER
    FOSTER SON
    FOSTER FATHER
    FOSTER MOTHER
    GRANDFATHER
    GRANDMOTHER
    GREAT-GRANDFATHER
    GREAT-GRANDMOTHER
    HUSBAND
    MATER
    MATERNAL ANCESTOR
    MATRIARCH

MOTHER	WIFE
MOTHER-IN-LAW	MARITAL *adj.* pertaining to husband, but more often simply to marriage itself.
NEPHEW	
NIECE	
PATER	MATERNAL *adj.* pertaining to mother, and esp. to motherly feelings and attitudes.
PATERNAL ANCESTOR	
PATRIARCH	
PROGENITOR	**Morganatic**
PROGENITRESS or PROGENITRIX	NEPOTAL *adj.* pertaining to nephew.
SON	
SON-IN-LAW	**Orbate**
SIRE	PATERNAL *adj.* pertaining to father.
SISTER	
SISTER-IN-LAW	SORORAL *adj.* pertaining to sister.
Stepchild	SPOUSE *n.* wife or husband.
STEPDAUGHTER	UXORIAL *adj.* pertaining to wife.
STEPFATHER	UXORIOUS refers to overfondness for a wife; UXORICIDE refers to a wife-killer, or to the crime of wife-killing itself.
STEPMOTHER	
STEPSON	
UNCLE	

Affinity A busily expressive word today, AFFINITY began its career long before Caesar was stabbed in Rome. The Latin word *finis*, for 'finish,' had been producing our AFFINITY, as well as our 'definition, fines (settled payments) and finance.' For *finis* means either an 'end' or a 'border,' and when either two ends meet or two borders touch, there is 'mutuality' and 'interest.' And by extension, there is 'natural attraction,' which is the modern meaning of AFFINITY. This natural attraction may refer to a more or less spiritual relationship between two people, but more often than not AFFINITY is used specifically in connection with the 'romantic attraction' between the sexes.

This sentimental connotation of AFFINITY is in one sense scandalously at odds with the word's origin and yet, perhaps, curiously correct. AFFINITY originally, in distinction to 'consanguinity (blood-relationship),' designated that other kind of kinship, a relationship by marriage. The Latin *affinitas* means literally 'nearness,' and hence also close agreement and mutual attraction. But it so happened that *affinitas* has its adjective, *affinis*, just as our own AFFINITY has its adjective, 'affinitive,' meaning 'having or tending to AFFINITY.' And *affinis* took on the additional meaning of 'partaking,' then of 'complicity,' finally of 'guilt.' Though this unfortunate sense has failed to contaminate our 'affinitive,' we still may wonder with some historical reason, whether our AFFINITY, with its connotations of love and romantic passion, is faithfully cognate with its Latin original, or whether it, too, has a hint of 'complicity.'

Consanguineous   Of the same blood, related. CONSANGUINEOUS comes from the Latin *con*, 'together,' plus *sanguis*, 'blood.'

German and **Germane**   We owe GERMANE to Hamlet, who fancifully used the word GERMAN, meaning 'akin to' in family relationships, as if it could refer also to things and affairs. And so Hamlet gave us a new adjective, meaning 'relevant.' He was commenting on a phrase of advice at a critical time, and remarked that the phrase would be more GERMAN to the matter if only they had brought along some cannon. Shakespeare practically saved the life of the original word, which had come from the Latin *germanus*, meaning 'closely akin to,' and survives now only in two rather needless compounds—'brothers-german' ('brothers by the same parents') and 'cousins-german' ('first cousins, having the same grandparents').

In English, GERMAN was formerly spelled 'germain,' so Hamlet's GERMANE acquired that pronunciation while improving somewhat upon the spelling. GERMAN with a big 'G,' referring to the Germans, also came from Latin *germanus*. But that was evidently a secondary form of *germanus*, built on a similar word of the Gauls describing the Germans, or one tribe of them, as their neighbors. The original *germanus*, related to the word 'germ,' meant literally 'of the same seed.'

Morganatic   A MORGANATIC marriage was quite a cautious nuptial transaction in ancient Germany, in which the *Morgengabe*, the 'groom's gift' to the bride on the morning after the marriage, was conferred without its acquiring for the groom any proprietorship over the person or chattels of the bride. It was a methodical Teutonic sort of trial marriage, favoring the bride. Then the Romans got hold of the idea, and called it, aping the Germans, *matrimonium in morganatica*. At long last, and from Germany where the credo grew and persisted that no marriage of unequals could ever be perfect, the custom spread through the royal families of Europe for use by husbands who completely outshone their fiancées in rank. The original proviso was reversed. The commoner wife cannot now share her husband's wealth or title, nor can her children inherit his title, real estate or sometimes even his personal property. But this MORGANATIC marriage is wholly legitimate and monogamous.

Orbate ORBATE means 'fatherless.' It is related to 'orphan,' which comes from the Greek *orphonos,* via Latin *orphanus.* The root means 'bereft.' Though Webster calls this word obsolete, you may still use it in the sense of 'bereft,' as some Germans may feel without a strong Fatherland.

Stepchild This words suggests a 'foundling,' a child deserted by its parents, and found on someone's doorstep. But the 'step' in 'doorstep' is from Anglo-Saxon *steppan,* 'to step,' and the 'step' in STEPCHILD is from Anglo-Saxon *steop,* a prefix meaning 'orphaned.' A STEPCHILD, then, is a child of a wife or husband by a former marriage.

LANGUAGE

See also Grammar

Articulate & Enunciate
DIALECT *n.* the form of a language as it is spoken in a particular region.
DICTION *n.* the manner in which a language is pronounced; style of writing or speaking.
Enunciate see **Articulate & Enunciate**
Etymology see **Linguistics, Philology,** etc.
Idiom & Vernacular
LINGO *n.* a foreign or outlandish speech, such as JAZZ LINGO.
Linguistics, Philology, Etymology, Morphology, Semantics, Semasiology, Phonetics, Phonemics & Syntax
Localism
Malapropism
Matutinal, Prandial, etc.
Metonymy
Morphology see **Linguistics, Philology,** etc.

ORAL *adj.* refers to words and speech.
PATOIS *n.* a dialect, esp. as it is spoken by the common people.
Philological Terms
Phonemics see **Linguistics, Philology,** etc.
Phonetics see **Linguistics, Philology,** etc.
Phraseology & Rhetoric
Rhetoric see **Phraseology & Rhetoric**
Semantics see **Linguistics, Philology,** etc.
Semasiology see **Linguistics, Philology,** etc.
SLANG *n.* any kind of special speech that is not accepted as good usage.
SPEECH *n.* the act of uttering or saying a language; talk.
Syntax see **Linguistics, Philology,** etc.

Vernacular   see **Idiom & Vernacular**

VOCABULARY   *n.* all the words that one has and can use immediately in his reading, writing or speaking.

Articulate and **Enunciate**   ARTICULATE is a word that is becoming popular as an adjective. An ARTICULATE people is a group, a class, a community, which is 'self-expressive.' A group of artists or dancers is, for example, ARTICULATE; but normally ARTICULATE is used to describe people who use words easily and well. This does not merely mean that they are intelligent. It means that they have the talent and desire to express themselves, which they do intelligibly, coherently, adequately. They do not need a spokesman, that is, someone to speak for them.

Literally, to ARTICULATE means to put parts of words together neatly and systematically. It is almost equivalent to ENUNCIATE.

In general practice ENUNCIATE is used to describe how someone 'pronounces' his words. An Englishman ENUNCIATES 'bath,' for example, differently from most Americans. ARTICULATE, on the other hand, refers to the relative pronunciation of one syllable after another in the same word. 'Transubstantiation' may be difficult for some people to ARTICULATE; but, if they ENUNCIATE each syllable with approximately equal quantity, they will be saying it correctly. Like ARTICULATE, ENUNCIATE has a less specific use. A man ENUNCIATES an idea, a doctrine, a philosophical position. In contrast, a man ARTICULATES his ideas one after another. A good speaker, for example, has to ARTICULATE well, but he doesn't have to ENUNCIATE his beliefs.

Anything that is ARTICULATE is 'linked' or 'coupled,' like a train of cars. "The head articulates with the backbone at a point that rarely becomes dislocated." If you remember that ARTICULATE is usually based on an idea of one thing coming after another, you won't have trouble with this word.

Idiom and **Vernacular**   IDIOM means 'one's own.' IDIOM is either the distinctive language of a particular region or a kind of people, or it is the distinctive phrases, words, and meanings in one language when compared to another. IDIOM is, then, the VERNACULAR. VERNACULAR English is the English of native Englishmen and Americans as they themselves use it. It is naturally highly unaffected and very indigenous. VERNACULAR includes whatever is peculiar to our language. It includes, that is, the IDIOM.

More often than not we use the word IDIOM not in its collective sense but to refer to a single example, a single specimen of lingual peculiarity. Consider "Not much I won't," or the contradictory but equivalent "Not by a little bit will I!" and "Not by a great deal will I!". These make no sense to a foreigner. To us they somehow not only mean something, but are especially vivid. They are our emphatic ways of saying, "I won't." They are very IDIOMATIC and their total meaning does not depend on the definition of any individual word.

Linguistics, Philology, Etymology, Morphology, Semantics, Semasiology, Phonetics, Phonemics and Syntax LINGUISTICS is the 'study of language,' from Latin *lingua,* 'tongue,' or 'language.' A synonym for LINGUISTICS is PHILOLOGY, which comes from the Greek for 'word.' Usually a 'linguist' is a man who can speak several languages, while a 'philologist' is a student of comparative languages. ETYMOLOGY, from the Greek for 'true,' treats of the 'origin and history' of words. It was originally used to refer to the literal meaning of a word as shown by its derivation. MORPHOLOGY, from the Greek for 'form,' is a part of PHILOLOGY (though biology also has a department called MORPHOLOGY). It is the 'study of word structure' from the beginnings, and how these structures relate and how they affect the function of words. Specifically, MORPHOLOGY considers inflectional formations and their role in formulating language. SEMANTICS, from the Greek for 'significant,' from *sema,* a 'sign,' is the scientific 'study of the evolution of language' as revealed by sense development and by the psychological significance of words and phrases. It is at once a particularization and an elaboration of ETYMOLOGY. In one way SEMANTICS compares with ETYMOLOGY as the whole study of surnames compares with genealogy, or the tracing of family lines. In another way, it restricts the study of word histories to the psychological significance and idea content of words. It searches for, finds, records and classifies such phenomena as specializations, betterments and depreciations of meanings, as well as adaptations and associations of ideas, as demonstrated by LINGUISTIC evidence. It is a whole science rather than a particular study, and thus contrasts with PHONETICS, which 'investigates speech sounds.' SEMANTICS dates from 1887, in France, but SEMASIOLOGY was used in a similar sense before that, being a branch of 'sematology' (or 'semantology'), the 'science of signs.' PHONETICS, from the Greek for 'sound,' dates to 1797, when it was used for ancient writings representing sounds instead of pictures. About 1850 PHONETICS became the scientific 'study of sound changes in speech,' applicable especially to spelling. PHONEMICS is a division of PHONETICS treating of 'phonemes,' or the 'irreducible unit elements' of sound in common language. SYNTAX, meaning in the Greek 'arranged together,' is a division of grammer dealing with the formation of words into phrases, clauses and sentences—that is, with 'sentence structure.' Hence it is also the 'grammatical arrangement' of the parts of a sentence. SYNTAX has been described as the traffic laws of speaking and writing; it is, surely, the most vital and dynamic contribution to language that dry grammar can give us.

Localism LOCALISM is a term applying to small areas, to LOCALITIES —small, that is, in a relative sense. These LOCALITIES may be situated in either the provinces or the chief cities, but they are all similar in that the key note of each is 'familiarity.' When LOCALISM is narrowed to apply to the 'characteristic speech' of a LOCALITY, as compared with the *same* language spoken elsewhere, it relates to, but is not the same as, 'dialect.' For 'dialect' refers to the manner of speech of *all* the people in a LOCALITY, but LOCALISM designates the manner of speech of only a few people in a LOCALITY. Furthermore, LOCALISM properly applies to only a few words while 'dialect' refers to the way a whole language is spoken. For example, 'gloss' for 'glass' (of water) is a phonetic LOCALISM of New England, just as a flat 'a' in 'glass' is a LOCALISM of northern England. Shakespeare may have used the flat 'a' before that usage became a LOCALISM anywhere. And George III probably said 'gloss' for 'glass,' like the modern Bostonian, unaware or contemptuous of any existing LOCALISMS. Only just enough people pronounce 'glass' in this way for it to be a New England LOCALISM. On the other hand, 'dialect' words pass naturally and unquestioned everywhere within a district or class.

Malapropism Mrs. Malaprop was a contemporary of Mrs. Grundy. Mrs. Malaprop (from the French *mal à propos*, 'unproperly') is a famous character in *The Rivals* (1775), a noted play by Richard Brinsley Sheridan. Mrs. Grundy is a character in *Speed the Plough* (1798), by Thomas Morton. Mrs. Grundy quickly became famous as the representation of a busybody who passed judgment on all her neighbors and who consequently was feared by some men more than God. In an age in which society put much stock in literary airs, aphorisms, and the latest bon mots of the dramatists and poets, Mrs. Malaprop aped that kind of up-to-date erudition in a futile attempt to appear both stylish and intellectual. But being essentially ignorant, without that native shrewdness we see in Shakespeare's Dogberry, she was given to flowery blunders, like "as headstrong as an allegory on the banks of the Nile." Today she is probably not so well remembered as Mrs. Grundy;

but, as a prototype, she still deserves to be recalled. After all, we still hear MALAPROPISMS on all sides, especially when people become excited.

Matutinal, Prandial, etc. Adjectives ending in Anglo-Saxon 'ly' have enriched our language with special meanings, but they still leave a general void which we have filled up with more broadly descriptive words drawn whole, or almost whole, from our Latin heritage. For example, the 'motherly' in 'a motherly manner' is, of course, broad in its implications, and yet we can not very well speak of 'motherly obligations.' We feel, rather, that 'maternal obligations' is better. For 'maternal' relates to anything at all appertaining to mothers, from hairpins to duties. But 'motherly' connotes personal qualities.

Often, of course, we circumvent this need for non-English-born adjectives by the simple old method of using English nouns as adjectives. If, in describing the countryside, we mention the 'morning mists,' we have no need of going Latin by saying 'matutinal mists.' In fact, there is always something pedantic about classical words used where our own English suffices. Yet during the centuries that preceded our own there was a mighty war in our language between Latinity and nativity, and in general the learned mén, the ones whose minds lived in books, were on the side of Latin. Consequently there attaches even now to Latin words either a suggestion of the pedant or, if the words are familiar ones, a sound of something missing, that something being perhaps homely sentiment.

But sometimes when we have inherited no adjective at all from the Anglo-Saxons we must resort to our abundant continental patrimony. We have 'breakfasts, lunches (and brunches), suppers, dinners' and, of course, 'meals,' all English or early Anglicizations. But we have no English adjectives for any of them. So we are obliged to use the dull Latin 'prandial,' referring to 'any meal.' But perhaps 'prandial' is slightly enlivened (in spite of still more Latin!) by 'post-prandial chats,' meaning confabs over after-dinner coffee.

Metonymy "I was sitting quietly enough in my office when that awful mustache walked in on me." This is an instance of METONYMY, the symbolical use of a part for the whole.

But, technically, this is only a part of METONYMY called 'synecdoche,' which may include the use of the whole for a part ('the weather [for rain] prevented me from . . .'), the container for the thing contained ('forty skins' for 'forty cattle'), or vice versa. But nowadays we usually ignore 'synecdoche,' and include it in METONYMY, synecdochically using the whole term for the part. Actually, METONYMY is any use of an associated or suggested word for the literal word, like "The pen (meaning writing) is mightier than the sword (meaning force and war)." "She has a cold nature," is an example of METONYMY because coldness is not properly an attribute of people. In an expression like "That bit of bad luck was the ruination of us all," the 'bit of bad luck' was really the cause of our ruination and not the effect itself. But here, in this last example, you can easily see that METONYMY is also metaphorical. See METAPHOR.

Philological Terms   Even as an amateur you can't explore philology, the study of words, without encountering or needing special terms. The following few are offered just in case:

APHESIS: Loss of an unaccented first syllable, like 'squire' for 'esquire,' 'sport' for 'disport.'

ASSIMILATION: Just as words color each other's meanings when they are brought together in a sentence, so their component sounds, or even letters, influence each other. The 'd' in Hudson, as a surname, tends to become 't' before the 's'; frequently, therefore, the name becomes Hutson. The term for such changes is ASSIMILATION. A century ago one of the brothers Grimm, of fairy story fame, discovered a distinct pattern of consonantal changes in the historical development of European languages, occurring throughout medieval times. The pattern has been named Grimm's Law. Similar apparently systematic vowel changes occurred in early English.

DISSIMILATION: Practically, a faddish tendency to dissemble the familiar or to avoid its repetition. It chiefly affects the letters 'l,' 'n,' and 'r.' Thus, in surnames, Ranson, the son of Randolph, becomes Ransom; little Paul becomes Pollott (the 'ott' is a diminutive); Timothy somehow becomes Timbs, and Sevenoaks, Snooks. Many high names in society appear to have suffered this process deliberately.

DOUBLET: Ordinarily, a DOUBLET is just a pair or one of a pair. But in philology it is any of several words that have arrived at approximately the same meaning from the same source, but by different courses. 'Abridge' and 'abbreviate' are good examples; both stem from Latin *brevis* 'short.' When you 'abridge' a writing you 'shorten' it by leaving parts of it out, which is exactly what you do when you abbreviate 'company' to 'co.' But when the nucleus divided itself long ago, the two halves entered different channels of conversation and they are today different sizes. An 'abridgement' today suggests the use of bridges to quicken progress; there is no such suggestion in 'abbreviation.' 'Abridgement' also means an apparent shortening of time itself. 'Abbreviations' don't bother with such fanciful suggestions. DOUBLETS thus sometimes deviate in content; they say the same thing but each in its own way.

EPENTHESIS: Intrusion of a sound for purposes of euphony, as the 'i' in Canadian.

EPITHESIS: Very common in surnames but not unusual in other kinds of words. EPITHESIS is the addition of a rear consonant as, in baby talk, kitten may become kitting. The 'd' and 'b' are EPITHETIC in the surnames Neild and Plumb.

EXCRESCENCE: The 't' in the surname Derwent, once probably 'Darwin,' is EXCRESCENT. So also is the 'i' in Canadian and, in a broader sense, all the silent letters, like the 't' in French *mot* and the 'p' in raspberry.

FUNCTIONAL CHANGE: This refers to the use of a word as one part of speech when it is customarily or was first used as another. "Give me your hand," compared with "Hand me that hand glass." In the first example, 'hand' is a noun; in the second, it is used as a verb and as an adjective.

METATHESIS: The whimsical but factual interchanging of sounds within a word, as when the middle English *kers* became our modern 'cress.' In surnames, incidentally, Cripps is METATHETIC. It was once Crisp.

PRIVATIVE: PRIVATIVE refers to more than simple loss or negation. A PRIVATION is the actual absence of some substantial thing.

A PRIVATIVE prefix, as the 'in' in 'inglorious,' renders a positive word negative. So does the PRIVATIVE suffix 'less' in 'homeless.' These are negative affixes, but the dictionaries don't always call them that because PRIVATIVES are more than negatives even in grammar. Also, they are not the same as antonyms or opposites. They are a special kind of antonym. A PRIVATIVE adjective indicates the absence of something ordinarily possessed or present; 'blind' is an example since we inherently possess 'sight.' As a noun, PRIVATIVE is something, such as 'darkness,' which could not exist except in the absence of something else. 'Aftermaths' are not PRIVATIVE, because they are not essentially absences, but something new, a result. But the abolition of Christmas would most positively fill us with PRIVATIVE gloom, for it would truly be the absence of an accustomed spiritual light.

Phraseology and **Rhetoric** These two come from Greek words: PHRASEOLOGY from *phrasis*, a 'speech,' and RHETORIC from *rhetor*, 'orator.' PHRASEOLOGY is more than 'syntax,' which is the orderly and intelligible arrangement of words. PHRASEOLOGY is 'syntax' plus 'art' and 'RHETORIC.' It is, you might say, the art of expression with words. RHETORIC is primarily the power 'to please' or 'to persuade.' It achieves this power usually by an appeal to 'reason' and 'logic.' Sometimes we speak contemptuously of speeches as mere RHETORIC, that is, flowery, oratorical, or perhaps declamatory. This means that, in too enthusiastic an effort 'to persuade' or 'to please,' 'reason' and 'logic' have been forgotten.

But these two words are interesting in their relation to styles of expression—PHRASEOLOGY, especially, since it is a question of a choice of words. When you form a phrase, such as 'encircling the world like a twofold rainbow,' you must choose words that smoothly express the idea within the narrow compass of a few words. You must therefore choose words that exactly convey your idea because in language an idea is more beautiful than simply the pretty sound of a word. For example, in the phrase cited, the word 'circle' conveys the main idea; its verbal adjective, 'circling,' reinforced by the directive prefix, provides the exact motion necessary to complete the image of a rainbow.

The formation of individual words has usually been a long and complicated process. 'Fustian,' for example, which we commonly use as meaning 'bombast or bombastic,' was first an Arabian name for a 'suburb' of Cairo. But coarse cloth was made there, and in time almost any cheap cloth was called 'fustian.' Corduroy and velveteen cloths, with some sheen and some pretentiousness, were particularly called 'fustian.' So the meanings crept forward figuratively on many fronts. 'Fustian' today is not merely 'bombast,' but also 'pompous or pretentious cheapness' as well as 'plain, coarse cheapness,' in diction. Yet sometimes whole phrases may have been improvised in an instant on someone's lips, and have stuck as securely in our language as the common words listed in dictionaries. Other phrases were thoughtfully constructed by writers, and have proved equally permanent and indispensable. Both colloquial and literary phrases have to some extent been compiled into reference books, but the vast body of them is floating loose, as it were, in our daily talk and writing. Collectively they constitute the so-called 'idiom' of our language. They illustrate infinitely the ways we string words together, often in defiance of literal or individual meanings. They are our PHRASEOLOGY, and they reflect our RHETORIC. See IDIOM and VERNACULAR; LINGUISTICS, PHILOLOGY, etc.

LAW

See also Rule; Government; and Politics

ACT *n.* a law; statute.

Attestation see **Imprecation & Attestation**

ATTORNEY *n.* a lawyer; anyone legally qualified to act for another person.

BAR *n.* the legal profession; the court of law itself.

BENCH *n.* the bench on which a judge sits; hence a court of law.

BYLAW or BYELAW *n.* a law made by a locality or organization for regulation of local or organizational affairs.

CANON *n.* ecclesiastical law or laws.

Chancellor see **Justice, Equity, etc.**

Chancery see **Justice, Equity, etc.**

CODIFICATION *n.* a reduction of all laws into one system, more or less harmonious.

COMMON LAW *n.* the English system of law, as distinct from Roman law; also unwritten or uncodified law.

CONSTITUTIONAL *adj.* of or pertaining to a constitution; hence, in accordance with a constitution.

COUNSELOR *n.* a lawyer.

COURT *n.* any assembly where justice is rendered according to law.

CRIMINAL *adj.* against the law; pertaining to crime. *n.* CRIME an offense against the law.

DECREE *n.* a declaration of a rule or law made by the proper authorities or by anyone in power; a judicial decision. *v.* to enact or promulgate a law.

EDICT *n.* a decree issued by a king or a person possessing supreme power; hence, a command.

Exculpate

FELONY *n.* a crime, usually of a serious nature and more serious than a misdemeanor.

FIAT *n.* a decree or command; an authoritative sanction or consent.

Fiduciary

GRAND JURY *n.* a jury, usually of more than twelve persons, assembled to decide whether or not there is sufficient evidence to bring an accusation into court.

HEARING *n.* a court proceeding; a trial.

HIS HONOR *n.* the judge.

ILLEGAL *adj.* against the law, as an ILLEGAL act.

ILLICIT *adj.* illegal.

Imprecation & Attestation

INFRACTION *n.* a breaking of the law or rules.

JUDGE *n.* the presiding officer in a court of law.

JUDICIARY *adj.* pertaining to court judgments.

Jurist

JUROR *n.* a member of a jury.

JURY *n.* a group of persons who are assembled to hear and render an opinion on whatever material is submitted to them; thus, in law, a JURY is required to render a verdict on evidence concerning a crime or a suit.

JURYMAN *n.* a juror.

Just

Justice, Equity, Chancellor & Chancery

LAW *n.* a rule which officially regulates the conduct of persons living in an organized society; hence any regulation issued by an official constituted authority or recognized by custom.

LAWFUL *adj.* according to law; legal.

LAWSUIT *n.* the prosecution of a case in a court of law.

LAWYER *n.* the person, learned in the law, who is legally entitled to give counsel concerning the law and to act in a court of law on behalf of others.

LEGALITY *n.* the state of being in conformity to the law. *adj.* LEGAL, according to law; conformable to law.

LEGISLATURE *n.* a body of men established to enact law. *adj.* legislative.

LICIT *adj.* conformable to law; legal; lawful.

Lien

LITIGATION *n.* a proceeding, usually civil, in court.

MAGISTRATE *n.* a judge, usually a minor civil official who administers certain civil laws. *adj.* magisterial.

ORDINANCE *n.* a public regulation; decree.

PANEL *n.* a group of persons, required to attend a court, from whom a jury is selected.

Penal & Punitive

PETTY JURY *n.* the jury which renders the final verdict in a lawsuit, as distinguished from a grand jury.

Pre-empt

PRESCRIPT *n.* a regulation; ordinance.

Punitive see **Penal & Punitive**

REGULATION *n.* a rule designed to enforce a standard of conduct.

RULE *n.* a principle, precept, or command which orders or guides.

SOLICITOR *n.* a person who takes charge of legal business.

STATUTE *n.* a law; ordinance.

STATUTORY *adj.* referring to the nature of statutes; according to statute.

SUBPOENA *n.* an order commanding a person to appear in court.

SUMMONS *n.* a subpoena.

TALESMAN *n.* a member of a panel.

Tenets

Tenor

TRANSGRESSION *n.* a crime; usually a minor offense against the law.

TRIAL *n.* the proceedings in
court when a case is presented
before a judge or jury or both.
TRIBUNAL *n.* a court.

UNCONSTITUTIONAL *n.* not in conformity with a constitution.
VIOLATION *n.* a transgression of
the law.

Exculpate This ugly sounding word means 'to free from blame.'
If you are 'indicted' ('formally accused of a crime'), and 'arraigned,'
('called before a court or judge'), you may be 'acquitted' ('freed or
cleared') and 'exonerated' (literally, 'relieved of the burden of blame').
But these words are legalistic. Plenty of times we may wish to speak
formally of a freeing from blame when no connection with the law
exists. EXCULPATION is not too learned a word to use in a personal letter.

Fiduciary FIDUCIARY comes from the Latin for 'faith.' It means 'confidential,' in the sense of 'trustworthy,' and is used almost exclusively
in connection with legal trusts in the hands of trust officers.

Imprecation and **Attestation** IMPRECATION is a word for 'swearing'
in the sense of downright cursing. Evolving from the simple word
'pray' it avoids the implications of obscenity. An IMPRECATOR need
not be a foul-mouthed reviler. He prays evil upon his enemy. Swearing,
of course, depends for its connotations on the prepositions that follow
it. The kind of swearing you do *on* a Bible differs radically from the
kind you do *at* an enemy. And the swearing you do *to* a fact is ATTESTA-
TION. But strictly speaking a TESTATOR (or the feminine, 'testatrix') is
one who makes a will. A person who has made a will dies 'testate.'
Otherwise he dies 'intestate.'

Jurist A JURIST is not a judge or a juror or even a lawyer exactly.
He is an authority on law and its principles, especially one who expounds them.

Just No one will deny that this is a very important word. All we
have to remember is the power and dignity of the Nine Old Men
ceremonially robed. Yet no one will deny, either, that sometimes it is
JUST a little word. At these times it means 'merely, simply, only.' And
in this difference lies a tale.

JUST goes back beyond the ancient Mediterranean tongues, whether
Latin or Greek, to the Sanskrit of India. There its root was JUST two
letters, *ya*, meaning 'join, bind.' From the 'joining' of things came the
'fitness' of things, and their 'rightness.' From that came a 'fairness to
all,' what we call JUSTICE, or JUSTNESS, from the Latin *jus*, meaning

either 'law' or 'right.' The JUST man today is either 'upright in character' or 'fair minded.' And from that human quality came the more impersonal idea of 'reasonableness,' like in a JUST (that is, a logically nice and equable) opinion. Yet these ethical ideas are not behind such expressions as, "I was just thinking that . . . ," "He just caught the bus," "He was just on time," "He is feeling just dandy." The reason probably is, that the mere idea of 'fitness' has colloquially merged into 'approximation,' into 'exactness' and hence even into 'completeness.' Thus the sentences read, "I was thinking only a moment ago . . . ," "He barely caught the bus," or "He caught the bus only a moment ago," "He was exactly on time," and "He is feeling completely dandy."

But this is not the whole story. Even among the Romans the sense of JUSTNESS was erratic. The old Sanskrit root had given the Romans not only JUSTICE but also their plainer word for 'to join,' *jungere*. The base of this verb then gave them their adverb *juxta*, meaning 'close to, nearby, against.' That in turn produced in the late, loose Latin a verb *juxtare*, meaning to 'approach,' especially belligerently. Upon this word, appropriate for a special purpose, the Old French seized. Thus they obtained their word *jouter*, 'to joust,' for a tilting of arms 'against' (*juxta*) an adversary. But the English turned *jouter* back again into JUST, and so our surnamed Justers are the true English 'jousters.' And when we speak of something's being 'just against (touching) the wall,' or 'just behind the counter,' or even 'just even,' who knows whether we are thinking, etymologically, more of 'fitness' or of 'fighting'?

Justice, Equity, Chancellor and Chancery Basically, JUSTICE is moral law in action. The base is Latin *jus*, 'law.' The French built the word from the adjective of *jus*, which was *justus*, meaning 'just.' 'Judge' came from the same base, via *judex* (*jus* plus *dico*, 'to speak'). But if you have a just cause and your neighbor has a just cause neither is a criminal before the law, though a mutual grievance may exist. JUSTICE condemns neither, but the principles of JUSTICE must still be applied to the dispute. EQUITY means 'equal JUSTICE'—JUSTICE as a fair arbiter. The courts of EQUITY, meaning of 'equality,' take care of cases like the one above where collateral law must reconcile the differences. They are called courts of CHANCERY, and the judges that preside over them are CHANCELLORS. In early Europe the CHANCELLORS were only ushers or glorified clerks of a law court. The Roman emperors instituted them. Later they were given judicial powers and became in time exalted, with authoritative jurisdiction over the form and style of official writing in the courts and governments of kings. So they became the keepers of the Great Seal. Prelates followed the suit of kings, and also had their CHANCELLORS. In the field of learning there are CHANCELLORS—some today are mere teachers' aides and others are heads of universities.

Lien This is French for a 'band.' In English it means figuratively but practically a legal claim on property as potential indemnity against a risk.

Penal and Punitive The Latin word for punishment is *poena*, which came from the Greek for a 'penalty.' The middle vowel became 'u' in the verb. The meanings of PENAL and PUNITIVE derive from the same source, but the different applications of the words have given them different emphasis. PENAL, softened in France, is now the abjecter word, referring to 'legal punishment.' PUNITIVE suggests a 'punishing' blow in the boxing ring, with much 'vindictiveness.' It connotes 'revenge.'

Pre-empt Means literally a 'pre-buying'; legally, to secure the right of preference in the purchase of public land. But in the course of human events, 'buying,' then 'appropriating' and finally 'occupying' are often within a few steps of each other. PRE-EMPT has become especially useful since we have no other word for 'pre-occupy' in just the active sense which PRE-EMPT, by customary application, has achieved. The professor might be pre-occupied with his mathematical problems, and the problems might pre-possess his mind, claiming priority. But the predominant sense in 'pre-occupy' or 'pre-possess' is of *present* possession rather than of *prior* intent to possess. When the thought involves 'premeditation' and 'scheming,' PRE-EMPT is the apposite word.

Tenets "These things we hold to be true—." TENETS are the things we hold to be true (*teneo*, 'I hold'), whether they are articles of faith in a creed, planks in a political platform or the propositions of an accepted doctrine. 'Doctrines' are things taught and presumably believed.

Tenor Forgetting the high voice, TENOR is the general course or purport of anything, as the TENOR of our communal life is reflected in our folklore. As a legal term it is clearly defined as the 'substance and effect' of a law.

LIGHT

BEAM *n.* a ray of light; concentrated light.

BLARE *n.* dazzling brilliance.

BLAZE *v.* to burn or shine with a bright or dazzling light.

Bleak

BRIGHT *adj.* pertaining to intense or concentrated color or light; brilliant.

BRILLIANT *adj.* sparkling; shining; reflecting a great deal of light or color.

CLEAR *adj.* not dark; bright; transparent.

Crepuscular

DARK *adj.* without light; hard to perceive; dim.

Diaphanous

DIM *adj.* dark; with little light; faintly lit.

DUSK *n.* that part of the day, just after sunset, before night falls. *adj.* DUSKY, dim; without much light; partly dark; gloomy.

EFFULGENT *adj.* brilliant; blazing.

FLASH *v.* to shine or blaze forth suddenly and shortly.

GLARE *n.* a bright light that hurts the eyes.

GLEAM *v.* to shine; reflect light.

GLINT *v.* to sparkle; to flash; to reflect light momentarily, as "The dime glinted from the sidewalk when I passed."

GLOOMY *adj.* dark; dim.

GLOW *n.* a soft light; haze. *v.* to shine forth with a soft light.

Iridescent & Opalescent

LAMBENT *adj.* softly shining; luminous.

Lighted & Lit

LIMPID *adj.* clear; transparent.

Lit see **Lighted & Lit**

Lucent see **Lucid & Lucent**

LUCERNAL *adj.* refers to artificial light.

Lucid & Lucent

LUMINOUS *adj.* glowing; showing a soft light.

LUSTER *n.* the glow or shine from reflected light. *adj.* LUSTROUS

MURKY *adj.* dark; dim; foggy.

Obfuscate

OBSCURE *adj.* dim; hidden by the dark, as an OBSCURE figure.

Opalescent see **Iridescent & Opalescent**

OPAQUE *adj.* dark; not to be seen through, as a wall is OPAQUE.

Pallid

PELLUCID *adj.* transparent, like the PELLUCID waters of a mountain stream.

PHOTIC *adj.* refers to light.

RADIANT *adj.* brightly shining.

RAY *n.* a beam.

Refulgent

SHADE *n.* dusk caused when light is interrupted, as "The shade in the room was the result of bamboo blinds drawn over all the windows."

SHINE   *n.* a gleam or glint. *v.* to glow; to reflect light.

SPARKLE   *v.* to shine forth brilliantly or brightly.

Translucent   see **Transparent & Translucent**

Transparent & Translucent

Bleak   BLEAK means 'exposed to wind and weather'; 'windswept and desolate'; hence, by extension, 'dismal and depressing'; as a BLEAK prospect. It is surprising to learn that a word with such gloomy connotations originally meant 'bright, shining,' and that it is directly related to the verb 'bleach.'

Crepuscular   This long word refers to 'twilight,' that time just before (or just after) dark.

Diaphanous   You can see through something 'transparent,' and light can pass through something 'translucent.' For example, window glass is 'transparent,' and ground glass is 'translucent.' Both are possible with something DIAPHANOUS. Anything made fine or delicate enough to see through or to let light through is DIAPHANOUS. The word sounds light and airy. It is most commonly used to describe silks, clouds, and even non-material things, like manners and excuses.

It is a fine, poetic word. "Behold the daybreak! The little light fades the immense and diaphanous shadows."—Walt Whitman.

Iridescent and **Opalescent**   IRIDESCENT refers to all the colors of the rainbow, but it is used loosely to mean 'softly and richly vari-colored.' It is therefore confused sometimes with OPALESCENT, which describes an opal's especial IRIDESCENCE, in which there is a delicate play of pearly colors.

Lighted and **Lit**   He LIT the fire, or he LIGHTED it. It doesn't matter which. Likewise, the fire was LIGHTED, or it was LIT. LIT and LIGHTED serve equally for the past participle, as they do for the past tense. Nevertheless, customary usage does sometimes make a choice, especially when the forms are used as adjectives: "Bring me that lighted candle," he said, probably without the slightest temptation of saying, "Bring me that lit candle." But note the poet Browning's words: "The sin I impute to each frustrate ghost, is the ungirt loin and the unlit lamp." UNLIT has a little length, but LIT has less than little. LIT is sometimes just too picayune a word to prefer.

These more or less cryptic remarks apply also to the other meaning of LIGHTED and LIT. Having LIT, you have LIGHTED; or having LIGHTED, you have LIT. A spark LIT on your dress; a bird LIGHTED on a bough. You can use two syllables or one, just as your ear prefers.

Lucid and **Lucent**   LUCID means 'bright and clear.' A pane of glass may be LUCID, but custom reserves the word for inanimate things that are moving or capable of motion like a sparkling stream or a sheet of clear water. A tumbling green sea is not LUCID but a still clear pool in the moonlight invariably is. Figuratively, a man can be LUCID in his character; but more often we use the word to refer to his mind, thought or speech. In this respect LUCID has lost its connotations of 'light,' and has become suggestive of 'sanity.' The LUCID pool is clear to our eyes, but only faintly on its own part is it radiant. If the moonlight makes it 'brilliant' or 'radiant,' we can better use a variant of LUCID, with identical parentage, namely LUCENT.

Obfuscate   Literally OBFUSCATE means 'to darken, becloud.' But now we use the word to indicate a mind 'confused' or 'bewildered' by a dim or blurred vision. OBFUSCATION results from 'obscuration.' When an issue is obscured people are automatically OBFUSCATED, confused. They are obliged to grope their way to a clear understanding. The word applies properly only to persons: you are OBFUSCATED, your meaning is obscured.

Pallid   PALLID is the adjective for 'pallor,' which is a pale or wan appearance. PALLID emphasizes the actual 'sadness' or 'weakness' of something rather than its faint color. Pastel colors are pale but they aren't PALLID because they still have an actual definite color. But a PALLID moon refers to more than dim moonlight: it suggests that the moon is kind of sick and ghastly.

Refulgent   This is a popular word with sportswriters. Anything that is 'brilliant' in sports, such as a star performer or a scintillating play, is REFULGENT. While the word means 'to shine back,' it is not a brilliant sounding word in itself. A star receiving the plaudits of the fans is REFULGENT, he shines with splendor. But his actual feats were not so much REFULGENT as 'dazzling.'

Transparent and **Translucent**   TRANSPARENT means 'see through,' and TRANSLUCENT means 'shine through.' The air is TRANSPARENT, but a thinnish cloud is TRANSLUCENT.

LITERARY TERMS

See also Language; Grammar; the Written Word

ACADEMIC *adj.* pertaining to the university; thus, sometimes, not practical or down-to-earth but rather theoretical or speculative.

AMBIGUITY *n.* state of doubtfulness or vagueness, esp. in ideas, theories, writing or speeches. Often AMBIGUITY implies a conflict between two ideas or theories. "His speech was full of ambiguity: I don't know whether he finally said 'Yes' or 'No' to my proposal." *adj.* AMBIGUOUS.

Ana

Analogy see **Metaphor, Simile,** etc.

Assonance

Attitude see **Posture & Attitude**

Attribute

BARDIC *adj.* pertaining to poetry or to the poet (bard).

BOMBAST *n.* language full of hot air, extravagant words and exaggerated ideas.

Burlesque see **Travesty, Parody,** etc.

Caricature see **Travesty, Parody,** etc.

CHAPTERAL *adj.* pertaining to chapter, as of a book.

CLASSIC *adj.* pertaining to the classical periods of culture; thus, first of class or first rank; accepted by most people as very superior, applied esp. to the arts.

CLIMAX *n.* the highest point; the most important idea; the most intense emotion, as in writing and music. *adj.* CLIMACTERIC.

Concise see **Succinct, Terse,** etc.

Connote & Denote

CONSTRUE *v.* to interpret; translate.

Context

DECLAMATORY *adj.* pertaining to bombast, esp. in speeches. It suggests a kind of oratory where the manner of delivery has more force than sense.

Denote see **Connote & Denote**

DIALECTIC *adj.* pertaining to the art of discussion or reasoning. It also means controversial.

DIDACTIC *adj.* pertaining to teaching, or to instructive explanation. Usually it is used in an unfavorable sense of dogmatism or overbearing authority. "His didactic speech insulted his intelligent audience."

Edit & Redact

ELEGIAC *adj.* pertaining to sad meditation, as in an ELEGY.

ELLIPTICAL *adj.* ambiguous, esp. in the sense of something having been left out or of the main subject never having been discussed.

EPITHET *n.* a term, often an adjective, applied to a person or thing as part of its name, like STONEWALL Jackson. *adj.* EPITHETIC or EPITHETICAL.

ERISTIC *adj.* pertaining to disputations.

Euphemism see Euphony, Euphemism, etc.

Euphony, Euphemism & Euphuism

Euphuism see Euphony, Euphemism, etc.

Expository

Farce see Travesty, Parody, etc.

FIGURE *n.* a metaphor.

FORENSIC *adj.* pertaining to argument.

GLOSS *v.* to make a false or superficial explanation of something. (Frequently followed by 'over.')

GRAPHIC *adj.* pertaining to writing or illustrating. Hence, in a general sense it means vividly descriptive.

HERMENEUTIC *adj.* pertaining to interpretation, esp. of the Scriptures.

Hyperbole

IMAGERY *n.* the imaginary pictures any kind of writing brings to mind. *adj.* IMAGINAL.

Incidence

Infer & Imply

Imply see Infer & Imply

IRONY *n.* a kind of sarcasm or humor in which the real meaning is exactly opposite to the meaning expressed literally.

LABORED *adj.* refers to an artistic style that seems much worked over; thus, unnatural; unspontaneous.

LEXICONICAL *adj.* pertaining to dictionary.

Logomachy

LUCIDITY *n.* the clearness and comprehensibility of something. *adj.* LUCID.

Metaphor, Simile & Analogy

MODERN *adj.* up-to-date; current, as MODERN writing.

NEBULOUS *adj.* cloudy; vague; not lucid; not easily understandable.

OBSCURITY *n.* confusion or lack of clarity as in art or writing; the opposite of lucidity. *adj.* OBSCURE.

ODIC *adj.* pertaining to ODE.

Onamatopoeia

PANEGYRICAL *adj.* refers to the singing of praises.

Parody see Travesty, Parody, etc.

Periphrasis

PERSPICUITY *n.* a penetrating intelligence or eye; thus, the state of seeing clearly and deeply into things, as the PERSPICUITY of a good sermon. *adj.* PERSPICACIOUS.

PITHY *adj.* having substance; full of good ideas; expressed concisely.

Plagiarism

Posture & Attitude

Precious see Preciosity & Precious

Precocity

Preciosity & Precious

PREGNANT *adj.* full of meaning or importance, as a PREGNANT idea.

PROLIXITY *n.* verbosity.

PROSAIC *adj.* pertaining to prose.

Redact see **Edit & Redact**

RHETORIC *n.* artful exression, in prose especially.

SATIRE *n.* a kind of writing full of scorn and sarcasm for vice, stupidity, or other undesirable traits.

SENTENTIOUS *adj.* pithy; full of maxims or moral statements; thus, often shallow writing.

Simile see **Metaphor, Simile**, etc.

STANZIC or STANZAIC *adj.* pertaining to STANZA.

Succinct, Terse & Concise

SYMBOL *n.* a figure or image that carries many unexpressible connotations or meanings, as a flag is a SYMBOL of patriotism.

Tautology

Terse see **Succinct, Terse**, etc.

Thrasonical

Travesty, Parody, Burlesque, Caricature & Farce

TRENCHANT *adj.* penetrating; forceful; as a TRENCHANT observation.

TROCHAIC *adj.* pertaining to trochee, a kind of metrical foot in poetry.

TROPE *n.* the use of words or phrases in a figurative way. *adj.* TROPAL or TROPICAL.

TURGIDITY *n.* bombast. *adj.* TURGID.

VALEDICTORY *adj.* refers to a farewell speech. *n.* VALEDICTION.

Verbiage

Verbose

Verse

Ana 'Literary notes or a miscellany.' It is also used as a suffix, for example Lincolniana, where it signifies 'personal things,' usually literary, like letters, clippings, notes, speeches, anecdotes, etc. Sometimes it is preceded by an 'i' to assist the tongue, as in the example.

Assonance 'Sounding alike.' If you are not listening closely the words 'main,' 'came' and 'rave,' or 'roam' and 'rove,' or 'fool' and 'full' may all sound nearly alike. The medial vowel sounds do the trick. If medial vowels are alike and are stressed in longer words, the words may be ASSONANT, especially if the consonants resemble each other.

The examples given are not true English rimes because the vowel-sounds and the consonant-sounds are not identical. If two words begin with different consonant-sounds and all subsequent vowel-sounds and consonant-sounds are similar, then you have a true rime. For example, 'sand' and 'land' rime. ASSONANCE and rime depend on sound, not spelling. Consequently, 'so' and 'though' are true rimes.

In verse ASSONANCE has played a leading role. It was the basis of Romance poetry, especially Provençal poetry, and still characterizes the lighter verse of the Italians and Spanish, where the sound plays around the concluding vowels of the lines, whether stressed or unstressed.

ASSONANCE occurs if the last stressed vowel and any ensuing vowels are alike, though the consonants may be 'dissonant.' Sometimes the reverse relationship is considered ASSONANT, the consonants agreeing, as in 'mad' and 'maid.' Philologically, ASSONANCE depends usually on the use of the *same* vowel in different words. The word itself means, roughly, 'of similar or converging sound,' from 'to' (represented by the prefix 'as') plus 'sound.' Thus it can indicate 'transliteration.' The English versions of Polish or Chinese names are approximations of those names in their original languages, which use sounds and symbols not existing in English. But these transliterations are ASSONANT if the sounds are similar.

ASSONANCE is not confined to words. ASSONANCES may be harmonizations of color, taste or suggestion. For example, the pictures on your wall may be ASSONANT with each other, or with the whole room.

Attribute   An ATTRIBUTE is a 'characteristic or distinguishing mark, a symbol.' For example, in great art there are certain themes which are ATTRIBUTES of an epoch's prevailing philosophy.

This noun comes from a very plain verb meaning, originally, 'to allot to.' If you ATTRIBUTE your rheumatism to rain, you 'assign, or allot,' to the weather your pain. An ancient work of art ATTRIBUTED to Phidias means that this ancient sculptor is supposed to be its creator. An adjective ATTRIBUTES qualities to a noun, so it is called an ATTRIBUTE. A word used ATTRIBUTIVELY is simply a word used as an adjective, or its equivalent.

But not only adjectives are ATTRIBUTIVE. Curses, for example, ATTRIBUTE all the worst things to the offender. Even the Romans used the verb in this sweeping way. They had it mean 'to grant, to pay, to bestow, or to assign.' An ATTRIBUTE is clearly a trait, a quality or merit (with no questions asked as to how it came into your possession), an ascribed distinction, a capability, an assigned function, an earmark.

This is one of those tricky words whose pronunciation changes with its use. As a noun the accent falls on the first syllable: 'AT-tribute.' But as a verb it shifts to the middle syllable: 'at-TRIB-ute.' Also, it is 'at-TRIB-utive.'

Connote and **Denote**   A statement DENOTES your meaning just as a pointing finger designates an object that you can see wholly and clearly. A suggestive word, like 'glamorous' or 'valorous,' CONNOTES thoughts, feelings and other extra meanings associated with the object or quality it DENOTES. The 'con' means 'with.' All the extras come along 'with' the word's meaning. CONNOTATIONS are perhaps half of any language.

Context Primarily a literary term referring to the developing content in writing, its imagery, its facts, its story, its thought. A passage quoted out of its CONTEXT may make sense, but it will never make the same sense as it does in CONTEXT.

The complexity conveyed by the word comes, of course, from its derivation. In the beginning it meant a 'weaving together,' a close combining of all the threads of a fabric, from Latin *con*, 'together,' plus *texere*, 'to weave.'

Edit and **Redact** When a manuscript or typescript is EDITED it is prepared for publication. To EDIT means to make an author's writing readable in every way. It involves the correction of bad grammar and faulty logic.

REDACTION is more drastic. REDACT comes from the Latin *agere*, 'to drive,' and is the complete shaping and kneading of copy before it goes to press. It includes all necessary editorial improvements with an eye to expense. Sometimes, being inclusive. REDACTION is a titular term for a publisher's entire editorial staff. REDACTED copy is also called a REDACTION.

Euphony, Euphemism, and **Euphuism** EUPHONY is 'harmony of sound.' But in the adjective EUPHONIOUS, the meaning is 'melodious.' A one syllable word like 'bell' can be called EUPHONIOUS because it is so sweet sounding. But from a strict point of view, 'bell' is not an example of EUPHONY since there is nothing for it to be 'in harmony with' but, perhaps, itself or our ears. As in all three of these words, the element 'eu' means 'well,' in Greek. The second element in EUPHONY is, of course, the one we recognize in 'phonetics, 'phone, phonograph,' etc. Smooth diction is EUPHONIOUS, because it sounds 'well.' It has been said that the most EUPHONIOUS word in English is 'hush.' But every lover of words has his favorites.

EUPHEMISM is the saying of things in a 'softly disguised and indirect way.' We learned very early to shun what we dislike or what hurts us. As the Irishman expresses it, if we only knew where we are going to die, "We'd niver go near the place." EUPHEMISM probably stems chiefly from this feeling. In part it may originally have indicated a tactful regard for the feelings of others. In part it may represent artistry, because art is often a kind of escape from harsh reality by making things beautiful. But more basically EUPHEMISM is probably a result of dislikes. The caveman who carelessly dropped a rock on his big toe probably did not want to mention rocks for a while. There are countless such reasons why early people wanted to substitute a soft word for a blunt, unpleasant word. The 'dead' became merely the 'departed,' and 'death' itself was only, vaguely, 'a passing away.' Some primitive tribes even today will never utter aloud the names of their gods. The ancient Hebrews did not allow themselves to think even of the real name of the Deity, and so they had many substitute names, such as Jahveh or Yahue, whence our Jehovah. Some primitive people will not even speak their own names, because they believe their real names are part of themselves, like their blood, and if their names are spoken, they believe evil spirits will get hold of their names and cast bad spells on them. So they use nicknames, which are EUPHEMISMS. You might amuse yourself by writing down all the EUPHEMISMS you can think of for the word 'money.' For some reason, most people think money is offensive, so there are hundreds of ways to refer to it in a pleasantly indirect way.

A Mrs. Malaprop (see MALAPROPISM) will inevitably confuse EU-PHEMISM with EUPHUISM, though the definitions are very different. Both words pivot around the same 'well' that characterizes EUPHONY, but the ensuing elements of the two words differ radically. The 'phem' in EUPHEMISM remains equivalent to the 'phon' in EUPHONY—'speak,' instead of 'sound,' and so 'well-spoken' instead of 'well-sounding.' But the 'phu' is far broader and vaguer. It is almost solely the product of an eccentric writer of Shakespeare's day, John Lyly, who, besides some sprightly and graceful comedies, wrote two books about an ideal man modelled on the perfect man of classical Greece. The Greek's name is Euphues, meaning 'well-grown.' He was the perfect man grown above the common man. Though this Euphues was an intellectual marvel, it seems his forte was urbanity. He was a paragon of verbal manners, of cultural phrases and flowery compliments. The courtiers of the Elizabethan court took Euphues as their model. Queen Elizabeth herself doted on him. The court adopted the flowery language, which it called the new English. But it didn't last very long, for it abounded in fantastic similes involving fabulous animals that Lyly had adopted from the medieval imagination. But these fancies softened the still rather harsh English. It is not unlikely that this rage for decoration in literary style left its mark on Shakespeare, who still knew how in his better plays, to redeem it from grotesque excess. EUPHUISM now means 'preciosity' in writing, and an affected, flashy manner in talking. See PRECIOSITY and PRECIOUS.

Expository 'Explanatory,' in the sense of 'showing or exposing the meaning.' "The person who writes a simple but accurate exposition of Einstein's theory of relativity has done a difficult job indeed."

Hyperbole Not to be confused with a 'hyperbola,' a 'geometrical curve.' For HYPERBOLE is not mathematical but poetical. It is an extravagant expression, an exaggerated statement. The word has come commonly to mean 'overpraise,' usually 'flowery overpraise.' HYPERBOLE usually abounds in sweeping statements and fulsome, rather than subtle, praise or exaggeration.

Incidence A technical word frequently borrowed from the sciences for common or literary purposes, like 'technique' in the 'technique of a prize fighter.' INCIDENCE literally means a 'falling upon.' Compare with an 'incident,' something that 'befalls us.' Narrowed, INCIDENCE means the 'direction' of the falling, like the angle of INCIDENCE of a sunbeam on the floor. It may suggest the act of falling or even striking. The INCIDENCE of a popular idea is broad in scope; it strikes upon many minds. The INCIDENCE of an advertisement is roughly the measure of its effectiveness. "The incidence of childhood disease has dropped markedly in civilized countries."

Infer and **Imply** I IMPLY something when I speak, and you INFER from my remarks what I have IMPLIED. In writing, of course, the point of view is sometimes lost sight of because a passage stands, in a sense, independently of both reader and author. Thus an author's IMPLICATION is in a passage, and so is the INFERENCE that the reader gets out of it. INFERENCE and IMPLICATION then become alike.

Logomachy LOGOMACHY is a 'bickering over words,' as purists, academicians, legalists or pettifogging negotiators in general might bicker. LOGOMACHY also refers to any word-constructing game, like anagrams. In Greek the word means 'to fight over the wording.' The adjective, 'logomachic,' could be useful.

Metaphor, Simile and **Analogy** Grammatically, a METAPHOR is a figure of speech which implies 'indirectly' some fact of resemblance. "That child is a little hog at the table," is an example of METAPHOR. A SIMILE is a 'direct' statement of resemblance. "The child eats like a hog," is an example of SIMILE. Most SIMILES are introduced by 'like' and 'as.'

You may think, "Surely the metaphor is the stronger of the two expressions because it is worse to *be* a hog than to be *like* one. And doesn't the definition say the metaphor only *implies* the resemblance?" But the point is, the METAPHOR doesn't directly allude to the resemblance at all. When you say, "A child is a little hog at the table," you know immediately he isn't literally a hog. Your imagination must be at work to see in what way the child is being piggish. The exact point of resemblance is not stated. But in, "The child eats like a hog," you know by a direct statement in what respect a resemblance to a pig exists.

SIMILES, also figures of speech, are famous for their extravagant imagery. They are poetic comparisons, not literal ones. "Tom is like his brother Ned," is not a SIMILE. A SIMILE compares two different kinds of things. And if SIMILES fall short of METAPHORS in amazing effects, it is only because they must keep one foot on the ground, by always reminding us with a 'like' or an 'as' that only a resemblance is involved. "My love is like a red, red rose," is perhaps as famous and as beautiful a SIMILE as one could find in poetry.

ANALOGIES have only one thing in common with SIMILES and META-PHORS, that they also appertain to 'resemblances.' But they are not figures of speech. They are the 'resemblances and relations themselves.' An ANALOGY refers to the relation between two things, but a SIMILE or METAPHOR suggests a comparison of things. The comparison may exist only to help explain or describe something: "A child eats like a hog," helps describe the child's deplorable manners. But in "There is an analogy between the eating of a hog and the eating of that child," there is no implication which of the two animals is worse, which is being compared to which, etc. All that the latter example implies is that there is a relation of some kind between the two creatures. The word naturally lends itself to the sciences, where the relationships between things are important but where the value of one thing to another is not so important. For example, "An analogy exists between the motion of the moon around the earth and the motion of the earth around the sun." Here a relationship is pointed out: the relationship is a similarity in the motion of the moon around the earth to the motion of the earth around the sun. But there is no suggestion that one is more grand, more precise, more anything-at-all than the other. There is no comparison involved. But in "The motion of the moon is like the motion of the earth," the suggestion is that the moon's motion takes on some of the vast, cosmological significances of the earth's motion. In philology, for example, ANALOGY explains the 't' in 'egotism': it is there from ANALOGY with 'despotism' and 'nepotism.'

People simply inserted it in one word because it existed in other words, performing a similar function.

METAPHOR and ANALOGY are Greek. The former means literally a 'transference,' having derived from *meta-morphosis* in which the *meta* implies a 'change,' rather like Latin *trans* in our 'trans-Atlantic,' and the rest refers to 'form.' ANALOGY means literally 'according to ratio or proportion.' SIMILE is from Latin *similis,* 'the same (thing).'

Onomatopoeia With millions of vocables (pronounceable syllables) to choose from, we still had to adopt one of the longest words the Greek had, instead of constructing a short one of our own. Yet there may be some wisdom in using such a word in this case. Literally, the word means 'name-making.' Actually, it means using sounds we hear for the names of things that make these sounds. ONOMATOPOEIC words constitute our imitative terminology. No one knows just how many such words there are. 'Buzz, hiss, and boo' are ONOMATOPOEIC, and so was the Danish *hvirre* which gave us 'whir.' And so may have been the Icelandic *skraekja* and *skrija,* both meaning 'shriek,' which gave us both 'screech' and 'shriek.' 'Roar,' even, that came from Anglo-Saxon *rarian,* may have been imitative. On the other hand, 'scream' derives from Icelandic *scraema,* which meant merely 'to scare'; etymologically, the effect preceded the sound. But as so many words, and especially short ones, are clearly imitative, the process itself is worth a word of its own. 'Chirp, bleat, coo, baa, crack, boom, tick, maa, click, and its variant clink, moo, pop, whizz, splash and Bobwhite' are all imitative. Even the word 're-iterate' shows how we value sound as conveying sense. It repeats sound twice as much as 'repeat' does; and the sense of both is 'repetition.'

Periphrasis Notice the 'e' and the first 'i.' For if you would 'paraphrase' ('express in other words') a statement, you would not necessarily PERIPHRASE it ('re-render it in a roundabout way'). PERIPHRASIS is the art of 'circumlocution.'

Plagiarism Literally, from the Greek, a 'kidnapping of other people's ideas,' from the basic idea of 'catching in a net.' It is no wonder, therefore, that the meaning has spread, like a net, to catch many innocent authors, inventors and innovators who had no design, on their part, to take other people's ideas. Ambrose Bierce has remarked, with wry sarcasm, that to PLAGIARIZE is to take the thoughts or style of authors you have never read.

PLAGIARISM is now to steal deliberately, and to use as one's own, the ideas or the writings of another. It is also the actual stolen idea, passage, design, invention, etc.

Posture and **Attitude** POSTURE is a useful word from the French. Its use as the position of one's body is already widespread. Mothers are always saying to their children "Straighten up—your posture is terrible." But this word can be stretched to serve special areas, chiefly artistic, literary and scientific. POSTURE may mean a 'mental ATTITUDE' as well as 'physical position.' You can picture the mind as standing gracefully or at attention, facing this subject or that. Such uses are of course figurative because with the use of the word POSTURE you must picture some definite position or pose which the mind, for example, can only assume figuratively.

The dictionaries will tell you that POSTURE means the 'visible disposition' of the parts of a thing. Thus the meaning is more explicit than in ATTITUDE. An ATTITUDE is only a 'general facing' toward something or someone, with nothing particular about it. In art the ATTITUDE of a painter is not the same as the POSTURE. Several paintings of a carnival scene may all indicate one ATTITUDE toward the occasion, though the arrangements on the canvases may all be of different POSTURES. What we call the composition of a picture is its POSTURE.

Precocity This word derives from Latin *praecox*, meaning 'early-ripe.' An early spring is PRECOCIOUS, and so is a prodigy who enters Harvard in his eleventh year.

Preciosity and **Precious** PRECIOSITY is 'overniceness.' It is fastidiousness in speech or writing for artistic reasons, not for showy or foppish reasons. The purist endued with PRECIOSITY cherishes his words, selecting those of special beauty or meaning which are endeared to him for academic reasons. He is invariably a littérateur or a scholar. But as the fastidious man tends to become foppish, so the man who regards words as PRECIOUS possessions tends to become insipid. His words act a pretty but an empty drama.

Thus arises our word PRECIOUS as it serves in literary criticism. PRECIOUS has other, more common meaning, but its use in literary criticism is exceptionally expressive. Molière made his reputation ridiculing the seventeenth century Parisian women of the salons. They were the *précieuses*, 'the precious ones,' and doted on archaisms and other affectations. The masculine counterpart is *précieux*, from which our PRECIOUS. A PRECIOUS literary style is one where the author, perhaps for sincere reasons, overvalues words and style for their own sake so that the final result is mighty artificial, without dramatic, intellectual, or human content.

Succinct, Terse and Concise SUCCINCT means 'compressed but distinct.' The root is *cingere*, 'to gird,' and the 'suc' was *sub*, 'under.' Like TERSE, it is used almost entirely of language. Basically, SUCCINCT language is tightly cinched.

TERSE remarks are SUCCINCT, but the emphasis now is less on 'extent' and 'compression' than 'polish.' TERSE comes from the Latin for 'rub.' TERSE talk is therefore vigorous. But, like SUCCINCT, TERSE suggests compactness, the absence of flowery phrase. A TERSE remark is a pointed remark.

But if a sentence is cut away to the bare core, to the expression simply of essence, then it is CONCISE. A CONCISE statement lacks details, but a SUCCINCT statement has details, though conveyed in as few words as possible. A TERSE statement may be either, but it is also expressed with vigor and polish. It is pithy.

Tautology A taut literary style is, despite the assonance, free of TAUTOLOGY. 'Taut' means 'terse.' See SUCCINCT, TERSE, and CONCISE. But TAUTOLOGY meant in Greek 'saying the same things,' in other words, 'repetition.' Even if you repeat the same thoughts in different words, you are TAUTOLOGICAL.

Thrasonical Perhaps because it is literary, this word carries fine pointed connotations. Shakespeare used it: "Caesar's thrasonical brag of I *came*, I *saw*, I *overcame*." Its root is in the Greek word *thrasys*, meaning 'bold, spirited,' which includes also the root of our own word 'dare.' But the Roman playwright, Terence, successfully made a mock of its meaning, naming a soldier in one of his comedies Thraso. The soldier was a braggart and swaggerer; he may have been brave but he surely was not seemly. There is a certain effective sarcasm, now, in describing such false or offending heroes, or their acts, with the long euphonious THRASONICAL.

Travesty, Parody, Burlesque, Caricature and Farce These are words that we commonly confuse one with another. Actually, there are differences in their meanings that we should know. Though they are all words that refer to imitation, they can be applied in different ways to different subjects.

TRAVESTIES are essentially 'disguises,' from the Latin *trans*, 'over,' plus *vestire,* 'to clothe.' In literature and drama, serious and elevated works are sometimes 'disguised' with ludicrous or extravagant language, often for comic effect. Suppose, for example, that Hamlet were played by an actor who at every grand and profound soliloquy overemphasized the lines or used ridiculously extravagant language. This man's acting would be a TRAVESTY of how Hamlet should be played. PARODIES are the opposite. In this kind of imitation, the style and form of really serious art is used for a trivial idea. For example, suppose the kind of poetry, the same sort of words, and the general method of delivery that constitutes one of Hamlet's soliloquies is used to convey a silly idea, then you have a PARODY of Shakespeare. A PARODY has more intentional wit and mockery than a TRAVESTY. The pure incompetence of musicians may produce a rendition that is a TRAVESTY of the composer's symphony. But PARODIES do not happen by accident or chance. They are intentional.

A BURLESQUE resembles either a TRAVESTY, a PARODY or both at once. It ridicules the serious and inflates the inane. It is a zanily satirical imitation of life itself. It depends largely on language and pantomime for its effect, which, like a PARODY, is always intentional. A BURLESQUE depends on exaggeration, but sometimes the exaggerations work in a narrowing way. For example, a BURLESQUE of a general giving orders to attack the enemy, might be created by showing a general giving orders to his orderly about how to attack bedbugs. In this example, the BURLESQUE depends on the exaggerated importance given to a small subject. But sometimes a small subject is treated grandly, and that also is a BURLESQUE.

BURLESQUES lead to CARICATURES, which are 'imitations,' usually drawings, but represent a very real art. They are exaggerations, like BURLESQUES, but they are essentially true, not incongruous. They exaggerate salient features of a situation, or perhaps of a person, and are usually funny. For example, a CARICATURE of President Roosevelt always includes an exaggerated representation of his cigarette and cigarette-holder, and a CARICATURE of Prime Minister Churchill always employs a tremendous cigar.

FARCES, of course, rear up in every corner of life. Their name, which is French, implies it. In Latin, they meant 'stuffings'; in the theater today they mean what is 'stuffed' between the acts of a serious play. Thus, in ordinary life, a futile action is also a FARCE. A board meeting that accomplishes nothing (that is mere 'stuffing') is a FARCE. In a sense FARCES have been stuffed themselves sometimes, with spicy ingredients, and some word historians believe that it was that sense which accounts for their modern meaning. For the root word in Latin meant 'to stuff viands,' as with spices, and the medieval *comedies farcies*, which engendered our theatrical forms, were most certainly stuffed full of risqué ingredients. But probably it was the idea of interpolation in the old Latin verb which produced the term for these theatrical performances, the earliest of which were buffooning interludes in, quite oddly, religious dramas.

On the stage, of course, and at their best, FARCES are light and madcap BURLESQUES. They borrow from BURLESQUE the trick of exaggeration for comical effect. On the whole, a FARCE is a lighter form of comedy than those represented by its four companion words because it is made out of all the ludicrous aspects of the completely impossible. It is making the completely futile funny, and of course the completely futile doesn't exist.

Verbiage A noun referring to words collectively, 'wordage.' But more often VERBIAGE refers to a 'wordy style or diction.'

Verbose 'Wordy; too wordy; prolix.' "His verbosity was beyond belief; words seemed to propagate themselves coming up his throat."

Verse Ogden Nash's whimsical *Versus* as a title for a book of poetry is not simply amusing phonetics. 'Versus' and VERSES are cousins ancestrally and so, under their skins, in sense. When you are 'versus' a proposition you are 'turned *against* it'; but to be *against* anything you must have turned *toward* it. The Romans used *versus* as an adverb and preposition meaning 'toward,' but its beginning was in their verb *vertere*, 'to turn.' And they used that verb with all the twists of sense that 'to turn' can suggest. The Romans called a furrow in ploughing a *versus* because they turned from one furrow to another. Eventually any line became a *versus*, including a line of writing or of poetry. So it was easy for literary VERSES to become the numbered passages or paragraphs in the Bible, and for the metrical VERSES to become a stanza, then a group of VERSES and, finally, poetry itself.

LOGIC

A POSTERIORI *adj.* pertaining to knowledge deduced from experience.

A PRIORI *adj.* pertaining to knowledge arrived at previous to an experience which might support it.

ASSUMPTION *n.* a supposition; a

proposition or idea adopted for the purpose of examining its effects even though its ultimate truth may not be established.

BASIS *n.* a fundamental principle; the principle, ground or argument upon which subsequent ideas are raised.

DEMONSTRATION *n.* the process by which a conclusion is established or "proved" by logic.

DILEMMA *n.* a situation in which one is confronted by two opposed and, usually, unfavorable alternatives, one of which must be chosen.

HYPOTHESIS *n.* an assumption; a theory advanced as a possible basis for an argument; a possible explanation of known facts.

LEMMA *n.* a subsidiary proposition used in the midst of a demonstration to prove another proposition which is essential to the course of the argument.

MAJOR PREMISE *n.* in a syllogism, the premise which contains the major term.

MINOR PREMISE *n.* in a syllogism, the premise which contains the minor term.

POSTULATE *n.* an assumption; a prerequisite or necessary condition; esp. the first assumption in an argument.

PREMISE *n.* an assumption or proposition on which an argument is based; specifically, one of the first two propositions of a syllogism.

PRINCIPLE *n.* a statement of truth on which subsequent arguments or conclusions are based.

PROPOSITION *n.* an assertion or argument proposed as the basis for one's logical position or belief. "As I understand your argument, the proposition is that the earth is flat and that if you go close to the edge, you are likely to fall off into space."

Syllogism

Term

THEOREM *n.* a statement which is not obviously true but which can be demonstrated to be true.

THESIS *n.* the general direction or significance of an argument, as "You don't prove your thesis that all men are naturally good."

Syllogism　In logic, a SYLLOGISM is the stock pattern or formula for argument. It consists of three propositions: (1) It's going to rain today; (2) Rain is ruinous to picnics; (3) We won't go picnicking today. The scheme is to set forth two ideas which determine a third and concluding one.

Term　A TERM is not just any name. It is a particular name for a special use. Thus we speak of the 'terminology' of a science, meaning the words it uses for the tools, special ideas or objects it deals with.

The same TERM may have another name for ordinary purposes. Or a TERM may be used, just as it is, in ordinary ways, though in this case it usually has a slightly different emphasis. 'Tort' is a legal TERM for a wrong. 'Fair' is a meteorological TERM for clear weather.

MAN

Anybody see **Anyone & Anybody**

Anyone & Anybody

BEING *n.* person; life; a living thing.

BODY *n.* person.

Human

FELLOW *n.* man; a male person; as "Do you see that fellow over there?"

INDIVIDUAL *n.* one person; a single person, esp. in the sense of one out of many, as "I am talking about that individual there at the edge of the crowd."

Man

MORTAL *n.* a human being.

None see **No one & None**

No one & None

ONE *n.* man; a person; esp. in the sense of individual, as "Which one of you threw that piece of chalk?"

Person

PERSONAGE *n.* individual, esp. in the sense of an outstanding individual.

SOUL *n.* a being.

Anyone and **Anybody** ANYONE may be written 'any one,' but ANYBODY should always be one word. This is because ANYBODY has referred to persons only. When we stopped speaking starkly of persons as 'bodies,' as in "Gin a body kiss a body, need a body cry?" we naturally joined 'any' and 'body' into one solid word. But ANYONE is a more general word. It is a contraction of 'any one thing' or 'any one person.' Now ANYONE, however, applies only to a person.

The same reasons apply to the spelling of 'somebody' and 'busybody.' And 'anyhow' and 'anyway' are naturally single words. ('Anyways' is a more popular word for 'anywise.') Verbal pairs tend to join when they define a single idea or object and when that idea or object is widely spoken of. At first the component words use a hyphen, which is eventually dropped to form a solid word. In the public mind a blueprint has not yet quite gotten away from the separate ideas of a print and of something blue. The 'blue-penciling' of manuscripts and reports has now taken on a new singleness and uses a hyphen, as if the color of the pencil no longer matters much. 'Bluebirds,' however, though they are still very blue, is now solidly spelled. And so is Bluebeard, the wife-killer! But usually such spelling matters are difficult to settle. Sometimes a dictionary is a good aid; but only in long-established instances, like ANYONE and ANYBODY, can we feel sure.

Human A word attesting, indirectly, to the immortality of dictionaries, because every generation of lexicographers expects posterity, eons hence, to read a statement of what it thinks of itself. If our lexicographers did otherwise, it must appear that we today still do not know what we are, or what we are like.

From the beginning we have taken our own image and cast it into any number of shapes animate or inanimate, according to personality, to opinion, and to wisdom. There is, for instance, 'humanism,' which represents variously the state of being HUMAN or the existence of HUMAN beings. 'Humanism' also represents more narrowly the quality of HUMAN living, as HUMAN beings are supposed to live, interested in one another, and kindly and merciful. Narrower still, and in reference to the HUMAN mind, 'humanism' also means a polite or liberal education, which especially includes the classics. Within recent years, 'humanism,' considering all at once HUMAN nature, HUMAN intellect and HUMAN soul with respect to other creatures and to God, has become a so-called religious philosophy. This philosophy holds that, not dogma, but only the recognition of man's unique ethical will can, and should, refute skepticism. This humanistic philosophy is a revival of earlier humanistic beliefs exalting man but now leading (as the main dictionaries conclude) naturally toward agnosticism and the transference of faith from God to man himself. Has not Mencken adjured us to cheer his soul, after his death, by winking at a homely girl?

Perhaps the emergence of this 'neo-humanism' explains in part the apparent culmination, in the present, of the many ups and downs the noun HUMAN has endured in the past. We used to be at much pains to speak of ourselves with some dignity, as HUMAN beings, or entities higher than mere creatures. We reserved the shorter expression, HUMANS, for jocular or less respectful usage. But now at last the trend seems to be toward reinvesting the word HUMAN with dignity—a dignity it once enjoyed in literature and philosophy of the ancient and golden age of humanity.

A glance at the history of the word HUMAN throws some light on its multiplicity of meanings. Most historians trace it to the Latin *humanus,* its ultimate root, the Latin *homo,* 'man.' But *homo* himself was a creature of the earth—that is, of Latin *humus,* the same word that has come down to us, decaying through the centuries, as the rotted vegetable matter we now esteem in our horticulture. So humanity is really of earthy substance. It was only through imitating the Roman use of their word *humanitas,* which refers to 'HUMAN conduct and education,' that our word HUMAN developed into 'philosophical humanism.' Furthermore it was not definitely until the eighteenth century that HUMAN took on the ideal meanings that refer to the qualities a nearly perfect man should have. 'Humanitarianism' (helpfulness to humanity, philanthropy, kindness and mercifulness) as an explicit doctrine then developed.

HUMAN was spelled 'human,' 'humaine' and 'humane,' indifferently, prior to about 1700. But when the adjective acquired its new moral sense the final 'e' was retained only to designate *that* moral sense. HUMAN itself, as an adjective, has really acquired another meaning. Though it always distinguished us from divinity on the one hand and from beasts on the other, it has also come to distinguish *most* of us from the few paragons or perfect people among us. So now we often say, "But that is only human," meaning that though we may be weak and imperfect, we still belong to that class of creatures closest to God. Thus the word HUMAN reaches this way and that: "We are *only* human," or, "We are the only human animals." Succinctly, we are HUMANS— the addition of the 'beings' is redundant.

Man MAN has been wryly defined by a celebrated wit as the animal whose chief occupation is the extermination of both other animals and himself, but whose numbers nevertheless infest the whole habitable earth. It is the latter part of this cynic's definition which interests us most etymologically since it attests to both the importance and the prevalence of the word MAN.

Probably in the beginning MAN referred simply to the individual and then, as 'man-kin,' to 'mankind,' or to the whole race. Today when this broader sense is intended we usually drop the article, saying, "Man is great," not "*The* man is great." But when we say, "He is every inch a man," the sense of MAN is not only intensive but generic as well. Thus this man both really and truly stands on his own two feet, and is also a fine representative of all mankind. In comparison with the more pretentious term, 'gentleman,' MAN has retained its dignity and acquired a certain humbleness of tone. Perhaps 'gentleman' has proved too flattering a term to escape suspicion. Probably several decades of warfare, exalting the braver qualities of manhood, have had their influence on the word MAN. The youth of our age are very sensitive about not being MEN. Rampant hoodlumism is, in part, a distorted result of the respect we still pay, perhaps more now than ever before, to the underlying and essential implications of this ageless word.

No one and **None** "What difference does it make? No one will care." Surely, nobody in this case would say "None will care." Or almost nobody, since a few still do, including a few metropolitan newspaper editors. But NO ONE shrank to NONE for a purpose. Now we can use NONE for either things or persons. But NO ONE is used only for 'no person.' It seems foolish to ban NO ONE because those two old words clarify the meaning and often improve the style. Though it looks as if NONE came from a shrinking of NO ONE, the merging actually took place in Old English when 'one' was *an* and 'no' was *ne*.

Person "Gin a *body* meet a *body*, comin thro the rye . . ." sounds quaint and a little ridiculous to us now. But, after all, aren't we using PERSON pretty hard? The word does escape some work when we say 'people' for PERSONS, "There were only two people there." But the word 'people' primarily means a population. Unfortunately we have given PERSON so general a referent that its specific meanings are losing their significance. Aside from the terminology of grammar, law, science and religion, a PERSON is rightly one of three things: a human being, a self or personality, or the body of a human being. You can say: "There was not a single person in the room"; or, "He was there in person" (in the flesh); or, "He is immaculate, as if he respects his own person," though this use of PERSON does include his clothes. But just as 'body' has lost its significance in 'somebody' and 'anybody,' so both 'body' and 'individuality' have lost their sense in our common use of PERSON. The word is useful because it includes both sexes and all ages. Perhaps no all-round and serviceable synonym exists. But at least we could use PERSON with more discretion, with more respect for its several exact senses.

MIND AND ITS PROCESSES

See also Perceptions

ACCOUNT FOR *v.* to explain, as "The suspect accounted for all his activities on the day of the murder."

ACUMEN *n.* penetrating intelligence.

ANALYZE *v.* to reduce something, usually a proposition or idea, to its constituent elements; to take something apart in order to understand it, as "I analyzed what she told me and decided she was lying."

BELIEF *n.* mental consent to the truth of something, as a BELIEF in God.

Believe see **Guess & Believe**

CERTAIN *adj.* without doubt; absolutely sure, as "He is always certain he is right."

Choice & Option

CLAIRVOYANCE *n.* intuition; insight. "Her clairvoyance taught her that he was in love long before he knew it himself."

Clarify

COGITATE *v.* to think; speculate; ponder; as "The riddle caused them to cogitate all that afternoon."

COMPREHEND *v.* to understand; take in or absorb mentally. *n.* COMPREHENSION.

CONCEIVE *v.* to imagine or visualize something, as "They conceived a foolproof way to murder the old man." *n.* CONCEPTION.

CONCLUDE *v.* to finish; come to an end; esp. in the sense of arriving at a belief or opinion, as "He concluded that she was a cheat." *n.* CONCLUSION.

Conjecture see **Guess & Conjecture**

CONSIDER *v.* to ponder; contemplate; discuss; as "The thieves considered every possible way of entering the palace treasury."

CONSTRUE *v.* to interpret; as "She construed what he told her in any way that pleased her at the moment."

CONTEMPLATE *v.* to ponder; speculate; consider.

Decided & Decisive

Decisive see **Decided & Decisive**

Deduction & Induction

DELIBERATE *v.* to ponder; analyze.

Discernment & Discriminate

Discriminate see **Discernment & Discriminate**

DISSECT *v.* to analyze, as "If you dissect your problems, you will often find them not so bad after all."

DIVINATION *n.* a guess; explanation; prophecy. *v.* DIVINE, to foretell; guess; as "It is necessary in bridge to divine your opponent's plan before he plays it."

DOUBTFUL *adj.* without certainty; uncertain; suspicious, as "He has doubtful morals."

DUBIOUS *adj.* doubtful; uncertain; questionable; vague.

ELUCIDATE *v.* to explain; to clarify.

EXPLAIN *v.* to make someone understand something by describing it or analyzing it.

EXPLICATE *v.* to analyze or to untangle something in order to arrive at its meaning, esp. in the sense, "He explicated the difficult passage in Eliot's poem." *n.* EXPLICATION.

EXPOUND *v.* to explain; esp. to teach, as "The professor expounds his theories with great vigor."

Guess & Believe

Guess & Conjecture

HEURETIC *adj.* (in logic) pertaining to discovery. HEURISTIC means serving to find out, like a guide book, or even a hint.

IMAGINE *v.* to form in one's mind

a mental picture; to visualize. *n.* IMAGINATION.

Induction see **Deduction & Induction**

INSIGHT *n.* clairvoyance; intuitive understanding; a perception of something beneath the surface, as "He had an insight into her heart."

INTELLECT *n.* all the faculties of man which enable him to reason, think and imagine. See also INTELLIGENCE.

INTELLIGENCE *n.* the faculty of thinking, etc.; esp. in the sense of thinking clearly or reasoning well. "He has intelligence" means, "He is wise, brainy."

INTERPRET *v.* to explain, esp. to express something foreign in a new way, as "It is difficult to interpret the Oriental mind to a Westerner."

LUCIFEROUS *adj.* means affording mental illumination.

MEDITATE *v.* to ponder; contemplate; plan.

MIND *n.* intellect; reasoning power; memory.

MNEMONIC or MNESTIC *adj.* refer to memory.

MUSE *v.* to think; ponder; reminisce.

Musing
Nescience
Noetic

OPINION *n.* a belief, esp. one concerning a matter upon which there is general disagreement or uncertainty.

Option see **Choice & Option**

PERCEPTION *n.* understanding; also the faculty of comprehending something quickly and completely. *adj.* PERCEPTIVE.

PERSPICACITY *n.* keenness and clearness of understanding. *adj.* PERSPICACIOUS.

PHRENIC *adj.* pertains to mind.

PONDER *v.* to think; meditate; esp. to weigh or judge something, as "The jury pondered the case for a long time."

PROGNOSTIC *adj.* refers to prediction.

RATIOCINATION *n.* reasoning; the process of figuring things out or of arriving at an understanding. *v.* RATIOCINATE. See RATIONALIZE.

Rationalize

REASON *n.* the thinking faculty.

RESOLVE *v.* to decide; agree. "They resolved upon a plan of living without working hard."

REVOLVE *v.* to ponder, as "He revolved the story in his mind until he understood where it was false."

RUMINATE *v.* to muse.

Sagacious see **Sage & Sagacious**
Sage & Sagacious
Socratic

SPECULATE *v.* to guess; wonder; cogitate; think.

SURE *adj.* certain.

SURMISE *n.* guess, as "It was my surmise that he had plenty of money to begin with."

UNDERSTAND *v.* to comprehend; to absorb something into the mind.

VIEW *n.* opinion; a way of thinking about something, as "It is my view that you are mistaken."

WEIGH *v.* ponder.

Choice and **Option** Both are general words, when compared with 'alternative,' which refers to a CHOICE between only two items. The noun CHOICE is Teutonic (though cognate with the Latin that gave us 'gusto' and 'gustatory'), and it comes from all over Europe, from the Goths, Norsemen, our own Saxon forebears, as well as from the mellifluent Old French. It says: You can take anything you see and want. OPTION is ancient Latin, probably a work-a-day word compared with the martial-sounding 'alternative,' also Latin. It says: You can take that or these, or leave them all.

Both words have provided useful adjectives, with CHOICE having the richer meanings, not surprising since Shakespeare had a hand in elaborating them. That which is OPTIONAL is left entirely open to your wishes; you can take it, leave it or select part of it. CHOICE, as an adjective, is more selective. A CHOICE bit of turkey on the table is above all worthy of being selected. In this sense the word is unusually expressive. A CHOICE gift has been chosen with care, it is especially appropriate and fine.

Clarify One of the clearest, prettiest sounds in English is the sound of 'ar' when the 'a' is short as in 'charity' and in CLARIFY. It is not a common sound. Usually the 'a' droops, as in 'far.' In 'Mary,' it is neither clear and short as in 'merry,' or long as in 'bare,' or rather as in 'base,' for an 'a' is practically never long before an 'r.'

CLARIFY means to 'clear-ify'—both it and 'clear' come from the Latin *clarus*, the former via the Old French verb *clarifier*. It describes the sparkling atmosphere that April showers have washed and CLARIFIED. "He is a very good professor—he can clarify the most difficult mathematical problems." This is a word that, in the interests of good talking and writing, you cannot afford to pass by.

Decided and **Decisive** Of course, used as a participle, for example, "I have decided to buy that blue suit," this word retains all its original force. But as an adjective, DECIDED has lost some of the sharpness of 'decide,' literally 'to cut from.' It now primarily means 'free from uncertainty,' and hence 'beyond question or dispute.' DECISIVE, however, goes further; it has a note of finality in it. Primarily it now means 'an end to uncertainty, delay or argument.' For example, "I have a decided opinion that fresh water swimming is more healthful than salt water swimming," simply means that I have made up my mind about the merits of fresh water swimming. My opinion can conceivably be changed by new evidence and I tacitly admit there might be arguments relative to the excellence of salt water that I have not heard. But, "My decisive conclusion is that salt water swimming is harmful and that fresh water swimming is healthful," definitely means that I can not conceive of my ever changing my mind. You may DECIDEDLY hope some particular person will be at a party you are going to, yet that person's presence may not be the DECISIVE factor in your own going to the party. A horse that wins a race by twelve lengths achieves a DECIDED victory, but the winning of the Kentucky Derby, even by a nose, is DECISIVE, because the winner becomes a champion.

As all things can be described either objectively or subjectively, both these words have taken on a secondary meaning that refers essentially to personality. Business executives and military men are noted for their DECISIVE actions and hence for their DECISIVE manners, even character. They are strongminded and positive, while most dreamers and sentimentalists are INDECISIVE in their actions and character. Similarly, we speak of DECIDED airs or types. "He was a very decided young individual." Doubtless we even endow the color blue with some personality when we speak of a dress being a very DECIDED blue. On the other hand, the usual meaning of DECIDED is quite objective. Often it only means 'obvious.' "He looked decidedly the worse for wear."

Deduction and **Induction**   Many nouns derived from verbs literally summarize the action in themselves until they become simply results of actions, like 'bundle,' from old English *binden*, 'to bind.' But many other nouns continue distinctly to repeat the action of their verbs. DEDUCTION and INDUCTION are nouns of this sort.

They derive from Latin *ducere*, 'to lead.' When a military leader (*dux* in Latin, *duc* in French, 'duke' in English) leads his men it is taken for granted that he leads them *into* battle or *forward* to new glories. But for more general or abstract uses it was thought necessary to make explicit the direction *ducere* might take. Thus Latin has *inducere*, 'to lead into,' and *deducere*, 'to lead out of.' From the past participle *inductus* we get our verb 'to induct,' meaning 'to introduce or lead into formally,' as to induct into the army. There is also the word 'induce.' Its action is mild, tentative, often indirect. You induce (almost tempt) someone to do something. The Latin *inducere* produced the noun *inductio*, from which our INDUCTION derives. In logic INDUCTION is a 'bringing or leading in.' It is opposed to DEDUCTION (from *deductio*), which is a 'drawing down,' a sort of 'eliciting.'

When we DEDUCE something we start from proved or known principles. Then we 'lead away' from them to a point which at first sight doesn't seem connected with the principles but actually is. If, for example, we know on principle that criminals like to visit unsavory dives, and if we can prove that a certain suspect in a particular crime also visits unsavory dives, we may infer—that is, DEDUCE from the principle —that he is very probably a criminal.

On the contrary, when we make an INDUCTION we construct in our minds, or discover, a particular principle which we suspect certain facts imply. We do this by marshalling these facts and 'leading them on, or into,' the very principle we seek. For example, when white men came to America they encountered savages with whom it was difficult and dangerous to deal. Some good principle for dealing with them had to be discovered. Certain facts suggested a principle of killing them off: dead Indians were good Indians. Another principle was suggested by observing Indian traits. It was observed they were inordinately fond of trinkets, and they also revered the giving of gifts as tokens of good will. Moreover, they liked whiskey. Thus an alternate principle was arrived at, by INDUCTION.

Discernment and **Discriminate** DISCERNMENT is a nice word, as it intends to be, in the sense of 'delicately exact.' See NICE. DISCERNMENT is 'exactness of perception' that involves also 'judgment.' You cannot judge fairly without seeing clearly. DISCRIMINATE means 'to separate with true judgment,' to distinguish one thing from another on the basis of intelligence. Sometimes DISCRIMINATE means 'to favor one thing above another.' Thus a judge must not DISCRIMINATE against the accused, but he must DISCRIMINATE between right and wrong, and between the relevant and the irrelevant. DISCERNMENT is perceiving these distinctions. The truly DISCERNING person does not merely see things in their material proportions. He also sees them in their true lights, as they appear to people of nice tastes and real justice.

Guess and **Believe** As the shadow before substance, the model before criterion, so GUESS is to BELIEVE. GUESS in its own substance is solid enough and means basically 'to get.' When you GUESS what I mean you 'get' my meaning. See GUESS and CONJECTURE. But its minor figurative usage, now probably conveying its commonest sense, as "I guess (suppose) that is true," relates itself to the extensive connotations of BELIEVE.

BELIEVE is a word of many meanings compactly integrated in two successive fundamental senses. Historically, it stipulated that you must first 'like' a person, then 'love' him, before you BELIEVE him. The root is common Teutonic, and it gave us the German word *lieben*, 'to love,' and our own word 'love.' Its continuous essence has been 'approval.' So when we BELIEVE something today we BELIEVE it, not by conjecture, but by faith and respect. Of course, this sense has broadened by now, till the faith sometimes approaches fancy, or in practical matters, becomes quite hardheaded. What we BELIEVE we accept either on faith in some authority, like our eyesight, or respect for its character, which we determine perhaps by investigation or study. Sometimes we BELIEVE instinctively, whether on the basis of a higher insight than the mind's, or on the basis of the mind's incapacity for freeing itself from prejudice or ignorance.

This basic meaning in BELIEVE is quite different from 'supposing' something is true, or from 'getting' the truth by hook or by crook, that is, from GUESSING. Yet in this modern, scientific world the intellectual process of arriving at BELIEF now seems commonest. BELIEF is primarily an aspect of the mind, while trust partakes of love and respect. Yet, the bestowal of respect and love, when we BELIEVE in a friend, is still typical of the word in its origin and development.

In the United States especially we use GUESS very loosely, not only in the sense of 'supposing' or 'thinking,' but also in the sense of BELIEVING. And worse than that, we use BELIEVE in the sense of 'suppose.' GUESS itself does not really mean 'to guess at,' which might imply some 'inspiration.' It is proper to GUESS a riddle because you 'solve' it, you 'get' the answer, the practical chore is positively done. But it is not strictly proper to say "I guess your age is twenty-five," because now GUESS doesn't mean 'to get' or 'to acquire' your age. It means 'to suppose' your age. You can make this example strictly correct by saying, "I tried to guess your age," which means I tried to 'find out' your age. When we use GUESS as a synonym for 'suppose' we are not 'reasoning out' an observation so much as we are relying on 'luck or inspiration' for a good observation. But in the beginning any GUESSWORK was quite rational. Its inception was probably in an Icelandic word meaning 'acute and ingenious.' In Chaucer's time it meant 'to GUESS' or 'to think,' but also 'to estimate, appraise.' There may still be some 'calculation' in our GUESSES, since colloquially 'calculate' can convey the vague meaning of 'suppose.' "I cal'late there'll be quite a crowd attendin'." But this is an accident of usage. On the whole it might be good to return GUESS to its ancient and useful meaning.

Guess and **Conjecture** When you say you 'get' the meaning of a remark you mean, historically, that you GUESS it. GUESS comes from Middle English *gessen*, meaning 'to estimate,' from Early English *geten*, 'to get.' CONJECTURE had an equally solid beginning, and has held fast to its original meaning more than has GUESS. See GUESS and BELIEVE. From Latin *con* and *jacere* it meant 'to throw with or together.' A CONJECTURAL opinion may still mean a judgment from assembled information. CONJECTURE serves nicely when you wish to imply you are GUESSING not only with thought but with 'extra' consideration. It is a deliberate GUESS.

Musing To amuse yourself leisurely with your own thoughts is what MUSING means. Sometimes you MUSE one certain thing, as does the villain in books who MUSES an evil idea that comes to him as another person talks. The word doesn't derive from the Muses or from music, but from the Old French *muser;* 'to sniff about, to nuzzle.'

Nescience A bookish word whose adjective 'nescient' is rather neat, especially as it can substitute in some degree for 'ignorant,' which has unpleasant or insulting implications. NESCIENCE is, in fact, a vague and vast word for 'ignorance' as well as for the 'unknowable.' In philosophy, it declares that God and His Kingdom are too vast and vague to be known by mortals. Agnostics are sometimes called NESCIENTS, because they incline to this philosophy. NESCIENCE means 'inability to know,' or the 'state of being unable to know.' Animals are NESCIENT of our inner or fuller lives; we are NESCIENT of theirs.

Noetic A philosophical word meaning, roughly, 'pertaining to the intellect.' Loosely, NOETIC is sometimes used as a synonym for 'intuitive,' probably because intuitions are mysterious, and the truly NOETIC is certainly mysterious. Its noun is NOESIS, meaning the 'highest form of knowledge.' NOESIS is the apprehension by the intellect alone of imperishable truths, the highest ones, which are purely ideas. In NOESIS the ideal transcends all sensations.

The word NOETIC comes by stages from the Greek word for mind, *nous.* NOETIC thinking is not simply pure reasoning. The NOETIC thinker contemplates the abstract, his thoughts relating only indirectly to physical and visible matter.

Rationalize To RATIONALIZE is quite commonly used in the sense of 'to excuse,' referring especially to one's own misdeeds. "He rationalized (explained away) his bad behaviour by saying it all came from his poverty, which wasn't his fault." This sense of the word derives from the usage of psychologists, much as the slangy use of 'alibi' is derived from its legal meaning. To psychologists RATIONALIZATION is a reflexive personal sophistry, conscious or unconscious, plausibly but superficially explaining one's conduct, attitude or feelings.

RATIONALIZATION has also its uses in theology where it is antonymous to inspiration and places reason above revelation. In philosophy,

RATIONALISM is a somewhat misrepresented German doctrine that is the foil of sensationalism or sensism, and consequently of empiricism. It holds that reason supplies something without which experience is impossible.

Normally, to RATIONALIZE means to explain something in terms of reason, as you might explain to a child that thunder does not growl from rage or ill-humor but because air makes a noise when it vibrates from the suddenness of the lightning. At bottom, the meaning is simply to make RATIONAL or sane, to make into sense.

Sage and Sagacious   SAGE is one of our words that comes from the French but doesn't look like it. Ultimately, though, it comes from the Latin *salvus,* 'safe.' It means 'eminently wise,' especially the wisdom that comes from a long life. The straight Latin equivalent is SAGACIOUS, with a very hard and accented 'g,' from the Latin *sagire,* 'to perceive.' A SAGE person, therefore, being SAGACIOUS, is also a seer, but he is no idle visionary because he is 'safe' too. Anyhow, a SAGE remark is not only a wise statement but also somewhat prophetic. "The doctor sagely said that if I broke my bad habits, I'd live longer."

Socratic   An adjective referring to the Athenian philosopher Socrates, who, some two and twenty centuries ago, left us a philosophic method celebrating his name. SOCRATIC refers, in general, to the discovery of truth by questions and answers. But SOCRATIC refers not only to this dialectical method but also to a distinctive characteristic of that method. With apparent innocence Socrates would lead the discussion to positions where disbelief in his basic proposition was impossible. Hence SOCRATIC also implies 'socratic irony.'

MORALITY AND IMMORALITY

Abet

ALTRUISTIC *adj.* unselfish; characterized by an interest in or devotion to others.

Amoral, Immoral & Unmoral

CHASTE *adj.* pure; innocent.

CONTEMPTIBLE *adj.* extremely bad or hateful; despised; beneath notice.

DECADENT *adj.* evidencing ruin or decay, particularly mental or moral ruin.

Ethical & Moral

EVIL *adj.* very bad; esp. in an intentional, malicious, devilish way.

HONORABLE *adj.* worthy of honor or respect.

Immoral see **Amoral, Immoral,** etc.

Impious & Infamous

Infamous see **Impious & Infamous**

MAGNANIMOUS *adj.* generous; noble; showing a high morality and great spirit.

MANLY *adj.* having the virtues of a man, such as bravery and strength.

Moral see **Ethical & Moral**

NOBLE *adj.* possessing especially good and elevated qualities.

Profligate

PURE *adj.* chaste; innocent; free from guilt; as a PURE mind.

RECREANT *adj.* cowardly; esp. in the sense of being false to a principle, cause or person.

REPREHENSIBLE *adj.* blameworthy; guilty; as a REPREHENSIBLE act.

RIGHTEOUS *adj.* free from wrong; given to good acts.

SUBLIME *adj.* noble; very exalted; of the very best quality; out of ordinary reach.

UNIMPEACHABLE *adj.* without suspicion or fault.

Unmoral see **Amoral, Immoral,** etc.

UNSELFISH *adj.* generous; not concerned with oneself.

Veracious

VICIOUS *adj.* ruthless; malicious; mean; wicked.

VIRTUOUS *adj.* showing virtue; being good; esp. in the sense of pure and chaste.

Abet This word is used loosely these days, usually as a flapping appendage in the phrase 'to aid and abet,' said almost invariably of something criminal or wrong. It sometimes means 'to incite,' and sometimes 'to originate.' When we ABET an action we commence or craftily further it. So today the action has been narrowed down to an evil scheme, and our part in it has become furtive.

Amoral, Immoral and **Unmoral** "He is a moral man," means that he is 'ethically good.' But we have come to regard morals as good, bad or indifferent, or, loosely, as few or many, meaning, of course, few or many moral principles. For example, "He has few morals," means that he does what he wants, and he wants ethically unacceptable things. In the old days when morals were considered usually good, IMMORAL simply meant the 'absense' of morals. An IMMORAL man was thus bad because he had 'no' morals. But now IMMORAL refers to actual morals, but bad ones.

Partly to supply another word for the old meanings of IMMORAL, AMORAL was coined in modern times in imitation of certain Greek derived words using the same privative prefix. The 'a' in AMORAL stands for 'absense.' To be AMORAL is, literally, 'to be without morals.' The truly AMORAL creature does not recognize morals either in others or itself. It is simply non-moral. Some people think animals in general are good illustrations of AMORAL creatures. Loosely, we speak sometimes of an AMORAL man, one who can not distinguish between right and wrong. But generally any mentally normal man is either moral or IMMORAL.

Instead of AMORAL we might have used UNMORAL. 'Un' is an English prefix meaning in its original sense 'not,' just like Latin *non*. UNMORAL primarily means 'having no sense of right or wrong,' or exactly what AMORAL means. Why, then, with a choice of Latin, English and Greek did we choose Greek? Perhaps because AMORAL is the shortest and best sounding after all.

A secondary meaning of UNMORAL describes, not the absence of morals, but the having anything at all to do with morals in the first place. AMORAL after all implies a system of morals which is absent. A man can be AMORAL because most men are either moral or IMMORAL. But a machine can not be discussed in terms of morals. Therefore it is not AMORAL; it is UNMORAL.

Ethical and **Moral** ETHICS is a moral science, or, perhaps more properly, a science of morals seen as social duties. The word is Greek and means 'character.' Etymologically, MORALS are less lofty, deriving from the common Roman *mores*, or 'laws governing manners.' But the Roman word mushroomed. Today you are very IMMORAL if you murder some one, but only slightly or reminiscently IMMORAL if you speak out of turn in polite society. While the word ETHICAL has been tightening itself and narrowing itself to a code, the word MORAL has spread itself to cover everything that pertains to right and wrong at every level. See AMORAL, IMMORAL, and UNMORAL.

Impious and **Infamous** IMPIOUS is no mild negative. No one becomes IMPIOUS through inactivity. It means 'lack of piety,' but a man is rarely called IMPIOUS until he really acts badly, until his lack of respect for God shows itself in a really reprehensible life. Once begun, his iniquity usually grows quickly. Automatically he begins to become INFAMOUS. INFAMOUS has gathered all the aspects of 'ill fame' into one word. It is difficult to conceive of a man's being bad enough to be called INFAMOUS without his also being IMPIOUS.

Profligate What the original word exactly meant is moot. Scholars contradict each other about it. While agreeing that it meant in effect 'to wreck or destroy,' they interpret its constituents variously. The 'pro' might stand for 'before,' 'forth,' or 'forward'; the Latin *fligare* might mean 'to dash someone back' or 'to strike him down.' You can see an enemy horde routed and driven away, or you can see a personal opponent dashed down to the ground before you, right at your feet. It is significant that an obsolete meaning of the word in English was 'overwhelmed, defeated.' PROFLIGATE is, in any case, a dramatic, descriptive word, albeit no longer a tragic one because in tragedy there must be sympathy or at least some grandeur. To the warlike Romans *profligare* meant 'to dash or strike forth, to drive forward,' like the enemy in an harassing pursuit. Hence, it meant 'to rout, ruin, destroy.' The PROFLIGATE man is derived from the past participle of that verb, and he thus becomes a Lucifer—he is driven from Heaven, he is dashed down to a carnal wasteland. But unlike Lucifer he is singularly devoid of majesty. Today a PROFLIGATE has wantonly abandoned himself to evil. A man who gives himself up to complete dissipation is a PROFLIGATE.

In another sense, a PROFLIGATE is a 'self-exhibiting prodigal, a wastrel.' Thus we use the word to describe extravagances which are too free and wasteful to excite admiration, such as the exuberant use of long or lurid words in writing or the PROFLIGATE use of bright colors in a garish picture.

Veracious This word means 'habitually truthful.' Adjectives ending in 'ious,' like 'VERACIOUS, audacious, ferocious, voracious,' are commonly subjective, denoting a state of personal being. But since we generally act as we feel, these adjectives become active themselves. If you are VERACIOUS, you are not only 'disposed' to be truthful but are 'actually' truth-telling. Likewise, if you are 'mendacious' you are 'lie-telling.' Incidentally, adjectives ending in 'some' are wholly objective, and denote the effects of external things on us; for example, 'gruesome' and 'awesome.' Occasionally such an adjective will be appropriated by ourselves: 'lonesome' now refers to a feeling in us.

Figuratively VERACIOUS sometimes refers to inanimate things. A VERACIOUS report is truthful.

MOTION

ADVANCE *n.* forward progress; as "The enemy's advance was halted by our tanks." *v.* to go forward; to proceed; as "Our troops advanced their line."

AMBAGIOUS *adj.* pertaining to a roundabout or winding way; hence to an indirect proceeding. *n.* AMBAGE.
Approach

ATTAIN *v.* to reach; to gain; to arrive at; as to ATTAIN a goal.

BACK UP *v.* to move backward; to go in an opposite direction; to retreat, as "The railroad engine backed up to the cars on the siding."

BALLISTIC *adj.* pertaining to the motion and impact of missiles. See the category SCIENCE.

CAREER *n.* a quick charge or advance.

CHANGE *n.* a movement from one situation to another. *v.* to make different; to exchange or substitute; to vary.

Circuitous

COURSE *n.* path; forward movement; the direction a movement takes; as "Our course lies directly east until we meet the main road."

DECAMP *v.* to leave suddenly; to depart quickly.

DEPART *v.* to go away, sometimes in the sense of to die. *n.* DEPARTURE.

DIGRESS *v.* to turn off the main course; to wander.

Divagate

Drag see **Draw & Drag**

Draw & Drag

DRIFT *v.* to be carried along, as to DRIFT with the crowd.

Encounter

FLIGHT *n.* a running away; departure.

FLIT *v.* to move quickly and lightly from one thing to another. "She flits about the house, doing nothing, all the day long."

FLOW *n.* a movement; hence, a stream, as a FLOW of water. *v.* to move along, as "The crowd flows down the street."

GESTIC or GESTICAL *adj.* pertaining to gestures or bodily motion, esp. as in or of dancing.

GLIDE *v.* to flow; to move from place to place, esp. in a silent and unobtrusive way. "The attacking Indians glided through the forest, surprising the settlers at dawn."

Go

HAUL *v.* to drag along; pull.

ISSUE *v.* to come forth, as "The Indians issued from the woods in great numbers."

Jump

LEAVE *v.* to depart; go away.

LOCOMOTION *n.* movement; the ability to move.

MOVE *v.* to go from one place to another; to change the position of something.

MOVE TOWARD *v.* to advance.

PASS *v.* to make one's way through something, as to PASS through a city; to move; go.

PROCEED *v.* to advance; make progress.

PROGRESS *n.* a going forward, esp. in the sense of a change for the better; improvement. *v.* to advance; grow; develop.

QUIT *v.* to depart; leave.

RAMBLE *v.* to wander here and there; to go from place to place slowly; to walk aimlessly.

RETIRE *v.* to retreat; move backward; withdraw, as to RETIRE to bed.

RETREAT *v.* to go back; withdraw; retire.

RETURN *n.* an arrival at a place previously vacated. *v.* to come back to a starting point, as "A man leaves home for work in the morning and returns in the evening."

ROLL *v.* to turn on itself, as a ball ROLLS along the floor.

ROVE *v.* to wander; ramble; to go from place to place, more or less aimlessly. "Sailors rove the world." See also the category TRAVEL.

SALLY *v.* to advance quickly; to issue suddenly.

SALTATORY or SALTATORIAL *adj.* pertaining to dancing, esp. dancing with much leaping.

SHEER OFF *v.* to turn aside, as "The car, to avoid a smash, sheered off the road."

SHIFT *v.* to change the position of something.

STEER FOR *v.* to head in a particular direction, as to STEER FOR a lighthouse.

STREAM *v.* to flow.

SWEEP ALONG *v.* to drift very quickly, as "The wind swept the leaves along the road."

SWERVE OFF *v.* to sheer off; to go off the course suddenly.

TOW *v.* to drag; pull.

TWIST *v.* to turn on itself without forward movement; to spin, usually very slowly.

VOLAR *adj.* pertaining to flight.

VORTEX *n.* a whirling motion, esp. of water, like a whirlpool, or of air, like a whirlwind. *adj.* VORTICAL.

WANDER *v.* to rove; ramble; stray.

WITHDRAW *v.* to retire; draw back; leave.

Approach It is both transitive and intransitive as a verb, and it can also be a noun. "The horseman approaches the corral," "The enemy approaches rapidly," and "The enemy's approach was by way of the swamp." The word has unlimited figurative uses. You can APPROACH your destination on a highway, or you can APPROACH the point of your argument in a debate. An APPROACH suggests 'deliberation' and usually 'slow motion.' APPROACHING doom seems grim and inevitable. Your APPROACH shot, in golf, is careful. When you 'near' a town you simply go closer to it. When you APPROACH a town you make a tactical maneuver, and look for signposts. When you APPROACH the enemy you move cautiously. If you are a novelist, your APPROACH to your climax must be studied, you must move with intelligent deliberation.

Circuitous 'Circling, indirect, roundabout.' But the base of this word is not 'circle' but 'circuit.' A 'circuit' can be a 'lap,' as on a race track, and the track is often oval, not round. A 'circuit' can also be almost a straight course, as sometimes the itinerary of a circuit court.

The meaning is in the 'circu,' the curtailed *circum,* 'around' of the original word, *circumire.* The little *ire* meant 'to go.' When you reconnoiter an enemy's outpost you approach CIRCUITOUSLY. You purposely vary your course for reasons of caution. You use the same strategy in reaching your point in a debate, or in a business transaction.

Divagate DIVAGATE means 'to stray aimlessly.' An author usually DIVAGATES when he wanders all over his subject without coming to a point. Of course, there is a purpose in most things if we but knew it. At any rate, a butterfly is an excellent example of a DIVAGATING creature.

Draw and Drag These are practically the same words. The Teutonic 'g' in Anglo-Saxon *dragan* became Middle English 'w' to give us DRAW, though it stuck through the centuries in DRAG. But when words change their costumes they sometimes change their dispositions, and in this case both words, but especially DRAW, assumed an amazing variety of meanings.

DRAG can mean to dredge, to harrow, to draw along heavily and slowly, or to move as if so drawn. It can also mean to travel along the ground not heavily but flappingly, like a rope's end dangling from a car; or, it can mean figuratively to lag behind like a loiterer, first on one foot, then another, like a tired pedestrian. As a noun DRAG may still refer to a coach behind four horses, a brake on a vehicle, anything that ships DRAG to slow them up, a wooden frame for smoothing ground, a net for DRAGGING a stream's bottom or any slowness or obstruction of motion, progress or pleasure. Thus, in slang, a girl you take to a party is a DRAG.

DRAW is used in more ways than DRAG. You DRAW a prize, even if there is no DRAWING of lots or pulling prizes from a bag. You DRAW a picture even though you 'push' a pencil. You DRAW ruin down upon yourself. You DRAW money from a bank. You DRAW information from an almanac, and DRAW a conclusion from other data. You DRAW a fowl quite literally when you disembowel it. Likewise, you physically DRAW a cork from a bottle or a gun from your pocket. But when you DRAW your weekly pay you don't extract it, like a tooth, from your employer. And when you, technically, DRAW steel things you temper them. When you DRAW near a town you approach it, but when you are DRAWN to a person, you like him. Intransitively, a chimney DRAWS well when all the smoke goes up it. Woolen fabrics DRAW when they shrink. Drawbridges DRAW when they are pulled upward. This is the opposite of a 'drawback,' which is usually an obstruction of some kind. In a race, when two contestants arrive at the finish in the same moment, the result is a DRAW, probably on account of the stakes that are 'withdrawn' in the event of a tie. Don't forget the 'withdrawing' rooms to which the gentlefolk 'withdrew' for privacy long before the Victorians assembled in 'drawing rooms' for social activity. Elizabethan bums and thieves probably originated DRAWERS, in their slang, as garments that are pulled on, because the idea of 'pulling' is found in most of DRAW's imaginative uses. Finally, when you DRAW up a document or a will you presumably are DRAWING all things to a conclusion, or at least to a definitive point.

Encounter ENCOUNTER is a good vocabulary-building word. It is expressive, referring to all the things you meet by design or chance, physically or spiritually. The 'count' in it was *contra,* 'against.' What you ENCOUNTER you 'come up against.' You have to confront it. You may ENCOUNTER good luck, but you come face to face with it. If you ENCOUNTER a mad bull, he is your adversary, he is against you; you confront his mad existence whether or not you yourself stand to fight.

Go Since we can GO ahead, back, up, around, down, to, into, through and among, it would seem that here we have the elemental verb of all motion. Yet the sober truth is that while GO is, in itself, a round little cannon ball of a word, still it acquired its scope to a great extent from what might be called a very happy accident in the formation of our present language. For when English began to dispense with its inherited nounal inflexions, and to use the same form for subject, object and indirect object, new demands were made upon the verbs themselves. These demands they could not meet without aid. So, in their need, they enlisted all the prepositions and adverbs they could find. GO went the limit, as indeed it had to, and so today it can GO in all directions and manner.

But of course GO was always, from its nature, a dynamic word. Did it not help produce our 'yachts,' literally, speedboats or hunters, and our awful word 'gang,' meaning an evil going-together? And does not 'going together' also mean, romantically, 'to keep company as lovers?' Then we can GO batty or berserk, GO adrift, GO shopping, GO great guns, GO kerflop, GO sit on a tack, or GO cahoots (equal partners) with some others. We can GO by the board, or, rather mysteriously, GO 'along with you.' We GO high hat, GO religious, or GO democratic. Or just GO to it, GO at it, or GO off it. Who could want a more accommodating verb?

Still we must recognize that the secret of its strength lies largely in its acquisitions. As men grow great by employing the best assistants, so GO's efficiency rests widely on its adjuncts. When in pre-Shakespearean times it found it could no longer rely on nouns to describe its situation it began collecting brief connectives for its own use. And, experimenting, GO hooked these connectives to everything in sight, still considering them, nevertheless, as arms of its own. So today the world GOES round in a thousand senses, by means of GO and its army of assistants.

Jump The famous feat of the cow that JUMPED over the moon takes on extra marvelousness when you examine the word JUMP. The word itself is no older than Shakespeare, in English, and prior to his time had all manner of queer forms in other countries, such as *tzumpe* in the north of Italy, *gumpa* in Sweden, *jopo* in Spain, *zhope* in France, *dzumba* in Naples, *gumpen* in Holland and *jumpei* in Sardinia. But all evidently rendered the sound you make when you JUMP with your feet close together and then land with a thump. In spite of this restricted sense JUMP quickly took hold in English, and has in time almost entirely replaced the less definite words 'leap,' 'spring' and 'bound.' The bovine high jumper who bounded over the moon with all her feet close together must have landed back on earth with an incredible thump. We could hardly call her a mere bounder.

Which all goes to show that when certain words catch our fancy we don't care too much about their exact sense. Today we see fish JUMP that have no legs at all, and how do you account for "I nearly jumped out of my skin?" And we have many other extravagances: Jumping Jesus'es, those intrepid chaplains who leap with the paratroopers; Jumping Jacks and Jills, who are jitterbugs; and the Jumping Off Place, that last stop before nothingness. There is the JUMP of a gun when it is fired, especially the 'up-jump' of its muzzle. We refer to the JUMPING of game in a thicket, that may in their turn JUMP our guns. We have JUMP heads in newspapers, that is, the headlines of JUMP stories that start on one page and then JUMP to a page farther on. All these usages are obviously imaginative, and most of them are colloquial. Humor leavens them all.

The literary sense of 'to jump with,' meaning 'to coincide with,' as in Scott's "Good advice is easy to follow when it jumps with our own interests," is obviously derived from the basic meaning. Shakespeare extended this sense, he went further and used JUMP as an adverb: the ghost in Hamlet arrived "jump at this dead hour." Basic is also the colloquial sense of making a general calculation (somewhat like 'jumping to a conclusion') as in 'jumping' the dressed weight of a hog.

But the nautical jacket we call a JUMPER has nothing to do with all this, though in English it was first called a JUMP and was any short coat. Probably the 'm' just came in through the nose, by a nasalizing of French *jupe* for a 'skirt' or 'kilt.' The origin of *jupe* was in Arabia where, if sailors wore it at all, they probably were riding camels, the ships of the desert. It came West as *jibbah,* whence also the 'gippos' or 'gyps' worn by servants at Cambridge: 'short jackets.' Perhaps influenced by 'gypsy' (from 'gypcian,' or 'Egyptian') it gave us our verb 'to gyp.'

MYSTERY

AMBIGUOUS *adj.* uncertain; vague; open to more than one interpretation.

AMULET *n.* a token or object worn because it is supposed to have magical power to ward off evil.

ANAGRAM *n.* a word or phrase formed by the transposition of letters from another word or phrase, as 'rave' from 'aver.'

CHARADE *n.* a parlor game in which a player or players act out in pantomime a word or phrase which the others try to guess.

CHARM *n.* an amulet; a talisman.

Circe

CONUNDRUM *n.* a riddle; a puzzle, usually involving a pun or a play on words.

Cryptic & Grotesque

EQUIVOCAL *adj.* ambiguous; having several possible meanings.

Enigma

Fetish

Grotesque see Cryptic & Grotesque

LABYRINTH *n.* a maze; any place that is crisscrossed by many twisting streets or passages.

Myth

OBSCURE *adj.* dim; vague; not easily understood, as an OBSCURE passage in a book.

Occult

OMINOUS *adj.* pertaining to omen.

ORACULAR *adj.* pertaining to prophecy, esp. when pompous.

Paradox

PUZZLE *n.* confusion; uncertainty; a difficult question or matter that needs solving; hence, a toy or game which must be solved or untangled by cleverness.

RIDDLE *n.* a puzzle; esp. a question asked in such a way as to obscure the answer.

Rune

SORCERY *n.* magic, particularly black magic; spells; the art of casting spells and calling up evil spirits. *adj.* SORCEROUS.

SPHINX *n.* a mythological monster which proposed riddles; hence; a person who asks riddles, or whose reticence is baffling, like a riddle.

Talisman

THAUMATURGIC *adj.* pertaining to the working of miracles.

VAGUE *adj.* obscure; ambiguous.

VATIC *adj.* pertaining to a seer or a prophet. Hence, oracular; prophetic; inspired.

X

Circe Figuratively, a CIRCE is a 'sorceress.' The adjective is CIRCEAN from the Homeric enchantress who, while bewitching men, enslaved and corrupted them. Sorcery is that kind of enchantment.

Cryptic and **Grotesque** These two words were born as one, but they exhibit, philologically, an interesting instance of a DOUBLET. See PHILOLOGICAL TERMS. As far back as scholars can see, these words were first, in Greece, a suggestive verb meaning 'to hide, conceal.' Becoming in time a noun meaning an 'underground cell, a hidden cave, a hideout,' they passed into the Latin and later divided. *Crypta* remained what we now call a 'crypt,' but *grupta*, a lowly corruption, gave us ultimately Italian *grotta*, whence our 'grotto,' a 'picturesque natural or artificial cave.'

CRYPTIC, from *crypta*, inherits the mystery of the original concealment, and means, literally 'hidden in mystery.' GROTESQUE, from *grupta*, having taken on meanings the Italians gave to it, refers to the 'fantastic in appearance,' especially in the sense of 'oddly misshapen' or 'weirdly misproportioned.' The strange gnus or 'wildebeests' of South Africa are GROTESQUE, being part buffalo, part ass and part horse. In comparison, CRYPTIC things are strange for a different reason. It is obscurity, or figurative darkness, that produces the CRYPTIC. A CRYPTOGRAM is a writing in cipher, and its meaning is 'hidden' from our minds. A CRYPTIC remark puzzles us because its meaning is hidden in words.

Though GROTESQUE is a word of narrow applications, it is laden with collateral suggestions. GROTESQUE things are not only 'odd' to our eyes but also 'weird' to our imaginations. Hence, according to our viewpoint, they are in turn 'curious, ludicrous, crude, distorted, fantastic,' or, more often, all these at once. *Grottesca opera*, 'grotesque works,' was the Italian term for the antique art found in excavated grottoes and ancient buildings. In the former were crude mural paintings or shell-and-pebble designs on the walls. In the latter were mutilated bits of art. Hence 'grotesquery' may represent either rampant primitive imagination or the fact that primitives are not yet technicians in art. It also refers to any art that has been made ludicrous by disproportion.

Both words have architectural meanings. CRYPTS are subterranean cells, whether vaulted or not, used for burials or as chapels. CRYPTIC is their adjective. GROTESQUE architecture is a decorative style grouping animals and flowers in fanciful lines. It flourished in the Roman grottoes, and was revived in Renaissance Italy. In early France it reflected the art of ancient cave dwellers, and was later renamed 'baroque' from the Spanish. GROTESQUE is simply the French version of Italian grottesca.

Enigma   What is an ENIGMATIC man? He is one you can't for the life of you size up. And why is he called ENIGMATIC? Because an ENIGMA is, and since early Grecian times has been, a 'puzzle,' though in the very beginning it was only a 'tale.' "All women are enigmas to me." Or "The ending of that novel is an enigma to any ordinary man."

ENIGMATIC is a broad word. It classifies a man, or his manner, or anything about him that baffles you. Such words are useful. You need them for your every day vocabulary.

Fetish   A word used quite loosely, and fortunately so, on the whole. Though FETISH was no part of their vocabulary, savages are responsible for its popularity today. Portuguese and French fashioned it from broken-down Latin to indicate first the 'luck-charms' of sailors, and then objects of all sorts which were worshipped by primitive Africans as the abodes or symbols of spirits. The native words were probably too difficult for the whites, and so they took a word they already were used to.

Feitico, like our 'partitions,' derived from Latin *partitus*, 'sham, pretended.' *Feiticos* were worn by Portuguese sailors to ward off evil spirits. The savages, to secure their aims and to gain protection against misfortune, treated directly with sticks and stones, within which helpful spirits were believed to lurk. So when the French took over the word and, as *fetiche*, handed it on to us, there was a strong flavor of superstition in it. But in general today FETISH means an image, idol, object of 'unreasoning devotion' or of 'blind affection.'

Myth   "I investigated the rumor and found it was only a myth," "His prowess became a myth in all the annals of sport."

Such usages suggest that a MYTH is, first, a 'fake' and, second, a 'mysterious ghost of fame.' In fact, this is true on both counts but with some important qualifications! For some lies, though partly fake, are intrinsically true; and behind all mysteries there is also truth. To the Greeks a MYTH was a 'word,' and it was soon extended to a 'legend.' Now MYTH may be a 'made-up' story, without foundation in fact, passed off as history. Another meaning of MYTH is a 'traditional' story, at first told by primitive people about supernatural things, to explain in some way the mysteries of creation or the incredible things of life. Hence, in some literary senses, a MYTH is also an 'allegory or parable,' like the fanciful tales Socrates used to clinch his arguments. A modern MYTH can be any story, true or false, that captures the popular imagination and commences to grow. Babe Ruth himself is now a MYTH, and so is Billy the Kid, two people, one good and one bad, who are popular heroes.

There is always some mystery in MYTHS. According to how literally we view them, they are fakes on the one hand and revelations on the other. This variability is represented in further types of MYTHS which we recognize and refer to. A 'culture MYTH,' for example, is one that fancifully explains how we obtained our arts, industries or the materials which make them possible. It represents them as coming from the gods, as gifts, or as resulting from the enterprising spirit of man himself. Prometheus stealing fire for man is a culture MYTH. Similarly, a 'nature MYTH' is one that explains some phenomenon of nature, such as how the bear lost his tail or the fox became sly in fables. How the winds came to blow fitfully or wrathfully is explained MYTHICALLY in terms of the moods and the temper of a diety, Aeolus. But the true MYTH, as distinguished from a 'legend,' is religious, and its heroes are gods, or else it is a fanciful story whose origin has been forgotten but whose significance has spread like a spirit through the minds of many people.

Occult As *occulere* in Latin meant 'to hide,' its past participle *occultus*, the progenitor of our word OCCULT, meant 'hidden.' So OCCULT came to mean, for us, 'mysterious and mystical'—the sense in which we most often use it. In more exact usage whatever is OCCULT is 'concealed.' It is concealed from ordinary observation and from common knowledge. It is not something immediately in sight. If you wish to understand it, you must investigate it. Which all comes around to the same thing: the mystery of concealment, the esoteric importance of the unseen.

Paradox A PARADOXICAL statement is one that is true for a given subject, yet apparently 'contradicts' all that is commonly believed about that subject. It is not, however, a mere believe-it-or-not, which is simply an amazing fact. PARADOXES are seldom factual though they are truthful. They are so vastly truthful, in fact, that the mind is repelled from the truth for a moment, appalled by an apparent incongruity or absurdity: "I'm never less alone than when I am alone."

And financiers sometimes speak PARADOXICALLY of a 'controlled panic.' If you analyze that phrase, you see that it is not equivalent to 'impending panic' or 'partial panic' or 'well-governed panic,' because panics after all are in their nature 'stampedes,' and they defy all control. You recognize that the phrase expresses a phenomenon that can be expressed only PARADOXICALLY.

Rune A character in an ancient alphabet of Northern Europe is a RUNE. Phonetic alphabets have used its remnants. The word itself is mysterious and romantic. It originally meant a 'secret,' sometimes a 'whisper,' and so today we use it for a 'cryptic poem or observation.' Sometimes RUNE means a 'mysterious mark' or a 'magical sign.' RUNES were more decorative than Roman letters, and RUNIC now refers to all the decorative art of the earliest Teutons. There is also a decorative printing type called RUNIC.

Talisman An Arabic word that meant a 'magical figure, a horoscope,' built upon the Greek word for a 'religious rite.' It was elaborated in old Spain where it became an 'amulet, luck-charm,' with vast and marvelous powers against death and disaster, because of its astrological connections. TALISMANS were representations on stones and metals of heavenly signs, constellations or planets. Unlike a mere amulet, which may consist only of words and is always personally worn or possessed, a TALISMAN is any object that is credited with supernatural powers of protection, as for example Aladdin's lamp, a horseshoe, or the Statue of Liberty.

X The 'X' in 'x-rays' is a symbol of the 'unknown,' like the symbol 'X' in algebra, which in the Middle Ages was adopted by scientists to represent the 'unknown quantity.' Actually, they crossed a Roman 'R' erratically, that it might thus remotely represent either *radix* or *res* in the Latin, that is, either a 'root' or just a 'thing.' But in 'Xmas' for Christmas, the 'X' is simply the Greek letter for 'ch.'

NUMBERS

AMOUNT *n.* sum; total.

BAKER'S DOZEN *n.* one more than a dozen, or thirteen, but reckoned as a dozen; thus, a dozen with one extra.

BRACE *n.* two things; pair; couple.

Cardinals see **Ordinals & Cardinals**

CENTESIMAL, QUADRAGESIMAL, etc.

adj. consisting of hundreds, forties, etc.; also, pertaining to one-one-hundredth, one-fortieth, etc. The forms BIENNIAL, TRIENNIAL, QUADRENNIAL, etc., mean occurring once in those numbers of years. SESQUI, as an element added to these words, means one and a half or a half-again. For example, SESQUICENTENNIAL (150 years).

CIPHER *n.* a number; also, the symbol for naught; *v.* to reckon or calculate with numbers.

COUNT *v.* to repeat the numerals, as one, two, three, four. To determine how many of something there is.

DECAGON *n.* a plane figure of ten angles and ten sides.

DELTA *n.* the fourth letter in the Greek alphabet; thus, the fourth one of anything.

DICHOTOMOUS *adj.* pertaining to division into two parts. *n.* DICHOTOMY.

DIGIT *n.* any number from 1 to 9.

DOUBLET *n.* pair; couple; two of a kind.

ENNEAD *n.* any group or set of nine things.

FEW *n.* a small number, as "A few students receive top grades."

FIFTY-FIFTY *adj.* & *adv.* pertaining to sharing something equally, as "Let's go fifty-fifty on this job."

FOURSCORE *n.* eighty, or twenty multiplied four times.

FOURSOME *n.* two couples; four people; esp. in golf.

FRACTION *n.* a part; usually in the sense of a part of one, as one-half, one-third.

Half

HALF & HALF *adj.* & *adv.* fifty-fifty; a mixture of two equal portions.

HALF A DOZEN *n.* six.

HEPTAD *n.* the number seven; any group or set of seven things.

HEPTAGON *n.* a plane figure with seven angles and seven sides.

HEXAD *n.* the number six; any group or set of six things.

HEXAGON *n.* a plane figure with six angles and six sides.

INTEGER *n.* an entity; thus any whole number, as one, two, three.

LONG DOZEN *n.* a baker's dozen.

MATCH *n.* an equality.

MILLESIMAL *adj.* pertaining to thousands.

MILLION *n.* a number written 1,000,000; thus, a thousand thousands.

    BILLION *n.* a thousand millions; 1,000,000,000.

    TRILLION *n.* a thousand billions; 1,000,000,000,000.

    QUADRILLION *n.* a thousand trillions.

    QUINTILLION *n.* a thousand quadrillions.

    SEXTILLION *n.* a thousand quintillions.

    SEPTILLION *n.* a thousand sextillions.

OCTILLION *n.* a thousand septillions.

NONILLION *n.* a thousand octillions.

DECILLION *n.* a thousand nonillions.

UNDECILLION *n.* a thousand decillions.

DUODECILLION *n.* a thousand undecillions.

TREDECILLION *n.* a thousand duodecillions.

QUATTUORDECILLION *n.* a thousand tredecillions.

QUINDECILLION *n.* a thousand quattuordecillions.

SEXDECILLION *n.* a thousand quindecillions.

SEPTENDECILLION *n.* a thousand sexdecillions.

OCTODECILLION *n.* a thousand septendecillions.

NOVEMDECILLION *n.* a thousand octodecillions.

VIGINTILLION *n.* a thousand novemdecillions; or 1 followed by sixty-three zeros.

ZILLION *n.* a huge undefined number, usually used in an humorous way.

Moiety

NAUGHT *n.* zero.

NONAGON *n.* a plane figure with nine angles and nine sides.

NOUGHT *n.* no value, as "All my work came to nought."

NOVENNIAL *adj.* occurring in the ninth year.

Number

OCTAGON *n.* a plane figure having eight angles and eight sides.

Ordinals & Cardinals
Pair

PENTAD *n.* the number five; any group or set of five things.

QUADRUPLET *n.* any group or set of four things; one of four children born at the same birth to the same mother.

QUARTET or QUARTETTE *n.* any group or set of four, as a QUARTET of singers.

QUINTET or QUINTETTE *n.* any group or set of five, as a QUINTET of basketball players.

QUINTUPLET *n.* any group or set of five things; one of five children born at the same birth to the same mother.

RECKON *v.* to compute or cipher, as "The waiter reckoned the bill."

SCORE *n.* twenty; an account kept of points in a game.

SEVERAL *n.* a few.

SEXTUPLET *n.* a group or set of six things.

SUM *n.* a total, as "The sum of two and two is four."

TALLY *n.* sum; total; a record of numbers; score.

TETRAD *n.* the number four; any group or set of four things.

TREY *n.* three, esp. a three of any suit in cards.

TRIAD *n.* the number three; any group or set of three things.

TRICHOTOMOUS *adj.* pertaining to division into three parts. *n.* TRICHOTOMY.

TRIO *n.* any group or set of three, as a TRIO of people.

TRIPLET *n.* any group or set of three things; one of three children born to the same mother at the same birth.

TWAIN *n.* two. *adj.* In TWAIN means in two parts, as cut in TWAIN.

TWO or THREE *n.* a very few.

UNAL *adj.* pertaining to one, or a unit. UNAL is a companion to DUAL and MULTIPLE. For examples, note UNAL opinion, or UNAL controls, as in an airplane.

VICENARY *adj.* pertaining to twenty.

VICESIMAL *adj.* pertaining to twentieth; divided into twenties or into twenty parts.

Half Everybody knows what HALF means, but it has a few tricks. While 'not half bad' means logically and quite liberally 'rather good,' and 'half-and-half' means 'half of one thing and half of another,' HALF can nevertheless play hide-and-seek with the definite article in 'a HALF mile' and throw us into a quagmire of confusion. When we say 'a million and a half, and a half again,' what do we mean? Do we mean 2 millions? Or do we mean a million and a half plus half that much, making 2¼ millions?

Fowler, in his *Dictionary of Modern English Usage*, deplores the 'two-and-a-half millions' as against the more euphonious 'two millions and a half.' Of course, he admits that '2½' can eliminate three printed words. But a loose adjectival fraction before an invisible noun really talks doubly. We have to remember that 'two millions and a HALF' means 'two million plus a HALF a million,' which is expressed unmistakably in '2½ millions' and almost unmistakably in 'two-and-a-half millions.'

Moiety A French product that languishes for the most part in our dictionaries where it is usually given two half-lines of space. It means only 'one half,' so perhaps that's all right. At the table, it is easier to say, "Yes, but only a speck more, please," than to divide up the interior vowels of MOIETY and use that word. The first syllable simply rhymes with 'boy.' It is interesting to note that the reason MOIETY is used for 'speck' or 'a little bit' is because a half of anything is, loosely speaking, almost nothing at all.

Number Grammatically, NUMBER is a singular noun. Sometimes it is used as a collective singular noun. But since NUMBER may refer to the figure 9, or to a variety of things, the question arises, should NUMBER sometimes drop its singular verb and take a plural?

"A number of guests were seated around the room when I came in." Well, if the guests were sitting in a huddle, it would be easy to think of them as a single group. "A number of them *was* sitting in the room." But when they are scattered, they draw attention away from NUMBER. NUMBER consequently becomes, in effect, only a noun in an adjectival phrase, meaning "Several guests were seated about the room." Grammar must sometimes make accommodations for sense, and "A number of guests were . . ." is, as it sounds, correct. When, of course, a NUMBER refers simply to a word or a symbol, like the numeral 9, then a singular verb is correct.

Ordinals and Cardinals 'First, second, third' are ORDINALS; 'one, two, three' are CARDINALS.

Pair The clerk who writes down 'two pair shoes,' 'three pair pajamas' is half right. PAIR was originally a plural noun: Latin *para,* 'equals, peers.' This old sense survives in a 'newly wedded pair.' But the final 'a' of *para* dropped off in France, and compensation was made with an interior 'i.' Still, this didn't suit the English and now we add an 's' to indicate doubly the plural sense of the word. An exception is when we speak of a 'pair of steps,' meaning a 'flight of stairs,' in which there might be twenty or thirty pairs of steps.

OCCUPATIONS

ABBOT *n.* the head of a monastery.

ACCOUNTANT *n.* a person who can keep accounts or financial records and who is further qualified to inspect or audit them.

APIARIST *n.* a beekeeper.

Apostle see Disciple & Apostle

ANCILLARY *adj.* pertaining to a main servant; hence, helping, auxiliary.

BARBER *n.* haircutter; beardtrimmer.

Boniface

BOOKKEEPER *n.* a person who keeps financial accounts or records.

BUCOLIC or PASTORAL *adj.* pertaining to a shepherd, or a rustic and his habitat.

CABINETMAKER *n.* a person who makes fine things, such as superior furniture, out of wood.

CARTOGRAPHER *n.* map maker.

CHIEFTAIN *n.* the chief, or head, of a tribe, clan, group.

CLERK *n.* one who keeps records and handles letters in a business office.

COSMETOLOGIST *n.* a person professionally skilled in the use and application of cosmetics.

DEAN *n.* a university official, usually head of a college or a department of the student body, as the DEAN for women. *adj.* DECANAL.

DIETICIAN *n.* one who applies the science of nutrition to the feeding of people.

DIPLOMAT or DIPLOMATIST *n.* one who conducts state affairs between nations.

Disciple & Apostle

DRAFTSMAN *n.* one who draws plans or sketches to guide builders, engineers or machinists.

DROVER *n.* one who drives animals to market; hence, a cattle dealer.

DUENNA *n.* a Spanish chaperon.

Eremite & Recluse

Esne see **Ryot, Esne,** etc.

Factotum

Ganymede

Haberdasher

Jockey

LAMA *n.* a Tibetan priest.

LUMBERJACK *n.* one who deals in lumber or who cuts timber in forests.

MANAGER *n.* one who manages, or directs, a project, enterprise.

MASON *n.* one who uses brick or stone for building, as "A mason built our fireplace."

MASSEUR *n. masc.,* a man who gives massages, a treatment of the body by rubbing, kneading, slapping. *fem.* MASSEUSE.

Matador

MECHANIC *n.* one who works with machines, esp. engines, such as an automobile MECHANIC.

MENIAL *adj.* pertaining to a servant and to his work. Hence, often, servile or slavish.

MIDWIFE *n.* a woman who helps deliver babies.

MINISTER *n.* a person who is authorized to conduct religious services; also a government official of high rank, as a MINISTER for foreign affairs.

MORTICIAN *n.* an undertaker; a man who prepares for burial, and buries, the dead.

Mountebank

NOTORIAL *adj.* pertaining to notary.

OBSTETRICS *n.* the branch of medicine that deals with the care of women before, during, and after childbirth; in earlier times, midwifery.

OCULIST *n.* a doctor who specialized in diseases of the eye. Compare OPTOMETRIST.

OPTOMETRIST *n.* a man who gives eye examinations with the purpose of correcting mechanical faults. Compare OCULIST.

PASTORAL *adj.* pertaining to a minister having charge of a congregation.

Peon see **Ryot, Esne,** etc.

PROFESSOR *n.* a teacher, esp. at a college or university. *adj.* PROFESSORIAL.

Publican see **Publicist & Publican**

Publicist & Publican

Pupil & Student

Recluse see **Eremite & Recluse**

Robot

Ryot, Esne & Peon

SARTORIAL *adj.* pertaining to a tailor or to tailoring.

Secretary

SHEPHERD *n.* a tender of sheep.

Steward

Tiler

TILLER *n.* a farmer; one who grows things.

TONSORIAL *adj.* pertaining to barbering.

VICAR *n.* minister, esp. one who in some way substitutes for another minister or priest. *adj.*

VICARIAL.

VOCATIONAL *adj.* pertaining to line of work, to vocation.

WARDEN *n.* a person who guards; hence, the chief official of a prison.

Boniface 'Inn keeper'; 'tavern or hotel host.' From a famous fictional character in Farquhar's comedy *The Beaux' Stratagem.*

Disciple and **Apostle** The former is 'taught' and the latter, having been taught, is sent out in turn 'to teach' the truth he has learned. Plato had DISCIPLES, who learned his philosophy; but Christ had APOSTLES, who were explicitly enjoined to go through the world teaching Christianity.

Eremite and **Recluse** An EREMITE is a hermit, from the Greek for 'lonely,' and is by connotation 'austere and wise,' and he lives in bare lands. 'Hermit' is a doublet of EREMITE. (See DOUBLET.) In Greek it means 'solitary.' He is akin to a RECLUSE, who is a 'voluntary shut-in,' preferring to live in seclusion. RECLUSE as an adjective means 'solitary, secluded.' RECLUSE haunts may be woodland dales.

Factotum Once an imperative phrase, 'do everything' (Latin *fac* plus *totus*). The phrase became a term for 'busybody,' someone who loves to do everything without being told to. Today a FACTOTUM is a jack-of-all-jobs, employed perhaps to run errands, milk the cow, drive your car, answer the phone and bring your mail. He is necessarily a versatile fellow.

Ganymede Figuratively, a 'cup-bearer, a personal servant.' GANYMEDE is the name of the beautiful youth in classical mythology who was carried to heaven by Jove's eagle to serve the gods their wine.

Haberdasher HABERDASHERS are common enough, but where did they come from? This is a question that puts HABERDASHER into almost every reference book on words. Even the exact present meaning of the word is somewhat moot. Does a HABERDASHERY ('men's furnishing shop') sell only shirts, ties and underwear, or does it also go in for notions like needles and threads? And if you say HABERDASH for the noun, instead of HABERDASHER, is that a colloquialism, or was the dealer really first a HABERDASH?

There are many answers, in the main confusing because no one knows where or how the word began. It is interesting. You hear it came from Germany where it was jocularly "Habt ihr das, hier?" or perhaps "Habt Ihr dass, Herr?" roughly, "Have you this or that?" supposedly asked of shopkeepers. But then this idea is pooh-poohed. Shakespeare's contemporaries had a word 'mercerot,' defined as a 'peddler' or 'paltry HABERDASHER.' Quite probably the first HABERDASHER *was* a 'mercer,' now a dealer in silks, woolens, etc. But the 'mercer' in Latin, as later in English, used to be just a dealer in merchandise, especially in small wares. And in the Anglo-French such a dealer was called a *hapertas*, which the Oxford sees as the beginning of modern HABERDASHER. Others think *hapertas* was hat material, whence HABERDASH, for small wares, and HABERDASH or HABERDASHER for the one who sold them.

But then you hear: HABERDASH, from the Icelandic word *hapurtask*, 'haversack.' And Ernest Weekley, with his usual exquisite combination of acumen with caution, suggests that HABERDASH might be historically 'to have' (compare avoirdupois, 'to have weight') plus a Provençal word for a 'board,' on which a dealer would naturally spread out his wares.

So you can have HABERDASHER just about any way you want it—like hash. Some dictionaries give up, and don't give you any derivation at all.

Jockey Appropriately, to admirers of the Robin Hood tales, from Jackey, the diminutive of Jack. When Robin Hood named his giant henchman "Littlejohn," he simply meant, ironically, that he was no JOCKEY. But JOCKIES have given us an expressive verb. Before races were started from a gate divided into stalls, the matter of aligning the horses on an open track, keeping them alert, yet not too conscious of their neighbors, and then of getting them off briskly, was a very ticklish and important job. Most business deals involve a JOCKEYING for a start, too. "Candidates for the senatorial nominations jockey for the best political advantage months before the state conventions."

Matador Bullfight enthusiasts may feel mixed emotions if they regard MATADOR etymologically. He is, on any grounds, a killer, coming from the Latin *mactare*, 'to kill.' But to the Romans *mactare* only incidentally meant 'to kill.' Behind that it meant 'to make a sacrifice to,' as when a lamb was sacrificed to the gods. And before that it meant 'to worship.' *Mactus* meant 'venerated,' and *macte*, through emotional developments, meant 'bravo!'

Mountebank   The original 'soapbox orator,' especially if selling quack medicines. The 'bank' was Old German for a 'bench,' on which he probably stood. By extension, MOUNTEBANK now refers to any 'quack' who has a slick tongue.

Publicist and **Publican**   A PUBLICIST is a writer on international law or other broad matters of public interest. Sometimes he is a promoter of public welfare. A PUBLICAN keeps a public house. He is an innkeeper or a hotel manager.

Pupil and **Student**   You are a PUPIL when you are being taught. Studying PUPILS automatically are STUDENTS. But STUDENTS are those who seek knowledge by largely their own effort.

Robot   A mechanical man, as introduced in a play by the Bohemian playwright Karel Čapek in 1921. Hence any 'automaton' or 'insensate drudge.' The Czech word for work is *robota*.

Ryot, Esne and **Peon**   Respectively, a 'peasant' in India, an Anglo-Saxon 'serf or farmhand,' and a 'common laborer or servant.' In Mexico the PEON is bound to service by debt, and is virtually a slave. In South America he is specifically a muleteer. In India a PEON is not the same as a RYOT, but is an orderly or a constable.

Secretary   This word derives from Late Latin *secretarius*, a 'confidential officer,' or 'notary,' from earlier Latin *secretum*, a 'secret.' Now a SECRETARY conducts correspondence and records proceedings for societies, executives or professional workers. The SECRETARY is no common employee but one who represents a type of humanity. This type, now predominantly feminine, is so characterized by graces, tact, and an efficient service that the old conception of a close-mouthed scribe with a quill pen thrust behind his ears is disappearing. Modern SECRETARIES connote, first of all, social SECRETARIES, then business SECRETARIES. In fact, the connotations are almost glamorous. But only a few generations ago a most awful looking African bird, that stands perhaps three feet high and feeds on snakes resembling its own long neck, was named a 'secretary bird,' presumably because some feathers stick out behind its ears, like penholders.

Steward A word that certainly has elevated itself, and in some reaches actually ennobled itself. In early English the first syllable was *stig* and stood for 'sty,' which we now take to mean a 'pigpen' but which then signified a 'farmyard.' The second syllable was a 'caretaker or warden.' But to care for a farmyard certainly meant to look after the livestock, and to provide the food for the owner. Thus, the STEWARD worked his way into the kitchen, then the pantry, and over it. He became a 'caterer' and a 'major-domo.' A STEWARD is the 'manager' of an estate or of someone's financial affairs. The English royal family name Stuart, Stewart, or Steuart comes from a family which held for several generations the office of high STEWARD of Scotland.

Tiler Originally a 'coverer,' in the Latin. In medieval times he was a 'roofer or floorer.' Now he is a maker and layer of tiles, or a doorkeeper in a Masonic temple. But TILER has taken on other capacities. He is a cat who prowls over roofs, a pickpocket's aid who makes off with the loot, and a stovepipe silk hat.

ODORS

AMBROSIAL *adj.* pertaining to a delightful taste or smell; fragrant.

AROMA *n.* an agreeable odor, such as that coming from spices, cooking foods or perfume. *adj.* AROMATIC.

BOUQUET *n.* a pleasant perfume or aroma that some wines possess.

ESSENCE *n.* perfume; scent; esp. the volatile aroma that comes from perfume.

EXHALATION *n.* the odor which is emitted by something, esp. the odor EXHALED by swamps or decaying matter. *v.* EXHALE.

FETID *adj.* having an offensive or disagreeable smell; stinking.

FRAGRANCE *n.* a sweet or pleasant odor; the odor from a flower or spice. *adj.* FRAGRANT.

FUME *n.* a smoky or perhaps invisible exhalation that stifles or chokes one.

FUSTY *adj.* fetid; rank; musty.

HEADY *adj.* pertaining to an odor, usually an aroma, that effects one in the head with a dizzy sensation.

INCENSE *n.* any aromatic substance, as gums or spices; the aroma coming from certain burning substances, as frankincense.

Malodorous

MUSCHATE *adj.* musky. MUSK is used in perfumery.

MUSTY *adj.* having an old, stale or sour odor, as MUSTY rags.

Noisome

ODORIFEROUS *adj.* giving off an odor, usually sweet and pleasant, as an ODORIFEROUS bakery.

ODOROUS *adj.* odoriferous.

PERFUME *n.* essence, esp. a volatile liquid made from a concentrated oil pressed from flowers or derived from chemicals both of which emit fragrance. *adj.* PERFUMED, fragrant; sweet-smelling. "She sent perfumed letters."

PUNGENT *adj.* pertaining to a sharp or piercing odor.

PUTRID *adj.* pertaining to a state of decay or corruption; thus, fetid.

RANCID *adj.* fetid; musty; referring to any odor very offensive or sickening.

RANK *adj.* strong or very pungent, as the RANK jungle.

REDOLENCE *n.* fragrance; perfume.

Reek see **Smoke & Reek**

SCENT *n.* perfume; aroma. *adj.* SCENTED, referring to something with a pleasant aroma, as a SCENTED soap.

SMELL *n.* an odor or scent, usually a bad or offensive odor. *adj.* SMELLY.

Smoke & Reek

SPICE *n.* an aromatic or pungent material, esp. an herb used for cooking. *adj.* SPICY.

STENCH *n.* an unpleasant odor.

STINK *n.* a stench. *adj.* STINKING, fetid; rank.

WHIFF *n.* a puff of odoriferous air.

Malodorous In this day of much advertised DEODORANTS we see a deterioration in the meaning of the word 'smell,' while the robust, not to say ribald, old stand-bys, 'stench' and 'stink' are now unthinkable in polite usage. That leaves us with a vacuum which soft sounding MALODOROUS can easily fill. We still have, of course, the round Roman word 'odor,' and hence 'odorous.' But ODOR has that repugnant association with DEODORANT, so we may well take the cue of the advertisers, and bury the ODOR in MALODOROUS.

Noisome This word means 'disgustingly offensive.' NOISOME is a strong word, especially as it is usually used to refer to a strong smell. Incidentally, 'noise,' which comes from the French word for 'quarrel,' is not etymologically related to NOISOME. NOISOME is kin to the word 'annoy.'

Smoke and Reek When Prometheus stole fire from the heavens for use on this planet he was probably thinking little of SMOKE, and not at all of 'tobacco.' But today SMOKE first of all suggests 'tobacco,' which, incidentally, is now said *not* to have been one of the sixteen 'herbs' sniffed, chewed and smoked by our Indians when Columbus first made their acquaintance. It quickly became a favorite after it was planted in Jamestown in 1612, having been borrowed, presumably, from some Spanish colony elsewhere. In England it was first popularly used as snuff. But when Shakespeare was a boy SMOKING already was known in England, and he probably heard it spoken of as 'drinking tobacco.' Within his life time the intransitive verb, to SMOKE, without predicative additions, became fairly common.

SMOKE has superseded, except in Scotland, its Anglo-Saxon companion, REEK, leaving that unfortunate word to denote 'real stenches.' Sometimes REEK refers weakly to mere 'steam or vapor.' Only the vilest cigars now REEK. We are using strong language when we say someone's manner is REEKING with something we don't like. "That man reeks with power," certainly conveys disgust both of power and of that man.

THE OTHER WORLD

APPARITION n. a ghost; specter; phantom.

BODILESS adj. without substance; ghostly.

DISCARNATE adj. without flesh; as DISCARNATE bones.

DISEMBODIED adj. discarnate; without corporeal existence, as DISEMBODIED ghosts.

EERIE adj. mysterious; weird; frightening; as "How eerie the woods appear in the moonlight!"

EXTRAMUNDANE adj. above or beyond worldly limits; beyond physical or material spheres.

FETCH n. an apparition; a wraith.

GHOST n. spirit; soul; apparition; esp. in the sense of SPECTER. adj. GHOSTLY or GHOSTLIKE.

HAUNT n. a ghost, esp. a local spirit (Colloq.).

INCORPOREAL adj. without substance or body.

PHANTASM n. apparition; specter; also, a fantastic idea; illusion.

PHANTOM n. phantasm. adj. illusory; vague; dim; as a PHANTOM memory.

PRETERNATURAL adj. extraordinary; beyond the natural; as a PRETERNATURAL ability.

Seance

Seraph

SHADE n. soul; spirit; ghost.

Specter see Spectral & Specter

Spectral & Specter

SPIRIT n. soul; an animating or life-giving force, as the SPIRIT of man; any invisible force or being.

SPOOK n. ghost; usually in a humorous sense.

SUPERNATURAL adj. above the

natural; not like anything natural. See also PRETERNATURAL.

Undine

WRAITH *n.* an apparition of a person who is actually alive but in another place. *adj.* WRAITH-LIKE, describes a person who doesn't look quite himself, who is thin or ill-looking.

Seance A SEANCE was originally a 'sitting,' from obsolete French *soir,* 'to sit,' from Latin *sedere.* It was a solemn word, designating a meeting of learned men. Perhaps it was tinged with humor, like the lingering scholarly phrase, 'to sit under' some famous teacher, meaning to sit on the benches below his raised desk. But about 1845 a spectacular lot of learneds came along, strange metaphysicians called 'spiritualists,' who claimed to be able to talk with the dead. They were given to holding meetings or sessions ('sittings'). SEANCE occured to them as having impressive connotations, and they adopted it. They filled it with new and mysterious meanings. Almost any secret meeting now, where weighty and mysterious matters are discussed, can be a SEANCE.

Seraph An angel of the highest order, attending the throne of God. In Hebrew the name meant 'burning.' SERAPHS at the outset were the fiery and fast-flying couriers from the Lord Jehovah to humans on earth.

Spectral & Specter A SPECTER is, etymologically, a 'vision.' Consequently anything that is SPECTRAL is sure to be ghostly. A SPECTER is any 'ghostly phantasm.'

Undine One of the fabled 'water nymphs,' whose only hope of ever possessing a soul was to marry a mortal. From Latin *unda,* 'wave.'

PARTS AND THE WHOLE

ALL *adj.* pertaining to the whole quantity or number of something; as ALL history, or ALL the children.

ATOM *n.* the smallest part of an element that enters into the composition of molecules; also, a very small particle, a minute quantity.

BALE *n.* a large bundle or package, usually wrapped and corded or banded. Its contents are usually compressed.

Bevy & Bunch

Bunch see **Bevy & Bunch**

BUNDLE *n.* several things bound together; a package or several packages tied together for easy carrying.

Clastic

Compact

COMPONENT *n.* an essential part of a whole thing, as "One component of concrete is cement." *adj.* pertaining to a part or an element of any whole.

CONSTITUENT *n.* whatever serves as a part of an organic whole, as "Symmetry is a constituent of beauty."

Cortege see **Ménage, Entourage,** etc.

COVEY *n.* a flock or group of game birds, esp. partridges.

DETAIL *n.* a distinct part; a particular; a small or unimportant fact. "He forgot the details of the theory, though he could remember the general argument."

Divers see **Divert, Divers,** etc.

Divert, Divers, etc.

DOT *n.* point, speck, or spot on something.

Dregs & Lees

DROVE *n.* a flock of sheep, cattle, swine, driven in a body.

ELEMENT *n.* a constituent; a fundamental part of anything; a part that cannot be divided into any components.

ENTIRE *adj.* having all its parts; whole, complete.

Entourage see **Ménage, Entourage,** etc.

Extraneous

FACTOR *n.* a part, or an influence, that contributes to a given result.

FARDEL *n.* a bundle.

FLIGHT *n.* a group of any birds flying together, usually migrating birds.

FLOCK *n.* a group, chiefly of birds, wild or domestic, sheep or goats. FLOCK suggests a large company or crowds.

FRACTION *n.* a part of a whole, esp. in the sense of a fragment.

Friable

GAGGLE *n.* a group or flock, esp. of geese on water.

GROSS *n.* whole; total; without any deductions; as the GROSS amount of money earned.

HERD *n.* a group or collection, chiefly of sheep, cattle, or other hoofed animals, or of whales or seals, massed together.

INGREDIENT *n.* a constituent; component part.

Iota see **Modicum, Iota,** etc.

ITEM *n.* a detail.

JOT *n.* a point; iota.

Lees see **Dregs & Lees**

MANIFOLD *adj.* many; numerous; varied; as the MANIFOLD fall colors.

MANY *n.* a large number, as "Many have read this book." *adj.* numerous; manifold.

Ménage, Entourage, Cortege & Retinue

Minutiae

Miscellaneous & Multifarious

Modicum, Iota & Morsel

MOLECULE *n.* a small particle of matter—the smallest that keeps its identity with the substance in mass; also, any small particle of matter, as "Little molecules of water formed a jeweled pattern on the iced glass."

Morsel see **Modicum, Iota,** etc.

MOTE *n.* dot; speck; as a MOTE of dust.

Multifarious see **Miscellaneous & Multifarious**

MULTIFOLD *adj.* manifold; folded or covered over many times, as the MULTIFOLD petals of some flowers.

Multitudinous

NUMEROUS *adj.* many; in great numbers.

Olio

PACK *n.* a group, esp. of hounds or wolves when they hunt together for game or food.

PACKAGE *n.* a bundle; esp. a small BUNDLE in one container, easy to carry.

PACKET *n.* a small package or parcel.

PARCEL *n.* bundle; package.

Part

PARTICLE *n.* atom; speck; mote.

Personnel

PIECE *n.* part; component; often in the sense of fragment.

PORTION *n.* a share or part of anything; piece; as a PORTION of food.

Retinue see **Ménage, Entourage,** etc.

SCHOOL *n.* a group, esp. in the sense of shoal.

SECTION *n.* segment; portion; part; as a SECTION of land.

SEGMENT *n.* section; esp. a natural division, as "That segment of my property is worthless marsh."

Several

SHOAL *n.* a group, esp. of fish or aquatic animals.

Snippet

SPECK *n.* a very small spot or particle, as a SPECK of sand.

SWARM *n.* a mass or large group, esp. of insects in motion.

Torso

VARIOUS *adj.* manifold.

Bevy and **Bunch** BEVY is said to be from the Old French *beveye,* a company of good fellows at a 'drinking party.' BUNCH is from Icelandic *bunki,* a 'heap.' BUNCH refers to a collection of usually 'unharmonious or unalike objects,' such as quarreling birds or a mixture of people. "Look, at that bunch of sight-seers in front of the statue." BEVY, perhaps because of its softer sound, usually signifies a collection of 'harmonious or attractive beings,' such as flowers or young girls. "All those butterflies over there look like a bevy of dancing flowers." It is your ear and good taste that will determine which word to use. A hint: BEVY is almost never used to indicate 'inanimate' things.

Clastic A termological adjective meaning 'can be taken apart.' Anatomical models with detachable parts are CLASTIC. The term is also used in geology. Conglomerate rock, composed of bits of older and various rocks, is CLASTIC.

Compact The snow in a hard snowball is COMPACT, and the snowball itself is COMPACT. So is a business office of six efficient workers in comparison with one in which the same work is spread out among ten. Your thoughts are COMPACT when you concentrate. Your style of speaking or writing is then COMPACT. The word COMPACT is honest and prosaic. 'Com' means 'together,' and 'pact' from Latin *pangere*, means 'to fasten.' In the verb the fastening has been generalized, but in the noun and adjective the meaning is nearer its old self. A COMPACT agreement is a 'close and binding' one. It fastens you and the other fellow together, with obligations.

Divert, Divers, etc. You can DIVERT ('turn aside') an attack of ennui when you DIVERT ('amuse') yourself with a good book. For DIVERS ('several or various') reasons such a book will probably be DIVERSIFIED ('variegated') reading. For DIVERSE ('opposite, distinctly different') reasons a book to be studied must be solid and homogeneous. A DIVERTISSEMENT is an extraneous little entertainment between the ordinary acts of a play. With one less 's' it is any diversion or amusement. All these words stem from the Roman *divertere,* 'apart' plus 'turn.'

Dregs and Lees The DREGS of our sorrow, the LEES of our grief. These are equivalent phrases, only in one we are speaking English, in the other Latin. DREGS is Middle English *dregges,* for 'settlings' or 'sediment' ('sorrow' is early English). LEES are Latin for 'settlings' or 'sediment' ('grief' is Latin *gravis,* 'heavy').

Extraneous EXTRANEOUS is the opposite of 'necessary to,' 'essential,' or 'native.' *Obiter dicta* are EXTRANEOUS remarks scattered through a text. They are not essential parts of it; they are 'foreign' to the general subject. Though they may be cleverly integrated with the text, they are not 'intrinsic' or 'germane.' More practically, imported wheat is EXTRANEOUS. It 'comes from the outside,' but it is not exactly external. It is strange in the sense that foreigners are strangers.

Friable Not an uncommon word in books. It is found sometimes in newspapers, but we could use it more often in our every day speech. It is an adjective, and means 'crumbling,' like sandstone, or 'falling to pieces,' like old paper, or 'reducible to powder.'

Ménage, Entourage, Cortege, and **Retinue** These are all collective nouns from the French. MÉNAGE means the collective members of a household. Hence it can mean 'housekeeping.' The emphasis is domestic, bourgeois or familiar. An indirect way of asking whether someone is living with a woman—wife, mother, sister, mistress—is, "Do you have a ménage?" In distinction, an ENTOURAGE or a RETINUE is the 'aggrandized MÉNAGE' of an important person. It follows him when he travels or goes to war. It may consist collectively of his associates, colleagues, companions, followers, henchmen and retainers. When they travel they may constitute a CORTEGE. A CORTEGE is a procession or train of people usually belonging to an ENTOURAGE.

Inferentially, an ENTOURAGE may be simply an 'environment,' and a RETINUE may be figuratively a 'train of events.' "A retinue of pleasant memories may follow a vacation."

Minutiae Small and often meaningless details.

Miscellaneous and **Multifarious** MISCELLANEOUS refers to 'various, usually unrelated, parts,' mixed together. MULTIFARIOUS signifies 'many parts,' always of different or unrelated sorts. "That man has a miscellaneous collection of playing records." "Every adult woman has a multifarious personality which shows a new facet every time she meets another man."

Modicum, Iota and **Morsel** Each of these words signifies 'small particles or amounts.' A MODICUM was to the Romans a 'measure' *modus*. Time has permanently shrunk it. Now MODICUM means a 'single measure,' like *one* lump of sugar per cup. An IOTA is simply the Greek name for the smallest letter 'i.' It means a 'small quantity.' A *morsellum* in Latin was a 'bite, mouthful.' Consequently, a MORSEL today is not only a small quantity of food, a mouthful of choice tidbit, but also a small, solid chunk, of anything at all.

Multitudinous This is certainly a descriptive and sonorous word. It was new in the literature of John Milton, that master of Latinized words. It is structurally almost identical with *multitudo*, a 'crowd.' If the cares of the day press and crowd you in countless numbers, what word better describes the confusion than MULTITUDINOUS?

Olio A 'medley,' especially of songs or musical numbers in a performance, is an OLIO. Unlike the combining form 'oleo,' OLIO has nothing to do with oil or butter, like 'oleomargarine.' A 'medley,' like a 'meddler,' comes via Old French from Latin *misceo,* 'to mix.' OLIO was the 'pot,' *olla,* in which probably they did the mixing. OLIO is any 'mixture' or 'miscellany.'

Part PART means any 'fraction of a whole,' but this fraction has come to mean a whole in itself. There is a discussion in which several individuals are involved. Each individual can say that, 'on his part,' he considers this is the truth. This usage is equivalent to saying 'in his opinion,' 'from his point of view,' or 'as for him.' In most cases, a preposition can be used to replace the cumbersome PART. "I am only speaking (on his part) (for him)." "Think of how much energy is wasted (on the part of) (by) youth!"

Personnel A government of the people, by the people and for the people would certainly suggest an extensive PERSONNEL. But Lincoln would never have used that word. It was the French who first realized that governments must concern themselves separately with persons and things. They therefore employed two complementary words to express the separate categories: *personnel* and *matériel.* We adopted both words, especially in the army. PERSONNEL is used for 'employees collectively,' or simply for 'manpower.' 'Matériel' is used for 'stock,' animate or inert, whether horses, houses, appliances, or what not.

But PERSONNEL, since it consists of persons, is not in practice solely a category, since employees naturally conceive of themselves as personages. So a term that represents them as mere correlatives of nails, axes and stationery has its shortcomings. PERSONNEL is sacrilegious of persons. 'Persons' were first, etymologically, megaphone-mouthed masks worn by Greek actors, but they became everybody, including 'parsons' who preached the word of God. 'Person' is derived from *per,* 'through,' plus *sonare,* 'to sound.' The actors spoke through their masks. And until quite recently 'person' was pronounced 'parson,' as 'clerk' was 'clark.' The word PERSONNEL seems ingratiating, but usage refutes it, and we don't like persons being catalogued. Yet the hard fact is that we adopted the word because we had no other one for it.

The substitute should be a collective noun, but one not too general to apply to small groups of people. The word 'force,' as in an 'office force,' suggests itself; but a government's 'force' would sound dangerous because of the association with 'air force,' 'police force,' etc. 'Help' would be a poor choice, and so would 'hands'; both words signify co-operative workers but they have acquired a menial bias. 'Staff' is too particular since it refers only to officials. And the French don't have a better word either!

Several Sometimes SEVERAL is used in the sense of 'separate,' which was its original meaning. "The several members of a law firm and their several opinions all conflicted." But the common meaning of SEVERAL today is 'two or three,' 'a very few.' "Several boys are going camping overnight."

Snippet Not a bad word to remember. As SNIPPET tries to tell you, it means a small piece 'snipped' off from something. Whence quite naturally comes its colloquial sense, of a 'small or unimportant person.'

Torso TORSO, the stem of a human being, not including the limbs and head, comes ultimately from the ivy-wreathed wand of the Bacchantes, the 'thyrsus.' Even in ancient Greece the word came to mean any 'straight stem or rod.' The Romans borrowed it, then the Italians, and finally we. To the Italians it had on the one hand as little significance as a 'cabbage-stump' or a 'flower stalk,' but it grew again in dignity to mean the 'trunk of a statue.' Since dug-up statues in architectural ruins are usually headless and limbless, TORSO has now a figurative use referring to any fragmentary object, especially an unfinished or mutilated one, which conveys an idea of the whole. Sometimes TORSO means the whole human figure, or even the personality which that figure represents.

PEACE

ARMISTICE *n.* a suspension of hostilities on the basis of a temporary agreement; truce.

CALM *n.* stillness; without motion; peace; tranquillity. *adj.* quiet.

CONCILIATION *n.* the act of putting into harmony or agreement opposing or hostile persons or parties. *v.* CONCILIATE. *adj.* CONCILIATORY. See also **Propitiate & Conciliate.**

HARMONIOUS *adj.* pertaining to harmony, agreement, lack of discord.

HUSH *n.* stillness; quietness. *v.* to make quiet, as "The fog hushed the city traffic."

PACIFIC *adj.* pertaining to peace or to lack of discord or hostility; conciliatory.

Pacify see **Placate & Pacify**
Palliate

PEACEFUL *adj.* pacific; esp. in sense of calm.

Placate & Pacify

PLACIDITY *n.* state of being peaceful or calm and tranquil in disposition and manner. *adj.* PLACID, free from disturbance, as "How placid lies the lake in moonlight!"

Propitiate & Conciliate

QUIET *n.* stillness; peace. *adj.* tranquil; free from noise, as "At noon the forest is full of sleepy quiet."

RECONCILIATION *n.* the act of bringing together in peace and agreement persons or parties once friendly but now hostile.

REPOSE *n.* state of sleep or rest. *v.* to rest or to spend some time at a place, as "They reposed during the summer at the shore."

SERENITY *n.* placidity; calm; tranquility.

SHUSH *v.* to quiet, as "The mother shushed the fretful baby to sleep."

SILENCE *n.* quietness; freedom from noise.

STILL *n.* silence; quietness; as the STILL of the night. *adj.* quiet.

Tranquil

TRUCE *n.* an agreement to stop fighting for a specified time, often short. *adj.* TRUCIAL.

Palliate A word that is a good deal in demand, along with others like it, suggesting 'easement,' 'abatement' or 'remedies' in a world which is, as things happen, full of illness and evil. PALLIATE is, at bottom, quite specific, as is shown by its still persisting, though archaic, meaning of 'to hide or conceal something.' The Romans developed this sense from their matter-of-fact word for 'cloak,' *pallium.* Hence today we speak commonly of PALLIATING a crime, meaning to make it appear less awful, though we still more commonly use PALLIATE with a newer sense of 'abatement,' as in PALLIATING ('lessening') pain.

If we compare PALLIATE with some of its near synonyms, we can find the distinctive meaning in it. 'To excuse' something implies, really, the granting of a plea, no matter what the plea might have offered or argued in extenuation. On the other hand 'to extenuate' is argumentative, advancing reasons in the light of which a misdeed is less blameworthy. But PALLIATION, if it is argumentative at all, is sophistically so. It does not soften a crime, but seeks to extenuate it by misrepresenting or concealing its worst features. It is odd, therefore, that our chief usage of PALLIATION is for 'abatement.'

Placate and **Pacify** PLACATE is a staccato word, yet it is equivalent to the soft PACIFY. It is in fact softer and more limited in meaning than PACIFY. You PLACATE ('appease') a wrathful man, you PACIFY ('calm') a turbulent or violent mob. When, however, you reverse yourself the word's sense stiffens up. When you are '*im*placable' you are 'unyielding, adamant.' If you are PLACABLE, the word softens again:

you are 'amenable.' 'To PACIFY' implies action and force. But to
PLACATE simply suggests 'good temper.' You can PLACATE a grumbler
with soft reasoning. But if you fail and the grumbler growls, then
you have to PACIFY him.

Propitiate and **Conciliate** PROPITIATE means to appease someone
who, presumably, feels offended. With the assumption that whoever is
offended is justified in his grievance the word then means 'to make
atonement, to expiate an offense.' A PROPITIATORY gesture is therefore
not the same as a CONCILIATORY one, in which your main object is
to reason with or to tame someone lest he become a troublemaker.
PROPITIATE thus sticks close to the Latin meaning, 'to appease.' While
CONCILIATION consists of 'peaceful persuasion' and 'reasonable con-
cessions,' PROPITIATION suggests unworthy ingratiation and the offering
of bribes. Yet PROPITIATION can sometimes be a token of true contriteness. "I conciliate my enemy, and I propitiate my King," says that I
take the trouble to keep the peace and that I take pains, by gifts or
service, to have the King's pardon for my past offenses and indulgence
for my future mistakes.

Tranquil The state which this word describes is so well-known
that some dictionaries will give you two or three common synonyms
for TRANQUIL and there let the matter rest. Which is not inappropriate
since the word itself virtually means 'at rest.'

Yet there is something in the sound of the word, especially when it
expands into the noun, TRANQUILITY, which its synonyms lack. Sometimes these synonyms have been generally used in such a specific way
that their connotations have narrowed. 'Peaceful,' for example, is a
foil to 'warlike,' and so there is always a suggestion of impending
turbulence in it. 'Composed,' 'unruffled,' 'calm,' 'sedate,' and 'un-
disturbed' all suggest some mental effort, some self-control or sedative,
to attain the meaning of TRANQUILITY, which itself exists by virtue
of a natural right, without effort. Perhaps the 'serenity' of a landscape,
or the 'calm' of a seascape best describes this intrinsic inevitability of
TRANQUILITY. The second syllable of TRANQUIL is virtually our word
'quiet' and the 'tran' has the force of 'through and through,' as well as of
'over,' 'across' and 'beyond.'

PERCEPTIONS

See also Mind and Its Processes

BEHOLD *v.* to see; to observe or watch with wonder. "They beheld the rising dawn."

Curious

Cursory see **Peruse & Cursory**

DESCRY *v.* to perceive, esp. in the sense of to discover by seeing or looking, as to DESCRY a distant bird.

DISCERN *v.* to distinguish or comprehend by using either one's eyes or mind.

Envisage see **Visualize, Envisage, etc.**

Envision see **Visualize, Envisage, etc.**

ESPY *v.* to descry.

EXAMINE *v.* to look something over carefully, as to EXAMINE a jewel.

GAPE *v.* to look at something open-mouthed; to stare.

GLANCE *n.* a quick look. *v.* to look quickly at something, as to GLANCE at a book.

GLIMPSE *n.* & *v.* glance.

Inquisitiveness

INSPECT *v.* to examine; look around. *n.* INSPECTION.

Look

MACROSCOPIC *adj.* visible to the naked eye. Its antonym is MICROSCOPIC.

NOTE *v.* to perceive; observe.

NOTICE *n.* the act of observing or paying attention. *v.* to observe.

Observe

PEEK *v.* to look slyly, esp. around corners or through crevices.

PEEP *v.* to peek.

PERCEIVE *v.* to see something, esp. in the sense of comprehending what is seen.

Peruse & Cursory

REMARK *v.* to notice.

SCAN *v.* to look over or about, as to SCAN the horizon.

Scrutinize

SEE *v.* to look; to distinguish light and dark, color and form, with the eyes.

Sense

SIGHT *n.* the ability to see.

Squint

SURVEY *n.* scan.

VIEW *v.* to look at something, esp. a spectacle, as to VIEW a picture.

Visualize, Envisage, Envision

Curious This word has sunk itself into two usages. "He is curious about the origins of our solar system," and "Isn't it curious how the giraffe can run, with its long neck?" In the first case, the word means, of course, filled with the urge to ask questions. In the second case, it means 'peculiar.' The word came to us from the Old French, but back of that it meant bluntly, in the Latin, 'care.' Our imaginations have built on the idea of 'care.' Not so long ago we spoke of fine or subtle passages in literature as CURIOSITIES, meaning 'niceties,' specimens of exquisitely careful and exact literary workmanship. It is probably by such a development that the sense of eccentricity developed in CURIOUS. "He is a curious sort of person." We still read in the older books of fabrics woven CURIOUSLY or with CURIOUS skill. This idea of 'meticulous care' came to be applied to the seekers of CURIOSITIES. In other words, if you go around hunting for CURIOUS things, you're inquisitive. See INQUISITIVENESS.

Inquisitiveness INQUISITIVENESS can be both a serious nuisance and a potent factor in human progress. It means a tendency to poke into things, to examine and search out the nature of things, to inquire about matters that are possibly none of your business. In the intellectual sphere, it rewards the acumen it requires, for INQUISITIVENESS has led to many scientific discoveries and philosophic concepts. INQUISITIVENESS differs from curiosity in this respect, that the former is the act of prying or of hunting for answers, while the latter is a state of mind. See CURIOUS.

Look There is no reason LOOK should not be a nice word, but it hardly is any more. Even if someone says that you are 'good-looking,' there is the uncomfortable reflection that, similarly, wild ducks are good eating. There are other indignities heaped upon LOOKING in general. There is 'look-see' for a 'lamping' or a 'once-over' of anything at all, and the 'lookies,' or television, with its 'lookers-in,' or audience. 'Lookit' and 'looka' for the already annoying 'look here,' and 'swell looker,' for someone who LOOKS like a million dollars, are the poorest sort of slang because they aren't even colorful. Not all of these expressions are modern, of course; but all of them are emasculations of the old Saxon word that began as 'Behold.' It gave us our 'lookouts' on mastheads and mountain tops, and the warning we are neglecting today, to 'Look out!' lest we lose the flavor of an old word.

Observe The verb OBSERVE is expansible and contractible in its meaning. You can OBSERVE a scene, such as a football game being played, in the simple sense of 'seeing' it, 'noting' it or 'watching' it attentively. On the other hand, if you are a player, you can OBSERVE the rules of the game: your attentiveness becomes a devotion, an adherence. In this sense you OBSERVE—that is, appropriately 'keep' or 'celebrate'—a national holiday. In a little different direction the word serves scholars and scientists: they can OBSERVE a theory critically and closely for its truth. And then OBSERVE is used intransitively. "'This is a matter that requires some thought,' he observed." In this usage, OBSERVE is a synonym for 'remark,' which, incidentally, is 're,' an intensive, plus 'mark,' which means 'OBSERVE, perceive.'

Peruse and **Cursory** A PERUSAL is a 'light reading,' presumably 'for a purpose.' The 'use' in PERUSE means 'use.' The 'per,' which means 'through,' suggests 'use' without lingering. A CURSORY reading is the same thing, a 'rapid reading.' CURSORY literally means 'running.'

Scrutinize Though we don't often realize it, this word can be a real comedy-character. SCRUTINIZE suggests a pre-Yuletide Scrooge among his treasures. When he examines his ledger he screws up his face and lowers it with mean deliberation to within an inch or two of the page. Thus he SCRUTINIZES the page, item by item, as if his two eyes were two microscopes. But the word can be used seriously. SCRUTINIZE simply means 'to examine closely, to inspect with minute care.' In these days of false reports and scare headlines we would all do well to SCRUTINIZE the newspapers before we make our conclusions.

Sense One of our favorite verbal conveniences is turning nouns into verbs. But some nouns, and especially the more inclusive and elastic ones, we habitually neglect to apply. SENSE is one. We forget how much it can say as a verb. If we SENSE danger, for example, we feel it not with our fingers, not with our minds, not even in our bones, but with any or all of our SENSES. We feel it, that is, with all the powers of perception we possess. In a narrower way of course, we can also SENSE things with our skins, as, for instance, a caterpillar crawling up our necks. 'Sensate,' an adjective, means 'perceived' or 'felt' by the SENSES, like an injury or insult, especially a slap in the face.

Squint This is an expressive word for a 'squeezed-up glance.' Originally *asquint,* 'sidelong,' usually from reasons of suspicion, SQUINT now chiefly expresses screwed-up eyes, like sighting a gun or in trying to look at the sun.

No one knows where *asquint* came from. Perhaps from Old English *swink* meaning a 'wink'; *swinka* from Swedish, 'to shrink up'; or from Dutch *schuin* and *schuinen,* 'oblique' and 'to slant,' usually mentioned as its probable source, though of late origin, leaving the earlier prefix 'a' dubiously attributable to Old English 'an.' Anyway, SQUINT has been free to be appropriated by various groups. To the medicos it now means 'cross-eyed.' Literary people have exploited its pristine 'sidelong-ness' in a sense that is synonymous with 'hint.' "These extravagant sentiments squint at heresy," for example.

But in the main the word itself has exploited the 'reasons' for a glance askance. 'To SQUINT' now usually connotes some 'shrewdness,' and 'comedy.' We say "Let me have a squint at that," and mean "Let me have a quick look at that." But the truer connotation is revealed humorously by the shrewd scout SQUINTING over a log, or the fox SQUINTING through fence slats at chickens. SQUINTS are not necessarily furtive and suspicious. They can be sly and covetous. And being sly their exact motives are masked. Puckered up eyes can be piercing, frightened or tense. The most we can say is, that SQUINTS are intent, if only for an instant, and peculiar. They have motives behind them, unless a pair of glasses is needed.

Visualize, Envisage and **Envision**   Three companion verbs that still can divide their labor skillfully. You can see the faces of things (EN-VISAGE them) or you can just seem to see them, in your mind's eye (VIS-UALIZE them). The meanings intertwine, of course, because their uses are figurative. If you VISUALIZE the facts of a case, you are momentarily a 'seer,' and ENVISION them; and still more if you VISUALIZE the face of a lost friend, you may ENVISAGE it less than you ENVISION it. When you VISUALIZE something you are 'conjuring' it pictorially in your mind or making a representation by writing, painting, carving, etc. "An actor visualizes the person he is portraying before he goes on the stage." When you ENVISAGE something your eyes actually expect to 'confront' it. "When I tell her parents that we want to get married I envisage a terrible squall." Often ENVISAGE is used as a synonym for VISUALIZE. ENVISION means, like VISUALIZE, to have a mental picture in your mind of something, but this picture is the representation of something that will come in the future. "He envisions a heaven on earth."

PHILOSOPHY

DUALISM   *n.* any philosophical system based on a two-fold, or double, principle, such as a system that reduces everything to body and soul.

Dynamism

EMPIRICISM   *n.* the philosophical systems which hold that all knowledge is derived from experience.

EVOLUTIONISM n. any philosophy which holds that change, esp. change in a direction, is invariably present in all reality.

Hedonism

HUMANISM n. any philosophy generally oriented towards human ideals, interests and limitations.

IDEALISM n. any philosophy which holds that the ideal, the spiritual and the mental realms are the ultimate realities.

MATERIALISM n. any philosophical system which holds there is only one reality, matter, and that all can be explained in its terms.

MONISM n. any philosophical system which maintains there is only one ultimate reality or principle.

MORALISM n. any philosophy or way of life, which emphasizes morality over religion.

NOMINALISM n. the belief that only in language can a universal be expressed, that *in reality* there is no universal essence, and a mental image of a universal essence can not be formed. *adj.* NOMINALISTIC.

MYSTICISM n. the practice or doctrine of putting oneself in direct, unmediated relationship with God.

PHILOSOPHY n. the science which deals with the facts or principles of all reality.

AESTHETICS n. the study of beauty and art.

EPISTEMOLOGY n. the study of knowledge; its source, validity.

ETHICS n. the study of moral human conduct.

LOGIC n. a science which treats of formal reasoning.

METAPHYSICS n. the study of ultimate reality, first principles.

PSYCHOLOGY n. the study of human personality, behavior and mind.

POSITIVISM n. a philosophy, usually associated with Auguste Comte, which accepts only scientific facts, and dismisses as useless any study of metaphysics.

RATIONALISM n. a doctrine that reason is a source of knowledge. Compare SENSATIONALISM.

SENSATIONALISM n. a doctrine that sensation, or sense perceptions, provide us with all our knowledge.

Transcendentalism

Dynamism Any doctrine that holds that the universe is merely a realization of forces. Derivative concepts are common, like the theory that matter itself is an embodiment of energy. The DYNAMISM of the Nazis took the form of ceaselessly progressive aggression.

Hedonism Ethically, HEDONISM is a self-interested, self-indulgent philosophy. Commonly it is the feeling or belief that pleasure, however or wherever found, is the chief good in life. HEDONISM at its best is a highly selective and intelligent approach to the pleasure principle. This was the doctrine of the Greek philosophy of HEDONISM.

Transcendentalism It has been said that TRANSCENDENTALISM is fading out. The word now survives mostly in its adjectival form 'transcendental.' TRANSCENDENTALISM is now often used to name those ideas of 'surpassing ordinary limits,' or of 'exceeding bounds,' or of 'greatness,' that the adjective 'transcendent' has always conveyed. Hence TRANSCENDENTALISM now loosely means 'supernatural, incomprehensible, obscure, fantastic.' The philosophy itself, the quiet moral philosophy of Emerson and his followers, has been all but obliterated by the human consternation that the excitement of a century of science and warfare has brought. There is no Concord group today which is influencing novelists, orators, editors, preachers, philosophers, poets, essayists and dinner-table sages, and which is spreading a gospel of insight into the spiritual existence of things as a substitute for the dependence we are accustomed to place upon knowledge gained from material experience. It is quite possible that TRANSCENDENTALISM deserves not yet to be forgotten.

Emerson's philosophy was expressed in his essay, *Nature,* in which he offered little information on his subject but conveyed the idea that man, through his intuitions, is one with all men, that all men are one with nature, and that nature is one with God. Thus, he thought, man should depend more upon his spiritual insights than upon knowledge gained from history or science. Here Emerson was rebelling against the tyranny of the formal philosophies of his time, as others had already rebelled in England. This idealism had its vague inception in the TRANSCENDENTALISM of Kant in Germany, who sought to reconcile science with religion and to show that knowledge was not reality in itself, but only derived from something 'transcendent,' which he depicted as the 'processes' of the human mind. But TRANSCENDENTALISM in America carried the step onward, asserting not only the dignity of the individual but his spiritual oneness with all nature, including God. To 'feel' nature rather than to 'know' nature may seem fantastic today; yet no censorship can exist over feelings, and feelings are perhaps more acute than thought.

PHRASES AND EXPRESSIONS

Alright & All Right
As For & As To
Cockles
Dead
Deal
Don't
Ex Parte
Fait Accompli
Foregoing
Foreign Words and Phrases
  AD HOC
  ANENT
  ERGO
  ET ALTERA and ET ALTERI
  EXEMPLI GRATIA or E.G.
  IN RE, or simply RE
  INTER ALIA
  MIRABILE DICTU
  NON SEQUITUR or NON SEQ
  NON VULT
  OBITER DICTA
  RAISON D'ÊTRE
  SANS
  SERIATIM
  SIC
  SIC PASSIM, or just PASSIM
  VIDE or QUOD VIDE
  VIDELICET
  VIS-À-VIS
Good Taste
Heart
However
Jingo

Kind & Sort
Likely & Apt; also Liable
Loan & Lend
Lot
Madcap
Mean
Mine
Mot
Mumbo Jumbo
Namby-pamby
Need
Non
Open Sesame & Shibboleth
Perfect
Quiddity
Quidnunc
Scot-free
Simon Pure
Soi-disant
Soubriquet or Sobriquet
Spick-and-span & Brand-new
Take-off
Tempt & Tender
That
Tip-off
Tit for Tat
Touch
Whilom & Erstwhile
Yahoo
Ye
Yes
Zigzag

Alright and All Right   The first is all wrong. It was ALL RIGHT several centuries ago, but this early English spelling is now incorrect. Its excuse for remaining around is twofold. First 'already' and 'altogether' are correctly spelled as one word with one 'l.' Then, of course, the shorter spelling saves time.

As For and **As To** AS is an unbelievably busy little Anglo-Saxon adverb, shrunk to one-third its original size. It serves us easily in idiomatic phrases either as adverb, preposition, conjunction or relative pronoun. Fortunately it is so familiar our ear can usually tell us the correct usage. A few of its special uses do seem ambiguous, for example AS FOR and AS TO. Few dictionaries make any clear distinction between them. They may often be equivalents, but sometimes you can catch the individuality of each when it is used most distinctly. Either of them often occurs in an emphatic phrase at the beginning of a sentence: "As for me, I am going to stay right here," or "As to that, I am not quite certain." In either case the translation could be: 'concerning,' 'about' or 'as regarding.' But the first case, unlike the second, suggests another use of AS, "As a member of the family, he spoke with some assurance." Consequently we could render the 'AS for me' not only 'AS concerning me,' but, more specifically, 'so far AS I am concerned.' In other words, this double emphasis of the subject of the sentence seems to sound better with AS FOR than with AS TO. "As for the flowers, they are beautiful this year." But, "As to the flowers, well, I worked hard on them this year."

Cockles We ought perhaps to be displeased with this word, or with ourselves for using it, because we do not know what it actually means. But it enables us to tell others that something has pleased us wonderfully. Something has warmed the very COCKLES of our heart. COCKLES appertains only to our heart, and is customarily used only in the expression, ". . . warmed the very cockles of one's heart."

What these COCKLES are, is anybody's guess, and many people *have* guessed. Most people connect them with a French word, *coquille*, compounded from the French *coque*, 'shell.' This is because if you hold lengthwise one valve of a mussel, which lives in a shell, it looks a little like a heart. But there is more in the analogy than that. There is another French *coquille*, said to be derived from the first one, that is used in French cooking. This *coquille* refers to 'blistered pastry,' with its creases and crinkles, and to serrated edges, like piecrusts—or like the fringes of mussel shells. Presumably, *coquille* suggests the kindly wrinkles we might imagine in a cheerful heart.

But the clews do not all come from the French. There are other words that contribute possible explanations. The very sound of the word COCKLE seems to have attracted our ears, and we have COCKLES of this kind and that from a variety of sources. There is an old English COCKLE that comes from the Scandinavian, meaning 'to pucker up' or 'to be uneven, be cockled up.' Then there are the Old English COCKLES or 'tares,' which now are corn cockles and other nuisance weeds that grow in grain. They may be the roots of agricultural evil, as COCKLES are the roots of our heart. Though this contribution may be far-fetched, it points aptly in the right direction, namely, inward. For it is not the shell of our heart that is warmed or cheered, but the very interior. The Standard Dictionary pictures a furnace with a dome or fire-chamber. From this COCKLE (the dome's name) came, it says, the inner chambers of our heart. Still other explanations go back to the 'snail,' the Latin *cochlea*. This, they say, is related to 'conch.' The conch has a spiral shell, so it is now our name, in anatomy, for a twisting part of the inner ear, the hideaway of our auditory nerves. Hence, they say (and they are very definite), in 1660 came the COCKLES, or the winding cavities, of our heart. Nor do the conjectures and declarations stop there. There was Saint James the Apostle, and his shrine, a medieval mecca in Spain. Were not the hearts of the pilgrimaging palmers warmed, and their souls content, when they returned from the slopes of Mount Pedrosa, wearing a part of a 'cockleshell,' one valve of it, on their hats, as a testimonial of their Christian love?

In any event, 'the COCKLES of our heart' is one of those deeply rooted, colorful phrases that our language will not lose simply because its origins are obscure.

Dead Perhaps no adjective in English is so common and perennial, especially in compounds, as DEAD. Whether we are fascinated by the dreadful idea of death itself, or whether we are tempted by bravado to find some drollery in it, doesn't matter. From 'Deadwood,' North Dakota, to 'Deadeye Dick,' the sailor, and the spectacularly named race horses, 'Drop Dead' and 'Strike-Em-Dead,' we can go through all the vocations and all kinds of persiflage, and find a DEAD thing here and a DEAD thing there. Consider, for example, 'dead letter,' which signifies an 'unrepealed but inoperative law,' a 'dead weight,' which is 'an inert lump,' or 'dead men' and 'dead soldiers,' which are terms for an 'empty beer or liquor bottle.'

Especially, of course, the moribunds flourish in slang. A 'dead pan' is an 'expressionless face,' such as poker players wear. A 'dead heat,' originally just a 'dead,' an inconclusive result that can be cast out, is a 'tie' in a race. A 'dead beat' is 'someone unable to meet his liabilities,' or else 'someone completely beaten, a down-and-outer, an idler, a bum.' But a 'dead beat' is also a 'deadhead,' meaning upwards of twenty other things, including an 'unresponsive audience, a dunderhead, a poor companion on a date, an empty car, an empty train, a hawser post on a wharf.'

Out of this welter of slang many DEAD compounds have staked permanent claims in dictionaries. 'Dead broke,' 'dead set' and 'dead gone,' for example, convey a sense of 'complete death.' 'Deadwood' is quite literally 'DEAD branches still on a tree,' but figuratively it is a 'solid block' used to strengthen a ship's keel. A 'deadlock' is a graphic expression for an 'impasse,' suggesting horns so locked in combat that neither deer can accomplish anything. Deer locked so firmly together frequently die of starvation. Originally, it was a wrestler's term: neither man dared to let go. DEAD often suggests a 'standstill,' as in the 'deadlock' on a door, worked with a handle on one side and a key on the other. But it also means 'deadly,' as in a 'deadfall,' a trap that kills or disables big game. A 'dead letter' is one that lies unclaimed in a postal morgue, though at first this term referred to an 'alphabetical letter' and later to a 'law.' 'Dead water' is an 'eddy' under a ship's stern. A 'dead light' is a 'storm shutter over a porthole.' 'Dead reckoning' is estimating a ship's position without aid of the stars, that is, only from the compass and the records of the log. In this example, DEAD is probably an abbreviation of 'deduce,' i.e., deduced from the log. A 'dead well' is a 'reservoir for waste waters.' 'Dead-alive' referred first to 'places,' probably like Podunk; now 'dullards' are 'dead-alive' too, a contemptuous version of 'living-death.' 'Deadman' as a surname may be from Debenham in England, or it may be from an old-clothes man, 'dudman.' But 'deadeye' was an authentic 'deadman's eye,' almost as old as Chaucer. Centuries earlier Piers the Plowman remarked: "As dead as a door-nail." The obsessing idea persists inevitably. We are 'dead certain,' 'dead shots,' take 'dead aim' or are 'dead game.' Something happens in the 'dead of night.' It is probably the notion that something happens, something inconceivable happens, that accounts for the insistence of this word.

Deal Like all languages, English is very idiomatic. In fact, idioms very largely make a language by constantly enriching it. "He caused me a good deal of trouble." "He got a good deal in cards last night," or "By George! I made a good deal in business over lunch yesterday." In each of these usages the word DEAL conveys a sense of a 'part' or a 'share,' which is the early English meaning. It has always stood for something practical and universal, and has its cognates all over northern Europe. Now it has its uses in nearly all spheres of life.

Don't DON'T is death on stiltedness, and so is welcome in conversation and informal writing. It is even welcome in artistic or oratorical writing when the measured sound of 'do not' interferes with the rhythm. But it should never be used for 'doesn't.' If someone says: "Doesn't he like you?", DON'T say, "No, he don't." Remember, anything that can be replaced by 'he,' 'she' or 'it' takes 'doesn't'; but all else takes DON'T.

Ex Parte This means 'from one side only,' and, specifically, when the other side is inactive or absent. An EX PARTE argument emanates from 'one side,' relates only to that side or its views.

Fait Accompli This is a French phrase that means a 'thing done' or a 'thing completed.' We use it often in English. "The newest revolution in South America is already a FAIT ACCOMPLI."

Foregoing There seems to be some confusion in the minds of quite a few authors who refer you to the 'above-mentioned,' or the 'above,' passage, which we eventually discover on a later page. To avoid this confusion we might remember FOREGOING, which conveniently covers everything we have already written, up to the latest period.

Foreign Words and Phrases Many fragments and phrases of foreign languages are serviceable and expressive. Sometimes we abbreviate even these bits, like 'i.e.' for the Latin ID EST, 'it is,' which means for us 'that is,' 'for example,' 'specifically,' etc. Sometimes these expressions succinctly express an idea which our own language has no equally good word or phrase for, like SERIATIM and NON SEQUITUR. Though most of these might be most useful only in books, their classic coloring needn't disturb anyone; everyone knows what 'via' means, though he may not realize it is the Latin equivalent for 'by way of.' Only custom, or the style demanded by a particular writing job can tell you whether these foreign phrases should be italicized or whether you may let them stand like any English word. The tendency in all writing, except the most academic, is to handle these common foreign expressions just as though they were English.

AD HOC: Latin, 'in respect to this exact thing.' A useful designation of emphasis.

ANENT: Anglo-Saxon, *onefen,* 'on' plus 'even,' means 'pertaining to' or 'regarding.'

ERGO: Latin, 'therefore.'

ET ALTERA and ET ALTERI: Latin, 'and other things' and 'and other persons.' The first is practically the same as ET CETERA, though there is the suggestion that the ALTERA, or 'things,' may vary from the cited things. The ALTERI are a kind of 'also rans' or 'also present.'

EXEMPLI GRATIA or E.G.: Latin, 'for example.' The abbreviation is third fiddle to 'i.e.' and 'viz'; but, if you have many examples to mention, you might employ it, for variety's sake.

IN RE, or simply RE: Latin, thing' or 'affair.' This is a time-saving device that no one who pushes a pencil can afford to forget. We use it in English to mean 'in regard to the thing' in question. It is incomparably shorter than either 'pertaining to' or 'concerning.' The most practical person needn't mind its Latin looks. "Re library books, you owe ten cents."

INTER ALIA: Latin, 'among other things.'

MIRABILE DICTU: Latin, 'marvelous to be told.'

NON SEQUITUR or NON SEQ: Latin, 'it does not follow.' Most things that are nonsense are 'non secks.' If they don't make sense, they don't follow from what does. Conclusions from arguments that don't click are NON SEQUITURS.

NON VULT: Latin, 'not guilty.'

OBITER DICTA: Latin, 'thing said by the way.' These are remarks not necessarily off the record, but off the subject for the moment. They are things said in passing, but usually with remarkable deliberation and point.

RAISON D'ÊTRE: French, 'excuse for existing,' 'reason for being.' "The raison d'être of Reno is divorce and gambling." Foreign phrases mystify us a little, take on connotations, and thus prove useful. This phrase, which literally says no more than our 'reason for being,' is used because our own lacks prestige.

SANS: French, 'without.'

SERIATIM: Latin, 'done after another,' 'serially in order.' Like our word 'respectively' SERIATIM is a useful co-ordinator. However, the two words 'in order' serve the same purpose. 'Respectively' is unique; it carries and co-ordinates two or more threads or lists at once: "Cats, dogs and cows are feline, canine and bovine respectively."

SIC: Latin, 'thus or so' or 'like this.' SIC is very useful in parentheses after a word or phrase whose meaning or spelling may seem doubtful.

SIC PASSIM or just PASSIM: Latin, 'thus everywhere.' Usually PASSIM is used in parentheses as equivalent roughly to a distributive et cetera, meaning 'such instances are found everywhere.' "The author has errors on pp. 7, 10, 25, passim."

VIDE or QUOD VIDE: Latin, 'which see.' This word saves encyclopedias thousands of words. If you are requested to look under another entry, you may see ". . . of Tolstoi (q.v.)."

VIDELICET: Latin, 'to wit,' 'namely,' 'that is to say.' It is commonly abbreviated to 'viz.'

VIS-À-VIS: French, 'face-to-face.'

Good taste A desk dictionary may give you ten or fifteen different meanings of the adjective 'good' and as many more of the noun 'taste' but the meaning of the combination GOOD TASTE is unique. Yet in spite of this uniqueness some say that the phrase is losing caste, is being commercialized, or hackneyed into hardness, as the word 'gentleman' is.

This is a pity, and the more so since it leads us to analyze a phrase that has served us indispensably for ages, and to find that it is, after all, shaky in its foundations. Because in the first place the word 'good' in this phrase is redundant, a mere intensive casting question on the competency of 'taste,' which, as Webster's tells you, also undertakes to express the same meaning as GOOD TASTE, all by itself. In the second place, viewed objectively, the common wholesome word 'good' possesses none of the fine discriminating ability we associate with GOOD TASTE. In the third place, while 'taste' is an epicurean word, it lacks that wide association with the contents of the world from which GOOD TASTE deduces its judgments. A 'taste' is, first of all, simply a 'touch of the tongue, a sip, a savoring, sampling.'

But when all this has been said what still will the English-speaking world do when GOOD TASTE is expunged from its language? Will it rely all the more on the single word 'taste,' which has other meanings? There is no doubt that GOOD TASTE is different from BAD or POOR TASTE. GOOD TASTE is essential to any civilized society.

Heart Sometimes we speak of getting down to the HEART of a matter ('its center or core'). But to us the HEART is not usually the center of anything, unless it be an affair of the affections. As a matter of fact, the HEART is not the center of our bodies. Our physiological center is somewhere in the viscera where the soul was once supposed to reside. Ancient men held particular interest in the internals of animals, in which the gods were supposed to have left signs for the guidance of mortals. Barnyard fowls were religiously disemboweled, and their insides examined for portents. Finally it dawned upon humans that the HEART, as the vital center of the blood supply, was more worthy of worship and more instructive than the intestines. Men noticed that their own blood pressures rose with the excitation of their affections and antipathies. So the HEART presently became important for a new reason. It no longer simply represented the essence or center of everything, like the 'core' of an apple, the 'pith' of a proposition, or the 'hub' of activities; but it represented also the 'seat' of emotions. Today we think of the HEART as especially the symbol for love. A stony-hearted person does not have love and compassion for his fellows. A hard-hearted person does not admit that love has any place in the affairs of the world.

However As an adverb, HOWEVER qualifies an adjective or another adverb: "However ('no matter how') meanly he nags you, hold your temper;" or, "However beautiful she is, she hasn't brains enough for a butterfly." But HOWEVER's most common and useful service is as a conjunction, especially in connecting whole sentences with previous sentences: "That may all be true. However, I still think you're wrong." This is not the best example of usage. It is in longer sentences and in more formal or urbane diction that HOWEVER has its chief place. It replaces the abrupt 'but.' In the example above either 'but' or 'never-theless' would have served better, because 'but' is briefer and more explicit, and 'nevertheless' is more emphatic. The point is that HOW-EVER has a way of pulling a number of ideas together and posing them all for a moment at the outset of a sentence. It is also soft-sounding, not too abrupt.

Jingo A merry sounding word suggesting 'jingle,' and hence 'tinkle' and other merry sounds. Actually it probably means Jesus, Who can hardly be said to have led a merry life.

Whether we are blaspheming or not when we say "By Jingo" is moot. The origin of JINGO is obscure. It is thought JINGO, like its common synonym 'chauvinism,' originated in a god. In the case of 'chauvinism' the god was Napoleon, one of whose most loyal supporters, Chauvin, sang his praises so loudly he became a public joke, giving his name as a new term for an 'overzealous patriot.' However, the JINGO god, JINKO, was not French but Basque, and was none other than our own God. The English of the seventeenth century were in the habit of employing Basque sailors as harpooners on whalers, and evidently they overheard the word and liked it. Probably they gleaned its meaning, but were tricked by its phonetics, interpreting it as Jesus.

It took still some centuries before, like Chauvin, JINGO was cele-brated on the comedy stage and acquired a political bias. In 1878 Russia was then, as now, a fear in the public mind, and a music hall ballad in England ran: "We don't want to fight but, by Jingo, if we do, we've got the ships, we've got the men, we've got the money too." The phrase, 'by Jingo,' immediately became a warlike slogan; but when the war fever abated JINGOISM appeared excessive, and JINGOISTS became synonymous with 'chauvinists.' The usage, meaning 'rash action in the name of patriotism,' seems now to be waning. JINGOISM has no longer its original popular force.

Yet there is still a touch of magic in JINGO. "By Jingo," quoth Panurge, "the man talks something like!" That was not what Rabelais wrote (he wrote, *par diem*), but the way he was later translated suggests, perhaps, something of the conjurer's "Hey Jingo!" that astonishingly produced rabbits from hats. ("Hey Presto!" made them disappear.) All such extravagant expressions are spiritually akin to our own 'high jinks.' Today JINGO seems to us to convey good spirits and an animated manner. It suggests the opposite of 'jinx,' which means 'bad luck.'

Kind and **Sort**   Certainly we use SORT and KIND in every variety of loose ways. Often with a little care we could be more specific. SORT refers to a 'particularizing principle,' and though KIND once referred specifically to our 'kindred,' it has now a general but precise meaning. For example, the candy in a box of assorted chocolates is, of course, diversified in a way; but more accurately it consists of several varieties of one KIND of candy, namely, chocolate. It is called 'assorted' chocolate because it has been SORTED. Presumably, the varieties you buy in the box have been SORTED from a greater number of possible varieties. Whether the other varieties are then sold in a different box, or are wholly hypothetical, need not concern us. The idea is that all the specimens of chocolate have been spread out, and that certain specimens have been chosen. A SORTING is a particularizing, and therefore SORTS may be chosen on the basis of excellence, inferiority, size, cost, or any value whatever. A SORT is, literally speaking, merely a 'part of anything at all.'

Scientists speak of phyla, classes, families, genera and species: those are all in one way or another SORTS and KINDS. We, who are laymen, like the old words, and use them overgenerously. Especially in colloquial usage, where 'sort of' and 'kind of' are easygoing modifiers of our thought. We use these two expressions to 'tone down' or 'dampen' an exaggeration or a humorous statement. "It sort of made me sick to see him making a fool of himself;" or "He sort of stumbled out of the starting stall and continued to shuffle his feet around the race track." In fact, 'sort of' and 'kind of' are practically compounds (whether adverbial or adjectival) equivalent to 'seeming' or 'seemingly,' 'like' or 'as if,' 'resembling,' 'almost,' 'somewhat,' 'rather,' 'in some way,' 'to some degree,' 'as it were' and even 'paradoxically.' "The kid looked kind of sorry, in spite of saying he was no such thing." In other words, he looked as if he might, perhaps, be smiling.

We sometimes lose sight of the specific meaning of KIND altogether. In "Those kinds of things are delightful," the demonstrative 'those' modifies 'things,' though KINDS is actually the basic noun of the clause. Furthermore, 'those' is almost a synonym here for KIND. It is enough to say, "Those things are delightful." If you want to emphasize the type or class of things, you should say, "Things of this kind are delightful."

At any rate the expressiveness of 'sort of' and 'kind of' cannot be denied. What they do, really, is to extract from the nouns KIND and SORT all their intimations of similarity and approximation, and they tag them with 'of,' in order that we may have four phrases, two adverbial and two adjectival, to use when we want to be fanciful or inexplicit.

This convenient blurring of the senses of SORT can be analyzed in other uses of that word. For the noun partly originated our verb, and gave it an inference of 'good selection.' The verb is also rooted in Latin *sortire*, which often implied a 'setting of things in good order.' Thus, in Tudor times a 'man of sorts' was a 'man of quality,' and conversely a man 'out of sorts' was ill. Today we look down on a 'thing of sorts,' or 'thing of a sort.' The emphasis has reversed itself, but the reference is still to quality. Anyhow, when we speak of 'sort of doing something' we have, as it were, historical license for playing with the senses of SORT.

Likely and **Apt**; also **Liable**   "It is likely to rain and I am likely to get wet;" not, "It is apt to rain and I am apt to get wet." LIKELY conveys the sense that 'something will probably happen shortly.' But APT means that 'something is very possible at *any* time.' "It is likely to rain when the sky becomes cloudy and threatening, and whenever rain does come everybody, even farmers, are apt to seek shelter."

But in these examples both APT and LIKELY are adjectives. When LIKELY is used as an adverb, for example, "All this trouble will likely blow over in a day or two," it is synonymous with APT. "All this trouble is apt to blow over in a day or two," or "All this trouble will probably blow over in a day or two."

LIABLE is an adjective, and is synonymous with the two others only in its latest derived sense of 'probability.' At bottom it means, from the Latin, 'bound' or 'tied,' implying 'obligation' and 'responsibility.' "You are liable for the consequences of your crime." By a further extension of sense, "You are liable to suffer," or "An occurrence is liable to cause suffering." Through association the meaning of LIABLE equates with the meaning of LIKELY, but *in an unfavorable sense.* "Unfortunately, he is liable to change his mind"; "She is not liable to agree with us." This modern derived meaning of LIABLE is very commonly used now, and consequently is APT to come first in recent dictionaries.

Loan and **Lend**   There is some question about the propriety of using the noun LOAN for the verb LEND: "Loan me your lawn mower," for "Lend me it." This functional aggrandizement of LOAN is possibly in the interest of euphony, though LEND itself earlier had no 'd,' adopting one only to suit speech convenience. At any rate, the LOAN usage has become popular in the United States, and the more conservative British content themselves with saying merely that Americans no longer hesitate to use LOAN as a verb. LOAN isn't a native part of LEND anyhow. We adopted it from the Scandinavian version of Old English *læn.* LEND on its part has quite forgotten that it was originally only that same Old English *læn,* and a noun. If LEND was so lazy as to borrow a form for its noun, what is to prevent this more energetic LOAN from taking over the whole usage?

Lot   If you are tempted to say that someone is a bad LOT, you ought to be thinking of the auction room, for that is where the phrase originated. But the fact is that ever since Shakespeare's time, when LOT first took on its quantitative meaning, we have conceived of it, singular or plural, as a 'large amount of anything at all.' Prior to that, of course, and continuing along with it, a LOT was just an 'object used for the drawing of chances,' especially for the division of plunder. Hence came our realty LOTS, originally assigned by allotment, and our cutting across 'backlots.'

LOT has piled up in our slang. "A lot of good that will do you," says someone, and we cannot deny the ironic force of the comment. But what of a 'lot of honey,' or a 'lotta hooey?' Or a 'lotta mush, monkeydoodle or phooey?' Or, crawling up from slang, a 'lot of things' to do today, and 'lots of love,' and a 'lot of worry?' Only when a plural noun follows either 'a lot of' or 'lots of' do we use a plural verb: "There *are* lots of knives and forks, but there *is* a lot of time." Or, "There *are* a lot of knives, but there *is* lots of time." Must we always say, "There *are* a lot of knives," and never, "There *is* a lot of them?" The latter looks like the more grammatical form, but this quantitative LOT is a collective noun.

Madcap   "With madcap glee. . . ." Have you ever thought that phrases like this are tinsel—and often very pretty tinsel—in your talk?

Besides, there is never really any substitute for genuine merriness in any conversation. Wit with all its dexterity must always be a bit clumsy when it attempts to masquerade as mirth.

Mean "I mean to say, he's really mean!" The second MEAN meant 'common,' in Old English, whence, as a poor commentary on the man in the streets, it came to mean a variety of things, all derogatory, such as 'stingy, petty, base, low, vile, malicious, ignoble, degraded, sordid, pitiful, humble, ordinary, insignificant, and lacking in ability, intelligence or honor.' Some of these senses are colloquial, but all these condemnatory meanings have proved almost as indispensable as the verb 'to MEAN,' which is also Old English, meaning from the outset, 'to intend.'

The Latin-derived adjective MEAN is not so useful. It is equivalent to 'average,' but the sense is narrower. It refers specifically to something 'midway between two extremes,' while 'average' may connote simply the 'ordinary' or 'usual' in type or kind. This MEAN comes from Latin *medius*, 'middle.' Although it has that general meaning of 'moderate,' its chief connotations reflect the various senses of the noun 'medium.'

Mine The student colloquy, "Jeet-yet?" "No. Jew?" "Did you eat yet?" "No, did you?" illustrates our tendency to alter words, especially by contractions. These alterations are often permanent, like those in the history of MINE. MINE was the early English genitive of either 'me' or 'I,' and so it meant 'of me,' 'my.' But in common speech, like the 'jew' above, MINE lost little time in reducing itself to 'my.' But for some time the four-letter form was used before a following vowel, like, 'mine eyes.' Nowadays, though, we say: "I couldn't believe my eyes." As a predicate adjective MINE still is used: "This house is mine." 'My,' not content with reducing itself, has also cast off some of its escorting words. "Oh my!" we say, meaning "Oh! my Heavens," or "Oh! my poor aching heart." So students are more students than they think. They have learned the wisdom of the past.

Mot French for 'word,' in English we use it to mean the 'witty word, the phrase or scintillating observation we can't forget.' "Oscar Wilde is especially famous for his social charm and his extraordinary wit, both largely the result of his sense of the mot."

Mumbo Jumbo There is more in MUMBO JUMBO than you might think. There is in it color, pomp and a kind of terrorism, in addition to its sense of 'meaningless incantation.' Today when we capitalize the word it is concrete, being an 'object of superstitious homage or fear, a fetish-like bugaboo.' But we don't stop to think that it has an exotic history, that it is the name of a tutelary genius of certain romantic African tribes along the Senegal River in the Western Sudan. This MUMBO JUMBO is represented by an imposing masquerader wearing a headdress of pompons (bunched ornamental feathers) designed to awe females into humility and good behavior, and especially to ward off evil spirits that corrupt virtuous wives.

Among these Mandingo tribes the word MUMBO JUMBO is said to have been the name of a tree, *mama jomba,* to which refractory wives were tied, in terror, by the masquerader. But Webster's gives the derivation more soberly, as from *mama dyambo,* in which the *mama* means an ancestor and the *dyambo* is a wearer of pompons.

Namby-pamby Unlike Humpty Dumpty, NAMBY-PAMBY was a real person. He did not live in nursery rhymes, but was memoralized by the derision of Alexander Pope and his coterie. Ambrose Philips's particular failing was the writing of insipid but flowery felicitations to the newly born offspring of the nobility. It was a kind of literary toadyism which exposed him to the ridicule of better poets like Alexander Pope.

This derivation is helpful in usage because today 'lackadaisical' can also mean 'weakly or affectedly sentimental.' But 'lackadaisical' came from 'alackaday,' which was an expression of 'regret' or of 'woe.' It is quite foreign to any sense of 'felicitations.' But NAMBY-PAMBY was overly fond of 'felicitation,' and has suffered a lasting retribution because of exactly that. His only luck is that his real name no longer appears in print. We only remember him by the playful, though still derisive, corruption of Ambrose Philips, contrived by the poet Carey, after such jingles as Georgy-Porgy.

Need Colloquial language is naturally erratic. Usually it clips words and shortens sentences in order to make them easier and quicker to say. But sometimes it paradoxically lengthens formal diction.

Conversationally we say, "She thinks she needs to put on airs or she won't be noticed," unnecessarily adding an 's' in NEEDS and putting a 'to' before 'put.' In formal usage, the sentence would be, "She thinks she need put on airs."

Formal usage makes NEED an auxiliary to a verb, as above. Often, in questions and in negative sentences, formal diction eliminates the verb 'to do,' which informal usage keeps. "Need I hurry?" compared to "Do I need to hurry?" "You need not hurry," and "You don't need to hurry."

Non Shakespeare said, "To be or not to be," which might be another way of saying, "To think or not to think." Anyhow we usually choose not to think, at least, to the extent of not thinking up an antonym for a word. It is much easier to place a NON before a word, and let it go at that: 'nonskid, nonstop, noncombattant, nonresistant.' The habit is an old one, as witness 'nonsense,' 'nonchalant,' and 'nondescript.' Sometimes the NON was French, usually it was Latin, but now it is straight English or American because we compel any word, native or adopted, to accept it. The number of such improvised negatives and antonyms now in use is so great that no ordinary sized dictionary can encompass them. Yet the idea of using them is often good. How could you express 'nonexistent' without using the weaker 'unexisting' or an explanatory phrase?

Open Sesame and **Shibboleth** OPEN SESAME is a magical double compound. It is an automatic password and key. Its first job was to open the robbers' cave in the Arabian Nights' Tales. Now it is a conjuration to gain access to locked and secret places of all sorts.

A SHIBBOLETH is a test word and therefore a password. It has become a kind of 'party motto' or 'verbal tartan,' for clan, society, class or country. It originated in Biblical times when the Euphraimites were running for their lives from the Galeadites. They came to the fords in the Jordan River. The enemy was there before them, stopping all travelers suspiciously. It happened that the Euphraimites were unable to pronounce the 'sh' in the word SHIBBOLETH, which meant a river. It was an easy matter for the sentries to ask leading questions, so exposing the refugees. Foreigners today have the same difficulty with the English 'th,' as in 'thy' and 'thigh.'

But not only distinctive words and eccentricities of speech can be SHIBBOLETHS. Native traits, customs and popular ideas are SHIBBOLETHS. Club mottos and college slang are SHIBBOLETHS. The SHIBBOLETHS of infancy are baby talk, and one SHIBBOLETH of beggars is "Can you spare a dime?"

Perfect "I thank you so much! No more perfect gift could ever have been found!" No, it couldn't, for PERFECTION cannot be improved on. PERFECTION is that state or quality of a thing so right that any change in it mars it. Of course you can't make anything 'more PERFECT,' or more anything, without changing it. To change PERFECTION is to make it not less PERFECT or more PERFECT but 'imperfect.' And to be very logical and grammatical PERFECTION can never be really attained. It is an ideal conception, like infinity. So you should say, "No more nearly perfect gift could be found."

But this is dogmatic nonsense. Everyday speech simply changes the sense of PERFECT. This is a practice which all peoples have been adept in since the dawn of etymological history. In the example cited above the PERFECT is simply an intensive; it doesn't matter whether or not it is actually a superlative. It simply suggests that the speaker's feelings know no bounds. In the interests of a living language we must be prepared to accept popular usage as correct.

This admission of change is not to say that we should accept blindly every alteration of meaning. For example, PERFECT has been actually debased in, "That man is a perfect stranger to me." There is no suggestion of perfectibility here. This, too, may fill a need; but it would be better to find another superlative than to destroy completely the meaning of a good word.

Quiddity   A QUIDDITY is an 'oddity' so characteristic of something that it distinguishes it from everything else. It is an 'intensive shibboleth' (see OPEN SESAME and SHIBBOLETH), distinguishing not one individual from another, but distinguishing one person from *all* others. It is thus an essential characteristic that serves to answer the questions "What is it?" or "Who, or what exactly, is he?"

But when this has been said the definition is still radically incomplete. Though a characteristic is usually an oddity, QUIDDITY is basically the 'essential identifying characteristic.' It is the 'essence itself, the ultimate nature.' Thus the true QUIDDITY of music, as distinguished from mere sound, is 'harmony.'

All this is indicated in the word's inception. In scholastic Latin, where it originated, a *quid,* 'what,' was folded over both the *qual* and the *quan* of *qualitas* and *quantitas,* 'quality' and 'quantity,' to produce a meaning combining 'oddity' and 'entirety.' But, as happens with words conveying 'quality,' fancy took hold of the element of 'oddity,' producing several tangential meanings.

Thus, in spite of its literary look, the word is quite human today. When QUIDDITY demeans itself it is first an excessively nice distinction and hence, in common parlance, a cavil or a quibble. Next, it allows itself to become a mere trifle, a next-to-nothingness, a passing quip or fad, like the comic birthday cards in a novelty shop. QUIDDITY today is also a person's predilection for such trifles, or his disposition to cavil, or his practiced ability along any of these lines. It may even be used to mean 'subtlety of mind.' For example, unimaginative persons are devoid of all QUIDDITY, with nothing to distinguish them intellectually from the everyday person of common perception.

Quidnunc Literally, the Latin for 'what now.' In other words, a QUIDNUNC is an 'inquisitive busybody.'

Scot-free The 'scot' doesn't mean Scottish; it is an Old Norse word, *skot*, which became Old English *scot*, meaning a 'contribution' hence a 'tribute,' a 'levy,' a 'tax.' So SCOT-FREE means free of assessments of any kind, and 'to go scot-free' is, as we might say, to get off without any strings attached, without arrears hanging over.

Simon Pure This word means the real thing, no imitation, genuine in the sense of genuinely good, like real Scotch whisky. There may be much in a name, but this pure 'Simon' bears no relation to the Galilean fisherman later known as the apostle Peter. Nor, on the other hand, to the minor Biblical character, Simon Magnus, who tried to purchase the power of conferring the Holy Spirit and succeeded only in giving us our word 'simony.' This 'Simon' came fictionally from a poor Quaker, named SIMON PURE, in a Horatio Alger-like play popular some years before George Washington's lifetime. A clever Colonel, symbolically named Feignwell, impersonated Simon and married an heiress, but the humble hero eventually succeeded in proving that he was the one and only SIMON PURE. The author was Suzanna Centlivre, a pioneer female playwright.

Soi-disant "He is only a would-be tennis player," we say, with a disparaging implication both of the player's ability and of his ambitions. If we should wish to be less hard on him, we might say he was a SOI-DISANT player. For SOI-DISANT in the French means literally 'self-saying,' but not in the sense of 'he says so himself,' but in the sense of 'in his own conceited opinion.' 'Self-styled' is our nearest English synonym, but it has also some of the meaning of our less specific phrase 'so-called.' If we say, "He calls himself a tennis player," we are saying, "He is a soi-disant player." Perhaps because we have such colorful expressions of our own, SOI-DISANT is dropping out of our language.

Soubriquet or **Sobriquet** A French word taken by us to mean 'nickname.' It has a certain usefulness for us since 'nickname' sounds juvenile, or else prosaic. The emphasis in SOUBRIQUET is on 'fancy' and 'humor,' touched usually with 'scurrility.'

In Shakespeare's time it meant, in the French, 'a jest broken on a man,' or a 'mock or a flout,' or a 'byword.' And since a 'byword' is itself a protean thing, a nondescript proverb or saying with usually a disrespectful implication, SOUBRIQUET lost no time in becoming a 'nickname.' Originally, in the Old French of Chaucer's time, it was a 'chuck under the chin,' the first syllable equivalent to *sub*, 'under' and *briquet*, apparently meaning the 'chin' as an adjunct of the nose (beak). Modern Italian still has *sotto-becca*, 'chuck under the chin.'

Spick-and-span and **Brand-new** That which is SPICK-AND-SPAN is, literally, BRAND-NEW. BRAND-NEW means 'as good, or as attractive, as new.' Both 'spick' and 'span' originally expressed 'clean and sparkling newness,' like a splinter from newly cut wood or like a new nail. Compare our phrase 'neat as a pin.' Chaucer said: "This tale ay was spannewe to beginne;" and 'spick' came into English in the sixteenth century from archaic Dutch, where it was related to *spijker*, 'nail,' and where it occurred in a compound equivalent to SPICK-AND-SPAN. BRAND-NEW referred originally to a metal that was new from the forge; 'firenew' was a synonymous compound.

Take-off There was a fairly recent day when a TAKE-OFF was well-known as a 'burlesque,' a 'ridiculous mimicry' of some person's manner or of some performance. The two syllables were then evenly stressed. Sometimes when we now mean some one of the many meanings of TAKE-OFF we stress one or the other word. If you surprise a burglar in your house, he will probably TAKE-OFF as quickly as he can, regardless of how much more booty he would like to TAKE-OFF. He won't stop to TAKE-OFF his hat, if you are a lady, in the hope that you will TAKE-OFF something for good behavior if he is caught.

When the expression becomes a noun the emphasis shifts to 'take.' Thus in athletics the broad jumper notes a spot on the ground where he must TAKE-OFF in his flight through the air. Airplanes made TAKE-OFF grow enormously in importance. Now it represents any point not only of rushing departure or of beginning flight, but of any beginning of a line of action. Air schedules state the TAKE-OFF times of planes. And note this: "When are we going to take-off for our Sunday ride?" Since we are so used to hearing TAKE-OFF used in this sense for airplanes, it almost sounds as if our autos can fly too.

Tempt and **Tender** TEMPT and TENDER, strange to say, are both rooted in the concept of 'holding.' But if you keep on 'holding' some-

thing, and probably 'pulling' on it, you will 'stretch' it. When it is
'stretched' it becomes 'thin,' like a stretched rubber band you can see
through. This idea of 'thinness' led to TENDER, literally, 'stretched to
the breaking point,' and hence 'delicate.' The idea of 'stretching' led
to the idea of 'attempting,' and hence of TEMPTING, literally, 'trying
something to see how strong it is.'

It is interesting to see what has happened etymologically to these
two words rooted in Latin *tenere*, 'to hold.' The frequentative was
tendere, 'to stretch,' which gave *tentare* or *temptare*, 'to tempt' or 'try.'
Both the 'trying' and the 'tempting' were an 'endeavor,' an 'attempt,' but
the TEMPTING took on assorted other meanings, such as 'to handle, touch,
feel'; 'to prove, to attack, to urge, to disturb, to excite.' Some think the
'm' got into the word through analogy with Latin *tempus*, 'time,' to give
us our TEMPT. 'To TEMPT' is a '*timely* trying' for an urgent occasion, a
'testing.' Today how often does TEMPTING imply an intention of testing
someone's integrity or strength? Rather, the word has become sly. A
TEMPTER is no longer honest, and only a TEMPTING dish is free from the
sinister. But most of the other meanings of *temptare* give our word
TEMPT many areas of suggestion.

And so also with TENDER. To the Roman, as *tener*, it meant much
more than 'thin.' It also meant 'soft, delicate, effeminate, young, gentle,
inexperienced, weak.' It meant 'merciful,' and so in all was well prepared to become our own TENDER. But today what does it say first? It
does not say, for example, that your skin is 'soft to the touch' or 'thin,'
but that it is 'sensitive.' And a TENDER heart is not 'weak' or 'effeminate'
but is 'merciful.' We have elected another word from the same Latin
root for 'delicate thinness,' namely 'tenuous.' Since we have 'soft' and
'gentle' also, our TENDER is free for its special, and sensitive, mingling
of mercy and love. (See TAUNT.)

That This is the oldest relative in the language. In Shakespeare's
time, when Latin was adored and its flexible pronouns were particularly admired, 'who' and 'which' began to assume some of the functions
of THAT. But 'who' and 'which' are both very ancient words, descending through the Proto-Germanic, or Teutonic, and the Anglo-Saxon
from that parent language, Indo-European, grandfather of the most
important languages in the world. Today we use all three relatives:
"The house that is brown is the one I like," "The clown is that man who
has a painted face," and "What did you do with the book which was
placed on this table?"

But in Old English 'who' and 'which' were only interrogatives ("Who
are you?" and "Which is it?"). However, they lent themselves to in-

flection, and we have 'whose' and 'whom' from 'of which,' and 'who.' THAT, which was only nominative or accusative, became even stiffer. You can't say, "The house of that I told you."

Nevertheless, though THAT lost prestige for a while as a relative, it exploited its assets so effectively that at times, it serves as a pronoun, adjective, conjunction, noun or adverb. Consequently it is possible that that 'THAT' that that pen of yours writes may mean various things, each necessary for the moment. The only unfortunate thing is that the versatile actor never changes his costume. A certain novelist not long ago attempted to remedy this failing by giving THAT, as a conjunction, two 't's' at the end, making three in all. The publisher obliged, and suffered long tribulation.

THAT's virtue lies in its universality. While 'who' and 'which' have come to some sort of an agreement respecting their reference to things and persons ("The man who lived next door," "The house which he lived in," and "The infant who (or which) was his"), THAT refers conveniently and without prejudice to anything animate or inanimate. In the very beginning it was a demonstrative, and produced the definite article 'the,' which is somewhat less definite than THAT is. "The house there is very old," compared to "That house is very old." Then THAT was sometimes used as a noun, modified by a clause which followed it, "He saw that, (namely) the people were restless." Gradually the emphasis shifted from THAT used as a predicate object to the illustrative clause itself, and THAT became a mere connective, or conjunction, "He saw that the people were restless." For a while THAT was sometimes used in addition to a conjunction, and with only an echoing force, as in Shakespeare's "When that the poor have cried, Caesar hath wept." Adverbially, THAT is substandard: "He was THAT tired he didn't open his mouth all evening." However, there is much to be said for the colorful expression "He never even thanked me, he was just that rude!" In this example, THAT is used as an adverb, but it also suggests its demonstrative use, as in the example "That house is very old." Therefore, it has more force than the adverbial 'so.' "He never thanked me, he was so rude!" THAT, partly because of its early and continued use as a demonstrative and partly because of its quick, flat sound, has a real emphasis about it, "That's that!" has a finality we never mistake.

Tip-off 'A bit of secret information,' especially in advance of a happening disclosing an opportunity for profit, is a TIP-OFF. Yet that has not been enough for Americans. When is such information most valuable? Probably when danger threatens. So TIP-OFFS are very often 'warnings.'

Tit for Tat A 'blow for a blow'; more exactly, a 'TIP for a TAP.' But notice that TIT for TAT does not represent the stern justice of revenge, like 'an eye for an eye, or a tooth for a tooth,' because TIP was less than a TAP. In early usage a TIP was a light TAP. TIP itself came obscurely from the dim past associated with, but not assuredly cognate with, 'top.' Its earliest English usage was in 'tiptoe,' as we might say, on the 'tip-top' of the toes. 'Tap' came via Old French from a Teutonic word meaning 'to grope,' also 'to hit a blow,' or 'fumble'; there is a Low German word, *tappe*, for a 'paw.' Possibly both 'tip' and 'tap' were imitative in origin.

Touch You might think a TOUCH is only a 'light tap' or a 'soft stroke' of one's fingers. But what do you mean when you TOUCH a friend for a small loan? And there is something much more than a caress when you are TOUCHED to tears by a poignantly pathetic story. If you look into the reasons for these emphases, you will find that the first TOUCH really was a 'stroke' or a 'blow,' which still reverberates in the first syllable of 'tocsin,' an alarm bell.

TOUCH broke early down into many meanings. When we can't TOUCH an expert in golf we mean only that we can't compare with his skill. In geometry a tangent briefly TOUCHES another line, and a tennis player's TOUCH is the way he 'feels' or handles the ball in the brief second before it bounces out of his racket. In slang a TOUCH may refer to getting money by trickery, a swindle, or pickpocketing. If you can't TOUCH the golf expert, you can TOUCH (match) others. So the battle between the two egos of TOUCH is unceasing. A picture is TOUCHED with light deft strokes, a cloud is TOUCHED at sundown with soft reflected light, and we are TOUCHED with emotion. But then we can be TOUCHED also to the quick, and hurt horribly, by a mean personal remark.

Slang has made all kinds of tough or trivial things out of TOUCH. A 'theft' or a 'racket'; 'booty' or 'illicit goods'; a 'fake sale' or a 'cheap auction'; an 'imitation article' or one that is sure to sell at a certain low price; a 'dupe' or an 'easy-mark'; a 'clever trick' or a 'fastie'; when the tables are turned, a 'mean or petty trick'; a 'side-line,' a 'short-time loan,' a 'try-out' or 'trial'; and, of course, a 'nip,' a 'slight swig'; all these are TOUCHES. Perhaps the fullest force of the original is felt in a cowboy expression of utter contempt: 'to touch leather,' meaning to grab the saddle or the saddle horn to keep from being thrown off a bucking broncho.

Whilom and **Erstwhile** WHILOM as an adverb means 'formerly,' and as an adjective it means 'former' or 'once-upon-a-time.' Sometimes it means 'off and on,' as in the expression, 'your whilom friend.' It is occasionally equivalent to the literary adjective 'sometime.' "He was (a) sometime (at some time in the past) president of the society." ERST, or as we now have it, ERSTWHILE, is also Anglo-Saxon, and the superlative of the Saxon word for 'before.' Compare the poetical word 'ere.' It means literally 'in the beginning' or 'long ago,' but it is now equivalent to WHILOM, meaning 'former' or 'formerly.'

Yahoo You may think this word, sounding like a drunken yell, is slang. But it comes from very fanciful and classic English literature, where we are told a race of men, stupid and vicious, are subjects in an imaginary land of wise and benevolent masters, who are horses. Of course, this occurs in Dean Swift's famous satire, *Gulliver's Travels*. Swift describes the ascendency of a race of noble horses, endowed with reason and real justice over degraded human beings, who are more bestial than human. But the irony of it is that linguistically the Houyhnhnms, so named from their neighings, has given us no lasting general word for Christian virtue, but the YAHOOS, or human beasts, lent their name (without the capital) to any 'low and vicious person'— or, at least, to 'persons rough, coarse or uncouth.' In this country the YAHOOS are almost civilized, being 'country bumpkins' or 'yokels.' Probably this is, in part, an independent germination of the word, for at least one dictionary frankly calls it slang. But if it *is* American slang it still pays lip service to those imaginary humans who were so low in the animal social scale.

Ye In Old English YE was the subject or nominative form, and 'you' was the object or accusative form, of our 'you.' Both were always plural. In Chaucer's time their functions were still properly the same, though they had become somewhat mixed in people's minds, and were sometimes used interchangeably. The confusion was so rampant by Shakespeare's time that he says: 'Throw me that (which) you have about ye," with 'you,' not YE, as subject, and YE only an object in a phrase. By this time Danish 'thou' (nominative) and 'thee' (accusative) had challenged YE and 'you,' but were already fading out. YE faded out with them, though lingering, in the inferior objective capacity, in 'thankee,' for 'thank ye.' 'You' then took over both functions and also extended itself to include the singular. And thanks to the eighteenth century grammarians there is no verbal clue as to whether 'you' is used in the singular or the plural. It is impossible to say correctly that 'you *is*,' though Webster himself while he was alive stoutly defended 'you *was*.'

Nor has YE fared any better functioning as 'the,' like 'Ye Olde Wine Shoppe.' When the Normans came to England and began to write English in the French way they threw out the English letter called 'thorn' which had represented 'th.' In careless calligraphy the thorn letter could look like a 'y.' The 'thorn' hung on for a long while in the north of England, though modified in form, and looking more and more like a 'y.' So when printing came in some centuries later it was sometimes printed as a 'y.'

Yes When someone tells you you are more handsome than you know you are, and you think "Oh yeah?", you are only copying our very ancient Anglo-Saxon ancestors. For their *gēa* ('g' like 'y') didn't mean much, either, as an affirmative. For a stronger expression they had *gēse*, a contraction of *gēa swā*, or 'yes so,' which in time became our YES.

But in succeeding centuries it must have fallen into disuse, because you can look through the Authorized Edition of the Bible and find, as yet, not a single YES. Even Shakespeare, the arch innovator of those times, uses YES specially and pointedly as in answer to a negative question: "You did not then converse with him?" "Yes," equivalent to our present, "Why, yes, I did!" After a negative, the French also use their *si*, 'so' or *mais si*, 'but so,' for an emphatic *oui*, 'yes' or *mais oui*, 'but yes.' Similar also is our inserting the Latin, *sic*, 'thus, so,' in brackets after a dubious statement, as if saying to the reader, "This is so, just as you see it."

But it is interesting that Congress takes four kinds of votes on questions, the most serious and formal being a vote of 'yeas and nays.' In this vote the members do not answer 'yea,' but, as in the simplest vote, 'aye.' That 'aye,' pronounced like the pronoun 'I,' may have been an early spelling of the pronoun. If you can answer a roll by proclaiming yourself, probably you could likewise proclaim your affirmation of a proposition. Or perhaps 'aye,' sometimes spelled 'ay,' originally was that Old English word *ay*, rhyming with 'lay,' and meaning 'ever.' If we use 'never' as an emphatic 'no,' why don't we use 'ever' as an emphatic YES?

Zigzag A word that, for once, justifies the shape of letter 'z.' It is French, as all former doughboys and G.I.'s in France probably know; like *malade*, it is slang for 'drunkenness,' or at least was, not so long ago.

But longer ago it was German *zick-zack*, a reduplication of *zache*, a 'tooth,' of the kind in *zachen-werk*, 'notched-work.' And at this point we begin to see that ZIGZAG, though rather an idle and often a facetious word today, really has important connections with considerable sections of our language. For though modern Germans have *zick-zack segeln*, for 'tacking' in sailing, we derive the word more directly from the German or Friesian *takken*, 'to notch.' The idea expanded from an 'indentation' to a 'prong,' or tine, hence a 'nail' (compare our 'tack,' a little nail), or any fastening that serves a particular purpose, as specifically the 'tacks,' or fastening ropes, of sails which are shifted to alter the course of the craft. Note then when a sailing boat tacks it ZIGZAGS. Meanwhile, the 'tack' which was originally any pointed thing, initiated other particular forms in related tongues, like 'peg,' 'nail,' 'twig,' etc., which in time provided new English usages. And in addition to all this the root word found vast outlets through 'attach' and 'attack': it is not merely that we 'attach' a mat to the floor with little nails we call 'tacks,' but that when an 'attack' is made the battle is, as we also say, 'joined'—i.e. 'attached.' The word 'attack' is derived directly from the Italian, but it is cognate with the Teutonic, and Italian *attaccare* means 'to fasten or attach,' just as 'tack ropes' fasten sails.

POLITICS

See also Government; Law; and Rule

Gerrymander

JOBBERY *n.* corruption of public affairs, esp. graft.

LEFT *adj.* refers to persons who hold radical, highly progressive or socialistic ideas.

Liberalism

Maverick

Mugwump

Nepotism

PARTIES *n.* political organizations that try to control the government by electing its candidates to office.

CONSERVATIVES *n.* a party which holds that social institutions are in general better as they now exist than if they were changed.

DEMOCRATS *n.* a political party in the United States.

Dixiecrats

LIBERALS *n.* a party which does not feel itself bound by existing social institutions and doctrines.

PROGRESSIVES *n.* a party which encourages wide changes in the existing social order.

RADICALS *n.* a party that presses for immediate and sweeping changes in the social order.

REPUBLICANS *n.* a political
party in the United States.
SOCIALISTS *n.* a party which
holds that certain governmental control over the

production of certain basic
goods and services is
essential.
Spoils System
Tory

Dixiecrat A DIXIECRAT is a 'Dixie-Democrat.' The term applies to those Democrats in the U.S. who opposed the movement towards civil rights in the 1940's. 'Dixie' is a magical word as indefinite, in a specifically geographical sense, as it is vital emotionally. Whether originally it referred merely to the states south of the Mason and Dixon (hence 'Dixie') line, or whether it really originated in the nostalgic songs of negro slaves in the South, 'Dixie' is uniquely symbolic of the Old South now. It is said that these songs commemorate a holding-plantation on Manhattan Island in New York where a Mr. Dixie lavished comparative love and goodwill on all his slaves before they were shipped South to work. Incidentally, these Dixie songs predate Emmett's rallying song of 1859, "Dixie," by perhaps fifty years.

Gerrymander Politics and alchemy have something in common. Paracelsus, a Swiss alchemist born only one year after America was discovered, postulated a genius or spirit that inhabited fire, and named it 'salamander.' GERRYMANDER means not only to arrange voting districts favorably for a particular party but also to conduct any political affairs with an unfair party bias. The word itself dates back to 1812 when Governor Gerry of Massachusetts, paying less attention to the war with England than he should have, zealously re-districted his state for the benefit of his own political party. It happened that the county of Essex came out of the reshuffle in the shape of a 'salamander.' A journalist friend astutely telescoped two terms, and gave us our GERRYMANDER. Today we can GERRYMANDER many things, including plans which we wish to misrepresent for our own advantage and speeches which we can profitably garble.

Liberalism One might say that 'conservatism' is cozy, that it clings to the familiar and traditional while LIBERALISM exceeds all bounds, leading us to an unknown void. Such a definition of political and social sentiment is much too simple to be equitable. But the fact remains that the word LIBERAL hardly knows any bounds, having begun life meaning 'free.' It is impossible to express exactly the actions or feelings that LIBERALISM consists of. Fundamentally, it is a reaction against everything that is conforming. Consequently, LIBERALISM is always defined in part by what it is reacting from. Thus, in a sense, it has no fixed, or absolute definition. This distinguishes it from 'radicalism,' for the latter may have, and practically must have, its dogma. LIBERALISM is not necessarily progressive, for freedom is its own self, and may stand still if it so wishes, or move forwards or backwards. But meanwhile it is freedom, either of thought or of action.

All the connotations of LIBERALISM arise not so much from the fact of freedom itself as from the uses which humans have made of freedom. A LIBERAL disposition, for example, may be a 'generous' disposition; 'generosity' goes back to the 'genus' (or clan·) where it meant 'of high birth.' We still speak of 'generous' old port wine. But in those times only persons of high birth were 'free.' Thus LIBERALITY in a man is associated with the flair for 'giving' plus the tolerant culture that only the rich could once afford.

As another example, the LIBERAL man may be 'frank.' 'Frankness' comes from the German tribes that conquered Gaul, naming it France. The frank man was a member of a ruling race, he was 'free,' he was 'frank,' etc. Though usages have thus endowed the word LIBERAL with specific implications, you can test all the usages and find in them an underlying idea of 'unorthodoxy.' Even politically, LIBERALISM in England first bore the suggestion of foreign lawlessness, and of Jacobinism. But gradually political LIBERALISM is moderating its original reputation and attaining the true meaning of LIBERAL, 'open-minded, free-spirited.'

It is worth noticing that a LIBERAL education has been unaffected by confusing senses. A LIBERAL education is simply an excellent, albeit a general, education, one fit for a 'gentleman,' as that individual was formerly distinguished from a 'professional man' and from what we now call a 'technician.' It is not necessarily, what its name might imply, a broad, lavish or unscholastic education.

Maverick   Politics not only generates words of its own but appropriates and exploits other words, especially those that have already gained popularity with the public. MAVERICK, coined perhaps a century ago, was particularly attractive to politicians because it was first an epithet, and because, where there is political contention, there is perennial need for labeling-words that are, if possible, fresh and powerful.

MAVERICK was a real man (first name Samuel), who lived in Texas, was a civil engineer, and owned so many cattle he couldn't possibly keep an eye on them all. So, of course, some of the cattle ran wild, unbranded, and in return, branded him with a reputation he didn't deserve, a reputation for carelessness and independence. But it is his roving steers that we remember now in the term MAVERICK. A MAVERICK is any 'wandering outcast' without dependents, who is free to do what he pleases, and usually pleases to do just that. Since such individuals are seldom popular in politics, the term is derisive there, like the term 'mugwump.' A 'mugwump' is a sullen or stubborn obstructionist while a MAVERICK, like the young steer on the loose, is much more of an annoyance and a destroyer. On the other hand (and to extend the metaphor), he is also something of a Bull Moose—not always an agitator and a bothersome innovator but sometimes a real progressive in politics.

Mugwump   All great leaders are supposed to possess independence, and *mugquomps* among the Algonquin Indians were high chieftains and leaders. And when the Bible was translated into Algonquin by John Eliot in 1663 the terms 'captain, duke, centurion, etc.,' were rendered by *mugquomp*. But when the term MUGWUMP came into our politics in the 1880's, such 'independent leadership' was not very much admired by politicians in general. So it happened they used the term ironically for a boss, eventually fixing it chiefly and permanently upon anyone who thwarted political proceedings by stubbornly standing aloof. Now you will find MUGWUMP defined sarcastically in *The Devil's Dictionary* as, in politics, someone who is afflicted with self-respect and who is, therefore, addicted to independence. It is a term of contempt. In common parlance, however, the term refers more reasonably to political obstructionists who are pigheaded or old-fashioned.

Nepotism   NEPOTISM is the political practice of favoring your relatives when you are in office, with the idea especially of strengthening or prolonging your personal influence and perpetuating your policies. The adjective relating to NEPOTISM is 'nepotic.' A high officeholder guilty of NEPOTISM is a 'nepotist,' and the things he does along this line are 'nepotistical.'

Spoils System   Originally SPOILS were the stripped off hides of animals taken as game. Old Hickory's political motto, "To the victors the spoils," expressed something like our later but already obsolete phrase, 'to skin 'em alive.' Old Hickory was Andrew Jackson, who got elected in 1828 on the first Democratic landslide and who inaugurated the SPOILS SYSTEM in government.

Tory   From an Irish word for a 'pursuer,' *toiridhe*. In the 18th century the English called the Irish (especially Catholic) outlaws,

TORIES. The Duke of York was a Catholic, and while efforts were being made to prevent his becoming James II, debaters in Parliament who opposed the efforts were called TORIES, the purpose being to connect them in the popular mind with the outlaws in the Irish bogs. Properly, the old Irish word did mean the 'pursuer,' with affinities with the Old French for 'progress' and 'pursuit.' But in Ireland—it had come to mean the 'hunted one, the robber.'

POSITION

About   see **Around & About,** etc.

Above   see **Around & About,** etc.

ABREAST   *adj. & adv.* side by side, and headed in the same direction, as "The soldiers stayed abreast of each other as they searched the jungle."

ACROSS   *adv. & prep.* on the opposite or other side of, as "Across the river stands an old mill," "He stepped across the street."

AGAINST   *prep.* in opposition to or in opposite direction from, as to be AGAINST tyranny, or to walk AGAINST the wind.

Aloft

ALONGSIDE   *adv. & prep.* side by side; along the side of; by the side of, as "Alongside the Cadillac stood a Model-T."

AMID   *prep.* in the middle of; among; in the midst of; as "See that red flower amid all the white ones?"

Among   see **Center, Middle,** etc.

Antipodes & Antithesis

Antithesis   see **Antipodes & Antithesis**

APICAL   *adj.* at the top (apex).

APPOSITION   *n.* the state of being opposite or before something.

Around & About; Over & Above

ASIDE   *adv.* to the side; at a short distance; as to turn ASIDE.

ASLANT   *adj., adv. & prep.* in a sloping or oblique direction.

AT HAND   *adj.* near; next to; close; as "Where is my umbrella? It was at hand a moment ago."

ATHWART   *adv. & prep.* crosswise; aslant; directly in the way, as "The tree fell athwart the forest path."

BASAL   *adj.* pertaining to 'base.' BASAL is a broader and deeper word than BASIC, just as BASIS refers to a more profound, less concrete foundation than BASE.

BELOW   *adv. & prep.* beneath; in a lower position; as "My house is just below yours on the hill."

BENEATH   *adv. & prep.* below; esp. with reference to something overhead or in the air, as BENEATH a tree, or BENEATH the stars.

BESIDE   *prep.* next to; near, at the side of; as "He sat beside me on the bench."

BETWEEN *prep*. anywhere in the space that separates two objects, as "The girl walked between us."

BETWIXT *prep*. between.

Bevel & Cant

Cant see **Bevel & Cant**

Center, Middle & Among

CLOSE *adj*. near; next to; as "The child kept close to her father during their nightly walk."

Contiguous

CORE *n*. the center or fundamental part of a thing, as "The core of the problem was really simple to understand."

Crossways see **Crosswise & Crossways**

Crosswise & Crossways

DEEP *adj*. pertaining to whatever goes far downward, as a DEEP well.

Diametrical

DISTAL *adj*. pertaining to an extremity, to something away from the center, like a finger tip or the rim of a wheel.

DISTANT *adj*. remote; far off; as the DISTANT horizon.

EQUIDISTANCE *n*. equal distance. *adj*. EQUIDISTANT.

ERECT *adj*. raised; upright; standing.

FACE TO FACE *adj*. facing each other; in a confronting position.

FARAWAY *adj*. distant

FLAT *adj*. level; smooth; as FLAT land.

HALFWAY *adj*. & *adv*. equidistant; midway; as "They met each other halfway."

HEART *n*. the center or core of anything, as the HEART of his argument.

HIGH *adj*. having great distance upwards; far from the ground; as the HIGH airplane.

HORIZONTAL *adj*. flat.

JUXTAPOSITION *n*. state of being placed side by side, abreast or adjoining.

KERNEL *n*. core; heart.

LEVEL *adj*. flat; not aslant.

LOW *adj*. situated below or beneath, as LOW mountains among high mountains.

MEDIAL or MEDIAN *adj*. pertaining to the middle.

Medium

Middle see **Center, Middle, etc.**

MIDWAY *adv*. & *adj*. pertaining to the middle; equidistant; as "Midway between the poles lies the equator."

NEAR *adj*. close; next to.

NIGH *adv*. & *prep*. close; at hand; near.

NUCLEUS *n*. heart; core.

OPPOSITE *adj*. on the other side, as the OPPOSITE side of the river.

Over see **Around & About, etc.**

OVERHEAD *adj*. pertaining to something above one's head in the direction of the zenith.

PENULTIMATE *adj*. next to the last, like a syllable of a word or an event in a series.

PERPENDICULAR *adj*. erect; a position such that if it were extended it would pass through the center of the earth.

PROXIMITY *n*. closeness; nearness.

REMOTE *adj.* distant, as REMOTE seas.

RIGHT AND LEFT *adv.* on all sides; to the right and left; as "They looked right and left for the lost book."

SIDE BY SIDE *adj.* in juxtaposition; next to each other, as "The couple stood side by side before the priest."

Slant

STRAIGHT *adj.* without a turn, bump or bend, as a STRAIGHT road or line.

TILTED *adj.* slanted.

UNDER *prep.* beneath; below.

UNDERNEATH *adv.* & *prep.* under, as "Underneath the stove lived ants."

UPWARDS *adj.* & *adv.* in the direction of over head; in the upper parts. "The bird flew upwards to a tall elm."

VERTICAL *adj.* upright; perpendicular.

VICINITY *v.* proximity, as in the VICINITY of the graveyard.

ZENITH *n.* the spot directly overhead; a point in the sky equidistant from the four directions.

Aloft There is a lift in ALOFT that makes it expressive. Although 'above' serves us in three adverbial senses, and 'over' in thirteen more, not mentioning the more than a score of meanings these words have as nouns and prepositions, ALOFT itself has also plenty of everyday uses in addition to its poetic use. ALOFT is as old as the Norsemen, and as free and alive as those unhampered Vikings to whom it meant the 'top of the skies' or, at least, 'high up' in the vast air overhead. Later, sailors associated it with 'high mastheads,' but even in this use ALOFT carries the full force of 'on high' that makes a drab descriptive word like 'above' seem quite often inadequate. As a matter of fact, it was the Norsemen's phrase for 'on high,' *a lopt.* Their word for 'to lift,' *lupta,* was almost the same as their word for 'sky,' *lopt.* The 'p' in them both was pronounced 'f.'

With the passing of sailing ships ALOFT waned in common usage. It echoes faintly in 'haylofts,' 'lofts' (the upper floors of warehouses) and the 'lofting shots' of golf. Yet even the outwardly unromantic English persisted in calling tall buildings LOFTY, with a poetic suggestion of the Alps, and now air travel, far more romantic than even the early coursing of the seas, is bringing about a renaissance of ALOFT. The activities on an airfield are terrestrial, but what happens in the planes when they take to the air happens 'ALOFT.'

Antipodes and **Antithesis** ANTIPODES is the Greek phrase for 'opposite the foot,' used by us as a single word commonly referring to Australia and other regions on the opposite side of the world. But anything situated remotely and exactly on the 'opposite' side of anything is ANTIPODAL. Likewise, an antonym is figuratively ANTIPODAL, like 'white' is to 'black.' 'Cloudy' days are ANTIPODAL to 'bright' ones.

More intellectually, ANTIPODES (it is used in the plural, like 'the blues') are equivalent to ANTITHESIS, in which the 'anti' means 'against,' as it does in 'antipathy,' and the root is 'place.' ANTITHESIS implies a contrasting of 'extremes,' or a comparison of 'extremely different' things, like Parisian fashions and Quaker clothes. In a narrow sense it means 'one of the two factors in a contrast.' 'Dark clouds' are the AN-TITHESIS of a 'serene sky.' As ANTIPODES is the diametrically opposite pole, so ANTITHESIS is the directly contrary type or kind. This is an important distinction: ANTIPODES refer to 'position' and ANTITHESIS refers to 'quality.' The ANTITHESIS of 'hot' is 'cold'; the ANTIPODES of a 'tower' is a 'well.' In figurative use, of course, this distinction disappears.

In rhetoric, ANTITHESIS is the balancing of contrasted words or ideas against each other: "The dog barked his indignation, the cat hissed her complaints." ANTITHETIC is the adjective.

Around and **About; Over** and **Above**   AROUND is not really a twin of ABOUT, nor is OVER of ABOVE. ABOUT is from an Old English form that said literally 'on by outside,' which is a consolidation of auxiliaries into one adverb that at first meant 'in the neighborhood of.' AROUND came probably about 1750 from the French en ronde, with an original sense best illustrated in, "Call me around five o'clock." ABOVE is another product made of Old English fragments, meaning, literally, 'by upward.' A prefix was added later to imitate the 'a' in ABOUT. OVER is also Old English, but it is a solid Teutonic word, common nearly everywhere in Europe. Compare German uber. It is even cognate with Latin super. OVER is also more coherently descriptive than the others, being a comparative degree of the word 'up,' that is, 'more up.'

It is easy to see why these four words have developed four senses which never entirely coincide. Nor do they ever exactly agree in any particular sense. Though the words of either pair are often used interchangeably, we should be careful not to assume identical meanings where, in fact, none exist. One characteristic of OVER, for example, that is not shared by ABOVE, is its suggestion of 'two-dimensional space.' Anything that is OVER us has 'length' and 'breadth.' The sky OVER us, for example, stretches from horizon to horizon in every direction. But whatever is ABOVE us is directly 'overhead,' a phrase that limits OVER to a point where it loses its spatial connotations. The sky ABOVE us, for example, is the zenith. ABOVE expresses 'altitude' and 'perpendicularity,' OVER expresses 'extent' and 'sweep.' A church spire points ABOVE, not OVER, and is definitely directional. It may even suggest motion, like a rocket's. But a sky or cloud that hangs OVER is extensive, and suspended. An airplane is ten thousand feet ABOVE the ground, but it goes two hundred miles an hour OVER the earth.

In addition, OVER can suggest reversal, "Turn the thing over and let's look at its under side." The upper side easily revolves to the lower. But not so with ABOVE. It is 'overhead,' and stays stationary. Pebbles may be scattered all OVER the seaside, but the stars that are ABOVE us are, each one, at a vertical height. When both words are used very figuratively they sometimes coalesce in sense, like 'over-exertion' and 'above-normal' where they agree in expressing 'excess.' Even 'above-normal' suggests something of the superiority in "He is above deceit." When we get OVER a cold it is not so much that we rise ABOVE it, like a master ABOVE his slave, as that we put it behind us. To clinch this distinction, consider Bernard Shaw. Others before him had attempted to translate Nietzsche's *Ubermensch,* a 'godlike he-man.' They had tried 'beyondman' and 'overman.' Neither took hold, though they were pure and robust Anglo-Saxon. Shaw produced a hybrid by mixing English and Latin to coin 'superman.' It not only took hold; but it littered the language with imitations, from super-colossal to super-elite to super-ultra.

The distinctions between AROUND and ABOUT are more obvious, perhaps, than those between OVER and ABOVE, but basically the first two words are closer than the latter two. You can say several men were standing idly AROUND, or you can say they were standing idly ABOUT, and in either case the sense is the same. Basically the original sense of both AROUND and ABOUT was 'in the vicinity.' The exact usage here is said to be colloquial American, and it does add a dispersive sense to the original. The men are not merely in the neighborhood but are scattered AROUND and ABOUT it.

Of course the meanings vary slightly as either word is used as a preposition, adverb, or adjective. You wrap a scarf either AROUND or ABOUT your neck. You ask if the janitor is AROUND or (slightly British) ABOUT. You might say a track is a mile AROUND or (more British) ABOUT. You can look AROUND for signs of game, or look ABOUT. You can wander AROUND the room or ABOUT it, though the AROUND might here simply imply going AROUND the walls, as you would AROUND the circumference of a circle. You can meet someone AROUND ten o'clock tomorrow, or ABOUT ten. You can turn AROUND or face ABOUT. You can pass candy AROUND, as in a circle, or (with some weakening of the sense) pass it ABOUT. You can be hemmed AROUND by the enemy, or hemmed ABOUT. The enemy can press AROUND you or (closely) ABOUT you. You can go AROUND the block or AROUND an obstacle or, literally, ABOUT them.

But though you can say "Turn and turn about!", "The best thing about him is his honesty," "That's all I can say about him," or "You go about your business," you cannot substitute AROUND in any of those phrases. If you ask someone, "Have you a pin about you?" you show how all the senses in the previous paragraph are derived. For 'on by outside' is the literal translation of ABOUT. You might dispense with the 'by outside' and ask, "Have you a pin on you?" Likewise AROUND is 'on ("a" as in "afoot" for "on" foot) round.' 'Round' goes all the way back through Latin *rotundus*, 'round,' to *rotae*, 'wheels' and the In-do-Germanic root *ret*, 'to roll.' When you gaze AROUND you glance outward in all directions as the spokes in a wheel go out from the hub. In AROUND the action is centrifugal; but in ABOUT the action is toward the center, 'on by outside.' When you are ABOUT thirty years of age you are closing in on the thirty. When you are ABOUT your business you are surrounding it.

'Round' is a variant form of AROUND, but its sense is more confined to an encircling motion or a circuitous course. It is in favor more in England than here.

Bevel and **Cant**   BEVEL is both a noun and a verb. BEVEL is the 'slant' or 'inclination' of one surface compared to another. 'To BEVEL' means 'to cut a BEVEL angle.' CANT has two meanings, and in each may be both a verb and a noun. (1) CANT is an inclination, a slope, a tilt, or tipping to one side. 'To CANT' means 'to give a tilt or slope' to something. (2) CANT is also an affected or insincere manner of talking or singing, but more often in this second meaning CANT refers to the peculiar language of any exclusive group, such as the jargon of thieves or tramps, or the private language of sportsmen or entertainers. 'To CANT' means 'to talk with a whine,' or 'to talk hypocritically.'

Center, Middle and **Among**   You probably could find the CENTER of any MIDDLE, but you would be a genius if you could map the MID-DLE of a CENTER. A CENTER is a 'spot, point, core, nucleus.' Even figuratively it is always a 'point' of concentration. If you are the CENTER of attraction in a crowd, you are much more than 'amidst' the crowd, though 'amidst' is an intensive or superlative form of 'in the middle of.' A stage star is a CENTER of attraction both figuratively and physically when he stands in a limelight, whether or not he is somewhere in the MIDDLE of the stage.

Only in a linear sense is a MIDDLE a point, 'half way between two ends.' Of course the line may be a figurative one, like a line of action, where the MIDDLE point expands itself into a period of time. MIDDLE is Teutonic, and no doubt the ancient Germans, including the early English, were not so precise as the more highly conditioned Romans, who gave us CENTER. MIDDLE comports more with our Latin derived 'medium'; they both suggest 'intermediate.' Theoretically, MIDDLE is any part 'halfway' between two extremes, or any part 'intervening' between two main parts. We use it pretty much to suit our imaginations, just as we expand the CENTER of things far beyond the original meaning of that word in Greek where it pointedly means a spike.

AMONG is not so shifty. The 'a' means 'in' and the 'mong' means a 'crowd.' Yet, we have managed to give it three other much contracted special meanings. They suggest 'co-operation,' 'time' and 'distribution,' like (1) "Among us all we should be able to think of something"; (2) "Among savages, learning had no repute"; (3) "He divided it among his men."

Contiguous Like 'contact' it comes from Latin *contingere,* 'to touch.' It usually suggests an 'edge' or 'boundary.' Two adjacent or adjoining fields, for example, are CONTIGUOUS. Figuratively, two lines of thought may be CONTIGUOUS too.

Crosswise, Crossways and other **Wises** and **Ways** These compounds appear to be punsters when you investigate their histories. For the noun WISE, meaning in early English 'wisdom' or 'skill,' came to mean a WAY, that is, a WAY of doing things, like 'in this wise.' "After having been taught the new steps, we danced in this wise all night." And the very ancient word WAY, which probably originated in prehistoric Aryan cart tracks across Europe, took on the meaning in our middle English of 'wisdom,' or 'wise method,' like 'ways and means.' Even today when we arrive at a conclusion by WAY of a line of reasoning there is a suggestion of 'wisdom,' because the WAY is not any old method but a good one. So when the two nouns came to be used as adverbial suffixes you could practically take your choice. What was WISE was WAYS, and WAYS were WISE. Now you can sit or move 'sidewise' or 'sideways.' They mean the same.

The same, that is, with some differences, depending on what form of speech or what word it attaches itself to. Collectively, both can suggest 'position, direction, design, method, manner, character or even degree.' It is the use, or shall we say, custom, that determines the exact meaning.

Diametrical "His house is diametrically opposite the hotel." From its source, DIAMETER means 'the measure across.' Consequently it is commonly the distance from one side of a circle 'straight across' to the opposite side, that is, the longest straight distance within the circle. So DIAMETRICAL has two meanings. "My opinions are diametrically opposed to yours," which is a kind of figurative use of DIAMETRICAL, depending on its literal meaning. And "The diametrical distance of the earth is 7918 miles."

Medium This is a word that has run wild in our newspapers and over our radios. The fact is that MEDIUM, originally meaning 'middle,' Latin *medius*, has acquired not so much several variant meanings as many precise applications of its one very broad meaning. Consequently dictionary definitions are inadequate, since the present variant meanings are still so broad that their definition also fits a number of other common words, such as agency, instrumentality, intermediary, inter-agent, vehicle, channel, and, most particularly, means. Incidentally, 'means,' a word we use to refer to anything which accomplishes something, was first the adjective 'mean,' or 'average,' and is cognate with MEDIUM. A 'golden mean' is a 'happy medium' between excesses, Horace's *aurea mediocritas*.

Consequently, it is the usages that now practically determine the meanings of MEDIUM. It seems that we are free to use the word in any sense not prohibited by the given broad definition. The result is our present chaos, with MEDIUMS, or sometimes MEDIA, becoming favorite jargon for newspaper and radio commentators, who often misuse the word or fail to employ it when they profitably could.

At bottom and always, a MEDIUM is a 'middle ground.' One of its earliest meanings in English was a 'mathematical average,' a sense that still lingers in our 'happy medium.' But a 'middle ground' between excesses is inevitably an 'arena' where things happen. It is a site of co-operation, stalemate, agreement or conflict. And, of course, it is an area of 'communication' and 'co-operation.' Thus the middle ground, or MEDIUM, becomes any intervening visible or invisible space, or any intermediary substance or person, by which or through which anything is accomplished. It may be as immaterial as air. It is anything that *exists between* and can *aid action*, like the sunlight that is a MEDIUM in the growth of plants.

The services that MEDIUMS perform are not trivial. 'Transmission' is one service. For example, a message is conveyed through the MEDIUM of telegraphy. A MEDIUM is often some sort of 'inert ingredient' which is nevertheless necessary to the whole product. Such a service, for instance, oil performs when pigment is mixed with it to produce paint. In this category, water color itself, or oil paint, chalk, marble, clay are all MEDIUMS in which a work of art is composed. But most often a MEDIUM is an 'active ingredient.' The gelatin used for the experimental cultivation of bacteria in laboratories is a MEDIUM. 'Spiritualism' illustrates another active meaning of MEDIUM. Since the eighteen-nineties certain persons who profess to aid us in communicating with the next world are called MEDIUMS. And, incidentally, we cannot use the Latin plural, *media*, for them, though all other MEDIUMS may be either MEDIA or MEDIUMS.

At any rate, this word is used much too often. You must ask yourself when you are about to use MEDIUM whether it precisely conveys in your sentence an idea of essential service. You will find in almost every instance that another word or perhaps a concise explanatory sentence will clarify your thought.

Slant   Except for a common colloquial usage, which some dictionaries still regard as slang, SLANT gets little attention in the smaller lexicons. They are content to say, in effect, that it means a 'slope.' Sometimes they add that it can also be an inclination away from a straight line, as an auto must SLANT to one side to pass another in front of it.

But that colloquial usage in which SLANT refers to a 'mental disposition' and hence a 'habitual way' of looking at something, is giving SLANT quite a stature. Its strict sense is maltreated, of course, as it always is in slang. We ask, "What is your slant on this?" when we mean only, "What is your opinion of this?" The suggestion is, however, that opinions may change soon, but a person's SLANT is a little more fixed. Thus this use of SLANT assumes some real importance. It can be an index to the man's mental make-up, which will determine his reaction to the whole of life.

The danger is that the word will always imply some bias, and sometimes we think of bias as unintelligent. Most bias is unintelligent; but everyone has to have a certain perspective, or way of looking at things, and that is his SLANT.

POVERTY

BANKRUPTCY   *n.* failure of business; inability to pay off debts.

BEGGARY   *n.* the state of extreme want or poverty, typified by a beggar.

Desolate & Destitute

Destitute, Devoid, Lacking, Indi-

gent, Needy & Penurious. See
also Desolate & Destitute

Devoid see Destitute, Devoid,
etc.

Eke

Frugal

HUNGRY *adj.* having a strong appetite; the discomfort felt from going without food.

IMPECUNIOUS *adj.* without money; poor.

IMPOVERISHED *adj.* pertaining to the condition of increasing poverty, as "The impoverished people are again in the midst of a famine."

Indigent see Destitute, Devoid, etc.

INSOLVENCY *n.* bankruptcy.

Lacking see Destitute, Devoid, etc.

Needy see Destitute, Devoid, etc.

PAUPERISM *n.* the condition of poverty or complete destitution which requires outside aid.

PENNILESS *adj.* without money.

Penurious see Destitute, Devoid, etc.

Poor & Wanting

Privation

STARVELING *n.* a person in great hunger; thus, a poor, thin person.

Starving

Wanting see Poor & Wanting

Desolate and **Destitute** Two gloomy words that can better be contrasted than compared. When you are DESTITUTE, in the common sense, you are economically 'down and out.' As the Romans had it, you are 'put down.' Here, it would seem, is a hard and dry word that says bluntly: "You've got nothing." DESOLATE, on the other hand, is a soft and enchanting word, a surprising heritage from the traditionally war helmeted Romans. It means, literally, 'all alone,' or, 'left all alone.' It expresses a feeling of inconsolable grief. When your heart is DESOLATE you feel bereft of everything human. DESOLATE is more heart-rending than DESTITUTE.

We have assiduously built up DESTITUTE so that it refers to the loss of not only means and money but also all ambitions. Sometimes a person is DESTITUTE of an entertaining personality or of an intelligent mind. One can be destitute of morals, too. Concurrently, we have widened and modified DESOLATE. Now even financial prospects may appear DESOLATE. But the word still carries its mournful content. Uttermost bleak peaks, above the timberline, are DESOLATE. It, of course, can also serve as a verb. When you kill all the inhabitants of a land you DESOLATE it. "She so much loved him that, on his death, she was desolated in heart and mind for the rest of her life."

Destitute, Devoid, Lacking, Indigent, Needy, Penurious These six words are all quite specific in their meanings. They differ from one another in spite of the lack of discrimination, with which they are commonly used. What each of them really does, is to emphasize some certain sense of two other more general words, 'poor,' and 'wanting.' See POOR and WANTING.

There is, for example, a note in DESTITUTE that goes beyond NEEDY and LACKING, towards 'hopelessness.' It is the 'hopelessness' that accompanies 'wretched loneliness,' for it comes from the Latin *destituere*, 'to forsake, abandon.' But DESTITUTE does not suggest the 'utter emptiness' that DEVOID means. If you are DESTITUTE, you may have a spark of energy, spirituality, or even hope, that encourages you, but if you are DEVOID of all, then you are indeed forsaken. DEVOID means 'emptied,' a corruption of Latin *vacuus*, 'empty.' Both of these words hint at a former prosperity, which has been lost. And when we are 'in need'— that is, are NEEDY—we may also be without what we want, what we formerly had or what we are used to. Yet it is usually the 'necessities of life,' in the form of concrete things, that now are most often intentionally implied in the word NEEDY. 'Necessity' was the first meaning of NEED, yet NEED did acquire a spiritual yearning through confusion in the late Anglo-Saxon with *neod*, meaning 'desire.' At that time NEED was spelled *nied* or *nyd*. INDIGENT is simply the Latin form of NEEDY; it is the present participle of Latin *indigere*, 'to be in want.' It is prosaic, and really implies no dire NEED but rather 'reduced circumstances.' A student who has used up his allowance too soon is INDIGENT. In periods of economic depression unemployed people are called INDIGENTS. The word has thus come to mean practically 'penniless.' Yet people who are actually poverty-stricken, are better described as DESTITUTE if they are forsaken, utterly out-of-luck or despairing.

We might call penniless people PENURIOUS, since PENURY is simply 'poverty' with its hard Latin origin undisguised. It comes from Latin *penuria*. But PENURIOUS has taken on additional meanings which now supersede that of pecuniary NEED. A PENURIOUS person is now more 'parsimonious' than 'impecunious,' more 'stingy' than 'poverty-stricken.' He is perhaps greedy or grasping, since the word reflects the worst and seemingly inevitable by-products of poverty. "That man is destitute and his character is penurious." Things and conditions, also, are PENURIOUS, "That certainly is a penurious science textbook: it has no exciting photographs and the description of the experiments sound as though they came out of an old, stuffy laboratory manual."

And within all these words there lies a LACKING; the adjective LACKING thus approaches the generality of 'poor' and 'wanting.' Long ago it missed the boat when the Angles and the Saxons invaded England. It stayed behind among the Frisians where it is still found, carrying inherently a specific note which these other adjectives have either lost before they came into English or never had—a note of 'censure.' The Dutch today have *lac*, meaning 'blemish' or a 'stain.' When we ourselves say "He just hasn't got it," we imply this hidden blame. "Something is lacking in his sense of square dealing," something, that is, which he certainly ought to have. LACKING is the present participle (used as an adjective) of the intransitive verb LACK, meaning 'to be deficient or wanting,' or 'to fail.' 'Failure' and 'fault' is its historic essence. In the Frisian the word suggested 'damage, harm, even attack.' In English, where it finally arrived in Chaucer's era, it still denoted 'failure.' Though we now use the word LACKING casually, still the old woes of the word return in their pristine plaintiveness when we say "Alas and alack," expressing 'unhappiness' first and then 'blame, sorrow or surprise.'

Eke This verb used to mean 'to increase, enlarge, lengthen.' Now it means 'to supply whatever is lacking,' or 'to increase or make barely sufficient by adding onto.' "One ekes out his small income by doing odd jobs."

Frugal 'Liberality' is a much used word, and FRUGALITY, which is its antonym, is little used. It refers to the practice of very strict economy. A FRUGAL meal is a meager one. "After the late World War the British people had to be frugal until their national economy recovered from its war losses."

Poor and **Wanting** It is the privative force of both POOR and WANTING that account for their universality. See PHILOLOGICAL TERMS. Both of these words achieve their power ultimately from the things they suggest by inference. For example, POOR has force because it immediately contrasts itself with 'rich,' and with all the self-satisfaction that goes with having enough. POOR is much used and in many ways; WANTING is seldom used, but it can say a mindful. A literary style that is WANTING lacks something that is needed. You never use the word WANTING for the absence of something unimportant or unnecessary. "She is wanting warmth and love in her heart." Don't say, "There is a page wanting in this book," because this is debasing WANTING. Simply say "There is a page missing." The verb 'to want' has, of course, taken the additional meaning of 'to wish.' When we are conscious of a WANT we 'wish' to supply it.

As for POOR, which is a child of Latin *pauper*, 'poor,' and Old French *povre* or *poure*, it was, we might say, a natural. Meaning 'ill-provided,' and sounding soft, it was assured of popularity. Consequently, it has many extended usages. So from POOR that describes 'poverty,' which is aggressive, to POOR that means 'humble,' there is included all the things we might have had and didn't. Note these applications of POOR: Anything 'badly done'; a lean horse, with little flesh on his bones; the man of mean spirit; a miserable man; whatever lacks strength, fineness or beauty; harvests that are scant; soil that is barren; bad luck or opportunity, like a POOR chance of success; any living creature that is unfortunate.

Privation PRIVATION is a bleak word stemming, as the cozier word 'private' does, from the austere sense of 'to separate.' It refers to 'something missing,' something that is 'wanting.' When we think in our PRIVATION of our more happy days we speak of a 'deprivation,' because the 'de' emphasizes the 'taking away from' which is implicit in our loss.

'Privative' meant simply 'depriving, causing destitution.' Logicians have come to use it as a label to denote PRIVATION. At first suggesting a lack, 'privative' has come to mean a 'negative.' See PHILOLOGICAL TERMS.

Starving STARVING is a vivid word that lends itself readily to figurative uses. We can be extravagantly STARVING for affection, for attention or for anything at all nowadays.

Normally one STARVES for 'solid food.' We have no word whatever for STARVING for 'liquids,' and are obliged to 'perish' from thirst, or to 'die' for a drink.

PRAISE

(*adjectives*)

ADMIRABLE fine; excellent; estimable.

ANGELIC like an angel.

ASSIDUOUS pertaining to concentration, application, and diligence; persistent; attentive.

AUTHENTIC genuine; reliable; legal; credible; true.

BEWITCHING entrancing; enchanting; charming.

BLAMELESS without blame; free from guilt.

BONA FIDE genuine; authentic.

BRIGHT shining; brilliant; intelligent.

CALM peaceful; quiet; motionless; still.

CHAMPION best; top-notch; of high caliber; unexcelled.

CHARMING pleasing; delightful; fascinating.

CHOICE superior; worthy of being selected.

CLEAN free from dirt or grime.

CLEVER witty; intelligent; shrewd.

CULTIVATED educated; well-mannered.

CULTURED cultivated.

DAINTY delicate; exquisite; nice.

DECENT upright; modest; respectable.

DELIGHTFUL pleasant.

DEPENDABLE steady; reliable, as a DEPENDABLE doctor.

DILIGENT hard-working; attentive; assiduous.

DISCRIMINATING displaying good taste or a keen intelligence.

DOWNRIGHT forthright; candid.

Élan see **Verve & Élan**

ENCHANTING bewitching.

ENGAGING attractive; charming.

ESTIMABLE worthy of esteem, good opinion, respect.

EXCELLENT of high quality; first-rate.

EXQUISITE beautiful; lovely; of or pertaining to rare and delicate workmanship.

EXUBERANT full of life; luxuriant; richly abundant; effusive; lavish.

FAULTLESS without fault; perfect; without wrong or guilt.

FELICITOUS apt; fortunate; particularly fitting, as a FELICITOUS expression.

FIRST-RATE excellent; superior; the first in degree of any sort.

FORTHRIGHT in a direct manner; immediately; down-to-earth; outspoken.

FRESH unspoiled; ripe; new.

GENUINE pure; authentic.

GLORIOUS illustrious; splendid; worthy of great honor and applause.

GORGEOUS splendid; magnificent; sumptuous; showy; colorful.

GRAND big and sweeping; magnificent; stately; imposing.

HALE healthy; hearty; robust.

HEALTHY free of disease; strong.

HONORABLE worthy of respect; estimable.

IMMACULATE clean; free of stain.

INDUSTRIOUS diligent; hard-working.

Irenic or **Irenical**

JUDICIOUS careful of thought; showing judgment.

JUST fair; right; well-founded.

KEEN eager; sharp; pertaining to penetrating sight or mind, as "His keen intelligence solved the mystery quickly."

LAVISH extravagant; in great abundance; rich in effect, as a LAVISH display.

LIKABLE friendly; attractive.

LOVELY pretty; charming.

LUSH profuse; lavish; juicy; tender.

LUSTY vigorous; exuberant; robust.

Luxuriant see **Luxurious & Luxuriant**

Luxurious & Luxuriant

MAGNIFICENT imposing; great in size; splendid; grand.

MAJESTIC stately; possessing

royal dignity and bearing; imposing.

MATCHLESS not to be equaled, as the MATCHLESS color of her dress.

MERITORIOUS worthy of reward; good.

MODEST humble; reserved; chaste; decent; without show or extravagance, as a MODEST house.

NATURAL unaffected; acting in a spontaneous manner.

Nice

OPULENT wealthy; rich.

PEERLESS without match or equal; very superior.

PERFECT the very best; flawless; faultless.

PLACID calm.

PLEASANT attractive; agreeable; friendly, as a PLEASANT personality.

PREPOSSESSING pleasing; making a good impression, esp. on first appearance.

PRODIGAL wasteful; lavish.

PROMPT on time; without delay, as a PROMPT answer to my letter.

PRUDENT careful; wise; judicious.

RADIANT full of light; shining; gleaming; bright with hope or joy.

RAVISHING very attractive or captivating.

REFINED cultured; cultivated; very polite or well-mannered.

RESPLENDENT brilliantly lighted; splendid; gorgeous.

ROBUST healthy, as a ROBUST plant.

SAGE wise.

SANE of or pertaining to a sound mind.

SCRUPULOUS honest; carefully following the rules.

SEDULOUS diligent; given to constant application.

SELECT choice; superior.

SENSIBLE wise; judicious; referring to common sense.

SERAPHIC angelic.

SERENE calm; peaceful.

SMART intelligent; quick-witted; also chic or fashionable.

SOUND free from imperfections; healthy.

Splendid & Splendor

Splendor see Splendid & Splendor

STALWART strong and steadfast; valiant.

STATELY imposing; grand.

STERLING of high character and repute.

STOUT heavy; strong; brave.

STURDY firm; strong; robust.

SUBLIME lofty; exalted; pertaining to the noblest, as SUBLIME emotion.

Sumptuous

SUPERB splendid; excellent; first-rate.

TIPTOP first-rate; the best (of anything).

TOP-NOTCH tiptop.

TRANQUIL calm; peaceful; still.

UNPARALLELED matchless; without equal.

UPRIGHT honest; respectable.

Verve & Élan

VIGOROUS strong; healthy; resolute.

WINNING charming; captivating;   WISE very intelligent; capable of
attractive.   judicious decisions.

Irenic or **Irenical** This word comes from Irene, Greek goddess of peace. It is often misunderstood for 'serene,' but it means 'pacific' in the sense of 'conciliatory.' It is a good word to suggest the promotion of peace, as IRENIC overtures to the enemy, or IRENIC counsel to disputants.

Luxurious and **Luxuriant** The verb to 'luxuriate' spreads out its two arms of meaning and gathers in with each the foliage of associated ideas: from one arm we have the adjective LUXURIOUS, referring to 'luxury' and connoting subtle things, and from the other we have the adjective LUXURIANT, suggesting 'abundance' and 'rich growth.'

There was a time when LUXURIOUS and LUXURIANT were synonymous, both referring to 'rank growth.' There was more particularly a long time when LUXURIOUS meant 'lustful,' 'excessive' and 'outrageous.' But through figurative usages the words separated, each finding a characteristic meaning. LUXURIOUS purged itself of passion, and became symbolical of what gives deep, rich comfort. LUXURIANT retained its first allegiance to profuse abundance. But LUXURIANT also suggests 'exuberance.' LUXURIANT things run wild.

Nice Among philologists NICE is a wonder word. Many adjectives develop or degenerate amazingly, especially those with emotional or humorous meanings, but NICE has taken up ideas from everywhere, and has done so for centuries. Originally it was Latin and meant, astonishingly to us, 'ignorant'—from *nescius,* 'not knowing': *ne,* for 'no,' plus *scire,* to 'know.' In the Old French it still referred to 'fools,' and it came into our Middle English associated with many attributes of fools. A NICE boy could be 'ignorant' or 'stupid,' but he also could be 'silly' or worse. He could be 'wanton, irresponsible, lewd.' But after Chaucer's time, the meaning was narrowed and took on a lasting bias, a bias that persisted through many vicissitudes and a long period of desuetude after the Shakespearean era. After Chaucer it had come to denote predominately a 'fussiness' about little, unnecessary things. But the Elizabethans, with their multifarious interests and their lively minds, made it mean many things, including 'coy, shy, reserved.' Still this trend from 'finicalness' to 'fastidiousness' to 'good taste and discrimination' continued, and some centuries later NICE reappeared as a popular word referring to anything that was 'exacting in taste, delicate or delicious.'

Henceforth its future was assured. One of Jane Austen's heroes, in perhaps 1806, was appalled by all the common meanings that NICE had taken on. Originally, he said, he supposed it referred only to 'neatness and delicacy,' for example, in dress or in sentiments; but now anything could be NICE. And the fact is, anything still can be, provided it pleases us at all. There is just that much demand for a NICE word for all the NICE things in the world. That the word also has specific meanings, 'scrupulous exactness, exquisite skill, social refinement, punctilio,' is also natural. It is only a pity that NICE must share the ubiquity and careless popularity of 'okay,' but the circumstances of its long struggle seem to have made it arbiter of its own fate.

Some scholars think NICE's general meaning arose with comparative suddenness from scientific experiments whose precision was NICE, that is, 'foolish,' as regarded by laymen. When the scientists won out they gave us the meaning: 'discriminative,' hence of 'good taste, NICE.' This may be. But it seems more probable that when the trend between Chaucer's and Shakespeare's time was once set up it continued up to the present day.

Splendid and **Splendor**   There are two ways of using descriptive words: first, quickly and carelessly, and second, with a deliberate desire to let the word speak for itself. More than that it is our custom to reserve some particular form of a word for this second, more special usage.

For example: "That will be splendid," we may say, or ". . . perfectly splendid," or ". . . perfectly splendid and I can't wait till it happens," —from which anyone can easily infer that we feel sure something fine is in the cards. On the other hand there is Kipling's sunrise that came up from Mandalay, across the bay. No doubt it, too, was SPLENDID, and yet even the commonest of us, seeing it, might have said, with almost formal fervor: "I have never seen such splendor in all my life!"

Thus the word SPLENDOR, unassisted by adjectives and perhaps even without emphasis of voice, speaks its whole meaning, which is all that we wish to express. It is like the glory that was Greece, or the grandeur that was Rome; it is reserved for special, rhetorical use.

Sumptuous   The basis of the word is 'buying.' A SUMPTUOUS meal is not merely one that is lavishly prepared. It is one that is fit to be consumed with a luxurious relish. The woefully hard core of the word is still exposed in the adjective 'sumptuary,' pertaining to the 'spending of money,' like 'sumptuary laws.'

Verve and Élan The lilt of a melody is the delicate counterpart of the VERVE in a military march. The lilt is dainty but animating, and the VERVE is exciting yet fine.

ÉLAN is French, the long 'e' allows the accent to fall forward, on 'lahn,' and the word means a 'dash forward,' like the dash of cavalry troops into battle, with their excitement, vehemence and brilliance. ÉLAN is any sensational manifestation of such spirit in motion. ÉLAN refers to the dash of color and seasoning that some people have in their personalities.

VERVE is French too. The dictionary calls it the 'excitement of imagination and feeling' which attends artistic production. It has a suggestion of music or eloquence, while ÉLAN connotes the military or the athlete. Thus it is more a quality than an action. The vigor VERVE produces in any action may resemble ÉLAN, but in itself it is more a sustained and ringing sincerity, an exhilarating fervor that quickens the hearts of all as it sometimes quickens the pace of oratory. Since VERVE rhymes with 'nerve,' perhaps we think of a certain firm courage when we use VERVE. The VERVE, or daring, of a trapeze artist high in the air certainly has something of the courageous about it.

The origin of VERVE is moot. Webster's thinks it comes from the French way of pronouncing the Latin *verba*, 'words.' Presumably the idea lies in a rush or gush of words. Other authorities directly derive VERVE from the Late Latin *verva*, a 'sculptured ram's head,' which makes sense since 'caper' and 'caprice' were both fathered by a goat. *Caper* is Latin for 'goat,' just as *vervex* is for 'ram.'

REACTIONS

ACT   *v.* to move; to effect some change; to accomplish something; often in the sense of responding to a particular stimulis, as "After he saw what the other fellow was doing, he acted quickly."

ARISE   *v.* to appear; originate; come into existence.

BACKLASH   *n.* a sudden movement backwards from a movement forwards; recoil.

BEHAVE   *v.* to act, esp. in a certain way, as "As soon as he saw her again, he started to behave badly."

BOOMERANG   *v.* to come back on itself; esp. in the sense of turning on itself, as "The pills boomeranged; instead of making him feel better, they made him worse."

BOUND BACK   *v.* to react; bounce; spring back.

DERIVE *v.* to come out of something; to originate; as "Bridge derives from whist."

Ensue

EXCHANGE *v.* to swap; to give something away while receiving something else.

FLY BACK *v.* to recoil; bound back.

FUNCTION *v.* to perform; esp. to move according to nature or destiny, as "Man functions as a thinking creature."

ISSUE *v.* to originate; arise; as "History issues from oblivion."

KICK BACK *v.* to recoil; bounce.

ORIGINATE *v.* to come from someplace or something, as "His novel originated in his own experiences as a child."

React

REBOUND *v.* to recoil; bounce.

RECIPROCATE *v.* to exchange; to do something in return for something done.

RECOIL *v.* to draw or spring back suddenly, as "He expected the gun to recoil."

REPERCUSSION *n.* the backeffect of an act or force; "The repercussion to my speech was immediate: I was branded a fool."

Reprisal see **Requital & Reprisal**

Requital & Reprisal

RETALIATION *n.* a return of evil for evil suffered.

RETORT *n.* a sharp answer, as "Her retort was 'No!'"

REVENGE *n.* retaliation; the desire or act of hurting someone for the harm he did to begin with.

REVULSION *n.* an instinctive impulse to recoil because of deep disgust, as "I felt revulsion for his dirty thoughts."

RISE *v.* to originate, as "Mysticism arose in the Orient."

SPRING BACK *v.* to bounce; recoil.

STEM *v.* to rise; to come from.

VENGEANCE *n.* retaliation.

Ensue ENSUE is a soft-sounding word. There is a rich though muted sonority in its second syllable. It means 'to follow after,' from the Latin *insequi*, which also produced our 'sequence' and 'consequence.' ENSUE commonly refers to events that follow other events. Sometimes these 'following events' are emphasized as 'consequences' or 'results.' "In the ensuing silence our nerves were put to an even harder test." The euphony of ENSUE is not the real reason for its having preference over the good old Anglo-Saxon word 'follow,' which is a romantic word itself. But 'follow' has sacrificed its present participle to the needs of business. "The following examples (or just 'the following') will illustrate our point." A word that is worked so often in such a specialized way often loses its general usefulness.

React In chemistry, a REACTION is the mutual action of chemical agents (they put on a combined show), and in physics it is a counteracting force. But, in general, the word's meaning is multifarious because it represents the 'responses' to anything. You can, of course, simply RE-ACT, or 'repeat,' a performance; but the word would have withered long ago without its other and more elastic, intransitive senses. You can REACT in the sense of 'retracing' your steps or of 'reversing' your action; REACTIONARIES, such as Tories, are nominally 'backtrackers.' But usually you REACT more often in the sense of 'responding' to influences or urgencies—to stimuli, as the scientists say. The world is one big bundle of responses. REACT commonly means 'to respond by showing a change.' The way you REACT to praise and reproof, or to shock and privation is manifested by their visible effect upon you, by your alteration of attitude and conduct. When you say a client REACTED to your proposition you mean he showed a 'response,' no matter how small it may have been. But, of course, REACTIONS may be big too. "It has been shown that after sudden disasters, like tornadoes, explosions, and floods, the citizens of a community react in uniform ways that may, with probable success, be predicted and utilized in the case of national emergency." A big sentence, but it elevates REACT to a position of importance in this, our world of international threats.

Requital and Reprisal REQUITAL comes from the French word *quitter*, originally meaning 'to release' and later 'to depart,' preceded by the Latin preposition *re*, meaning 'back.' *Quitter* also gave us our verb 'quit' in its sense of 'paying back,' as 'to quit a debt.' A REQUITAL is a paying back of either 'good with good,' or 'evil with evil.' A REPRISAL, stemming through the French to Latin *re* plus *prehendo*, 'seize,' means paying back 'evil with more evil.'

RELIGION
See also The Other World

ABBATIAL *adj.* pertains to abbot, abbey.

AISLE *n.* in a church, a long passage on each side of the nave and transept, set off from both by pillars.

ALTAR *n.* a raised table on which religious sacrifices are made or offered; a communion table.

APSE *n.* the projecting end of a cathedral, usually semicircular.

BANDS *n.* a bond; tie; as the BANDS of matrimony; thus, often in the sense of imposing mutual obligations.

BELFRY *n.* a bell tower of a church; the room where the bells are hung.

Bethel

BREVIARY *n.* a book containing the daily offices or prayers.

CATECHISM *n.* a manual or a set

of formal questions used for purposes of teaching, esp. religious teaching.

CATHEDRAL *n.* the church which contains the bishop's chair; any important or large church.

CHAPEL *n.* a small Christian church or sanctuary other than a parish or cathedral church.

CHAPLAIN *n.* a clergyman serving a public institution, a family, a royal court or in the armed services.

CHAPTERAL *adj.* pertaining to a branch of a society, a body of clergymen or the house either meets in. *n.* CHAPTER or CHAPTER HOUSE.

CHURCH *n.* a building set aside for religious worship, esp. Christian worship.

CIBORIUM *n.* a container for the consecrated bread, for the Eucharist.

CLERICAL *adj.* pertaining to clerk; esp. to clergy.

CLOISTERS *n.* a monastery or convent; esp. a covered walk bordering a court or garden, found often in monasteries or convents.

CREED *n.* a brief formula of doctrine, usually religious.

CRYPT *n.* a vault or cellar underground, as under the floor of a church.

CURÉ *n.* a parish priest.

DEANERY *n.* a dean's official residence. DEAN, the head of a religious chapter. See also the category OCCUPATIONS.

DIACONAL *adj.* pertaining to a deacon.

DOCTRINE *n.* a set of principles, or a statement, which is taught.

DOGMA *n.* a formal or official doctrine, proclaimed by authority.

ECCLESIASTIC *adj.* pertains to the clergy or the church.

EPISCOPACY *n.* a form of church government by a hierarchy, which includes deacons, priests, and bishops.

EVANGELICAL *adj.* pertaining to the Four Gospels, or to belief in or teaching of them. Hence, spiritual-minded.

EXODIC *adj.* pertaining to the Exodus.

Ferial

FONT *n.* a bowl or container of water used for baptism.

FORMULARY *n.* a book of authoritative forms, such as prayers, etc.

FRIAR *n.* a member of a monastic mendicant order. *adj.* FRIARY.

HERETICAL *adj.* pertaining to HERESY or to a HERETIC.

HIERARCHY *n.* a body, esp. religious, of people organized in ranks and grades.

HIEROCRACY *n.* a government by a hierarchy; by extension, government by ecclesiastics.

HOLY *adj.* sacred; worthy of worship; etc.

ICON *n.* a picture or illustration, usually commemorative; in the Eastern Church, a holy picture or image.

INVOCATION *n.* the act of calling on God; prayers.

LAIC or LAICAL *adj.* pertaining to laymen, non-clergymen. Broadly the LAITY comprises everyone who does not have a given profession.

LITANY *n.* a form of prayer, or religious service, characterized by alternate responses of clergy and congregation.

LITURGY *n.* the services of the Christian churches. *adj.* LITURGICAL.

MANSE *n.* a clergyman's home.

MEETINGHOUSE *n.* a place used for religious worship.

MINISTRY *n.* the clerical profession.

MISSAL *n.* a book containing the service of the Mass for every day in the year.

MITRE *n.* a bishop's crown.

MONASTIC *adj.* pertaining to a monk or to a monastery. Hence, also, withdrawn or austerely secluded.

NAVE *n.* the main, or highest, part of the church, with the aisles flanking it.

PARSON *n.* a clergyman.

PARSONAGE *n.* a clergyman's home.

PECTORAL CROSS *n.* a large cross worn on the breast by bishops, abbots and sometimes canons.

PIETISTIC *adj.* pertaining to piety.

PRELATE *n.* an ecclesiastic of high rank. *n.* PRELACY, the office of a PRELATE.

PRESBYTER *n.* an elder in a church; a minister. *n.* PRESBYTERY, a court composed of ministers and elders.

Providence

RITUAL *n.* the form or prescribed method of conducting religious services.

ROOD *n.* the cross; also a crucifix.

ROSARY *n.* beads used in counting prayers; the prayers of the ROSARY.

Sacerdotal

SACRAL *adj.* pertaining to sacred rites.

SACRAMENT *n.* certain religious ceremonies that are said to have been instituted by Christ. *adj.* SACRAMENTAL.

SECT *n.* a dissenting religious group.

SECULAR *adj.* laic.

SHRINE *n.* a holy place.

Sodality

SYNAGOGAL *adj.* pertaining to a synagogue.

SYNODICAL or SYNODIC adj. pertaining to a SYNOD, or church council.

THEOLOGY *n.* broadly, the study of religions and religious doctrine.

TIARA *n.* the Pope's crown.

TRANSEPT *n.* that part of a church that crosses at right angles to the nave.

VICARAGE *n.* the vicar's or clergyman's house.

TRIFORIUM *n.* the gallery over the aisles of a church.

Yoga

Bethel A 'sailor's chapel,' on ship or ashore. Or BETHEL is any 'house of God,' which is the word's meaning in Hebrew.

Ferial This adjective refers to any 'holiday,' or 'public day.' Its ecclesiastical meaning is any 'weekday,' which is not a special fast day or festival. "Ferial music is opposed to festal music."

Providence Primitive peoples often possess in their languages sacred words which they never utter. They use rough synonyms for them, or else invent phrases of circumlocution. In our own tongue PROVIDENCE, which originated from the verb 'to provide,' is a somewhat similar substitute. It represents the Supreme Being's concern for and management of the universe. Especially anything good that happens to us can be attributed to PROVIDENCE. More than that, the word represents the Deity Himself.

Strange enough, besides using the adjectives PROVIDENT and PROVIDENTIAL in the cosmic sense, we also use them to refer to the prudently economical. "He was a provident man," because he laid aside pennies for the future. "Habitually his dealings were cautious and providential." Instead of PROVIDENTIAL we might have used either 'provisional,' had it not been warped out of shape to mean something like 'temporary,' or 'provisionary,' had it not been tinctured so highly with the idea of 'stipulations,' like in 'the provisions of a charter or a law.' Incidentally, most disasters are not PROVIDENTIAL, but the burning down of London in 1666 was PROVIDENTIAL, because it checked the plague.

Sacerdotal Pertaining to 'priests or priesthood.'

Sodality In a broad sense, this word means 'brotherhood, fellowship, even friendship.' Specifically, SODALITY is a lay organization for a religious or philanthropic purpose. Still more specifically, in the Roman Catholic Church, it is a brotherhood for devotional or charitable purposes. From *sodales,* who among the Romans was any 'comrade, boon companion, mate (even in crime) or a member of some corporation.'

Yoga Like 'voodoo' and other words indicating mystical practices, YOGA is hard to understand or to explain. There is a tendency to judge it by some of its aspects and to confuse it with the means by which it exists. Webster's plunges right in by defining YOGA as a Hindu mental discipline enjoining intense concentration upon some object (whether concrete like the tip of your nose or abstract like a Supreme Deity) and for the purpose of actually merging one's own consciousness of existence with the existing object itself. It then goes on to state some of the requirements and means of attaining this merger, and some of its results, including a union with the Universal Spirit. Thus the primary emphasis is on the discipline and its methods, an emphasis echoed by some other authorities. One goes so far as to say that the word itself means, in the Sanskrit, 'concentration,' though the philological concensus is that it means 'union,' that is, union of the soul with the Godhead.

The fact seems to be that YOGA is a mystical and religious philosophy based on the belief that the primordial soul existed even before the most primeval matter. From them both arose the Spirit of Life which now gives us not only contentment and virtue but also magical power. Consequently, to merge one's own consciousness with either the concrete or the abstract restores the primordial soul in its infinite power. But since this merging is no offhand or easy accomplishment the devotee, or YOGI, must be capable of the severest self-discipline. He must practice the exacting exercises prescribed by the system, such as the holding of the breath or strained, but motionless, posing. But if, by this ascetic practice, the desired union, or *samadhi*, is attained, then it is claimed that the YOGI acquires occult powers and can, for example, understand the languages of all animals, foretell the future or at will float through the air. He can also read the thoughts of others, and thus what we would call 'self-hypnotism' results in 'clairvoyance.' It is little wonder that YOGA connotes to us, who are not Hindus, not a spiritual philosophy but a kind of jiujitsu of the mind.

Etymologically, YOGA is related to English 'yoke,' and to the Latin root of 'conjugal,' referring to the 'matrimonial yoke.' Did you note that YOGA is the discipline, and YOGI the man who follows it?

RESTRAINT AND PROHIBITION

Abstain see **Refrain, Restrain,** etc.

ARREST *n.* a check or stoppage; forcible seizure. *v.* to stop; capture; restrain; as to ARREST its motion.

AVERSE *adj.* having a dislike or unwillingness, as AVERSE to flying. *n.* AVERSION.

BAFFLE *v.* to check or frustrate; as to BAFFLE one's pursuers.

BALK *v.* to baffle; stop; hinder.

BAN *n.* a prohibition. *v.* to prohibit; forbid.

BAR *n.* a limit; barrier. *v.* to exclude, as "The club barred poor people from membership."

BLOCK *n.* an obstacle, such as an

antitank BLOCK. *v.* to prevent; to obstruct; as to BLOCK a hole.

BRIDLE *n.* a restraint; curb. *v.* to check or control; restrain.

CHECK *n.* a rebuff; reprimand, as "Our troops suffered a momentary check." *v.* to curb; restrain; as to CHECK one's temper.

CLOG *n.* an encumbrance; block. *v.* to block or check, as to CLOG a leak in the roof.

Constrain see **Obligate, Oblige,** etc.

CURB *n.* a restraint; bar; barrier. *v.* to restrain; govern.

DAM *n.* a check; barrier, as a water DAM. *v.* to stop; check; block.

DENY *v.* to refuse a request or a grant, as "He denied her the right even to think for herself." *n.* DENIAL.

Depress see **Repress, Depress,** etc.

EMBARGO *n.* a prohibition, esp. on the flow of goods, as an EMBARGO on trade.

ENJOIN *v.* to prohibit.

FETTER *n.* a bond; curb; shackle. *v.* to shackle, or put FETTERS upon.

FOIL *n.* bafflement; frustration. *v.* to baffle.

FORBID *v.* to prohibit; bar; to command that something shall not be done.

FORESTALL *v.* to hinder or prevent; esp. in the sense of doing something before someone else can.

FRUSTRATE *v.* to prevent; esp. in the sense of rendering ineffectual all attempts at something.

HAMPER *v.* to balk; hinder.

HINDER *v.* to obstruct; block; esp. in the sense of putting obstacles in the way.

Impede

Inhibition & Prohibition

INJUNCTION *n.* a command against something, as an INJUNCTION against travel.

INTERDICT *n.* a prohibition; esp. an official or formal order of prohibition.

Jim Crow

MANACLE *n.* a fetter.

Maroon

Obligate, Oblige, Constrain & Restrain

Oblige see **Obligate, Oblige,** etc.

OBSTRUCT *v.* to block; clog.

PREVENT *v.* to frustrate; to act in such a way as to keep something from happening.

PROHIBIT *v.* to command that something shall not happen. *n.*

Prohibition see **Inhibition & Prohibition**

PROSCRIPTION *n.* an interdict; a prohibition; a restriction or exclusion.

Refrain, Restrain & Abstain

Reluctance

Repress, Depress & Suppress

Resistive see **Resistless & Resistive**

Resistless & Resistive

Restrain see **Refrain, Restrain,** etc. See also **Obligate, Oblige,** etc.

SHACKLE *v.* to chain people together; thus, to restrain.

Stymie

Subdued

Suppress see **Repress, Depress,** etc.

Taboo & Totem

THWART *v.* to block; to frustrate.

Totem see **Taboo & Totem**

VETO *v.* to say "no" to; to prohibit.

Impede The 'pede' is of course the Latin, *pes, pedis,* 'foot,' that occurs in 'pedal,' which you work with your foot. It is a graphic word. Whatever IMPEDES you is somehow in the way of your foot. In IMPEDIMENT the meaning, though still strong, shifts. Latin *impedimenta* means the 'baggage' you carry when traveling on foot. It therefore not only is a 'burden,' which in itself restrains your progress, but it also IMPEDES your movement.

Inhibition and Prohibition INHIBITION can mean PROHIBITION. The body of both PROHIBIT and INHIBIT means 'to hold,' but the 'pro' means 'before' and the 'in' should mean 'in.' When you PROHIBIT something you 'block' it by acting 'antecedently.' When INHIBIT means PROHIBIT, the 'in' obliges by also meaning 'before.'

When INHIBITION is generally used, however, it is the cause and influence that compels us to 'hold *in*' and suppress any thoughts, feelings or actions that we would like to indulge. If a dog bit you when you were a child, he may have instilled in you an INHIBITION that stops you from liking dogs. Though INHIBITIONS are primarily psychological, inanimate things can INHIBIT and be INHIBITED. Home office directives can INHIBIT your free action in the field.

Jim Crow His real name may have been Tom Rice, and he may never have been a Negro. Or JIM CROW may have been a real name and, though a Negro born in the South, he may have died a rich man in London. Early in the nineteenth century James Crow of Richmond died in England. Was Thomas D. Rice, the famous white minstrel, thinking of him when he sang his bestseller song of 1835, "Jump, Jim Crow?" Hardly, it seems. The second line of the song says: "I'se just from Tucky hoe," and the fourth says: "My name's Jim Crow." Or was that appellation for a Negro already in common use? If neither Tom nor Jim originated it, who or what did? No one knows.

But today JIM CROW is a full-fledged noun. When it is not capitalized, it refers to 'various tools,' like the one used for straightening railroad rails. JIM-CROW is a serviceable adjective, too, and even a verb. 'To

JIM-CROW' is 'to discriminate' against Negroes. Even in his minstrel days JIM CROW was nearly a verb. The refrain ran: "Everytime I wheel around (in his dance) I jump Jim Crow." As an adjective or minor noun JIM CROW is now sometimes 'trifling' or 'ignominious,' like Broadway's 'jim-crow (chocolate) sodas' and the lumbermen's 'jim-crow,' a miserable little tie not worth selling. In England JIM CROW is a 'street singer or dancer.' No matter how much the term has since degenerated, JIM CROW in his early days was extraordinarily popular on the stage.

Maroon If a mendicant sailor had buttonholed Shakespeare for a bite to eat, offering the explanation that he had been MAROONED, probably the bard would have blinked at him in bewilderment. For, so far as we know, sailors did not use the term MAROONED in the sense of 'being bereft' on a desert island (and hence in any inhospitable place) until the time of Defoe's *Robinson Crusoe,* which was a hundred years later. The full original word was French, *cimarron,* 'wild, untamed, feral.' But it was applied at an early date, probably long before Defoe's day, to fugitive slaves in the West Indies, and so became a verb both transitive and intransitive. "They marooned the sailor on an uninhabited coast." "They have been marooned for twenty years."

But the color MAROON comes from a different French word, *marron,* 'chestnut.' Consequently chestnut horses should all be called 'maroon horses' too, but they are not. For MAROON has departed from its original color while chestnut doesn't always recall the chestnut either. MAROON now varies from 'reddish blue' to 'reddish yellow,' though perhaps its commonest hue is the color of a dark macaroon, a French cake. It is dull and not, as chestnut can be, golden. And MAROONS, with the same derivation, are also a kind of fireworks, as *marrons* are in France, presumably because roasting chestnuts often pop.

In the South, MAROONING is 'camping out,' or 'picnicking' for several days at a time.

Obligate, Oblige, Constrain and Restrain Like its work a day synonym, OBLIGE, OBLIGATE stems from Latin *obligare,* 'about' plus 'bind.' When you are OBLIGATED you are 'bound,' whether by legal requirements or by moral duty. We usually use the word in the passive tense, but you can OBLIGATE ('hold') someone to a duty. "When you become a soldier you are obligated to defend your country." "A uniform obligates you to act with military courtesy." OBLIGE gets around more in daily life and does smaller jobs. All sorts of considerations OBLIGE ('bind, constrain') us to do this thing or that. "Since you wanted to raise a family,

you are now obliged to stay home nights to watch over your children."
But notice this use of OBLIGE means to CONSTRAIN, not to RESTRAIN.
We must act within limits, to do nothing but what is required. When
we are RESTRAINED we are 'prevented' from doing something, but when
we are CONSTRAINED we are 'compelled' to act in a certain way. "The
law is a restraint against crime; religion is a constraint to live morally."
See REFRAIN, RESTRAIN and ABSTAIN.

Refrain, Restrain and Abstain   You should REFRAIN from bad company or from doing evil. That is, you should 'hold yourself back' from
bad company, you should 'control or curb' your bad impulses. REFRAIN
comes ultimately from the Latin word for a 'rein,' *frenum*. But REFRAIN
is also related to Old French *refraindre*, 'to resound,' which gave us the
REFRAINS in songs. *Refraindre* is derived from Latin *refringere*, 'to break
up,' but in early times, it meant much the same as our verb REFRAIN.
You can still break up a party by REFRAINING from going.

Formerly you could also, if you wished, REFRAIN others as well as
yourself; but now we RESTRAIN others. We can also RESTRAIN ourselves,
and do, when we REFRAIN. Etymologically, RESTRAIN means 'to draw
tight, constrict,' from Latin *restringere*. It is a severer word than RE-
FRAIN. "I restrained the dog from jumping at the throat of the stranger."
"He restrained his anger at the soldier's stupidity, because an officer
never breaks down before his man." See OBLIGATE, OBLIGE, CONSTRAIN
and RESTRAIN.

We REFRAIN because we wish to. We also act voluntarily when we
ABSTAIN from something. If we ABSTAIN from enough things, or habitually enough, we become ABSTEMIOUS, a favorite adjective in the description of religious men. The word comes via France from the Latin
verb 'to hold,' *tenere*. When you ABSTAIN from something there is a
distinct suggestion either of 'disdain' or of 'fanaticism.' When you RE-
FRAIN you convey quite an opposite urge of 'canniness' or 'prudence.'
You ABSTAIN from voting when you wish to invoke a plague upon both
parties, but you REFRAIN when you think it might be wise politics to do
so.

All three of these Latin words flowered in France, but RESTRAIN was
common in England in an earlier form from Chaucer's day until Shakespeare's.

Reluctance   Though RELUCTANCE implies 'resistance,' which in various ways can be unpleasant, it is nevertheless a rather polite and useful word. In the beginning it meant 'to struggle or strive against,' but

now it indicates a 'disinclination,' at times a churlish one. On the whole, RELUCTANCE has considerable dignity. Inwardly you may be struggling against a dislike, let us say, of cats, when outwardly you are RELUCTANTLY petting one. There is some dignity, even stubbornness, but also an expressive hesitancy that bespeaks your feelings. When you reply to a questionable proposition, "I am reluctant to accede to it," there is a polite rebuke in your tone. People may be RELUCTANT for diverse reasons. They need not always be stubborn or disobliging.

Repress, Depress and **Suppress** Anyone can, in some fashion, express his impressions, because he knows what those two words, 'express' and 'impression,' mean. But these three words are more obscure to him, and he may never use them except, of course, to say occasionally that he is DEPRESSED (literally, 'pressed down') on a humid day by the heat. SUPPRESS is a stronger word, and means 'to press *down* and *under*.' A revolt SUPPRESSED is a revolt quelled. A SUPPRESSED newspaper is banned. An emotion SUPPRESSED is an emotion denied expression. Or else it is an emotion submerged in the lower fathoms of our psyche. But a REPRESSED emotion is one merely 'held back.' The idea is fundamentally similar to that in 'restraint.' See OBLIGATE, OBLIGE, CONSTRAIN and RESTRAIN. REPRESS is often used in the sense of 'crush.' "The dictator ruthlessly repressed all opposing opinion."

Resistless and **Resistive** RESISTLESS has two mutually contradictory meanings: having no power or inclination to resist, or having so much strength that nothing can resist it. Fortunately, we can often use 'listless' as a substitute for the first meaning, and there is a second word, RESISTIVE, which serves in the direction of the other meaning. But RESISTIVE means 'inclined to oppose,' rather than 'inclined to RESIST.' Its 'resistance' is more 'obstructive' than 'defensive.' Despotic tendencies in a government are opposed, and blocked, by the RESISTIVE forces of a liberal-minded citizenry.

Stymie A word with plenty of possibilities for general use. No one seems to know where it came from before golf got hold of it. Back of golf it was probably an old Scotch word, *styme,* meaning a 'glimpse.' But somehow even the 'glimpse' disappeared. 'To see not a styme,' was practically 'to see nothing at all'; hence the non-see-er, or any fumbler, became a STYMIE. But where the *styme* came from, nobody knows. In golf any obstruction became a STYMIE. Sports, being full of action, excellently illustrate our verbs of action, and so there is no reason why they shouldn't originate some or invigorate old ones. Anyone who plays golf knows what a path-block to his own ball can do to his temper. So now you will find in some dictionaries that STYMIE can mean simply 'to hinder,' like a STYMIE in golf, where your opponent's ball blocks the course of your own on a green. More than that, lexicographers now allow us to say that something STYMIES us when it 'hinders us completely.' A STYMIE is one big frustration.

Subdued Whatever is SUBDUED is either subjugated ('completely conquered'), or merely 'tamed, modified, lowered, softened.' Wild lands are SUBDUED by cultivation. This is another of those adaptable words, like 'pursuit' and 'capture,' which have proved plastic in the mouths of phrase-makers. Our feelings are SUBDUED when we are contrite. Politicians are SUBDUED when they are chagrined. Ambition is SUBDUED by adversity.

Taboo and Totem In the Mohammedan paradise there are ten animals. All others are TABOO. This is mixing religions since TABOOS originated in the ancestor worship of the South Sea Islanders. Anyhow the word has been absorbed into Christian English. The essential meaning of TABOO is a 'forbidding of something for religious reasons.' A TABOOED object is excluded from sight or from speech. The exclusion is for two mutually opposite reasons, both of them still religious: first, because the thing is bad and should be excluded even from the mind, and secondly because the thing is good and it should be kept reverently in mind. In short, those things that are TABOO are either too bad or too good to have about.

To illustrate this meaning with animals is not impertinent. For, in a sense, the antonym of TABOO is the American Indian TOTEM, in which animals often appear as gods. It is not uncommon for primitive peoples to believe that they are descended from animal ancestors, who afford them—and them only—preternatural protection. Hence, particular animals are depicted or inscribed on the TOTEMS. The first 't' in the word presumably says that those animals were the 'tribe's own': it is said to represent the last sound of a possessive pronoun that preceded their word *aouton,* for the monolithic tribal sign before their homes. Another version is that the word was coined as *totam* by a missionary to express the 'total' protection afforded by the animals or by other supernatural agencies. Nor is there agreement about the word itself, its meaning, native form and origin. Thus, while a tribe might kill a panther with savage joy, it would revere a bear, whose silent effigy on the top of a TOTEM pole would hold their spirits in awe. When they were in trouble they would look to that carven image for spiritual leadership, for it symbolized to them victory over disaster, guidance and good cheer. Thus, it was the opposite of a TABOO, which might also be an object bearing marks or symbols that declare it should be kept apart from all others and not resorted to. Even men are so marked, and become like the lowest caste in India, untouchable, TABOO.

The idolizing of animals is like the idolizing of dead ancestors. The inner life of animals, being unscrutable to man, impressed the primitive mind, and so the creatures were deified. Likewise the human dead, gone beyond this life to the gods, became divinely mysterious and were worshiped by the living. And here began that amazing confusion of religious do's and don't's that primitive beliefs have handed down to us as our TOTEMS and TABOOS. Among the Polynesians and the Javanese the TABOOS say that the dead may not be mentioned nor even the favorite words of the dead, to the bewilderment of philologists because of inevitable substitutes that arise endlessly in usage. And along with these inconveniences there exist TABOOS upon iniquities, together with a system of penalties to insure their enforcement.

This powerful influence of the dead and the past is not confined to the South Seas: it is universal. The Alaskan Indians have their inspiring TOTEMS. The Navajos may not even speak to their mothers-in-law. The British recoil from the word 'bloody' ('By Our Lady,' probably—there is said to be no sanguinary prejudice). Straw hats are TABOO before May fifteenth. Reverence, superstition, whimsey and custom all combine to impose TABOOS upon us, down to our most trivial concerns. And yet behind them all lie those primitive TABOOS whose violations in the South Seas still are sometimes atoned for painfully by suicide or by terrible ritual purifications.

RULE

See Law; Government; and Politics

BID *v.* to make a more or less formal request, with an implication of command.

COMMAND *v.* to make a formal or official demand, or request, not subject to contradiction, that something be done. *n.* COMMAND.

CONTROL *v.* to regulate or rule; to guide.

DIRECT *v.* to instruct, with the sense of command, as "The teacher directed her students to study hard for the examination."

Dynast

ENFORCE v. to see that laws are obeyed; to compel.

ENJOIN v. to issue a command that implies admonition, as "She enjoined her husband to come directly home after work."

GOVERNOR n. a ruler; a high official of a state who sees that laws are enforced and the affairs of government properly managed. adj. GUBERNATORIAL.

MANAGE v. to rule; govern. n. MANAGER. adj. MANAGERIAL.

MANDATE n. a command from the very highest authority.

ORDER v. to make a peremptory, even arbitrary, command. n. ORDER a command, usually from a superior, which implies instructions.

RULE v. to control; guide; manage; esp. in the sense of governing a nation. n. control; government; dominion.

> BENIGN adj. gentle; kindly; as a BENIGN ruler.
>
> CLEMENT adj. easy going; lenient; forgiving, as a CLEMENT king.
>
> COERCIVE adj. serving to rule or control by the use of force; repressive.

Despotic & Tyrannical

DICTATORIAL adj. pertaining to the methods of a government controlled by one man; thus, imperious; absolute.

Dominate & Domineer

Domineer see **Dominate & Domineer**

IMPERATORIAL adj. pertaining to a commander, general or emperor, thus, absolute, as "A general often has an imperatorial manner."

IMPERIOUS adj. imperatorial.

MILD adj. gentle; clement; moderate.

MODERATE adj. keeping to a middle way that avoids all extremes, as a MODERATE government.

OVERBEARING adj. imperious; dominating.

RUTHLESS adj. without mercy; unforgiving.

TOLERANT adj. unwilling to interfere.

Tyrannical see **Despotic & Tyrannical**

Despotic and Tyrannical DESPOTIC is an excellent, much needed synonym for the overworked adjective, TYRANNICAL. Moreover, it is a delightfully mean word to apply to all minor forms of TYRANNY. TYRANT, though common in Roman conversation as *tyrannus,* came from Greece and meant a 'master.' We might imagine he was an 'overseer,' a Simon Legree. A TYRANT today is a 'brutal and formidable boss,' whether of whole peoples or of individuals. A DESPOT, in Greece, was also a 'master.' But his growth has been held more closely within legal bounds. Like a TYRANT he was an 'absolute ruler.' He became an 'autocrat' and an 'absolute monarch.' Like these he became TYRANNICAL. But he may still be only an autocrat, and an autocrat may still rule only a breakfast-table. A TYRANT, however, was from the outset often an *illegal* absolute ruler. Therefore TYRANT came more quickly to stand for 'brutal authority.'

Dominate and **Domineer**   Roman words full of the pristine Roman power. Politically, 'to DOMINATE' is 'to rule.' But the power necessary for governing can be conferred upon you or it can be acquired by yourself. In the latter case, you DOMINATE ('prevail over') the governed. The DOMINATING must therefore start with a 'conquering.' If you are to be an absolute ruler, you must be not only DOMINANT but PREDOMINANT (DOMINANT above all others).

When this word spread from Rome to the provinces it naturally had its terror. DOMINATION is not a pleasant word, even today. Consequently, the early French, who not long since had been Gauls and Franks under mighty Roman DOMINION, intensified the word into DOMINEER: 'to rule arrogantly and insolently.'

In due course this more violent word narrowed, and was made personal. Applied to petty tyrants, perhaps Gallic, it lost its connection with empires. Today only individuals DOMINEER. "That executive has a domineering wife, but away from home, especially in the office, he dominates everyone else."

Dynast   A 'ruler,' especially a 'monarch.' This word has the same origin as DYNASTY, a prolonged sovereignty of one family descent. Napoleon was a DYNAST. The Hapsburgs are an example of a DYNASTY.

SCIENCE

ACOUSTICS   *n.* the science of sound.

AERONAUTICS   *n.* the science of operating airplanes and other aircraft.

Agrarianism   see **Agronomy & Agrarianism**

Agronomy & Agrarianism

ANATOMY   *n.* the science that deals with animal and plant structure.

ASTRONOMY   *n.* the science of celestial phenomena.

BALLISTICS   *n.* the science which deals with the motion and effects of projectiles.

BIOLOGY   *n.* the science of living things.

BOTANY *n.* the science of plants.

CARTOGRAPHY *n.* the science of map-making.

Chromatics

CHRONOMETRY *n.* the science of measurement of time.

COSMOLOGY *n.* a metaphysics which treats of the nature of the universe in a systematic way.

Cultures

CYTOLOGY *n.* the science of cell structures.

DERMATOLOGY *n.* the science which deals with the skin and its diseases.

DYNAMICS *n.* the science which deals with force as producing or affecting motion.

ECCRINOLOGY *n.* the science of the secretions and excretions of physiological organs.

ECOLOGY *n.* the science of environment in relation to biological life.

EMBRYOLOGY *n.* the science dealing with the first stages of individual life.

GASTROENTEROLOGY *n.* the study of the structure and diseases of the stomach and intestines.

GENETICS *n.* the science of heredity.

GEODETICS *n.* the science dealing with the mathematical plotting of the earth's surface.

GEOGRAPHY *n.* the science of the earth.

GEOPHYSICS *n.* the science which treats of the mechanics of the earth's behavior.

GERONTOLOGY *n.* the study of old age.

HISTOLOGY *n.* the science of animal and plant tissue.

HYDRAULICS *n.* the science of the behavior of liquids in motion and their use in engineering.

HYETOLOGY *n.* the science which studies precipitation.

KINEMATICS *n.* the science which treats of the behavior of motions isolated from their causes and effects.

KINETICS *n.* the science which treats of the behavior of motions in relation to their causes and effects.

MALACOLOGY *n.* the science, or branch of zoology, which treats of mollusks.

MATHEMATICS *n.* the science of numbers and quantitative relationships.

MECHANICS *n.* the science which treats of the motion of physical bodies influenced by forces.

METALLURGY *n.* the science of metals; esp. their extraction and refinement.

METAPHYSICS *n.* the part of philosophy which studies ultimate reality and cosmology.

METROLOGY *n.* the science of weight and measure.

MINERALOGY *n.* the science of minerals.

Morphology

MUSICOLOGY *n.* the systematic study of all music.

NAVIGATION *n.* the science of sailing or steering a ship or airplane.

NEPHOLOGY *n.* the study of clouds.

NEUROLOGY *n.* the science of the nervous system.

OCEANOGRAPHY *n.* the science of the ocean.

'ologies

ONTOLOGY *n.* the study of essence, philosophical nature, or ultimate reality.

PALEONTOLOGY *n.* the science of the earth's history, based in part on the study of fossils.

Parallax

PHYSICS *n.* the science of physical, in distinction from chemical, behavior in the inanimate world.

PHYSIOLOGY *n.* the science of the living processes of animals and plants. A branch of biology. See also ANATOMY.

PNEUMATICS *n.* the science of the physical behavior of gases.

PSYCHOLOGY *n.* the science of the mind and of personality.

STATICS *n.* the study of motion held in equilibrium. Compare DYNAMICS.

THEOLOGY *n.* the study of God.

THERMODYNAMICS *n.* the study of the relations between heat and mechanical energy or work.

TOPOGRAPHY *n.* the science of land-surface description.

ZOOLOGY *n.* the science of animals.

Agronomy and **Agrarianism** AGRONOMY refers to the application of scientific principles to agriculture, especially to field crops. An AGRONOMIST is the man who does this. Do not confuse AGRONOMY with 'agrimony,' which is a common yellow-flowered plant formerly used in medicine. AGRARIANISM advocates equal distribution of land and reforms in land tenures. AGRARIAN is the adjective and the practitioner. You can say, "He is an agrarian," and "He holds agrarian politics."

Chromatics 'The science of colors.' CHROMATIC as an adjective means 'pertaining to colors' or, in music, 'proceeding by half-tones.'

Cultures Formal names for some CULTURES and minor industries frequently elude us. For example, 'husbandry,' includes agriculture, economic management of any sort, especially domestic. Literally, the 'husband' is the thrifty manager of a marriage. 'Animal husbandry' is the breeding and raising of livestock. A few other CULTURES may be mentioned: 'Pisciculture,' fish; 'horticulture,' gardens; 'sericulture,' silk worms; 'pomiculture,' apples; 'apiculture,' beekeeping; 'hirudiniculture,' leeches; 'ostreiculture,' oysters; 'aviculture,' birds; 'galliculture,' cocks; 'viticulture,' grapes; 'floriculture,' flowers; 'puericulture,' children, the art of rearing them well, the matter of training them; 'silviculture,' forests; 'agriculture,' field-crops.

Morphology This word has nothing to do with death. It refers to that part of biology that treats of 'form' and 'structure,' of anatomy and the flesh. Hence, in any science, the study of the shape and build of things.

'Ologies Everyone knows what biology is, but among probably thousands of other 'OLOGIES some curious ones get into common print that are worth recognizing. -LOGY usually means 'a science.' Thus 'agrology' means the science, or study of soils. There are, for example, the following:

ANEMOLOGY: winds.

ANTHOLOGY: not a science at all but concretely a collection of literary extracts.

APICOLOGY: honey-bees.

ASTROLOGY: sun, moon and stars as occultly affecting human affairs.

BRYOLOGY: mosses.

CAMPANOLOGY: bell-ringing and bell-making, as arts.

CARPOLOGY: fruits.

CHIROLOGY: sign-language, with hands and fingers. But CHIROPODY is the care of the hands and feet, PODIATRY is the care of the feet and PEDIATRICS is the care of children's health.

CONCHOLOGY: shells.

CRANIOLOGY: skulls.

DENDROLOGY: the natural history of trees.

ENTOMOLOGY: insects.

EPISTEMOLOGY: philosophic study of the truth, proofs, nature and limits of human knowledge.

EPISTOLOGY: epistles or letters.

EROTOLOGY: love; compare erotic.

ESCHATOLOGY: theology as it considers immortality and the Beyond.

ETIOLOGY: scientific study of causes, as of diseases.

ETYMOLOGY: the study of word derivations.

EUDEMONOLOGY: the study of happiness—in spite of the second and third syllables.

FILICOLOGY: ferns.

GRAPHOLOGY: hand-writing, esp. as indicating character.

GYNECOLOGY: women's diseases.

HERPETOLOGY: reptiles and amphibians. See ANIMALS.

HOROLOGY: clocks, and hence time.

HYPNOLOGY: sleep.

ICHTHYOLOGY: fishes.

METHODOLOGY: the theoretical study of method; in logic it is the study of ways in which theory can result in knowledge.

MYCOLOGY: fungi.

NEALOGY: study of the early adolescence of animals.

NECROLOGY: literally, a study of corpses, from the Greek nekros and logia, but now an obituary notice or a list of deaths.

NEOLOGY: a new theory or doctrine but more specifically a new use of a word or a new meaning, or the new word or meaning itself.

NIDOLOGY: bird nests.

ONCOLOGY: tumors.

ORNITHOLOGY: birds.

OROLOGY: the science of mountains.

OSTEOLOGY: bones of living vertebrates.

OTOLOGY: ear.

PATHOLOGY: diseases.

PEDOLOGY: children.

PENOLOGY: punishment and prison management.

PETROLOGY: rocks.

PHRENOLOGY: character reading from the shape of skulls.

SELENOLOGY: the moon.

SOMATOLOGY: a combination of physiology and anatomy.

TERATOLOGY: the study of physical monstrosities and abnormal growths, in plants as well as animals. In early times the existence of freaks created horrifying superstitions and the wildest rumors.

TRICHOLOGY: the science of treating hair.

Parallax If you look at a certain star after supper and then again before you go to bed, its position is of course different. The earth has revolved under it, carrying you along with it, so your viewpoint is different. This 'apparent difference' in the star's position is its PARALLAX, called in this case its 'diurnal (daily) PARALLAX.' If you look at the star in September and again in November, its position will be different. The earth has moved along in its orbit around the sun, and you see the star from a different angle. This is 'annual PARALLAX.' Thirdly, any similar 'apparent displacement' (for the star itself was practically stationary), is a PARALLAX. Life seen in youth and then in maturity is PARALLACTIC.

SEARCH

Detect

EXPLORE *v.* to search through; examine thoroughly; esp. with the sense of discovering something new or of covering a large area. *n.* EXPLORATION.

FERRET OUT *v.* search out; hunt out; esp. in the sense of driving out into the open a hidden thing.

FORAGE *v.* to hunt around; to explore for food; hence, to explore for anything.

HUNT *v.* to search; to look for, esp. in the sense of to HUNT for something lost.

INSPECT *v.* to examine; to look something over carefully. *n.* INSPECTION.

NOSE OUT *v.* to ferret out.

PROBE *v.* to examine; investigate.

PRY *v.* to peer inquisitively; to poke one's nose into something.

QUEST *v.* to search; to hunt; esp. in the sense of following a trail, as the QUEST for the Holy Grail.

RAKE *v.* to ransack or search through something thoroughly, esp. in the sense of having to clear things away to get at what is wanted.

RANSACK *v.* to rake.

RUMMAGE *v.* to hunt around, as to RUMMAGE through a closet.

SCOUR *v.* to search quickly; to explore widely and quickly.

Seek

Snoop

Detect Everyone knows what a detective is. But DETECTION, and that keen little word DETECT, are curiously little used. There is sharp suggestiveness in DETECT. It says you not only 'see' something but 'discover' it, and with keenly discerning eye. "I detected a malign gleam of sarcasm in his smile." How flat 'noticed' would be, and how utterly inadequate 'saw.' DETECTION is not mere observation. An observing man may notice everything in a room, but that won't make him a detective. A detective is after something in particular. You DETECT an odd noise in your car's motor. In a business letter, in spite of a persuasive tone, you DETECT a wry note, or an omission. Also you DETECT a delicate perfume.

Seek This is a Teutonic word, with a strong Norse flavor, in which you would not expect to find sophistication. To the Anglo-Saxons it meant bluntly not only 'to seek out' but 'to come to,' in order either 'to visit' or 'to attack.' In some usages, especially military ones, we still convey a hostile intent. "Go seek the enemy and smite him." But the marvel of the word now is its expansion from the basic idea of 'searching' for something. It still is, except in its softened, South-of-England derivative 'beseech,' a word of action—of many actions now. Colloquially it has shed its plainer senses to common phrases, 'to search for, hunt for, look for.' We would blush to say, "I am seeking my lost handkerchief." But this reserve opens the way for SEEK's own ambitions, and it has become a skillfully competent word.

When we SEEK something now we still try to find it, but it is seldom a simple thing like a lost article. It is usually something large but intangible, like aid, comfort, advice or power. Such things are not easily located, and so the emphasis in SEEKING has slipped slowly but impressively to the 'will' which guides the 'search.' To SEEK now often means 'to attempt, to want, to scheme, to plan for, or to ask for.' A new President may SEEK a lowering of taxes, or you may SEEK a favor from a friend.

When we break down these sophisticated senses we find a variety of motives, even emotions, dominating the meanings. But the actual method of search becomes vague. A man SEEKS the theater as a solace to his worries. How he SEEKS doesn't matter. He may SEEK his bed when he is tired, but he knows where the bed is, having only to drop into it. What he really SEEKS, or desires, is rest. Nations may SEEK peace, but the 'how' is unfortunately much too vague. Intransitively, when a bird dog retrieves a bird he SEEKS.

Snoop As we use it, SNOOP is a colloquial word, but very expressive. Anyone who pries into your affairs is a fox and his nose is probably sharp, like his eyes. Anyone who prowls about in order to pry is more or less fox-like. But a SNOOPER, though he pries some and may prowl, is more domestic. He is soft-footed, no doubt, and yet rather slow-moving; he is inquisitive and none too well bred. In his own estimation he may be only looking around. There is, in fact, something in his nature faintly suggestive of a fumbling Dutchman, and the word *snoepen*, from which he is supposed to have come, is wholly Dutch, picked up by the English in New Amsterdam. Only, it has long since lost its exact native meaning, which was 'to eat in secret,' presumably as children might steal in the pantry. Some think SNOOP is only a variant of an obsolete word 'snook,' which also came from old Dutch. It not inappropriately meant 'to sniff,' and then in English 'to lurk in ambush' and, finally, 'to search, to pry about.' In any case, a SNOOPER is now something less than a common sneak.

SERIES

See also Beginnings; Ends

ARRAY *n.* an ordered display of things.

CATENATION *n.* a regular connection of things in a series.

CHAIN *n.* things linked together one after another.

COMING (or FOLLOWING) AFTER *n.* a chain; a succession of events or things, in more or less loose order.

Continual & Continuous

Continuance & Continuation

Continuation see **Continuance & Continuation**

Continuous see **Continual & Continuous**

FILE *n.* a line of things or persons, as a FILE of soldiers.

LINE *n.* an array formed by placing one thing after another in a long series.

QUEUE *n.* a line of people, usually waiting for service.

RANK *n.* a file.

ROUND *n.* a recurring series of events or things, as "One New Year's Eve we made a round of the parties."

RUN *n.* a continuous passage or course of events or things, as "We've had a run of bad days this month."

Sequence & Series

Series see **Sequence & Series**

STRING *n.* a chain; things one after another, as a STRING of misfortunes.

SUCCESSION *n.* the following, or coming one after another, of events or things.

TRAIN *n.* a succession; a procession.

Continual and **Continuous** Of course you know what these two words mean, but good writers use them carefully and so should you. Only roughly are they synonymous. If you say it has rained CONTINUALLY all week, you needn't have your tongue in your cheek. CONTINUAL allows for gaps, for periods of cessation. But CONTINUOUS permits no ceasing. A CONTINUOUS downpour, for perhaps an hour, is like a CONTINUOUS unbroken line.

Continuance and **Continuation** A good pair to illustrate the sense of our rather few words ending in 'ance,' especially when they are compared with those that end with 'ation' or 'tion.' CONTINUATION means the 'going on' of a line or an act. For example, "The continuation of the battle means more casualties," or "The continuation of the rain will insure good crops." In this usage the emphasis is on the extension of a 'single' act that has a recognizable 'beginning.'

CONTINUANCE is a rounder word; it envisages what is contained in CONTINUATION. It therefore becomes a duration of time, and its emphasis is on the 'condition obtaining within' that duration. "During the continuance of the war, social barriers were broken down." We often abbreviate the sense of CONTINUANCE to "For the duration . . ." At any rate, CONTINUANCE suggests the perpetual extension of a process or form of life whose beginning is not clearly defined. "In old age the continuance of days leaves one weary," or "The continuance of turtles is a striking example of the persistence of life."

Sequence and **Series** SEQUENCE emphasizes the 'motion' or 'progression' in a SERIES. Ordinarily, we think of a SERIES as a unit, not as a moving chain. A World's Series is a single thing, a row of games. A SERIES of numbers is a unit, let us say, from one to ten. "What a series of rainy days we've had!" emphasizes the whole block of rainy days instead of one day coming after another. But a SEQUENCE of events is a 'succession of events.' It is the following of one after another in progressive fashion. A SEQUENCE of numbers rises or descends. A SEQUENCE of days may be dry, wet, hot, and cold. "Well, she's enjoyed a sequence of love affairs!" suggests that she was happy and unhappy by turns.

SHAKING

DITHER   n. a shaking; a trembling; hence, a state of bewilderment or confusion caused by excitement.

FLUTTER   v. to flap quickly, as to FLUTTER wings; to vibrate; to flit.

Palpitate   see **Pulsate, Palpitate,** etc.

Pulsate, Palpitate & **Throb**

QUAKE   v. to shake; to shiver; esp. in the sense of a deep-rooted shudder.

Quaver   see **Quiver, Quaver,** etc.

Quiver, Quaver & Shiver

SHAKE   v. to vibrate; quiver; tremble.

SHIMMY   v. to vibrate unnaturally and rapidly.

Shiver   see **Quiver, Quaver,** etc.

SHUDDER   v. to quiver or quake, esp. in the sense of a profound disturbance.

Throb   see **Pulsate, Palpitate,** etc.

TOTTER   v. to tremble as if about to fall; to teeter.

TREMBLE   n. a shaking; pulsation;

vibration. *v.* to shake, esp. in an involuntary way, as to TREMBLE from fear.

TREMOLO *n.* a rapid vibration or flutter of a musical sound.

WAGGLE *v.* to wave; move from side to side; wag.

WAVER *v.* to fluctuate; to vacillate slowly, as a flag WAVERS in the breeze.

WOBBLE *v.* to waggle; esp. in the sense of moving weakly from side to side, as "A sick man wobbles in his walk."

Pulsate, Palpitate and **Throb**   The origins of PULSATE and PALPITATE are both Latin, 'to beat' and 'to pant.' Commonly both our pulses and our hearts PULSATE ('beat') and our hearts PALPITATE ('pant') when they beat hard. PULSATION is 'rhythmic throbbing.'

The little Middle English word THROB (its ultimate origins are doubtful; we first know it as *throbben*) is expressive. An entire community may THROB with interest when a scandal breaks. THROB is a synonym for PULSATE; but the former, perhaps because it belongs to the more primitive parts of our language, has an everyday or poetic use while the latter, like many Latin words, is reserved for clinical or abstract use. You would never say, "I'm pulsating with excitement"; but "I'm throbbing with excitement," is very appropriate.

Quiver, Quaver and **Shiver**   The Anglo-Saxons had two words for shake, *sceacan* and *cwacian*. These gave us, respectively, 'shake' and 'quake.' Those in turn gave us QUAVER and QUIVER. QUAVER has lost all ambition. It is used only to describe an old man's voice or a waver in singing. In musical terminology QUAVER denotes an eight note.

But QUIVER is still a very alive and sensitive word. You can QUIVER all over from rage or disgust, your heart can QUIVER inside you with joy. And conversely, your voice QUIVERS miserably when you QUAVER, yet you yourself QUIVER with excitement when you are vibrant with animation. You can QUIVER with fear or indignation as noticeably as you can SHIVER from cold. While 'quaking' and 'shaking' are awkward, QUIVERING is discreet. It serves cowardice as well as it serves enthusiasm.

SHIVER is of course more prosaic. It stems honestly from Middle English *shiveran*. Only slightly groomed, it has done its routine job since Chaucer's day. SHIVER is used almost exclusively to describe the effects of cold. But note, 'to shiver in one's boots,' is still a standard circumlocution for 'fear.'

SHELTERS

ARK *n.* any huge uncomfortable building. (U.S. colloq.)

BARRACKS *n. pl.* any building, often barn-like, which houses soldiers.

BOOTH *n.* a small, temporary shed, used at circuses and fairs for displays.

BUNGALOW *n.* a small house; a cottage, properly, of one story.

CABIN *n.* a small house, often of logs or otherwise rough and rustic.

Caravansary & Hostelry

CELL *n.* a small, enclosed space; a small room.

CHALET *n.* a mountain cabin, esp. one designed according to the Swiss style.

CLOISTER *n.* a monastery or convent; esp. the colonnaded and covered passages around the sides of a court or garden.

Cottage, Coterie & Croft

Coterie see **Cottage, Coterie, etc.**

Croft see **Cottage, Coterie, etc.**

DUGOUT *n.* a cave; any low trench-like shelter, as a baseball DUGOUT.

DUPLEX *n.* a two-story apartment.

GRANGE *n.* a farmhouse with its stables, barns, and other farm buildings.

Harbor & Haven

Haven see **Harbor & Haven**

HERMITAGE *n.* a hermit's house; thus, a very isolated or shut-in house.

Home

HOSPICE *n.* an inn.

Hostelry see **Caravansary & Hostelry**

HOUSE *n.* a building in which people live.

HUT *n.* a very small, temporary house, usually primitive.

INN *n.* a public shelter for travelers where they can get food and bed.

Kiosk

LEAN-TO *n.* a more or less rough shelter made by placing one edge of the roof on the ground and the opposite edge on poles or against trees or some other support.

LODGE *n.* a house for special purposes; as a LODGE for the meetings of an organization; a game-keeper's LODGE.

Manse

MANSION *n.* any large house.

Seraglio

STALL *n.* a booth.

TENT *n.* a shelter made of canvas.

Tepee & Wigwam

Vestibule Train & Vestibule School

VILLA *n.* a country house, usually near the ocean and used esp. for vacationing.

Wigwam see **Tepee & Wigwam**

Xanadu

Caravansary and **Hostelry** A CARAVANSARY is an 'Oriental inn.' In Persia it is a 'tavern' for caravans, built around an open space in which the camels can rest. HOSTELRY is from old French HOSTEL, just as 'hotel' is, and for that matter 'hospitality' and 'hospital.' HOSTELRY is synonymous with 'hotel,' and is chiefly interesting from its archaic flavor, which attracted Sir Walter Scott. He is chiefly responsible for reviving this word in the nineteenth century. Anyhow, HOSTELRY is related to one of the most amazing broods of words and meanings in all etymology.

In early Roman times there was a word for 'stranger,' which began to grow in devious ways to reflect all that a people's curiosity can find in a stranger. So this word *hostis* came to mean an 'enemy,' then it grew to suggest 'ability' and 'lordship,' and shrunk again for convenience into *hospes*, a 'guest.' But after that the word denoted a 'guest lord,' then a 'lord,' and then a lord as an 'entertainer' and a 'host.' Then the 'host' simply became one upon whom soldiers are quartered. But, of course, the relationship was confused, so that each accommodated soldier became likewise a *hospes*. And finally it arrived in England as 'host,' and in Shakespeare's England the 'host' was a 'landlord.'

In the meantime, it spread into Teutonic tongues, or perhaps the root had existed there all along, the Latin and Teutonic words having a common Indo-European ancestor. Again it meant a 'stranger,' then an 'enemy,' and it proceeds as it did in Italy. But it possessed a northern initial, so that in early English it appears as the prototype of our word 'guest.'

And while all these permutations are taking place, longer words were growing from the Latin *hospes* to give us 'hostage' (from pledges given on receiving and vouching for strangers), 'hospital' (originally a place for guests, and still in Europe often a charitable refuge), 'hospice' (a charitable foundation, originally an inn, like the ones the Knights Hospitalers established in Jerusalem for poor pilgrims), 'hotel' (originally, in France, either a mansion or inn, and sidewise growing into Hôtel-Dieu, or hospital, and Hôtel de Ville, or town hall, and arriving in England during our Revolution as a rival of 'inn,' or a place to stay 'in') and, finally, 'hospitality' (which gathers up most of the meanings into an expansive graciousness).

Cottage, Coterie and **Croft** A 'cote' is a 'sheep-pen' or any 'place of shelter,' from Anglo-Saxon *cot*, 'den,' whence our COTTAGE. Whence, in turn, comes our COTERIE, via the French, where it means a 'society.' But COTERIE's connotation of 'cozy clique' comes from its origin, because it was at first an amicable association of 'cotters,' or as we would say, 'cottagers.' A CROFT is a 'little field' near a house, also from the Anglo-Saxon. A 'crofter' is a tenant farmer who tills a CROFT.

Harbor and **Haven** Though it looks like one, HARBOR is not a Roman word, like 'arbor, labor, etc.' Actually, it is Scandinavian, and in spite of its beneficent sound today, it has been historically a military term, closely related to the martial devastation originally denoted by our horrific verb 'to harry.' In the beginning HARBOR might have meant merely a 'shelter,' especially in the sense of 'lodging.' But the first element of the word derives from the words for an 'army' not only in the Old Norse but also in the Old English, Old French and Old German. The meaning seems clearly to have been both military and utilitarian, like a 'shelter' for troops. But as the word developed it acquired two variants, 'harborough' and 'harbrow.' There is a theory that these variants became oddly confused with the word 'ardor' from the Latin, giving us the form of our present word. At any rate, a HARBOR did not remain a mere barracks or camp.

The word began to be used fancifully. A wild animal's 'lair' became his HARBOR, an 'inn' was a HARBOR, even the stars in their fixed 'positions' or 'houses' were said to be in their HARBORS. And to support the confusion with 'ardor' (Latin *ardor*, 'burning, fire') there is a chest which glassmakers use, holding fusible materials, which is called a HARBOR. While these derivatives in the main preserve the idea of usefulness they indicate that the word was spiritually on the move.

Today a HARBOR connotes much more to us than a mere 'shelter.' It is a 'refuge, a sanctuary, a broad anchorage' safe from the storms, while a shelter may denote only a pup tent or an umbrella. The true merger of sense is with that of HARBOR's maritime companion in the Old Norse, HAVEN, a 'sheltered anchorage.' The nautical reference of HARBOR appeared early. To the father of English poetry, Chaucer, it was already common usage. But the meanings of both words have advanced from land and sea to the ethereal, and Heaven itself is now figuratively the ideal HAVEN and the ultimate HARBOR.

But it happened otherwise with the verb arising belatedly from HARBOR. A century after Chaucer, Tyndale's Bible could still say with beatific inference: "I was herbeorlesse and ye lodged me." Today we principally HARBOR grudges, unkindly intentions, or a criminal at the risk of legal penalty. This is indeed a curious example of one kind of tendency evident in the evolution of all words—the tendency to specialize.

Home This is a word which is, in its sentimental or emotional sense, characteristically, if not uniquely, our own. The French, for example, have no precise equivalent to it. It grew from the early English *ham* (pronounced quite hollowly, 'hom') to the lugubrious looking Middle English *hoom,* pronounced 'hawm,' and then to the full musical syllable we now use. The meaning grew in consonance with the form and sound. From meaning merely a 'structure' in which humans resided or sought shelter, the word has come to mean anything which provides 'material and spiritual shelter.'

Our house is our HOME, our village is our HOME, and our country is our HOME. It is no wonder that this word has integrated itself into the whole fabric of our language so that we can hardly use more than a certain small number of other words, on any subject, without ultimately using this one also. Whether we are speaking or writing of ourselves, of our friends, of politics, of wars, or of whatnot, the word HOME somehow enters the discussion.

When we need to refer to a dwelling without recognition of its spiritual qualities we have other words for it, like 'house' or 'abode.' But these other words have only momentary convenience. For back of the word HOME is the idea of 'permanence,' of both 'refuge and security.' The root of it can be found even in the Sanskrit, where it meant 'to dwell, abide,' but where it produced also a noun meaning 'safety.' In many tongues, as in English, the word HOME came also to mean a permanent town, as in Stoneham.

We who speak English may feel that this word belongs to us. Yet there is the German (and also Jewish) word *heim,* which can take on almost a meaning of 'spiritual welfare' or a 'blessing.' Nor is our own poignant expression 'homesickness,' basically ours. 'Homesickness' came to us as late as Colonial times, and from the faraway Alps, by Swiss mercenaries who had compounded their expression *heimweh* for the nostalgic longing they felt for their native hills.

Kiosk In Turkey, a 'summerhouse'; here, a 'newsdealer's shack' on the sidewalk, or the 'hood' over a subway entrance.

Manse A 'parsonage.' Sometimes, a MANSE is any landowner's house. Like mansion, it comes from Latin via Old French.

Seraglio The Turkish sultan's palace, but especially its feature, the 'harem,' is a SERAGLIO. Hence it means any 'harem.' The sense is derived from to 'lock up.'

Tepee and **Wigwam** Respectively, Indian tents in the Western plains, and tents or lodges in the Eastern forests. TEPEES are conical and of cloth, though they used to be made of skins. A 'wickiup' is a temporary TEPEE constructed of boughs and matted reeds. WIGWAM probably comes from the Massachusetts Indians, and means 'big house.' Colloquially, today a WIGWAM is a public building, or a lodge house.

Vestibule Train and **Vestibule School** A VESTIBULE is literally a 'forecourt' to a house, something separated from the main living quarters. Through adaptation it is now the small enclosure outside a front door. The term 'VESTIBULE (or VESTIBULED) TRAIN' refers to those trains whose platforms between cars are enclosed for the comfort of passengers passing through to the diner. The British go farther, calling them 'corridor trains,' which only incidentally refers to the platforms, since the whole train then becomes one corridor.

In an industrial plant a VESTIBULE SCHOOL is an introductory or training department for new workers. Figuratively, the new worker goes through initiatory exercises in the VESTIBULE before beginning work in the shop proper.

Xanadu The palace of the Mongol emperor Kublai Khan, son of the monstrous Genghis Khan who scourged Eurasia in the thirteenth century. But XANADU is a misspelling of XAMDU. Samuel Purchas, whose own name seems to have lacked a letter, thus misspelled it, perhaps by candlelight mistaking the 'm' for an 'na.' But the travel stories he was compiling were not ruined by his spelling, and two centuries later the one about Xanadu inspired Samuel Coleridge to write his most magical and musical poem, called "Kubla Khan." "In Xanadu did Kubla Khan/ a stately pleasure-dome decree . . ."

SLEEP

Doze & Drowse
Drowse see **Doze**
EXHAUST *v.* to tire; wear out; fatigue. *n.* EXHAUSTION.
FAG *v.* to work until tired. "Chopping wood fagged him completely."

FATIGUE *n.* tiredness; exhaustion.
Languor
Lassitude
LETHARGY *n.* laziness; tiredness; esp. in the sense of being physically weak from heat or boredom.

Loll

NAP *n.* a short sleep. *v.* to sleep for a short time.

NOD *v.* to show drowsiness by NODDING the head.

OSCITANT *adj.* yawning with great drowsiness; hence, also, gaping, drowsy, sluggish.

SLEEPY *adj.* pertaining to sleep; tired enough to sleep; drowsy.

Slumber

Snooze

SOMNAMBULISM *n.* sleepwalking. *adj.* SOMNAMBULISTIC.

SOMNOLENT *adj.* sleepy.

STUPOR *n.* lethargy; a dazed half-conscious condition.

TIRE *v.* to wear out; exhaust.

TORPOR *v.* lethargy; drowsiness; sluggishness.

TUCKER OUT *v.* to tire.

WEARY *adj.* tired; fatigued.

Doze and **Drowse** Your wife DOZES, and you DROWSE before the fire. But hold on to your chairs, because DOZE probably gave us our 'dizzy' and DROWSE originally meant in the Anglo-Saxon 'to fall or sink.' Anyhow, both words now say about the same thing, a 'light, short sleep,' sometimes simply to pass time. DROWSY is a good adjective, and DOZY, though it isn't heard often, is in the dictionary.

Languor Haven't you often felt the sheer luxury of lying long in bed on a cold morning? And can you remember the lazy, satisfying after-dinner naps you take in the summer? This is LANGUOR, that expressive word with the softly rolling 'or' on the end and the long, slow relaxing syllable to begin it. Note these other words we like (in spite of some of their meanings) to say with relish: rancor, candor, sapor, valor and squalor. This 'or' sound is especially effective in English, which is so often spoken in a flat uninteresting way.

The adjective LANGUID which denotes about the same feeling as LANGUOR, has been associated too long with 'ailments' and 'laziness' to retain many attractive connotations. But LANGUOROUS, another adjective for LANGUOR, is really a substantial word for all its lingering. We often think of LANGUOROUS in connection with a beautiful but dangerously seductive woman. The verb LANGUISH is another cousin—these words arise from Latin *languere,* 'to be faint or weak.' There is a flux in the meaning of LANGUISH that gives it a resisting peculiarity. It represents always a 'continuous waning.' Thus we LANGUISH when we become dull or weak to the point of almost extinction. Sometimes we LANGUISH from the lack of something we want very much, like the young girl who casts LANGUISHING eyes upon a new evening dress. We LANGUISH in prison, from unrequited love, from physical ailments, or from hunger. Flowers LANGUISH when they droop, and even the scenes of our childhood LANGUISH in our minds with the passage of time.

Lassitude Though originally it was 'faintness,' LASSITUDE is now a 'state of listlessness' amounting to laxness. LASSITUDE conveys a suggestion of reprehensible LANGUOR. See LANGUOR. "One often and necessarily feels languor in the tropics, but when he keeps up his indolent habits in London or New York his lassitude is blamable."

Loll 'To sit over the fire,' as the Dutch had it. But today in English it means to move around in a lazy, indolent way. Respectable people don't LOLL, for it has a suggestion of idle irresponsibility. LOLL also means 'to hang loosely.' "A dog's tongue lolls on a hot day."

Slumber SLUMBER is a longer and slower word than 'sleep.' It comes to us out of the Gothic forests of the remote past. SLUMBER, which is Old English and beyond, never meant anything but simply 'sleep.' It is queer that we use such an expressive word so little. We don't even use that sleep-inducing adjective SLUMBEROUS. But SLUMBER is used in a figurative way perhaps more than 'sleep.' "The slumbering sea seemed ready to erupt into a tremendous storm."

Snooze Facetious words are often slighted in dictionaries, even when they are truly humorous. The humor in SNOOZE is delicious: it is soft but playful, light but expressive. In fact, the Standard calls SNOOZE imitative, presumable of a light snoring. At any rate SNOOZE is a tasteful and tactful word for 'snoring.' We always smile when someone says he's just had a SNOOZE, because sleep is such a gentle, universal delight. Perhaps that is why our other words for a short sleep are also humorous: nap, cat nap, or kitten nap.

SOCIAL, POLITICAL AND CULTURAL DESIGNATIONS

See also Politics; Government; Areas and Measurements

Borough

BURGESS *n.* a citizen.

CANTON *n.* an administrative division of a country, as the CANTONS of Switzerland.

CHAUVINISM *n.* extravagant or exaggerated patriotism.

CITIZEN *n.* a person who enjoys full legal status in a nation, receiving protection and the rights specified in its law in return for his allegiance.

CIVIC *adj.* pertaining to a citizen, a community, or the public.

COMMON WELFARE n. the general good of all citizens.

COMMUNE n. the common people; an administrative division in France.

Cosmopolitan

COUNTY n. a subdivision of all U.S. states but Louisiana, which has parishes instead.

Denizen

DIOCESE n. the administrative area of a bishop.

Enclave

Endemic

Ethnic

FREEDMAN n. a former slave set free.

GENERAL WELFARE n. common welfare.

GHETTO n. formerly a section of a city restricted to Jews.

Highbrow, Middlebrow & Lowbrow

Laic see **Secular & Laic**

Lowbrow see **Highbrow, Middlebrow**, etc.

Metropolis

Middlebrow see **Highbrow, Middlebrow**, etc.

MUNICIPALITY n. a city or town.

PARISH n. a section, of land or of people, served by an individual church. See also COUNTY.

PRECINCT n. a district created for administrative reasons, as a police PRECINCT.

Province

PUBLIC n. the people. adj. pertaining to all citizens.

PUBLIC WELFARE n. common welfare.

RURAL adj. pertaining to the country as opposed to the city.

Secular & Laic

SHIRE n. an English territorial division, as YorkSHIRE.

Street & Its Collaterals

SUBURB n. a residential area around a city.

TOWN n. a small city, usually not incorporated as a city.

TOWNSHIP n. usually a subdivision of a county.

Borough An 'incorporated town.' Originally BOROUGH, 'burgh,' 'bury,' 'burg,' and 'borg' were all one: something like a 'castle' or 'stronghold.' The 'borg' is Scandinavian, the 'burgh' is Scotch and the 'burg' is German. 'Burgh' is disguised in the Irish surname, Burke. 'Berg' is something else again, a 'hill.' An iceberg is a hill or mountain of ice.

Cosmopolitan A 'metropolis' is a vast city. If you live in one, you soon see it as a whole world in miniature, a microcosm. In that sense, any metropolitan is a COSMOPOLITAN. The 'cosmos' is a 'world' or 'universe,' and the immediate universe, for people, is our planet. Anyone who has lived all over the world, or is truly worldly in his knowledge, is a COSMOPOLITAN. In an austere sense, the true COSMOPOLITAN is a man without a country.

Denizen An inhabitant, usually of the back country, or the wilds, as distinct from a city, rural area or the state at large. A Scot Highlander is a DENIZEN of the Highlands as a deer is a DENIZEN of the forests.

Enclave Plainly speaking, an ENCLAVE is an 'earth-bound island.' It is a spot of foreign territory within a country's borders. For example, if Illinois was situated in Canada, it would be an ENCLAVE. The noun derives from the verb, 'to surround a region thusly.'

Endemic A companion word to 'epidemic.' ENDEMIC in the original Greek meant 'native.' It is our formal way of saying something is native to a particular country or people. "Penguins are endemic to Antarctica." It is usually used to refer to a disease whose origin can be traced to a particular geographic location. ENDEMIC has excellent figurative possibilities. For example, "Evil is endemic to man."

Ethnic This word is distinguished from 'ethic' by the letter 'n,' which might represent 'nation,' since the originating Greek word was *ethnos,* meaning 'nation.' ETHNIC means pertaining to race or to peoples, sometimes simply to pagan peoples. It is a terminological adjective chiefly referring to a branch of anthropology.

Highbrow, Middlebrow and **Lowbrow** These terms are vivid in themselves, but unfortunately in their applications they are vague and disturbing. The towering white brow, or forehead, of Edgar Allan Poe was called beautiful and lofty in his own time, but no one thought of calling him a HIGHBROW. Some self-styled HIGHBROWS today may adore their own fronts, but millions of LOWBROWS ridicule the former. Conversely, of course, LOWBROWS and MIDDLEBROWS are often snubbed by more high-standing heads. Moreover, at times a member of one category may yearn to be included in another. The erudite and sophisticated HIGHBROW may yearn for the relatively easygoing simplicity of the average person, while these LOWBROWS may at the same time yearn for the power and magic of educated or superlative minds.

Linguistically, and hence sociologically, these terms are important but deplorable. Social enmities are fostered by these slang designations that were selected to differentiate intellectual classes. Like 'white-collar,' these artificial but sense-laden terms have become instruments of offense and defense in an undeclared sociological warfare. What after all is the conflict? It is the poignant and pathetic struggle of human minds to make themselves understood in the idiom of others and yet be understood in their own. It is the struggle for universal intelligibility, with the ways and means hotly and harshly debated. Frustration and pride obscure criteria as fast as they are established. Note the slyness of these agitating words, alternately loyal or unfaithful to either side. The dictionary says: "Highbrow. Noun—person so highly educated as to lack interest in the commonplace; an intellectual snob;" and "Adjective—intellectual; cultured." That is if you are HIGHBROW you may be proud of it. But beware; there are millions who call a HIGHBROW a snob. Then the dictionary again: "Lowbrow. Noun—one of low mentality and coarse tastes; one incapable of, or without pretensions to, culture;" and "Adjective—incapable of culture; lacking good taste." Notice the bluntness: not lacking *in* good taste, but lacking *all* good taste. If you are a LOWBROW you are damned, presumably too ignorant and prideless to be even indignant. But note it is the HIGHBROWS who are writing down these definitions. They are the custodians of our language. No imputation of unfairness is here attached to them, and the force of good usage supports them. But the force of their definition is so strong, and the distinctions are so sharp, that a new, or compromise group, the MIDDLEBROWS, is forming. The MIDDLEBROWS blunt the conflict by bridging the gap between HIGHBROW and LOWBROW. The MIDDLEBROWS are not yet in the dictionaries, but their essence is that, unlike the true LOWBROW, they have aspirations upwards.

But we must remember that the formation of new words, no matter how unsavory their meaning, is a healthy sign of the vigor of both society and language. There is, in a sense, a liberation of languages when it grows continually, and perhaps, after all, it is a social liberation as well to see certain distinctions in graphic language. When distinctions are brought into the open it is easier to determine their value.

Metropolis A METROPOLIS is a 'mother city'; it comes from the Greek. In Western Europe a METROPOLITAN was formerly a 'bishop.' He held a certain authority over other bishops within a province, and his see was in a METROPOLIS. But now a METROPOLIS connotes a vast hurly-burly and all the latest things in worldly fashion. From being a capital in ancient Greece, it has become merely a mammoth city.

Province PROVINCES are divisions of territory, remote from the central government, and usually designated for the purpose of administration. The adjective PROVINCIAL consequently carries a connotation of 'narrowness' or 'rusticity.' A PROVINCIAL person—or simply a 'PROVINCIAL.'—is marked by the peculiarities of his PROVINCE.

No one knows where the meaning in the word PROVINCE began, but probably it was a part of our word 'Friday,' cognate with an old Gothic word for a 'lord and master.' The German *frau,* 'housewife,' is a related word. Thus the Roman *provincia* was at first a word for a governor's office, and later it was extended to the regions they ruled (*pro,* 'before' plus *vincere,* 'to conquer'). These Roman PROVINCES were the antecedents of the great half-independent PROVINCES that constituted early France, and, through imitation, of the English PROVINCES as distinct from the great city of London.

The figurative use of PROVINCE takes on grandeur from this political tradition. Thus, a PROVINCE may be one's own domain, an area where you have special knowledge or power. "A general's province is war, but a statesman's province is peace."

Secular and **Laic**   Most of us know what a layman is. He is the non-professional man, not being a lawyer, doctor, clergyman, etc. LAIC is his adjective, and LAITY is his collective noun. The words come, like democracy, from a Greek word meaning 'people,' *laos,* in this case, and *demos* in the case of democracy. SECULAR comes from the Latin synonym of LAIC. Its source is *saeculum,* 'age,' hence 'worldliness,' and consequently stresses the 'nonreligious.'

Street and Its Collaterals   The first STREETS were not English, as they sound, and they traversed not towns but whole countrysides. And they were always paved. STREET is derived from Latin *stratae viae,* 'paved ways,' which were roads.

Meanwhile in the Middle Ages ROAD was even less definite than ROUTE is now. They were merely the 'ways (directions)' in which you rode, hence becoming places for riding, and distinguished from WAY, which was chiefly for vehicles. ROADWAY now combines them. Both were distinct from PATH which was reserved for pedestrians.

But thanks to Roman engineering STREETS became universal at an early date (compare German *strasse,* Spanish *estraded,* etc.). Inevitably different kinds of STREETS were eventually recognized. AVENUE and BOULEVARD are now broad and imposing, partly because of the buildings that border them, and the statuary and trees that adorn them. BOULEVARDS can run into the country, and if they are landscaped, or 'parked,' they become PARKWAYS. A tiny STREET clings to the rural term LANE, though in town a small street is usually an ALLEY. Yet, in France, an ALLEY is still a miniature of AVENUE; an *allée* is a path down a long garden, or greensward, marked with shrubbery or ornamental trees. It is from French *aller,* 'to go,' as AVENUE is from French *venir,* 'to come.'

Historically, BOULEVARD represents a Gallic capacity for resurrection with capacious spirit and art. The word was first German and war-born: *bulwerk* meant a promenade roughly constructed of logs on the ramparts of ruined fortresses. The English took their word 'bulwark' from it, using it both for earthen ramparts and for the wall around a ship's dock. But many of the razed fortresses were in France, and in time the French endowed the term with a peaceful and proud meaning. BOULEVARDS, large and splendid, now accommodate all traffic.

CAUSEWAY is also a built up word. It was 'causey,' a beaten (trodden) path, the French having first beaten down the Latin *calx* or *calc*, 'heel,' to something softer to the ear, in *caucie*. Or perhaps it comes from the other Latin *calx*, 'lime,' because many CAUSEWAYS are still shell roads, literally lime roads.

HIGHWAYS are utterly English. They are 'high' because 'high authority' (Parliament) ordained them, and royal command controlled them. They were the King's High Ways and the main roads, their true descendents are our SUPER-HIGHWAYS. TURNPIKE contains the idea of spears, or pikes, on a crossbar to cavalry, presumably conceived by Dutch infantry in the fifteenth century to stop mounted Spanish troops. As HIGHWAYS with tollgates, TURNPIKES came in early enough to get into Dr. Johnson's dictionary.

The development of ROUTE is fascinating. It was Latin *via rupta*, 'a broken way.' *Rupta* was the past participle of *rumpere*, 'to break,' and the warlike Romans made it mean a 'defeat, a flying body of troops, a rout.' Our own army still rhymes ROUTE with 'shout.' After that, it meant a 'way,' as through a forest, broken out by such a troop, or by any troop. Our modern ROUTE is thus the same word as 'rout,' a demoralizing defeat, and even in Shakespeare's day it had both meanings.

SOUNDS

ARIOSE *adj.* song-like; characterized by melody.

BABEL *n.* a confusion of noises or of many languages spoken at once.

BAWL *v.* to shout or cry out; to howl; to weep loudly.

BEDLAM *n.* a place of great uproar and confusion.

Bellow

BLARE *v.* to shout; to make a loud, penetrating noise.

BLAST *n.* an explosion or burst of sound. *v.* to shout or call loudly and suddenly.

BLATANT *adj.* noisy; blaring.

Bleat (Baa & Maa)

BOISTEROUS *adj.* loud and noisy.

BRAY *n.* the cry of a donkey or ass; hence, a harsh cry. *v.* to make such a sound.

CALL *n.* a shout or cry; often the cry of a bird or animal, as the CALL of a moose. *v.* to cry or sound off.

CAROL *n.* a sweet and melodious song, esp. a song expressing joy.

CATERWAUL *n.* specifically the howling of cats; hence, any noisy quarreling.

CHATTER *n.* very rapid talk; non-sensical noise like rapid talk, as the CHATTER of squirrels.

CHITTER *n.* & *v.* to twitter; tweet.

CHORUS *n.* several people, animals or things singing or making a noise together.

CLACK *n.* the sharp noise of two things brought together suddenly; chatter, as the CLACK of a typewriter.

Clamor & Clangor

CLANK *n.* a heavy brief sound made by dropping heavy metal.

CLASH *n.* the sound made by a collision or the sound of conflict, as the CLASH of armies.

Clatter

CLINK *n.* a light brief sound made usually by dropping a light piece of metal, such as a coin. Compare CLANK.

CLUCK *n.* a hen's call. *v.* to make the sound of a hen's call, usually done with the tongue.

Crepitant

CROAK *n.* a noise made deep in the throat, like a frog's call. *v.* to make a CROAK.

CRY *n.* a shout; esp. in the sense of a distress call, as a CRY of pain; any plaintive call, as the CRY of sea birds. *v.* to CRY.

DIN *n.* racket; a heavy, continuous noise.

Dirge

GABBLE *v.* to chatter.

GOBBLE *n.* the sound of a turkey, hence *v.* to make such a sound or a guttural chatter.

GROAN *n.* a moan; any sound expressive of grief or pain. *v.* to moan.

GRUMBLE *n.* a verbal complaint. *v.* to complain; rumble.

HONK *n.* a nasal noise, like the call of geese. *v.* to make such a noise.

HUBBUB *n.* din.

HULLABALOO *n.* noisy confusion.

MELIC *adj.* pertaining to melody or song.

MUGIENT *adj.* lowing or bellowing.

NOISE *n.* an unharmonious or unpleasant sound.

OBSTREPEROUS *adj.* very noisy; rebelliously noisy.

Pandemonium

PIPE *v.* to make whistling sounds with musical pipes.

Purl

PURR *n.* a low, throaty murmur or chatter, like the PURR of a contented cat. *v.* to PURR.

RACKET *n.* a din.

RING *n.* a clear, often musical sound made by vibrating metal, as the RING of a bell.

ROAR *n.* a loud, windy sound, like

the ROAR of the ocean or the ROAR of a bull; a bellow.

SCREAM   n. a cry at the top of the voice, indicating great distress. v. to make such a cry.

SCREECH   n. a loud, harsh, shrill sound, such as the cry of a hawk; scream. v. to make such a sound.

SHOUT   n. a loud call; a burst of noise, as the SHOUT of a crowd. v. to make such a call.

SHRIEK   n. scream; a loud, hysterical call. v. to scream.

Shrill

Silence

SING   v. to make music, or harmonious and very pleasant sounds, with the voice.

SNARL   n. a low, ferocious sound of anger or meanness. v. to SNARL.

Snivel   see Snuffle

Snuffle & Snivel

SQUEAL   n. a sharp, shrill cry. v. to utter such a cry.

Staccato

STRIDENT   adj. harsh; loud; grating.

TESSERAL   adj. song-like, ariose.

TRILL   n. a sound made by vibrating the tongue, the lips, or the uvula; a rapid alternation of pitch. v. to make such a sound, as "Some Frenchmen trill their 'r's."

TOOT   n. a short blast on a whistle. v. to play a whistle, or horn.

TUMULT   n. hubbub.

TWEET   n. a low, repeating chirp.

Ululant

UPROAR   n. din.

VOCIFEROUS   adj. loud; noisy.

WARBLE   n. a throaty and melodious sound made by certain birds. v. to sing.

YELL   n. a shout; cry. v. to shout; to cry.

Bellow   You wouldn't think it, but bells BELLOW. Both words come from the Anglo-Saxon for 'roar.' Generally, bulls now BELLOW; but in fiction an irate father or an infuriated mob often BELLOW. Perhaps the word is related to the Anglo-Saxon *below*, 'bag,' which gives us our 'bellows.' In any case, it is a serviceable word for a 'deep, powerful roar.' We should use it more often. "All night long, whipped to a frenzy by the wind, the seas bellowed against the shores."

Bleat (Baa & Maa)   A sheep BAAS, a goat MAAS. But both BLEAT.

Clamor and Clangor   CLAMOR is an 'outcry.' It comes from the Latin, and has that full-throated classical sound that seems appropriate for a word meaning a 'continuous noise.'

CLANGOR is also Roman, and rings with its own authority. It is a 'repeated or long-ringing clanging.' Sunday chimes make a CLANGOR, but usually a CLANGOR is not melodious. The sound of alarm or victory bells is real CLANGOR. 'Clang' and CLANGOR have the same meaning; but while 'clang' is sometimes a verb CLANGOR never is. "At sea the bells clanged dolefully through the fog."

Clatter A din is a loud, confusing and continuous noise, sometimes full of clamor and sometimes full of CLATTER. The CLATTER is what makes it 'rattle.' See CLAMOR and CLANGOR.

Crepitant 'Crackling,' like a fire on the hearth. Old stairs can CREPITATE, too. So can your bones in your 'decrepitude.' The base is the frequentative of Latin *crepare*, 'creak.'

Dirge This word has always sounded its part, a 'mournful chant of grief,' whether oral, rhetorical or musical. It started in the litany of a funeral hymn, being the first word. "*Dirige*," addressed in Latin to the Lord: "Oh, direct us, Thou." It is like a muted moan and a muffled drum. It is, in fact, so solemn and so mournful we have little use for it. But when occasion does arise, it is the exact word.

Pandemonium Milton gave us this word; he made it up. The 'pan,' as in Pan-American, gives it scope, and all the syllables, sonorous in different keys, give it sound. When PANDEMONIUM breaks out in a crowd everything is 'noise and confusion.' Ear-splitting noise and utter confusion.

And well it should be. The PANDEMONIUM which Milton described was in Hell. It is a palace built expressly at the order of Satan to house demons. Inside it, is perpetual wild uproar. Milton's palace was classically built, and majestic; as someone has suggested, PANDEMONIUM has become a mere rowdy tenement.

Purl A continuous babbling or murmuring sound; an audible rippling, as of a brook.

Shrill This word is worth a moment's thought. At first it was probably imitative of the cries of some birds. But like migrating birds, it flew far and wide, as witness Norwegian *skryla*, Scotch *shirl*, German *schrill*, and not a few others. Coming into English presumably from the Low German, it did not confine itself to sounds, but meant also 'sharp,' as 'keen' and 'bright' suggest 'sharp.' But it soon surpassed all other words in describing 'high-pitched sounds,' piercing and wild. But a SHRILL sound doesn't have to be unusual, like the sound in 'shriek' or 'scream.'

A strident voice may be high-pitched and loud, but its excitement is nervous and grating. The SHRILL voice is startling in its high pene-trating clearness. Poets still speak of birds SHRILLING their cries, and crickets SHRILL insistently on the hearth. What is SHRILL is the com-plete opposite of what is 'muffled.'

Silence SILENCE is a favorite word, because of the beauty of its sound, as well as its message. Yet it can be a very stern word, the antithesis of life. When the guns of the enemy are SILENCED they are conquered or killed. When anything SILENCES us we are likewise, per-haps forever, conquered or dead.

The SILENT strong men of the movies may be less SILENT than 'taci-turn,' which means 'habitually reserved,' both for purposes of business and, probably, by nature. But even in the beginning 'to be silent' meant, as of persons, to keep SILENCE; to act, and not to speak: *silere,* the Latin verb, which was not vernacular but classical, and stronger than *tacere,* which has given us 'taciturn.' When the Romans called for a SILENCE they cried, "Tacete! Tacete!" equivalent to our "Quiet! Quiet!" But one of their most solemn figures of speech for the dead was *silentes,* the 'silent ones.'

The full sweep of SILENCE probably antedates even the Romans, for there was Gothic *anasilon,* 'to be silent,' no doubt describing the vast forests in which the Goths lived. SILENCE early took the meaning of tranquility and repose, even perfectness. But it did not wholly resist contamination. To be SILENT was to keep a secret, and hence to be secretive; but always it meant also 'not to be garrulous,' 'untrustworthy.' SILENCE thus assumes, or perhaps reassumes, a meaning of perfection. "Silence is the word," whisper conspirators, and for them it is the perfect word. We also are SILENT when we are above gossip. And the SILENCE of the night is for poetry.

Snuffle and **Snivel** Though they can be synonymous, a SNUFFLE is a respectable SNIVEL. Normally, SNUFFLE means to breathe with difficulty through the nose, being a frequentative of 'snuff' or 'sniff.' A SNUFFLER may be annoying, but he probably has a cold. A SNIVELER may have a cold too, but he doesn't use his handkerchief. 'Sniff' and 'snuff' are from active and honorable verbs (Danish and Dutch); but SNIVEL comes from the Anglo-Saxon word for 'mucus.' No wonder we don't like a SNIVELER.

Staccato The sharp clickings of typewriters are STACCATO. So STACCATO or music played STACCATO (the adjective and adverb are identical) is disconnected and abrupt in manner, differing generally from syncopation in having no rhythm. STACCATO tones are sharply emphatic. STACCATO replies or remarks are abruptly positive.

Ululant Possibly the hoot owl gave us this word. 'Ulula' was the Roman word for that creature, imitating its wailing or howling. Today ULULATION is, as it sounds, a 'wailing.' ULULANT is the adjective. "The ululant sound of wind through the fir trees at night is ghostly."

STATEMENTS

ADDRESS *n.* a speech; an informal talk.

AFFIRM *v.* to state; to agree; to assert.

ALLEGATION *n.* an unverified assertion; a formal statement. *v.* ALLEGE, to make an ALLEGATION.

Allege & Assert

ANNOUNCE *v.* to state or assert; to give notice, as "They announced his death in the papers."

ANNUNCIATE *v.* to announce.

Assert see **Allege & Assert**

ASSERTION *n.* a statement; allegation.

Asseverate see **Aver & Asseverate**

Aver & Asseverate

AVOUCH *v.* to assert emphatically; to avow.

COMMENT *n.* an opinion or relevant statement.

DECLARE *v.* to state boldly and openly.

DEPOSITION *n.* an opinion or statement set down, usually in writing, for anyone to examine at any time.

Diction see **Parlance & Diction**

DICTUM *n.* a maxim; dogma.

DISCOURSE *n.* informal talk or conversation; a lecture.

Drawl

Ejaculate

ENUNCIATE *v.* to state something in its last and definite form; to articulate distinctly.

EXPRESSION *n.* a statement, or perhaps only a word, which represents an opinion, feeling, emotion, as an EXPRESSION of grief.

Gabble

Garrulous

Gobbledegook

Grandiloquence

HARANGUE *n.* a ranting speech. *v.* to make a speech in an offensively bold manner.

Import & Purport

LECTURE *n.* a discourse designed especially to instruct, as a professor's LECTURE.

MOUTH *v.* to talk, or say words, esp. in an unnatural or affected manner.

Parlance & Diction

PERORATE *v.* to harangue; to lecture, esp. in a long and monotonous way; to sum up a discourse.

PLATITUDE *n.* a commonplace thought or remark. *adj.* PLATITUDINOUS.

Pontificate

PREDICATE *v.* to state; affirm.

PROFESS *v.* to affirm; avow, as with personal pretension.

PROTEST *n.* a statement against some act or measure. *v.* to make a PROTEST, to assert, esp. against opposition.

Purport see **Import & Purport**

Screed

Sententious

Soliloquy

STATE *n.* to say; allege; affirm.

UTTERANCE *n.* speech.

WARRANT *v.* to state or declare with positiveness.

Allege and **Assert** To ASSERT an opinion, for example, is comparatively easy: you need simply be bold enough to say it. The origin of ASSERT's meaning is to set free a slave or to enslave a free person by declaration, and consequently today to ASSERT something is 'to declare with boldness your intentions.'

But when you ALLEGE something you must take care what you are doing, for, owing to much uncertainty about the word in the past, its purport today is by no means clear. To ALLEGE is less than to ASSERT. "I assert that this man has stolen my watch," means that you probably can, on request, provide strong proof of the man's guilt. "I allege that this man has stolen my watch," means that you strongly suspect the man, but have no substantial proof of his guilt. When we use the word impersonally, or in the passive, "That man is the alleged thief of your watch," the implication that the man is guilty is even less than when the word is used as an active verb. The ALLEGE here is studiously objective, and emphasizes the lack of proof. That the word concerns itself chiefly with misdoings is traceable to certain legalistic beginnings. Like the law itself, it aims to be impartial. But the odd point is, that there are counter forces within it which suggest a certain definite charge or bias such as exists in ASSERT.

Aver and **Asseverate** AVER is from Latin *verus,* 'true.' When you AVER something you state it confidently as a 'fact,' you 'affirm it.' ASSEVERATE is, you might say, the intensive of AVER. The Latin root of it is *severus,* 'serious.' When you ASSEVERATE a truth you 'solemnly AVER' it.

Drawl DRAWL is the frequentative of 'draw.' If you DRAWL in your speech, you 'draw' your words out and out and out. But the essence of its meaning lies in its cause: listlessness, laziness or just habitual deliberation. Time can DRAWL its dreary days along.

Ejaculate 'To speak out spurtingly,' usually a single remark, and with the suddenness of an explosion. The base is Latin *jacere,* 'to throw.' The 'e,' which means 'out,' confines the sense to 'away from' the speaker.

Gabble Like babble, cackle, jabber and gobble, GABBLE is imitative or senseless or discordant sounds in nature. But in common with 'gobble' (and 'jabber' is etymologically a variant of both) it has picked up some sense from old words that relate more specifically than it does to the mouth.

Probably GABBLE began only as a 'gab-gabbing,' as of geese, like 'babble' that began with a baby's 'ba-ba.' But before we had the 'gift of gab' we had the 'gift of gob' (Scotch and Irish for 'mouth,' Gaelic for 'beak'). Sometimes the mouth just hung wide open, and became a 'gape.' There was also the Old French, *gobe,* for a 'mouthful' of food or (disgustingly) of phlegm, which we have inherited with only the loss of one letter. It is possible that that old word gave us our 'gobble,' not the turkey cock's 'gobble,' which is only a sonorous version of his hen's GABBLE, but 'gobble' in the distasteful sense of devouring food greedily and loud. Some even think it gave us the sailor's nickname 'gob,' which others attribute to English imitations of similar-sounding French or Chinese terms for 'sailor.' But 'to *gabben*' in Middle English meant 'to mock,' from another Old French word meaning that, and probably related. Still another old sense of 'gabbing' was 'boasting.'

The result of it all is our own GABBLE of today, still made with the mouth, and as noisy and senseless as a goose's GABBLE. It is an infatuation with one's own words. Or should it be said, with one's own sounds?

Garrulous 'Talkative; long-winded in conversation.' In Latin, it meant 'chattering.'

Gobbledegook A new arrival in dictionaries, which variously spell the penultimate syllable with an 'e,' or an 'i,' or a 'y.' Its origin has been debated to no result. But, in all common sense a turkey gobbler, being pompous, must have had a voice in it. For GOBBLEDEGOOK is writing, or talk, that is obscured by excessive technical terms, long words and clumsy sentences. For example, 'thirty-six calendar months' is GOBBLEDEGOOK for three years, 'in short supply' is GOBBLEDEGOOK for 'scarce.' Government reports and college catalogues are famous for this fault.

Nevertheless, out of GOBBLEDEGOOK we do occasionally get a new short-cut word, squeezed into existence by pressure of all the other words. 'Decontrol' seems valuable, and so does 'disinflation.' The prefix 'dis' carries a suggestion of 'action reversed' or 'undone' (i.e., 'done back again'). Therefore, 'disinflation' suggests something different from 'deflation.'

Grandiloquence Grand 'eloquence.' Grandiose ideas are usually on a grand (big) scale. Grand manners may attempt to be genteel but their sweep is always a little ridiculous. When the grand manner is supported by 'flowery speech' and 'grandiose ideas' you have GRANDILOQUENCE.

Import and **Purport** An exporting and importing firm would undoubtedly say that an IMPORT is important. Certainly it is rhetorically as well as economically. IMPORT and 'IMPORTANCE' can be synonymous. More often IMPORT means 'meaning.' The IMPORT of a long letter may simply be 'yes.' But in usage this sense is usually narrowed and emphasized. The IMPORT of a letter is its significance, its truest meaning, its spiritual message, its intended truth, its most striking implication.

PURPORT can mean the same thing, but it was so softened down in the Old French it can now also mean little more than a 'rumor.' It might be defined as an 'intended and plainly visible IMPORT.' It may be the 'purpose' behind an act. The PURPORT of a play is necessarily important, but it is plain. Sometimes a PURPORT is simply the 'gist' of something. The PURPORT of a long report may be simply that a company is in debt. In this case, it is equivalent to what we add after "In other words, . . ." As a verb it may mean merely 'to profess,' "He purports to be an expert," or to 'rumor,' "He is purported to be an expert." Here 'to PURPORT' is a few pegs less definite than 'to report.'

Parlance and **Diction** PARLANCE is not parlor talk but rather the opposite. It is 'colloquial or conversational DICTION.' DICTION itself, though including common speech, is the formal word for 'expressed language.'

Pontificate 'To PONTIFICATE' means 'to talk like a pope,' but perhaps the Pope is the only living speaker who has the authority to PONTIFICATE. When lesser folk attempt it, their talk is pompous. So if you ever PONTIFICATE on your pet subject, you may be sure you are making yourself a colossal bore.

Screed This is a curious Old English word with a tinge of pedantry and quaintness. But authentically a SCREED is now a piece of emphatic writing of an argumentative type. It may be a 'tirade' or a long ranting speech. The latter usage is less frequent; both usages are strained enough from the original meaning of simply a 'shred.' A shred is a long strip of anything, even of land, or of cloth wrapped around a cap, but especially of something to write a long list on. Plasterers still use wooden or plaster measuring strips called SCREEDS, and the Scots still apply the word to cloth. The idea was always of a strip torn off something to use for some purpose. But now this purpose predominates, and a SCREED is sometimes a 'vitriolic discourse' in which the speaker may think he is arguing but cares more about expounding his own pet phobias. The quaint sound of the word is illusory, since SCREED has little in common with patient 'scribes.'

Sententious This is an adjective that refers to a person habitually given to 'pithy language.' The Latin root is 'opinion,' but today the opinion is usually someone else's, conveyed tersely in axioms or maxims. "'Cleanliness is next to godliness,' the teacher sententiously said to her first-graders."

Soliloquy SOLILOQUIES occur in literature, especially in dramas, where a playwright composes them for a chief character, who is supposed to be dramatically thinking aloud. However, since everybody is free to SOLILOQUIZE, or to talk oratorically to himself, it is well to reflect on the connotations of the word.

SOLILOQUIES are certainly speeches: they are more than monologues, though less in dignity, perhaps, than declamations. They are egotistical; they are the solitary utterances of the ego itself, under some kind of stress. When Hamlet SOLILOQUIZES, for example, he believes himself completely alone. But of course the audience listens, or else there wouldn't be a play.

SOLILOQUY comes from St. Augustine, who made it up from Late Latin *soliloquium,* comprising *solus* for 'alone,' and *loqui,* 'to speak,' and meaning literally 'to talk to one's self.'

TALK AGAINST

Admonition & Admonishment
Admonishment   see **Admonition & Admonishment**
Animadversion
Badgering   see **Badinage & Badgering**

Badinage & Badgering
BANTER   *n.* light ridicule; chaff. *v.* to poke fun at; to joke lightly.
Captious & Carping
Carping   see **Captious & Carping**
CAVIL   *v.* to bring up unimportant

objections; to harass by carping. *adj.* CAVILING.

CENSORIOUS *adj.* faultfinding; severe.

CHAFF *n.* banter; jesting talk; teasing. *v.* to tease or lightly ridicule.

CHIDE *v.* to scold; to reprimand lightly.

CONFUTE *v.* to reduce to nothing by superior argument; to refute; to confuse.

Contemn

CONTRADICT *v.* to assert the opposite.

CONTROVERSIAL *adj.* pertaining to argument or controversy; open to question; polemical.

CONTROVERT *v.* to contradict; to refute or oppose an argument.

CRITICIZE *v.* to find fault with.

Denounce

DENY *v.* to contradict; to say that something is not true.

DERIDE *v.* to chaff; mock; laugh at; scorn.

DISPROVE *v.* to disagree with; to refute. An earlier meaning was to disapprove or find fault with.

ERISTIC *adj.* pertaining to arguments. From the Greek word for strife.

FLEER *v.* to laugh or sneer at; to deride.

GAINSAY *v.* to deny; dispute; contradict.

FLOUT see the category ANGER.

GIBE *v.* to rail; sneer; scoff; esp. in the sense of sarcastic name-calling.

IMPUGN *v.* to question or call something false.

Invective see **Inveighing & Invective**

Inveighing & Invective

JEER *v.* to gibe; to scoff.

JIBE see GIBE

MOCK *v.* to jeer; to make fun of, usually in a sarcastic, taunting way.

Persiflage

Polemic & Polemical

Polemical see **Polemic & Polemical**

QUIZ *v.* to worry or pester; to chaff.

RAILLERY *n.* bitter or sarcastic taunting; heavy ridicule; sometimes also good-humored banter.

RALLY *n.* to banter; scoff.

Rasp

REBUKE *v.* to reprimand severely.

Rebuff

Rebut

REFUTE *v.* to destroy or nullify an argument, as "I refuted all the reasons she advanced for not marrying me."

REPRIMAND *v.* to scold sharply; to score someone's mistakes; to blame someone sharply for his errors.

REPROVE *v.* to reprimand.

RIDICULE *v.* to cast sarcasm upon; to mock; to laugh at.

SCOFF *v.* to ridicule.

SNEER *v.* to laugh with contempt or scorn.

Taunt

Admonition and **Admonishment** Basically, both words mean an 'advising.' Without the *ad*, 'to' they would still mean an 'advising' because this prefix simply emphasizes 'before.' It is advice given, like a tip-off, 'before' something unpleasant happens. This advice is a timely warning or a reproof.

The words suggest conscientious, if not kindly, counsel. For this reason, probably, they are not much used with respect to awful things. ADMONISHMENT, the longer word, is the lighter. An ADMONISHMENT may be a single word or a phrase, but an ADMONITION could be quite a speech.

Animadversion If you 'advert *to*' something, you turn your mind to it, perhaps you talk about it. When you 'ANIMADVERT *upon*' something you do almost the same at more length. But in this case your mind criticizes, even censures, whatever has engaged its attention, and then you definitely express your criticism. "His animadversions upon the subject were so clearly biased that I blushed for his lack of intelligence." ANIMADVERSIONS are always an 'unfavorable' comment; but the intransitive verb used with 'on' or 'upon' may mean as little as 'to remark upon' something. "He animadverted for a while on the beauty of the sunset."

The word is slightly distorted. *Animus* in Latin means in general 'the mind.' But it also means 'the intent of the mind,' 'the animating purpose and spirit,' 'the temper.' Hence to the Romans it meant 'courage' and, with a little shift, 'hostile courage,' whence our word 'animosity.' In our word 'animus' we have also kept its original connotation of 'hostility' or 'enmity.'

Badinage and **Badgering** BADINAGE is 'banter' or 'playful raillery.' BADINAGE borders on BADGERING, which is 'baiting' or 'persecuting' in a pestering way. It is a polite heckling, while BADGERING may go beyond heckling to the throwing of rotten eggs. BADINAGE comes from an Old French word for a 'joker,' with antecedents in Provençal and, before that, in vulgar Latin, where it meant merely 'to gape,' *batere*. Our word 'to bay,' like a hound, has the same origin. BADGER comes, apparently, from the cruel sport of 'badger-baiting.'

BADINAGE, like 'persiflage' and 'banter,' is a happy word, and its keynote is good humor. There may be a touch of 'taunting' in it but its lightness suggests delicacy rather than frivolity or flippancy. But BADGER is an unhappy word, like 'scoff, deride and rail.' People who BADGER other people take a malicious pleasure in their cruelty. See PERSIFLAGE.

Captious and **Carping** A CAPTIOUS person is the opposite of an 'appreciative' person. He isn't looking for the good in anything. He always complains of the faults he finds. The point about a CAPTIOUS person is that he always goes out of his way to catch you in a fault or to trap you in a mistake. "He always asks me captious questions, knowing I will embarrass myself by answering wrongly."

The CARPING person is congenitally an extrovert. Among the hardy, ancient Icelanders he was a 'boaster.' Apparently, he degenerated into a 'barker.' Nowadays he barks at everything you say, to shut you up or just to nag you. He is a crude, unreasonable 'faultfinder.'

Contemn A useful but little used verb, companion to the noun 'contempt.' Some of contempt's intensity is lost when you use this unfamiliar and bookish verb, but it takes on connotations from its assonance with 'condemn.' If you CONTEMN someone's actions, you 'scorn' or 'despise' them. "A brave man contemns death."

Denounce If you want to show someone you disapprove his actions, you 'reprove' him. If you are angry and speak bluntly, you 'rebuke' him. If you reprove him with serious indignation and on moral grounds, or from a sense of personal injury or grievous regret, you 'reproach' him. If you scold him, you 'reprehend' him. If you rebuke him threateningly and authoritatively, you 'reprimand' him. You *don't* 'reprove,' 'rebuke,' 'reproach,' 'reprehend' or 'reprimand' the acts themselves but only the persons who perform them. But DENOUNCE is a more embracive word. You can DENOUNCE 'acts' as well as 'persons,' provided you utterly disapprove them. DENOUNCE means literally 'to announce-down, decry.' But it is a strong word, and sometimes a bitter one. If you DENOUNCE a friend, you repudiate him, you abrogate a friendship. And you do it directly to him, openly and positively.

Inveighing and **Invective** When you are in trouble you may INVEIGH against the fates that oppress you. Always you INVEIGH *against* something, and that shows you the character of the word. When you are 'against' something you do not merely resist or disapprove it. You 'deny' or 'dispute' it. When you do so with real vigor you INVEIGH against the thing. INVEIGHING is almost INVECTIVE. Both words probably come from the Latin one for 'scolding,' though INVECTIVE by-passed the sound-softening Old French. INVECTIVE is a very violent 'denunciation' or 'accusation,' usually accompanied by profanity.

Persiflage A French word meaning light talk or writing in an airy or flippant manner. It is an effeminate version of 'repartee.' It was compounded from *per,* 'through' plus *siffler,* 'hiss, whistle.' PERSIFLAGE is sometimes slightly derisive, like 'banter.'

Polemic or **Polemical**   From a Greek word for 'war,' only the war is now a battle of words. Controversial writers are POLEMICAL. So are both parties in a dispute.

Rasp   In the Old High German RASP meant 'to scrape together.' But in the Old French the word lost its sense of two things RASPING each other, and assumed the meaning of one thing, presumably rough, scraping against a second thing, presumably smooth. "Her argumentative manner rasps his placid nature."

Rebuff   REBUFF is a blunt word. When you REBUFF someone you 'repel' his advances or 'reject' his proposals suddenly and almost with violence. "I felt rebuffed by his hostile tones." Also the fox when he doubles back REBUFFS the hounds that come suddenly to the end of a trail, and are 'thrown back,' as it were, on their haunches.

REBUFF comes from the Old French and the Italian for 'a chiding or checking.' But the word may go beyond itself and indicate a 'counterattack,' 'a driving or beating back,' and consequently a 'defeating.' An army that is REBUFFED may in varying circumstances be checked, routed or defeated. Somewhat in this same sense a REBUFF can be a 'retort.' Milton spoke of the loud REBUFF of a cloud, presumably meaning a blast of thunder, a repercussion. But commonly a REBUFF is a curt and usually a rude 'repulse,' especially to anyone asking you a favor or trying to sell you something. "I was rebuffed in my advances by a slap on the face." This is an especially good word for you to know and use often.

Rebut   REBUT is a short way of saying 'to make a rebuttal.' REBUT is both transitive and intransitive. You can REBUT an argument, or you can just REBUT. In either case, you talk back with the purpose of 'refuting.' It is a good word to remember because it has more force in its sound than its synonym 'refute.' One of the meanings of 'butt' is a sudden 'push or blow,' such as a goat gives you when he 'butts' you with lowered head.

Taunt   TAUNTS are favorite gibes bullies use to provoke a fight. They differ from 'jeers' and 'scoffs' in their ability to provoke hostilities. Consequently, an upright man may at times TAUNT a bigger adversary in order to settle things once and for all. Thus, sometimes TAUNT is defiant, but more often it is just ignoble. Usually TAUNTS are 'insolent dares.'

Though perhaps born in the same Roman cradle as our word 'tempt,' TAUNT has carried tempting to the extreme point of 'provocation.' The first 'tempting' was a tentative effort to determine merit or strength, but TAUNT's 'tempting' is a downright baiting. Sarcastic insults, mockery and contempt are the property of TAUNT.

Literally, TAUNT is a 'paying back.' It is commonly supposed to have come from the French phrase *tant pour tant*, equivalent to our 'tit-for-tat.' The *tant* (also spelled *taunt*) was from Latin *tantum*, 'so much, this much, this great, etc.' But another Old French word undoubtedly influenced TAUNT. It was *tanter*, a variant of *tenter*; and *tenter* traces back to the Latin original of our word 'tempt.' This combination gives us a 'tempting' and 'testing,' which leads inevitably to suspicion, faults, displeasure and reproach. By the early seventeenth century the French word had come to mean not only 'to tempt,' but also 'to try,' 'to prove,' 'to suggest,' and 'to excite to evil.' Meanwhile, in the English Shakespeare's 'taunt my faults,' or 'cast them in my teeth,' 'censure me scornfully with them,' is surely different from *tant pour tant*. Other old meanings, some persisting in dialect, bear out this fusion: to 'answer back' banteringly, to 'quip' or to 'tease'; to 'dare,' to 'tempt' another, or to 'rebuke' or 'scold' him.

TIME

Age see **Eon, Era,** etc.

AGO *adj.* & *adv.* in the past.

ANCIENT *adj.* very old; aged.

Anile see **Senile & Anile**

Antecedents

ANTEDILUVIAN *adj.* before the flood; ancient.

ANTIQUE *adj.* old; in an outdated style.

Archaic see **Obsolete, Archaic,** etc.

Atavism

BEFORE *adv.* previously; at an earlier point in time.

BYGONE *adj.* in the past; referring to times past, as BYGONE ages.

Coeval see **Simultaneous, Concurrent,** etc.

Contemporary see **Simultaneous, Concurrent,** etc.

Concurrent see **Simultaneous, Concurrent,** etc.

CYCLE *n.* a recurring period of time, like a week, month, year, as in an annual CYCLE.

Date

EARLY *adv.* near the beginning, as of the day, month or history.

EOLITHIC *adj.* pertaining to the earliest stone age.

Eon, Era, Age & Epoch

Epoch see **Eon, Era,** etc.

Era see **Eon, Era,** etc.

GENERATION *n.* cycle; esp. a stage in genealogical history, as brothers, sisters and cousins belong to one generation, while parents, aunts and uncles belong to another.

HITHERTO *adv.* up till now, as "Hitherto his bark has been worse than his bite, but be careful!"

IMMEMORIAL *adj.* going beyond memory, as from times IMMEMORIAL.

JUVENILE *adj.* pertaining to youth.

LATE *adj.* the opposite of early; occurring near the end.

LONGEVITY *n.* length of life.

Medieval

MINOR *adj.* under legal age; in English public school usage, lesser in age or school standing (of two boys with the same surname).

Modern

Obsolescent see **Obsolete, Archaic,** etc.

Obsolete, Archaic, Obsolescent & Rare

OLD *adj.* ancient; pertaining to things in time past; advanced in years.

PAST *adj.* pertaining to time gone by.

Posterity

PREVIOUS *adj.* coming or occurring before, as PREVIOUS weeks, PREVIOUS times.

PRIMEVAL *adj.* of or pertaining to the earliest or very first ages; hence, primitive.

Rare see **Obsolete, Archaic,** etc.

RECENT *adj.* close to the present, as RECENT days.

Reminiscent

Retroactive

Retrospective

SCIATHERIC *adj.* pertaining to a sundial.

Senile & Anile

Simultaneous, Concurrent, Contemporary & Coeval

Sometime

SUPERANNUATED *adj.* old; out-of-date.

Time

ANNUAL *adj.* yearly.

ANTEDILUVIAN *adj.* primitively ancient or out-of-date. Literally, it refers to times before the Flood.

ANTEMERIDIAN *adj.* before noon; hence (*n.*), the morning. It is abbreviated: A.M.

AUTUMNAL *adj.* of or pertaining to fall.

CENTURY *n.* one hundred years. *adj.* CENTURIAL.

DAY *n.* twenty-four hours. *adjs.* DAILY and DIURNAL.

DECADE *n.* ten years. *adj.* DECADAL.

EONIAN *adj.* pertaining to eon, which is sometimes used to suggest eternity.

ERAL *adj.* pertaining to era.

ESTIVAL *adj.* pertaining to summer or appropriate to it.

HEBDOMADAL *adj.* weekly.

HIEMAL, HIBERNAL or BRUMAL *adjs.* pertaining to winter.

HODIERNAL   *adj.* of the present day.

HOUR   *n.* sixty minutes. *adj.* HORAL.

MATINAL   *adj.* of or pertaining to matins or to the morning.

MATUTINAL   *adj.* of or pertaining to the morning.

MENSAL   *adj.* pertaining to month. This adjective can also mean once a month, as MENSTRUAL means recurring monthly.

MERIDIAN   *n.* noon; *adj.* of or pertaining to noon.

MILLENNIUM   *n.* a thousand years. Used also to mean an indeterminate long time.

MINUTE   *n.* sixty seconds; a very short time; *adj.* prepared in a very short time.

MOMENT   *n.* any very short period of time, such as a portion of a minute.

MONTH   *n.* about thirty days; one-twelfth of the year.

NEOTERIC   *adj.* pertaining to the present time; modern.

NOCTURNAL   *adj.* pertaining to the night.

PASCHAL   *adj.* pertaining to Passover, or Easter.

POSTMERIDIAN   *adj.* after noon; hence (*n.*), the afternoon. It is abbreviated: P.M.

QUARTER   *n.* three months.

SABBATICAL   *adj.* pertaining to Sunday; also to a seventh year, often a year of rest or study granted to college professors. Among the ancient Jews, the seventh year was for resting, and for the enriching of the soil by letting it lie fallow.

SECOND   *n.* the sixtieth part of a minute; any small unit of time; a moment or instant.

SECULAR   *adj.* pertaining to a generation or a long time. Hence, the opposite of PERIODIC. In the ecclesiastical sense it refers to life on earth and to the laity—not to Heaven and the clergy.

SEMESTER   *n.* six months; or, one of the two periods of about eighteen weeks into which the academic year is divided.

VERNAL   *adj.* pertaining to spring.

VESPER   *adj.* pertaining to evening or to vespers.

VESPERIAN   *adj.* pertaining to evening or to the evening star.

WEEK   *n.* seven days.

YEAR   *n.* twelve months, or about 365 days.

Today
Tradition

Age   A mite of a word that does our bidding in so many ways. In fact, it seems to refer to about any number of years you want it to.

You are not of AGE until you have lived about eighteen years. But, "My dear, I haven't seen you for an age!" means that I haven't seen you for a long time, possibly six months. On the other hand, your whole life is your AGE, but when you are AGED, it is only the latter part of your adult life that counts. A century is also an AGE. Any large or distinct part of history is an AGE, especially of the earth's history. You AGE when you grow old, and liquor AGES merely when it matures.

The rudiments of this little word, which never until modern times had less than two syllables, and sometimes had four, go back beyond the Greeks and the Goths to that ancient Aryan tongue which is the parent of most European languages. Invariably these rudiments connoted 'life' itself, and then some 'period' of life.

Antecedents The things that happen 'before' are ANTECEDENTS, from *ante*, 'before,' not *anti*, 'against.' Commonly they are the things that happened in someone's life 'before' you knew him, or in your own life 'before' someone knew you. They form a background, but backgrounds can move along as you advance. In a novel, they follow you as you read. They are the threads your hindsight carries along to interpret what is occurring next. They are ANTECEDENT (the adjective is also useful), but they are paradoxically a progressive accumulation of results.

Less commonly the noun ANTECEDENT is a figurative synonym for 'ancestor.' In grammar an ANTECEDENT is the thing that a relative pronoun refers to: "The glory that was Greece . . . ," 'glory' is the ANTECEDENT of 'that.'

Atavism From Latin *avus*, 'grandfather,' this word means a 'return to ancestral types.' For example, if your next door neighbor beats his wife continually, his brutality probably is an ATAVISM, or a recurrence in modern times of ancient animalistic behavior. But, of course, it is difficult to define what is primitive behavior and what is modern behavior, so ATAVISM is better illustrated by a scientific example. It is possible to breed animals in such a selective way that a primitive type reappears. This is an ATAVISM. It is very interesting that sometimes a child will have traits, such as a manner of walking, which is inherited from a grandfather but which did not appear in either parent. This also is an ATAVISM.

Date With equal facility we can DATE a letter or DATE a girl. When we DATE a letter, we are noting on it the day, month, and year; but when we DATE a girl, though it may be a memorable day, we're simply taking her out, or, more simply, entertaining her. In these two examples DATE is used as a verb, but usually it is a noun. For example, the girl becomes the man's DATE, and her escort becomes her DATE; both enjoy their DATE. Now a DATER meets a DATEE, who is also called a 'meetee.' In her mother's girlhood, the participle DATED currently possessed a modified meaning of *passé*, or 'out-of-date.' For example, a play was said to be, and still is, DATED when it is no longer modern.

Gone is the official austerity of a DATE from Latin *dare*, 'to give': '*Datum Romae*' and the day, which means, 'given at Rome on this day.' At last the word is 'up-to-date,' though it is to centuries of plodding bookkeepers that we owe thanks for this cliché 'up-to-date.'

Eon, Era, Age and **Epoch** An EON is an incalculable period of time, an AGE without known beginning or end, sometimes an eternity. An ERA is more definite. It is a long period, but it has a starting point called an EPOCH, which in Greek meant a 'stopping-place,' or 'check-mark.' Commonly, ERAS and EPOCHS are synonymous, one or the other used according to custom. We usually speak of the Christian ERA and, conversely, of the EPOCHS which comprise geological time. EPOCHS of modern times are generally determined by the 'advent' of a new order, like the Reformation or the invention of the steam engine. AGES, in a stricter sense, are arbitrary periods set off by exact dates. The AGE of Pericles would extend from the day he was born, if it were known, until 429 B.C., when he supposedly died.

Medieval Literally, in the Latin, MEDIEVAL means 'of the middle age.' Hence it is an adjective referring, ever since it was coined in the nineteenth century, to the so-called Middle Ages, extending approximately from the fifth to the sixteenth centuries A.D. Figuratively, it refers to anything old fashioned. "Why don't you buy a new car? Yours is medieval!"

But don't confuse the 'middle' in MEDIEVAL with the one in Middle English, which is the English of only the last three and one-half centuries of the Middle Ages. Nor is the MEDIEVAL age simply the Dark Ages. The Dark Ages cover the earlier part of the Middle Ages from the downfall of Rome to little past the beginning of Chaucer's Middle English. Chaucer died in 1400, but his era was from about 1150 to about 1500. The Dark Ages thus include the period of Old English or Anglo-Saxon (from the fifth century to about 1150), and extend on to about 1200.

Modern   When the Romans wanted to say something had happened just a while ago or just now, they said it happened *modo,* with the same brevity with which we now say something happened 'pronto.' And after the lapse of some twenty centuries their word is still with us in our MODERN. MODERN fashions are things that are in fashion 'just now,' or 'just a while ago.' There is, therefore, more immediacy in the word than we often realize.

Obsolete, Archaic or Obsolescent, and Rare   A word is OBSOLETE when it is no longer used, like 'brenne' or 'bryn' ('to burn'). Meanings also become OBSOLETE though the words live on; 'sly' once meant 'skilled.' Objects, ideas, and practices become OBSOLETE.

Everything is born with the seeds of OBSOLESCENCE in it. Everything grows old and eventually is discarded. When a word or custom is on the way out, it is OBSOLESCENT. Customarily, we call OBSOLESCENT words ARCHAIC. However, a word on the way back (and very few ever succeed in coming back, in a popular sense) is also ARCHAIC. An ARCHAIC word has become OBSOLETE, and then been rescued momentarily by perhaps a handful of reputable writers or speakers who have fetched it up from oblivion.

When a word has never enjoyed popularity, so far as we know, and occurs only sporadically in print, the dictionaries say that it is RARE. Sometimes RARE words include provincial and dialectal words which seldom get into print except in regional writing.

Etymologically, OBSOLETE and ARCHAIC differ radically from each other. ARCHAIC is Greek for 'the beginning,' from which we have inferred the old, the antiquated, that which belongs to an earlier era. On the other hand, there is no hope for life in OBSOLETE, for it is etymologically not only the end, but 'a dead-end.'

Posterity   POSTERITY is literally that which is 'posterior' or 'behind,' like a postern gate. But we have made it a collective noun referring to succeeding generations of persons. Usually POSTERITY is the whole of the conceivable future, as ancestry is that other part of *all* the progenitor's descendants down to the present.

Reminiscent   REMINISCENT is a 'musing back over,' as when with a friend you recollect the past, and discuss the good old days. Often REMINISCENCE occurs in revery, or dreaming, when you conjure the happier days of your youth. REMINISCENT is the adjective. "When he was an old man he moved to a little country village that was reminiscent of his boyhood home."

Retroactive This word means 'acting back over,' in the sense that certain forces or influences in the present and the future can still have an effect in the past. Certain laws, for example, are made RETROACTIVE so that they 'reach back' in their effect to a date before they were enacted. It is an adjective.

Retrospective This adjective refers to a 'looking back over.' For example, a RETROSPECTIVE show in an art gallery is one that takes you back over some portion of the past.

Senile and **Anile** Respectively, 'old-mannish' and 'old-womanish.' The words refer especially to the kind of infirm childishness that very old people often display. SENILE is often used to refer to 'old women' as well as 'old men.' Sometimes SENILE simply suggests any characteristic of old age. "That baby looks quite senile: no teeth, no hair on its head, and all wrinkled in the face."

Simultaneous, Concurrent, Contemporary and **Coeval** Two boxers may both land blows SIMULTANEOUSLY ('at the same instant'). Peace may reign in one country while in another war reigns CONCURRENTLY ('at the same time'). The Italian Renaissance was COEVAL ('occurring in the same age') with the opulent Chinese civilization discovered by Marco Polo. Notice, however, that COEVAL refers not to a 'period' but to an 'age,' usually a remote one. Things existing in the same period are CONTEMPORARY (usually the 'modern period'), just as people living in the same house are 'cohabitant.' Things, or people, living together (and necessarily at the same time) are 'coexistent,' or CONTEMPORARIES.

Sometime Note that this is not 'sometimes.' SOMETIME means 'once' or 'formerly.' "The sometime champion of the links," means champion for a time in the past.

Time At the outset, TIME was eclectic, denoting chiefly the 'apt' or 'best' TIME for doing something, much as we speak now of a 'wonderful time' or of the 'proper (exact) time' for planting beans. Such phrases as the 'nick of time' or 'in good times,' have this same sense of a propitious moment. The general word for TIME was then 'tide,' which lingers in 'Yuletide,' 'tidings' and 'tidy,' which earlier meant 'timely' or 'seasonable.'

It is interesting that the penological slang, 'the big stretch,' which means a 'long TIME' to serve in prison, preserves the earliest sense-core of TIME. The root *ti* means 'to stretch.'

Of course, now TIME can refer to any length of existence, a moment, hour, day, month, year, etc. It also can be bad as well as good. The word has so many uses you have to leave it to the context to define the exact meaning.

Today It is a fact that so far as strict grammar is concerned, we need not use TODAY in the sense of 'of TODAY' and 'as of TODAY' as often as we do. Actually the tense of the verb is usually enough.

"People think cleanliness is very important," is enough unless you want to infer that in the old days people did not think cleanliness is important. Then you say, "Today people think . . . ," which sets up a contrast between the present and the past. It is just these emphases in speech that strict grammar doesn't pay any attention to, so to be repetitious, let us admit, is often helpful. Note that TODAY is now spelled without a hyphen.

Tradition Etymologically, TRADITION is 'treason' that has redeemed itself. The two words were one word in the Latin, meaning most often 'treason,' in the sense of 'treacherous betrayal.' Literally, the prototype word meant a 'handing over,' like handing someone, even a friend, over to the authorities. But it also had the meaning of 'handing down,' so that when the word was absorbed later into English it took on the sense of things 'bequeathed' from generation to generation. In France, the word kept its sense of 'betrayal,' eventually giving us 'treason.'

TRADITION has practically no derogatory usages now. Its literal meaning of a 'handing down' or a 'handing across' suggests now the transmission of knowledge, opinions, beliefs, customs, practices and even information from one age to another, originally by word of mouth. Hence, TRADITION includes any segment of this heritage, like the traditions of New England or of Yale. Sometimes the TRADITION may be very specific, like the hazing of students, or the rendition of 'mama' with an 'r' (mommer).

TITLES OF RANK

ARCHDUKE *n.* a prince of the Austrian royalty.

BARON *n.* a member of the lowest grade in the English peerage; a nobleman of similar rank on the Continent or in Japan.

BARONET *n.* a member of a British hereditary order, next in rank below a baron and above a knight.

BEGUM *n.* in India, a Moslem lady of high rank.

CALIPH *n.* a successor (originally of Mohammed). The title has been adopted by many rulers in Moslem countries.

CAVALIER *n.* a knight; a courtier of Charles I of England, hence, a Royalist in distinction to a Roundhead.

CHEVALIER *n.* a member of the lowest rank in the French nobility; a member of certain honorary orders; in general, a knight.

COUNT *n.* a Continental nobleman, corresponding to an earl in the English peerage.

COUNTESS *n.* the wife or widow of an English earl; the wife of a count; a woman who enjoys in her own right the rank of a count.

CZAR *n.* a king, as the CZAR of Russia. Also spelled TZAR, TSAR.

CZAREVNA or TSAREVNA *n.* a daughter of a Czar of Russia.

CZARINA or TSARINA *n.* the wife of a czar.

DAME *n.* an English woman of title, corresponding to a knight.

DOGE *n.* the chief magistrate of the old republics of Genoa and Venice.

Don see **Grandee & Don**

DOWAGER *n.* in England a widow holding a title or substantial property from her marriage.

DUCHESS *n.* the wife or widow of a duke; a woman who holds in her own right the rank of a duke.

DUKE *n.* a nobleman of high hereditary rank, in England of the highest rank below a prince. DUCHY is the domain of a DUKE or duchess. *adj.* DUCAL refers to either DUKE or DUCHY.

EARL *n.* in England, a nobleman corresponding to a count on the Continent and ranking next below a marquis and above a viscount.

EMIR *n.* an Arabian chieftain or prince (the title of the descendants of Mohammed's daughter, Fatima).

EMPEROR *n.* the king of an empire.

EMPRESS *n.* an emperor's wife; the queen of an empire.

Equerry

GENTLEMAN *n.* a well-born man, ranking above a yeoman; today, any well-bred man.

GRAND DUKE *n.* a sovereign Continental duke, ranking just below a king.

Grandee & Don

HIDALGO *n.* A spanish lower-grade nobleman.

IMAM *n.* a Moslem chief, esp. a religious leader.

INFANTA *n.* a daughter of a Spanish or Portuguese king.

KAISER *n.* an emperor.

KING *n.* a male monarch or sovereign.

KNIGHT *n.* a man of special military and chivalrous rank; a man holding a rank of special honor.

Kulak see **Moujik & Kulak**

LADY *n.* a woman of title, corresponding to a Lord; the wife of any member of the English peerage.

LORD *n.* a titled nobleman.

Madam

MANDARIN *n.* a public official in the Chinese empire.

MARCHIONESS *n.* a wife or widow of a marquis. Also spelled MARQUISE.

MARQUIS *n.* in England and France a nobleman just below a duke and above an earl in rank.

MIKADO *n.* the emperor of Japan.

MIRZA *n.* in Persia, a royal prince or one so-called as a title of honor.

Moujik & **Kulak**

Mullah

NOBLE *n.* a person of high rank; a peer.

NOMINAL *adj.* pertaining to name, title; also, existing only in name, and hence, by implication, not real, unimportant.

PASHA *n.* in former times, an officer of high rank in Turkey. The title was an honorary one and placed after the name.

Paladin

PATRICIAN *n.* a noble or aristocrat.

PATROON *n.* a Dutch manor owner in Colonial New York.

PEER *n.* a nobleman; in England, one of the five ranks of nobility: duke, marquis, earl, viscount and baron.

PEERESS *n.* the wife of a peer; a woman who holds her own title in the peerage.

Pendragon

PRINCE *n.* a male member of the highest rank of nobility; also a male member of royalty, as the King of England's first son is the PRINCE of Wales.

PRINCESS *n.* a female member of a royal family; a woman holding the rank of Prince.

Rani

REGAL *adj.* kingly.

REGINAL *adj.* queenly.

Sahib

SAYID *n.* a Moslem lord or prince. The title is applied to descendants of Mohammed.

SEIGNIORIAL *adj.* pertaining to the lord of the manor. Often spelled SEIGNORIAL.

SHEIK *n.* an Arab elder or chief.

SIGNOR *n.* an Italian lord or gentleman.

SOVEREIGN *n.* a monarch.

SQUIRE *n.* an Englishman of a rank just below knight and above gentleman.

SULTAN *n.* a ruler, esp. in a Moslem state.

SULTANA *n.* a close female relative of a sultan.

TITULAR *adj.* pertaining to title.

Veep

VICEREGAL *adj.* pertaining to viceroy, a person appointed, usually by a king, to rule a country or territory.

VISCOUNT *n.* an English nobleman whose rank is just below that of an earl and above that of a baron.

Yeoman

Equerry   In royal households an EQUERRY is any officer in the department of the Master of the Horse. He has considerable prestige and is close to the sovereign or his son.

Grandee and **Don**   A GRANDEE is a 'Spanish nobleman'; the 'grand' means 'great.' A DON in Spain is simply a 'gentleman,' as a 'donna' is a 'lady.' In England a DON is a college dignitary or instructor.

Madam   A maligned word, being so often cheapened to 'ma'am,' and even chopped down to " 'm," though intrinsically it means 'My Lady.' It once was applied most especially to queens, having originally been the feminine form, *domina,* of Latin *dominus,* for 'lord.' There are still times when MADAM, spoken not by a hurried clerk but by a very earnest gentleman, rings true because of the formality of the occasion or of the underlying respect which the word implies.

Moujik and **Kulak**   Both these words are Russian. MOUJIK at first were just 'men,' or sometimes 'husbands,' but now the word means 'peasant.' KULAKS were just 'peasants,' but now they are rich, or comparatively rich, peasants. Today KULAKS are regarded by the Communists as 'politically uncooperative peasants,' but MOUJIKS are considered compliant. KULAK was a Tatar word meaning a 'fist,' and it was applied at first, in Russia, to peasants who exploited their poorer neighbors. They were probably both hard-fisted and close-fisted. But MOUJIK (or *muzhik,* in the Russian) is a broader word. It is ultimately cognate with 'male,' and was a diminutive of the Russian word *muzh,* 'man.' It was quoted in England in Shakespeare's time as *mousik, mowsike* and *musick.* Spelling was then erratic enough with English words, but it ran riot with foreign ones.

Mullah   MULLAHS sound soft and mild; but they are to be reckoned with, not only by the millions whom they teach and judge in Moslem countries, but by everyone who deals with those countries. The word goes back to the Arabic, where some say it meant a 'judge' and some a 'teacher.' It is said to have expressed originally a certain legal bond connecting slave-owners with the slaves whom they had freed. What that bond may have consisted of is important today only in its implications, for the MULLAHS possess an extraordinary influence over people. The MULLAHS are Islam's learned men, those who are experts in the sacred laws and dogmas. In recent history they have at times exercised an influence over populaces comparable to that of kings. The Mad

Mullah of Swat led the frontier uprising in India in the 1890's, and another Mad Mullah followed suit in Somaliland. Yet in India the term is sometimes applied to humble Moslem school teachers. MULLAH is a title of respect not only for the most exalted, but also for learning itself, especially sacred learning. An understanding of this may clarify modern history. Only recently there appeared a headline in the news: 'Mullah Warns U.S. to Quit Iran Influence.'

Paladin Any one of the twelve peers of Charlemagne was a PALADIN. Hence a PALADIN in Chaucer's language was a "parfit gentil" knight. Today he is a noble and fearless man.

Pendragon Welsh for 'head leader.' In early Briton, a PENDRAGON was appointed in times of dire danger. Two legendary British kings were also named PENDRAGON. They were brothers, and one of them sired King Arthur. His first name was Uther.

Rani In India and the Malayan peninsula a RANI is a queen, princess or rajah's consort.

Sahib Like *effendi* in the Near East, *tuan* in the Dutch East Indies and *baas* (whence our 'boss') in South Africa, SAHIB is a title of respect in India. But it is not exactly an empty or general title. In its original Arabic it meant first a 'friend' or 'companion' but then a 'lord' or 'master.' So, as used by Hindus in speaking to white men, it meant 'lord' or 'master' or, at least, 'gentleman,' 'sir' or 'mister.' And to the Englishman in the Indian services it meant commonly himself, that is, a white man, with all the distinctions belonging to that term in those lands.

Veep In case anyone doesn't know and can't guess, a VEEP is a 'vice-president.' We used to be content with simply saying the initials: the Grand Old Party (the Republican) is the G.O.P., the Grand Army of the Republic, recently disbanded by the death of its last remaining member, is the G.A.R., and S.R.O. is Standing Room Only. But now, perhaps to save time, we like to say a short word. Since there is no available initial vowel in vice-president, we spelled out only the 'V.' Perhaps this is intelligent, since the 'vice,' practically meaning 'assistant,' is colloquially more significant in 'vice-president' than is the word 'president.' Actually, the 'vice' means 'substitute' (literally, 'in the place of'), while in Roman times a president, *praesidis,* not only 'sat before' a meeting but also was a guardian, defender and protector.

VIP has also arrived among us within the last decade. It conforms to the modern structural pattern. It stands for Very Important Person.

Yeoman   This word is as British as beefsteaks and yoicks, and connotes traditional English stalwartness and honest service. In our own minds, YEOMAN is tinged with the menial and the plebeian, even in the Navy where, incidentally, the usage is a derived one. As a term in English history YEOMAN progressively designated various ranks and occupations, principally on land. The first YEOMAN was a subordinate or attendant, and became through service, chiefly military, a small landowner in his own right, comparable on a reduced scale to a squire. But in the main, from the Middle Ages onward, he composed that great middle class of England which had no counterpart on the mainland, the European peasant submitting *en masse* to feudal slavery. Thus through the ages, from the long bows of Chaucer's time to the indomitable industry of recent days, he has been a backbone of England, representing an honest union of loyalty and independence.

When knighthood was in flower the YEOMAN ranked just above the knave or common fighting man and just below the squire, who attended the knight. But there were YEOMEN in many services, including the households of nobles. Hangmen's assistants were once waggishly called 'yeomen of the cord,' as Henry the Seventh's 'Yeomen of the Guard' are now colloquially called Beefeaters. These Beefeaters are the only YEOMEN left in the Queen's personal service.

The source of the word is in some doubt. The first syllable may suggest 'youth,' or it may indicate 'locality' or 'land.' There is supposed to have been an Anglo-Saxon word *gea-mann,* of which no record remains, though *gea* occurs as a final element in place names. Across the Channel in the Low Countries there was a word *gaman,* meaning a 'villager.' German *gau,* also in place names, is cognate, and means 'region.' Yet Danish *yong* and Anglo-Saxon *geng* suggests 'young' for the 'yeo.' In Elizabethan England YEOMEN could be a synonym for French *valet,* or 'junior vassal,' though the equation may have depended merely on the sense of secondary. As for today's odd spelling, that was a poor attempt to include both Chaucerian spellings, 'yemen' and 'yoman.'

TRAVEL

AIRCRAFT *n.* any airplane or dirigible.

AMPHIBIAN *n.* an airplane which can land on water as well as land.

BICYCLE *n.* any two-wheeled vehicle which is propelled by pushing pedals with the feet.

BIPLANE *n.* an airplane with two sets of wings, one above the other.

CANOE *n.* a small narrow boat, propelled by paddles.

CARRIAGE *n.* any vehicle on wheels used to carry people or goods; esp. such a vehicle drawn by horses.

CLIPPER *n.* a sailing ship, with a slim hull and many sails.

COACH *n.* a carriage of four wheels pulled by horses; also a railway car filled with seats for passengers.

COURSE *n.* the path or route that a conveyance takes; esp. that of ships and aircraft.

CUTTER *n.* a small vessel, now powered and, in the coast guard, armed.

Excursion

EXPRESS *n.* a train which passes by local stations, stopping only at large ones.

FREIGHTER *n.* a ship used to transport mainly goods or cargo.

Galleon

Hansom

ITINERARY *n.* the route or course of a journey.

JOURNEY *n.* a trip; a traveling or passage from one place to another.

KETCH *n.* a certain type of sailing vessel.

LIMITED *n.* a train which carries only first-class passengers at a higher fare.

LINER *n.* a large steamship or motorship designed chiefly to transport passengers and operating on a regular schedule.

LITTER *n.* a couch or bed-like conveyance, carried by means of poles on the shoulders of men.

LORRY *n.* a truck.

Macadam

MONOPLANE *n.* an airplane with one set of wings.

NAUTICAL *adj.* pertaining to ships, seamen or navigation.

OMNIBUS *n.* a bus.

PACKET *n.* a vessel, usually designed to carry both passengers and cargo, which makes scheduled trips, frequently between only two points.

Palanquin

PASSAGE *n.* a journey by water.

Peregrinate

PILGRIMAGE *n.* a journey for special purposes, esp. to a religious shrine.

Plod & Slog

RAFT *n.* logs or timber tied together to provide a floating surface.

Rove
Safari
Saunter
Schooner & Sloop
SIGHT-SEER   *n.* one who travels chiefly to see places of cultural, historical or natural interest.
SLED   *n.* a conveyance which moves on runners over snow and ice.
SLEIGH   *n.* a sled drawn by horses.
Slog   see **Plod & Slog**
Sloop   see **Schooner & Sloop**
STEAMER   *n.* a vessel which is powered by steam; often a liner, but a steamer may proceed without schedule.
TANDEM   *n.* a bicycle constructed for use by two people at once.

TOUR   *n.* a journey, esp. a trip devoted to sight-seeing and ending at the starting point.
TOURIST   *n.* one who makes a tour.
TREK   *n.* a journey, esp. a migration made with difficulty.
TRIP   *n.* a journey, esp. a short one.
VEHICULAR   *adj.* pertaining to a vehicle.
VELIC   *adj.* pertaining to sails. VELARY is a rare variant.
VIATIC   *adj.* pertaining to a journey, or journeying.
VOYAGE   *n.* a journey by sea.
YACHT   *n.* a private pleasure ship, usually small.
Xebec or Zebec

Excursion   EXCURSION does not necessarily refer to a river boat. Theoretically, we can make EXCURSIONS anywhere, even into the world of the imagination. "The college professor took a quick excursion into the business world, but soon strategically withdrew to the university." The word means 'to run forth.' Possibly one reason why it has been so popular a tag, like 'excursion boat,' 'excursion train,' 'excursion ticket,' is its sonority and rhythm. It goes with 'most any word.

Galleon   Typically, a big three- or four-decker merchant or naval ship used by the Spaniards and other Mediterraneans from roughly Chaucer's death (1400) to George Washington's birth (1732).

Hansom   In the days of horse-drawn vehicles the adjectival term 'one-horse' was derogative, meaning 'second-rate.' A 'one-horse' town was really a backwater place. But the one-horse HANSOM cab was something else again. Of all public conveyances it was perhaps the smartest, though oddest, with its narrow seat for two persons under a projecting roof, and a driver on display at the rear of the roof, erect in a box like an elephant's howdah, flourishing a long willowy whip to the skies. There was something quaint about the contraption invented in 1834 by a man named Hansom. Specimens still exist, and some are in use. Anyhow no one can ride in one without feeling distinguished.

Macadam MACADAM roads are mottled gray and black, being crushed granite, basalt or the like, packed hard. They were, you might say, a Scotch-American invention that first gave respectable and durable surfaces to the awful English highways of the early nineteenth century, and then spread around the world. John Loudon McAdam of Scotland (you will only occasionally find his name spelled with the Gaelic 'Mac') came to New York, made a fortune in business and returned to his home, all a number of years before George Washington died. His interest in highways led him to experiment with surfacings. Before he died in 1836 he became surveyor-general of all British roads and introduced his system of applying broken stones to them.

Palanquin An Oriental conveyance, like a portable bed, carried on men's shoulders.

Peregrinate Literally, 'through,' from Latin *per,* plus *ager,* 'land.' PEREGRINATE means 'to travel from country to country.' The word suggests a leisurely traveling with plenty of stopovers.

Plod and **Slog** These words are so small we might forget to use them. PLOD means 'to walk heavily,' not necessarily because of exhaustion but because a full day's work makes one put his foot down deliberately, seriously, without, as it were, any dancing around. Figuratively, the word refers to any dull, unimaginative work or worker. "The work on the new parkway plodded along so slowly that drivers began to wonder whether it would ever be done." PLOD is Gaelic, deriving from 'pool,' perhaps with sloppy ground around it. SLOG, meaning 'to hit hard,' is British sporting slang, perhaps derived from 'slug.' SLOG also means 'to PLOD,' but especially in marshy ground where you have to splash through water, making a squelchy sound.

Rove ROVE is a wild word, the prowling cousin of 'roam.' Probably pirates started it. Anyhow, it meant a 'robber' to the early Dutch, and hence a 'wanderer.' From this noun we coined the verb. "Some sea birds rove the shores looking for dead fish to eat."

Safari In Arabic, a 'caravan,' from a verb, *safari,* 'to travel.' Hence, a SAFARI is a 'long procession,' like a single file of natives in Africa, carrying supplies. By extension, therefore, it is an 'expedition, hunting trip, journey.'

Saunter When you SAUNTER forth in the morning you venture forth, you are adventurous. Both SAUNTER and 'adventure' were born of the same parents in ancient Rome. Both reached us via the Old French. But SAUNTER was appreciably softened. 'Adventure' was originally *ad* plus *venire*, 'to come to.' The French made another word of it. The reflexive *s'aventurer*, 'to come yourself to or along,' gave us SAUNTER.

It is a pleasant and expressive word, as leisurely but not so lazy as 'meander.' "The young couple, obviously just in love, sauntered through the park hand-in-hand." Sometimes even the seasons SAUNTER, June lingering into July. Your mind SAUNTERS through a placid, slow-paced novel.

Schooner and **Sloop** A SLOOP slips over the water, a SCHOONER skims over it, like a flat stone thrown so as to skim (or 'scoon,' a word still used in Scotland) over the surface. SLOOP is Dutch *sloep*, probably from Low German *slupen*, 'to glide,' originally 'to slip.' 'To slip' became *slippen* in Dutch, so now the SLOOP should really glide. And the SCHOONER (which the Dutch adopted from the English, changing the spelling of it) also glides, but swiftly. When the first one was launched, in New England in 1713, somebody cried, "Oh, see how she scoons!" 'Scoon' was then still dialectal here, meaning 'to glide swiftly.' Its origin is probably Scandinavian, but both its application to ships and its extension, for some odd reason, to a large, tall glass of beer is American.

The French call the SCHOONER a 'tern,' or at least one kind of seagull, *goélette*, which skims over the water. The same idea, and probably the root of the same 'scoon' are in our modern 'scooters.' But the French took their word *chaloupe*, directly from the Dutch, and we took it over from them for good measure in 'shallop,' a 'small light open boat.' In the Navy, a SLOOP is any warship with guns on only one deck, provided it is larger than a gunboat.

Xebec or **Zebec** These are worth noticing as a curiosity. It is said to be the only word in our language which begins with an 'x' and isn't both learned and of Greek origin. It designates a small three-master with both square and triangular sails. It is Arabic, via the Turks and French.

TREACHERY AND STRATAGEMS

Ambush
ARTIFICE *n.* a subtle or artful stratagem.

BETRAYAL *n.* a breaking of trust or faith, esp. in the sense of delivering someone to his enemies.

Canard see **Petard & Canard**

Capture & Catch

Catch see **Capture & Catch**

CHICANERY *n.* legal trickery that looks honest and is therefore treachery; illegal or under-handed practice.

Collude see **Connive, Suborn,** etc.

Connive, Suborn & Collude

DECEIT *n.* a deception; deliber-ate concealment of true mo-tive.

DECEPTION *n.* a cheating; fraud; false front. *adj.* DECEPTIVE.

Dissemble & Dissimulate

Dissimulate see **Dissemble & Dissimulate**

DODGE *n.* a chicanery; evasion; trick. *v.* to avoid obligation; to take the easy course.

DOUBLE-DEALING *n.* false or de-ceptive dealing or business.

DUPLICITY *n.* double-dealing; also, changing one's motives and sentiments to suit the occa-sion.

Elusive see **Evasive, Elusive,** etc.

Evasive, Elusive & Furtive

Factitious

FEINT *n.* a trick; a false appear-ance or motive used to hide an evil purpose.

FORGED *adj.* pertaining to a false copy; an imitation, as a FORGED signature.

FRAUD *n.* deceit; deception.

Furtive see **Evasive, Elusive,** etc.

GUILE *n.* treachery; cunning.

INSIDIOUS *adj.* treacherous; in-tended to entrap by foul means, as an INSIDIOUS plot.

INTRIGUE *n.* a plot. *v.* to trick; to try to snare or trap by chican-cry.

Lurk see **Skulk & Lurk**

Machinate

Marplot

PERFIDY *n.* a breaking of one's promise; falsity. *adj.* PERFIDIOUS, double-dealing; treacherous.

Petard & Canard

PLOT *n.* a scheme; plan; esp. in the sense of a secret project. *v.* to form such a scheme or proj-ect.

SCHEMER *n.* one who plots.

Skulk & Lurk

SPURIOUS *adj.* false, as SPURIOUS money.

Strategy & Tactics

Suborn see **Connive, Suborn,** etc.

Surreptitious

Tactics see **Strategy & Tactics**

TRICK *n.* a stratagem; esp. a scheme to cheat.

WILE *n.* deceit.

Ambush We have coined verbs to express our reaction to certain situations. When the British are lost or confused they say they are 'bushed.' The reference is to the trackless wastes of the Australian bush. AMBUSH is Old High German for 'to go into the woods.' Especially in unexplored forests unexpected and catastrophic events may always be imminent. Probably from these tragedies came a feeling that sudden catastrophe can be always associated with primeval darkness, with feral passions, and so the modern meaning of AMBUSH evolved. AMBUSH now means 'to attack an enemy by surprise and treachery'; by extension, it is any sort of 'trap.' The word is grim, its force heightened by its suggestions of 'treachery' and 'unfairness': "The ambush hit the soldiers without warning; many died before they knew what had happened." The word lends itself especially to figurative usage. A business man may feel bitterly that he has been AMBUSHED when his business has been wrecked by adroit and rapacious competitors.

Capture and **Catch**   Usually we CATCH timid creatures that easily, like rabbits, run, and CAPTURE the ferocious animals, like tigers. But in the Latin both CAPTURE and CATCH meant 'to take.' We still speak of the 'take,' meaning the 'kill' in a hunting season.

But, with usage, the two words have deviated. CATCHING a man's eye is quite a different process from CAPTURING his affections. CAPTURE, of course, is the less colloquial word, comparing with CATCH as 'purchase' compares with 'buy.' CAPTURE is an imaginative word. It is a pretty word, too. Even if you CAPTURE a gorilla, you must seem to do it gracefully.

CAPTURE has also an intellectual cousin whom we have taught to flirt: 'captivate.' 'Captivate' is classically Roman in sound, more so than CAPTURE and far more so than CATCH, which sounds like an Anglo-Saxon monosyllable, like 'batch,' It means 'to CAPTURE by charm' and, in the meanwhile, 'to fascinate.' CAPTIVATE means 'to win' in the sense of 'win over.' 'Captivity' is, of course, the doleful ultimate of all these words. It is any state of mind, heart or body in 'bondage.'

Connive, Suborn and **Collude**   When you CONNIVE at something, you wink at it, you purposely don't notice, for example, a crime that you know is being committed. Perhaps you overlook the crime, or make light of it, condone it or dismiss it from your mind. In other words you contrive to ignore or belittle a crime when you CONNIVE at it. "Her father connived at her elopement; her mother was the only surprised person in town."

When you SUBORN someone you induce him in one way or another to bear false witness. SUBORN can be used to persuade anyone to do evil, especially to perjure themselves by concealing the truth. When two people COLLUDE (literally, 'play together') they co-operate clandestinely in a plot. CONNIVANCE, SUBORNING, and COLLUSION all relate to a shady or sinister action, but it may not be a question of breaking the law.

Dissemble and Dissimulate DISSEMBLE is a two-barreled word, meaning either 'to disguise' or 'to feign.' Its two meanings almost coalesce in DISSIMULATE. Both words come from the same Latin seeds meaning roughly 'not alike.'

DISSEMBLE means to disguise in the sense of 'altering' in appearance, or 'falsifying,' a situation, perhaps even a person. It is a softer, more subtle word than 'disguise,' not having that word's suggestion of a visible mask. For example, the snake that tempted Eve was not in 'disguise,' but it did DISSEMBLE, or 'hide' its true, wicked intentions. Thus the word is naturally used about a person's thoughts, feelings, intentions: "He dissembled the real purpose of his call as he prattled endlessly about the weather." A filibuster in the Senate is in a sense a DISSEMBLING. But remember that the word works both ways. For example, while the gentleman above was DISSEMBLING the purpose of his call, he was also DISSEMBLING ('pretending') an interest in what he was prattling about. DISSEMBLING does not so much misrepresent as it misleads, artfully and by degrees. 'Camouflage,' a chromatic misrepresentation, DISSEMBLES by artfully misleading the eye. If a soldier 'disguises' himself he takes off his uniform and masks himself by putting on civilian clothes, or perhaps women's clothes. But if a soldier 'camouflages' himself, he tries to 'resemble,' or 'become like' the background. Thus, if a man DISSEMBLES the facts of a subject, he talks round and about the subject; but, if he 'disguises' the facts, he actually changes them.

In DISSIMULATION where the intent is not actually to conceal a purpose, or to feign another, but to manipulate emphasis, real skill is required, though a rather mean one. DISSIMULATION mutes a main purpose by emphasizing an aspect of the aim. The art of advertising consists basically of DISSIMULATION. We know the advertiser wants to sell his product; there is no use trying to disguise that fact. But, in some way, he must make us feel that he advertises only out of admiration for his own product; it is the best in the market and he wants us to know about it. He DISSIMULATES his motives. He isn't lying; he just makes things look agreeably different.

Incidentally, DISSEMBLE and DISSIMULATE are intransitive verbs also. You can simply DISSEMBLE, with no mention of what you DISSEMBLE. Thus, by extension, DISSEMBLE can also mean 'to ignore,' as when you DISSEMBLE a headache at a party. These words are all good words to add to your vocabulary. Their distinctions, though fine, are very practical in this world of ours where we so often encounter every shade of deceit.

Evasive, Elusive, and **Furtive** If you avoid trouble by wiles, shifts, and stealthy dodges, you are employing EVASIVE methods. Usually, you are blamed for using them because it is assumed you would be more courageous, more upright if you confronted a bad situation. But many matters can be EVADED on good conscience. EVADE means literally 'to go from,' but in usage it invariably implies a 'subterfuge,' a substitution of one issue for another, a concealment of motives. We call a man EVASIVE if, when we ask him questions, he replies with indirect, irrelevant, or vague explanations. Under such circumstances it is only courtesy, or the laws of libel, that restrain us from calling him a 'sneak' or a 'liar.' He thinks he is simply dodging.

But ELUSIVE is held to be more honorable. It implies a chase on the one hand, and an escape on the other. "That fox is perhaps the most elusive of all animals; I've been hunting him a week now, and he's escaped my dogs a half dozen times." An ELUSIVE creature is not merely 'shifty,' like an EVASIVE creature; he is an expert dodger, slippery, fast, and intelligent. He has many hideaways. ELUSIVE is a short lively word. Ideas ELUDE you in a pinch. You can't put your finger on an ELUSIVE fellow. You can't assess an ELUSIVE man's capabilities, intentions, character or worth.

A FURTIVE creature is perhaps best illustrated by a slinking weasel threading his way along a stone wall in the moonlight and glancing behind him at every few steps. Its glances are quick and sidelong, as if it feared a long, direct look would attract an enemy. Its whole attitude is FURTIVE, and we attribute its guilt to its bad conscience, that of a professional outlaw. FURTIVE comes, significantly, from Latin *fur*, 'a thief.' Actually all hunted wild creatures are FURTIVE. It is a reaction to the unknown, it is an ever-alerting dread. To the primitive man the roar of thunder is the audible wrath of an unseen but awful deity. This fear that comes from ignorance, and self-guilt, always produces a FURTIVE manner.

Factitious FACTITIOUS means 'affected, put-on, trumped-up, improvised for spurious effect, sham.' The opposite of 'genuine, natural, true,' FACTITIOUS is applied only to immaterial things, such as explanations and excuses. FACTITIOUS is not to be confused with 'fortuitous.' See ADVENTITIOUS and FORTUITOUS. FACTITIOUS comes (with animadversions along the way) from Latin *factus*, 'fact.'

Machinate To contrive and execute secretly a sinister scheme with, by inference, the precision of a machine, is to MACHINATE. Palace plots of old, and some recent political plots are examples of MACHINATIONS. "Her whole family helped her: they entered enthusiastically into her machinations, and at last they were rewarded when she finally succeeded in marrying the rich young man from the other side of town."

Marplot   An expressive noun: a MARPLOT is one who interferes with our plans and so mars them. Its only unfortunate note is the intimation that we ourselves are in mischief by plotting. Still, even conspirators feel the right to complain about a meddler.

Petard and **Canard**   You have probably heard the expression, "He was hoisted by his own petard," meaning he was caught in his own 'trap,' or frustrated by his own 'stratagems.' A PETARD (Old French) was an explosive device to breach a wall in warfare. A CANARD has nothing to do with a cannon, but it is also explosive. It is a sensational blast of news in a newspaper, a wholly invented hoax. Since a CANARD is almost inevitably malicious, disparaging or disrespectful, it has come to mean any 'extravagantly slanderous public jibe.'

Skulk and **Lurk**   Probably two Scandinavian words (Danish and Swedish respectively), SKULK and LURK appeal to imaginative writers. Like 'slink' and 'prowl' they may originally have suggested only fierce fauna, but their sinister sound has lessened only a little through long and special application to humans. A SKULKING man may be a prowling burglar, both sly and sneaky; but there is no real mystery about him. LURK is mysterious. Wolves as well as men can LURK, and wolves have mysterious habits. The common meaning of LURK is to lie hidden near some spot, or to hang around it unnoticed, in order to spy or to attack. But the suggestion of an 'ambush' or, in the case of an animal, of an 'attack,' is not strong in LURK. On the other hand SKULK is a mean and treacherous sounding word: a SKULKER is unquestionably a sneak, and he is foxy. In fact, a troop of foxes is called a SKULK.

Strategy and **Tactics**   Both STRATEGY and TACTICS are Greek. STRATEGY was military from the start; even in modern Greek the word for a 'general' is *stratevma*. The original meaning was 'generalship,' or the 'direction' of a military force. Devious Ulysses, an archetype of a Greek leader, might have originated the idea. For the job of a chieftain was never simple since it required both planning and artifices. STRATEGY today is the art of generalship required in a campaign, and STRATAGEMS are the necessary artifices STRATEGY invents. Once, when a Chinese general feared to enter a forest with his troops lest they be ambushed, he told his men to throw stones into the trees. If birds flew out, no enemy was there, and it would be safe to proceed. The stones were thrown and the birds flew out. The army proceeded, and was ambushed. The opposing general had anticipated the STRATAGEM and employed a counter-STRATAGEM. When the stones came in his men liberated birds they had previously caught for that purpose. But back of both STRATAGEMS lay intelligence and planning—STRATEGY.

When STRATEGY is thought of in a somewhat narrower and more active sense it becomes STRATEGICS, which are in a sense TACTICS, being practical methods (as STRATAGEMS are often the means) of attaining an end. But true TACTICS, in the martial sense, imply a maneuvering of forces, against an enemy's forces in the field. Both a general and a captain study TACTICS, but the former invents real STRATEGY. A general may be the head of a 'stratocracy': 'military rule, government or despotism.' In contrast, TACTICS began from a 'fitness of things' that provided us with our word 'tact.' TACTICS is a literal rendering of the early Greek for 'an arranging of matters.' In both TACTICS and 'tact' the real connotation is 'skill,' whether in managing a battle, or in pleasing our friends. Needless to say, 'tact' is the more civilized word.

Surreptitious SURREPTITIOUSNESS is stealth. The beginning of the word was Latin *rapere*, 'to seize' or 'to snatch,' with an additional meaning of 'carrying away hastily.' When this verb was built upon, a new verb appeared, meaning to 'take away secretly.' From the past participle *surreptus* of that synthetic verb arose an adjective meaning 'stolen' or, at best, 'taken by stealth.' With almost the same meaning that adjective has come down to us in SURREPTITIOUS.

There is in this word a sense both of thievery and of taking liberties. If you insert in a speech a passage which you would like people to think is your own, such a fraud is SURREPTITIOUS. A clandestine understanding between two members of a group of three in a business deal is SURREPTITIOUS—it is a 'stealthy' act. 'Stealth' suggests not so much a criminal act as a sneaky act. People who do things they know they shouldn't do but which are not so very bad, act SURREPTITIOUSLY. "He surreptitiously cut a piece of cake which his mother was saving for supper." But, of course, SURREPTITIOUS can also refer to downright 'illegal' acts.

UNDERWORLD

Abduct

Abscond

Accost

Blackmail   see **Mail** & **Blackmail**

BOOTY   *n.* plunder; loot; spoils.

BRIG   *n.* jail; guardhouse; esp. a place of confinement in a vessel.

Brigand, Bandit & **Gangster**

Buccaneer, Corsair & **Freebooter**

BURGLAR   *n.* thief; robber; esp. housebreaker.

Corsair   see **Buccaneer, Corsair,** etc.

CRIB   *n.* a trifling theft; plagiarism; often a translation which students improperly use to aid them in foreign language studies. *v.* to steal.

DELINQUENCY   *n.* guilt; mistake; moral fault. *adj.* DELINQUENT. Also *n.* DELINQUENT, one who is DELINQUENT.

DESPERADO   *n.* a desperate, dangerous man; a reckless criminal.

DUNGEON   *n.* prison or cell, esp. one underground.

EXTORTION   *n.* the act of forcing someone by threats to give up his possessions.

FENCE   *n.* a receiver of stolen goods.

FILCHER   *n.* a thief. *v.* to filch.

Footpad   see **Padlock** & **Footpad**

Freebooter   see **Buccaneer, Corsair,** etc.

Gangster   see **Brigand, Bandit,** etc.

Gaol & **Jail**

Hanged & **Hung**

HIGHWAYMAN   *n.* one who holds up and robs on a public highway.

HOLDUP   *n.* a forcible attack on a person for the purpose of stealing his possessions.

HOODLUM   *n.* a delinquent; a ruffian; a petty gangster.

Hung   see **Hanged** & **Hung**

Incorrigible, Intractable & **Refractory**

Intractable   see **Incorrigible, Intractable,** etc.

Jail   see **Gaol** & **Jail**

Jolly-boat   see **Jolly Roger** & **Jolly-boat**

Jolly Roger & **Jolly-boat**

LOOT   *n.* plunder; booty; any illegally gotten gain.

Mail & **Blackmail**

MALFEASANCE   *n.* an illegal or immoral act.

Nefarious & **Notorious**

Notorious   see **Nefarious** & **Notorious**

Padlock & **Footpad**

Peculate

PILFERER   *n.* a petty thief.

PLUNDER   *n.* loot.

POACHER   *n.* one who traps or shoots game illegally.

Privateers

PROWLER   *n.* one who hunts or searches for something to steal.

PURLOIN   *v.* to take; steal; thieve.

Refractory   see **Incorrigible, Intractable,** etc.

RIFLE *v.* to ransack and steal; to carry off.

SMUGGLE *v.* to bring something into a country illegally and secretly; hence, to convey anything secretly.

SPOILS *n.* loot.

THUG *n.* a desperado; a murderer.

TOUGH *n.* a TOUGH person; a roughneck; a bully; a marauder.

TURPITUDE *n.* depravity; grave fault and immorality; wickedness.

VICE *n.* immorality; depravity; turpitude.

Wetback

WORKHOUSE *n.* a prison.

Abduct 'To kidnap.' Perhaps we could get along with the one word, and dispense with the more formal ABDUCT. For 'kidnap' is plenty old enough to have wide authority. Yet ABDUCT remains on the books, and we should know the reasons why. There are two reasons. First, since it literally means 'to lead away,' ABDUCT can and does now mean 'to carry away forcibly and unlawfully,' and so is broad enough to cover both kidnapping and rape in its earlier, and still literary, sense. Secondly, the medical profession uses ABDUCT, applying it principally to muscles and specifically to those muscles that draw parts of the body away from its axis or center, as distinguished from others that pull them in the opposite direction, or '*ad*duct' them. Broadly, however, physiological ABDUCTION is moving parts away from their usual positions.

Abscond 'To run away and hide.' Originally it was simply 'to hide.' The 'running away' is modern, but it has become the main idea in the word. A bank official juggles some figures, pockets a hidden profit, and ABSCONDS.

The verb was at first transitive; you ABSCONDED something, hid it away. Later, persons began ABSCONDING themselves, and from this reflexive form came the present intransitive use.

Accost Have you ever been ACCOSTED on the street—hailed and spoken to? The point is, the ACCOSTER may be a friend, but he is more probably a suspicious character. Not one whom you suspect, but one who suspects you. He may want to investigate you or he may want to 'rib' you. He 'coasts' up to your side and addresses you. 'Coast' and ACCOST both contain vestiges of the Latin *costa*, 'rib'; a 'rib' is, figuratively, your 'side.' A revenue cutter in nautical terms ACCOSTS a rumrunner. It comes up alongside of it.

Brigand, Bandit and **Gangster** A BRIGAND is a BANDIT. In the plural they both refer to 'banded outlaws' and 'robbers.' Perhaps because of the wide use of these words in literature and folklore, they suggest a romantic, not unpleasant life. BRIGAND, which comes from Italian *briganti*, which in turn comes from a verb meaning 'to fight,' is perhaps the more romantic. Its root is eventually traced to Celtic origin, *briga*, 'strife,' comparing the Gaelic *brigh*, 'power,' and Old Irish *brig*, 'importance.' So the original BRIGANDS were probably 'chieftains.' The authentic ones today live in bands in mountain hideouts along the Mediterranean. So do the real BANDITS, though the emphasis in their name is on 'outlawry,' *banditti* being 'outlaws.'

Both words are less harsh than GANGSTER. For true GANGSTERS are not GANGSTERS because they belong to a 'gang,' but because they form a gang for a purpose. The purpose is to 'gang up' on a victim. *Gang* itself is an old Anglo-Saxon word meaning a 'going.' It has equivalents in Dutch, German and Danish, and is akin to Gothic and Old Norse words meaning a 'thoroughfare.' The idea seems to have been of a 'going along together.' But GANGSTER is a word we in America apply to ruthless criminals, and because of this close, real everyday use, it is an unpleasant word.

Buccaneer, Corsair and **Freebooter**   A BUCCANEER is a pirate but not necessarily ship-borne. Originally he was a French colonist of Haiti who acquired the sobriquet BUCCANEER because (1) he lived largely on the flesh of wild cattle and (2) he cooked it as the natives did on a *bucan*, a grill for smoking meat. But the Spanish drove these colonists out of Hispaniola (Haiti) in the seventeenth century, and the roving Frenchmen became CORSAIRS, quite naturally devoting their special attention to Spanish ships off the Spanish coast of South America (the Spanish Main). Meanwhile, the term BUCCANEER became general, applying even to petty practitioners of piracy, such as common rogues.

A CORSAIR, from Latin *cursus*, 'a running, a course,' roves, of course, the sea, and is also a FREEBOOTER, or pirate. But he first practiced in Persian waters in antiquity. Both words were touched up by the French before the English took them over. FREEBOOTER is Dutch, *vri-buit* plus *er*, for 'free-booty-er,' that is, a 'roving robber.'

Gaol and **Jail**   One and the same word, even in pronunciation. GAOL is the English form of JAIL; but since normally 'G' is hard before an 'a,' JAIL, which is pronounced as its spelling indicates, has become current now in England, except in official usage. Yet both spellings are only mangled remains of an ancient word. The Old French had *gaiole* from late Latin, which had altered the Latin *cavea*, 'cage,' to *gabia*, and then a diminutive of it, at first *caveola,* and then *gabiola.* Today the coop is larger, but the birds are still in it—our 'jailbirds.' Actually 'jailbird' refers also to former convicts. In Roman days, however, the *cavea* could also be any enclosure, even a theater. By extension, it could designate an audience in the theater. But originally it was a hollow in the ground, whence our 'cave.'

Hanged and **Hung** Nothing is ever HANGED *but* a man. For anything else we say HUNG, including even a man who simply caught his clothes on the limb of a tree, and HUNG there until help came. The point is that both HANGED and HUNG are the past tense forms of 'hang,' but HANGED is used only for one circumstance. A man is HANGED by a rope from a scaffold until dead. For example, we are HUNG up (not HANGED up) in the office when we can't be home for dinner. Figuratively, of course, we can be HANGED, as in effigy: "I'll be hanged if I will," is an ejaculation that would not sound natural with HUNG. On this side of the Atlantic, however, there is a growing tendency to say, "The prisoner was hung," just as he himself might have said, when he was alive, that his clothes had been HUNG on the line.

Incorrigible, Intractable and **Refractory** INCORRIGIBLE is an adjective that means incapable of being law abiding or reformed in any way. "That man is an incorrigible liar; he'll never tell the truth." Unfortunately, INCORRIGIBLE is too often applied only to bad boys. Actually everyone is INCORRIGIBLE in one way or another. "My aunt is an incorrigible talker." "My wife is an incorrigible spender . . . I never have a cent in the bank."

INTRACTABLE is a more specific word. If the INCORRIGIBLE boy is stubborn, positively refusing all correction, he becomes INTRACTABLE. It is true an INCORRIGIBLE person cannot be reformed, but at the same time he is not actively rebellious, or even obstinate. An INTRACTABLE person won't even make a try at reform.

REFRACTORY is even a stronger word. From Latin *re,* 'back,' plus *frangere,* 'to break,' REFRACTORY means 'to break from control, to be completely unmanageable.' A REFRACTORY member of a committee, for example, is always obstructive and probably obnoxiously so.

The connotations of both REFRACTORY and INTRACTABLE reflect their application to inorganic objects. Tough substances, like rocks, are said to be INTRACTABLE. You cannot mold them with your hands. Ore that cannot be easily reduced is said to be REFRACTORY. It resists the extraction of its metal, such as gold or aluminum, and so it seems mean or obstructive.

Jolly Roger and **Jolly-boat**   JOLLY ROGER is a 'pirate's flag.' It is no relation to a JOLLY-BOAT, a 'small ship's boat,' from Danish *jolle,* 'yawl.' The origin of JOLLY ROGER is a mystery.

Mail and **Blackmail**   There is no etymological connection between these two words, just as there is no connection between their meanings. MAIL comes directly from the old French *male,* 'bag,' and postmen carry MAIL in bags. But BLACKMAIL's origin and development are more spectacular.

The 'mail' in BLACKMAIL is a Viking word that had to do with 'speech,' and hence with 'agreement.' It came to mean in the North of the British Isles, 'payment, tax, rent.' A rent paying tenant is still called a 'mailer' in Scotland. But it was in Scotland too that the word began its scandalous career.

There were different kinds of rent or 'mail,' but chiefly only two: 'white mail,' that was paid in white money (silver), and BLACK MAIL, that was paid in work, produce, black cattle or perhaps darker money, such as copper. And here the marauding Highland chiefs come into the picture. They exacted a new kind of BLACKMAIL from the Low Country landholders. They demanded protection money, and in return scrupulously refrained from further raiding, and 'protected' the payee from other marauders. And it happened that in these respects they resembled the Arabian sheiks who took tribute from Englishmen crossing their lands. So the British began calling both practices BLACK-MAIL.

So the use of the word has spread to include the extortion of money by threats of pressure from unscrupulous persons (at first usually officials). In 1868 the *New York Herald* first used BLACKMAILER in its present specific sense of one who extorts money by threat of damaging publicity. No doubt its dark sound promoted this usage.

Nefarious and **Notorious**   NOTORIETY is supposed to be vulgar today. The word itself derives from the Latin *notorious,* 'making known.' But we insist on a sinister interpretation. Something NOTORIOUS is not only public knowledge but also subject to disapproval. NEFARIOUS to the Latins meant 'utterly bad.' The NEFARIOUS man engages in all sorts of wicked activities, but he may not be NOTORIOUS. If a man's NEFARIOUS business is revealed to the public, he will then become NOTORIOUS.

Padlock and **Footpad**   'Pad' is an old word for 'highwayman.' FOOTPADS traveled on foot, especially on city streets, while bold highwaymen robbed on the King's highways. PADLOCKS were designed to keep FOOTPADS out of your house.

Peculate This word means 'to pilfer, embezzle.' Specifically, it refers to the taking of public property for your own use. Even using an official car for your Sunday pleasure drive is a small PECULATION.

Privateers Most commonly they are ships 'privately' fitted out to prey on enemy vessels in wartime, like the American PRIVATEERS in the War of 1812. But the captains and crews are also called PRIVATEERS. Sometimes, after the wars were concluded, these PRIVATEERS would turn outlaw and pirate. Thus you occasionally see PRIVATEER used in the sense of 'pirate.'

Wetbacks Mexicans who cross the border illegally to work in the United States are called WETBACKS. About a half a million of these all-wet swimmers of the Rio Grande are sent back to Mexico annually. They are transported chiefly by aeroplane because they jump off trains, and because the Mexican soldiers and officials don't like the job of herding them to the interior where they are less likely to slip back here.

UNIVERSAL AND SPIRITUAL TERMS

ABSTRACT *n.* the essence, or the concentration of the essential qualities, of something; thus, also, the summary or epitome of the substance of a book or discourse. *v.* to withdraw or remove something, as to ABSTRACT one's attention; to derive a general idea from particulars.

CATHOLIC *n.* a member of the universal Christian church; a member of the Roman Catholic Church. *adj.* universal, all-embracing; pertaining to breadth of mind, liberality of spirit.

CELESTIAL *adj.* pertaining to the visible heaven, or the sky; heavenly, thus of superior quality.

COMMON *adj.* pertaining to all, as the COMMON good, or the COMMON safety or the COMMON law; pertaining to things equally, as "Patriotism is common to Democrats and Republicans."

COSMIC *adj.* of or pertaining to the universe, or to universal harmony.

COSMOPOLITAN *n.* a person who has no or few national or local prejudices; one who has no fixed residence. *adj.* belonging to all parts of the world; free from local or national prejudices, ideas and manners.

DIVINE *adj.* pertaining to God; religious, sacred; proceeding from God or the gods.

ECUMENICAL (or OECUMENICAL) *adj.* general, universal; belonging to the entire Christian church.

EMPYREAL *adj.* formed of pure fire or light. Refers to the purest and highest region of heaven.

ETHEREAL *adj.* heavenly, celestial, spiritual; having the characteristics of air.

GENERAL *adj.* pertaining or applicable to all or almost all the objects of one class; pertaining to the whole rather than the part.

GENERIC *adj.* pertaining to the nature or the mark of a genus; thus, to the qualities that distinguish a part from the whole.

HEAVENLY *adj.* pertaining to heaven; fit for or characteristic of heaven.

HOLY *adj.* consecrated; set apart for religious use; of a religious or saintly character.

IDEAL *n.* that which exists only in an idea; hence, a standard or model of perfection. *adj.* of or pertaining to ideas; thus, to whatever is virtually perfect.

INDESCRIBABLE *adj.* surpassing description; beyond words.

Ineffable

INENARRABLE *adj.* incapable of being narrated or told.

INEXPRESSIBLE *adj.* above or beyond the power of words.

SACRED *adj.* holy; set aside for religious use; hallowed, consecrated.

SPIRITUAL *adj.* pertaining to the soul; incorporeal.

Ubiquitous see **Universal & Ubiquitous**

Universal & Ubiquitous

UNSPEAKABLE *adj.* surpassing the power of words. Often used about obscene or horrible things.

UNUTTERABLE *adj.* incapable of being expressed. Often used about something mysterious.

Ineffable This adjective refers to whatever is beyond the power of words to express. A woman's beauty may be INEFFABLE.

Universal and **Ubiquitous** These two words illustrate that synonyms usually partake of the same meaning, but are not identical in meaning. UBIQUITOUS is the expanded Latin word *ubique,* 'everywhere.' A friend whom we are always meeting is, or seems to be, UBIQUITOUS—he appears 'everywhere.' But while UBIQUITOUS has retained only this simple adverbial force, UNIVERSAL, which comes from Latin *unus,* 'one,' plus *vertere,* 'to turn to,' has etched out in usage both a broader and yet a more exact application for itself. Thus samples and specimens are UBIQUITOUS when they exist or appear 'everywhere.' But less tangible or less visible things are UNIVERSAL when they pervade 'all things everywhere' or because they exist 'every place,' including the human mind. The UBIQUITOUS samples, as they integrate themselves with the world, become UNIVERSAL. Everything which is UNIVERSAL necessarily exists or shows itself 'everywhere,' and is therefore UBIQUITOUS. The synonyms are mates, not twins.

UNPLEASANTNESS

See also Talk Against

Abomination

ANNOY v. to pester; molest; irritate. n. ANNOYANCE.

BADGER v. to annoy; bait; tease; nag.

BAIT v. to harass; to worry; esp. in the sense of physical attack or goading.

DEFORMITY n. any part, aspect, or form of a man which is in an unnatural condition; a disfiguration.

Delude see **Ludicrous, Delude,** etc.

Deride see **Ludicrous, Delude,** etc.

DISAGREEABLE adj. unpleasant; distasteful.

Discomfiture

Disgruntled

DISGUST n. a strong, almost physical revulsion against an unpleasant experience. v. to cause or arouse disgust. adj. DISGUSTING.

DISMAL adj. dreadful; gloomy; used esp. in the sense of depressed or unpleasant spirits.

Execrable see **Inexorable & Execrable**

GHASTLY adj. deathlike; terrible; very pale; as a GHASTLY complexion.

GRUESOME adj. repulsive, esp. in the sense of exciting fear.

HARASS v. to annoy; to pester; esp. in the sense of wearying another person to the point of breakdown; also, to attack continually; to raid.

HECKLE v. to question continually; gibe; taunt.

HIDEOUS adj. very ugly or repugnant; esp. in the sense of creating a shock, as a HIDEOUS sight.

HORRID adj. unpleasant; objectionable. Orig. and strictly, hideous.

Inexorable & Execrable

IRRITATE v. to annoy; exasperate.

LOATHSOME adj. disgusting.

Ludicrous, Delude, Ridiculous & Deride

MELANCHOLY n. depressed spirits; dejection.

Mendacious

Mischief

Misgiving

NUISANCE *n.* an annoyance.

Obloquy

OFFENSIVE *adj.* causing displeasure or disgust; as an OFFENSIVE joke.

Peremptory

PESTER *v.* to annoy.

Pestilential

PLAGUE *n.* a pestilence; hence, any nuisance or irritation.

Prurient & Purulent

Purulent see Prurient & Purulent

Ridiculous see Ludicrous, Delude, etc.

Sad, Sack & Sadsack

SCOURGE *n.* a whipping; punishment. *v.* to punish; to lash.

Scowl

Slattern see Sloven & Slattern

Sloven & Slattern

SQUALID *adj.* poor; neglected; dirty.

Sycophantic

Terrible

TORMENT *n.* torture; very great pain; punishment. *v.* to cause TORMENT.

Tough

Umbrage

VEXATION *n.* annoyance. *v.* VEX, to annoy.

WOE *n.* grief.

Abomination An ABOMINATION excites both hatred and disgust. The explosive second syllable expels it like a lungful of loathing. ABOMINATION has gathered force through the ages. It stems from the Latin *abominari,* 'to deprecate as being ominous.' The origin of 'omen' is shrouded in mystery, arising vaguely in the Greek from 'feelings of presentiment.' Thus there is a touch of 'shrinking fear' in an ABOMINATION.

Discomfiture We do not succeed in dissociating this word from 'discomfort.' Properly DISCOMFITURE means 'defeat,' which implies, if you wish, 'discomfort.' Perhaps we can settle for a compromise, and let DISCOMFITURE stand for the 'superlative' of discomfort.

Disgruntled A DISGRUNTLED man is dissatisfied and displeased, and is disposed to grunt about it. He is also disposed to be disagreeable, distempered. DISGRUNTLED was, believe it or not, very likely formed from 'dis' plus 'gruntle,' the frequentive of 'grunt.' And apparently 'grunt' is in its ancient source an imitative word—probably imitative of a DISGRUNTLED man. But this explanation is going round in circles.

Inexorable and Execrable When something is INEXORABLE ('implacable, unrelenting') it is probably EXECRABLE ('deserving to be cursed'). Literally, EXECRABLE means 'too worthless to be respected,' from *ex*, 'out,' plus *sacer*, 'sacred.' It probably has connotations derived from that malodorous word 'excrement,' for which, quite inconsistently, we use the drier and decenter word 'dung' when it applies to animals.

INEXORABLE is a powerful word. Its strength is understandable. We may curse the gods, but our swearing is futile. No amount of threats has an effect on the gods—they are INEXORABLE. We commonly think of fate in the same way. We are pawns in the INEXORABLE moves of our destinies. Thus, we speak also of the INEXORABLENESS of natural laws. Naturally, when we use the word of a mere mortal, the effect is stupendous. A prospective father-in-law looking with disfavor upon his daughter's suitor is often INEXORABLE.

Ludicrous, Delude, Ridiculous and **Deride**   LUDICROUS is loosely used as a synonym for 'comical' or 'RIDICULOUS.' It comes directly from the Latin *ludere*, 'to play,' which, preceded by *de*, 'off,' came to mean 'to beguile,' hence 'to deceive,' or as the word now stands, 'to DELUDE.' Thus from its antecedents LUDICROUS is still, though rather clumsily, a frolicsome word.

RIDICULOUS began as a simple 'jest,' *ridiculum*. The Latin verb *ridere*, 'to laugh,' preceded by *de*, also gave us DERIDE. But here the *de* was an intensive, making the laugh a 'horselaugh,' which accounts for 'derisive.'

Mendacious   This has always been quite a word because even when it was young and little, among the Romans, as *mendax*, it meant 'lying, false, deceitful, counterfeit.' Each of these synonyms has a meaning which none of the others can touch. It is small wonder then that Ambrose Bierce, in his *Devil's Dictionary*, flippantly asserts that MENDACIOUS means 'addicted to rhetoric.'

It is probably in oratory that MENDACIOUS has its commonest use. Seldom in a personal quarrel do we speak of MENDACITY. In a personal quarrel our passions are hotter, so we use such sharp words as 'fraud, deceit, lying, betrayal.'

MENDACIOUS is a literary word because of its length and elasticity. Its length safeguards it from too hasty use, yet it always talks positively, deliberately and clearly. Nor does its versatility weaken it. It assumes its strength from its context. "Of all the explanations I have ever heard, this fellow's is the most mendacious." Here the word pulls out all its stops, using the full gamut of its senses. "This company report is, to say the least, mendacious." It is not only inaccurate but intentionally misleading. "I know he's mendacious," I know he lies. And besides all this MENDACIOUS, from its unusualness, may be used softly. 'Liar, cheat, deceiver and falsifier' are real positive words in their own right. But, since MENDACIOUS depends upon its context for power, it can formally call a man a 'liar' without his becoming too angry.

Mischief Too often these days we call petty crime MISCHIEF, and so excuse it by some sort of 'boys will be boys' reasoning. Perhaps we are only fooling ourselves because MISCHIEF may mean more than we know. Originally it was the offspring of a French verb *meschever*, 'to come to grief.' So, while MISCHIEF is almost a playful word now, it really was born from some tragic occurrence.

Misgiving An expressive noun because it retains an early sense of the word 'give,' a sense of 'suggesting,' as in "My heart gyveth me that [matters will not mend]." So, with the 'mis' connoting 'unhappy,' as in 'misfortune,' when your heart MISGIVES you it suggests 'unhappy things.' The result is, as the dictionaries say, a feeling of doubt and of anxious uneasiness; of apprehension and foreboding, of presentiment, premonition, and loss of courage and confidence. "At the last minute she felt misgivings about marrying such an eccentric man." The word is sometimes a verb, usually used only with mind or heart. "Some sixth sense warned the pilot too late: his heart misgave him just before the crash."

Obloquy OBLOQUY is that 'spiteful blame' heaped by envious men on successful men. Behind OBLOQUY is an attempt to assassinate character. OBLOQUY, which means literally 'to speak against,' is also the state of shame in which the culprit or victim finds himself.

Peremptory This word means dictatorial; arbitrarily abrupt and decisive. A single act may be PEREMPTORY, but a series of events is rarely so. The basis of the word is Latin *perimere*, 'to annihilate.' "Her father gave me a peremptory 'no' when I asked him if I might marry his only daughter."

Pestilential Like 'pest' and 'pester,' it comes from the Latin for 'plague,' but unlike those others it has kept its horrific meaning. A mosquito may be pestiferous, and pester and plague you; but only germ-carrying females of some species are said to be PESTILENTIAL. Figuratively, a certain person in your parlor may be a PESTILENTIAL presence among your guests. He may poison the atmosphere of your party.

Prurient and **Purulent** PRURIENT comes from the Latin for 'itching,' and thence, via 'craving,' means 'impurity of mind and desires.' The 'pur' in PURULENT means 'pus.' Both nouns for these adjectives end in either 'ence' or 'ency.'

Sad, Sack and **Sadsack** It is a question whether Sgt. Butler's pencil was mightier than his philological sense, or vice versa. At any rate two more remarkable and vocal words could hardly have been found for the sobriquet SADSACK, that poor bewildered private in the army, blundering his way through the vexations, vicissitudes and miles and miles of military redtape. When we speak now of a pretty SAD sort of party, or a pretty SAD theatrical performance, meaning they were dull and a flop, we use the word SAD in its original sense. Not only in English but in all Teutonic tongues, it meant 'heavy with saturation.' Soon after, it came to mean 'dull.' Gradually SAD redeemed itself, via the senses of 'settled,' 'orderly' and 'sober,' until at last it was touched and ennobled with pathos. Today SAD connotes a calm grief, a gloomy disposition, or a mournful aspect.

And even older, and more universal than SAD, is the word SACK, for a 'bag.' Anglo-Saxon *sacc*, French *sac*, Latin *sacus*, and also in Greek, Hebrew, and most European languages, including Celtic and Slavic. It is in the Biblical 'sackcloth' of goat's or camel's hair. As a bag, probably to hold the stolen goods in, SACK became a synonym for 'plunder.' "The pirates sacked the peaceful coastal town." In England SACK is a slang word like our 'fire,' meaning to be discharged from a job. "My boss sacked me yesterday, but he'll hire me again tomorrow." Truly a SADSACK is a bundle of woe.

Scowl A word that is not only malignant looking but aggressive sounding. You can SCOWL upon someone's hopes, or SCOWL your wife to tears. As a noun, a SCOWL is a 'threatening frown.'

Sloven and **Slattern** These two words are mates. The first is usually a man, the second is always a woman. SLOVEN is probably a mixture from Dutch *alof*, 'careless,' and Flemish *sloef*, 'dirty.' SLATTERN is from dialectal 'slatter' meaning 'to slop, waste.'

SLOVEN is almost archaic now, especially as an adjective. But the adjectival function is performed by the adverb SLOVENLY. A girl who is SLOVENLY will have a difficult time getting married. A SLOVEN is careless in habits, dress or work, or in all of them. His carelessness comes partly from laziness and partly from indifference to the niceties of life. Therefore, a SLOVEN is sometimes dirty. A clumsy manner of moving may be called SLOVENLY, with only a slight implication of laziness or lack of pride, and a SLOVENLY mind may be only tired or half-asleep.

An inveterate female SLOVEN is a SLATTERN. She is such a poor house-keeper she is no housekeeper at all. She lives in squalor, and frequently, by imputation, in vice. A SLOVEN may possibly be unaware of his untidiness. He may be a professor of philosophy and his mind may be wrapt in abstract fancies. But a SLATTERN is defiantly SLOVENLY. In a way, she glories in her condition.

Sycophantic A SYCOPHANT is obsequious, but historically he is also a scallywag. In ancient Athens it once happened that laws were being flouted, and so inducements were offered to informers. The original SYCOPHANTS were those 'informers.' Specifically they concerned themselves especially with illegal exporting of figs, whence their names—'fig' plus 'show.' On the one hand they were spies, and on the other, to the party in power, they were servile and obsequious. And always they were slanderers, bearers of false witness, and after something for their private gain. Though some men are false or tricky by nature, these men, who gave us our adjective, were known not only by their nature but specifically by their trade, and it is that which should logically have characterized the adjective. Yet as their progeny moved down toward our day, and the original conditions were forgotten, it was the 'obsequiousness' that clung, so that today SYCOPHANTIC and 'obsequious' are practically synonymous. Nevertheless, in view of all the circumstances, SYCOPHANTIC is by all odds the broader and stronger word.

Terrible "I'm terribly sorry," we say, quite affably, which is certainly pulling the claws from a ferocious adjective. But fortunately, if we must express awful things, the noun TERROR has lost none of its force. For TERROR itself is a truly TERRIBLE thing, sometimes rampaging through a crowd, stampeding it, or sometimes putting merely one man into a panic. In its early history it was simply a 'great fear.' So when we fell to using TERRIBLE for a mere 'extreme unpleasantness,' like the buzzing of mosquitoes when we are half-asleep, we are being ironical. Irony is the saying of one thing in order to mean the opposite. Thus, a TERRIBLE dinner served by a young bride is simply a way of saying it wasn't so bad after all. In this sort of usage, the word's original meaning is implied in a negative way.

Tough No matter how nice the people are, if you find it close and hot at a cocktail party, you will feel that the occasion is TOUGH. And if you look back into the history of TOUGH, you will discover it had in the oldest early English a companion, whose meaning it considerably absorbed. This other word meant simply 'oppressive.' That affinity was possible because TOUGH's own earliest meaning, in ancient Germany, was 'close together.' From this union we have all of TOUGH's meanings today, from 'firmness' and, hence, 'strength of texture' to the 'tough neighborhood' or America's 'tough guy,' now invading British diction to the consternation of critics there.

The permutations of TOUGH are quite considerable. It is all a question of 'closeness of texture.' The objects themselves must always remain flexible; you think of TOUGH leather but not of TOUGH iron or steel. We speak technically, yet fancifully, of some clays or sticky tars as being TOUGH. In figurative use the emphasis is not so much on close texture and flexibility, both of which produce great strength, as on plain 'difficulty.' The TOUGH problems in arithmetic are difficult to solve, the TOUGH battles on the gridiron take firm resolution to ensure victory, and the TOUGHS, or ruffians, are almost impossible to manage. Incidentally, the TOUGH which is a 'tough guy,' is the only use as a noun this word has. It may derive from a corruption that followed the extension of 'rough' into 'roughneck.'

Umbrage UMBRAGE is a noun meaning 'resentment' or 'offense.' *Umbra* was the Latin word for 'shade.' We can still use UMBRAGE to mean 'shade,' or the act of affording shade. But commonly, the UM-BRAGE you take when you feel insulted does not resemble ordinary shade. "The student took umbrage at his friend's success in earning a good mark." This suggests that the student felt a shadow was cast on his own abilities to make a high mark. Thus UMBRAGE usually suggests a 'slight' or 'pique.'

WAR

Alarm
Alert
Belligerency
BLOCKADE *n.* the closing off of an area or a country; esp. the BLOCKADE of a country by means of naval patrols, thus preventing the inflow of goods and matériel.
BRIGADE *n.* the largest unit of an army division, usually composed of two or more regiments.

CAMPAIGN *n.* military maneuvers considered in the light of one mission, as the Pacific CAMPAIGN in World War II, or the CAMPAIGN against Paris.
COHORT *n.* a company or any band of soldiers.

COMBAT *n.* a battle; fight; conflict. *v.* to fight; to give battle.

Combatant

CONFLICT *n.* a struggle; battle.

CORPS *n.* a tactical unit of an army, larger than a division; a very large branch of an armed force, as the Signal CORPS.

COURT MARTIAL *n.* a military court.

Displaced Persons

FOE *n.* enemy.

FORAY *n.* a sudden attack, often of an exploratory or foraging nature.

GARRISON *n.* a body of soldiers who are stationed in and guard a city or fort.

HOSTILITIES *n. pl.* acts of warfare.

INSURRECTION *n.* rebellion.

Martial

MILITANT *adj.* warlike; aggressive.

MILITIA *n.* citizens, not on active duty, who belong to a military organization under regular training.

Mission

MOBILIZE *v.* to muster an army; to prepare an army or a country, for active military duty.

MUTINY *n.* a rebellion in military service against the constituted authority.

OBSIDIONAL *adj.* pertaining to the act of besieging; or to a siege.

PATROL *n.* a man or group of men who guard an area or installation by making appointed rounds; a squad of soldiers sent into advance areas for purposes of reconnaissance.

PICKET *n.* a special group of men who are posted around a camp to guard against surprise attacks.

Rebel

RECONNOITER *v.* to look a place over; to make preliminary investigations.

SALLY *n.* a rushing advance; a light charge, as a SALLY of horsemen.

SCIAMACHOUS *adj.* pertaining to an imaginary struggle; literally, to a battle with shadows. *n.* SCIAMACHY. The spelling of the adjective is not formalized.

SENTRY *n.* a watchman; guard.

SIEGE *n.* a blockade or assault designed to capture a fortified place or starve it into submission.

SKIRMISH *n.* a sally; a small fight as a part of a battle.

SOLDIER *n.* a man in military service. Note the following:

> ARTILLERYMAN *n.* a soldier in the artillery, which is in charge of heavy, usually mounted guns.
>
> BOMBARDIER *n.* a soldier in the air corps whose duty is to guide a bomber over the target and release the bombs.
>
> CAVALRYMAN *n.* a soldier in the cavalry, which is a part of an army mounted on horse.
>
> DRAGOON *n.* a cavalryman.
>
> ENGINEER *n.* a soldier in the Corps of Engineers.

INFANTRYMAN *n.* a foot-soldier.

SAPPER *n.* an engineer engaged in undermining enemy fortifications.

SHARPSHOOTER *n.* a soldier who is a good marksman; hence, a sniper; also one of a picked group of marksmen.

Tirailleur

TROOPS *n. pl.* any armed group.

VANGUARD *n.* the first troops to engage the enemy; troops at the front.

War

WARFARE *n.* the state of being at war; the actual hostilities.

Note the following distinctions:

AERIAL WARFARE
CHEMICAL "
DESERT "
GUERILLA "
MINE "
MOBILE "
MOUNTAIN "
NAVAL "
PSYCHOLOG-
    ICAL "
TRENCH "

Alarm A pretty word that rings powerfully. In the Old French it meant "To arms," "À *l'arme*," as it also did, before that, in Italian. A mouse might scare you, but a loose lion ALARMS a whole town. ALARMING news is worse than scare headlines. It suggests disaster.

Alert War planes have reminded us enough of this word, except in its important finer senses. An ALERT man is not necessarily always on the watch. But he must be truly alive, truly aware that life is worth living. An ALERT man has all his senses timed to the world around him.

Belligerency A formal word for 'warfare' or a 'state of war,' and by extension a state of 'preparedness' or 'desire' for war. The 'belli' was of course the Latin *bellum*, 'war,' and the second syllable is from *gero*, 'to carry on.' BELLIGERENCY originally referred only to 'active warfare,' but now its meaning has been extended, in the word 'belligerent,' to include the neighborhood 'bully.'

Combatant Literally, 'beating together, contending, fighting.' COMBATANT is both an adjective and a noun. As an adjective it means 'prepared or disposed to fight,' or 'intended for fighting purposes.' As a noun it is a soldier who participates in the actual fighting. 'Combative' is a synonymous adjective but retains the full animus of combat. Thus if you are 'combative,' you are either fighting or wanting to fight.

Displaced Persons A tragic term coined by the harsh circumstances of modern war. It was applied first to inhabitants who had to flee from their native countries because of military action. But it was generalized to include all persons forced by any calamity to leave their homes. At the same time, it has narrowed to mean civilians who are deported as slave laborers.

Martial An ADJECTIVE deriving from Mars, the Roman god of war. Therefore, MARTIAL now suggests military, naval, aerial, and perhaps chemical warfare though it retains its original emphasis on hand-to-hand combat. "The general was a tough, old soldier: his martial air challenged the enemy personally although actually he was too valuable a man for front-line duty." Incidentally, we have not yet any single adjectives, corresponding to 'naval' and 'military,' for aerial or chemical warfare. A naval man, for example, is distinctly not an ordinary mariner, but an airman may pilot either a bomber or a commercial airliner.

Mission Mythology tells us that Mercury, the flying messenger of the gods, captured the imagination of ancient people perhaps as no greater god did. According to Tacitus, even the barbarous Germans accepted him from the Romans, and so admired him they made human sacrifices to him on certain days.

This may explain how the word MISSION, meaning the 'sending of word, of negotiators or of apostles,' is today so widely used, always flying forward to new meanings.

A venerable meaning of MISSION refers to 'envoys,' or 'special embassies,' sent somewhere, usually abroad, to perform any service. This sense has been extended by the United States to mean a 'permanent foreign embassy' or 'legation.' But aside from this usage, and aside from the religious utilization of the word to refer to 'missionaries' and their establishments, MISSION has retained its ideological connections with Mercury. For example, many MISSIONS are now flown at top speeds, and they have an implacable purpose, like messages from willful gods. The MISSION of a group of airplanes may be to bomb an enemy installation. In this sense MISSIONS must be specified and definite tasks, whether reconnaissance, observation or bombing. At any rate, the word is always looking outward and onward, extending its meaning in countless areas. Now it appears that any goal in life is a MISSION one must personally achieve.

Rebel Because of the Revolutionary and Civil Wars, REBELLION and REBELS are still familiar nouns in America. But REBEL, the verb, with the accent on 'bel,' is seldom used. It is both blunt and clear, and therefore expressive. By origin, it almost means "To arms!" from Latin *re* and *bellare*, 'to make war again!'

Tirailleur (Borrowed from the French, pronounced tee-ra-yur, the accents on the first and third syllables). Basically, a TIRAILLEUR is a 'skirmisher,' though in American military usage the term designates a 'sharpshooter.' TIRAILLEURS, in France, are troops of light infantry organized for skirmishing duty. See TIRADE.

War WAR, regrettably one of our commonest and most powerful words, grew from a word meaning a 'quarrel,' with an admixture of 'scandal.' The word comes from the Anglo-Saxon *werre*, identical with *werre* in the northern dialects of the Old French, which received it from the Old High German *werre*, a 'quarrel' or 'sedition.' This old German noun derived from a verb meaning 'to mix, confound,' akin to the present German *wirren* and *verwirren* meaning 'to disturb' and 'to embroil.' The Romans and the Greeks had similar words that conveyed the ideas of perishing, vanishing, and being dragged or swept away. The Latin verb was *verrere;* but the late Latin *warra* was not Roman at all. It was a Teutonic synonym for the regular Latin word for 'WAR,' *bellum*, which the Gauls confused with Latin *bellus*, 'beautiful.' Later, in the Old French, the 'w' became 'gu,' and the French word for WAR is still *guerre*, as the French for William is *Guillaume*.

WAYS AND MEANS

Ability, Capability & Capacity

Accomplish see Obtain, Attain, etc.

Achieve see Obtain, Attain, etc.

AFFORD *v.* to supply, furnish, provide; as, "The sunny day afforded him an excuse to play golf."

AGENT *n.* a person, means, tool or force used to obtain certain results.

APTITUDE *n.* talent, skill, capacity; quick intelligence; state of being readily trained.

Attain see Obtain, Attain, etc.

Capability see Ability, Capability, etc.

Capacity see Ability, Capability, etc.

COMPASS *v.* to attain, achieve, accomplish; to contrive.

COMPETENCE *n.* state of being suitable for some task.
adj. COMPETENT, well-qualified.

Contrive & Devise

Devise see Contrive & Devise

DISCHARGE *v.* to perform, fulfill

or accomplish a duty, task or obligation.

EFFECT v. to see that something is done; to make happen, as "The general effected his son's promotion to captain."

Endeavor

ENFORCE v. to make sure by force that something is done, as "By threats the bully enforced his demands on the smaller children on the block."

EXECUTE v. perform; carry out; accomplish.

FACULTY n. skill; talent; an ability to do certain things well, as a FACULTY for card-playing.

FASHION n. manner; way; mode.

IMPLEMENT v. to execute, perform, finish up or carry out a piece of work or a job.

IMPOTENCE n. state or quality of weakness; inability to do something. adj. IMPOTENT, powerless.

Ingenious

INSTRUMENT n. a tool or device; an agent or means by which something is done, as "A tyrant uses the police as an instrument of injustice."

Intelligible & Practicable

MANAGE v. to do something, esp. in the sense of getting a special job done. "He managed to get himself fired from his job after only a week of work."

MANNER n. way or means of getting something done.

MEANS n. pl. instrument; method; agent.

METHOD n. a mode of doing things; a kind of procedure. "His method of work was slow but very accurate."

MODE n. method; a way of effecting things; manner.

Obtain, Attain, Achieve & Accomplish

ORGAN n. instrument; means, as "An important organ of government is the judiciary."

PERFORM v. to accomplish; do; execute.

POWERLESS adj. without power or means of doing something.

Practicable see **Intelligible & Practicable**

REACH v. to attain; to arrive at, as of some goal.

SKILL n. talent; faculty; training.

SYSTEM n. manner; mode. "His system of ball playing was unlike anything New Yorkers had seen before."

TALENT n. a faculty; a special ability for doing certain things, as a TALENT for making enemies.

Ability, Capability and **Capacity** These three words illustrate the growth of an idea. All three form a union that expresses variously our powers for thought and action.

ABILITY was built from Latin *habilis,* meaning not only 'expert' or 'skillful,' but a host of other things now echoing in CAPABILITY and CAPACITY. For example, *habilis* took on the subjective sense of 'aptness,' and hence also of 'nimbleness,' discernible today in the proficiency of a CAPABLE person. But ABILITY's derivative senses have been predominantly alert ones: 'to handle, to use, to manage, and even to find out and know.' And so when we think of ABILITY today we think of something positive (not merely potential). We think of a reservoir of power, perhaps, yet it is power 'ready' for instant use, as the general ABILITY you may have in practical matters and the particular ABILITY you show in your business.

CAPABILITY and CAPACITY grew from the Latin verb *capere*, 'to take, hold.' The verb was amazingly alive, penetrating into all phases of life, martial and peaceful. One of its meanings was 'to take captive,' thence 'to captivate,' 'to allure' and finally 'to delude' or 'betray'; in another direction it meant 'to acquire' and hence 'to occupy.'

CAPABILITY came to mean 'CAPACITY for active power,' and CAPACITY took on the meaning of 'talent,' and then of a 'role' (we still speak of acting in the CAPACITY of a teacher). Finally, it has assumed the meaning of a general ABILITY, as the CAPACITY you might have for defending yourself against your enemies. But basically behind these two other words is the meaning of ABILITY, its suggestion of the simple power of 'possessing' and of 'retaining,' of 'having' and of 'holding,' of 'existing' and of 'subsisting.'

Contrive and **Devise** When you CONTRIVE to make ends meet on an inadequate salary, you find a way of doing something difficult. The idea in CONTRIVE is 'find,' from the French *trouver*. You don't CONTRIVE a way to walk down a road because your path lies clear before you. But you do CONTRIVE a way to climb a cliff. To CONTRIVE means 'to find a plan for doing something,' and it consequently implies 'ingenuity' and 'cleverness.' But there are various degrees of planning. If your planning is relatively simple, involving only a choice among a few alternatives, then you are CONTRIVING a way. "Soldiers quickly contrive to be as comfortable as possible when sleeping outdoors."

But if you have to lay deep plans in order to achieve your objective, you DEVISE a way of doing it. The exact meaning is a little ambiguous. The word first meant, in Latin, 'to divide.' At any rate you conquer a problem when you DEVISE an answer to it, and your method is probably complex. In practice, the difference between CONTRIVE and DEVISE is this: the former has a specific application, the latter a general application. "The thief, in order to break into the house, contrived a way by entering through the roof." "The thief had devised a method of house entering that always worked."

'Devices' and 'contrivances' may be anything from fanciful ideas to everyday tools. But they are always meant for a special use or purpose. 'Contrivances' tend to become instruments and artifices. 'Devices' include patterns, incidental ornaments and, in heraldry, symbols.

Endeavor This word often sounds stilted. "I'll endeavor to see you Tuesday," sounds stiff and silly unless the meeting were very important or difficult to manage. In that case, this long word reinforces its seriousness. ENDEAVOR basically suggests 'duty.' It is French *en,* 'in,' plus *devoir,* 'duty.'

Ingenious It was a rather dull word to begin with, meaning 'pertaining to an innate quality,' but it is vivacious enough today to describe any manner of inventiveness. "The boy ingeniously contrived stairs out of boxes so he could reach the cooky jar." "That is an ingenious method you suggest for lowering taxes, but we senators can take care of it ourselves, thank you."

Intelligible and **Practicable** These are good examples of some 'ible' and 'able' words we don't fully appreciate. Literally, INTELLIGENCE is a 'knowing.' If you are INTELLIGENT, you 'know' things. And if you then express what you know clearly enough for others to know it too, you speak INTELLIGIBLY. To speak INTELLIGIBLY is not the same as speaking INTELLIGENTLY, i.e. from 'known' facts. If you revise a word to make your speech clear and exact, you make it INTELLIGIBLE.

A PRACTICABLE plan is one that will actually 'achieve' some goal. A PRACTICABLE plan is not the same as a PRACTICAL plan. The latter means that the plan simply is *not* 'fanciful.' "It is more practical to save your money, than to expect a windfall whenever you are broke; a practicable method of saving is to have money for Savings Bonds taken from your salary regularly."

Obtain, Attain, Achieve and **Accomplish** When you OBTAIN something you just 'get' or 'receive' it. The statement is matter-of-fact, and not too particular. The thing you OBTAIN is usually quite concrete, like a lawn mower you borrow from your neighbor. With the lawn mower you may also OBTAIN an advantage, but this abstract acquirement is part of the concrete object.

The emphasis of OBTAIN is not on the effort you made to acquire something. But when you ATTAIN something, you have clearly 'directed your efforts' toward a goal which you have reached. As a rule, this goal is abstract like advantage, public esteem or success.

When you ACHIEVE something you ATTAIN it after 'overcoming difficulties.' The thing ACHIEVED is usually a task, an enterprise or an ambition. It is abstract, but it includes many things less abstract, such as some sort of reward. ACHIEVEMENTS are always 'triumphs.'

When you ACCOMPLISH something, you 'complete the doing of it,' whether it is a wood carving or a career. ACCOMPLISH conveys a sense of real effort and solid work. ACCOMPLISHMENTS imply a skill and artistry that accompanies the effort. We speak of an ACCOMPLISHED musician, for example, who has worked hard but who is talented to begin with.

OBTAIN is a workhorse. By simply making it over into an intransitive verb we have a new and singularly useful word. When something simply OBTAINS it is established and prevails, like, for example, a law which is in effect. When we say something *still* OBTAINS, we mean it still holds good, is not obsolete in any way. This one word does the work of a phrase or clause.

WEAKNESS

ANEMIA *n.* a condition of physical weakness induced by thinness of the blood, reduction of the red corpuscles, or deficiency of hemoglobin; pallor.

ATHENIC *adj.* refers to general debility. It is a pathological term from the Greek for 'without strength.' The initial 'a' in many Greek words means without. Do not confuse this adjective with Athenian, for Athens.

COWARDLY *adj.* without courage; timid. *n.* COWARDICE.

CRAVEN *adj.* cowardly; afraid.

DASTARDLY *adj.* cowardly in a mean or malicious way.

DEBILITY *n.* weakness.

DECREPITUDE *n.* state of being worn out, weak, broken down, esp. by infirmity or old age.

Desultory

Emaciate

Emasculate

Enervate

FEARFUL *adj.* without courage; timid.

Feckless

FEEBLE *adj.* weak.

FRAIL *adj.* weak; thin; delicate.

HELPLESS *adj.* weak; incompetent.

IMPOTENCE *n.* weakness; lacking strength or vigor; esp. sexual weakness. *adj.* IMPOTENT.

INFIRMITY *n.* weakness, esp. because of disease or old age.

Macerate

POLTROONERY *n.* cowardice.

POWERLESS *adj.* without strength or power.

Pusillanimous

SAP *v.* to weaken someone or something, as "Poor food saps a person."

Vitiate

WEAKEN *v.* to lose one's strength; to sap.

Weary

Desultory DESULTORY gunfire is fitful, discontinuous and irregular. But the basis of the word DESULTORY is Latin *saltire*, 'to leap.' DESULTORY talk 'leaps around' from one subject to another, though actually the leaping is listless.

Emaciate As a verb, EMACIATE means 'to make lean, to take almost all the flesh off.' "A fashionable woman nowadays emaciates herself by eating hardly enough to stay alive." Its near synonym 'to starve' is more popular, but the past participle, EMACIATED, used as an adjective, is widely heard today. "The modern fashions make a woman look emaciated," or " 'Escapees' from concentration camps are invariably emaciated."

Emasculate Literally, 'to castrate.' But EMASCULATE is a synonym for 'to weaken, to rob of strength.'

Enervate Hot humid weather is ENERVATING. It makes you feel listless and weak, it dulls your nerves by weakening them. 'Nerve' is the root of the word.

Feckless An adjective meaning 'ineffectual' or 'ne'er-do-well.' The 'feck' (still going strong in Scotland) meant 'strong, vigorous, hardy.' The antonym, 'feckful,' is still a dictionary word.

Macerate This word means 'to soften' by steeping, or soaking in water. But it may also mean 'to harden' in the sense of making lean, as by fasting. But with the loss of fat goes a 'loss or softening' of muscle, and a 'wasting away.'

Pusillanimous To the Romans *animus* meant, in part, 'courage.' At any rate, that is the cue we took in PUSILLANIMOUS, for today that word means 'cowardly.' It is a long word for us to handle, but the 'pusil' lingers on an effective sardonic note. By itself, it once meant very little. Hooked up here with 'animus,' which had a score of meanings allied with 'courage,' it gives us a single word for 'meanly faint-hearted, contemptibly cautious.'

Vitiate This word sounds almost vicious, and 'viciousness' does tinge it. When a business concern is struck by ill fortune or bad management it is VITIATED. Whether the business becomes bad itself or is a victim of bad circumstances, there is 'viciousness' somewhere in the mess. The basis of the word is a Latin word for 'fault.' When you VITIATE anything you 'impair' it. You especially 'mar' it. If it is anything that runs, like a machine or a course of events, you 'block' or 'stop' it. A good name can also be VITIATED ('debased' or 'destroyed') by slander. A good character can be VITIATED by bad influences.

Weary At least etymologically, when you are WEARY you are not 'worn out' in the sense of 'used up.' You are not 'worn' in any sense, but you are 'tired.' 'Wear' and WEARY are *not* cognates. Perhaps the first WEARY Anglo-Saxon had been tramping, *worian*, 'to wander, tramp about, travel,' in a *wōr*, 'a moor, a swampy, leg-tiring place.' And WEARY comes from an Anglo-Saxon word *wērig*, 'weary.' *Wērig* and *worian* and *wōr* all were cognates. It was no unusual trick in the Old English for an 'o' before an 'r' to contract itself thus, into an 'e.'

THE WEATHER

AIRY *adj.* pertaining to air; breezy.

AUSTRAL *adj.* pertaining to the south wind, or simply to the south.

BLASTY *adj.* blusterous.

BLEAK *adj.* cold; penetrating; sharp; as a BLEAK day.

BLOWY *adj.* windy.

BLUSTEROUS *adj.* windy; characterized by fitful or sudden bursts of wind; stormy.

BLUSTERY *adj.* blusterous.

BOREAL *adj.* pertaining to the north wind, or simply to the north.

BREEZY *adj.* pertaining to gentle, or moderate, winds.

BRUMOUS *adj.* pertaining to wintry fog and to lowering skies.

CIRROUS *adj.* pertaining to high fleecy clouds (CIRRUS).

Climate & Weather

CLIME *n.* climate; by extension, a certain area or district, as a remote CLIME.

CLOUDY *adj.* full of clouds; overcast.

DIRTY *adj.* referring to bad weather; stormy; wet; bleak.

DOG DAYS *n. pl.* the very hot, sultry days toward the end of summer.

DOWNFALL *n.* rain.

DRIZZLE *n.* steady, light rain.

Dry see **Wet & Dry**

EOLIAN *adj.* pertains to any wind, or all winds.

EURUSIAN *adj.* pertaining to the east wind (or possibly southeast wind).

FAVORIAN *adj.* pertaining to the west wind.

FOG *n.* a cloudy or murky atmosphere at or near ground level. *adj.* FOGGY.

GUSTY *adj.* blusterous.

Halcyon

HAZY *adj.* pertaining to a murky or shimmering atmosphere.

HYALINE *adj.* pertaining to the atmosphere or sea when smooth (poetic).

HYPERBOREAN *adj.* pertaining to the north wind, but esp. to the extreme north in any respect.

MIST *n.* a kind of light fog or steam that obscures the atmosphere at or near ground level. *adj.* MISTY.

NEBULAR *adj.* pertaining to cloudlike masses of gaseous matter or stars which occur at great distances, far beyond our solar system. Hence, also, hazy or cloudy, both in a literal and figurative sense.

NIVAL or NIVEOUS *adj.* pertaining to snow.

OVERCAST *adj.* cloudy.

PLUVIOUS or PLUVIAL *adj.* rainy or pertaining to rain. HYETAL refers more to rainfall or to rainy regions.

PRECIPITATION *n.* rain, snow, sleet, hail.

RAW *adj.* bleak; wet and cold; as a RAW wind.

RORIC *adj.* pertaining to dew.

SHOWER *n.* a short, sudden rain.

Slosh, Slush & Sludge

Sludge see Slosh, Slush, etc.

Slush see Slosh, Slush, etc.

SOUPY *adj.* foggy.

SPRINKLE *n.* a light shower.

SQUALL *n.* a violent burst of wind, often accompanied by some precipitation. *adj.* SQUALLY.

STORM *n.* a more or less violent atmospheric disturbance, nearly always accompanied by winds and precipitation.

BLIZZARD *n.* a heavy and long snowstorm.

BLOW *n.* a hurricane; any storm with high winds.

CLOUDBURST *n.* a sudden, very heavy rain.

CYCLONE *n.* a storm with heavy winds blowing with a circular motion and covering a large area. *adj.* CYCLONIC.

DELUGE *n.* a flood.

DOWNPOUR *n.* a moderately heavy rain.

GALE *n.* high winds.

HURRICANE *n.* a cyclone that travels hundreds of miles.

SANDSTORM *n.* a windstorm in the desert that carries great clouds of sand.

TEMPEST *n.* a violent storm, with wind, rain, lightning.

THUNDER SQUALL *n.* a thunderstorm.

THUNDERSTORM *n.* a storm with thunder and lightning, and nearly always rain.

TORNADO *n.* a compact, whirling wind, accompanied by a funnel-shaped cloud, and moving over a narrow path with great force.

TWISTER *n.* a tornado.
TYPHOON *n.* a South Pacific cyclone.
Sultry & Swelter
Swelter see **Sultry & Swelter**
TEMPESTUOUS *adj.* stormy.

TORRENTIAL *adj.* pertains to TORRENT, a rush of water or a violent downpour of rain.
Weather see **Climate & Weather**
Wet & Dry

Climate and **Weather** Generally speaking, WEATHER is local and transitory; CLIMATE is regional and year-round.

More particularly, WEATHER refers to the earth's atmosphere only. CLIMATE suggests *any* atmosphere, terrestrial, intellectual or moral. The intellectual CLIMATE of a college town differs from that of a manufacturing town. The moral CLIMATE of Hitler's Germany differed from that of nineteenth-century Germany. However, the verb 'to WEATHER' helps us WEATHER not only a storm but also adversity in general. In this sense, WEATHER means to 'stand up against' something, or to 'endure.'

Etymologically, WEATHER is the wind, CLIMATE is the slope of the earth. WEATHER not only *was* in its source but actually *is* 'variable,' like the wind, even reversible and contradictory. Its root is the Lithuanian's word for 'storm'; it also appears in the Russian's word for 'fair WEATHER.' In the very beginning, the Aryan word signified a 'blowing.' This is another example that Lithuanian is probably closer to that parent-language than any other European tongue. While English is of course a comparatively new tongue, the same root produced 'wither,' an effect that might follow from either sunshine or hard WEATHER.

On the other hand CLIMATE is no more unsteady than the earth is— at least etymologically. Our words 'climbing,' 'inclination' and 'climax' are all offshoots of CLIMATE's root because they also pertain to 'slope.' The Greeks had a notion the earth sloped down to the Arctic, and that the WEATHER grew worse and worse the farther you went in that direction. Hence there were successive CLIMATES, or prevailing regional weathers.

Incidentally, you can be either 'WEATHER-beaten' or 'WEATHER-bitten.' But you must take the words literally: in one case you are 'beaten' and, in the other, 'bitten.'

Halcyon In the hectic days of modern life the word HALCYON has a picturesque appeal. The HALCYON days of Indian Summer are inevitably associated with quiet scenes in the country, as the HALCYON days of sea voyaging refer to fair weather and a calm, beautiful sea.

It is a pity to distort these pictures in the least, but the fact is that the word HALCYON is something of a hoax. It is the mangled name of a noisy bird, the 'kingfisher,' that long-billed fish-eater with a harsh chatter. Worse than that there is probably an 'auk' in the word, by an etymological relationship. Without necessarily punning, there are probably no awkwarder or more ill-adjusted-looking birds anywhere than the 'auks.' Specifically, the Greek word for 'kingfisher' is *alkyon*, whence Latin *alcedo*, probably akin to the Old Norse for an 'auk.' But *alkyon* was poetically pulled to pieces. The new word was *halskyon*, meaning, not a kingfisher now, but vaguely 'sea-conceiving.' For it had been reported that the female kingfisher laid her eggs at sea on a floating nest her mate had built, and that the eggs always hatched out during a fortnight of fair weather. No waves lapped over the cradle and all was peaceful and serene. Such days deserved a name for themselves, and through these circumstances they obtained it.

Slosh, Slush and **Sludge** Perhaps these were all the same word originally, from the Norwegian dialect *sluss* or *slusk*, 'mire.' But nobody knows for certain. SLUSH, a noun, usually means to us 'muddy, melting snow,' and we SLOSH, a verb, or SLUDGE through it. SLUDGE is an informal modification of 'trudge,' formed for just this sort of winter walking. But on shipboard SLUSH is 'refuse grease,' and a ship's cook is disrespectfully called a 'slushy,' at least by English sailors. More seriously SLUSH is a greasy mixture for oiling or protecting machinery or for filling in chinks in masonry. Colloquially SLUSH is used as a verb to indicate the dashing of water over objects to clean them. This use becomes confused with 'sluice,' a distinct word deriving from the Old French *escluse*, for a 'floodgate.' The colloquial noun SLUSH is of course just 'gush,' only less hurried, or more silly or sloppy. SLOSH really means to flounder splashingly through water, hence just 'to splash.' Some say SLUDGE comes directly from Middle English *sluche*, in turn from an Old Norse word for 'greasy.' It means SLUSH or 'mire,' including 'sticky mud' or 'mixed muddy snow and ice.' It extends its uses to mean anything like that, such as refuses in refining oil or washing ores. In these extended uses SLUDGE becomes a synonym for 'muck.'

Sultry and **Swelter** SULTRY is probably derived from an obsolete form of SWELTER. SWELTER in Old English meant 'to die.' Today when we are like-to-die in a packed and perspiring crowd on a hot day we say we are SWELTERING, which means more we are 'perspiring' than we are 'expiring.' Likewise a SULTRY day is 'oppressively hot,' and makes us sweat. A SULTRY woman is warming enough to make us, figuratively, sweat.

Wet and Dry WET is all it says it is, being closely related to 'water' itself, as can be seen from their ancestors, Icelandic *vātr*, 'wet' and *vantn*, 'water.' But like its opposite, DRY, WET has captured the imagination, and now we use it in all sorts of colloquial expressions. "Oh no," we say, "he's all wet," meaning "He's 'all wrong.' " The equating of 'wetness' with 'wrongness' is a pure tour de force of slang. On the other hand, we say: "Kansas is dry" as if the state had no water. The reference is of course to legislation prohibiting the sale of liquors. It obliges us to describe the Sahara desert as 'arid,' lest we confuse what liquid is scarce. DRY is Old English *dryge:* but it exists in altered forms in Dutch and German (*droog* and *trochen*), and it may have originated in Icelandic *drauge*, 'dry log.' When a cow is DRY she is unable to give milk; sometimes we say we are DRY when we cannot shed tears. Wine is DRY when it is not sweet. When humor is DRY it is without a show of feeling. A book is DRY when it hasn't any humor or real interest in it. DRY work can cause us to be thirsty, but it also means that it can be dull work. A prize fight is DRY when no blood flows, and in military parlance DRY fire is shooting without live ammunition. Which leaves us wondering again what is 'wetness' after all, when such things are DRY.

WORDS OFTEN CONFUSED

Accept & Except
Access & Excess
Advise & Advice
Allure & Lure
Allusion & Illusion
Annular & Annual
Aptitude & Ineptitude
Arrogate & Abrogate
Ascetic, Aesthetic & Acetic
Averse & Adverse
Caret, Carat & Carrot
Carnage & Carnival
Complimentary & Complementary

Council & Counsel
Dam & Damn
Deadly & Deathly
Dear & Dearth, also Deer
Deliberate & Elaborate
Differ & Defer
Distinct, Distinctive & Distinguished
Efficiency, Proficiency & Efficacy
Elect & Select
Emanate & Eminent
Endue & Endow
Evoke, Provoke & Invoke
Exercise & Exorcise

Explicit & Implicit
Felicity & Facility
Fervent & Fervid
Gentle & Genteel
Imbue, Imbrue & Imbibe
Immanent & Imminent
Immolate & Emulate
Immunity & Impunity
Impart & Impact
Impinge & Infringe
Intent & Attent
Linage & Lineage
Mettle & Fettle
Mortify & Mortuary
Muddle & Meddle
Neb & Nib
Ocular & Oracular
Oppose & Appose
Pediatrics & Pedagogue
Personable & Personage
Perspicuous & Perspicacious
Phase & Faze
Practice & Practise

Prescribe & Proscribe
Pretense & Pretext
Proceed & Precede
Produce & Adduce
Recur & Occur
Refragable, Infrangible & Refrangible
Relegate & Delegate
Remiss & Amiss
Serape & Etape
Shallop & Shallot
Shuffle & Scuffle
Slick & Sleek
Solecism & Sciolism
Sordid & Morbid
Suffragette & Suffragist
Ted & Tat
Tepid & Trepid
Tonsorial & Sartorial
Torrid & Horrid
Trip & Trap
Yell & Yelp

Accept and **Except**   These are two very different words in spite of their similar look. As a matter of fact, though these words are both verbs, EXCEPT may also be used as a preposition. Much too often ACCEPT and EXCEPT are confused, possibly because EXCEPT is used as a preposition more often than either word as a verb.

Actually, the prefixes 'ac' and 'ex' have opposite meanings. They mean 'to' and 'from,' with the same directional connotations as in "I walked to the corner," and "I came from the corner." They are the familiar Latin preposition *ad* and *ex*. But the *ad* was not changed to 'ac' by the English. Early Romans changed it when they combined it with *capere,* 'to take,' to form the verb *accipere,* 'to receive.' Later Romans created the frequentative *acceptare,* whence French *accepter* and our ACCEPT, meaning not merely 'to receive' but, as it were, 'doubly to receive,' hence 'to receive with gratitude.'

EXCEPT was formed for an opposite purpose, not to 'take to one's self,' but to 'take out.' Hence transitively it means today 'to exclude' or 'to omit,' as when the names of lesser personages are EXCEPTED in a list of notables. Very infrequently EXCEPT is used intransitively, with 'to' or 'against,' in the sense of 'objecting to.' But usually we express this intransitive thought differently. We make what is really a new frequentative, in view of the Latin 'take' that already exists in EXCEPT. "Mr. Chairman, I take exception to the last speaker's remarks." 'Take exception to' has become standard idiom in English.

Access and **Excess**   The noun ACCESS refers to an approach, or a means of obtaining admission, to something. "Passengers do not have access to the captain's bridge on most steamers." EXCESS, on the other hand refers to an overabundance of anything. "She has an excess of fat on her hips."

Advise and **Advice**   This entry ADVISES you that the noun ADVICE, like in 'good advice,' is spelled with a 'c.' But also it suggests that ADVICE is a more important word than we often suppose. And consequently, so is ADVISE.

It is only human that we should disfavor unsolicited ADVICE. But the dictionaries will tell you that ADVICE can actually, at times, mean 'encouragement.' This sense seems odd, until you reflect that ADVICE is an opinion offered either to dissuade you from doing something, or to encourage you to do something. That is, ADVICE is often constructive. In one usage 'to ADVISE' is completely neutral. It may merely 'apprise or notify' you of something. "This letter is to advise you that your payment of the last telephone bill is long overdue." The noun naturally follows suit, you receive ADVICE that you should pay your bill. ADVICE and ADVISE in this sense are cold and formal words.

In the Old French ADVICE was *avis*, a contraction of *à vis*, 'in or according to my opinion.' In the Latin, it was a solidification of *ad visum*, 'according to what looks good to me.' The noun was formed to express 'opinion,' but it came to mean also 'admonishment,' and finally 'notification.' But the main meaning, 'to proffer a critical opinion,' has remained, and both ADVICE and ADVISE (the difference in spelling is purely artificial) go back to the Latin verb *videre*, 'to see.' The first meaning of ADVISE was 'to look at' or, reflexively, 'to consider.' Compare French *aviser*, 'to perceive, spy, consider.' So when someone ADVISES us today about something, he has not merely observed our plight but has reflected upon it.

Allure and **Lure**   Two words rich in overtones. One hints at the ineffable, and the other conveys our imagination down to some mystery of peril and doom. Yet both words, in the sense in which we use them today, were born of a common bunch of feathers.

A medieval LURE or 'bait,' was a feather decoy, used by falconers to entice hawks back to the hand. It so happens, however, that falcons are obedient birds, even affectionate, with a doglike respect for their masters. During their novitiate real meat was wrapped in a LURE, but soon the birds by habit came down at a mere glimpse of feathers— and only feathers—on the ground.

Thus a LURE was an 'illusion' from the start. And as illusions include all the mysteries of life, good and evil, the sense of the word was bound to expand. When the alliterative 'al' (really 'a,' meaning 'to') was prefixed to LURE, a new word was born with especially manifold suggestions. LURES themselves had already become 'enticements' and 'temptings.' The verb 'to ALLURE' came to mean 'to attract onward,' as by flattery. It quickly assumes the sense of 'to fascinate' or 'to charm.' It is this meaning that adjective ALLURING conveys. The plainer verb, to LURE, has remained quite faithful to the simpler meaning of 'to entice, attract.'

An obsolete meaning of ALLURE was a 'manner,' even a manner of moving, a gait. So an ALLURING manner today may, though it is 'attractive, enticing' because of its charm and fascination, has no suggestion of physical danger in it. But a LURING manner is purposely planned to tempt someone to misfortune or evil. It is a snare designed to trap. Behind it is a malevolent intelligence.

Allusion and Illusion These two words are often confused. Aside from their formal similarity, perhaps the reason for this confusion is, that both the words are vague, or at least evasive, in their import. When we ALLUDE to something we 'mention it quickly in passing.' Consequently, ALLUSIONS are evanescent things, fleeting noticings of things. This definition places them close to ILLUSIONS, which are 'mirages,' things that 'seem to exist but do not.' Thus ILLUSIONS, like ALLUSIONS, are elusive, and the confusion of the words starts at this point.

Annular and Annual Christmas is ANNUAL because it comes 'yearly,' but eclipses of sun are not ANNUAL since they occur at various intervals. But a solar eclipse may be ANNULAR, and may occur when the moon is at its greatest distance from the earth, directly between an observer on the earth and the sun. Because the moon is further away, it cannot cover the sun completely, and a 'ring' of light shows all the way around the moon. ANNULAR refers to 'ring or rings.' It also refers to a 'ring's shape,' and to 'ring-like markings.' ANNUAL is from Latin *annus*, 'year.' ANNULAR is from *annulus*, 'ring.'

Aptitude and **Ineptitude** The little seed of APTITUDE was Latin *apere*, 'to fasten, fit.' From the participle, *aptus*, 'fitted,' came our much abused dwarf adjective APT. If we are APT to do something, we are 'likely' to do it, because we are good at doing such a thing, 'fitted,' to do it. APTNESS is a 'natural tendency' or a 'quickness to learn or to act.' It is *'demonstrated* readiness,' you show your APTNESS in action. APTITUDE is *'potential* readiness,' a state of fitness, and always for some specific activity. For example "He has an aptitude, or talent, for music." Naturally, the idea of 'skillfulness' has been added.

The negative of APTNESS is INEPTNESS (the 'a' was simply pressed upon and shrunk), which inevitably carries a suggestion of clumsiness, lack of skill, etc. The negative of APTITUDE is INEPTITUDE. INEPTITUDE is the 'constitutional inability to say or do the appropriate thing.'

Arrogate and **Abrogate** The dictionaries give you for ARROGATE: 'to take, assume or demand unduly; to claim with presumptious pride; to usurp; to demand unreasonably.' The verb is transitive, and has given us both ARROGATION ('unwarrantable assumption' or the 'act of usurpation'), and ARROGANCE ('an aggressive haughtiness'). 'To ARROGATE rights' is therefore 'to claim them as your own' on the assumption that other persons are inferior to yourself. You are interested in possessing their rights, and you assume in advance that your obtaining those rights will be proof enough of your superiority. ARROGANCE is thus the expression of pride in its more fatuous, unhampered form. It never bothers to scorn or to criticize those whom it affronts.

ABROGATION is an 'authoritative rescinding of public acts,' such as laws. It has no nounal companion, as ARROGATION has in ARROGANCE, nor has it given us any adjective comparable to ARROGANT. In a sense it is a companion to ARROGATE, because AGGRESSORS who ARROGATE the authority of others naturally ABROGATE ('repeal') the laws of those others. Both are built on Latin *rogare*, 'to call, ask' or, specifically 'to propose a law.' In this latter sense *rogare* acquired a reversing negative, the affix *ab*, 'from.' That negative gives us ABROGATE. The prefix of ARROGATE means not 'from' but 'to.' It was *ad* in Latin, changed to 'ar' to form *arrogare*, 'to assume.' Since a little bit of 'assumption' is a dangerous thing, we now have ARROGANCE, or 'insolent assumption.'

Ascetic, Aesthetic and **Acetic** ASCETIC is not by any means to be confused with AESTHETIC, for they are spiritual opposites. But both are Greek. AESTHETIC meant 'perceptive,' and as the Greek continually sought to perceive the beautiful, it came to mean 'devoted or pertaining to the arts,' which are supposedly dedicated to beauty. ASCETIC meant 'gymnastics,' then it referred to the 'strenuous,' was narrowed to the 'rigorous,' and finally to bitter 'self-denial.' Its connotations are religious, and it is typified by a person who retreats from the material everyday world to a life of spiritual contemplation. An ASCETIC is abstinent to an extreme. A vegetarian is only mildly ASCETIC; his abstinence does not regiment his whole life. ASCETICISM can be a relentless creed, not merely an exacting principle.

ACETIC is a practical word. It means 'sour.' Its base is Latin *acer*, 'sharp, sour.' Vinegar is partly ACETIC acid.

Averse and **Adverse**   Both these adjectives are born of Latin *vertere*, 'to turn.' One acquired the prefix *ad*, 'toward,' and the other acquired the prefix *a*, 'away.'

AVERSE means 'unfavorable, ill disposed toward, reluctant.' "Her mother was averse to her staying out late." AVERSE always results from a dislike, it is a question of will. You can *not* say, "The sun was averse to shining today," because the sun has no free will. Perhaps a cat doesn't have free will either; but we usually think animals have responsible behavior, so you can say, "The cat is averse to petting."

ADVERSE means 'opposed to,' whence our word ADVERSITY. "The adverse winds made it impossible to sail upstream," means that the winds were coming from upstream and thus opposed the boat's progress. ADVERSE usually means 'antagonistic.' "His adverse remarks threw the debate into disorder." "She reacted adversely to his proposal of marriage."

Caret, Carat and **Carrot**   A CARET is the inverted 'v' in writing or printing that indicates the site of an omission. CARET is the third person singular, present indicative of Latin *carere*, meaning 'it is wanting.' A CARAT is twofold; either one twenty-fourth of gold in an alloy, or a unit of weight in gems, 3.086 grains troy. It comes via France and Italy, from ancient Greece where it was a carob bean that was used (or its shell was, as other small shells were), as a measure of weight. A CARROT, the vegetable, is just Gallicized and Latinized Greek for the same thing.

Carnage and **Carnival**   CARNAGE is a fleshy word for 'slaughter,' suggesting also the 'corpse' and the bloody aftermath as well as the actual massacre. It sometimes denotes simply the 'collective slain,' as a hunter speaks of dead game on the ground as the 'take.' Lightly used, CARNAGE can be humorous "Well, look at the carnage these children have made of my house." CARNIVAL is related to CARNAGE; they both come from Latin *caro*, 'flesh.' But CARNIVAL also has the word *levare*, 'to lift.' In this case, the 'lift' meant 'to put away.' The word probably first applied to the last three days before Lent, when people 'put away' the cares of the flesh while they enjoyed themselves for the last time before the sacrifice for the Lenten season. Now CARNIVAL means any 'happy occasion,' though specifically it is a synonym for 'circus.'

Complimentary and **Complementary** Everybody knows what COMPLIMENTS are, and we appreciate them enough to use often the word COMPLIMENTARY. But a heavy responsibility rests on the tiny 'i.' When an 'e' slips into its place all the pleasant persiflage goes out of the word. It becomes calculative. 'To COMPLEMENT' means 'to make complete,' from the Latin *plere*, 'to refill,' preceded by the intensive *com*, 'to fill to the brim'—as we would say.

In common usage today a COMPLEMENT is an "addition,' specifically the 'addition necessary to complete a thing.' Consequently, to COMPLEMENT a thing is 'to provide that addition.' A 'supplement' is something added *after* completion. However, COMPLEMENTARY is used loosely as the equivalent of 'corresponding.' Two COMPLEMENTARY (corresponding) parts complete a whole, as may two fields on opposite sides of the road that constitute your property.

Oddly, COMPLIMENTARY derives from COMPLEMENTARY and is probably related to Latin *imber*, 'rain.'

Council and **Counsel** The medial 'c' and 's' are far from being insignificant. They were there in the time of Julius Caesar, and before that, to distinguish one word from the other. The *concilium* was a 'political assembly.' The *consilium* (from a different root) was an 'advisory board,' and more commonly simply a 'deliberation, sitting together for advice, planning, judgment.'

The basis of a COUNCIL is a 'calling together,' and that of a COUNSEL is a 'consulting.' When today a father COUNSELS his son to be good, or gives him wise COUNSEL, he speaks as the experienced man. Professionally a COUNSELOR is now a 'lawyer,' who usually gives us his COUNSEL in private, and may have no official relation to public affairs. But a COUNCILMAN belongs to a 'political COUNCIL.'

COUNSEL may be a verb or noun, but COUNCIL is only a noun.

Dam and **Damn** All little words with a punch aren't Anglo-Saxon. DAM doesn't appear in Old English, and DAMN is pure Latin. DAMN is, of course, much the stronger of the two, though we have used it so profligately upon the slightest of annoyances, that it has lost much of its intensive and vindictive strength. Today it usually expresses only 'vehement disapproval,' but for such mild purposes the Romans used quite a different word, our present word 'explode.' When an actor was hissed off the stage he was not DAMNED but 'exploded.' DAMNED, to the Romans, was a more prosaic word. It meant 'condemned,' as by a court, to a penalty, with *damnum,* 'loss or injury,' as its basis. We have this root still in our word 'damage.' It was not until Chaucer's time that DAMN took on its theological connotations, and the Puritans gave it a depth of terror peculiarly their own. Inherently, of course, it is far more forceful than any hissing, since even at the outset it implied 'punishment.'

The other word DAM has two meanings, an 'obstruction or dike,' as in Rotterdam, and the 'mother of a quadruped.' In its maternal sense it is just 'dame,' from the feminine *domina* of Latin *dominus,* 'lord.' But in Elizabethan times it separated from 'dame' in usage, and was used for a female parent, especially of animals. 'Sire' has had a similar development. It comes from Latin *senior,* 'older,' and is used for a person of noble or authoritative status. But 'sire' is now often used for a male parent of animals, particularly of horses.

In its sense of a containing wall DAM is Teutonic, with many European counterparts. It did not occur in Old English except as a derived verb *for-damman,* 'to dam up.' Even that was just a sizable slice of the Gothic original *four-dammjan.* Our remnant is simply a convenience.

Deadly and **Deathly**   Roughly, the difference between 'doing' and 'feeling.' A DEATHLY fear will come over you if you see someone taking DEADLY aim at you with an automatic gun. Mortal diseases are DEADLY, but the atmosphere of a plague-stricken town is DEATHLY. When DEADLY becomes qualitative, attesting more to our feelings, we often shorten it to 'dead.' "There was a dead silence." This is somewhat the same as a DEATHLY silence, but it differs in stress. In our minds, death is a 'finality,' and hence of 'completion.' A 'dead silence' is a 'complete silence.' It is, therefore, to a degree, DEATHLY. But it is not DEADLY.

Dear and **Dearth,** also **Deer**   When there is a DEARTH, a 'scarcity,' *not* an 'absence,' of potatoes, for example, then potatoes become DEAR, that is, 'expensive.' But historically the relationship was the reverse. The exact roots of DEARTH are in doubt, but the sense seems to have stemmed from a very ancient idea in Teutonic tongues, of 'superiority, glory, even fierceness.' These traits were probably wishes, which had value so that the word soon represented 'costliness.' This far it got in the Anglo-Saxon; but later it acquired a 'th,' after the manner of 'health' from 'heal' and 'warmth' from 'warm,' and DEARTH came to mean a 'scarcity.' This is not strange when you consider that all costly things are scarce, comparatively speaking.

DEARTH is full of expressive undertones, being intimately related to our adjective DEAR, which, from meaning 'costly,' came to mean 'precious' and, finally, 'beloved.' Even the beautiful animals we call DEER may have been related in antiquity to DEAR, although the roots of the two words have been always confused by their sheer similarity and by our ancestors' mixed-up spelling. All animals were once called DEER, as witness Shakespeare's "mice and rats and such small deer." But the DEER that hunters were forever chasing, and that tasted so good, eventually assumed the word to themselves.

Deliberate and **Elaborate**   When we speak of doing something with a DELIBERATE purpose we retain some, but far from all, the manifold meanings of the verb 'to DELIBERATE,' or 'to consider, ponder over, discuss.' When we say a man walks with a DELIBERATE step or that his manner is DELIBERATE two other connotations of this sadly neglected verb creep in: 'slowness' and 'contemplation.' Unfortunately, when we use the adverb we forget the range of the verb almost entirely. "You did that deliberately," which implies only 'on purpose.'

The adjective ELABORATE has suffered the same fate as the adjective DELIBERATE. We use ELABORATE to suggest 'fancy' or 'fantastic,' with a touch of 'grandioseness' or 'size.' But the verb 'to ELABORATE' means to work something out with thoroughness and exactness, to produce a product which is actually complete and carefully worked over. This product may be incidentally fantastic or grandiose but it is not necessarily so. Occasionally we do speak of 'ELABORATING our ideas,' but usually with only the meaning of 'explaining them more fully' to some dunderhead who doesn't understand them. Though we do speak of 'ELABORATING on a subject,' of 'enlarging it by explanation,' still the adjective belittles itself in ordinary speech. In other words, when you say, "What an elaborate house you have!" you are not getting the full use of a good adjective.

Differ and **Defer**   There is a temptation to say, "My house is different *than* my neighbor's house," instead of more correctly saying, "My house is different *from* my neighbor's house." The correct usage is made clear by comparing DIFFER with DEFER.

The common meaning of 'to DEFER' is 'to put something off, to delay some action.' DEFER in this sense comes from Latin *dis*, 'apart,' plus *ferre,* 'to carry.' Hence it means 'to bear things in different directions or ways,' which naturally means you are 'delayed' or 'get nowhere.'

The word DIFFER, whence 'different,' has precisely the same origin. Both 'dif' and 'de' were once *dis.* When you DIFFER with someone you both go in different directions; naturally you 'don't agree.' When you DIFFER from someone in point of resemblance the separation is still more distinct—you 'depart *from* him.' Hence DIFFER implies less comparison, calling for *than,* than separation, calling for *from.*

DEFER has a second meaning. "I defer to your better judgment and will do as you suggest." In this sense, DEFER means 'submission,' and it is another word altogether. Its prefix was Latin *de,* 'down,' and not *dis,* 'apart'; but its root is again *ferre,* 'to carry.' Thus it meant 'to bear or bring down,' and ultimately 'to lay something down before someone.' In the Old French it meant 'to admit or give way to an appeal.' Now when you DEFER you submit yourself respectfully to some other person's authority or judgment.

Distinct, Distinctive and **Distinguished** Whatever is DISTINCT is 'clearly defined or outlined.' "That is a distinct photograph of his face even though it is so small." It means more than 'visibility.' A house, for example, is visible even against a background of trees. But if it were on the horizon, with the sky behind it, then its silhouette would be visibly DISTINCT. Mothers DISTINCTLY tell their children to come right home after school. If things are made DISTINCT, there can be no mistakes.

Nevertheless, a house might stand out against any background if its features were unusual enough to catch the eye. In that case its shape, color, size, etc., would be its DISTINCTIVE features. Something DISTINCTIVE is always 'unique,' but something DISTINCT may be very common. And here the word DISTINGUISHED comes in. It comes from a verb that means to recognize something that is 'separate' from other things. "He distinguished right from wrong like no other six-year-old." This verb suggests the actual process of 'separating' one thing out of many. "Through his microscope the scientist finally distinguished the two germs he was hunting for." The adjective DISTINGUISHED therefore refers to whatever 'stands out' from a crowd by virtue of DISTINCT or DISTINCTIVE characteristic.

Both DISTINCTIVE and DISTINGUISHED have acquired extended uses that apply to qualities of people or things rather than to their concrete characteristics. "A DISTINCTIVE aspect of her mind is her logic," suggests that this woman has a 'unique quality.' And because this woman has logic, "She is a truly distinguished woman." She stands above her kind, she is outstanding. That is our meaning when we refer to honored or public people as DISTINGUISHED.

Efficiency, Proficiency and Efficacy EFFICIENCY is simply 'effectiveness.' The word comes from the Latin for 'make from,' that is, to produce a desired result. EFFICIENCY is used especially to denote the most economical way of getting things done. "The short-order cook worked efficiently: he didn't waste a move."

PROFICIENCY is literally 'making progress,' from the Latin for 'to make forward,' and it refers to 'skill,' or the 'ability to make things move forward.' "He was proficient in repairing automobiles, so he did not mind crossing the country in an old car."

EFFICACY is the 'power or state of being effective.' Almost invariably it has the connotation of 'being effective *enough*,' that is, 'effectual.' It is used principally of things, such as remedies or stratagems. "My friend's advice was certainly efficacious; he told me to stop spending money on my girl, I did, and so then she finally married me."

Elect and Select Both words mean 'to choose with discrimination.' But their emphasis differs. Usually, SELECT means to choose what is 'best', the 'finest' or the 'most fitting.' SELECT usually implies a nice or tasteful choice. In contrast, ELECT implies a choice of what is the 'most useful.' You ELECT a course in a curriculum or ELECT a good president. You SELECT a good place for a picnic, a place you will enjoy. SELECT is the broader word. It includes the narrower meaning of ELECT.

Incidentally, of course, when we ELECT a president the verb ELECT says more than 'choose.' Its direct implication is of the process (voting) which expresses our choice.

Emanate and Eminent EMANATE means 'to flow forth.' "Life emanates from that great Mother of all, the sun." Do not confuse EMANATE with EMINENT, which refers to 'distinguished persons' or 'outstanding ideas.' "William Faulkner made an eminent statement when he received the Nobel Prize for Literature."

Endue and Endow If you were rich, you might ENDOW a college; but you yourself must first be ENDUED with the spirit of generosity. ENDOW means 'to furnish with money,' or, more usually 'to enrich something from your own stores.' "He endowed their marriage with inexhaustible patience." ENDUE, though it may mean ENDOW, usually suggests a power or quality that 'emanates from within.' "She is endued with remarkable grace."

Evoke, Provoke and **Invoke**   EVOKE is a short word, unduly theatrical, but replacing a long phrase: 'to summon up, as from the past.' EVOCATIVE passages in a book intend, by their rhetorical excellence, to recreate as nearly as possible a sentiment from the past. An EVOCATION need not always refer to the past. It may simply draw up from deep inside you some feeling or thought that does not dwell on the surface of your personality.

PROVOKE means 'to cause or incite.' "He provokes her to anger." Its suggestion is always that of 'arousing' someone's emotional pitch. Usually it means 'to incite to anger.' "She is a provoking child."

An INVOCATION is a rather ritualistic affair. You can INVOKE ('supplicate') the Muses, or the aid of friends. To INVOKE is 'to address yourself to,' which implies something of a forum and some forensic ability. INVOKE usually implies an appeal for aid addressed to powers greater than your own. "The priest invokes God's blessing."

Exercise and **Exorcise**   These words look so much alike, but what a difference there is between them: 'to use something briskly,' and 'to expel live spirits.'

While the two words share a common prefix *ex,* 'out,' their roots are different. Perhaps if we could go far enough back, we would find their roots converging. For EXERCISE is built from a Latin word *arcere,* 'to enclose' or 'to confine,' like cattle in a corral. EXORCISE began in Greece by building on the word 'oath.' But that word *horkos,* was akin to another, *herkos,* a 'wall, fence, court.'

EXERCISE in the Latin took on a meaning of 'diligence' and 'perseverance,' of 'plugging on' or of 'keeping at it.' The conversion from that sense to the modern sense was a natural process.

The modern meanings are varied, but most of them suggest a 'continual movement' or 'work for a resulting benefit.' "She exercises daily so that her figure remains trim." "He does his Latin exercise so that he may someday read this ancient language." When we EXERCISE our wits we keep them busy, true enough, but it is more for the sake of present activity than of future benefit. When we EXERCISE our authority we simply carry out our duty even if it is unpleasant. When we EXERCISE an influence over someone we exert an influence over him. At any rate, no matter how we use EXERCISE, there is behind it a sense of freedom of movement which derives from its very roots.

EXORCISE is chiefly useful to us in more or less fanciful ways. In the past, EXORCISE referred to any kind of ritual or incantation that drove evil spirits out of a place or person. But since now most of us no longer believe in evil spirits in the same graphic sense as our ancestors used to, the word has assumed a figurative use. Now we use EXORCISE to refer to the act of 'expelling' any misfortune. "I exorcised my melancholy by seeing a comedy at the local theater."

Explicit and Implicit Both these words refer to ways in which something is described, communicated, or understood. You are EXPLICIT when you 'clearly specify' what you mean. But IMPLICIT means that something is merely 'suggested' or 'tacitly understood'—not expressed definitely. An implied thing is made known through its very nature and its total situation. It may, in fact, be more completely understood than that which is EXPLICIT. An IMPLICIT understanding may be unwritten. It is accepted on faith or intuition rather than on concrete knowledge. If you trust a person IMPLICITLY, you believe in him unquestioningly and faithfully.

Felicity and Facility FELICITY is an affected word for 'happiness'; but its adjective FELICITOUS can still be useful for certain aspects of happiness. When we speak of a 'happy' phrase in a speech we are really demeaning a beautiful word. A FELICITOUS phrase, meaning a pleasing one, conveys the oblique idea better.

FACILITY means 'ease.' By natural extension, FACILITY means 'skill, dexterity.' FACILITY is thus often used as a synonym for 'talent'; but that is rather putting the cart before the horse, because talent precedes practice, while FACILITY follows it. "He was born with great talent, but hard work was needed before he could play the piano with facility."

Fervent and Fervid It doesn't matter too much which one you use. As a rule one suggests 'boiling,' the other 'burning.' Both words express 'great warmth of feeling, intense ardency.'

Yet there is a difference of emphasis in them. FERVENT means boiling in the sense, primarily, of 'vehement, zealous, impatient, intense.' Secondly it means 'hot, glowing, burning' in an impassioned or even fierce sense. But by extension FERVENT can leap from 'vehemence' almost to 'violence,' just as a zealous person approaches the intensity of a fanatic. On the other hand, FERVID reverses the conditions. It begins in our minds with 'fiery zeal' or 'emotional passion,' waning in some usages to 'impetuousness' and in others to 'deep earnestness' or 'devotion.'

Customarily we think first of 'aspirations, zeal or piety' being FERVENT, and of 'eloquence, inspiration or ecstasy' being FERVID. And when intense devotion is expressed toward persons rather than, as in piety, toward God, the expression is more frequently FERVID than FERVENT.

Gentle and **Genteel** GENTLE is a word we generally fail to appreciate, not only in its modern and rather superficial sense but particularly in its historic breadth and depth. Its ultimate root gave us such specific and notable nouns as 'genius, king and gentleman' on the one hand, and such broad and common qualifiers as 'general, generous and congenial' on the other. A large number of our words have little more significance for us than labels have, because we do not understand how they came to us in flocks from antiquity, carrying connotations common to whole groups. In this instance, which is an excellent example, we have not only GENTLE and GENTEEL, with the six cognates mentioned above, but also 'genus, generic, progeny, generation, ingenuous, kindly, degenerate, congenital, kindred, indigenous, engender, genial, progenitor' and quite a few more. These are all closely related in their primeval origins and senses, some from the Latin *genus,* 'race' or 'tribe,' and others from its Teutonic equivalent, the Gothic *kuni,* giving us directly our 'kin' and 'king.' To which might be added a cognate Scandinavian word, now our lustily and almost obnoxiously prolific word 'get.' We still speak of the 'get,' that is the offspring, of a stallion, who is, of course, a progenitor of his own species.

But the Latin *gens,* 'clan,' from *genus,* 'tribe' or 'race,' was a human and social entity. It meant practically 'those of our own kind,' with all the force such a notion still conveys to us. So to be 'genuine' is to be 'of the true stock,' to be 'congenial' is to be 'sympathetically familiar,' and to be 'ingenuous,' or naively frank like children, meant originally to be 'open and honorable,' as you were, first of all, to your family. Even 'ingenious' reflects 'family pride,' for who is clever if it is not your own 'kin?' To 'degenerate' meant to sink below the standards of your own 'kind,' and now it means to fall below all standards. The word 'general' meant 'of the whole tribe,' and now it means of many or most things. Earlier it also meant 'of the representative of the whole tribe,' and hence of its leader, whence our military 'generals.'

And what has this to do with GENTLE and GENTEEL? Nothing, if you are in a hurry; almost everything if you are interested in backgrounds and believe that they give you perspective and understanding. For GENTLE meant in the first place 'of genuine'—that is, GENTLE—birth. Superlatively GENTLE referred to 'kingly' sentiments and character, for 'kings' are of the same etymological stock. 'Kingly' sentiment and character have 'genius,' or unique 'ingeniousness,' 'generosity,' or high birth, and 'kindliness,' which the ancients believed began at home among one's own 'kind.' From these ideas of what is both expected from and due to those who are closest to us arose the qualities connected with GENTLE, including 'gentility.' If there is a GENTLE shower in April, it is because it is warm and friendly. If a person of good breeding is GENTLE in his manner, it is because he respects you. If you stroke a kitten GENTLY, it must be because she belongs in the house, or is domestic.

Then what of GENTEEL? Unfortunately, you might almost as well ask, what of 'jaunty?' For 'jaunty' is a pure corruption of the Old French *gentil*, 'gentle,' which had budded from the Latin *gentilis*, 'of the family.' GENTEEL is a reconstruction of GENTLE in the belief, held by the 'ungenuine,' that it could be improved upon. Now it ironically denotes the quality of a 'fancy or polished gentility.' A GENTEEL manner may be GENTLE in a suave or polite way. It is an affectation of 'gentility,' a 'gentility' dressed up for show.

Imbue, Imbrue and **Imbibe**   IMBUE has two rich meanings: (1) 'To pervade,' which expresses both an action and its extensive effects, as when the spirit of an orator IMBUES the hearts of his auditors, who, in turn, are IMBUED (have absorbed) that spirit. (2) 'To tincture deeply,' as a sky IMBUED with the brilliant colors of a sunset, or as clothes IMBUED with the colors of the rainbow. This rather winsome word comes from the Latin for 'moisten,' and is probably related to the Latin *imber*, 'rain.' We still speak of brilliant skies 'drenched' with color. IMBUE can have the meaning of 'saturate.'

Its cousin, IMBRUE still means 'to wet or moisten,' or 'to drench or soak into,' from the Old French *embruer*, the *bruer* coming from *berre*, 'drink,' and probably tracing to the Latin for 'rain.' A sot is IMBRUED with whiskey, and anyone on a hot day may be IMBRUED with perspiration. Both IMBRUE and IMBUE are transitive.

But IMBIBE, which means 'to drink, absorb, soak,' can be intransitive. "He imbibed heartily." Of course, it is related to IMBUE and IMBRUE.

Immanent and **Imminent**   IMMANENT and IMMINENT are oceans apart in meaning, and always have been, though separated by only a single letter. They stem respectively from the Latin *manere* and *minere*, or 'to remain' and 'to project.' IMMANENT means 'in-dwelling, inherent.' The fear of starvation is IMMANENT in all creatures, but the love of barking is IMMANENT only in dogs. In IMMINENT the 'im' long ago modified the 'projecting' to a 'hanging.' An IMMINENT danger is one that 'hangs over you.' But an IMMINENT threat is worse than a merely 'impending peril.' It hangs right over your head, projecting itself, as it were, between the top of your head and the serene heavens. Also, it is worse than a threatening evil, because a threat need not eventuate. But anything impending or IMMINENT is, unfortunately, pretty sure to descend upon you, in the future if it is 'impending,' and immediately if it is IMMINENT.

Immolate and Emulate   EMULATION is 'ambitious and admiring imitation.' It is a result of a desire to equal a great man in some respect, but not to surpass or supplant him. Lucifer wasn't cast out of Heaven because he EMULATED the Lord. He sought to exceed His power. A crook may EMULATE a better crook, a young man may EMULATE an old man, an unknown man may EMULATE a famous man. In the beginning EMULATE meant simply 'to strive to equal.' Such striving is naturally associated with 'competition' and 'rivalry,' and both the latter with, at times, 'zeal.' EMULATION thus is often used in those sedate fields, like scholarship, where open competition is not considered gentlemanly. Nevertheless, both the Standard and Webster's dictionaries emphasize the idea of 'competition,' rather than of 'imitation,' in EMULATE.

IMMOLATION is 'sacrifice,' now usually 'self-sacrifice,' accompanied by tragic 'self-effacement' or 'self-denial.' But any sacrifice may be an IMMOLATION. You IMMOLATE your fondest hopes when you voluntarily submit to some other person's desires. Gradually, however, the verb has become so subjective it is now practically always reflexive, that is, we now seldom IMMOLATE anything but ourselves. Originally, it was the 'performing of a ceremony.' One sprinkled flour over a sacrificial victim, and so IMMOLATED him, even though he was only an ox whose throat was then immediately cut.

Immunity and Impunity   If you possess diplomatic IMMUNITY, you can with IMPUNITY do things in another country that you cannot safely do at home. At any rate, we can be IMMUNE to a million things besides diseases. IMMUNITY means 'exemption from a duty, a charge, a law, etc.,' or it means specifically 'the power to resist disease.' We can be IMMUNE to unjust criticisms if experience has toughened our skins and to the blandishments of ambition if we are earnest in our work.

IMPUNITY means 'safety from punishment.' In practice, of course, we use IMPUNITY figuratively for any kind of safety. "A bold man can act with impunity while a timid man always gets hurt."

Actually, the meanings of IMMUNITY and IMPUNITY impinge. In Latin, IMMUNITY meant simply 'exemption,' without specifying the thing from which we are exempted. And IMPUNITY can be freedom not only from a 'penalty' but from any 'undesired effects.'

Impart and **Impact** IMPART is always a verb, and it means 'to communicate, disclose or bestow something.' Its word comes from the Latin for 'to share,' and IMPART is a gentle word suggesting much good-will. "When he was an old man he imparted the philosophic secrets of a lifetime to his grandchildren."

But IMPACT, though it is sometimes a verb, is usually a noun. It is the sharp, quick blow of one thing on another. "The impact of the automobile crash was heard for nearly a mile." Figuratively, IMPACT means the definite impression something has on one's mind. "The impact of my professor's words lasted a lifetime." As a verb IMPACT means 'to drive or wedge.' "The dentist impacted gold in my cavity."

Impinge and **Infringe** IMPINGE, like INFRINGE, is a verb of motion. Its Latin root meant 'to strike,' but it also meant 'to fix or fasten.' INFRINGE's root, Latin *frangere,* meant 'to break.' INFRINGE is the more hostile word, though there is a definite meaning of clashing also in IMPINGE. "The sharp sound of a brass band impinges on your ears." But, generally we have damped IMPINGE. So when you IMPINGE on or against my rights you 'encroach' upon them. But if you INFRINGE them, you 'break' them, as you break a rule when you INFRINGE it. IMPINGE is usually intransitive, and INFRINGE is usually transitive.

Intent and **Attent** Reading a book, you are INTENT on what it says. When you listen to the radio you are ATTENT ('listening attentively or heedfully'). The difference between these adjectives is this, that in INTENT there is a suggestion of 'complete absorption' while in ATTENT your concentration is less focused, you are merely 'paying attention.'

As nouns, ATTENT means 'attention,' but INTENT is your 'purpose' as it affects other people. The INTENT of a letter you are writing, is what you want it to accomplish, no matter what it actually says.

Linage and **Lineage** Sometimes confused with each other, not so much because they look alike as because they are linked by 'lineal,' whose meaning overlaps that of 'linear.' Each of these words in one way or another refers to 'lines.' 'Linear' refers to 'line lines,' or to anything 'composed of lines.' 'Lineal' means the same, but also it means especially the figurative 'line of descent' in families. Thus, 'lineal' is the adjective for LINEAGE, which comes via French *lignage* from Latin *linea,* 'line.' LINEAGE means 'pedigree, descent from an ancestor and especially, proud descent.' "She is a lady of high lineage."

In contrast LINAGE is workaday, concerned with lines as they constitute a printed product. LINAGE is the 'number of lines' in a story, advertisement, column, etc. Hence, for convenience, LINAGE also refers to the 'rate of payment per line,' or the 'quantity of printed matter' determined on the basis of lines contained. But these are newspaper or printer terms. The word has also the meaning of 'alignment,' which is adjustment of formation into a line. The 'alignment' of ranks in a military drill may be so perfect as to suggest a printed page. Four nations may be so solidly 'aligned (or alined)' in their purposes as to present a straight front, like a headline. Thus we might speak of the LINAGE of a parade ground, or of powers that oppose each other on the international scene.

Mettle and Fettle It is customary but confusing, in English, to give words additional meanings without changing their spellings. Note 'table,' which has a myriad of meanings. But in the case of 'metal' we did bother to change the spelling when we gave it the highly fanciful and nonmetallic meaning of 'ardor' or 'spirit.' A METTLESOME ('high-spirited, fiery') horse may be gray and have muscles like steel, but those are his only physically metallic qualities. Shakespeare spelled the word in either way, but soon it had a definite spelling of its own. And now METTLE is sometimes confused with FETTLE, because it looks like it and because when you are in fine FETTLE (literally, 'in good condition, well-prepared') you are possibly also in fine (or high) METTLE.

The point of distinction lies in the perspective you choose. The high spirit of METTLE is 'heroic,' and the high spirit of FETTLE is 'exuberant.' When you are in fine FETTLE you are not only in 'good trim' but also 'frisky.' But if you are a person of high METTLE, you are 'courageous, ardent, persistent, faithful.' METTLE refers not simply to temperament but particularly to the stuff of one's disposition. But FETTLE partakes of temperament, and is affected by mental or spiritual health.

Mortify and Mortuary MORTIFY associates itself with MORTUARY, a place where the dead are stored for a while till burial. From its tinge of the macabre, it is suggestive and therefore useful. To be abashed is to be confused and embarrassed, but to be MORTIFIED is to be 'humiliated' and 'vexed.' Technically, and in reference to the body, MORTIFICATION is 'death,' or 'dying'; but even then it is usually used in a limited sense, that of a dying part of the body while the rest lives on. But the word has figurative uses. We can MORTIFY our passions by fasting.

As an adjective MORTUARY originally referred to the 'dead'; nowadays it pertains to the 'burial of the dead,' and hence to the 'dead as they are remembered.' As a noun, MORTUARIES are 'undertaker's parlors.'

Muddle and **Meddle** These two verbs are so expressive that we have almost forgotten what they came from, which was 'mud' in the one case and a 'mixing' in the other. When you are 'all mixed up' in your mind it is as if your thoughts had been MEDDLED with. MEDDLE comes from an earlier reflexive usage, "I medyll me with a thought," which in turn came from the Old French *"Je me mesle."* For, as usually happened in the Anglo-French, the 's' before an interior 'l' became a 'd,' and then in this case another 'd' was inserted, apparently under the influence of MUDDLE. The two words are associated in sense, in the same way that 'confusion' is like a 'mixing.'

But a greater debt was owed MEDDLE by MUDDLE. MUDDLE was merely a frequentative of 'mud,' to express the idea of 'muddying,' as water may be muddied by a duck rooting in it with his bill. But that usage existed later than the appearance of MEDDLE, for mud itself is not very old. Chaucer may have used the word occasionally, but the early English contains no record of it. So it was evidently from the 'mixing' in MEDDLING that MUDDLE acquired its sense of 'confusion.' Now we 'muddle through' a mess with a confused and rather chaotic determination.

Neb and **Nib** NEB is pure Old English for a 'bird's beak or bill.' NIB is a later alternative. Hence both may mean a 'point, projection or tip-end,' like the NIB of a pen.

Ocular and **Oracular** More than 'optical,' which refers directly to one's eyes (compare OCULIST), OCULAR refers to 'seeing and sight.' Its first reference is to the eye, but commonly anything that pertains to what we see or visualize is OCULAR, as for example OCULAR proof of a crime, or OCULAR uncertainties in gunnery.

The similar sounding ORACULAR pertains to 'oracles,' those classical founts of wisdom and prophecy. Modern prophets are ORACULAR too; but simple philosophers are often ORACULAR. The editorial pages of newspapers are typically ORACULAR. The word suggests a 'guiding wisdom.'

Oppose and **Appose** These words demand analysis. Perhaps no other two words in our language have in their history been so mixed with each other and with other words. To explain their differences requires a narration of their history; but here only an incomplete sketch is possible. They became very confused with each other in the Late Latin and the Old French, and afterwards with other words like 'pause' and 'pose,' which had evolved from the same roots. The confusion of two Latin verbs *ponere* and *pausare* in France started the worst of the trouble. Respectively they meant 'to put' and 'to pause.' But when something is 'put down' or 'placed,' it is, of course, 'set'; and when something 'pauses' or 'is stopped,' it also is 'set.' Given the slightest encouragement like this, words will often converge. These two did, taking up proximate starting positions for future development. But in their case two other verbs derived from *ponere* were already confused: *apponere*, in which the prefix was a variant of *ad*, 'to,' and *opponere*, whose prefix derives from *ob*, 'against.' Thus our word APPOSE began with an adulterated meaning at the outset. But meanwhile, and perhaps partly because the past participles of both *apponere* and *opponere* contained an 's,' a further confusion occurred with the verb *pausare*, a confusion which involved our word OPPOSE, since it also derived from *opponere*. Immediately, with two such similar words in the field, the battle of senses was on, and it carried over into England where it continued well into our modern English. At various times and in various places the two verbs have been used interchangeably. It is little wonder that today we don't observe very closely the distinctions between an OPPOSITION and an APPOSITION.

Pure OPPOSITION now needs no definition, whether it be 'obstructive' or 'aggressive.' When you 'set' something, such as an idea, or an argument or a roadblock 'against' anything they form an OPPOSITION. The OPPOSITION party in politics OPPOSES the policies of the party in power. Today OPPOSE refers to any action that forms an OPPOSITION, which is any 'restraint, disagreement, disapproval, resistance, or contrast,' either active or passive, to anything else. "In her mind she opposed what her husband was doing, but she kept silent." "Our troops bravely opposed the newest advance of the enemy with all the weapons at their command."

But the adjective, OPPOSITE is relatively quiet. It simply means 'standing against' where the 'against' is only positional. OPPOSITE suggests simply 'passive resistance,' in the sense in which we speak of our ideas being OPPOSED to other ideas. Yet at the bottom even this idea of location and contrast is only rhetorical. Your OPPOSITES are still 'adversaries.' The verb OPPOSE always refers to the idea of 'combating an enemy' in one way or another and that idea remains at the base of its apparently timid adjective.

But the meaning of APPOSE can be clarified by considering its adjective APPOSITE, which means 'appropriate or suitable' followed by 'to.' "His suggestions were quite apposite to the thought that was in my mind." APPOSITE's meaning differs from its synonyms in its pervading idea of real rightness. An APPOSITE thing is 'well put or applied,' and so when you APPOSE two statements, placing them figuratively or actually side by side, the inference is that there is exactly where they belong for the best view of them. This suggestion of 'aptness' is far stronger in the adjective APPOSITE than it is in the verb APPOSE. An APPOSITE answer to a question fits both the question and its whole occasion like a glove.

This suitability that belongs to APPOSE serves to distinguish APPOSING from 'comparing.' When we 'compare' two things we simply look at them 'together.' When we APPOSE them we not only note their 'differences' and 'similarities' but we 'appraise' them. The purpose is to place the two objects in juxtaposition in order to detect, or to determine, their suitability.

But note that if our purpose is to detect the differences or antagonisms between two objects, we have 'set up' an OPPOSITION.

Pediatrics and **Pedagogue** A 'pedometer' is a 'foot measure,' an instrument to record the distance traveled, and a 'pedant' and a PEDAGOGUE are, substantially, 'teachers,' who used to walk to and fro while teaching. But the original PEDAGOGUE was a slave who escorted his master's children to school, on foot, of course. All these words are from Latin *pes*, 'a foot.'

But PEDIATRICS is from Greek *pais*, or (in combinations) *paid*, 'child.' Children, teachers, slaves and the feet they walk on all seem mixed up, but PEDIATRICS has nothing to do with a child's foot. It is the kind of doctoring that specializes in 'children's disorders' (but not with his or her members). 'Pedology' is a synonymous, but properly, broader term, being the 'scientific and specialized study of childhood,' including the care of children and consequently, of course, PEDIATRICS proper.

Personable and **Personage** PERSONABLE refers to a 'likeable, attractive, sociable person.' It faintly reflects another word, PERSONAGE. A PERSONAGE is an 'important or well-known person.'

Perspicuous and **Perspicacious** Both are from the same root 'to look through.' PERSPICUOUS is just a long word for 'clear' or 'lucid.' It usually refers to the products of an intelligent or lucid mind rather than to the mind itself. An intelligent man's diction should be PERSPICUOUS, clear and easy for anyone to understand. Such clearness is distinct and explicit, so that anyone who is at all PERSPICACIOUS ('discerning') can comprehend it instantly.

For PERSPICACITY is a personal attribute. Hawks and detectives are PERSPICACIOUS. They possess the ability to see (and perhaps, see through) others. But in our sophisticated age we have tended to re-gard PERSPICACITY less as a faculty of quick-sighted observation than as 'mental penetration, appraisal, discernment.' The PERSPICACIOUS mind has a 'penetrating vision' that is both sagacious and acute.

Phase and **Faze** Commonly, a PHASE is a 'stage in development,' but its origin is in the Greek word for 'showing.' Properly, it is a 'partial view, aspect.' "I never understood that phase of the operation." It is no relation to FAZE, which is our own colloquial production for 'to worry,' 'scare' or 'upset.' "It never fazed him," that is, he didn't bat an eyelid.

Practice and **Practise** The verb can have either spelling but the noun is spelled only PRACTICE. You can PRACTICE, or you can PRACTISE, medicine without a difference of meaning, but then you can have only a PRACTICE. This whimsicality in the verb is less English than French. The Romans had only 'c's' in the word *practicare,* and they were both hard. At first the French rendered the Latin with fair consistency as *practiquer* and *pratiquer,* in which the 'qu' reproduced the hard 'c.' And the English tagged along with 'practic,' a word now archaic. Then the French varied their verb to *practiser,* and the English didn't know what to do, and still don't.

So you can use 's' in the verb, but not elsewhere, except in the ad-jective, which is merely the past participle of the verb used attribu-tively: his PRACTISED (or his PRACTICED) hand. But you can use either, worse luck, for one of its several nouns: 'practicer,' or 'practiser.' But for 'practitioner's' adjective, 'practice,' you must use a 'c.'

Incidentally, the earlier and more sensible form of 'practitioner' was 'practician,' which is a logical companion to 'dietician,' 'electrician,' etc.

Prescribe and **Proscribe** The doctor PRESCRIBES a remedy, and you take his PRESCRIPTION to a druggist. If the latter gives you the wrong medicine, his pharmaceutical brotherhood may PROSCRIBE ('banish, outlaw') him from its profession.

Pretense and **Pretext** "His pretense of gratitude afforded a pretext for his insidious addresses." But this example is a little loose at one end, for a PRETENSE may of course be a harmless and even a benevolent sham, while a PRETEXT is notoriously nefarious. A PRETEXT is a 'pre-tended motive, a bogus excuse,' and is always a tricky aspect of an evil purpose.

Historically, PRETENSES were stretched (Latin *tensus*) and PRETEXTS were woven (Latin *textus*). From the start, that is, a PRETENSE was more a mere 'stretching of a point,' while a PRETEXT displayed the 'complexity of a plot.' But naturally the meanings somewhat overlap. They did even in Roman times.

Proceed and **Precede** If you PROCEED ('go forward') fast enough, you will PRECEDE ('go ahead of') competitors. The profits of your successful business progress will then be your PROCEEDS (accent 'pro'). PROCEEDS may also be 'records' or 'minutes,' like those of a club meeting.

Produce and **Adduce** The noun PRODUCE bears mention as a specific substitute for 'production.' It is collective but concrete. For example, when you work in your garden the vegetables you grow are the 'production' of your toil. But the vegetables themselves are the PRODUCE, as individually they are 'products.'

Loosely we say we PRODUCE evidence when more exactly we mean to say we ADDUCE it. To ADDUCE means 'to bring something forward' as a pertinent example, and hence to present it as evidence.

Recur and **Occur** Uses for these verbs and their nouns, will OCCUR and RECUR to you often. "The continual recurrence of this trouble must be stopped." How else could you say that succinctly? OCCUR is little less helpful. "It occurred to me that . . . ," I happened to think that. "The occurrence of all these things in a single hour was bewildering."

Refragable, Infrangible and **Refrangible** Shatter-proof glass is INFRANGIBLE, 'unbreakable.' It is not 'irrefragable,' which means 'unanswerable, cannot be denied or proved wrong,' and is the negative of REFRAGABLE, which means 'refutable.' There is no word 'fragable'; the 're' in REFRAGABLE is simply reduplicative, and the root is the Latin for 'break.' From the same base comes REFRANGIBLE, which means 'capable of being bent or broken.' Usually, it refers to 'bending' or 'refracting,' as the rays of light are refracted, or as a pitched ball in baseball 'breaks.' The negative is 'irrefrangible.'

Relegate and **Delegate** These are fundamentally legal words, both from Latin *lex* 'law.' *Lex* produced *legare*, 'to commission or send'; a 'legate' is a 'commissioned' messenger. The prefixes 're' and 'de' steered the words into their separate uses. We have rather forgotten their authoritative force, but a DELEGATE is still an authenticated representative sent *from* his party or his company. But a broken armchair is, if not officially, at least ruthlessly, RELEGATED, or 'consigned,' *back* to the woodshed or attic. RELEGATION is the act or state of being sent back to comparative obscurity and remoteness from an important foreground.

Remiss and **Amiss**   You are not necessarily REMISS if you do something AMISS. If you hit a tennis ball out of bounds, you may have been careless and therefore REMISS. Your error may have resulted from REMISSNESS in that you were too lazy to swing your racket quickly enough. Nevertheless, you could have played AMISS through no negligence at all. AMISS indicates an 'error in execution.' REMISS implies a 'lack of earnestness or application,' some 'moral indifference.' If you don't thank someone soon for a Christmas gift, you are REMISS.

Serape and **Etape**   Respectively, a 'Mexican shawl (or blanket used as one),' and a 'public storehouse.' More notoriously, however, an ETAPE is a 'stockade' in Russia temporarily housing convicts on the long trek to Siberian exile.

Shallop and **Shallot**   A SHALLOP is a 'small open boat,' properly one rowed by two persons. But SHALLOT is an 'edible relative of the onion.'

Shuffle and **Scuffle**   Cousins, in sense, but Dutch or Low German in the first case, and Swedish or Scandinavian in the second. Both use the idea of 'shoving,' and in one instance, both describe about the same thing, that of a 'SHUFFLING way of walking' which is also a 'SCUFFLING along.' In the game 'shuffleboard' SHUFFLE is practically 'shove' itself because you give a disk a push with a stick that sends it sliding along a board. SCUFFLE is still a multifarious 'shoving' in a body-to-body fight, which is described also as a 'tussle,' meaning literally one that 'tousles the hair.' Some think that maybe SCUFFLE and 'shove' itself were telescoped to form SHUFFLE. Others think that SHUFFLE is a frequentative of 'shove' as SCUFFLE is of 'scuff,' from Swedish *skuffa*, 'to push.'

But the 'shoving' and 'pushing' in both words take on prodigious variations, as witness the SHUFFLING of a pack of cards, in which the cards do less shoving than SCUFFLING and mixing. And note the expressive SHUFFLING of many things, such as thoughts and plans. From SHUFFLING feet, suggesting a dragging movement and a holding back, we have inferred further meanings. A SHUFFLING way of doing things is a lazy way, or worse. It is a suspiciously reluctant way. So a SHUFFLING manner is an evasive but betraying manner. On the other hand, there is the SHUFFLE in dancing, not a lazy or a bad thing, but a lively one. This dance's SHUFFLE comes at rhythmic intervals; it doesn't drag with inertia but scrapes with energy.

The same reasoning holds with SCUFFLE. Just as 'tussling' is much more than hair-pulling ('tussle' goes back to German *zansen*, 'to pull'), so SCUFFLING denotes more confusion and struggle than mere pushing alone can account for.

Slick and Sleek SLEEK is dressed-up SLICK. It is a later variant of that word, probably fashioned to preserve a sense of shiny smoothness when SLICK became too common.

SLICK began as a verb, meaning 'to make smooth,' as when you might SLICK out a crumpled piece of paper. There is no doubt that the word has fallen upon evil days. The best that dictionaries can now seriously say for it is, that as a verb it still literally means 'to make smooth,' and that as an adjective it may, with an effort of mind, be taken to mean SLEEK, like SLICK hair for SLEEK hair. But overwhelmingly the adjective now conveys the qualities of the word's new slangy noun, not the raincoat, but the 'living' SLICKER, who is up to shrewd tricks and fake graces, and is so slyly greasy that suspicions slip off his SLEEK appearance. Perhaps even such SLICKNESS is something of a feat, and so any other deft and astonishing play, like in baseball, has become a SLICK play. And with the aid of 'up,' 'down' and 'out' SLICK retains other excellent colloquial uses. 'To slick up' implies not only 'to tidy' but 'to polish' and 'to prettify.' Water may be 'slicked down' with oil and become a SLICK. Troubles may be 'slicked out' in our minds.

Solecism and Sciolism SOLECISM is not a doctrine, as most 'isms' are: it is a 'barbarism in diction.' It comes from the Greek's contemptuous reference to the people of Soli in Asia Minor, an Athenian colony where people did not speak good Greek. It was an ancient counterpart of our jeering about Brooklynese. So a SOLECISM is now a bit of bad grammar or a rudely improper remark. "I done that," is a SOLECISM.

SCIOLISM is a prime cause, not of ignorant blunders in diction, but of inadequate knowledge passing for wisdom. SCIOLISM is a 'smattering of knowledge,' but it is known chiefly by its uses and effects. The true SCIOLIST is not nowadays some unfortunate fellow who is ill-schooled or lazy-minded, but that same fellow who is sharp enough, to everybody's detriment, to pretend to know more than he does, using his superficial supply as a display. Hence, if we do not watch him closely he may soon be practicing as a natural-born charlatan, and getting away with it handsomely.

The derivation is from late Latin *sciolus*, a 'smatterer,' a diminutive from *scius*, 'knowing,' from *scire*, 'to know.' But notice the word is no longer a diminutive. It is not now a case of little and dangerous, but of shallow and devastating, knowledge.

Sordid and **Morbid** Their sources are separate but alike. Literally, SORDID means 'filthy,' and MORBID means 'sick.' But their meanings have extended to keep pace with the larger conception our more or less hygienic modern sensibility conceives of the extent of filth and disease. MORBID, for example, now usually refers to 'gloomy or ill-humored disposition,' which reflects certain characteristics of the mentally ill. MORBID can still mean, specifically, 'pathological' or 'pertaining to disease.' Actuaries use the word MORBIDITY not only in that sense but also to mean a 'certain degree' of disease, as we speak of the humidity of the weather. But the derived meaning of MORBID is now its strongest. The MORBID mind is not merely pessimistic but is ill-conditioned. It is 'abnormally depressed' and 'subnormally obsessed' with unwholesome ideas. In short, it is under the baleful influence of black death itself.

SORDID naturally took the short step from 'dirtiness' to 'vileness.' Even a dirty trick has a strong connotation of minor villainy. Like MORBIDITY SORDIDNESS is on a low level, below the busy and wholesome upper level of life in general. Hence, like dirty tricks, it has attached itself specifically to 'meanness,' especially as it shows in a covetous or ignoble person. Politicians who are forever on the lookout for graft are SORDID. A SORDID mind is one that takes pleasure in pornography. A SORDID neighborhood is so economically depressed and physically filthy that no child can grow up in it with a healthy body and a wholesome mind.

Suffragette and **Suffragist** Earlier in this century SUFFRAGETTES were a good deal talked about. They were regarded as meddlers in men's politics, and that hurt the masculine vanity, which holds dearly to any belief that there are certain areas better managed by men alone. But the final laugh was on the men, and even before the SUFFRAGETTES won their point, in order that they might win their case, they had masculine supporters who, unable and unwilling to qualify as SUFFRAGETTES, accepted the lesser term SUFFRAGISTS. But this less definite term has practically absorbed the earlier word. Almost everyone is now, at least tacitly, a SUFFRAGIST, because in a sense it would be illegal not to be one. But almost no one is now a SUFFRAGETTE, because she was a special crusader, no longer needed in the United States. It is interesting to note, however, that in certain other countries, such as Egypt and

India, SUFFRAGETTES are working hard to gain for women the freedoms taken now for granted in America.

Ted and **Tat** 'To TED' is 'to spread for drying,' like hay. In Icelandic the word originally meant 'manure.' TATTING is a lacy handmade threadwork edging. The verb is 'to TAT.' It is also Icelandic, like 'tatters,' or rags, and meant 'to pick.'

Tepid and **Trepid** Your bath is TEPID when it is neither hot nor cold but 'lukewarm.' But TEPIDITY need not always refer to actual temperature. TEPID enthusiasm and TEPID amusement are simply 'mediocre' or 'weak.' TEPID tea may be weak tea as well as lukewarm tea. TEPID colors are not warmish colors but weak ones. A TEPID attempt is the opposite of an intrepid effort—it is weak, not bold.

The adjective TREPID is practically unknown to the public. It means 'trembling or quaking with fear.' Its noun TREPIDATION we continually couple with 'fear,' quite casually equating the two words in a phrase without noticing the quaking at all. But the negative of TREPID, 'intrepid,' is quite well-known. It means 'bold.'

Tonsorial and **Sartorial** The Romans called a barber a *tonsor*. The word lingers almost exclusively in the phrase 'a tonsorial artist.' The Roman tailors were patchers and menders, *sartores*, from *sarcire*, 'to patch.' So today we speak of the SARTORIAL art. But not only tailors but human thighs were called *sartores*, because tailors sat on them while they worked. Modern medicos call the thigh bone the 'sartorius.'

Torrid and **Horrid** Sometimes we say someone has a TORRID ('hot or burning') temper. But ordinarily the word TORRID stays within geography books where it refers to equatorial regions. But TORRID can be an impressive word for 'intense heat.' HORRID is also a forceful word. It is really the clipped and compacted form of 'horrible.' TORRID comes from Latin *torrere*, 'to parch.' HORRID, which also means 'rough or shaggy,' comes from *horrere*, 'to shudder' or 'to bristle.'

Trip and **Trap** A TRIP is a TRAP, and both are, or were, a 'tread,' a 'step.' The TRAP became a 'snare' when an animal stepped into a pitfall or, later, stepped on a catch and released it. When an anchor is TRIPPED it is freed from the snags and snares on the bottom and is then hoisted. The verb may have arisen in a general way from 'snags' and 'snares'; thus it would better be 'un-trip' or, more aboriginally, 'untrap,' an anchor. Anyhow when an anchor is TRIPPED the vessel begins her voyage. If it is her first voyage, it is her 'trial trip.' The initiating act of raising the anchor has been taken metaphorically to mean the whole voyage. The dictionaries give you TRIP as any short journey. But when we take TRIPS on land we are completing the circle back to the first 'tread' or 'step.' Furthermore, the word 'tramp' is cognate with TRAP and TRIP. Nor can we forget the now archaic 'tripping of a measure,' stepping lightly or gracefully, a quadrille, or square dance. This TRIPPING is Old French from older German for a 'skipping' or 'dancing'; but, like our TRIPPING over a curbstone, it probably relates back to the same 'misstep,' or 'broken step,' that first TRAPPED us.

Yell and Yelp   Both words are cognate with the 'gale' in 'nightingale,' which means 'singer,' from Old English *galan*, 'to sing.' In many words the Old English 'g' was sounded like our 'y,' and the 'y' sound remains from *galan* and *gielpan*, in YELL and YELP.

But YELL has come up in the world, and YELP has gone down. YELL was at first 'any sound,' like a screaming shout, and later it was an 'outcry' or 'resounding noise.' Perhaps our slang "It's nothing to yell about," contains this sense. Thus it didn't remain a mere sound, but became, on occasion, 'articulate.' Now a college YELL is a rhythmic cheer with, as a burden, words, or an approximation of them, which animals couldn't imitate. On the other hand, YELP, even among the Anglo-Saxons, was a 'loud talking or exalting.' It soon became a 'boasting,' but eventually it lost all touch with speech to become a 'quick, sharp bark,' made by dogs or other animals. Humans may still YELP, in slang usage. In that case they are not 'boasting' but 'complaining.'

Both words were probably imitative in their origins. YELP especially can be understood in its variants 'yap' and 'yawp,' which build on the mimicry. Tiny dogs, who haven't the stature to YELP, therefore 'yap.' When people 'yap' they continuously 'gabble, talk, complain, etc.' A 'yawp' is more uncouth; it is a loud ignorant complaint, or else a noisy yawn.

THE WRITTEN WORD

See also Literary Terms

ALBUM   *n.* a book in which visitors write their names; also, a book with blank pages on which photographs, postal cards or stamps are pasted.

ALMANAC   *n.* a book containing

a calendar, yearly statistics and general information.

Anagram

APPENDIX *n.* a section at the rear of some books giving more detailed information than can be found in the main text.

ARTICLE *n.* a relatively short written account of some factual matter, as an ARTICLE in an encyclopedia or magazine.

ATLAS *n.* a book of maps.

Bibelot

BIBLIOGRAPHY *n.* a list of books, articles, manuscripts, containing information on a given subject, such as a BIBLIOGRAPHY about bird watching.

Brochure see **Prospectus & Brochure**

CATALOGUE *n.* a list of separate items, such as a list of houses in a certain area, a list of courses offered by a university, a list of goods offered by a store.

Causerie

CHAPBOOK *n.* any small book, esp. a miscellany.

Coda & Codex

Codex see **Coda & Codex**

Colophon & Vignette

COLUMN *n.* a vertical section in a newspaper in which an article is printed.

CONSPECTUS *n.* synopsis; outline; esp. of a project.

DICTIONARY *n.* a list of words with their meanings and sometimes their derivations.

DISSERTATION *n.* an essay; thesis; esp. a full-sized formal written study of anything.

ENCYCLOPEDIA *n.* a book or set of books contains articles on various branches of knowledge.

Epitome

ESSAY *n.* a relatively short written discussion on any subject.

EXCERPT *n.* a passage removed from any written text, for separate use; a clipping.

Exegesis

GAZETTE *n.* a newspaper; journal.

Ghostwriting

GLOSSARY *n.* a list of words with their definitions and other explanations inserted at the end of a text to help the reader understand the text.

Hack

INDEX *n.* a list of the contents of a book, so that one may quickly find the pages on which a particular subject is discussed.

JOURNAL *n.* a newspaper; a book in which one records his thoughts and activities.

LEXICON *n.* a dictionary.

Manual

Manuscript

Minutes

Motto

Paleograph

Palimpsest

Palindrome

PAMPHLET *n.* a small book, with few pages.

Prospectus & Brochure

RÉSUMÉ *n.* a summation of a text.

SYLLABUS *n.* an abstract or summation of a course of instruction.

TABULAR *adj.* pertaining to a table, or to a tabulation or list.

THESAURUS *n.* a treasury or re-
pository; esp. of words.

THESIS *n.* an essay; theme; composition.

TRACT *n.* pamphlet, esp. one
written to persuade people.

Vignette see **Colophon & Vignette**

Anagram An ANAGRAM is a word that uses in a different sequence
letters from another word. 'Cask,' for example, is an anagram of 'sack.'
Sometimes it refers to a sentence similarly built from another sentence
or any figurative sense which comes from appropriating and reversing another sense. For example, a sophistical politician might use a
pork-barrel as a symbol of generosity. In the plural ANAGRAMS is a game
in which you construct words as rapidly and cleverly as you can from
separate letters each on a card. The adjective ANAGRAMMATIC could be
very useful in broad applications, except that the game, rather than
the old idea behind it, pre-empts our minds and confuses the meaning
of the word with the game.

Bibelot Any highly artistic trinket or curio is a BIBELOT. You might
be fooled in pronouncing this word. It is two syllables: bee-bloe.

Causerie A French word meaning a 'literary huddle,' an unfrivo-
lous and lightly critical tête-à-tête. Sometimes, a chatty, critical column
in a periodical is called a CAUSERIE.

Coda and **Codex** In music, a CODA is a concluding passage, especially a climactic one, recapitulating, as it were, the musical text
and theme. A CODEX is a code of laws, a collection of formulae or a manuscript in old uncial (big) letters.

Colophon and **Vignette** COLOPHON is from the Greek word meaning 'finishing stroke' or 'summit.' It is the emblem on the title page
or spine of a book, sometimes the artistic imprint of the publisher.
Formerly, a COLOPHON was an elaborate affair on the end piece of a
book, a kind of publisher's postscript, mentioning the author, the
illustrator, the printer and sometimes the circumstances of publication.
COLOPHONS are now rare because their function has been assumed by
blurbs and biographical sketches on the jacket flaps. VIGNETTE is etymologically the French diminutive of *vigne,* 'vine.' VIGNETTES on page
margins of books form an artistic accompaniment to the text, a shaded
fretwork or light drawings of leafy tendrils and the like. Occasionally
as headpieces or endpieces they are more prominent, approximating
COLOPHONS. On the other hand, a single letter can be VIGNETTED with

hairlines. Photographs can be VIGNETTED with shaded backgrounds and borders. Originally VIGNETTES were Gothic architectural columns VI-GNETTED with carven foliage.

Epitome An EPITOME is a compendium or condensed version of an account or writing.

Exegesis Greek for 'explanation.' As explanation of interpretation, it is often applied to the Bible. But EXEGESIS is commonly used for any exposition. The adjective is EXEGETIC.

Ghostwriting Writing for others is called GHOSTWRITING. The person who signs the writing is presumably not unable, but only too busy, to do his own writing.

Hack The HACKWRITER, or literary carpenter, has felt the yoke on his neck for at least two centuries. The HACKWRITER does any odd literary job, usually not of the highest quality but also usually for the lowest pay. Hired horses from Hackney in London had been in public service for centuries before that. And so had the carriages they drew and the coachmen who drove them: all called HACKS. From HACKS came our word HACKNEYED, or 'trite,' designating especially worn-out phrases in literature. It was Henry Fielding, the author of *Tom Jones*, the great English novel, who first complained: "I have no choice," he said, in a moment of discouragement, "but to be a hackney-writer or a hackney-coachman." *New Grub Street*, a famous novel by George Gissing, grimly portrays the base, futile lives of scholars and writers who have to do HACKWRITING to earn a living.

Manual A 'handbook,' from the Latin *manus*, 'hand.' A MANUAL can be carried, and presumably frequently consulted with profit.

Manuscript The question is now arising, should what is written by a typewriter be called a 'typescript.' Well, we still sail the seas in steamships. Odd words linger on, and we like to have them around. Many writers claim their best work is written by hand, and so MANUSCRIPT may never become completely archaic. But still, in an age when even many personal letters are written on the typewriter, 'typescript' is a word increasingly popular.

Minutes The MINUTES of a meeting, taken by a secretary, are not a complete record of the proceedings as they happened minute by minute but are simply notes, literally, small ('minute') recordings. We call them 'memoranda' in other situations. The mother of the author of Robinson Crusoe wrote in the family Bible MINUTES of queer dreams she had had.

Motto   The Romans had a word, probably imitative, for a 'grunt' or a 'mutter': *muttum.* From this word came MOTTOES, which are now brief quotations or maxims intended to keep some guiding thoughts crystal clear in our minds.

The force in the word MOTTO is shown in the French abbreviated form *mot,* simply 'word.' A MOTTO is the one and only word, or the phrase that says everything.

Nevertheless, nothing will keep words from wandering from their strict meanings. The sentimental bits of poetry children find printed on candy wrappers at parties are now MOTTOES. To the Elizabethans MOTTOES were literary poesies. And in heraldry, they still are single words or phrases among the bearings or emblems on a shield.

Paleograph   An ancient manuscript. Specifically a PALEOGRAPH is a manuscript written in a primitive way, like a stone tablet.

Palimpsest   This refers to parchment written on a second time. The first writing has worn off or been erased.

Palindrome   A PALINDROME is a word or sentence that says the same thing whether you read it forwards or backwards, like 'Anna' or that good old Irish word, 'dad.' Consider the greeting Adam gave to Eve the first time he saw her, "Madam, I'm Adam." See ANAGRAM.

Prospectus and **Brochure**   A PROSPECTUS is really important though it is used rather disrespectfully for the catalogs of mail-order houses and hotels. Its real meaning is a 'forward-directed survey,' like the view of a bird's eye as it flies forward. It is visualized expectations, published for everyone to read. Like its cousin, the word 'prospect,' which realtors have commercialized as a view from the front verandah, PROSPECTUS is an optimistic word. The contents of a PROSPECTUS may not prove to be of historic value, but there is a prophetic sound in the word itself. On the contrary, a BROCHURE, or 'stitched pamphlet,' from the French *brocher,* 'to stitch,' is by nature an ephemeral thing. In its right province it is merely a sketch of some subject of passing interest. This is not to say that BROCHURES may not be serious or even erudite.

APPENDIX

THE FORMS OF LIFE

Included here are lists of adjectives, each followed by the noun to which it has reference, dealing with the various forms of life. The nouns, of course, are not definitions of the adjectives, merely words to which the adjectives pertain. In certain cases, where there is not such a noun form, the adjective is followed by an actual definition, introduced by the word 'means.'

A

Birds
Fish
Insects and Other Invertebrates
Mammals
Reptiles
Animal Traits and Behavior

B

Man
    a. Head
    b. Limbs
    c. Torso
    d. General Terms

C

Flowers and Plants

D

Shapes

ADJECTIVES PERTAINING TO BIRDS

ACCIPITRAL any bird of prey.

ACCIPITRINE the short-winged hawks.

ALAUDINE lark.

ALCEDINE kingfisher.

ALCIDINE such three-toed birds as auks, puffins and murres.

ALCOID or perhaps ALCINE auk.

ALUCINE barn owl.

ANATINE duck.

ANSERINE goose. Used also for stupid or silly persons.

AQUILINE eagle, specifically the golden eagle.

BOTAURINE bittern.

CALLAEATINE or CORVOID Old World tree crows.

CAPRIMULGINE nightjars, which resemble whippoorwills.

CARINATE keeled breastbones, as of birds that fly; the flight muscles are attached to the keel.

CASUARINE cassowary; CASUAROID may include emus, and DROMADID is for the related crab plovers and cavaliers.

CATHARTINE American vulture; including turkey buzzard, king vulture, condor, black buzzard or carrion crow.

CHARADRINE plover, snipe.

CINCLOID water ouzels, which are oscines.

CICONINE stork; also jabiru, adjutant of Africa and adjutant stork of India.

CIRCAETINE Old World harrier, baleur and serpent eagles; bearded vulture and the lammergeir or fish-eagle.

CIRCINE harrier hawks or harriers, including the American marsh hawk.

CLAMATORIAL a suborder whose males crow, like the kingbird.

COCCOTHRAUSTINE grosbeak.

COCCYGINE or COCCYZINE cuckoo, including ani.

COLUMBINE dove, pigeon, dodo.

COLYMBOID grebe and loon.

CORACIOID roller, or trilling canary; also kingfisher or kirumba.

CORVINE crow, rook, raven; CORVOID includes relatives.

CROTOPHAGINE southern blackbird, or ani. See also COCCYGINE.

CUCULINE true cuckoo.

CYGNINE swan. 'Swan' is exact Anglo-Saxon. 'Cygnet,' now meaning 'a young swan,' is Greek via French.

CYPSELINE the swifts. CYPSELOID means 'like the swifts.'

DIDOID or, more broadly, COLUMBINE dodo. His name in Portuguese meant 'simpleton,' and his scientific agnomen (added

446

name) is *ineptus*. The dodo was easy prey, and for some 300 years it has been extinct.

DIOMEDEINE albatross.

DROMADID cavalier, crab plover.

FALCONIFORM (Latin *falx*, 'sickle,' here refers to the shape of the beak) birds of prey, except owls. The two suborders of these are the Falcones and the Cathartes, or, roughly, the hawks and the vultures, with FALCONOID and CATHARTOID as the adjectives.

FALCONINE used generally for hawks, but specifically for true falcons or the "noble," long-winged hawks best used for falconry.

FALCONOID means 'falcon-like.'

FRATERCULINE puffin.

FREGATOID man-of-war bird or frigate bird.

FRINGILLINE finches, including buntings, serins, grosbeaks, canaries, weaver-birds and some other OSCINE birds.

FULICINE coots, gallinules. The latter include moor and mud hens, and American scoters. Scoters are also popularly called 'surf ducks' or 'coots.'

FULIGULINE sea ducks, like scaups, canvasbacks, eiders. FULIGINOUS means 'sooty' or, as here adapted, 'sooty-colored.'

FURCULAR wishbone.

FURNARIDOID South American oven bird, ant bird, wood hewer.

GALLINE or GALLINACEOUS turkey, chicken, guinea fowl, and also grouse and partridge.

GARRULINE jay, magpie; they are also CORVINE.

GNOMISH when speaking of owls, this refers to the pygmy owl.

GRUINE crane.

HALIAEETINE American bald eagle.

HERODIAN or HERODIONINE stork, heron, ibis and other such wading birds, but not cranes or, commonly, flamingos.

HIRUNDINE or HIRUNDOUS swallow, martin.

IBIDINE ibis, also spoonbill.

ICTERINE oriole, which builds hanging nests; but also meadow lark, bobolink and American blackbird.

LANIOID shrike or 'shrieking' bird, with hooked and toothed beak, that pins its prey on thorns.

LARIDINE gull, tern.

LARINE gull, but not tern or jaegar.

LIMICOLINE shore birds, as snipe, plover. From Latin *limus*, 'mud.'

LUSCINIINE nightingale. Being thrushlike, its adjective may also be TURDINE; the thrush family loosely includes thrashers, mockingbirds, warblers, the redstarts of the Old World, wheatears, water ouzels, solitaires, bluebirds, and others.

MEGALAEMOID barbet.

MELEAGRINE wild or tame turkey.

MERGIN mergansers, certain

duck-like fish-eating birds, including smews.

MERULINE blackbird.

MICROPODINE swift, akin to hummingbird but resembling swallow.

MICROPOIDEAN swifts, nighthawks and hummingbirds.

MIMINE mockingbird, thrasher, catbird.

MUSCICAPINE flycatcher.

NESTORINE big parrots, like the keas and kakas of New Zealand.

NUMENINE or SCOLOPAROID curlew.

NUMIDINE guinea fowl.

ORIOLOID oriole.

OSCINE singing birds, like thrushes and larks.

OSSIFRAGUS osprey or ossifrage (a fish hawk)—literally, 'bonebreaker.'

OTIDINE bustard, related to crane and rail.

PARADISEINE bird of paradise.

PARINE bush tit, titmouse, chickadee.

PASSERINE sparrow, especially; but also other perching birds, as robin and crow.

PAVONINE peacock.

PHASIANINE pheasant; also barnyard fowl.

PHOENICOPTEROUS flamingo. The *phoeni* is Greek for 'red,' as *flamingo* is Latin via Portuguese for 'flame.'

PICARIAN any flying land bird not a passerine (percher), a fowl, or a bird of prey. From Latin *picus*, 'woodpecker.'

PICINE woodpecker; PICIFORM means like one.

PINNATE feather.

PLOCEOID weaver bird. It weaves its nest. More broadly, the adjective is FRIGILLINE.

PLATALEINE spoonbill.

PODICIPOID grebe.

PSITTACEOUS or PSITTACEAN parrot.

PYGOPODOUS loon, grebe, auk. It means 'with legs placed rearward for diving.'

RALLINE rail crakes; RALLID: rail, coot, gallinule.

RAPTORIAL bird of prey.

RATITE noncarinate birds, like emus, rheas, cassowaries, ostriches and moas that can't fly.

RHEOID rhea.

SAXICOLINE chats; they are also, like wheatears, TURDOID.

SCOLOPACINE snipe; also woodcock, sandpiper, redshank and other longbilled limocolous birds. SCOLOPACEOUS means 'snipelike.'

SCOPID umbrettas. Another adjective is ARDEOIDEAN.

SETOPHAGINE warbler.

SPHENISCINE penguin.

STERCORARIOID jaeger, skua or sea hawk.

STERNINE tern.

STRIGINE owl.

STRUTHIOUS or STRUTHIONINE ostrich.

STURNELLINE meadow lark.

STURNINE starling.

SYLVININE true or Old World warblers. Also American king-

lets and gnat catchers. SYLVI-
NINE, with its emphasis on
thrush-likeness, equates with
MUSCICAPINE for flycatchers.
SYLVIOID refers to any OSCINES
that are warblers.

TANAGRINE tanager.

TIMALINE modified thrush, like
babblers and bulbuls. In Persian *bulbul* means 'nightingale.'

TRINGINE sandpiper.

TROCHILIDINE hummingbird.

TROGLODYTINE or TROGLODYTIC
wren, and it may include mockingbird. TROGLODYTOID can include both mockingbird and
thrasher.

TROGONOID trogon.

TURDINE or ICTERINE thrush. See
also LUSCINIINE for thrush-like
birds.

TURNICINE button quail and similar birds.

TYRANNINE or MYIAGRINE flycatcher.

UPUPOID hoopoe.

URINATORIAL means, literally,
'diving.' In speaking of birds, it
may refer to the loon.

VIDUINE widow bird.

VIREONINE vireo.

VULTURINE Old World vultures,
including the cinerious vulture
from Gibraltar to India.

ADJECTIVES PERTAINING TO FISH

ALOPIOID thresher (very long-
tailed) shark.

AMIOID bowfin.

ANACANTHOUS spiny-finned fish.

ANGUILLIFORM common eel.

APODAL eels, including morays.

ARGENTINOID smelt.

BATOID ray.

BELONOID gar or gar pike.

BLENNIOID blennies.

BRAMOID pomfret and Ray's
breams.

CARCHARIOID hammerhead, tiger,
hound and tope sharks.

CATOSTOMOID American sucker.

CENTRARCHID fresh water sun-
fish; small-mouthed, large-
mouthed and Kentucky black
bass, Mississippi crappies.

CHONDROSTEAN sturgeon.

CLUPEOID herrings, shad, sprat,
sardines or pilchards, men-
haden.

CLUPEOIDEAN herrings, tarpons,
and their relatives.

COBITOID loaches.

COREGONOID whitefish, including
cisco.

COTTOID sculpin.

CYPRINOID carp (except toothed
carps), including common
shiners, European bream, gud-
geon, dace, goldfish, ide, roach,
loach, chub.

CYPRINOIDEAN the carps, catfish,
American suckers.

ELOPOID fish allied to the tarpons.

ESOCOID pike, gar, pickerel,
muskallonge.

ESOCINE pike.

ETHEOSTOMINE darters.

EXOCOETOID true flying fish.

GADOID common cod, haddock, burbot, ling, hake, pollack, forkbeards, and others.

GADOIDEAN cod, grenadier and their relatives.

GANOIDEAN sturgeon, gar pike, bowfin and paddlefish.

GOBIESOCIFORM clingfish.

HAPLOMOUS pike, toothed carp, mud minnow.

HETEROSOMATOUS flatfish.

HOLCONOTOID surf fish [and related forms].

HIPPOLGLOSSINE halibut.

ICTALURINE "naked" American catfish.

LABROID wrasse.

LAMNIOID maneater, porbeagle and basking sharks.

LEPIDOSTEOID gar, or gar pike.

LUTIANOID sea snapper.

MACROUROID grenadier or rattail.

MALACOPTERYGIAN rij; soft-finned fish.

MUGILOID mullets (often called suckers).

MULLID in Europe, still other mullets. In America, true suckers and other fishes are also called 'mullets.'

PEDICULATE anglers and batfish.

PERCID perches and pike-perches.

PERCOIDEAN perches, and many basses and their relatives.

PERIOPSOID trout-perches.

PISCINE, PISCATORY or PISCATORIAL fish.

PLEURONECTINE flounders or flukes.

POLYODONTOID paddlefish.

POMATOMID bluefish.

SALMONOID trouts and salmon.

SALVELINE chars and eastern brook trout.

SCIAENOID kingfish, drumfish and croakers.

SCOMBEROMORINE Spanish mackerel.

SCOMBROID mackerels or mackerel family.

SCOMBROIDEAN mackerels, spearfish, sailfish, swordfish, marlin.

SELACHIAN sharks, rays and dogfish.

SELACHOID sharks.

SERRANOID black sea bass.

SILUROID catfish.

SOLEID soles.

SPAROID porgies, scup, sheepshead (related to the grunts).

SPHYRAENOID barracuda.

SQUALOID dogfish. It also just means 'sharklike.'

STOLEPHEROID anchovy.

TELEOST fish of bony structure, not cartilaginous like sharks.

THYMALLOID lake trout and graylings.

TRACHINOID weaver, and perhaps Pacific coast whitefish.

TRUTTACEOUS trout.

ADJECTIVES PERTAINING TO INSECTS AND OTHER INVERTEBRATES

ACALEPHAN jellyfish.

ACARIDAL or ACARINE mite, tick.

ACRIDIAN the saltorial orthoptera, except crickets.

ANNELID or LUMBRICINE earthworm; ANNELID refers also to leech.

ANGUILLOID vinegar eel.

APIAN bee.

ARACHNIDAN spider, scorpion, mite ARACHNOID is for cobweb and, specifically, for the middle membrane of three enveloping the brain and spinal cord.

ARTHROPODOUS or ARTHROPODAL jointed-legged invertebrates, like crabs, spiders.

ASTEROIDAL or ASTEROIDEAN starfish.

BIVALVE or BIVALVULAR doubleshelled mollusks, like oysters and clams.

CARDIACEAN cockles or mussels, especially the heart-shaped ones you eat; hence the 'cockles of your heart,' and even, by analogy, a frail boat.

CARIDOID shrimp.

CEPHALOPODOUS octopus, and other such core-bodied mollusks, such as the squid, nautilus and cuttlefish.

CHELATE pincerlike claw, like a lobster claw.

CICADID cicada.

CIRRIPED barnacles, and other such crustaceans.

COELENTERATE means 'hollowbellied,' like jellyfish, coral, sea anemone.

COLEOPTERAL or COLEOPTEROUS beetle.

CORALLINE coral.

COREID squash bug.

CRINOID or ECHINAL certain stalked and flowerlike invertebrates.

CRUSTACEAN crust-shelled invertebrates, like lobster and shrimp.

CULICID gnat, mosquito.

CYNIPID gallfly.

DERMESTINE carpet beetle.

DIPTERAL flea, gnat.

DROMIOID sponge crab.

ECHINAL sea urchin.

ENTOMOLOGIC, INSECTEAN or INSECTIVAL any insect.

EPELROID common garden spider.

FORMIC ant.

FULGOROID lantern fly.

GASTROPOD snail, slug.

GEOMETRINE measuring worm.

GRILLID cricket.

GRILLINE the hopping orthoptera; hopper, locust, cricket.

HELMINTHIC worm, especially a parasitic one.

HEMIPTEROUS or HEMIPTERAL generally, all true bugs, as typified by such loathsome objects as bedbugs, stinkbugs, squash bugs and water bugs; but ticks are ARACHNIDS, which refers also to spiders, scorpions, daddy-long-legs or harvestmen and crabs.

HETEROCEROUS moth.

HIRUDINE leech.

HISTERID the hard-backed beetles in muck or treebark.

HOMARINE lobster.

HOMOPTEROUS or HOMOPTERAN cicada, leaf and tree hoppers, white and lantern flies, plant lice, scale insects.

HYMENOPTERAN four-wingers, like bees, wasps and ants.

LARID leaf and snout beetles.

LEPIDOPTEROUS or LEPIDOPTERAN moth, butterfly.

LIOTHELOID bird louse.

LOCUSTAL grasshopper.

MACRURAL lobster, shrimp, prawn.

MALLOPHAGOUS bird louse.

MELOID Spanish fly (blister beetle).

MEMBRACINE tree hopper.

MUSCID or MUSCIFORM housefly.

MYID clam.

MYRIAPODOUS or MYRIAPODAN centipedes, thousand-leggers and such. Or, SCOLOPENDRINE for centipedes, and CHILOPODOUS for the others: *chilo* is Greek for 'a thousand.'

NASSOID the gastropods, including the dog whelks.

ODONATOUS or LIBELLULOID dragonfly.

OPHIUROID brittle stars and basket fish (somewhat resembling starfish).

ORTHOPTEROUS or ORTHOPTERAL hard-and-soft winged creatures, like locusts, grasshoppers and crickets. The classification formerly included the roach. Beetles also have hard outer and webby inner wings, but the outer ones are not narrow like a roach's. Beetles belong to a separate order.

OSTREAL, OSTRACEAN or OSTRACEOUS oyster, which is also MICROPODAL.

PEDICULAR louse, 'lousy.'

PHYCITID flour and meal moths.

POLYPOUS coral and sea anemone.

PULICINE or PULICENE flea. PULICOSE means 'full of fleas.'

RHOPALOCEROUS butterfly (which is distinguished from the moth by the knobs on its antennae).

SEPIARY or SEPIOID cuttlefish.

SPHINGINE hawk moth.

TAENIAL or HELMINTHIC tapeworm.

TERMITID termite.

TINEINE cloth moth.

TRICHINOUS trichina, the parasitic worm that causes trichinosis, a disease of the muscles: *not* trichosis, which is any disease of the hair.

VERMICULAR worm, its shape or its tracks. VERMICULOUS or VERMICULOSE means 'wormy' or 'worm-eaten.' VERMIFORM means 'worm-shaped.'

VESPINE, VESPAL or VESPOID wasp.

ZOOID creature of the animal kingdom, including insects.

ZOOPHYTIC any plantlike animal, like coral.

ADJECTIVES PERTAINING TO MAMMALS

AGNINE lamb.

ALCINE moose, elk.

ALOPECOID fox. It is the Greek derived equivalent of VULPINE, which comes from the Latin.

ANTELOPINE antelope.

ANTHROPOID ape; also means 'manlike.'

APRINE wild boar.

ARIETINE ram.

ASININE donkey.

BESTIAL beast.

BISONTINE or BISONIC bison.

BOVINE ox, cow. Really refers to goats, sheep and other hollow-horned ruminants; and to wild sheep, goats and antelopes, but not to deer, which are solid-horned. Figuratively, BOVINE also means 'slow' and 'stupid' (ox-like).

CAMELINE camel.

CAMELOID camel, llama, alpaca.

CAMELOPARDAL or GIRAFFINE giraffe.

CANINE dog, jackal, wolf.

CAPRANTILOPINE combined characteristics of goat and antelope.

CAPREOLINE roe deer, i.e., true roebuck.

CASTEROID beaver.

CERVINE deer.

CETACEOUS whale; CETACEAN is the noun.

CHIROPTEROUS or VESPERTILIONINE bats, whether black or brown, though the latter, if European, are also SEROTINE.

CUNICULAR rabbit.

CYNOCEPHALOUS baboon. The 'cyno' is from Greek kunos, comparing with Latin canus, 'dog'; he is a dog-faced, big monkey, not an ape, for he has a tail.

DELOPHOCINE fur seal.

DELPHINE dolphin.

DELPHINOID toothed whales, except sperm and beaked.

DIDELPHINE or PEDIMANE opossum. PEDIMOUS means 'having handlike feet,' like those of monkeys. The PEDIMANES include lemurs and other marsupials with handlike rear feet.

DILAMBDODONT mole, shrew and other rodents with cross-ridged teeth.

DIPODOID jerboa, or Old World jumping mouse.

DIPROTODONT marsupials, referring to their teeth.

EDENTAL anteater, sloth, aardvark, ant bear, armadillo.

EDENTATE sloth.

ELEPHANTINE elephant. This adjective is frequently used to refer to anything of large size or of importance.

ELAPHINE red deer.

ENHYDRINE or MUSTELOID sea otter.

EQUINE or CABALLINE horse; also, EQUINE refers to ass, zebra.

ERINACEOUS hedgehog.

FAUNAL native animals of a region, or all animals of a geologic period; fauna.

FELINE cat; also tiger, leopard, lynx.

GLOBICEPHALINE pilot whale.

HERPESTINE mongoose.

HIPPOPOTAMIC hippopotamus.

HYENIC hyena.

HYLOBATINE gibbon.

HYSTRICINE porcupine.

LANIARY canine teeth, or whatever is adapted for tearing.

LEMURID lemurs.

LEMUROIDEAN lemur and tarsier.

LEONINE lion.

LEPORINE hare.

LUPINE wolf, which is also CANINE.

LUTRINE otter.

LYNCINE and, especially as meaning keen-eyed, LYNCEAN lynx, including Spanish lynx.

MACROPODINE kangaroo and wallaby.

MACROPOID kangaroo family.

MAMMALIAN mammals, as distinct from the rest of the animal kingdom that includes birds, fish and reptiles, as well as insects and other invertebrates.

MANATINE sea cow, or manatee.

MARMOTAN (probably) woodchucks, ground hogs, sometimes prairie dogs and even the larger spermophiles.

MARSUPIAL animals with skin pouches for carrying young.

MELINE badger or their close allies.

MEPHITINE skunk. Note the adjective MEPHITIC meaning 'foul,' 'noxious,' 'poisonous,' both morally and odoriferously.

MIDOID or HAPALOID marmoset.

MONOTREMATUS duckbill.

MOSCHINE musk deer.

MURINE or MURID mouse, rat.

MUSCARDINE dormouse.

MUSTELENINE weasel, mink, marten, glutton or wolverine.

MUSTELINE or MUSTELOID embracive adjectives for MELINE, MUSTELENOUS and MEPHITINE— i.e., for badgers, weasels, skunks and their relatives, including otters, ferrets, sables, honey badgers or ratels, ermines or stoats, and polecats.

NASUINE coati, of raccoon family.

ONDATRIAN (probably) muskrat.

OTARINE seal and sea lion.

OVINE sheep.

PANTHERINE panther.

PEDETINE jumping hare.

PHOCAENINE porpoise.

PHOCINE seal.

PINNEPEDIAN seals and walruses, referring to their flippers for legs.

PORCINE hog; also, pork.

PROBOSCIDIAN elephant, mastodon.

PROCYONINE raccoon.

RANGIFERINE reindeer.

RHESIAN hand-organ species of monkey [worshiped by Hindus] from India.

RUSINE deer, especially the Burmese antelope or sambar.

SACCOMYOID kangaroo rat.

SCIURINE squirrel.

SERVALINE African wildcat, or serval.

SIMIAN monkey, ape.

SIRENIAN manatees, and sea cows or dugongs.

SORICINE shrew; long-nosed mouse.

SORICOID shrew, mole.

SPERMOPHILINE gopher, chipmunk and other so-called ground-squirrels; the spermophiles.

SUILLINE means 'pig-like.'

TALPINE mole.

TAPIRINE tapir.

TARSIOID tarsier.

TARSIPEDINE tait (the mouselike marsupial of Australia).

TAURINE bull.

TENTACULAR tentacle or claw.

TIGRINE or TIGERINE tiger.

TRICHECHINE manatee. Formerly erroneously used for the walrus.

TROGLODYTIC incorrectly used for the higher or anthropoid ape, like the gorilla, chimpanzee. The 'troglo' refers to a cave, which presumably is their home. The adjective is used also for wrens, which live, theoretically, in holes.

URSINE bear. 'Bruin' is Dutch.

VACCINE cow. Compare French *vache*, from Latin *vacca*, 'cow.' Vaccination is inoculation with cowpox.

VERMILINGUAL anteater.

VITULINE calf; also veal.

VIVERRIFORM civets, including mongooses.

VIVERRINE civet cat.

VULPINE fox.

ZEBRINE or HIPPOTIGRINE zebra.

ZOIC all animals and their lives.

ZOID or ZOOID a more or less independent animal produced by fission or other asexual means.

Nouns corresponding to 'homicide' and 'suicide' can be formed from many of the adjectives that refer to living creatures. For example, 'vulpicide' means a killer (or the killing) of foxes.

ADJECTIVES PERTAINING TO REPTILES

ANGUINE or COLUBRINE snake.

CHELONIAN turtle, tortoise.

CHELONOID green turtle.

CROCODILIAN or EMYDOSAURIAN crocodile.

DERMOCHELYOID leatherback turtle.

DRACONIAN dragon.

GAVIALOID gavial.

LACERTIAN lizard, including alligator.

OPHIDIAN or OPHIC legless reptile; snake or serpent.

PYTHONIC python, but also means 'prophetic,' because serpents were supposed to be oracular in ancient Greece.

REPTILIAN reptile, including saurian and serpent. Variants: HERPETOID, HERPETIFORM.

SAURIAN 'lizard,' literally, from the Greek; but generally including any reptile with legs, such as an alligator or dinosaur.

SERPENTINE snake, especially a large one.

VIPERINE viper; also means 'venomous.'

ADJECTIVES PERTAINING TO ANIMAL TRAITS AND BEHAVIOR

ALATE means 'winged.'

ANADROMOUS going up river to spawn, like salmon.

ANTHROPOPHAGOUS or CANNIBALISTIC eating of human flesh. By extension, CANNIBALISTIC refers to any animal that eats its own kind.

ANUROUS means 'tailless.'

APODAL means 'footless.'

APTEROUS means 'wingless.'

ARENICOLOUS burrowing in sand, like the desert asp.

ARVICOLOUS or, more technically, ARVICOLINE means 'living in fields,' like meadow mice.

AURATED means 'eared.'

BRACCATE means 'with feet feathered.'

BRANCHIAL or BRANCHIATE gills.

CARCINOPHAGOUS feeding on crabs.

CARNIVOROUS meat-eating.

CIRRIGRADE moving by means of tendrils, like barnacles.

CURSORIAL running, as of horses or their limbs, in distinction from SCANSORIAL.

DIOECIOUS having male sex organs in one individual and female ones in another.

DIGITIGRADE walking on the toes, like cats and dogs.

ECHINATE means 'covered with spines or bristles,' like a porcupine or hedgehog.

EDENTATE toothless, like ant-eaters, sloths, armadillos, and infants.

EPICENE common to both sexes.

FOSSORIAL 'burrowing,' like foxes.

FRUGIVOROUS fruit-eating.

GRALLATORIAL wading, like herons.

GRANIVOROUS grain-eating.

GRESSORIAL walking, as of hens and not of snakes.

HERBIVOROUS plant-eating, in distinction from CARNIVOROUS.

IMPAROUS inability to have offspring.

LANIARY tearing, as a dog's tooth tears.

MARSUPIAL pouch, like a kangaroo's.

NATATORIAL swimming, like fish.

NIDULANT nestling.

OMNIVOROUS means both 'meat-eating' and 'plant-eating.' Hence, it also means 'gluttonous.'

ORYZIVOROUS means 'rice-eating.'

OSSIVOROUS means 'bone-eating.'

OVIPAROUS production of young by eggs.

PACHYDERMATOUS thick skin.

PALMIPED means 'web-footed.'

PALUDINOUS or PALUDINE means 'living in marshes.'

PEDIMANOUS or PEDIMANE hand-like feet.

PHOEOPHAGOUS means 'feeding on tree bark.'

PHYLLOPHAGOUS means 'leaf-eating.'

PLANTIGRADE means 'walking flat-footedly,' like a bear. This is a trait that shows bears belong neither to the dog nor the cat family.

PLUMIPED means 'feathered-footed.'

PREHENSILE means 'seizing,' as a claw or a monkey's tail can seize a limb of a tree.

PROBOSCIDAL elongated nose; trunk or proboscis.

RAPTORIAL means 'seizing,' in the sense of snatching away, as an eagle seizes its prey.

RASORIAL means 'ground-scratching,' like hens.

REPTANT means 'creeping,' like reptiles.

RIPICOLOUS means 'living among rocks.' It refers specifically to the 'cock of the rock.'

RODENT means 'gnawing,' as of rats and rabbits.

ROSTRATE means 'beaked.'

RUMINANT means 'cud-chewing.'

SALTATORY means 'leaping,' like crickets and grasshoppers.

SCANSORIAL means 'climbing,' like monkeys and some birds climb.

SECTARIAL means 'cutting,' like a tiger's tooth.

SEPICOLOUS means 'living in hedges,' like some birds.

SERPIGINOUS means creeping, like a skin blemish, vanishing here and reappearing there. It is a pathological term especially applied to ringworm, but is capable of extension, like SERPIGINOUS crab-grass.

SILVICOLOUS means 'living in woods.'

STERCORICOLOUS means 'living in dung,' like some insects and worms.

SUCTORIAL means 'sucking,' like butterflies, and some fish.

TARDIGRADE means 'slow-moving,' like sloths.

TEREBRANT means 'boring,' like termites.

TROGLODYTIC or, in anthropology, TROGLODYTAL means 'living in caves'; hence, also 'primitive,' 'barbarous.'

UNGUICULATE means having claws or nails rather than hoofs. UNGUICULAR or UNGUICULATED refers more to a single animal.

UNGULATE means 'hoofed.'

VERMIGRADE means 'creeping,' like a worm.

VERMIPAROUS means breeding worms.

VERMIVOROUS means eating worms, or grubs.

VIVIPAROUS refers to the production of live offspring. Not OVIPAROUS.

ADJECTIVES PERTAINING TO MAN

Head

ADENOIDAL the lymph glands from nose to throat.

AMYGDALINE tonsil; or another almond-shaped lobe behind the brain, or else the gray matter there.

AURAL or AURICULAR ear.

BRACHYCEPHALIC comparative breadth of head.

BUCCAL cheek or mouth.

CANINE biting teeth, the two upper eye-teeth, and their opposite companions, called 'stomach teeth,' on the lower jaw.

CEPHALIC or CAPITAL head; ACEPHALOUS means 'headless.'

CEREBELLAR coordinating lobe of brain below the rear or OCCIPITAL lobe; the cerebellum.

CEREBRAL or ENCEPHALIC brain.

CERUMINAL ear wax.

CERVICAL neck.

CILIARY eyelashes.

CORNEAL cornea, the front coating of the eyeball.

CORTICAL brain-covering, or outer layer of other organs, such as kidneys; cortex.

CRANIAL skull.

CRINAL hair; and sometimes CRINATORY, which also means made of hair. CRINICULTURAL pertains to the care or growth of hair. CAPILLACEOUS and CAPILLARY both refer to the hair, but in usage they refer more often to hairlike tubes such as those connecting arteries and veins.

DENTAL teeth; EDENTATE means 'toothless,' like sloths.

DOLICHOCEPHALIC narrowness of head, compared with front-to-back depth of skull.

EPIGLOTTAL epiglottis (the hatch over the windpipe, back of the tongue), which closes when you swallow.

FACIAL face, which derives from Latin. The adjective VISAGED is a figurative extension of vision —what we see, becomes its face.

FRONTAL forehead.

GENAL cheek.

HETERODONT means with ordinary mammalian teeth, including molars, canines and incisors.

HYOID u-shaped bone below tongue.

INCISOR cutting teeth, the squarish front ones.

INIAL medial ridge of crown; inion.

JUGULAR, GUTTURAL or GULAR throat; from Latin *jugulum, guttur* and *gula,* all meaning 'throat.'

LABIAL lips.

LABROSE means 'thick-lipped.'

LACHRYMAL or LACRIMAL tears; LACHRYMOSE or LACRIMOSE means 'weepy.'

LARYNGEAL larynx, upper wind-pipe, where the vocal cords are boxed; but the word is Greek for gullet.

LINGUAL tongue.

LOBULAR lobe.

MALAR cheek.

MANDICULAR lower jaws, or man-dibles, from the Latin for 'to chew.'

MASSETERIC or MASSETERINE the two masticatory muscles that raise the lower jaw.

MAXILLAR or MAXILLARY jaw.

MENTAL strange as it may seem, this adjective refers to the chin, being derived from the Latin *Mentum,* not *mentalis.*

MOLAR a back, or flat-crowned, tooth, a grinder; comes from Latin *molaris,* referring to a mill. Latin *moles,* 'mass,' gave us another adjectival MOLAR, pertaining to mass, as public opinion is MOLAR (acting in the mass).

MUCOUS mucus.

NARIAL nostrils, nares.

NASAL nose.

NEBAL nose, figuratively. Com-pare a bird's neb or beak.

NUCHAL nape of neck.

OCCIPITAL back of head.

OCULAR eye.

OLFACTORY lobe of the brain be-neath the forehead; seat or sense of smell.

OPHTHALMIC eye, especially in reference to inflammation.

OPISTHOGNATHOUS means 'with retreating jaws.'

ORAL mouth. When the mouth is gaping, RICTAL usually ap-plies.

ORBITAL eye-socket.

OSCULAR mouth.

OTIC ear, or its environs. See also PAROTID.

PALATAL palate.

PARIETAL the center wall-bones of the skull or the brain-lobe under them, i.e., between the frontal lobe where you do most of your thinking and the rear lobe.

PAROTID region of the ear; mumps gland.

PHARYNGEAL pharynx, which is the passage from the nose to the top of the gullet or wind-pipe. Here diphtheria attacks you, affecting both breathing and eating.

PINEAL a small cone-shaped vestigial gland in the brain, once suspected of housing the soul.

PITUITARY mucus, from the Latin for phlegm or spit. But the adjective now generally re-fers to the pituitary gland un-der the brain, one of whose lobes affects blood pressure and the other, body growth.

PORRIGINOUS dandruff.

PROGNATHOUS protruding jaws.

PUPILLARY pupil of eye.

RETINAL inner photographic coat of eye.

RHINAL nose. Compare 'rhinoc-eros.'

RICTAL width of open mouth, or gape. Hence, it also refers to the corners of the mouth.

SALIVARY saliva.

SCLEROTIC hard outer membrane of eyeball.

SINCIPITAL top of head.

SPHINCTERAL mouth muscle, or other muscles closing openings.

SUBLINGUAL salivary glands under tongue.

SUPERCILIARY eyebrows. Compare 'supercilious.'

TELAR brain tissue.

THYMIC self-eliminating thymus gland in neck and chest. As food, the thymus glands of calves and lambs, as well as the pancreas under their stomachs, are called 'sweetbreads.'

THYROID Greek for shield-shape; the thyroid, a ductless gland under windpipe affecting your growth. The gland sometimes grows into goiters.

TONSILLAR tonsil.

TRACHEAL trachea, or windpipe.

ULETIC gums.

UVEAL uvea, the colorful layer of the eye, including the iris.

UVULAR uvula, the flap of the soft palate.

VELAR velum, or the soft palate, behind the hard one.

VOMERINE bony central wall of the nose.

Limbs

ALAR wings, if we had any fleshly ones; ALATE means 'winged.'

ANCONEAL or ULNAR elbow.

AXILLAR or AXILLARY armpit.

BASILIC chief vein of arm.

BICIPITAL front upper arm flexors or biceps. Flexor muscles bend limbs or fingers; extensor muscles straighten or extend them. The quadriceps are extensors lying on the front side of the thigh. FLEXURAL and presumably EXTENSURAL are their adjectives.

BIFURCATE two-branched, as the lower part of man is.

BRACHIAL arm, especially upper arm.

CALCANEAL heel bone.

CARPAL wrist.

CONDYLAR knuckles.

CORNEOUS horn or a horny substance.

CRURAL leg, especially part between thigh and ankle; the shank.

DIGITTAL or DACTYLIC toes or fingers.

FEMORAL or CRURAL thigh.

HUMERAL shoulder.

MALLEOLAR ankle knob.

MANUAL or CHYRAL hand; AMANOUS means 'handless.'

MEMBRAL member, or limb.

METICARPAL back of hand, or the hand bones between wrist and fingers.

PALMAR palm.

PATELLAR knee; also the kneecap.

PEDAL feet; PEDATE means having feet.

PHALANGAL or PHALANGEAL the constituent bones of the fingers and toes. Hence, it refers also to the fingers or toes.

PLANTAR sole of foot.

POPLITEAL knee pit, and the area above and below it.

RADIAL forearm bone on front side.

SCAPHOID or NAVICULAR wrist bone on thumb side; or instep bone of foot.

SURAL or FIBULAR the outer and thinner of the two bones of the lower leg. Hence, it also refers to calf. See also TIBIAL.

TARSAL, TALARIC or ASTRAGULAR anklebones or ankle. 'Astragal,' or 'astragulus,' is taken from the Greek for the anklebone and

'talus' is from the Latin. *'Talus'* now refers specifically to man's main anklebone, which bears his weight. In many animals the anklebone is higher, being what we call the hipbone or hucklebone. Dice were made from those bones, so ASTRAGULAR is also an adjective for dice. TALARIC comes from 'talaria,' the wings on Mercury's feet.

TIBIAL, CNEMIAL or CRURAL shinbone or shin. The tibia, or shinbone, is the longer of the lower leg bones; the fibula is the shorter one behind it.

TRICIPITAL rear upper arm extensors, or triceps. See also BICIPITAL.

UNGUAL nail.

Torso

ABDOMINAL, CELIAC or (chiefly medical) ALVINE stomach or intestines. CELIAC is sometimes spelled COELIAC.

ADRENAL glands near kidneys. Compare RENAL.

ALIMENTARY nutrition. Hence it refers to the truncal food channel.

ANAL anus.

AORTIC main artery to the heart.

APPENDICULAR vermiform or worm-shaped appendix. APPENDICAL, or perhaps CAECAL, refers to the blind pouch, or *caecum,* at the end of the large intestine to which the appendix is appended. 'Blind,' in this instance, means open only at one end,

like a blind alley.

BILIARY or BILIOUS bile.

BRONCHIAL the main corridors to the lungs; bronchial tubes.

CAMERAL chamber of heart.

CARDIAC heart.

CAUDAL tail, if we had one.

CHOROID outer covering of fetus. It also refers to the coat of the eyeball, between the sclerotic and the retina.

CHYLOUS milky digestive fluid; chyle.

CLAVICULAR collarbone from shoulder to breastbone.

COLONIC large intestine or colon.

COSTAL ribs. Hence, it also refers to the side of the body.

COXAL hip, or hip joint.

DORSAL [applies to animals] back.

EPICARDIAL inner layer of pericardium.

EPIGASTRIC or EPIGASTRAL abdomen above stomach.

ESOPHAGEAL esophagus or gullet; tube from mouth to stomach.

FECAL, STERCORAL or EXCREMENTAL faeces or dung.

FETAL or FOETAL unborn young or fetus.

GASTRIC, STOMACHAL or STOMACHICAL stomach, which is Greek for mouth—quite inaptly suggestive when you are hungry.

GENITAL sex organ; AGAMOUS means without any.

GLUTEAL buttocks.

HEPATIC liver.

ILIAC hip, at the top. Not to be confused with ILEAC, which refers to the lower ⅗ of the small intestine, nor of course with its literal duplicate ILIAC, of ancient Troy.

INGUINAL groin.

LATERAL side.

LUMBAR loins. Compare lumbago.

OVARIAN ovary.

PANCREATIC pancreas.

PECTORAL or THORACIC chest.

PELVIC hips, or especially the basin formed by the hip bones. Those bones include the *sacrum* (with adjective SACRAL) at the rear of the pelvis; *acetabulum* (ACETABULAR) forming the socket for the thigh bone; *pubis* (PUBIC, which also means grown-up, as evidenced by PUBIC or groin hair), at the front of the pelvis; and *coccyx* (COCCYGEAL), the last tapering bone of the backbone.

PERICARDIAL membrane around the heart.

PERITONEAL membrane that covers abdominal contents; peritoneum.

PHRENIC or DIAPHRAGMATIC midriff, or diaphragm.

PLEURAL lining of the lung, esp. the membranes around the lungs.

PULMONARY or PNEUMONIC lung.

PYLORIC opening from stomach to small intestine.

RECTAL end of large intestine; rectum.

RENAL or NEPHRITIC kidney. The 'kid' in kidney is English for womb; the 'ney' is Icelandic for kidneys. The Latin *renes*, via Old French, gave us 'reins,' our 'innards' or 'kidneys.'

SCAPULAR collarbone at shoulder.

SCIATIC hip, or its nerves.

SPINAL backbone.

SPLANCHNIC bowels, and all internal organs.

STERNAL breastbone; hence, also, chest.

TESTICULAR testicle.

TRUNCAL trunk. 'Torso' seems to have no adjective of its own in English.

UMBILICAL navel.

URETIC duct from kidney to bladder.

URETHRAL duct leading out from bladder.

URIC, or less technically, URINOUS urine.

UTERINE womb.

VENTRAL stomach or front side; bottom side of bugs and beasts. The Latin for stomach or belly was either *venter* or *abdomen;* the English term was 'womb.' The 'womb' itself was Anglo-Saxon *cwith,* which became 'kid' in 'kidney.' English 'belly' was perhaps slangish for a bag, although it would seem that bags and bellies were synonymous throughout early Europe. Thus the bellies of man or beast may have been the first bags, with the term spreading to include sacks and wine-skins.

VENTRICULAR any of body cavities or hollow organs, like the ventricles of the heart.

VERTEBRAL spine; vertebrae.

VISCERAL and INTESTINAL the insides and the bowels.

General Terms

ADENOID or ADENOIDAL gland, especially one secreting lymph.

ANDROID the human shape or figure.

APONEUROTIC shiny fibrous covering of the muscles and their junctions, formed from the tendons.

APOSTEMATOUS abscess.

ARTERIAL arteries.

ARTICULAR joint. Compare with 'arthritis,' and with 'arthropods,' the term for jointed invertebrates.

CADAVEROUS corpse, cadaver; also, carcass, of animal.

CAPILLARY hairs, or hairlike tubes.

CARNEOUS flesh, as substance; CARNAL combines the senses of CARNEOUS and the adjective sensual, which refers to the body's appetites.

CARAPACIAL shell or carapace, as of a turtle or armadillo. But figuratively it refers to our own bodily integuments and to the 'shells' we stay in when we don't express ourselves.

CARTILAGINOUS cartilage or gristle.

CELLULAR cells.

CICATRICIAL scar, cicatric.

CILIARY fine hairs or cilia, as even on body cells.

CORPORAL, CORPOREAL or PHYSICAL the body, especially as distinguished from the mind or spirit.

CORPUSCULAR corpuscles.

CYSTIC sac or cyst.

DERIC skin.

DERMAL the real skin, as distinct from epidermis or cuticle. CUTICULAR is used figuratively of any outer covering. DERMAL also serves for CUTANEOUS. INTEGUMENTAL or INTEGUMEN-

TARY refers to skin as an over-all covering or envelope.

EPITHELIAL surface skin, or the cuticle as a whole.

ENZYMOTIC or ENZYMIC pepsin, and such natural catalytic substances, formerly called 'ferments'; enzyme.

FISTULAR holes or passages caused by disease; fistula.

FRACTURAL broken bones.

FURUNCULAR boil.

GANGLIAL secondary nerve centers, or ganglions.

GLANDULAR secreting organs, or glands. From the Greek for 'acorns.'

HEMAL, CRUORAL or SANGUINARY blood.

HEMOGLOBIN red corpuscles.

HERMAPHRODITIC means 'bisexual'; of both sexes.

HERPETIC means 'creeping,' like certain skin eruptions; formerly, ringworm and eczema.

LEUCOCYTIC white corpuscles.

LIGAMENTAL or LIGAMENTOUS tough fibrous tissues holding bones or organs in place and differing from contractile muscles which produce movements; ligaments.

LYMPHAL watery fluid, or lymph, in certain bodily vessels, like blood plasma.

MEDULLAR or MEDULLARY marrow.

MEMBROUS membrane.

MUCOUS mucus.

NEUROTIC or NERVAL nerve.

NEVOSE or NEVOID birthmark, mole or other blemish; NEVOSE also means 'spotted' or 'freckled.'

OSSEOUS bone.

OSSICULAR small or bony mass.

PLASMIC liquid part of blood; sticky part of cells; fluid in muscles; plasma.

PLEXAL plexis; a network of interlacing blood vessels or nerves.

PORAL pores.

PORRIGINOUS scurf.

PROTOPLASMIC chief mass of organic cellular matter; protoplasm.

PUSTULAR or PUSTATE pimple or pustule.

RUGOUS wrinkles. It means 'wrinkled.'

SCABROUS scab.

SEBACEOUS fat; grease.

SEROUS serum.

SPHYGMIC pulse.

STOMATAL minute pores; POROUS means 'full of pores.'

SUDORAL sweat.

SUTURAL juncture of notched bones; suture.

TELAR or HISTIC tissue.

TENDINOUS tendon.

TONIC muscles, and their condition.

TRAUMATIC wound or injury.

TROCHLEAR concave joint-part, as in elbow.

ULCEROUS ulcer.

VALVULAR valve.

VASCULAR ducts or vessels.

VENOUS vein.

VESICULAR small cavity or cyst; cell or vesicle. It also refers to the air cells of the lungs.

ADJECTIVES PERTAINING TO FLOWERS AND PLANTS

(Trees, grains, vegetables and fruits)

ACICULAR prickly bristle.

AGARIC fungus

AGARICOID edible common mushroom.

ALSINACEOUS chickweed.

ALGAL kelp, seaweed; algal.

ALLIACEOUS leek, onion, garlic; the odor of the latter two.

ALOETIC aloe.

APIACEOUS celery, parsley, carrot, dill.

ARACEOUS arums, like skunk cabbage, jack-in-the-pulpit.

ARALIACEOUS ginseng and English ivy.

ARBOREAL or SYLVAN trees. ARBOREAL also refers to living in trees.

  ABIETINEOUS fir.

  ACERACEOUS maple.

  ASHEN ashen.

  ASPEN or ASPINE aspen.

  BALSAMIC balsam.

  BOMBACACEOUS baobub and other trees of the bombax family.

  CASTANEAN, CASTANEOUS or, in chemistry, ESTULIC chestnut.

  CEDRINE cedar.

  CITRINE lemon, orange, citron, grapefruit, lime. CITROUS refers more to the fruits; and citrine to their color; CITRIC usually means derived from the fruits.

CONIFEROUS cone trees, such as the pines and firs.

CORTICAL tree bark.

CYPRINE cypress, not Cyprus, whose inhabitants are Cyprians or Cypriotes.

DECIDUOUS means capable of being shed periodically, like either leaves or horns. But trees themselves are either DECIDUOUS or EVERGREEN.

ELAEAGNACEOUS trees and shrubs of the oleaster or wild plum family.

FAGACEOUS trees and shrubs of the beech family.

FICOID or FICOIDAL trees, shrubs and vines of the fig family.

GERANIAL or GERANACEOUS plants of the geranium family.

ILICACEOUS trees and shrubs belonging to the holly family.

JUGLANDIC or JUGLANDACEOUS trees of the walnut and hickory family. Incidentally, the word 'walnut' is Anglo-Saxon and the 'wal' means 'foreign.' Ancient southern Germans applied it first to a Celtic tribe, and it was later affixed to Welshmen and the walnut.

LARCHEN larch.

LAURACEOUS laurel, sassafras, cinnamon.

MALIACEOUS mahogany.

MORACEOUS mulberry, breadfruit, fig, and others of the mulberry family.

MUSACEOUS banana.

OLIVACEOUS olive or olive-color. 'Olive oil' gives us OLEAGINOUS, meaning figuratively smooth or fawning.

PALMACEOUS, ARECACEOUS or PHOENICACEOUS palm.

PINACEOUS pine, fir.

POMACEOUS trees such as apple, pear, quince, hawthorn, which produce pomes.

QUERCINE oak.

RUTACEOUS rues. It sometimes also refers to rueful repentance.

SALICACEOUS trees of the willow family. SALICYLIC refers to willows as associated with SALICYLIC acid.

SAPOTACEOUS bully tree, and the chicle-yielding sapodilla.

TILIACEOUS linden or basswood.

ULMACEOUS trees and shrubs of the elm family.

AVENACEOUS oats, or similar grasses.

BACCATE berry.

BACCIFEROUS producing berries.

BRASSICACEOUS family of herbs which includes cabbage, turnip, radish, mustard.

BRYOPHYTIC or MUSCOID moss.

BULBOUS bulb.

CACTACEOUS cactus.

CEPACEOUS onion.

CEREAL grain.

CESPITOSE means growing in clumps or tufts.

CORTICAL fruit rind.

CUCURBITAL or CUCURBITACEOUS pumpkin, squash, cucumber, watermelon; the gourds.

CYNAREOUS burdock, thistle, artichoke.

CYPERACEOUS sedge.

FERULACEOUS reed.

FERULAR fennel.

FILICAL fern.

FLORAL flowers.

ACANTHINE acanthus. ACANTHOUS means spiny.

AMARANTHINE nonfading flowers.

ASTERACEOUS aster.

BRACTEAL stalk-leaf or bract; BRACTEOLATE is for little ones, or *bractedes*.

CAPRIFOLIACEOUS honeysuckle.

CARDUACEOUS aster, cosmos, chrysanthemum.

CICHORIACEOUS dandelion, chicory.

CROCINE crocus.

ERICACEOUS heath, including laurel, rhododendron.

HYACINTHINE hyacinth.

IRIDACEOUS iris, gladiolus, crocus.

LILIACEOUS lily.

MALVACEOUS mallow family.

ORCHIDACEOUS orchid.

PAPAVEROUS poppy.

PETALINE petal.

ROSACEOUS rose.

FRUCTIFEROUS fruit-bearing.

FRUMENTACEOUS cereals, like wheat.

FRUTICOSE shrub.

FUCOIDAL seaweed.

GEMMATE means having or producing buds.

GERMINAL seed.

GRANULAR grains, as of corn.

HERBACEOUS those seed plants that do not have woody, persistent tissue (as distinguished from shrubs and trees.)

JUNCACEOUS rushes.

LACTUCIC lettuce.

LEGUMINOUS peas or other legumes.

LEMNACEOUS duckweed, or the small plants which float on ponds.

LICHENOUS or LICHENACEOUS lichen.

MALIC apple. Used chiefly in chemistry.

MENTHACEOUS mint.

NATANT means 'swimming,' or more usually, 'floating,' like lily pads.

NEMOROSE growing in woods.

ORBICULAR means 'circular' like an ORBICULAR leaf or petal.

OXALIC sorrel.

PALUDOSE means growing in marshes.

PEDUNCULAR flower-stem.

PETIOLAR leaf-stem.

PHYLLOGENOUS means found on leaves, like fungus.

PHYLLOPHOROUS means bearing leaves, or the like.

PINEAL pine cone.

POACEOUS grass.

POMONIC fruit.

PRUNIFEROUS plum-bearing.

RADICAL root.

SEMINAL seed.

SESSILE stemless attachment, as of a leaf or a plant, at the base.

SOLANACEOUS the nightshade family, including the potato plant and eggplant.

SPHAGNOUS peat mosses.

SPINACEOUS spinach.

STAMINAL stamen. Sometimes it refers to stamina. STAMINEAL always refers to 'stamen.'

STELAR stele.

TUBERIFEROUS tubers, such as truffles, potatoes.

ULIGINOUS means growing in muddy places or in marshes. Hence it also means 'muddy.'

URTICACEOUS nettles or pellitory.

UVAL grape and similar fruits.

VEGETAL vegetables; or plants; or vegetables, plants, and animals generally, as mere organic things, in distinction from, in some cases, creatures of will and feeling.

VERDUROUS green grass, growing plants or the green freshness of them; verdure.

VIMINAL twigs, shoots.

VINACEOUS grape.

VIRGAL means made of twigs.

VITACEOUS grapevine.

XEROPHILOUS refers to ability to withstand dryness, as of desert plants.

ZOOPHITIC plantlike animals, such as coral.

ADJECTIVES PERTAINING TO SHAPES

ACEROSE needle shape. ACERATE refers to a needle's point, and ACEROUS means 'hornless,' or 'with few antennae.'

ACICULATE or ACICULAR needle shape. But they also mean 'sharp-pointed.' But ACERATE is more likely to be used figuratively, as in speaking of an ACERATE remark.

ACUMINATE means tapering to a point, whence ACUMINOUS, meaning 'sharp-witted,' 'having acumen.'

BACCATE berry shape.

BARBATE beard shape; it also means 'bearded.'

BOTRYOSE grape cluster, or the like.

CAMPANULATE bell shape.

CARINATE means 'full-chested,' like a robin. The opposite is RATITE for 'flat-chested.'

CIRCINATE means 'ring-shaped,' or 'spirally curled.'

COCHLEATE spiral twist, like some shells. Sometimes this adjective refers to the shape of those shells.

CORDATE heart shape.

CRENATE means 'scalloped-edged.'

CRISPATE means 'curled-looking.'

CRISTATE means 'crested'; or else it means CARINATE.

CRUCIATE cross shape.

CUCULLATE hood shape.

CULTRATE shape of a pruning-knife.

CUNEATE or SPHENOID wedge shape.

DIGITATE spread fingers, or the semblance of them.

ENATE means growing out, like horns.

ENSATE, GLADIATE or XIPHOID sword shape.

ERUCIFORM caterpillar shape.

FISSATE means 'divided,' or 'cleft,' as with deep fissures.

FLAGELLATE means with whip-like runners, or branches.

FLAGELLIFORM 'whiplash form.'

FURCATE means 'branched,' like two lines. FURCATE or FURCAL means 'forked' in anatomy.

FURCULAR or FURCIFORM fork or fork shape.

FUSIFORM spindle shape.

GALEATE helmet shape.

GENICULATE means with knobs, or knee-like joints.

GIBBOUS imperfect roundness, like the moon's shape when not quite full.

GLOBATE globe or sphere shape. Hence it can mean 'rounded,' 'complete.' GLOBAL not only means 'spherical' in shape but also refers to a globe itself or, to all the affairs on earth.

SPHERIC refers to the spheres or heavenly bodies collectively.

SPHEROID, as also GLOBOUS and GLOBOSE, means 'roughly spherical.' GLOBULAR may mean GLOBATE, or it may equate with GLOBULOUS, referring to a small sphere or to a mass of small spheres. GLOBERIFEROUS refers to things with GLOBULAR ends, like antennae.

HELICAL spiral shape.

LORATE strap shape.

LENTICULAR lentil shape.

LOBULAR shape of a small lobe.

LUNULAR small crescent. LUNATE also means 'crescent-shaped.'

NAPIFORM turnip shape.

NAVICULAR boat shape.

NODAL means 'knobby' or 'having swelled places,' like a plant's stem. Figuratively it may refer to the difficult spots in a story or play. In science it refers to nodes.

ORBICULAR refers to the shape of a globe, sphere, eye or orbit.

OVATE egg shape.

PEDATE foot shape.

PLICAL folds. PLICATE means 'folded,' like a fan.

RUGATE or RUGOUS means 'wrinkled' or 'corrugated.'

SCALARIFORM means 'ladder-like,' especially used for certain strips of cells in biology.

SCAPHOID boat shape.

SCOBIFORM refers to an object with looks or form of sawdust, like some seeds.

SCOPIFORM brush shape.

SCUTATE scale or sword shape. It pertains also to horny plates, like a covering.

SCUTELLATE or SCUTIFORM shield or platter shape.

SERRATE saw-toothed edge.

SPATULATE spatula shape or spoon shape.

SPICATE means arranged in spikes. As a zoological term it means 'spike-like.'

STROBILE cone shape, like some fruits.

TERATE tapered cylinder. Or it means 'round in cross-section.'

TORQUATE means having a collar.

VAGINATE sheath form. Also, it means 'sheathed.'

VERMICULATE a worm's winding motion. Hence it also means 'insinuating' or, more pleasantly, 'adorned with twisted markings.'

VIRGATE means 'rod-like.'

INDEX

abase, 30
abasement, 30
abash, 30
abashment, 30
abbatial, 315
abbot, 247
abdominal, 461
abduct, 387
abduction, 387
abet, 231
abhor, 10
abhorrence, 148
abietineous, 465
ability, 56, 404-405
abolish, 111
abomination, 394
about, 299-301
above, 299-301
abreast, 296
abrogate, 417
abscond, 387
absinthic, 116
abstain, 323
abstemious, 323
abstract, 391
absurd, 37
academic, 205
acanthine, 466
acanthous, 466
acaridal, 451
acarine, 451
accede, 75-76
accept, 414-415
access, 415
accident, 51
accipitral, 446
accipitrine, 446
acclaim, 113
accolade, 50
accomplish, 406
accomplishments, 407
accord, 76
accost, 387
accountant, 247
account for, 222
accrue, 44

accumulation, 23
acelephan, 451
aceraceous, 465
acerose, 468
acescent, 116
acetabular, 462
acetic, 417-418
achieve, 406
achievements, 406
achromatic, 60
acicular, 465, 468
aciculate, 468
acid, 37
acknowledge, 89
acme, 106
acoustics, 328
acquiesce, 75
acquiescence, 74
acquisitiveness, 152
acquit oneself, 68
acre, 21
acridian, 451
acrimonious, 7, 85
across, 296
act, 197, 313
actualities, 90
acumen, 222
acuminate, 468
address, 68, 354
adduce, 435
adenoid, 463
adenoidal, 458, 463
ad hoc, 270, 274
adipsous, 140
adjectival, 138
adjective, 138
administrative, 132-134
administrator, 132-134
admirable, 308
admiration, 148
admonishment, 360
admonition, 360
adrenal, 461
adulation, 114
advance, 233

advent, 32
adventitious, 52-53
adventurous, 142
adverb, 138
adverse, 418
adversity, 418
advice, 415
advise, 415
aerial warfare, 401
aeronautics, 328
aeruginous, 61
aesthetic, 417
aesthetics, 268
affable, 124
affection, 148
affection (disease), 1
affinity, 64, 187-188
affirm, 354
affluence, 44-45
affluent, 44-45
afford, 45, 403
affront, 96-97
against, 296
agamous, 462
agaric, 465
agaricoid, 465
age, 365-366, 367
agent, 403
aggravate, 97
aggregation, 23
aggressor, 8
agile, 142
agnation, 186
agnine, 453
ago, 363
agog, 166
agoraphobia, 104
agrarian, 127, 330
agrarianism, 330
agreeable, 124
agreement, 64, 74
agriculture, 330
agrology, 331
agronomist, 330
agronomy, 330

aguish, 1
ailing, 5
ailments, 1-5
aim, 106
air, 68
aircraft, 376
airy, 409
aisle, 315
ait, 129
alar, 460
alarm, 401
alate, 456
alaudine, 446
album, 440
alcedine, 446
alcidine, 446
alcine, 446, 453
alcoid, 446
alert, 142, 401
algal, 465
alienation, 148
alike, 64
alimentary, 461
all, 255
allegation, 354
allege, 354, 355
allegiance, 148
alleluia, 113
allergies, 1
alley, 348
alliaceous, 116, 465
alliance, 74
all right, 270
allure, 415-416
allusion, 416
alluvial, 127
almanac, 440-441
aloetic, 465
aloft, 298
alongside, 296
aloof, 72
alopecian, 1
alopecoid, 453
alopioid, 449
alphabet, 138
alright, 270
alsinaceous, 465

471

naive, 145-146
naivete, 145
namby-pamby, 282
nap, 343
napiform, 469
narcotic, 141
narial, 459
nasal, 459
nascent, 32
Nash, Ogden, 217
nassoid, 452
nasuine, 454
natant, 467
natatorial, 456
nation, 131
natty, 101
natural, 310
nature, 57
naught, 245
nausea, 5
nauseous, 3
nautical, 376
naval warfare, 401
nave, 317
navicular, 461, 469
navigation, 329
nealogy, 332
near, 297
neb, 431
nebal, 459
nebular, 410
nebulous, 206
necessary, 55
necessity, 52, 115
  and chance, 51-
  56
nectareous, 117
nectarial, 117
nectarine, 117
need, 282, 306
needful, 52
needy, 305, 306
nefarious, 390
neglectful, 85
negligee, 98
neighborhood, 19
nemesis, 115
nemorose, 467
neophobia, 104
neoteric, 365
nephew, 187
nephology, 330
nephritic, 462
nepotal, 187
nepotism, 295
nerval, 464
nervine, 141

nescience, 229
nescients, 229
nestorine, 448
nettle, 96
neurology, 330
neurotic, 464
nevoid, 464
nevose, 464
nib, 431
nice, 311-312
nidology, 332
nidulant, 456
niece, 187
nigh, 297
nigrescent, 61
nimble, 143
nincompoop, 161
nippy, 6
nival, 410
niveous, 410
noble, 231, 372
nocturnal, 365
nodal, 469
noetic, 229
noise, 350
noisome, 253
nominal, 138, 372
nominalism, 268
non, 283
nonagon, 245
nonchalant, 143
none, 222
nonillion, 245
non sequitur or non
  seq, 270, 275
non vult, 270, 275
no one, 222
norm, 93-94
nose infections, 2
nose out, 333
nostalgic, 3
notability, 113
note, 44, 264
notice, 264
notorial, 248
notoriety, 57
notorious, 390
nought, 245
noun, 138
nounal, 138
novemdecillion,
  245
novennial, 245
novice, 157
noxious, 81
nuchal, 459
nucleus, 297

nuisance, 394
number, 246-247
numbers, 243-247
numenine, 448
numerous, 257
numidine, 448
nuptial, 51
nutmeg, 118
nutritious, 141
nylon, 102

obeisance, 70
obfuscate, 204
obiter dicta, 270,
  275
object, 185
objective, 107
obligate, 322-323
oblige, 322-323
obliging, 124
obliterate, 111
obloquy, 396
obnoxious, 81
obscene, 38
obscure, 202, 239
obscurity, 206
obsequies, 49, 73
obsequious, 73
observance, 49
observe, 265-266
obsession, 104, 105
obsidional, 400
obsolescence, 368
obsolescent, 368
obsolete, 368
obstetrics, 248
obstreperous, 350
obstruct, 320
obtain, 406
obtuse, 146
obvious, 90, 91
occipital, 459
occult, 242
occupations, 247-
  252
occur, 435
oceanography, 330
octagon, 245
octillion, 245
octodecillion, 245
ocular, 431, 459
oculist, 248
odic, 206
odontalgic, 3
odonatous, 452
odoriferous, 253
odorous, 253

odors, 252-254
oecumenical, 392
offense, 6
offensive, 394
oily, 29
old, 364
oleaginous, 117,
  466
olfactory, 459
oligarchy, 132
olio, 259-260
olivaceous, 466
'ologies, 331-332
omega, 107
ominous, 115, 239
omnibus, 376
omnivorous, 456
oncology, 332
ondatrian, 454
one, 219
onerous, 38
onomatopoeia, 213
ontogeny, 16
ontology, 330
opalescent, 203
opaque, 202
open, 143
opening, 32
open sesame, 283
ophidian, 455
ophic, 455
ophiology, 16
ophiuroid, 452
ophthalmic, 459
opinion, 224
opisthognathous,
  459
oppose, 431-433
opposite, 297, 432
opposition, 432-433
opprobrium, 13
option, 225
optometrist, 248
opulence, 44-45
opulent, 310
oracular, 239, 431
oral, 189, 459
orbate, 189
orbicular, 467, 469
orbital, 459
orchidaceous, 467
order, 327
ordinals, 247
ordinance, 198
ordinate, 106
organ, 404
organize, 32

APOLLO EDITIONS

A1 Emerson's Essays $1.95
A2 God and the Soviets *Dr. Marcus Bach* $1.25
A3 The Lost Americans *Frank C. Hibben* $1.25
A4 Shakespeare's Plays in Digest Form *J. Walker McSpadden* $1.25
A5 The Shakespearean Review Book *Fannie Gross* $1.25
A6 The Shorter Plays of Bernard Shaw *George Bernard Shaw* $1.95
A7 The Insect World of J. Henri Fabre *Edwin Way Teale (Editor)* $1.95
A8 Laugh with Leacock *Stephen Leacock* $1.95
A9 Man's Emerging Mind *N. J. Berrill* $1.95
A10 How the Reformation Happened *Hilaire Belloc* $1.95
A11 Men Against Fire *S. L. A. Marshall* $1.50
A12 The Dark Eye in Africa *Laurens van der Post* $1.50
A13 The Reach of the Mind *J. B. Rhine* $1.95
A14 Emotional Problems and What You Can Do About Them
     William B. Terhune, M.D. $1.25
A15 Insects: Their Secret World *Evelyn Cheesman* $1.75
A16 King Solomon's Ring *Konrad Lorenz* $1.95
A18 Angry Harvest *Herman Field and Stanislaw Mierzenski* $1.95
A19 Grand Opera in Digest Form *J. Walker McSpadden* $1.95
A20 Faraday as a Discoverer *John Tyndall* $1.75
A21 Adventures in Nature *Edwin Way Teale* $1.95
A22 Golden Tales of Anatole France $1.95
A23 The Making of a Scientist *Anne Roe* $1.75
A24 The Wisdom of the Living Religions *Joseph Gaer* $1.95
A25 A Multitude of Living Things *Lorus J. and Margery J. Milne* $1.95
A26 The Twelve Seasons *Joseph Wood Krutch* $1.50
A27 The Role of Science in Our Modern World
     (*original title: What Man May Be*) *George Russell Harrison* $1.75
A28 Festivals of the Jewish Year *Theodor H. Gaster* $1.75
A29 Emile Zola *Angus Wilson* $1.50
A30 Coming of Age in Samoa *Margaret Mead* $1.75
A31 Thunder Out of China *Theodore H. White and Annalee Jacoby* $1.95
A32 Stephen Foster, America's Troubadour *John Tasker Howard* $1.95
A33 The Twelve Olympians *Charles Seltman* $1.95
A34 The Myth of Rome's Fall *Richard Mansfield Haywood* $1.50
A35 Introduction to Higher Mathematics *Constance Reid* $1.50
A36 A Treasury of Catholic Thinking *Compiled and edited by Ralph L. Woods*
     $1.95
A37 No More War *Linus Pauling* $1.75
A38 Strange Sects and Curious Cults *Marcus Bach* $1.75
A39 That's Me All Over *Cornelia Otis Skinner* $1.85
A40 Lewis and Clark *John Bakeless* $1.95
A41 The German Generals Talk— *B. H. Liddell Hart* $1.65
A42 New World of the Mind *J. B. Rhine* $1.95
A43 The Squeeze *Edward Higbee* $1.85
A44 Giovanni's Room *James Baldwin* $1.75
A45 The Dial: An Annual of Fiction $1.45
A46 Electrons Go To Work *J. Gordon Cook* $1.55
A48 Shiloh *Shelby Foote* $1.75